D1593982

Theodoret's People

TRANSFORMATION OF THE CLASSICAL HERITAGE
Peter Brown, General Editor

Theodoret's People

*Social Networks and Religious Conflict
in Late Roman Syria*

Adam M. Schor

UNIVERSITY OF CALIFORNIA PRESS

Berkeley   Los Angeles   London

University of California Press, one of the most distinguished university presses in the United States, enriches lives around the world by advancing scholarship in the humanities, social sciences, and natural sciences. Its activities are supported by the UC Press Foundation and by philanthropic contributions from individuals and institutions. For more information, visit www.ucpress.edu.

University of California Press
Berkeley and Los Angeles, California

University of California Press, Ltd.
London, England

Library of Congress Cataloging-in-Publication Data

Schor, Adam M., 1976–.
  Theodoret's people : social networks and religious conflict in late Roman Syria / Adam M. Schor.
      p.   cm.
  Includes bibliographical references and index.
  ISBN 978-0-520-26862-3 (cloth, alk. paper)
  1. Theodoret, Bishop of Cyrrhus—Friends and associates.   2. Christian sociology—Syria—History.   3. Syria—Church history.   4. Antiochian school.   I. Title.
  BR1720.T36S36   2010
  261.0939'4309015—dc22   2010025774

Manufactured in the United States of America

20   19   18   17   16   15   14   13   12
10   9   8   7   6   5   4   3   2   1

This book is printed on Cascades Enviro 100, a 100% post consumer waste, recycled, de-inked fiber. FSC recycled certified and processed chlorine free. It is acid free, Ecologo certified, and manufactured by BioGas energy.

CONTENTS

ILLUSTRATIONS

ACKNOWLEDGMENTS

This book is about the relationship between what people claim to believe and whom they know. Partly it concerns the history of religions, especially an epic doctrinal dispute known as the Christological controversy. Partly it concerns late Roman social relations, especially in "Greater Syria," also known as the Roman East. Different sections of this book feature prosopography, historiography, socio-historical survey, micro-historical narrative, theological analysis, and literary interpretation. My goal is to combine these various methods, with the aid of contemporary social theory, to better explain the social behavior that fostered religious communities in conflict.

My study of late Roman religious conflict has now lasted ten years. It began with a dissertation at the University of Michigan, which took form thanks to the generous financial support of the Mellon Foundation, the History Department, and the Rackham School of Graduate Studies. Some of the material in chapters 1 and 3 appeared in a different form as Schor, Adam M., Theodoret on the "School of Antioch": A Network Approach, *Journal of Early Christian Studies* 15:4 (2007), 517–62, © 2007 by Johns Hopkins University Press and the North American Patristics Society. It is reprinted with permission of The Johns Hopkins University Press. Some of the material in chapter 7 appeared in a different form as Schor, Adam M., Patronage Performance and Social Strategy in the Letters of Theodoret, Bishop of Cyrrhus, *Journal of Late Antiquity* 2:2 (2009), 274–99, © 2009 The Johns Hopkins University Press. It is reprinted with permission of The Johns Hopkins University Press.

With regards to this book, I offer my deep gratitude to the members of my dissertation committee, Ray Van Dam, John V. Fine, Jr., Traianos Gagos (now, alas, of blessed memory), and Susan Ashbrook Harvey. Their extensive comments on my thesis and manuscript have proven immeasurably helpful. I also thank other scholars who have commented on drafts of this book in full or in part: Peter Brown, David Olster, David Brakke, Ralph Mathisen, and Patrick Gray, as well as Stephanie Fay and Eric Schmidt at the University of California Press and four perceptive anonymous reviewers. Additional thanks go to Kevin Van Bladel for tutorial help with Syriac, and to George Bevan, Patrick Gray, Pauline Allen, Yannis Papadoyannakis, David Michelson, and Ray Van Dam for showing me early versions of their work on related topics. And let me thank Tara Thompson Stauch for her assistance with proofreading and indexing.

Finally, let me offer my heartfelt thanks to members of my family, my parents Robert and Deborah, my brother Ben, my son Micah (who is much younger than this tome) and my wife Leah. Their companionship, patience, intellectual conversation, and affection have grounded me as I exhume the textual remains of people more than 1500 years gone. "For love is stronger than death... it is a blazing flame" (Song of Songs 8:6).

ABBREVIATIONS AND REFERENCE INFORMATION

AB	*Analecta Bollandiana* (Brussels)
ACO	*Acta conciliorum oecumenicorum*, ed. E. Schwartz. (Berlin 1914–26)
Casiniensis	*Collectio Casiniensis = ACO* I.3–4
CCG	Corpus Christianorum series Graeca (Turnhout)
CCL	Corpus Christianorum series Latina (Turnhout)
CPG	*Clavis patrum Graecorum*. 5 vols. ed. M. Geerard (Turnhout, 1974–1996)
CPL	*Clavis patrum Latinorum*. ed. E. Dekkers and E. Gaar (Turnhout, 1995)
CSCO SS	Corpus scriptorum Christianorum Orientalium, scriptores Syri (Louvain)
CSEL	Corpus scriptorum ecclesiasticorum Latinorum (Vindobona)
CVatGr 1431	*Codex Vaticanus gr. 1431*. ed. E. Schwartz (Munich, 1927)
FC	Fontes Christiani (Rome)
Flemming	*Akten der ephesinischen Synod vom Jahre 449, Syrisch*. ed. J. Flemming (Berlin, 1917)
Fonti	Joannou, P. P., ed., *Fonti, Discipline générale antique* (Rome, 1962–63)
GCS	Die griechischen christlichen Schriftsteller der ersten drei Jahrhunderte (New series)
JECS	*Journal of Early Christian Studies*
JLA	*Journal of Late Antiquity*
JTS	*Journal of Theological Studies*

LCL	Loeb Classical Library (Cambridge, MA)
LRE	Jones, A. H. M. *The Later Roman Empire: A Social, Economic and Administrative Survey.* 2 vols. (Baltimore, 1986)
NPNF I	*A Select Library of Nicene and Post-Nicene Fathers of the Christian Church, First Series* (Grand Rapids, MI)
NPNF II	*A Select Library of Nicene and Post-Nicene Fathers of the Christian Church, Second Series* (Grand Rapids, MI)
NRSV	*New Revised Standard Version Bible* (New York, 1989)
Overbeck	*S. Ephraemi Syri, Rabulae episcopi Edesseni Balaei aliorumque opera selecta,* ed. J. Overbeck (Oxford, 1865)
Perry	*The Second Synod of Ephesus, English Version.* tr. S. G. F. Perry (Dartford, 1881)
PG	Patrologiae cursus completus, series Graeca. ed. J. Migne (Paris, 1857–)
PL	Patrologiae cursus completus, series Latina. ed. J. Migne (Paris, 1844–)
PO	Patrologia Orientalis (Rome)
PLRE II	*Prosopography of the Later Roman Empire, vol. 2, 395–527.* ed. J. R. Martindale (Cambridge, 1980)
SC	Sources chrétiennes (Paris)
ST	Studi e testi (Rome)
TU	Texte und Untersuchungen zur Geschichte der altchristliche Literatur

For additional clarity, references to Theodoret's letters use this new shorthand:

P = *Collectio Patmensis* (SC 40, formerly numbered inconsistently by Roman numerals)

S = *Collectio Sirmondiana* (SC 98, 111, formerly numbered by simple Arabic numerals)

C = *Collectio conciliaris* (SC 429, formerly numbered according to several systems) titled and numbered in this book according to *CPG*

References to Libanius's letters follow R. Foerster's numbering (= F).
References to Synesius of Cyrene's letters follow A. Garzya's numbering.
References to Ambrose of Milan's letters follow M. Zelzer's numbering (CSEL).
References to Firmus of Caesarea's letters follow M. Calvet-Sebasti's numbering (SC).
References to John Chrysostom's letters follow the numbering in PG 52.

References to all other letters and conciliar documents use titles and numbers from *CPG* and *CPL*.

Sessions at the Council of Chalcedon are numbered according to the Greek *acta*. (Note that Price and Gaddis, *Acts of Chalcedon*, number according to the Latin *acta*).

Except where otherwise indicated, all translations of source passages are my own.

Introduction

In the fall of 451, more than 350 bishops[1] gathered in Chalcedon, across the water from the Roman imperial palace, for a tense council. In theory these clerics led a single Christian church. Each week they preached a basic common message of brotherhood, love and faith. But most bishops were used to local authority. A gathering of so many chiefs strained the performance of Christian social ideals. On October eighth, the bishops entered the Church of St. Euphemia before a panel of imperial officials. Immediately they divided into two camps, one led by "Easterners" and the other by "Egyptians." The first activity, the reading of past minutes, sparked shouting matches that threatened to derail the meeting. One focus of hostility was Dioscorus, the bishop of Alexandria in Egypt. When he stood to speak he faced hissing from the opposing camp. All he could do to calm this reaction was to swear fidelity to Cyril, his more popular predecessor. An even sharper acrimony greeted Dioscorus's rival, Theodoret of Cyrrhus in Syria. All he had to do to cause offense was to enter the room:

> After the most pious bishop Theodoret was seated in their midst, the most pious Eastern bishops and those [allied] with them cried out: "He is worthy!"
>
> The most pious Egyptian bishops and those [allied] with them, shouted: "Do not call him a bishop! He is not a bishop! He is not a bishop! Cast out the attacker of God! Cast out the Jew! ... Cast out the one who insulted Christ! ... He anathematized Cyril!"
>
> The most pious Eastern bishops ... clamored: "Cast out the murderer, Disocorus!"
>
> The most pious Egyptian bishops ... shouted: "[Theodoret] has no right to speak! He was deposed by the whole synod!"
>
> Basil, the most pious bishop of Traianopolis, said: "Even we deposed Theodoret."

1

> The most pious Egyptian bishops ... cried out: "And Theodoret denounced Cyril! We throw away Cyril, if we accept Theodoret! The canons cast him out! God [Himself] turned away from this man!"

Shouts continued until halted by the imperial officials, who chided the bishops for their "vulgar clamorings."[2] Still, this verbal abuse actually marked an improvement. Two decades earlier, a council had descended into street riots. Two years earlier, a synod had culminated in a near-murderous manhandling.[3] This time, at Chalcedon, the lay officials intervened to forestall violence. They pushed the bishops to forge consensus on every major issue. By 451, however, the bishops had been feuding for twenty years. Hostility among clerics, monks, and laypeople proved possible to redirect but hard to resolve.

These scenes of clerical confrontation have fascinated scholars, and not just because bishops were behaving badly. The exchange over Theodoret at Chalcedon showcases an obvious feature of late Roman religious life: stark divisions over doctrine. On the right side of the church in Chalcedon sat a group of clerics mainly from Egypt, associated with Cyril and Dioscorus. On the left side sat a clique mainly from "Syria" (a.k.a. "the East"), associated with Theodoret.[4] These groups are traditionally defined by their answers to one theological question: how many "natures" (Greek: *physeis*) existed in Christ. Dioscorus's party preferred to speak of "one nature (incarnate)" and are usually called miaphysites (or monophysites).[5] Theodoret's party chose to speak of "two natures" and are labeled dyophysites (or "Antiochenes").[6] This doctrinal difference became the prime marker of intraclerical hostilities. But doctrinal partisanship was not the only factor in clerical relations. Friendship and mentorship linked bishop to bishop. Patronage ties bound bishops to people across late Roman society. Doctrinal alliances nurtured a sense of community that extended beyond the clergy. By 451, clerics were under pressure to curb their partisanship. By then, however, they had ignited a controversy that would eventually produce three separate Christian communities.

This book seeks to comprehend the Christological dispute by investigating the social dynamics that fostered alliance and conflict. It focuses on the dyophysites, a.k.a. the "Antiochenes," who assembled around Theodoret of Cyrrhus. Theodoret is best known as a hagiographer, a church historian, a Christian apologist, and a theologian. Yet he was also a social actor. He sought influence over a clerical coalition and across late Roman society. Here we shall investigate both Theodoret's doctrines and his social relations, as each influenced the other in turn.

To study Theodoret's social world, this book examines underutilized sources and takes a network approach to social history. Theodoret and his associates appear in varied sources, but their social relations are primarily illuminated by conciliar records and collected letters. These two archives showcase Theodoret's coalition in the act of communicating. They enable a rereading of Theodoret's other writings in richer context. To deal with all these sources requires an approach that integrates doctrinal, social, and cultural analysis. This study seeks such an approach through network theory. Theodoret's coalition can be seen as a socio-doctrinal network, a shifting cluster of mostly clerics bound by friendship and theological agreement. Theodoret's broader social relations can be seen as a patronage network, which included many doctrinal allies and linked them to clients, protectors, and friends. Each of these networks fostered certain attitudes and cultural practices. Together, I argue, they created a resonance between theology and social interaction, which encouraged religious certainty and conflict.

Before examining sources and arguments, however, let us survey the Christological dispute and the larger historical context. As we shall see, this clash has left unanswered questions that call for a fresh look.

THE CHRISTOLOGICAL DISPUTE:
A PUZZLING RELIGIOUS CONFLICT

The late Roman world had more than its share of religious conflict. Such, at least, is the impression one gets from our sources. During the fourth and fifth centuries, Christian leaders assembled arguments against Jews and pagans. They also made accusations of heresy as they discovered internal splits. The Christological dispute began with the words of a few clerics, but it drew more imperial involvement and sparked more riots than nearly any cultural struggle of the time. Generations of scholars have studied this dispute, which permanently fractured the Christian community. They have lacked neither sources nor knowledge of the historical context. Nevertheless the dispute remains puzzling for its intensity and its duration.

The Christological dispute began, like many religious conflicts, with the discovery of differences among allies. In the late fourth century Christian clerics were still arguing over the status of Christ as the Son of God.[7] Texts of the *New Testament* offered them conflicting signals, noting Christ's godlike powers in one passage and his human-like weakness in the next. A range of people sought to make sense of this matter. The active disputants assembled into loose parties, by signing ambiguous formulas and by labeling their foes. The Nicenes constituted one such amorphous coalition. Its members agreed that the divine Trinity was fully perfect and transcendent—that Christ the Son, despite his human attributes, was "of the same substance" as the Father. But this Nicene agreement masked a split between two groups with different ways of arguing their case.[8]

One set of Nicene clerics (centered in Antioch) sought explanations to dispel Scriptural paradox. They explained that Christ had a full humanity distinguishable from his Godhead. Thus when Christians read about Christ enduring suffering, they could ascribe it to his human component without impinging on the perfect God. Lists of Christ's human and divine attributes marked this approach.

So did the formula "Two natures (*dyo physeis*) in Christ," which, in the early fifth century, Theodore of Mopsuestia expressed most directly.[9]

A second set of Nicene clerics sought overt ways to express Scriptural paradox. This group emphasized that Christ was simply God the Word (a singular subject), who had decided to humble Himself by taking on human weakness. Thus, when Christians heard about Christ enduring suffering, they could see it as the mysterious act of an all-powerful Deity. Statements of "God suffering in the flesh" marked this approach; so did the formula "one nature (*mia physis*) incarnate of the Word of God," which Cyril of Alexandria stated most prominently.[10]

These two clerical groups taught for a generation without controversy, but starting in the late 420s they came into conflict. In 428, (the dyophysite) Nestorius was chosen as bishop of Constantinople. Famously he suggested that Christians should not call Mary the "One who bore God," (*Theotokos*), but more precisely the "One who bore Christ" (*Christotokos*). This statement sparked local hostilities.[11] And it offended Cyril, for it seemed to divide Jesus from the divine. Cyril denounced Nestorius and demanded he foreswear twelve specific doctrines. This demand offended Nestorius's allies; for it seemed to deny the impassibility of God.[12] In 431, Emperor Theodosius II called a council in Ephesus to settle the dispute. Cyril convened the summer meeting before Nestorius's supporters arrived. The two sides formed separate assemblies, and, amid street riots, each excommunicated the other. A colloquy that fall in Chalcedon failed to reach an accord. Regional schism now divided the Nicene church,[13] and soon this split involved not just clerics, but protesting crowds of monks and lay partisans.[14]

During the 430s the imperial court pushed the Eastern dyophysites to rejoin communion with Cyril and his associates. It sent mediators to run negotiations. It sought defectors and threatened holdouts with exile.[15] In 433, negotiators reached a settlement, a *Formula of Reunion* that excluded neither "one nature incarnate" nor "two natures in Christ." The agreement did accept the condemnation of Nestorius. Nearly half of the Eastern bishops initially refused to sign, though by 435 most were convinced to do so.[16] The *Formula of Reunion*, however, furnished only a truce. Dyophysites faced criticism from Cyril until his death in 444, and they remained suspect at court. And now, the church in Syria was divided; clerics, monks, and lay partisans waited to clash again.[17]

Then the doctrinal truce broke down. In 447 Theodoret wrote in defense of "two natures." He criticized certain monks (perhaps Eutyches of Constantinople) for denying Christ's humanity. In response some associates of the late Cyril accused Theodoret and his allies of heresy, among other crimes.[18] Theodoret and his partisans still pressed their claims. Eutyches was tried for heresy before Flavian of Constantinople. But by 449, Theodosius II was fed up with the Eastern dyophysites.[19] A Second Council of Ephesus convened in August under Dioscorus. After rehabilitating Eutyches, it condemned the dyophysite leaders, who were forced into exile.[20] Yet Dioscorus's victory was short-lived. After Theodosius II died suddenly in July 450, the new emperor Marcian shifted course. Theodoret and some allies were restored before a third big council.[21]

The Council of Chalcedon in the fall of 451 aimed at a final settlement. The council praised the late Cyril as a paragon of orthodoxy, even as it offered a generally dyophysite formula ("one *hypostasis* of Christ made known in two natures").[22] These decisions were ratified by all but a few attendees. But many clerics and monks protested; several cities responded with large riots.[23] Ultimately the council of Chalcedon magnified the conflict, leaving three factions in place of two, and eventually three self-identified churches across the Middle East.[24]

This Christological conflict has been studied thoroughly, but it remains puzzling. Why should a difference in theological language have caused so much bitterness? Why did the clerics of Syria become divided among the theological camps? Why did some monks and laypeople get so involved in this clerical conflict? And what turned small theological parties into large, self-conscious communities? It is hard to address these questions by merely comparing doctrines.

LATE ROMAN SYRIA: SOCIAL AND CULTURAL CONTEXT

To make sense of the Christological dispute, we must start by placing it in its wider context. Bishops like Theodoret argued from a specific social setting in the fifth-century, Eastern Roman world. Famously, church conflicts were tied to imperial politics, which largely (though not entirely) picked the winners. Equally, these conflicts were tied to the social order and the place of bishops therein. But the late Roman world was regionally heterogeneous. Theodoret's dyophysites were based primarily in Syria (which, in this study, means the eleven eastern Roman provinces between the Taurus mountains and the Sea of Galilee, whose clerics later answered to the patriarch of Antioch). In some ways, Syria was typical late Roman territory. But its landscape and varied past fostered local peculiarities, which influenced the course of religious conflict.

At first glance, the region of Syria looks like a microcosm of late Roman society. It includes mostly familiar Roman landscapes: fertile coastal plains, well-watered valleys, steep mountains, arable hills, semi-arable steppelands, and deserts.[25] It supported the usual range of Roman settlements, from Antioch (population circa 200,000), to more than one hundred smaller *poleis*, and thousands of villages.[26] But not every region followed the same demographic trajectory. Unlike western areas, Syria saw its population expand in the fourth and fifth centuries, especially in marginal lands.[27] Syria featured the usual late Roman social hierarchy. Landed wealth and privilege were concentrated in a small local notable class and a smaller senatorial order. But not all settlements were dominated by these elites. Much of

Syria hosted pastoralists and peasant proprietors, as well as tenant farmers and slaves.[28] In most respects, Syria featured the standard trappings of a coherent Eastern Roman government. Residents answered to municipal councilors and short-term governors (and their officers). The whole region answered to emperors and courtiers in Constantinople, aided by thousands of bureaucrats.[29] Again, however, geography mattered. Bordering Sassanid Persia, Syria supported a massive Roman army. It thus drew unusual levels of imperial attention, both military and legal. But unlike other frontier zones, Syria faced few fifth-century wars.[30] Other Roman regions endured crises; in Syria, the political and social order held firm.

Despite its typical political and social hierarchies, late Roman Syria was made distinctive by its diverse culture. Some variety came from past waves of migration, which brought the region its five major languages.[31] Some came from a complicated political heritage. In western Syria centuries of Hellenistic and Roman rule had a palpable impact on laws, architecture, and literary education.[32] In eastern Syria, local rule into the third century encouraged Syriac (and eventually Armenian) written culture alongside Greek.[33] Syrian society was not fractured by its diversity. But each district had its own mix of customs and influences.

Perhaps the surest mark of Syrian diversity was religion. Like many Roman regions, Syria boasted a wide range of traditional local cults.[34] It also hosted translocal religious communities: Magian, Manichaean, theurgic-pagan and Jewish.[35] By 450, the majority of Syrians probably practiced some form of Christianity,[36] but they still differed in cultic habits. Urban congregations lived under clerical oversight while many villages rarely saw priests.[37] Most Christian families lived much like their non-Christian forebears, a lifestyle rejected by the growing monastic movement.[38] Christian culture varied with the local language. It also varied with the preferred theology. In much of Syria, the Nicene clergy was a recent presence, not necessarily welcome.[39]

It is in this context that we must place the main participants in the Christological dispute: Theodoret and his fellow bishops. For bishops in Syria played a key social and cultural role. Some bishops were wealthy landowners; others were honored ascetics. Some rose through the local clergy, while others were recruited externally.[40] Whatever their background, the bishops took on important tasks for their communities. They arbitrated disputes, redistributed alms, hired subordinates, and cared for widows and orphans. They organized festivals, ran building projects, supported civic councils, and oversaw monasteries. Bishops still needed cooperation from other clerics and other sorts of notables.[41] But they were well placed to voice their concerns.

The life of Theodoret, in fact, exemplifies the complicated position of late Roman bishops. Born in 393 in Antioch, he was educated in Christian and sophistic (classical) traditions. As a monk (ca. 415–423), Theodoret studied Christian doctrine, but also non-Christian philosophy.[42] As bishop (423–460s) he presided over a small town near Antioch with a populous rural territory. He constantly courted its notables and toured its villages. At the same time, he befriended pagan teachers and Christian hermits, wealthy courtiers and tenant farmers, speakers of Greek and speakers of Aramaic. Theodoret was atypical, for his learning and connections.[43] But his performance as bishop had to fit the social context to give him hope of influence.

These features of late Roman Syria are familiar to historians, but they remain essential to understanding the conflict. Partisans in the Christological dispute were more than just doctrinal mouthpieces; they were participants in diverse regional communities. Everything they said or did had both theological and social implications. Usually, in premodern history, the links between doctrine and social life are obscure. For the Christological dispute, however, a closer look is possible.

SOURCES FOR THE CHRISTOLOGICAL DISPUTE AND ITS PARTICIPANTS

The clashes over Christology make for an unusual scholarly opportunity. No other episode in late Roman history is so richly documented. Like other religious disputes this conflict produced contrasting works of theology. Like other clashes it inspired hagiographic works and church histories. The Christological dispute, however, offers two caches of uncommon documents– transcripts from church councils, and collections of letters. These two archives present special interpretive problems, but they remain unequaled as records of ancient social interaction and religious controversy.

The largest cache of sources for the Christological dispute comes from church councils. These synods kept stenographic records. Their *acta* featured statements by delegates and witnesses and acclamations by attendees. The gatherings also assembled supporting documents—excerpts from treatises, sermons, and letters.[44] The First Council of Ephesus (431) produced two collections, one geared to support each party.[45] The Second Council of Ephesus (449) also produced two transcripts, each covering about half of the meeting.[46] Records from the Council of Chalcedon (451) were both more unified and more extensive, with transcripts of (nearly) every session and long excerpts from the *acta* of the prior synods.[47]

The second archive of sources for the dispute comprises collections of letters. Like most late Roman notables, the bishops conducted correspondence. They wrote to monks about lifestyle choices and to congregants about family issues. They wrote to wealthy notables about donations and to officials about taxes. Most often, the bishops wrote to one another, on everything from friendship to doctrine.[48] About six hundred letters[49] survive from the main participants in this controversy, grouped into various collections. More than half were kept as evidence in the conciliar records. Some of these were saved by miaphysite supporters of

Cyril, some by proponents of the Council of Chalcedon. The most important conciliar collection, for our purposes, was assembled by one man: the dyophysite exile Irenaeus of Tyre (in his *Tragedy*).[50] The rest of the letters come from personal collections. The largest personal set belongs to Theodoret, with nearly two hundred entries in two surviving manuscript traditions.[51] A smaller set comes from the miaphysite Firmus of Caesarea in Cappadocia, from one manuscript with forty-six letters.[52]

These two source archives have limitations. The *acta* and correspondence were first gathered by active disputants; often they show partisan agendas. For some sessions we have multiple contrasting records; for others, only one version. Official Chalcedonian records were kept in Greek, but some transcripts survive only in translation—miaphysite records in Syriac, Irenaeus's *Tragedy* in Latin. All of the conciliar records may have received later editing.[53] Personal letters, meanwhile, were assembled as examples of rhetoric or clerical conduct. These letters survive mostly in Greek (some conciliar letters, again, exist only in translation). Occasionally extant letters preserve both sides of a conversation. Often only one side remains. Some letters hint at a date of composition, but they are not evenly distributed in time. Theodoret's dateable notes, for instance, were mostly penned between 430 and 435 or between 443 and 450; just a few were written in the 420s and only one after 451. In any case, nearly a third of his letters can only be dated within ten years. Like the conciliar documents, the letters may have been edited. Assuredly they were selected and removed from their original context.[54]

There are, of course, other types of sources related to this dispute. Doctrinal treatises abound, especially from Cyril and Theodoret. These writings add arguments to basic theological formulas.[55] Biblical commentaries also abound, including a set by Theodoret. These works reveal how much doctrinal partisanship intertwined with the reading of Scripture.[56] Several authors wrote church histories during the conflict, including Theodoret. Such narratives provide both information about the disputes and competing visions of Christian community.[57] Several participants wrote hagiographies, from the anonymous *Life of Rabbula* to the *History of the Friends of God* by Theodoret. These works showcase the interplay between doctrinal alliance and ascetic affiliation.[58] Few artifacts, inscriptions, or papyri can be tied directly to this controversy. But the rich archaeology of certain portions of Syria helps to illuminate the social context.[59]

Yet it is the letters and council acts that enable unusual scholarship. No ancient gathering is so well documented as the church councils. No ancient conversation is so fully recorded.[60] Comparable letter collections come from other late Romans, including the bishop Basil of Caesarea, the sophist Libanius of Antioch, and the philosopher-bishop Synesius of Cyrene. But these letters and *acta* constitute a unique body of evidence. They feature two decades of socially embedded messages. They attest to hundreds of relationships, which form a context for reading other sources. No text will solve all puzzles of late Roman religious conflict, but together these texts surely help.

A NETWORK APPROACH TO RELIGIOUS CONFLICT

The Christological dispute thus presents enduring questions and fortuitous sources. But how should we use the sources to explore the social dynamics of religious conflict? Many scholars have studied the dispute and its participants. Until recently, most dealt either with doctrine or, separately, with social relations. The questions posed here, however, call for an integrative approach, which incorporates doctrine into social and cultural analysis. To craft such an approach, this study draws on recent trends in sociology, especially social network theory. Network theory features methods for analyzing personal interactions. It offers a framework for combining social concepts (such as patronage) with cultural concepts (such as performance). Network theory is no panacea but seems well suited to the sources and questions at hand.

The Christological dispute has received plenty of scholarly attention. The majority of studies have come from historical theologians. They have scrutinized the teachings of leading partisans. They have chronicled the development of doctrines from various influences.[61] Meanwhile, broader studies have come from social historians. These works have examined church-state politics and the shaping of religious institutions. They have looked at ecclesiastical resources, the social background of clerics, relations between clerics and monks, and the position of bishops in Roman communities.[62] Recent work has mostly taken the form of cultural studies. These efforts have explored the representation of bishops and ascetics within the sources. They have tied such depictions to the construction of religious authority and Christian identity.[63] Studies of Theodoret's vast corpus have also abounded. But they have likewise usually considered doctrine separately from culture and social relations.[64]

This book is indebted to generations of scholars who have examined the Christological dispute. The topic, however, could benefit from fresh approaches. Fifty years ago, historians and historical theologians tended to operate with contrasting assumptions. Most theologians assumed that clerics pursued theological truth. Most historians assumed that clerics pursued social authority.[65] Recently scholars have crossed disciplines more readily. Few, however, have dealt with this episode's full social complexity.[66] Perhaps this is due to intimidating sources; perhaps, to those contrasting assumptions.

This project seeks an integrative approach, which treats theology as a key factor in social relations. But how should we envision the social aspect of religion? Many theorists have made suggestions. Cultural anthropologists once defined religion as a "symbolic system" that both follows and affects social reality.[67] Poststructuralists cast religion as discourse, which constructs social boundaries and figures of authority.[68] Cognitivists treat religion as a mental phenomenon, produced by the same neural systems that manage social interaction.[69] In each case, the theorists have suggested a dynamic link between religion and social processes.

Recent studies suggest three specific ways in which religion, as a form of culture, interacts with social relations: through narration, through metaphorical reasoning, and through personal performance. First, many scholars cite the role that narratives play in building communities. According to Francesca Polletta, social movements tend to succeed when they offer communal stories in which members find their place.[70] Second, cognitive linguists stress the importance of deep metaphors (or "frames") in ideological affiliation. According to George Lakoff, ideological parties tend to succeed when they employ shared metaphors tied to basic social icons (such as family roles).[71] Finally, many sociologists now define social relations as the performance of cultural practices. Pierre Bourdieu linked social positioning to the learning of behavioral cues (habitus). Jeffrey Alexander notes how flexibly people display such cues, in order to link up with various communities.[72] All of these concepts are useful for the study of religious conflict. The letters and acta employ recurring stories and metaphors and can be seen as records of personal performance. But these concepts are insufficient unless they make sense of the relational interactions attested as central to this conflict.

One way to deal with such personal interactions is to use social network theory. Network theory pictures society as a web of relationships, which can be categorized, mapped, and modeled. Networks of relationships are assumed to be malleable. But even temporary social bonds transmit culture. In fact, these links only exist if participants communicate their attachment by trading cultural cues. In theory, the notion of a network fits any type of community, including religious movements.[73] In practice, scholars must set limits. Typically scholars concentrate on one category of relationship. They may focus on one central individual or a small core group.[74] This book uses another selection method. If individuals connect by performing certain words and gestures,[75] than a meaningful network can be identified by tracing exchanges of a shared set of these cues.

Network theory is built around a series of basic techniques for analyzing social data. One can map any network, with social "links" drawn between human "nodes." One can also measure quantities, such as the "density" of links, or the "centrality"[76] of nodes. One can look for relational patterns, such as central vs. peripheral locations, internal clusters, and "hubs." One can even map different types of relationships as overlapping networks. Thus one can distinguish simple from "multiplex" bonds and find "mediators" between disparate groups.[77]

In addition to analytical methods, network theory provides a helpful perspective on key concepts, such as leadership, friendship, and patronage. Network scholars treat these concepts as relational patterns, bound to culturally defined roles. Anthropologist Jeremy Boissevain defines patronage as "personal, asymmetrical, non-monetary, reciprocal" relationships. These links are, in his view, marked by the exchange of material favors for signs of loyalty. Boissevain distinguishes patronage from friendship, which aspires to emotional symmetry. He treats roles of patronage and friendship as situational. Patrons, clients, mediators, and companions are identified by their participation in a transactional network.[78] Boissevain also frames leadership as situational, based on relational positioning as well as official titles. Central figures can claim informal leadership, in his view, by asserting influence over contacts within the network.[79] This book draws on Boissevain's definitions, while retaining the significance of culture. The roles of patron, friend, and leader are situational, but to assume even temporary positions people must flesh out their roles by performing cultural cues.[80]

Network theory started in the 1960s with measurements and definitions. In recent years it has expanded into a "science," which theorizes about relational systems through observation and computer modeling. Scholars, such as Albert-László Barabási and Duncan Watts, have uncovered consistent patterns in the development of "self-organizing" networks. One general pattern, they note, tends to arise when a group steadily adds new members: the modular scale-free topology.[81] Modular scale-free networks feature cliques linked together by a handful of "hubs." They vary significantly, depending on the number of hubs and the way these hubs relate to one another (see figure 1). Simulated modular scale-free networks usually survive the random loss of members. They can, however, be reshaped if hubs change, and dismantled if a majority of hubs are removed.[82] This study uses Barabási's and Watt's models to interpret social outcomes that are already evident in the sources. As we shall see, some ancient networks look "modular" and "scale-free" and behaved accordingly.

Like any abstract construct, network theory has limitations in historical research. Some of these limitations are conceptually inherent. Social bonds are not objective facts, but the sum of temporary perceptions. They can only be traced when communicated intersubjectively. Networks, too, are not objective facts, but representations. People draw mental networks to represent their social relations. These mental networks, however, vary from person to person. They may include imagined social actors (such as God, dead saints, or demons). None of them can be expected to match the networks mapped out by scholars. Network maps always simplify social experience. They cannot capture all the differentials of authority, which shift with the cultural context. Further limitations of network theory have to do with the extant sources. Letters and *acta* supply patchy relational data. Inevitably they produce a social map that is incomplete and chronologically imprecise. Used incautiously, a network map might overemphasize certain relationships and miss others entirely. In order to do network analysis, this book deals in approximation. It distinguishes the *intersubjective networks* of ancient people from their

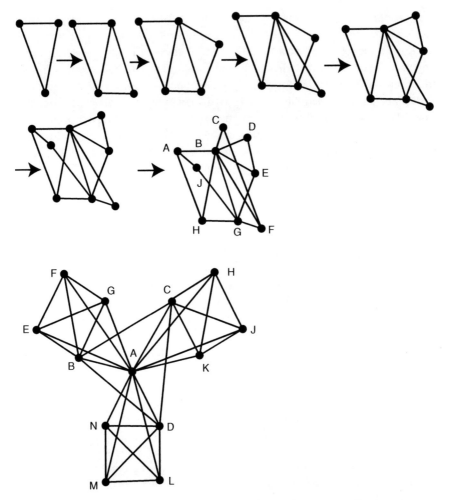

FIGURE 1. Network theory and the modular scale-free topology. A scale-free network (top) is here formed by steadily adding new nodes, each with 2 new links (the choice of partner is random but weighted toward nodes which are already well connected). A modular scale-free network (bottom) is formed similarly, if further links are occasionally added between those who already share acquaintances.

Network statistics: nodes = 9, links = 15, density = 0.417, diameter = 3. Connectivity: B = 7; G = 5; A, E, F, H = 3; C, D, J = 2. Centrality: B = 9; G = 11; A, E, F, H = 13; C, D = 15; J = 16. Remove both B and G to collapse the network.

Network statistics: nodes = 13, links = 33, density = 0.423, diameter = 2. Connectivity: A = 12; B, C, D = 6; E, F, G, H, J, K, L, M, N = 4. Centrality: A = 12; B, C, D = 18; E, F, G, H, J, K, L, M, N = 20. Remove A and either B, C, or D to collapse the network.

perceptual/mental networks, and both from the *network maps* of modern observers. It draws on network models for hypotheses, which must be confirmed in other ways.

Despite its limitations, network theory provides a practical framework for social and cultural history. Any society can be seen as a web of overlapping networks, which can be measured, modeled, and compared. Sources, such as letters and transcripts, give evidence for relationships. As modern observers, we will never discern every ancient social connection. But we can find meaningful networks by charting the exchange of socially resonant cues. Network maps can be drawn synchronically, to create a richer picture. They can also be studied over time, and compared to existing models. Network analysis might seem theoretically insular. In fact, it compliments cultural studies. Networks give context to people's performances, shape the models by which people reason metaphorically, and provide a basis for storytelling that builds community.

To study late Roman religious conflict, a network approach to social history is well suited. It makes the most of underutilized sources, and it allows persistent questions to be addressed. This study is hardly the first to do network history in a premodern context. Elizabeth Clark mapped the elite networks that contended in the Origenist controversy. Catherine Hezser employed network concepts to describe the early Rabbinic movement. Margaret Mullett used letters to map the social contacts of twelfth-century Bishop Theophylact of Ohrid. Each of these scholars combined network analysis with some form of cultural history.[83] More recently Giovanni Ruffini quantitatively analyzed networks evident in late Roman papyri.[84] My approach integrates recent theoretical developments, in network science and other fields.[85] Mainly it differs from prior efforts in how it manages the rich sources to draw out a small social world.

SUMMARY OF MAIN ARGUMENTS

The eight chapters of this book explore various aspects of Theodoret's associations. They are divided into two parts. Part I (chapters 1 to 5) looks at how Theodoret related to fellow clerics and other active disputants. Its main subject is the "Antiochene" doctrinal network. Part II (chapters 6 to 8) looks at Theodoret's patronage relations across late Roman society. Its subject is an amorphous transactional system, which overlapped the core of the Antiochene network.

The first chapter launches a synchronic investigation of interactions between Theodoret and his doctrinal allies. It surveys the ways in which clerics signaled social attachments through words and nonverbal practices. Extant letters and *acta* feature a consistent set of social cues, shared by Theodoret and his mostly clerical associates. It is this set of cues that allows us to identify an "Antiochene" network.

Chapter 2 continues the synchronic study of "Antiochene" interactions. Tracing the exchange of a characteristic set of cues, it maps and then analyzes Theodoret's doctrinal network. Our maps reveal the demographics of the network, as well as a basic form—modular and scale-free. Mere statistics and comparisons cannot tell us how this network developed. But they do suggest ways to interpret the patterns we see in a diachronic reading of the sources.

Chapter 3 begins that diachronic investigation. It explores the origins of the Antiochene network by analyzing the heritage that Theodoret depicted in works of history. Theodoret's writings celebrate his Nicene clerical forebears, including Diodore of Tarsus and Theodore of Mopsuestia. He narrates how these partisans recruited supporters and took over the churches of Syria. Theodoret's narrative must be placed in historiographical context. His depictions, however, make sense of developments in Antiochene doctrine and in Syrian clerical-ascetic relations. Here they receive consideration as an idealized description of a real network.

Chapter 4 addresses the social roots and effects of doctrinal conflict during the Nestorian controversy (429–435). It traces the social actions of Antiochene clerics, as they fractured and reassembled their network. Officially, the Antiochenes were divided over whether to accept a settlement with Cyril's side. But these internal divisions can be seen as a competition for network leadership. When Theodoret mediated an end to these feuds, his success can be credited to a well-timed rationale for reforming his community.

Chapter 5 follows the Antiochene network through a suppressed clash (435–440), a shaky truce (440–447), and a renewed controversy (447–450). It explores Theodoret's efforts, in the face of new threats, to preserve his Antiochene party. Partly his project involved personal networking, among clerics and across Roman society. Partly it involved new theological work and new narratives, both geared to foster Antiochene community. Theodoret's efforts, however, must be set against records of the Eutychean controversy, which show his network virtually collapsing. A close look at Antiochene relational patterns offers one way to explain so swift a social decline.

Chapter 6 begins a broader exploration of Syrian bishops' position in late Roman society. It synchronically surveys key figures in relations of patronage, and the potential for Syrian bishops to find a place in this transactional web. Late Roman society hosted a range of would-be patrons and mediators. Local civic notables and classical educators sought favors for clients, as did courtiers, government officials, senators, bureaucrats, generals, soldiers, synagogue leaders, rabbis, theurgists, heterodox clerics, and leading monks. Theodoret's letters reveal the roles sought by one Syrian bishop in relation to potential collaborators and in contrast to rivals. Comparisons highlight his pursuit of traditional niches as well as more unusual positions.

Chapter 7 turns from available roles of patronage to Theodoret's efforts to fulfill these roles. It interprets his patronage appeals as performances, tailored to encourage generosity and secure social connections. Theodoret's letters show a variety of tactics for establishing common ground, for keeping his personal distance, for directing appeals to multiple audiences, and for preserving relationships when requests failed. The letters also reveal the author's broader strategies for winning inclusion in patronage networks and for protecting himself in an acute doctrinal conflict.

Chapter 8 combines the two parts of this study. It seeks the interrelations between Theodoret's performances of patronage and his teachings about Christ. In his *Eranistes,* Theodoret sought to justify his claim that two natures existed in Christ. Thus he asserted that Jesus needed two natures to mediate between humans and God, to secure the distribution of salvation. This argument can be seen as metaphorical reasoning, based on the author's notions of human patronage. It is not clear how many allies endorsed this specific defense of dyophysitism. But the metaphor of patronage marks one of several ways in which Antiochene doctrine might resonate with specific social behaviors. The effects, I argue, were reinforcement of doctrinal certainties and reaffirmation of partisan bonds.

The book ends with a brief epilogue, surveying the legacy of this conflict during and after the Council of Chalcedon. The main conclusions of this book, however, are assembled progressively. The Christological dispute, I contend, was not just a mismatch of doctrines. Nor was it just a contest for authority. It was a crucial episode in the formation of partisan religious community.

PART I

Theodoret and His Antiochene Clerical Network

1

Traces of a Network

Friendship, Doctrine, and Clerical Communication, 423–451

It was a moment of complicated emotions as the clerics of Syria remembered their fallen godfather. Acacius, bishop of Beroea for nearly six decades, died in 437.[1] Several clerics expressed admiration for the departed.[2] Theodoret did so by commemorating him in the *History of the Friends of God.* Acacius had been a monastic student to great Syrian holy men. When the Nicene church needed him, however, he left his cell for the contentions of the urban clergy. It was then, according to Theodoret, that Acacius shone, revealing his "civic and ascetic virtues." "By taking the exactness (*akribeia*) of the latter with the flexibility (*oikonomia*) of the former, he put the extremes together in one."[3]

The memorializing of Acacius provides an entry point into the social world of fifth-century bishops. Theodoret had known Acacius for at least two decades. Like many Syrian prelates he claimed Acacius as a spiritual father, rivaled *in memoriam* only by Theodore of Mopsuestia.[4] While alive, Acacius had often courted controversy.[5] After his death, he symbolized brotherhood under consensual leadership.

The most intriguing aspect of this celebration of Acacius, however, has to be Theodoret's choice of words. When he spoke of Acacius's *akribeia* and *oikonomia*, it meant more than prudence and discipline. *Oikonomia* recalled the dispensation of the Lord, the heart of Christological teaching. And *akribeia* signified doctrinal precision, to which Theodoret and his friends aspired. With these words Theodoret did more than praise a shared hero. He called to mind a shared cultural experience.

Theodoret's praises of Acacius were powerful because they were part of a system of socially resonant communication. In late Roman Syria, as in any social setting, people demarcated relationships by performing certain cultural cues.

Theodoret sent cues in published books, like the *History of the Friends of God*. He sent cues all the more in conciliar statements and letters. Theodoret employed varied signals, tailored to a range of relationships. But some he kept for a special network of doctrinal allies and friends.

This distinct, mostly clerical network represents the focus of part one of this book, for it contended in the Christological dispute as the "Antiochene" party. Subsequent chapters in this book map the Antiochene network and chronicle its development prior to and during the controversy. Before we can trace this network, however, we need to identify it. Thus this chapter scrutinizes the records of clerical communication, in search of relevant cultural practices and an "Antiochene" set of cues.

As we shall see, certain clerics exchanged a key set of phrases and gestures that we can treat as idioms of an Antiochene network. These allies sent signals of emotional attachment and signs of doctrinal harmony. Thus they demonstrated intimate friendship and shared orthodoxy. To reinforce their mutual bonds, the clerics joined in rituals of cooperation. To verify bonds, they collected records and conducted surveillance. All this they did informally without declaring a special identity. All that was needed was regular communication, configured to show special affection and ask it in return.

THE LANGUAGE OF CLERICAL AFFECTION

When ancient Christian leaders imagined the church, they usually envisioned a tight, affectionate community. If clerics hoped to cooperate, they needed to communicate their emotional attachments, great and small. Greek words for attachments varied, from *agapē* (Christian familial love) and *adelphotēs* (brotherhood) to *philostorgia* (affection), *erōs* (desirous love) and *philia* (friendship).[6] Longer statements of affection also varied, though many Christian letters end with the farewell, "To you and whichever members of the brotherhood are with you, I and those with me send our highest regards." These words often inspire scholars to seek precise definitions, which have remained elusive.[7] The statements raise questions about emotional sincerity, which have proven difficult to resolve.[8] Such issues, however, matter less to this study than how clerics *used* their emotional terms. Every cleric offered certain words for attachment as basic social cues. Theodoret, and other Syrian clerics, employed the full Greek vocabulary to distinguish a variety of meaningful relationships.

The first touchstone of clerical affection in our sources is basic Christian terminology. Christian texts spoke of the love (*agapē*) that united believers as a single body or family (Romans 12:4, 12:9–10, I Corinthians 13:8–14:1, Colossians 3:14–16). The language of "love" pervaded quasi-normative guides, such as the *Apostolic Constitutions*.[9] It also pervaded clerical letters, including Theodoret's.[10] It could be expressed directly, or by the corollary of requesting mutual prayer.[11] These emotional expressions were common, but it was, in some sense, their commonness that gave them meaning. By declaring love, clerics signaled a shared moral ideal.

Agapē, however, could mean something narrower than universal love. Most obviously, the term was reinterpreted to accommodate the high status of the clergy. Such "clericalism" found scriptural support in the "special burdens" noted in I Corinthians 4, or the moral standards listed in the first chapter of the Epistle to Titus. It found expression in the letters carried by traveling clerics to certify their faith.[12] Theodoret, for his part, never failed to recognize a cleric as "Your Holiness" (*hagiotēs*), "Your Godliness" (*theiotēs*) or "Your Piety" (*eulabeia*). Monks were famous for their heightened sense of brotherhood. But it was their duty to shepherd souls that led John Chrysostom to rank clerics above monks as lovers of God and humanity.[13] *Agapē* was further modified to fit the clerical hierarchy. The *Apostolic Constitutions,* for instance, called bishops the new "priests and Levites," the new "prophets, rulers, governors, and kings," even "the voice of God." By contrast, priests were declared stand-ins, and deacons, mere assistants. "Let the bishop be honored among you as God," the *Constitutions* read, "and the deacon as his prophet."[14] Christian terms may appear to stand for "universal" love. But with each rank of clergy taking communion separately, all could see that the fabric of *agapē* had seams.

A second touchstone of affection in our sources was the classical vocabulary of friendship. Pre-Christian Greek and Roman writers used *philia* to signal preferential attachment. Plato celebrated pair-bonding (called both *erōs* and *philia*) as the keystone of happiness and the focus of personal desire (*epithymia*).[15] Aristotle spoke more of shared goals and morals than desire, but he kept things personal. *Philia,* in his view, was grounded in intimacy and reciprocity. It reached its pinnacle among pairs of true *philoi* (friends), ideally those of equal status and virtue.[16] Later Greeks and Romans continued to link *philia* with virtue, reciprocity, and desire. They merely added the medium of letters. Handbooks advised students how to write "Letters for Preserving *Philia,*" based on philosophic definitions. Pseudo-Demetrius urged correspondents to praise shared virtues, express desire, and avoid extraneous details, in order to reveal true emotions.[17] Late Roman elites clung to this *philia* tradition, especially in letters. Good letters encapsulated character (Greek: *ethos*), and as Synesius of Cyrene put it, "What possession is more beautiful than a friend who exhibits his pure character?"[18]

Expressions of *philia,* however, were not limited to particularist bonding. For fifth-century clerics, the term carried gradations of meaning. From philosophers and sophists, *philia* acquired a communal aspect. Inspired by the shared imitation of a teacher, philosophic *philia* was supposed to be as intimate as erotic love—and just as strong.[19] *Philia* acquired another meaning in elite circles, as a euphemism for patronage. Patrons might allow high-placed clients to call their bond a friendship, even though both knew that the implied "equality" was limited or non-existent.[20] By the fifth century, Christian leaders spoke of the communal *philia* of monastic communities.[21] They also spoke of their own *philia* with clerical subordinates (and superiors).[22] Yet reciprocal friendship remained an important connotation, especially when bishops wrote one another. Notionally bishops were all men of elite rank, bound by shared morals and learning. Their geographical scattering required letters, which expressed the mutual goodwill central to Christian identity. Most Christians found few problems with the concept of *philia*. Some even declared *philia* a divine gift—an image of the ideal relationship between people and God.[23] Conceptually, bishops were bound to the notion of *philia* in every ceremony and every letter—whenever they were called by the title "Most friendly with God" (*theophilestatos*).

When clerics of the fifth century expressed their social affinities, they used both Christian and classical terminology to craft shades of meaning. Some clerics preferred one set of terms. Firmus of Caesarea used *philia* almost exclusively.[24] Others intermixed *philia* and *agapē* to create tailored notions of affection. Consider, for example, one of Theodoret's letters to the clergy of neighboring Beroea. "I have come to know that it is with good reason that I am well disposed to Your Reverence," this letter began, "because the letter of Your Piety has reassured me that I love and am loved in return (*agapōn antagapomai*)." Theodoret then furthered the familial theme, calling their former "father" Acacius his own father and the current bishop "my true soul-sharing brother." But when he summed up their relations, he shifted terms: "[All] this is sufficient to give birth to friendship (*philia*) and once it is born, to make it grow." This he then compared to the bond between teacher and pupils. By the time Theodoret got to his advice, he had cited nearly every aspect of friendship and love.[25] The mix of terms signaled overlapping layers of affection, recognizing the complexities of distance and rank. Theodoret mixed terms with fellow bishops, with congregants, with governors and with generals. Each time he crafted a tailored expression that marked the grounds for a particular social bond.

Words of affection thus furnished a variety of cultural cues, which marked relationships. *Philia*, *agapē* and their derivatives recur frequently in communication. The various terms signaled social position, level of attachment, and the type of affection. Still, these direct expressions were of limited value—widely expected and easily given. When clerics sought lasting bonds, they had to add something more.

SIGNALS OF DOCTRINAL AFFINITY: TALKING "ANTIOCHENE"

Clerics marked out relationships by describing their mutual affection. They also signaled bonds by indicating their shared theology. When Theodoret conversed with other clerics, the "colophon of unity," he claimed, was "harmony of faith."[26]

But how could clerics know if they shared doctrine? Nothing was automatic; orthodoxy, like affection, had to be performed.[27] To signal shared faith, Late Roman clerics turned to doctrinal cues, both theological terms and less obvious turns of phrase. Doctrinal signals were riskier than signals of emotion; they could cause serious offense. But it was these cues that enabled bishops to find kindred spirits in orthodoxy.

It may seem odd to deal with theological doctrine as a matter of verbal cues. Most doctrinal specialists have looked for ancient theological systems, or "schools." In the case of "Antiochene" doctrine, scholars have noted at least four common markers found in the ancient texts: claims to offer "literal, historical" exegesis,[28] disdain for "allegory,"[29] efforts to match Old Testament "types" to New Testament "realities,"[30] and the recognition of two "voices," or "natures" (human and divine) in one "person" of Christ.[31] Scholars vigorously debate the meaning of these markers and their cultural roots.[32] Many have pondered whether these terms accurately describe what the authors were doing—just because a text claims that it interprets Scripture "literally" does not mean modern readers must agree. Some scholars have set Antiochene teachings in a broader context and questioned what, if anything, made them distinctly Antiochene.[33] Nearly every scholar in these debates, however, has treated the terminological markers as indicators of deeper religious thinking.

Searching for doctrinal thinking has both advantages and shortcomings. It works best when scholars do close readings of particular works and authors. Scholars have agreed with ancient writers that language could never adequately express theology.[34] Successful studies find not just surface words and images but underlying narratives and assumptions. The quest for "doctrinal thought" is less helpful when it comes to communities. Even intimate groups must share thoughts through gesture and language.

For the moment, then, let us set aside debates over the deeper meaning of terms such as "literal, historical" and "natures" (we shall return to them in later chapters). In order to explore the social dynamics of shared faith, let us instead treat doctrine as systems of symbolic communication. Such systems may include explicit verbal tropes, whether theological terms or analogies. They may also include references, watchwords, or generalities, with hidden connotations. Doctrinal meanings can even be encoded in non-verbal cues.[35] People may share doctrinal tropes in part, or in full, without sharing the same line of theological thinking. In fact, the more widely a set of terms and images is shared, the more likely interpretations would diverge. Words and symbols may change over time or in different cultural contexts. The main requirement for sharing faith, *on a social level,* is a consistent call and response of recognized cues.

But what were these doctrinal cues and how could they be used? The sharing of faith was complicated; it was easy for signals to be misread or to reveal too much.

Theodoret and his peers acknowledged one Nicene orthodoxy while nurturing various preferences. To bond effectively, clerics had to highlight only their common ground. Thus they conducted a careful ensemble performance. Each cleric read scripts of terms and references—just enough to signal orthodoxy without ruining the image of unity.

One basic source for communicating shared orthodoxy was the agreed set of Nicene terms. By the fifth century all official Eastern Roman clerics professed the Nicene Creed, augmented by the formula "one *ousia*" and "three *hypostases*." They also shared a list of doctrinal heroes, including Basil of Caesarea and Athanasius of Alexandria,[36] as well as a list of heretics, including Arius, Marcion, and Mani.[37] Clerics referred to all of these terms and figures in councils. With hallowed and ambiguous words, they inspired trust, while still allowing for silent interpretation. Clerics also used basic Nicene tropes in letters. For just as excessive details could interfere with true friendship, so they could obscure shared orthodoxy.

Nicene generalities pervaded fifth-century clerical communication. But doctrinal affinity in the midst of controversy often demanded more detail. This study seeks people with "Antiochene" preferences—those who somehow showed the four basic markers noted above (again, whether or not these tropes mark the same line of thought). But what did clerics say in company, or write in letters, to signal Antiochene preferences? As it turns out, we must look beyond the most commonly cited "Antiochene" doctrinal terms.

In fact, use of famous "Antiochene" doctrinal and exegetical markers was limited. Consider the familiar terms of Antiochene exegesis: "literal (*kata tēn lexin*), historical (*kata tēn historian*)," "sequence of thought (*akolouthia*)," and denunciation of "allegory." These phrases do appear in Diodore of Tarsus's fragmentary works and Theodore of Mopsuestia's commentaries.[38] By the 430s, however, Theodoret and his associates employed these words only rarely. Consider also the matching of biblical "types" and "realities." Theodoret made use of these tropes in a variety of works. But his choices here were not distinctive—most Christian writers did similarly.[39]

The technical vocabulary of "Antiochene" dyophysite Christology did find use in doctrinal formulas. But its prevalence in records of the 430s and 440s was sparser than we might expect. In several treatises, Theodoret embraced two "natures" (*physeis*), in one "person" (*prosōpon*). He also defended some of the formulas credited to Theodore of Mopsuestia. Nor was he alone; we see similar statements in several associates' treatises and sermons.[40] In a few letters Theodoret was as explicit, advocating "two natures and a difference between them, and a union without confusion."[41] And yet, more often in correspondence he was reluctant to deploy such specific terms. This reticence seems to have been standard

"Antiochene" practice. When one cleric (Nestorius) went public with dyophysite analysis, Theodoret and his allies advised him to retract his public statements, as Theodore had done before.[42]

Usually, when Theodoret and his allies needed to signal their doctrinal preferences, they turned to watchwords, innocuous to the outsider but meaningful to those in the know. One favorite trope noted the goal of all their doctrinal work: "exactness" (akribeia). This term appears repeatedly in Theodore's treatises and Theodoret's letters.[43] It also appears in conciliar acta. When John of Antioch assembled up to fifty-eight mostly Eastern bishops at the first council of Ephesus, he declared it improper to take any action "before the exact (akribēn) examination and confirmation of the pious faith of the holy and blessed fathers."[44] Another favorite trope urged tolerance of non-experts' theology. Theodoret and his associates touted their "condescension" (synkatabasis) as they accepted some outsiders' ambiguities.[45] Both akribeia and synkatabasis evoked shared doctrinal mastery. Neither risked causing theological offense.

Perhaps the most important Antiochene doctrinal cues were past clerics' names. Most clerics, of course, memorialized doctrinal heroes. Theodoret and his associates praised Diodore of Tarsus and Theodore of Mopsuestia, "the most holy and blessed fathers."[46] When these figures grew controversial, Theodoret took care in public,[47] but internally these names still served as a rallying cry. Clerics also remembered skilled orators and accomplished ascetics. Theodoret's group celebrated both John Chrysostom and Acacius of Beroea. They did so despite the fact that these two men fought bitterly, and showed some "doctrinal thinking" which scholars have not always viewed as Antiochene.[48] Perhaps most importantly, clerics recalled past enemies. Since the 380s, all Nicenes had officially denounced Arius, Eunomius, and Apollinarius.[49] Most fifth-century clerics focused on denouncing the first two. But Theodoret and his allies always included Apollinarius. Sometimes they equated enemies with all three arch-heretics at once.[50] In these names, Theodoret and his allies found a simple but effective code. While seeming to affirm the whole Nicene edifice, they could highlight treasured teachings and favorite villains, and thus a more particular "Antiochene" rapport.

Doctrinal language thus provided idioms for meaningful relationships. Some formulas and names served the whole Nicene church. Others served a smaller troupe—some phrases that explicitly marked Antiochene orthodoxy, and many that merely referred to its precision or its favorite heroes and heels. Theodoret and his allies did not keep to one line of thinking. They preferred slightly different Christological formulas and soteriological narratives, as we shall see.[51] What they shared, however, was important: an insider lingo of specific theological terms and seemingly innocuous cues.

DOCTRINE AND CLERICAL FRIENDSHIP
IN MULTIPLE LANGUAGES

Theodoret's relations with other clerics depended on verbal signals of emotional attachment and shared orthodoxy. The late Roman world, however, spoke more than one language. And despite the presence of bilinguals, linguistic boundaries formed semi-permeable social and cultural barriers. To reach beyond Greek-speakers, Theodoret and his allies made efforts at translation. At some point clerics found equivalents in Aramaic (more precisely, written Syriac), Armenian, and Latin for favored Greek cues. Translations raised the dangers of misunderstanding and hostility, but the promise of more Antiochene allies was apparently worth the risk.

The starting point of cross-linguistic relations was a (partially accepted) linguistic hierarchy. In the fifth-century Roman East, the top spot went to Greek. General councils did business in Greek; regional meetings in Roman Syria did likewise. Syriac/Aramaic, Armenian, and Latin found little use in these settings, despite their centrality to church life elsewhere.[52] Syrian letters were written in multiple languages, but only a few non-Greek specimens from the mid-fifth century survive. Many Syrian clerics were bilingual in Greek and Aramaic, including Theodoret.[53] But only east of the Euphrates did written Syriac play a prominent role in official church discourse. And only in the Persian-Armenian borderlands did Armenian come to the fore. Such linguistic choices reflected old patterns of elite preference. The surprise is that late Roman elites assigned significant value to any languages besides Greek and Latin.[54]

And yet, languages other than Greek had an impact. Language inspired no known separatism. Bilinguals served as social and cultural bridges. But the dynamics of contact were complicated. Writings passed from Greek to Syriac, from Syriac to Greek, and from both to Armenian.[55] Influences varied depending on proximity to channels of contact. Sometimes, residents of Syria treated language as a marker of identity. To Ephrem, Greek may have represented cultured paganism. To Theodoret, Aramaic may have signified semi-barbarian naiveté.[56] Displays of shared language could aid social connections. Equally, linguistic difference could become a barrier. But translation was itself a socio-cultural statement, which altered relations.

For Syrian clergymen, translation played a critical role in building doctrinal alliances. Statements of friendship were not as easy to make across linguistic lines. The connotations of *philia* and *agapē* differed from those of the Syriac *rehmatha* ("love," but linked to "compassion" and "mercy").[57] References to classical Greek concepts (or older Aramaic traditions) might go unrecognized. This made cross-linguistic connections more dependent on shared Christian doctrine. But if doctrinal expression already courted danger, translation heightened it. Stray notes of friendship might annoy a correspondent, but stray notes of theology seemed to risk offending God.

To preserve their sense of shared orthodoxy, Antiochene clerics came to rely on one type of translation: terminological equivalence. They offered symbolic phrases in Syriac and Armenian that they equated to cues in Greek. Translators, of course, chose from several approaches. Early translators in Syria preferred paraphrase so as to accurately convey meaning.[58] At some point in the fifth century, however, we see a transition, especially in East Syrian (i.e., pro-Antiochene) translations, to the search for a precise match for each word. Sometimes this effort involved claiming an existing term in the target language. Sometimes it demanded a neologism or a borrowing (usually from Greek).[59] Either approach raised problems, either stray connotations or unfamiliarity. No equivalence really matched meanings in two languages, and to us, the attempt might seem misguided. But fifth-century clerics judged differently. Even bilingual clerics valued precision, which enabled quick exchanges of social cues. Nicenes not only found Syriac equivalents for *ousia*, *hypostasis* and other theological terms.[60] They eventually sought "word-for-word" translations of Scripture to replace older, idiomatic renderings.[61]

The translation technique of equivalence saw use across the Mediterranean, but Antiochenes found it especially helpful for doctrinal formulas. Thus they chose Syriac equivalents for their favorite Greek terms. For *physis*/"nature" (or *dyo physeis*) the Antiochenes settled on *kyana* (or *tren kyane*), an existing word connected with notions of instinct. Initially, (*hen*) *prosōpon*/"(one) person" became *qnoma* (*had*), the common word for "(one)self." At some point, however, the Antiochenes grew dissatisfied with the connotations of *qnoma* and insisted on an import: *partsopa* (*had*).[62] Other phrases (e.g., "historical") were also rendered into Syriac (in this case, as *be-teshayatha*).[63] Armenian Antiochene works may have featured similar matching, though none have survived.

Again, however, overt doctrinal terms held limited utility. Already risky in Greek, in translation they could be explosive.[64] So Antiochenes found equivalents of their symbolic but inoffensive terms and names. In Syriac, *akribeia* ("exactness") became *hatitutha*, a term with the added sense of "sincerity."[65] *Oikonomia* ("flexibility" or "dispensation") was usually rendered as *mdabranutha* ("leadership").[66] Names proved even more useful, since they virtually sidestepped the translation dilemma. Theodoret and his allies celebrated Syriac authors like Ephrem.[67] More commonly, they championed familiar Greek teachers. Thus clerics in Edessa declared Theodore "the herald of truth" and Acacius "the noble [ascetic] brother in Christ."[68] Most helpful were condemnations of enemies, including Aramaic-speaking arch-heretics, such as Mani, but mostly Greek-speaking foes—Marcion, Arius, Eunomius, and Apollinarius.[69] Long after the Antiochenes' heroes became controversial, hatred of heretics remained.

Thus fifth-century Antiochenes built multilingual relationships via terminological equivalences. The timing and authorship of translated texts is often unclear, but East Syrian records from the 480s show well established matches.[70] In any case, cross-linguistic relations remained risky. Channels of communication were narrower between linguistic communities. Certain individuals played outsized roles in translating social cues.[71] Limited interaction fostered cultural difference. Idioms that spread readily in one language might diffuse more narrowly in others. Social cues, of course, could fail even in a monolingual setting, but translation sharpened contrasts and raised the chance of conflict. It is no coincidence that Theodore's work first inspired hostility on the Greek-Syriac-Armenian frontiers. Nor is it surprising that prominent translators (Mashdotz, Rabbula, and Hiba) engendered controversy.[72] More surprising is the persistence of translators, despite such controversy.

Language differences thus complicated the process of marking friendship and doctrinal alliance, but Antiochene clerics still sought multilingual relations. Linguistic differences also complicate, but do not negate, our attempts to read ancient social cues. Translation required conscious and unconscious choices. In some translated texts, these decisions were made by Antiochene clerics of the mid-fifth century. In others, the choices may have been made by outsiders, and as late as the mid-sixth century.[73] Oddly, it is Latin that presents the largest problem. A large fraction of our conciliar records come from a bilingual sixth-century deacon of Rome (Rusticus), who may have missed some connotations.[74] Still, sometimes the translation has unexpected value. When Rusticus read about the "exactness" of doctrine, he usually chose to transliterate (Latin: *acribia*).[75] Perhaps he did understand how meaningful such words had become.

THE SHORTHAND OF EPISCOPAL INTIMACY

Thus far, this chapter has focused on words and phrases, the basic cues by which Syrian clerics communicated rapport. Real relationships, however, demanded not just scattered symbols, but intricate rhetorical performances, customized to fit the situation. Letters show us some of the process of performing cues. Authors of letters intermixed terms and references. They told jokes and played off rhetorical formulas. Antiochene clerics used their rhetoric to categorize relationships. Thus they offered basic amity to many contacts but reserved "intimate" bonding for a closer circle of friends.

When a bishop like Theodoret wrote to distant connections, he offered a self-consciously formulaic performance of friendship and faith. An example can be found in Theodoret's first extant letter to Proclus, bishop of Constantinople from 434 to 446.

Now we, who reside in tiny and quite isolated small towns, often bear with ill grace that [small town] life, wearied as we are by those who approach us and ask us for some "favor" (*epikourias*). But Your Holiness, who inhabits a city, or rather a whole world that holds an ocean of people and receives flows like rivers from all directions, you exercise your forethought (*promethian*) not only for them, but also for people throughout our world. And if someone needs a letter for something, you set down to write, not in a simple fashion, as if it were [just one] amidst a mob of tasks, nor in some proper or polished manner, nor too precisely. Nay rather all things run together [naturally] in your letter: the beauty of words, the plethora of thoughts, the harmony of composition, and the honor that nourishes those who receive your letters, as well as the most beautiful of all good things, the modesty that blossoms in your words from prudence. On receiving such letters from Your Holiness, we marvel greatly at your apostolic mindset, and we see fit to apply to you that divine saying: "Our heart has been opened wide, there is no restriction in our affections for you" (II Corinthians 6:11–12).[76]

This note was, at base, a standard letter of friendship, following the rhetorical guidelines. Theodoret began with the common experience of patronage. Predictably he praised his correspondent for rhetorical skill. Theodoret wanted cordial relations, he claimed, because of Proclus's "apostolic" values. To prove that he shared such values, he cleverly quoted Paul.[77] By rhetorically involved sentences, Theodoret put his relationship within the broad framework of Christian Roman friendship. He featured his adherence to the formulas for friendly letters, exhibiting shared values while avoiding personal details. All he added was a note of Christian humility. He even suggested the ordinariness of his (hoped-for) connection by his scriptural reference. This safe approach made sense for an early contact between the bishops. As Theodoret and Proclus developed a bond, they could have related in more personalized ways. Actually, Theodoret *continued* to stick to the handbook, through twelve years of letters.[78] Theodoret's letter to Proclus reveals one shorthand for episcopal relations, marking an affectionate, but distant, functional rapport.

When Theodoret turned to regional colleagues, however, he gave a different, ostensibly less formulaic performance. An example of this can be found in one of his letters to Basil of Seleucia in Isauria.

While you carry on your tongue fountains of words, o pious one, claiming thirst you have collected some of our raindrops. It is as if someone said that the river of Egypt has need of a small trickle of water. Now, even a thin moisture [from you] brings me much utility, but to others Your Piety offers [whole] springs. Still, I praise your noble insatiability; for it has as its fruit divine blessing: "For blessed are those who hunger and thirst for justice, since they will have their fill." [Matthew 5:6] It is not easy to recount how much joy I took from your letter. For first you showed me the characteristics of your piety, and you kindled the flame of love. Then, the company of the one who brought it to me made my good state of mind greater. For the most pious fellow priest Domitianus is capable of scattering every sadness and substituting pleasantness in its stead. For he has a character sweeter than honey, and he carries around in him the wealth of the Holy Scriptures. He does not embellish himself with only the outer casing of your letters but uncovers the pearl hidden within them.[79]

To Basil, Theodoret fully demonstrated camaraderie, but the formula for friendship was tweaked in several ways. Here Theodoret employed oblique statements of praise. He began with a mocking accusation, followed by (expected) self-deprecation.[80] He feigned envy. Only then did he praise a shared value (insatiability) and mark it with a (silly) scriptural quotation. Theodoret next turned to personal emotions, such as the joy of rekindled friendship. He concluded by praising the bishops' envoy, personalizing their sense of affection. Theodoret covered similar ground in each letter. But here he operated less obviously, using jocular lines and rhetorical redirections. Most critically, Theodoret acknowledged a deeper context: a history of attachment and longing. This letter showed expectations not just of mutual aid, but of intimacy as well.

Such displays of intimacy pervade Theodoret's letters to many Syrian clerics. Here he found space to recall a shared experience, to make a joke, to play with expectations—to twist the standard epistolary formulas.[81] In context the signal was unmistakable: Theodoret informed some peers that he shared with them a special rapport. This is not a contrast between informal and formal correspondence. All his friendly letters employed templates and selected from the same affectionate terms. Nor is it a difference between reliable and unreliable friendships. While Proclus cooperated with Theodoret despite theological differences, Basil abandoned him in a crisis.[82] The distinction, rather, lies between two sorts of formalized friendliness. With most clerics Theodoret made formulaic style a source of rapport. With close colleagues, he accented standard elements to indicate deeper rapport.

Signals of intimacy thus served as a key social cue for Theodoret and certain colleagues. In fact, he set a tight boundary for these intimate relations. Consider Theodoret's letters to Irenaeus, a reliable ally who went from imperial office (to exile) to the bishopric of Tyre. When Irenaeus was a count, Theodoret offered him cautious notes of affection, filled with formal panegyric.[83] No letters to Irenaeus remain from his first exile (435–mid-440s). But after Irenaeus's ordination, the letters resume with more intimate cues. The transition was not instantaneous—at first Theodoret still praised Irenaeus's virtues. But later on he evoked brotherhood in passing remarks.[84] This transition shows us one key to the signals of intimacy. More than a signal of affection or alliance, Theodoret's relational shorthand distinguished a special fellowship, among some bishops and (as we shall see) a few other people.

In fact, it is this shorthand of intimacy that most reliably marks meaningful bonds among Syrian clergymen. *Philia* and *agapē* described feelings of affection. "Exactness," and "flexibility" coded for special orthodoxy. Equivalences carried cues across linguistic bounds. Any of these social idioms could signal a relationship. When a near full set of cues is traded, that indicates an Antiochene connection. But these shorthands go further, by showing how the cues could be combined in tighter, multiplex bonds. Theodoret had a close circle in which he traded signals of intimacy. Here his words stood for everything (friendship, doctrine, religious rank, experience) that the bishops shared. There was nothing particularly Syrian or "Antiochene" about expressing intimate bonds. Theodoret himself had a few intimate friends with different doctrinal preferences, or even non-Christian views.[85] But from a subset of bishops from Isauria to the Tigris, we see signals of deeper affection in virtually every mutual letter. Between basic and intimate modes of friendship lay a palpable boundary. When signs of intimacy were replaced with bare formulas, the bishops expressed pain.[86] Thus shorthands of intimacy served as a "colophon of unity" for the core Antiochene network.

RITUALS OF HARMONY: EPISCOPAL
VISITS AND COUNCILS

Verbal cues play an essential role in most human relations. They are, however, always enriched by equally symbolic practices. Weekly liturgies, festivals, collections, and distributions all lent context to words of clerical attachment. Two sets of practices require special attention. One concerns the conveyance and reception of letters (see below, this chapter). The other involves visits and councils, for such face-to-face meetings provided visible demonstration of an otherwise virtual community.

For all the interactions among Syrian clerics, nothing matched the intensity of church councils. Metropolitan bishops were supposed to hold provincial synods twice a year—just before Pentecost and in mid-October.[87] Regional councils convened less frequently, except during periods of controversy. Thus the years 430–436 featured a full cycle of Syrian synods.[88] Councils served doctrinal and administrative purposes. They affirmed orthodoxy and judged clerical improprieties. They also served overt social purposes. Simultaneous expressions of cordiality created a group dynamic that bishops could remember in times of isolation. In both doctrinal and social terms, attendance meant inclusion. It presented delegates with a map of accessible peer relationships. And it enabled them to stand together, before their subordinates.

Councils such as these were ritual performances.[89] They followed a standard order of activity. They began with doctrinal agreement, an "exact examination and confirmation of the Apostolic faith," followed by recognition of past orthodox fathers. Only then would the bishops hear accusations, take testimony, or examine finances.[90] Proceedings functioned by set hierarchy. The ranking metropolitan presided (and repeatedly interjected), while a full scoring of primacy determined the order of speaking.[91] Councils then pursued clerical harmony. Recent studies of councils have pondered the presence or absence of real debate.[92] Syrian records reveal serious deliberations, though not in official session.[93] But the goal was not to weigh competing positions. According to the *Apostolic Constitutions*, bishops were supposed to act "in unanimity, like the heavenly hosts."[94] Bishops might start with disagreements but had to end with acclamations. Judgments were not foreordained; even a suffragan like Theodoret could influence proceedings. But the general storyline was well understood. Those who could not join the acclamations almost always chose not to attend.[95]

At the heart of these conciliar performances lay a recitation of accepted doctrine. Councils were a poor setting for detailed expositions of faith. The number of attendees (so close in stature) brought dangers of disagreement. Syrian bishops had differences but were loath to raise them in session, if it would challenge the display of concord.[96] What councils provided was affirmation of doctrinal scripting. Key names and phrases, worked out elsewhere, were acclaimed by a council and thus transformed.[97] Thereafter the phrases recalled not just theology, but the experience of concord. Disagreeing bishops could skip councils, but then they distanced themselves from the harmonious ensemble.

Councils thus offered bishops a charged experience of contact. So did visits to nearby sees. During active conflicts, doctrinal consultations were often held in person. In calmer times bishops shared preaching, festivities, and administrative advice. Theodoret met regularly with the bishop of Antioch, and he visited Germanicea, Zeugma, and Apamea.[98] When his itinerary of travels became evidence of meddling, Theodoret could not deny them; all he could do was call such journeys normal.[99]

Whatever the main business, visits followed their own performative mode. They began with a ceremonious protocol. One Syriac source describes a welcoming ritual of torchlight parades and acclamations, reminiscent of an imperial *adventus*.[100] From there, bishops shared liturgical duties or even preaching.[101] All along they traded traditional gestures of hospitality (e.g., meal sharing).[102] Actual consultation required a less public setting, but rituals still framed the social interaction. They enabled bishops to show not just affection but mutual trust, particularly in terms of orthodoxy. They helped each bishop to aggrandize the other, more than each could aggrandize himself.

Both councils and visits contributed to the communication that cemented Theodoret's clerical network. Face-to-face interactions featured non-verbal elements of social performance. They invested linguistic tropes with greater significance, for they bound key phrases to experiences of mutual affirmation. Theodoret so valued face-to-face contact that when he missed a meeting, he expressed anguish. "I had hoped ... to give you the thinnest piece of honor that I owe," he wrote to a neighboring bishop, "to pass a few days [with you] and convey all that is due to you of fatherly affection." Having failed to connect he was "deprived of everything."[103] Such meetings remained infrequent, but rarity gave these performances their power. Under certain conditions personal contact itself became the definitive symbol of inclusion. As doctrinal tensions cut into relations, nothing marked a breach like the refusal of a visiting colleague, and nothing healed that breach like a personal embrace.[104]

PORTRAITS OF CAMARADERIE: CLERICAL PRACTICES OF LETTER WRITING

Visits and councils visibly demonstrated Syrian clerical relations. Most social interaction, though, still relied on written letters. And practices of letter exchange involved more than doctrinal codes and signals of intimacy. Individual letters had a rich symbolic life. Reciprocity guided their production. Stylistic expectations shaped their form. Meanings accrued over time, as letters were collected and reread. Letters not only communicated rapport; thanks to certain practices, they depicted it for ages to come.

All late Roman correspondence was governed by detailed expectations,[105] while Antiochenes set some special requirements. Theodoret and his allies were supposed to write several times a year, to keep a connection active. Moreover, in letters to each other, they were supposed to reply, to show friendship as reciprocal. Theodoret could be nonchalant with distant colleagues about frequency of contact; "Even if we have not received letters," he once wrote, "we still constantly delight in your praises."[106] He was less lenient within his own circle: when monks from a nearby diocese arrived carrying no letter from the bishop, Theodoret gave his colleague a rebuke.[107] Often bishops set expectations of contact higher than they could meet. Even in prolific exchanges they lamented not having written more often.[108] The sentiment was not mere contrivance. High frequency and higher expectation gave clerical relations a tension, which could only be broken by sending new letters.

Special expectations surrounded correspondence during festivals, particularly Easter. At these times bishops sent clerics and lay patrons short, cordial notes, called "festals." Scholars have generally ignored Syrian festals, since most follow a basic formula of just a few lines.[109] The Syrian notes seem meager compared to the thousand-line festals by bishops of Alexandria. Alexandrian festals provide specific advice for holiday preparation and preaching.[110] Syrian festals vaguely muse on seasonal "spiritual blessings" and the promise of salvation.[111] This comparison, however, is misleading. Syrian festals constitute a distinct genre. According to Theodoret, they were written to show that "every city, village, field, and frontier is filled with divine grace."[112] More to the point, these notes served specific social purposes.

Syrian festal letters provided tangible mementos of Christian community. Their short form communicated the safest sentiments, which any Christian could share. Their significance rose because of their timing. During Easter (or other major festivals) they showcased the breadth of simultaneous worship. At the same time, festals worked within particular relationships. General sentiments were received as objects, symbolizing the barest connections at the bishops' disposal. Thus the letters had to be short and formulaic. They had to present the author and occasion in a warm light. They had to evoke consensus of faith with no limiting specifics. Alexandrian festals resemble grand homilies from on high. Syrian festals resemble greeting cards.[113] But greeting cards were what met the need to demonstrate inclusion.

In addition to festals, clerics of Syria wrote many kinds of letters that served social ends. Several extant letters addressed whole monasteries or congregations. These epistles instructed recipients in doctrine or admonished them for moral failings. Other letters went to individuals, and while some requested practical cooperation, many asked only for friendship. Letters could be traded rapidly. The bishops sometimes wrote about such slight changes that their words only make sense amid a continuous exchange.[114] But this does not mean letters were quotidian. Theodoret once called correspondence the "adorable treasure of the fruits of love."[115] Like festals, personal letters gained significance because they displayed camaraderie.

Within particular relationships bishops' letters served as artifacts of emotional bonding. Bishops valued letters as individual objects. Letter exchange faced limitations, such as a shortage of materials or lack of envoys.[116] More important, it faced distance. Bishops formed a brotherhood of rank separated for most of the year. Each letter served as a window through that separation. Its arrival released feelings of affinity, which lingered as the object was saved. The bishops valued letters even more for their place in collections. By keeping copies of what was sent and received, they recorded their relations.[117] They then arranged archives—a whole social history.[118] The basic practices of collection rarely required comment. Only at the peak of doctrinal crisis did a colleague of Theodoret's cite his scrutiny of past letters.[119] But expectations shaped each letter. Correspondents wrote not just to send information, but also to create portraits of themselves, their relationships, and their network.

Letters thus led a rich private life within clerical relationships. They also led a public life by reaching secondary audiences. Bishops expected that their letters would be read aloud. Synesius of Cyrene once gave directions on how to read his letter properly.[120] Letters also reached new audiences through recopying. Syrian bishops requested copies of letters and sent copies unsolicited.[121] Generally the bishops did not regard copying or public reading as a breach of privacy. They assumed such sharing as they composed text. In fact, some letters appear to have grown in value with the number of hands touching them, since they showed broader camaraderie.[122]

Customs of collection and republication help to explain a puzzling aspect of late Roman letters: the use of handbook formulas. Rhetoricians offered templates for letter writing to fulfill dozens of social functions. Some scholars have treated these templates as limitations, which hindered honest communication.[123] But clerics *chose* to use handbook formulas that fit with their practices and goals. If bishops knew that letters were to be saved, they would tend to select representations of pure "character" over ephemeral details. If they knew they wrote for edited collections, they would work to show the development of rapport. If they anticipated wider audiences, they would exclude damaging intimations. Handbooks helped correspondents to create galleries of social bonds. In some ways letters did this more effectively than visits, since in correspondence the bishops could shed petty concerns and become better selves.

In any case, the rhetorical structure of letters did little to prevent Syrian bishops from trading gossip. The bishops tended to inquire about social shifts obliquely. When one bishop heard rumors of a personal tiff between his colleagues, he claimed that he would have refused to believe it, but for the trustworthiness of his source.[124] Sometimes the clerics accused each other directly, but they often refused to mention names.[125] This practice of reticence still allowed rumors to spread, but it channeled the rumors to preserve displays of camaraderie. In fact, some gossip mongering could reinforce the picture of cordiality, by reminding the bishops of just how close they stood.

From epistolary practices such as these, letters gained a significance beyond the written words. Letters still enabled necessary communication. If the formulas proved inadequate (such as during doctrinal negotiations) Theodoret and his colleagues set them aside. But even detailed doctrinal letters assumed certain customs of composition, reception, and republication.[126] And letters always furnished a basic social cue. Traded papyrus signaled reciprocal friendship; missing papyrus signaled a breach.[127]

ENVOYS, SURVEILLANCE, AND THE STAGING
OF CLERICAL RELATIONS

Customs of composition and collection thus shaped clerics' practice of letter exchange. So did customs of transmission. One of the most common features of Theodoret's letters was praise for letter bearers. Such recommendations could take just a few words, citing an envoy for his "kindness" and his "good, noble character."[128] Or the references could fill multiple lines. "I acquired an experience of his manners and the congregation had the benefit of his speaking," Theodoret said of one priest. Even though he "casts off but a few raindrops and leaves us thirsty ... it was a joy for me that he could be a procurer of the letters sent by Your Piety."[129] These recommendations are easy to ignore. As Theodoret noted to Proclus, bishops were hounded for a few kind words.[130] Envoys, however, contributed heavily to clerical communication. Beyond carrying letters, they served as an extra verbal channel, a responsive audience, an observant eye, and a helping hand. Symbolically, they became extensions of the bishops themselves.

Theodoret's recommendations reveal a functional context for the exchange of letters: the steady stream of traveling personnel. The *Apostolic Constitutions* demanded that bishops welcome authentic nonlocal clerics.[131] Since most envoys were clerical subordinates, recommendations authenticated them. Envoys might stay for several days, until the bishop could pen a reply. Or they might stay longer to assume regular duties.[132] Bishops used this exchange of clerics to share labor. Skilled orators and artisans were rare enough to be needed by several dioceses.[133] But the trading of personnel also served symbolic ends. Traveling envoys required greetings and farewells—the constant display of Christian hospitality. And a shared labor force reminded bishops of their ecclesiological ideal, the communal Christian life.

Beyond shared labor, the exchange of envoys played an expansive role in communication. Of course, envoys served as postmen. Eloquent letters were useless unless properly delivered. Unreliable couriers might leak information or alter written works. Without trustworthy couriers, bishops might not even read the letters that they received, for nothing differentiated those letters from forgeries.

Trusted envoys, however, did more than deliver letters; they often augmented what was written. For reasons of aesthetics and discretion, bishops preferred to keep certain details out of the text.[134] Envoys could then explain points only hinted at in writing. The presence of an envoy corroborating the text and a text backing up the envoy made communication more persuasive. Theodoret ended one letter to an ally with a vague imperative: "Persuade him who is able to give it to grant our request." If his colleague could not recall previous discussions, a trusted deacon was present to fill in the specifics.[135] The more sensitive the matter, the more bishops needed a dependable courier. For doctrinal negotiations, Theodoret and his colleagues relied not on priests, but on imperial tribunes and allied bishops.[136] This bathed the enterprise in statements of mutual respect and kept the record free of inconvenient details.

Not every relationship required so much discretion. But even ordinary contacts relied on both writing and oral supplements. Bishops wrote letters in various modes, from detailed appeals to unadorned recommendations. The choice of style was partly a matter of sensibility. As Synesius put it, "lengthiness in a letter argues for a lack of intimacy with the one conveying the letter." Nevertheless, as he then noted, sometimes this principle had to be set aside.[137] Among Syrian clerics, there were conventions. Theodoret once gave a priest this vague primer: "I salute your piety, using as a go-between for written letters the man who had brought us the unwritten words which you expressed concerning us. When you receive the letter, o pious one, send me writing for writing."[138] Some messages, it seems, could be sent orally, but others demanded writing. Most of Theodoret's letters imply some oral exegesis, the type and amount varying with the situation. In any case, both writing and supplementation served as key social signals.

Beyond oral supplements envoys augmented correspondence by setting the scene for the performance of social bonding. Whether or not they added words, envoys took part in letter reception, interacting with doormen, secretaries, and correspondents. Envoys served as authorial stand-ins, reference points for written messages and the emotions they inspired. Theodoret praised couriers as effusively as he praised colleagues. When celebrating these letter bearers, he linked the written words to their persons: "For the way we saw [the envoy Damian] is how you intimated in your letters."[139] Theodoret's praises were more than recommendations. Personal contact, even through a third party, felt closer to the clerics than any written letter.[140]

Envoys also served a less prestigious role in letter reception: scapegoat. If communication failed or proved offensive, bishops' friendships were at risk. But they could avoid severing contact if they blamed a faulty courier. Scapegoating played an essential role in sensitive doctrinal negotiations. Bishops unhappy at the results of a colloquy blamed envoys before blaming the negotiating leaders.[141] But even in lighter matters (like a botched travel schedule) Theodoret sometimes blamed his subordinates.[142] Envoys might symbolize the joy of epistolary friendship, but they remained available as instruments of expiation.

While envoys were treated as passive symbols in epistolary relations, they also had active duties, in the form of surveillance. Traveling couriers were able to observe ecclesiastical operations up and down the clerical ladder. Since most couriers worked for individual bishops, they were no doubt expected to report what they had heard and seen. Usually bishops were loath to acknowledge spying, which challenged bishops' traditional local prerogative. But they hinted at the state of mutual observation. Tellingly, Theodoret referred to clerics as *proxenoi* of other bishops. On the surface this meant "securers of benefit," but for an educated Roman, it carried classical connotations of "agent for a foreign power."[143] The implied analogy proves apt for periods of controversy, when agents started riots or reported to foes.[144] But even in calmer times, the social results were dramatic. Theodoret knew about problems in neighboring sees; so did some of his colleagues. Occasionally they used that knowledge to meddle with subordinates.[145] Clerical spying was common enough that it made a certain amount of intimacy involuntary. Acknowledged or not, surveillance actually tightened relations.

Through all their activities, envoys turned clerical communication into staged social performances. When letters arrived the envoys served as script readers and exegetes. They also served as the audience for bishops acting out their affections. For us letter writing may conjure up images of isolation. In the fifth century, the process was thoroughly social. Letters and envoys formed part of a larger theatrical system, where verbal messages were enhanced by observed actions and reported reactions.

ASSUMED AFFECTION: ANTIOCHENE
NETWORK AND COMMUNITY

This chapter has focused on the social interactions of the fifth-century Syrian clergy. Letters and conciliar documents feature expressions of affection and signals of shared orthodoxy. These cues served as elements of the rhetorical performances that Theodoret traded with his core allies. Letters and *acta* also reveal customs of clerical communication. Rituals of assembly and visitation, practices of letter writing and collection, and patterns of personnel exchange facilitated written and oral cues. Taken together these expressions and practices define a social experience that we may label "Antiochene." But how do we know that these social cues meant something to Theodoret and his associates? From a modern vantage point we cannot be certain. Nevertheless, the combination of practices and cues points toward a distinct network of relationships, and to an informal but palpable Antiochene community.

For starters, the social cues and customs noted in this chapter constitute more than a random set. Other clerics, of course, traded expressions of affection. Distant bishops still might share Nicene formulas, or even dyophysite terms.[146] Nothing about conciliar customs or epistolary practices was uniquely Syrian. Yet it is striking how all of these cues and practices run together in the records. We have seen how Theodoret mixed declarations of friendship with exclamations of "harmony of faith." We have also seen how his signals of intimacy hinted at past cooperation. Several key terms and symbols that appear in letters also arise in statements in the conciliar *acta*. All these verbal cues were then reinforced by the practices of record keeping and epistolary collection. Singular cues might be used in any clerical relationship. Nevertheless, this precise combination of tropes is unlikely to be found outside the Antiochene fold.

Antiochene social cues thus form a distinctive set. They also appear in a distinctive context: the clergy of one region. Theodoret traded notes of friendship with a range of colleagues. But almost all of his expressions of intimacy went to fellow Syrian clerics, Theodoret and his colleagues did not always employ every cue. But over time, the same set of clergymen employed overlapping subsets.

The set of social signals can thus be taken to indicate a distinguishable, regional network. But did this network form a meaningful community? Here the indications are less conclusive. Not all networks are formalized. Not all groups set clear boundaries. Some networks foster public identities; others remain private or unacknowledged. Theodoret and his peers were proud members of the Nicene clergy but claimed no party label. They only spoke of "like-minded bishops" at the height of controversy.[147]

And yet, the communication parameters of this network imply some communal sensibility. Even disorganized networks have figures of influence and gradual boundaries. Even unacknowledged networks create a sense of connection—a scene in which mutual affection is assumed. Within our extant records, some clerics were called orthodox based on a few names and coded phrases. Some colleagues were drafted for cooperative tasks with just a few kind words. Social cues went beyond the niceties of Christian brotherhood. And Theodoret expressed pain when these cues were removed. When Theodoret praised Acacius of Beroea in the *History of the Friends of God,* he was writing for a wide audience. But he knew that his work would be read first by close associates. Therein they would find deeper social messages that only they would understand.

2

———

Shape of a Network

Antiochene Relational Patterns

It was probably in 433 that Andreas of Samosata realized the full social cost of participating in doctrinal conflict. For three years this bishop had contributed to the debates. He wrote insistently against Cyril's *Twelve Anathemas against Nestorius.* Despite missing the council of Ephesus, he joined his colleagues' excommunication of the Egyptians. Meanwhile, he maintained key Syrian alliances, especially with Alexander of Hierapolis, John of Antioch, and Theodoret.[1] By late 432, it was clear that this trio was going to split. Alexander, John, and Theodoret argued over negotiating positions, while Andreas did shuttle diplomacy. He meddled enough to offend all three allies, and a neighbor who tried to oust him.[2] Still, Andreas pressed for reconciliations, with John and then Theodoret. Through them he won support from certain imperial officials, and he rebuilt links to bishops, lower clerics, and lay notables.[3] But Alexander refused to restore relations. "Consider the power of God," Andreas begged, "who reconciled... the heavens and the earth, who may join the divided limbs of the church, and who will give satisfaction to Your Holiness." It was to no avail. By 436, Andreas had settled into the core of his doctrinal network, but Alexander had been sent to the mines.[4]

The efforts of Andreas showcase the specific social context in which Syrian bishops worked and communicated. Andreas, like his colleagues, was enveloped by relationships. Belief and behavior depended on ephemeral arrangements of bonds. The pursuit of orthodox doctrine mattered to Antiochene bishops. But it was not abstractions that motivated Andreas to mediate; it was the pull of personal affections.

This second chapter is devoted to tracing out the Antiochene coalition in which Andreas and Theodoret were embedded. The exchange of social cues, noted in the first chapter, can be mapped, synchronically, to approximate an Antiochene network, as it was circa 436. This network map can then be analyzed and compared to scholarly models. The analysis offered here has limitations. It is constrained by the evidence, which is, at best, valid for a brief period of time. Network analysis, however, can help us to make sense of the social data, to contextualize individuals' actions (explored in subsequent chapters).

In fact, mapping the Antiochene coalition reveals some recognizable patterns. The mostly clerical network featured central hubs surrounded by a loose periphery, in a shape known to network analysts as the modular scale-free topology. This shape is hardly unusual; any group that recruits freely tends toward the same basic template. More noteworthy is the specific arrangement of Antiochene social links. At the center we find a tight clique of four bishops and one lay notable. On the periphery we find members stretched unevenly across Syria. These features prove little on their own, but they do furnish hypotheses, which can be tested against other evidence. The core structure suggests an informal but palpable order of leadership. The periphery suggests a group that, while claiming to represent the East, left room for opponents to arise.

METHODS FOR MAPPING ANTIOCHENE RELATIONS

We begin the mapping process with some methodology. Letters and conciliar transcripts record thousands of social interactions, interpersonal and collective. Mapping a network requires us to figure out which interactions signal meaningful relationships, and to decide which relationshps were "Antiochene." Any system of classification imposes on the evidence. Still, we must choose how to arrange the data and how to set thresholds for identifying a bond.

The first step to prepare for network analysis is to organize the social information. The simplest method would be to classify subjects by ecclesiastical rank: bishops, lower clerics, monks, and laypeople. This taxonomy fits with surviving church records, which understandably focus on bishops. It also fits with the institutional structure of the late Roman church. Lower clerics, monastic leaders, and lay figures all played roles in these disputes (as did the emperor). But it was bishops who laid claim to ritual and doctrinal authority—at least in sources that they controlled. Thus, this chapter will work in layers, expanding from purely episcopal interactions to bishops' dealings with lower clerics and monks, then to their contacts with laypeople.

Next, mapping social relations requires criteria for identifying personal bonds. Here we turn to the sorts of cues outlined in the first chapter. Nearly every extant letter features some nod to emotional attachment. Most include signals of shared orthodoxy. Individual instances of cue-giving tell us little about relationships. But the exchange of multiple cues and the recalling of past interactions do suggest an intersubjective bond. Throughout this process, we must remember the incompleteness of our evidence. A lack of cue-giving between people does not prove that a link did not exist. Nevertheless, by combining *all the signals sent within six years of 436*, we can get an approximation of this one portion of the late Roman social fabric.

Finally, mapping the Antiochene network demands a test for distinguishing internal from external bonds. Here we must make a stronger interpretive intervention. The previous chapter noted an "Antiochene" set of cues, including terms of emotional attachment (such as *philia* and *agapē*), doctrinal watchwords (such as "exactness," "Apollinarian" and "two natures"), oblique signals of intimacy, and modes of translation. Chapter 1 also noted an "Antiochene" set of practices, including communal rituals (during visits and councils), epistolary habits (during composition and collection), mutual recommendation, and even surveillance. (Please note, it is the *set*, not the individual cues, which are labeled as Antiochene). So, for purposes of drawing a map, let us set a reasonable threshold for inclusion. *For a relationship to be considered Antiochene, a sender and recipient must share* (that is, either personally exchange, collaboratively produce, or recall past instances when they exchanged or co-produced) *at least three different cues or habits* out of those listed in the first chapter, on more than one occasion, *including at least one specifically doctrinal cue.*

We could go further with this approach. We could grade bonds on the basis of numbers of attested interactions. We could also mark links that show special "intimacy" or distinguish personal contacts from communal ones. Occasionally this study will refer to such distinctions. For the sake of simplicity, they will not be visually represented.

A NETWORK OF BISHOPS

With interpretive methods set, we may now map and analyze the first layer of our network, relations among bishops. From the perspective of our sources, at least, bishops formed the backbone of the Antiochene network. Nearly all Nicene bishops could claim some official friendship and shared orthodoxy. Of the approximately six hundred letters in our archives, just over half were sent by bishops to other bishops. The communications, however, tend to involve a few repeated names. When sifted via the methods just mentioned, these records showcase a small core of noted Antiochenes reaching out to a regionally limited network.

Studying episcopal contacts involves the largest set of social data, and thus the fullest analytical process. We start with some prosopography, which comes mostly from conciliar *acta*. Records of the First Council of Ephesus in 431 list about 250 prelates, about 30 from between the Taurus mountains and the Sea of Galilee.[5] Regional and provincial councils in Syria add 24 more. The *Acts of the Second*

Council of Ephesus in 449 name at least 135 bishops, with just 22 from Syria.[6] But the list from Chalcedon (in 451) of more than 500 bishops includes about 128 Syrians.[7] Together, these *acta* trace the succession of bishops for hundreds of towns in the 430s and 440s, including about 50 Syrian sees.[8] Next we must identify the social links recorded in our archives. Here the conciliar documents and the personal letters each provide a set of data, which can be explored separately before the full pool is assembled. We start with the simpler of the two data sets, from Theodoret's collected correspondence.[9]

Theodoret's personal letter collection showcases two key features of Antiochene relations. On the one hand, it traces network links with a regional focus. Theodoret's friendly letters went to bishops in Anatolia, the Balkans, Constantinople, and Egypt. A few went to Persia and the city of Rome.[10] Relations that meet "Antiochene" criteria, however, fall almost entirely within the region of Syria. It was only with Syrians that Theodoret both acknowledged past exchanges of key signals and offered new cues. On the other hand, Theodoret's collection locates "intimate" bonds within a tighter area. The fullest sets of Antiochene social signals connect Theodoret with a handful of his neighboring peers. This collection is, of course, centered on one correspondent. It tells us little about the links among Theodoret's contacts. But we can compare its basic features to the larger data set from conciliar records (especially from Ireneaus's *Tragedy*).

In fact, conciliar letters and transcripts reinforce the impressions of Theodoret's correspondence. A few bishops (including Theodoret) are shown to have connections across the Mediterranean.[11] But for "Antiochene" bonds, the picture again centers on one region. Just six non-Syrian bishops gave or received Antiochene cues—and by 436 none of them still held a see. Meanwhile, the richest exchanges involve a small group of bishops. Theodoret's list of "intimate" contacts is slightly augmented by the conciliar documents. More importantly, these contacts are shown to form interlocking clusters. Conciliar records focus on several individuals. Still, they echo the basic pattern of Theodoret's collection: a network focused on Syria, with a smaller, densely woven core.

These two archives combine with other sources[12] to approximate an Antiochene episcopal network. Forty bishops meet our standards for attachment to this network; 34 of them had sees in Syria, and 30 (all Syrians) were running bishoprics in 436 (see figure 2). The network is dense (boasting 57 links and an overall density of 0.131). It is also tight (with an average path distance, or degree, of about three links). Areas of higher density alternate with "holes," which create a number of cliques and clusters. Individual members cut a range in terms of their connectivity. The majority had 1–3 links; several bishops had 4–5 links, with higher numbers of bonds reached by four prelates. These men (Acacius of Beroea, John of Antioch, Andreas, and Theodoret) are not only the most well connected members, but also the most central, with quickest access to the rest. Thus we can discern a shape to

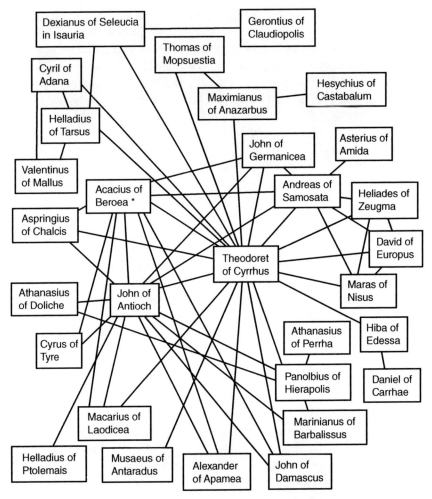

FIGURE 2. The Antiochene episcopal network, circa 436, according to letters and conciliar documents. Links approximate evident or implied exchange of 3 or more Antiochene social cues (including at least one doctrinal cue) within 7 years of 436 (more links may have existed).

Network statistics: nodes = 30, links = 58, density = 0.133, diameter = 4. Connectivity: Theodoret = 19, John of Antioch = 13, Acacius = 9, Andreas = 8, all others = 5 or fewer. Centrality: Theodoret = 39, John of Antioch = 43, Acacius = 50, Andreas = 55, all others = 60 or higher.

* Acacius of Beroea's death is here assumed to date to 437. See start of chapter 1.

the core members of this network, with an unambiguous center and a set of clusters leading outward to the periphery.

The basic shape of this network holds even if we speculate about links that the evidence may leave out. Records and methods are focused on the core membership. They have assuredly missed relationships and people, especially on the periphery. It is likely, for instance, that metropolitans (such as Helladius of Tarsus and Maximianus of Anazarbus) had links to additional bishops in their provinces. It is probable that central figures had further connections. Missing links might actually bridge some of the gaps that appear between cliques, or they might reveal whole new clusters that are barely attatched. But our map does make for a valid approximation, so long as our focus is the core itself. The smattering of missing figures is not likely to perturb the main pattern of relations surrounding the hubs.

The shape of this network matters because it conforms to a known relational architecture: the *modular scale-free topology*.[13] "Modular" refers to the clustering of members. "Scale-free" refers to the distribution of connectivity, with many ill-connected members and a few "hubs." Modular scale-free networks have certain properties. The structure allows for rapid communication, growth without central direction, and persistence despite localized losses. As we shall see, the modular scale-free pattern makes suggestions about the dynamics of network leadership and membership. Before we analyze further, however, we need to include other figures who joined in the network.

PARTICIPATION OF OTHER CLERICS AND ASCETICS

Surviving sources trace an Antiochene network centered on bishops, but these bishops were never alone. Their social position was defined, in part, by their relations with lower clerics (especially priests, deacons, deaconesses, country bishops, and *oikonomoi*) and monastic leaders (many of whom were also ordained). Just over one-eighth of the extant letters were addressed to lower clerics or ascetics. This count does not include clerics who served as envoys. Nor does it capture the constant interactions of bishops with their subordinates in liturgical, charitable, and personal settings. Our records cannot support a full network analysis of the Syrian clergy. But they do spotlight some additions to the Antiochene party. On the periphery they reveal a large pool of clergymen and monks; at the core they illuminate a few of the bishops' favorites.

Our treatment of broader clerical links must proceed differently from coverage of bishops because it starts from thinner prosopography. Syria's clergy included thousands of people—a hundred or more in each major city.[14] Quasi-normative sources list duties for each rank of the clergy, as well as for archimandrites, monks, and semi-ascetics (e.g., "covenanters").[15] Surviving documents, however, name just a few clerics and leading ascetics, not even one-hundredth of the likely total.

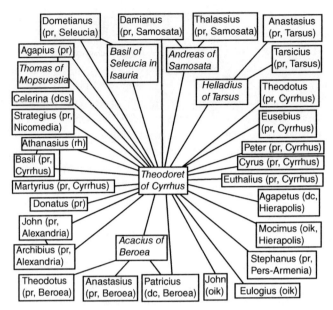

FIGURE 3. Subordinate clerics in the Antiochene network, circa 436, according to letters and conciliar documents. Links approximate evident or implied exchange of at least 1 Antiochene social cue within 7 years of 436 (more links may have existed). dc = deacon, dcs = deaconess, exm = exarch of the monasteries, oik = oikonomos, pr = priest, rh = orator.

What data do exist mostly come from Theodoret's collection. They cannot support conclusions about the region's clergy. But they do showcase where some priests and monks fit in the network.

Letters and *acta* reveal select clerics in significant Antiochene roles. Some of Theodoret's letters addressed priests like Agapius, engaged in tasks of recruitment.[16] Other letters gave clerics special missions; the *oikonomos* Mocimus, for instance, was asked to persuade his bishop (Alexander) to change positions in a dispute.[17] Many clerics only appear as couriers, but these envoys receive more signals of intimate friendship than almost anyone else.[18] Records place at least 23 clerics in an Antiochene relationship with Theodoret circa 436, (2 deacons, 1 deaconess, 3 *oikonomoi*, 15 priests, and a church orator). A few others are linked in similar fashion to other bishops (see figure 3). These clerics never rivaled bishops in numbers of links, but often they linked key members to one another, giving them some centrality.

The records offer a slightly different picture for inclusion of ascetics. Several archimandrites received attention from Theodoret, most in Syrian communities. Generally the letters signaled support; a few asked for specific cooperation.[19] Con-

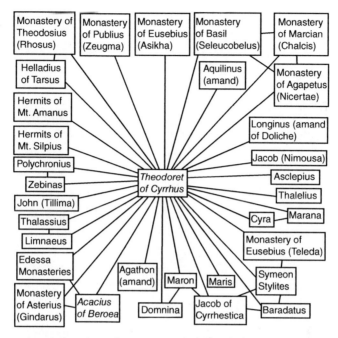

FIGURE 4. Ascetics and monasteries in the Antiochene network, circa 436, according to letters, the *HR*, and conciliar documents. Links approximate evident or implied exchange of at least 1 Antiochene social cue within 7 years of 436 (more links may have existed). amand = archimandrite.

ciliar documents augment the picture: three famous ascetics, Baradatus, Jacob of Cyrrhestica, and Symeon Stylites, were asked to mediate in multiple episodes of church conflict.[20] Hagiography also adds information. Theodoret's *History of the Friends of God* records 7 monasteries and 14 clusters of hermits with whom he had a relationship (see figure 4). The purpose of these connections is not instantly clear, but two quick possibilities arise: mobilization for charity or public protest, and recruitment to the priesthood and episcopate. Both possibilities find indirect support (see below, chapters 3 and 4). In any case, select monastic leaders won inclusion as mediating agents in the bishops' network.

Clerics and ascetics thus fill out the Antiochene social map, without altering its basic shape. Yet we must realize that the clerics and monks named in our records are not the rank and file on regular duty. Theodoret and his peers sometimes addressed groups of clerics and monks. They sent guidelines for doctrinal instruction and exhortations to "take greater care" of the flock.[21] But just one cleric is noted for service in the liturgy.[22] Just one monk is recorded as aiding in pastoral care.[23] No clerics are singled out for their management of finances or charity. The prayers of clerics and monks were treasured, but their labor may have been taken for granted.

Clerical and monastic records are too thin for broad conclusions, but they offer some suggestions. They posit at least two tiers of network participation. On the periphery stood ordinary clerics and monks. Performing basic duties, they leave little trace in the records. Closer to the core stood the bishops' favorites. They appear regularly as social mediators. It is not clear what portion of the clergy or leading monks found such favor. But from our (admittedly bishop-centric) sources, no clerics or monks seem to have rivaled the bishops as hubs.

PARTICIPATION OF THE LAITY

Theodoret and his associates constituted a clerical network, but not exclusively so. As church leaders they had to deal with sizable lay congregations. And they relied on specific lay notables, for loyalty, donations, and physical protection. About one-third of the extant letters in our archives were sent by or to non-clerics. Most of these involve imperial and local elites, not average members of lay congregations. Nevertheless, even these sparse records show certain patterns. Congregations clearly received cordial statements from bishops and reports on the conflict. Local notables were often called friends. Just a few laypeople appear involved in core Antiochene business. But one layman seems so involved that he represents a fifth hub of the network.

Relations between clerics and the laity require yet another study method because the prosopographical evidence varies. The majority of Syrian laypeople are personally hidden. A typical diocese hosted tens of thousands of ordinary congregants, some highly involved, some barely connected. The local notable class is less obscure. Decurions, professionals, and bureaucrats inevitably had dealings with bishops. Our sources, however, are constrained. In Syria, they name only a few notables from Cyrrhus, Edessa, and Antioch, and none from other towns. It is only at the level of senators and officials that we find detailed information to match the coverage of bishops.

Evidence for bishops' lay connections conforms to these gradations of social rank. For the majority of congregants we have only a general picture. Theodoret wrote (a few preserved) sermons. So did colleagues (notably Basil of Seleucia). The bishops also wrote letters to the people (*laoi* or *populus*) of various towns. Such collective communication was important. It allowed bishops to build community through shared reactions.[24] Collective address, however, had its limits. Preaching and liturgy were unlikely to bring whole congregations beyond the outer periphery of a doctrinal network.

Theodoret dealt more personally with notables, by offering pastoral care. He issued moral rebukes and wrote notes of consolation, locally and to other dio-

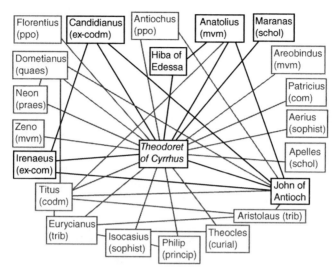

FIGURE 5. Lay notables in the Antiochene network, circa 436, according to letters and conciliar documents. Black links approximate evident or implied exchange of 3 or more Antiochene social cues within 7 years of 436 (more links may have existed). Grey links approximate evident or implied exchange of 2, or of non-Antiochene, cues (only those linked to multiple Antiochene associates are included). codm = count of the Domestici, com = count, curial = curialis, mvm = master of soldiers, ppo = praetorian prefect of the East, praes = provincial governor, princip = principalis, quaes = quaestor, schol = scholasticus, trib = imperial tribune.

ceses.[25] For most laypeople, Theodoret did his ministry orally. But letters brought the notable laity a sense of attachment. And pastoral care often led to greater cooperation.[26] Still, even prominent laypeople were kept at a distance. Only a few received multiple cues, and none the main signals of doctrinal affinity (see figure 5).[27] Many notables had personal ties to the bishops, but most were marginal to the doctrinal network.

The situation changes with regard to imperial officials and senators, a few of whom counted as Antiochene allies. Some contact with the political elite was required. Provincial governors had to be invited to festivals.[28] Grieving officials had to be comforted.[29] Prefects received updates on church business, personally and for the court. During doctrinal disputes some envoys were forced upon the bishops.[30] Still, a few connections went beyond obvious formalities. At least four high officials show signs of Antiochene affinity: Candidianus the count of the *Domestici*, Titus the count of the *Domestici*, Irenaeus the count (and future bishop), and Anatolius the master of soldiers. In fact, Anatolius won special inclusion. By 436 he had defended Theodoret's allies for six years. With his clerical contacts, and his brokering of further court contacts, he could be considered the fifth hub.

Laypeople clearly augmented the Antiochene network. Letters and council documents reveal a peripheral role for most congregants, whose precise involvement lies beyond view. But they establish personal links between bishops and many local notables. And they place a handful of powerful laymen within the core network. Lay participation does affect the shape of the network. It adds new mediating figures and another hub. As with clerics, the records have no doubt left out important lay participants, particularly notables from towns besides Cyrrhus. The overall network, however, retains a similar tightness and density and a modular scale-free form.

CENTRALITY AND INFLUENCE: THEODORET AND HIS INNER CIRCLE

So far, this chapter has traced basic membership patterns within the Antiochene network. Now we can go further, to analyze internal dynamics, starting with the distribution of influence. Influence was of serious concern to the bishops. Theodoret once worried to a colleague (sarcastically) that he was "looked down on rather than looking down on [others]" and "guided rather than guiding."[31] As we have noted, the network included five hubs. Network theorists stress the influence of these central figures, even if they lack institutional power. Late Roman Christian culture provided several models for assertion of authority. Theodoret's network followed none of them exclusively. Records reveal many figures acting as leaders—primates and metropolitans but also elders, ascetics, authors, and protégés. Even as these figures competed for influence, the relational pattern pushed them to cooperate.

Before examining social patterns, let us consider a more common way to explore the distribution of authority: rhetorical models. By models, I mean both the hierarchies of rank outlined in canons, and the rationales that bishops employed to get others to pay heed. The most obvious model of Christian authority was clerical rank. The *Apostolic Constitutions* repeatedly instructed laypeople and monks to join the clergy in obeying bishops.[32] Fifth-century bishops used this model whenever they commanded a priest or congregant, or patronizingly called one a friend.[33] Our network map clearly reflects the clerical hierarchy; the sources allow for nothing else. But clerical ranks could not help when it came to relations among bishops, or with powerful lay officials.

Regarding bishops, the late Roman church offered several models for deciding which should lead. One familiar model is primacy, the "customary privileges" accorded to "apostolic foundations" and other important cities.[34] In Egypt and

Southern Italy, bishops accepted one form of primacy: regional directorship. Alexandria and Rome made appointments and dogmatic statements with little room for dissent. In other places, see-based rankings took a less decisive form.[35] Syrian bishops accepted the primacy of Antioch: the right to preside at regional meetings and to consecrate bishops of important sees.[36] But when John of Antioch tried to assert supreme doctrinal authority, his efforts were rebuffed.[37] His successor Domnus accepted a more limited claim; though he spoke proudly of his "throne of Saint Peter," he also advocated "apostolic humility."[38]

More universal than regional primacy were the privileges tied to metropolitan sees (Seleucia in Isauria, Tarsus, Anazarbus, Hierapolis, Edessa, Amida, Apamea, Damascus, Bostra, and Tyre, as well as Antioch). The Council of Nicaea held that metropolitans were to call provincial synods and either to consecrate new bishops or to give written consent.[39] Theodoret reaffirmed this principle; he spoke of some actions as "ordered" by his metropolitan.[40] Yet Syrian metropolitan authority also had limits. The *Apostolic Constitutions* told metropolitans to "do nothing without the consent of all."[41] And Theodoret's discussion of orders was ironic, for he was talking about a meeting where suffragans had defied their superior. Like primacy, metropolitan privileges represented just one component of claims to authority.

Other rationales for leadership were connected with the person rather than the see. One was seniority. Throughout the Christian community, elderly bishops were treated with honor. Syria hosted an extreme example in the 430s, the centenarian Acacius of Beroea, who received deference from fellow bishops and even solicitation from the emperor.[42] Yet others also claimed years of experience and longer prospects. Another rationale was asceticism and monastic leadership. Here, too, Acacius had an advantage. But by the 430s his colleagues included several former monks and archimandrites.[43] A third rationale was evident doctrinal expertise.[44] In the 420s, Theodore of Mopsuestia had the longest list of treatises. By the late 430s, this honor went to Theodoret and Andreas in Greek, and possibly Hiba of Edessa in Syriac. A fourth rationale was connection to past heroes. Thus relative novices could claim the mantle of their mentors. And finally there was patronage. A number of bishops owed their positions to the hope that they would benefit those in their charge.[45] Many people could use at least one of these rationales to claim leadership. But mere claims cannot tell us who actually exercised authority.

It is here that our network map helps by charting the centrality of would-be leaders. Our Antiochene map presents multiple figures in positions of local centrality. With links to all the members of a cluster, they were placed well to manage communication. Four bishops (Theodoret, John of Antioch, Acacius of Beroea, and Andreas) are presented in positions of highest centrality, along with one layman (Anatolius). They had the greatest capacity to reshape social connections by adding or altering social cues. All scale-free networks have a few high-centrality hubs. The number and identity of the hubs, however, are matters of historical contingency. In this case, processes of growth and development put several people in favorable positions.

Our network map also helps to probe the distribution of influence by charting irreplaceability—the extent to which network relations rely on particular members. For this task we observe the hypothetical impact of selectively removing members. In our social map irreplaceability is fairly low. Single members or hubs could disappear without disrupting the network. Nonetheless certain losses would affect group tightness. Without John of Antioch, some members would grow distant. Without Theodoret nearly everyone would have a harder time communicating. Combination losses would mean greater changes. Without Andreas and Theodoret two clusters would be left hanging by a thread. Still, it would take the loss of four of the five hubs to collapse the network entirely. None of the members is thus truly irreplaceable; all of them faced limits in the quest for influence.

By combining network maps with rhetorical models we get a richer picture of clerical authority. Many Antiochenes had at least one viable rationale for claiming leadership. The central five had multiple rationales and various advantages. John of Antioch held the highest hierarchical title. Theodoret appears the most central (even if we ignore his personal letter collection). Anatolius had the most coercive power. But none of these men was positioned to hold ecclesiastical dominance. With so many claims to authority, we might expect conflict. Indeed, the Syrian bishops did contend for influence (see chapter 4). But multiple would-be leaders need not bring hostility. Communications reveal that the five central hubs worked to preserve cordial relations. They formed a high-density inner circle where notes of intimacy were common. Members of the inner circle publicly praised one another (hence Theodoret's eulogy for Acacius, noted in chapter 1). They defended one another to outsiders.[46] Most important, they found ways to avoid confrontation. Each lent public support to the others' decisions, despite their differences.[47] The leading positions of the five hubs were unequal and informal; but if the men stayed close, worries of confrontation might be set aside.

PERIPHERY AND FRINGE: NETWORK
INCLUSION AND EXCLUSION

Records of communication allow for an analysis of core relations in Theodoret's network, including the distribution of influence. They help in another way regarding the periphery. Core figures are named frequently in our records, but the majority of bishop members appear as minor players. Most clerics and laypeople are virtually invisible. Our map is, of course, incomplete, but it is suggestive about the effective limits of the core network. At ecumenical councils Theodoret and his associates spoke for "the East." Some churchmen, however, remained aloof; others were excluded. And while the bishops recognized no regional rivals, they seem to have left space for an opposition to form.

Theodoret and his allies made bold assertions about their control of the churches of Syria, supported by a careful performance. During and after the First Council of Ephesus, Theodoret and his associates called themselves "the Bishops of the East."[48] No doubt they meant the civil diocese of *Oriens,* but they hinted at a wider oversight, extending to Persia and beyond. This claim was not total fantasy. In the 430s the Antiochenes mobilized bishops across the region, including most of the metropolitans. At key moments they claimed the support of seventy-five or more Syrian bishops (the majority of those recognized by the Nicene church).[49] But more important than the numbers was how the bishops demonstrated their reach. Attendance at regional councils put geography on display. So did public correspondence. Not only did the bishops travel together to ecumenical councils; once present they tried to display unanimity. The performance had limits—it never included Cyprus or Palestine. But most allies and most opponents accepted the Antiochenes' regional label.

Our network map, however, challenges the performance of regional control. The seventy-five enumerated bishops leave out around forty or fifty (depending on when settlements gained bishoprics). Our list of member bishops includes just thirty actual names. Gaps can be found in every province, but Phoenicia I, Osrhoene, Mesopotamia, and Arabia seem especially underrepresented. None of these numbers include the thousands of clerics who never appear in correspondence. And even among the thirty stood peripheral figures whose links to the center may have been tenuous. The Antiochenes convinced some peers that they represented the East, but relational data do not support them.

One problem for the Antiochene network concerned clerics who kept their distance. Even big councils were missing bishops. Some protested their illness and named proxies.[50] Others gave no explanation (see figure 6). Some of the missing bishops may have been unsympathetic to the network. One way for dissenters to avoid conflict was not to write and not to attend. Even if a bishop did participate, his subordinates may have avoided involvement. The aloofness of lower clerics is hard to measure, but it must have been substantial.

Another problem for the network involved clerics who were actively excluded. Some member bishops publicly repudiated the cues of doctrine and memory. The most famous defector, Rabbula of Edessa, had just died in 436, but others would soon follow. In the meantime the allegiance of many bishops in Osrhoene province was uncertain.[51] Lower clerics and monastic leaders also defected. At least six in Antioch served as *proxenoi* for Cyril of Alexandria, staging protests into the 440s.[52] Then there were the members who had been cast out during doctrinal confrontations. By 436, at least nine Antiochene bishops had been deposed, including Nestorius and Alexander of Hierapolis (and every non-Syrian member prelate).

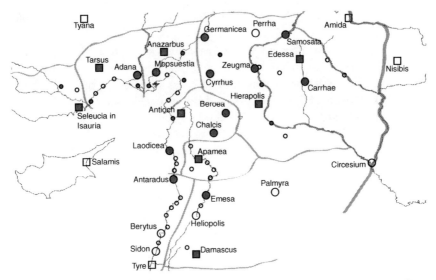

FIGURE 6. Map of Theodoret's known episcopal network, circa 436. Squares = metropolitan sees, large circles = major suffragan sees, small circles = minor suffragan sees, filled shapes = sees held by Antiochene members, empty shapes = non-members or unidentified bishops, thin lines = approximate provincial boundaries, thick line = approximate frontier of Roman Empire.

Several government allies now lived in exile, above all Count Irenaeus.[53] Some members kept contacts with their punished brethren. What we know of these contacts make them seem tenuous or downright hostile.[54]

It is thus startling that Theodoret and his peers acknowledged no organized resistance within the Nicene church. John of Antioch tolerated the priests who reported against him. Even the defector Rabbula was officially restored to communion before he died. The bishops did worry about heretics—the Arians, Manichaeans, and Marcionites who gathered in homes and distant villages.[55] But Nicene communities were treated publicly as partakers of concord. This may be a deliberate misrepresentation. As questionable clerics died or left, the bishops sought more reliable replacements. It also may stem from misperception. Most extant records come from core members, who may not have perceived how social life differed on the network fringe.[56]

It is also possible that in 436 there was no *organized* resistance so long as the Antiochene network appeared regionally dominant. Scale-free networks tend to persist in computer simulations. Multiple clusters and hubs make a network robust, so long as the inner circle remains united. They also tend to attract new nodes, which are clustered and drawn toward the hubs.[57] Such observations do not explain the rise of the Antiochene network, but they may explain its staying power. Sometimes modular scale-free networks have such success that they monopolize a social space.[58] Our network map leaves some scattered space for rivals, but it would take effort to link up these "gaps."

Yet our map of the Antiochene network does show vulnerabilities. Simulated scale-free networks can withstand losses but fail spectacularly if a force systematically eliminates the hubs. Our map reveals only minor weak points. Gaps appear between the bishops of Cilicia, for instance, and those of coastal Syria. But larger problems may loom beyond view, especially among the bishops of Osrhoene and Phoenicia I. These apparent gaps, of course, prove nothing; they may appear accidentally because of the spotty data. But they do suggest where the network reached limits, which other evidence may confirm.

If these regions were, indeed, "gaps" for the Antiochenes, then the problems could be magnified by later social developments. If one figure came to dominate the network, for instance, it would be easier to target him and thereby split the coalition. Or if disgruntled clerics could canvass thin spots in the social fabric, they might find people willing to switch sides. No synchronic social map could predict if a network would collapse. But our map shows us what it might take to overturn the Antiochenes: a coordinated attack on all the most central figures and an effort to unite people in the gaps of the network periphery (see chapter 5).

PATTERNS, IMPLICATIONS AND UNCERTAINTIES

Mapping and analyzing Antiochene relations thus yields some noteworthy results. Our data trace a singular network spanning the region. The results fit a modular scale-free template (a loose periphery, a gradation of well-connected hubs). At the same time they feature a specific social arrangement (a tight central clique that included all five hubs). This shape says something about Antiochene leadership. In place of a clear order of deference, we find informal would-be leaders. The shape also says something about network inclusion. In the Syrian clergy, we find only scattered non-Antiochene "gaps"—just enough space for opponents to potentially organize.

Such observations, of course, beg the question: how well do these patterns reflect social experience? All the elements of this map are approximations, and some are more noteworthy than others. Our maps are representations, based on limited, edited evidence. They gloss over variations in perception and processes of change. Some patterns likely arise from the selective nature of the social data. The emphasis on bishops, for instance, is hard to separate from the fact that they collected most of our sources. Other patterns are more reliable, if unsurprising. The modular scale-free form appears in both data sets. This template offers useful, but nonspecific, guidance, since it may be found in any growing network. The most important results have to do with the finer social details: the spotty reach of the Antiochene periphery and the tight core surrounding five (unequal) hubs. Strikingly, these features cut *against* the official claims of our sources. They also offer suggestions about the specific nature of this network.

The next three chapters shall return to our map, when its features illuminate certain social events. Here, we note just a few parameters of interpretation. Network maps do not offer certain predictions. Simulations suggest only what is possible or likely, when a similar arrangement is found. Consider the modular scale-free topology. Modular scale-free patterns arise in simulations when small networks experience steady growth. As they expand, these networks gradually become more dependent on hubs, and thus more prone to collapse. These networks may become less hub-dependent and less vulnerable, but only if they cease growing (and thus cease to be modular and scale-free).[59] These simulations tell us little about the origins of the Antiochene network, or the reasons for its virtual demise. They do not explain why certain members became hubs. They do suggest what it probably took to build the Antiochene network (steady growth). And they show us some of its possible futures.

Ultimately, the maps and models noted in this chapter merely beg further questions. How did Theodoret's network really form and grow? How did its members come to join and its leaders, to achieve centrality? How did the network deal with internal rivalries and external opposition? How reliable were its relationships? How potent was its sense of community? The next three chapters will address these questions, beginning with the network's historical roots.

3

Roots of a Network

Theodoret on the Antiochene Clerical Heritage

By all rights the spring of 448 should have been joyous for Theodoret. The season marked his twenty-fifth year as bishop and the eighth of relative calm in the church. Theodoret had recently completed a commentary on Paul's Epistles and a Christological dialogue. He could look forward to preaching in Antioch on these topics during his usual visit. The news of the season, however, put a damper on his routine. First came old accusations against allies, then an imperial letter relegating him to his diocese.[1] By the summer he was being called a crypto-Nestorian tyrant, with worse to come.

As confrontations intensified, other bishops of Syria reported to Theodoret to ask for advice. Domnus of Antioch, Theodoret's protégé, mentioned one source of hope: the emperor had called an ecumenical council. Theodoret, however, knew about past church struggles, when synods were no panacea. "Even at the great Council of Nicaea," he recalled, "the Arians voted with the Orthodox and swore by the apostolic creed." Emperors, in particular, had not always been reliable. Constantius II and Valens had compelled church leaders to compromise, deepening schisms and hindering proper faith. Luckily, the old struggles left another source of hope: crafty Syrian bishops. In the fourth century, he suggested, their ingenuity had saved Christian orthodoxy. Theodoret advised Domnus to gather "the most God-friendly, like-minded bishops," for a prolonged fight.[2] While his allies organized, however, Theodoret looked to the past for grounding. By the end of 449 he had turned his reflections into five books of church history.[3]

In the study of the Antiochene network, Theodoret's *Church History* (*Historia ecclesiastica* or *HE*) represents an inescapable text, for his narrative confronts the figures and events that shaped the fifth-century clerical world. His work was (most likely) the third church history written in the 440s. Socrates (between 438 and 443) and Sozomen (in 443 or 444) had already given their (Constantinople-centered) takes on the triumph of Nicene Orthodoxy.[4] Prior work by Rufinus of Aquileia and non-Nicene historians[5] had also found distribution. But Theodoret was unsatisfied; he needed to cover the "episodes of church history hitherto omitted." Theodoret played off existing historical and doctrinal writings.[6] He continually referenced his own *History of the Friends of God* (*Historia religiosa*, or *HR*) so that it would be read alongside the *HE*. He furnished prosopographic detail as he anointed new (mostly Syrian) honorees.[7] But more than an addendum, he offered a narrative thesis. Amid Trinitarian conflicts in Syria, especially in Antioch, Theodoret found the roots of his Nicene community. He sketched out its founders, supporters of Bishop Meletius, as they built a clerical party. He related how this party forged alliances and took the church back from heresy. Nicene victory owed something to emperors, he claimed, but it depended on past Syrian bishops.

This chapter evaluates the heritage that Theodoret depicted for his network. It traces Theodoret's account of his heroic predecessors and compares it to other historical sources. Theodoret wrote his narratives with definite purposes. He extolled Syria's orthodox pedigree, as he defended the symbols of his network. Theodoret's account is coherent and well informed. It helps to make sense of two important developments—the formation of Antiochene doctrine and the transformation of Syrian monasticism—as well as of traditions of informal clerical leadership. Other sources add (unpleasant) nuances to Theodoret's account without challenging its basic claims. In context, this history reveals some of the roots of the Antiochene scene.

THEODORET ON THE TROUBLES OF THE FOURTH-CENTURY CLERGY

Theodoret's account of the origins of his network began with a cry of sympathy. From the vantage point of the 440s, bishops of the fourth century seemed uncomfortably constrained. Part of this perception stemmed from decades of Christian growth. Theodoret was writing about bishops with smaller congregations and fewer resources. Part also came from changes in clerical authority. Theodoret and his peers expected life-long tenure, but fourth-century bishops were frequently unable to control their sees.

Theodoret's *Church History*, like the narratives of his contemporaries, centered on the Trinitarian controversy. And by the 360s, for a Nicene, the tale was getting depressing. Churches of the Roman East were growing more divided. Disputes and factions had been fluid until the 350s, but after 360, those with Nicene leanings were marginalized. Theodoret, of course, understood the phenomenon of doctrinal parties, the unstable coalitions that signed to common-denominator formulas and labeled one another as heretical. In the fourth century, the emperors' push for compromise helped to distinguish at least four such parties: the "Homoians" (who claimed that the Son was "similar" to the Father), the "Homoiousians" (who asserted that the Son was "similar in substance" to the Father), and the "Anomoians" (who held that the Son was "dissimilar" from the Father), as well as the "Nicenes." The Homoians took up most of Theodoret's annoyance, for they claimed imperial favor and controlled the most churches. They also taunted Nicene Christians for having a creed that was supposedly un-scriptural.[8] Late in his reign, Constantius II enforced his preferences by exiling recalcitrant bishops. After 368 Valens did likewise.[9] But court favor was not the only problem. For no imperial meddling caused the split in Laodicea between two circles of Nicenes.[10] In any case, Theodoret recorded the frustrating implications. By the 370s every major town in Syria hosted multiple claimants to episcopal office, unable to exercise their full charge.

Theodoret's *HE* did not hide the troubles of fourth-century clerics. In fact, it used these troubles to showcase church heroes who somehow, when faced with adversity, kept their nerve. One of Theodoret's favorites was Eusebius of Samosata, who defied emperors in the 360s to consecrate Nicene bishops. When Valens exiled him in 369, he supposedly told his flock not to resist, since "the apostolic law clearly instructs us to be subject to [civil] powers and authorities." So beloved was Eusebius by his congregants, we are told, that two replacements failed to pacify them.[11] But even Theodoret knew that such honor was cold comfort to the exiled.

It was in this context that Theodoret turned to Antioch. All the troubles that plagued the church in the 360s piled up there. One bishop, Euzoïus, usually had the support of the imperial court. A former priest from Egypt elected in 361, he clearly leaned Homoian. Meanwhile, two figures claimed the office under a Nicene banner: Paulinus and Meletius. Meletius had been a bishop in Roman Armenia. He was transferred to Antioch in 360 under a compromise between Homoian and Nicene bishops.[12] He was then deposed a few months later when his own (cryptic) doctrinal views came to light.[13] In 363 he declared his support for the Council of Nicaea, though Theodoret found signs of his prior loyalty.[14] Nevertheless, he had risen with the help of known anti-Nicenes. These links, coupled with his hesitancy to dogmatize, raised suspicions.[15] Paulinus, meanwhile, was an aged priest, who had been ordained by Eustathius of Antioch, the heroic Nicene confessor. Longtime leader of a separate "Eustathian" faction, Paulinus secured consecration in 363 from Roman Westerners who had come to survey the local Nicenes.[16] Eventually a fourth candidate was added. Vitalis, a priest under Meletius, was induced to break away and then consecrated by Apollinarius, the theologian-bishop of Laodicea.[17] Thus, Theodoret presents a confused competition for episcopal authority, in which most of the claimants considered themselves Nicene. As scholars have noted before, the result was instability.[18] Under Emperors Julian and Jovian, and initially under Valens, each of the three (not yet four) bishops controlled a subset of the personnel and churches. Each claimed external allies. None commanded universal regard within Syria or beyond. When Valens moved to Antioch in 370, Meletius was forced into exile (Vitalis was not yet consecrated, and Paulinus, not worth the bother).[19] Nonetheless, all claimants maintained local followings. Some even benefited from exile. After all, it was exile that bound Meletius to his biggest booster, Basil of Caesarea.[20]

At the same time, as Theodoret's account makes clear, the party balance could not erase the fear of factional disintegration. A few years earlier, in 358, the death of Bishop Leontius had turned the local clergy upside down. At that time, Eudoxius, hitherto bishop of Germanicea, came to claim Antioch for himself. He then ordained Aetius and Eunomius, who advanced an Anomoian doctrine that the other clerics reviled. The situation grew more confusing when repeated councils failed to choose a candidate acceptable to the emperor. In fact, it was because of this overall upheaval that Meletius had been chosen in the first place.[21] A kind of equilibrium returned under Emperor Julian, who had equal disregard for all clerical parties.[22] Still, one death had upended the factional balance, and a second one could do it again (see figure 7).

What Theodoret found lacking in Antioch and Syria of the 360s was a system of inter-see cooperation. Factionalism and rivalry hobbled church leadership. In some places (like Egypt) disputes were centralized, thanks to one bishop's primacy. But Syria lacked such a tradition, as Theodoret knew.[23] This absence of oversight created a more open episcopate. Any would-be bishop could find the two or three consecrators he effectively needed.[24] Once bishops were chosen, however, this openness held no benefit. For no bishop-claimant could ensure a heritable episcopate.

THEODORET ON THE TRIUMPH OF
MELETIUS'S NICENE PARTISANS

Then something changed. Starting in the 360s Theodoret found an assembling Nicene network, even in Antioch. Most leaders of this coalition were known from other histories. But Theodoret had his own tale to tell. In his judgment, it was the following of Meletius that led the Nicene triumph by taking over the Syrian episcopate.

At first this sort of triumph looked unlikely. By the 370s Meletius's authority was weakening. The Homoian party held Valens's support. They controlled the urban churches, relegating the Nicenes to an "army training ground."[25] The Homoians even managed an orderly succession when Euzoïus passed away.[26] As Meletius languished in exile, only his close supporters paid him attention.[27] How-

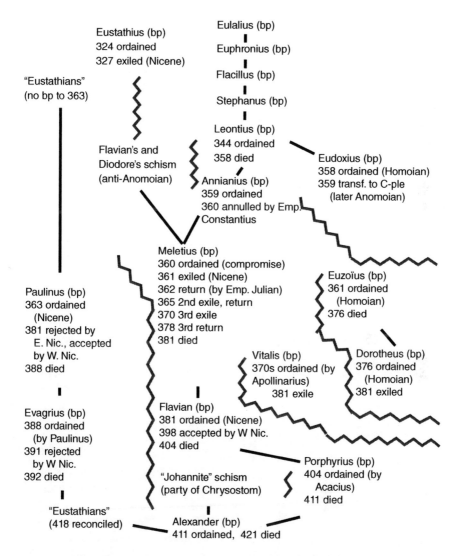

FIGURE 7. Episcopal factions in Antioch, 325–421, according to Theodoret's *HE*. Solid lines = partisan episcopal succession, broken lines = schisms.

ever, according to Theodoret, Meletius had a hidden advantage: two gifted partisans named Flavian and Diodore.

By the 360s Flavian and Diodore had already made names for themselves as lay patrons of the church. Even before Meletius arrived, both had demonstrated Nicene ardor, protesting Bishop Leontius and his "attacks against the faith."[28]

Famously they excelled in preaching and argument, a talent nourished through rhetorical education. Similarly they claimed crowd-control skills. Theodoret credited the pair with inventing the antiphonal chant, which they let loose in prayer meetings, on the streets, and even in Leontius's churches.[29] So strong was their following, we hear, that Leontius "did not think it safe to get in their way."[30] In 360 Meletius ordained Flavian and Diodore, but it was after his first exile that they came into their own. By 370 Flavian was serving as a proxy prelate, with Diodore at his side. Diodore researched arguments, we are told, while Flavian preached them to the crowds. This cooperation reportedly proved successful, despite Diodore's own departure (probably in 372).[31] Paulinus and Apollinarius were reportedly out-argued, and the "blasphemy of Arius" started to lose ground.[32]

Still, Flavian and Diodore succeeded, in Theodoret's judgment, as much because of their holy connections as their talents. Unlike other church historians, Theodoret drew no new attention to the *asketerion*, Diodore's schoolhouse for scriptural study and disciplined living.[33] Rather, he showcased Flavian and Diodore's ties to hermits and archimandrites. Such friends made good agents of persuasion at court. Theodoret noted, for example, how the hermit Aphraates rebuked an emperor face to face "for having cast these flames [of Arianism] upon the divine house."[34] Hermits also supplied their marvelous reputations. Julian Saba, we hear, won over the Nicenes with well-timed miracles of healing, including one for the count of the East.[35] This was "proof" of divine support that no party could deny. By the 370s, Theodoret claimed, Meletius's partisans were assembling a legion of ascetic allies.[36] This marked a turn of the tide.

According to Theodoret, this ascetic alliance was led by a new partisan, Acacius. A monk from a village near Antioch, Acacius was recognized for his ascetic regimen. While some monks treasured isolation, Acacius was more hospitable, accepting visitors with an open door.[37] But Theodoret cared less about his manners than his connections—to the monastic circle of Julian Saba.[38] According to Theodoret, Acacius befriended Flavian and Diodore in the 360s. Then he touted Meletius's cause to Julian Saba and his followers as "a way to serve God much more so than" in their caves.[39] Thanks to Acacius's travels Julian Saba, Aphraates, and their admirers filled the city. Needless to say, this made Meletius's partisans harder to ignore. Theodoret even suggests that cooperation proceeded with Ephrem, the Syriac hymn-writing deacon of Edessa, known to Greek-readers as a monastic leader.[40] Thus Theodoret depicted a monastic legion that spanned Syria's physical and linguistic landscape (see figure 8).

Between Flavian's preaching, Diodore's teaching, and Acacius's holy friends, Theodoret found his regional forebears gaining in popularity. He presented Meletius's faction as victorious, even before the court sided with the Nicenes. The new emperors Gratian and Theodosius, of course, did approve Meletius's return.[41] By Theodoret's account, the choice was providential: Theodosius had a dream in

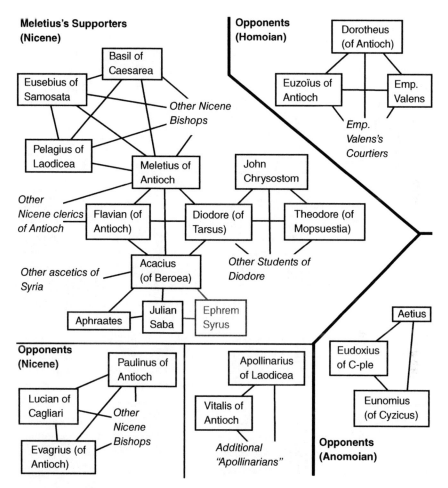

FIGURE 8. Meletius of Antioch's supporters and opponents, 360–378, according to Theodoret's *HE*. Note: Ephrem Syrus's link to the Antiochenes is only implied.

which Meletius crowned him and gave him the imperial robes.[42] In the *Church History*, this was a unique note of triumph. Many bishops were perseverant, but only Meletius appeared in imperial dreams.

At this point, we are told, Meletius chose to show magnanimity. In 380 Theodosius declared his support for the Council of Nicaea. He sent a delegation to Antioch to endorse one Nicene claimant.[43] Hence Meletius approached his rival Paulinus with a proposal. He offered to treat Paulinus as a colleague and link congregations, if it was agreed that whichever claimant died first would bequeath sole episcopacy to the other.[44] Reports vary as to the response. Socrates and Sozomen asserted that the offer was accepted.[45] Theodoret claimed that Paulinus refused. But even Theodoret could not deny the détente.[46] Meletius took hold of his old churches but respected Paulinus's following. Readers of Socrates would know that Meletius left for Constantinople, "because of the state of the church in Antioch,"[47] and Theodoret did not refute the point. But as Theodoret explained, what Meletius got in return was grand: deference to his leadership in Nicene councils[48] and acceptance of his ordinations in sees left "vacated" by the conflict. By 379 Meletius had placed Diodore in Tarsus and Acacius in Beroea. With imperial permission and help from Eusebius of Samosata, he put up candidates in Chalcis, Hierapolis, Apamea, Edessa, Carrhae, Doliche, and Cyrrhus.[49] These actions built up a Nicene presence in Syria. They also allowed Meletius's party to perpetuate itself.

When Meletius died in 381,[50] he had just started as president of the Council of Constantinople, and it was this gathering that began a second phase in the triumph of his party. For months Meletius had been preparing for the gathering; his passing brought disarray. First, the presidency was accorded to Gregory of Nazianzus. Gregory may have wanted to declare Paulinus the recognized episcopal heir. But luckily for Meletius's partisans he was persuaded to leave his position.[51] The next president, Nectarius, proved more pliant. A longtime friend to Diodore and Meletius anyway,[52] Nectarius accepted a request for delay. Then, after the council the Meletian bishops gathered in Antioch, where they put up Flavian for election. Consecrated by Diodore and Acacius, he soon received Nectarius's blessing.[53] Paulinus was upset, as were critics of Nectarius. Together they complained to western bishops, who took the message to the emperors.[54] Theodosius I called a new meeting in the capital. To Paulinus's disappointment, however, it confirmed both Nectarius and Flavian (it was, after all, filled with Meletius's friends).[55] This episode did not flatter Meletius's followers. Theodoret minimized the embarrassment by distancing his account of Flavian's ordination from his treatment of the council. Nevertheless, he acknowledged that Meletius's partisans pushed their rivals aside (see figure 9).

Still, the dispute with Paulinus continued and could not be ignored. After the councils Paulinus convinced the bishops of Italy and Egypt that he was the rightful prelate. In 388 he chose his own successor, Evagrius. And despite this non-traditional election Evagrius was embraced by the same set of colleagues. Theodoret seized upon Evagrius's ordination as a point of polemic. "[The apostles] did not allow a dying bishop to ordain another to take his place," he declared, "and they ordered all the bishops of the province to convene."[56] Even at the time supporters of Paulinus's party questioned Evagrius's status. In 391, a council of Italian bishops sided against Evagrius's claim. The dispute, however, had left an impression. Many Nicene bishops gave Flavian the cold shoulder, and the court threatened to intervene. It was only in 398 that he won belated acceptance. Even this took the support of the court, the oratory of John Chrysostom, and more visits by Acacius.[57]

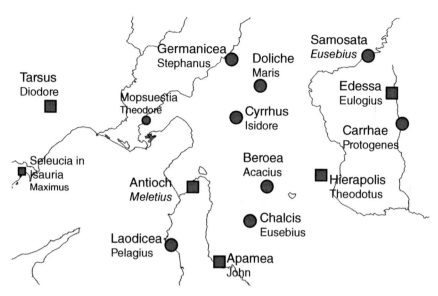

FIGURE 9. Map of Meletius's episcopal appointments, 378–381, according to Theodoret's *HE*, including appointments made by Meletius's ally, Eusebius of Samosata. Smaller shapes = additional appointments by Meletius's main allies, 381–393.

Theodoret could not deny this opposition, so he turned the affair into a test of character. According to Theodoret, Flavian met criticism by offering to abdicate in front of the emperor, a show of selflessness that impressed his majesty. In any case, Theodoret noted that Flavian was held in high regard within Syria (not surprising given Meletius's appointments).[58] Paulinus's followers held out until the 410s,[59] but Theodoret made it clear that Syria was in the hands of the proper Nicene party.

As to the significance of these episodes, Theodoret left little doubt: Meletius had launched a coup in the churches of Syria, extended by the machinations of his followers. It was, however, the long-term impact of these events that most concerned Theodoret. First, the rise of the Meletian party led to a more cooperative regional episcopate. Thanks to Meletius and Eusebius many Syrian bishops of the 380s claimed the same spiritual fathers. Theodoret credited these associates with unusual fidelity. Second, according to Theodoret, Meletius and his partisans stabilized episcopal selection. Like other church historians, Theodoret mentioned Diodore's students who became bishops, in particular John Chrysostom and Theodore of Mopsuestia.[60] He then listed many more bishops tied to Meletius and his following.[61] Third, according to Theodoret, Meletius and his protégés turned ascetic links to their advantage. As ascetics aided bishops in various causes,[62] bishops encouraged ascetics to found monasteries. In the *HR* Theodoret cited monastic groups that owed goodwill to Flavian, Diodore, and Acacius (see figure 10).

Map of monasteries linked to the Antiochene network

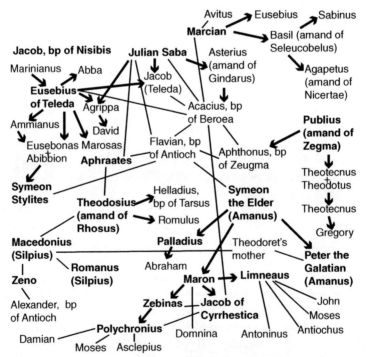

Relationships among ascetics linked to the Antiochene network

FIGURE 10. Ascetics and monasteries linked to the Antiochenes, 381–423, according to Theodoret's *HE* and *HR*. Thick arrows = mentorship links, thin lines = informal links, names in boldface = subjects of chapters of the *HR*.

Together these arrangements constituted a potent "Antiochene" legacy. For by the 420s they had fostered a network of clerics and ascetics, headed by a clique of bishops.[63]

Theodoret ended his *HE* in the late 420s with the deaths of Theodore and Theodotus of Antioch, as well as Polychronius of Apamea (Theodore's brother). Thus he confined his story to the *rise* of his Antiochene mentors. Theodoret's account, of course, cannot be simply accepted at face value. Nevertheless, it opens a window on the origins of his clerical community. Not only does it supply prosopography; it contextualizes several developments in Syrian Christianity. One of these has received limited attention: the peculiar distribution of authority among Syrian bishops. Another has been treated as part of a general trend: the establishment of coenobitic monasteries. This chapter will discuss both of these issues. First, however, let us consider a development that has long fascinated scholars: the formation of a "school" of doctrine.

"ARROWS OF INTELLIGENCE": ANTIOCHENE DOCTRINE IN CONTEXT

Theodoret's *HE* reserved a special place for his favorite teachers. Diodore he called "a great clear river," which overwhelmed the heretics of his day. Like many Nicene leaders, "He thought nothing of the brilliance of his birth, gladly enduring difficulty on behalf of the faith." But Diodore was no mere confessor. "At that time, he did not speak publicly in church gatherings, but provided an abundance of arguments and scriptural thoughts to the preachers. They in turn aimed their bows at the blasphemy of Arius, while he brought forth arrows from his intelligence as if from a quiver." His skills were such that he tore through heretical arguments as if they were "mere spider's webs."[64] Theodoret's affirmation of Theodore was just as pronounced. The final chapter of the *HE* called Theodore a "doctor of the whole church," who, after receiving the "spiritual streams" of Diodore, spent his episcopacy "battling the phalanx of Arius and Eunomius and struggling against the pirate-band of Apollinarius."[65] For Theodoret to praise these two men was hardly unexpected. He had already published *In Defense of Diodore and Theodore,* an apology for their orthodoxy. The *HE,* however, gave context to the work of these two authors. It assigned them the role of a theological research operation, a veritable "school of Antioch."

Theodoret's descriptions of Diodore and Theodore are intriguing because they give flesh to a hotly debated scholarly construct. The "School of Antioch," we recall, refers to the nexus of religious learning marked by four tropes: the "literal-historical" method of exegesis, the rejection of "allegory," the citing of "types" and "realities," and the distinction of Christ's divinity and humanity.[66] Scholars have differed over the meaning of these tropes. Many have searched for a system of thought behind Antiochene teachings.[67] Others, frustrated by shifting terms and lost texts, settled for Antiochene "tendencies."[68] Some looked for a lineage of teachers.[69] Others proposed broad cultural influences, from Aristotelian or Platonic philosophy to Jewish or Syriac modes of reading.[70] Thus scholars wrote many studies of doctrinal texts but they gave only vague explanations for the overall trend.

Recent research has reevaluated the Antiochene doctrinal phenomenon. Scholars now emphasize the similarity of Antiochene and Alexandrian exegesis.[71] They also challenge the notion of an Antiochene system, though most still acknowledge common concerns.[72] Some have situated Antiochene doctrine within a narrow cultural context: Greek sophistic education in Antioch.[73] Others have found inconsistencies between Greek and Syriac versions of Antiochene texts, enough to cast doubt on Diodore's and Theodore's positions.[74] Much of this reevaluation has been persuasive. Diodore, Theodore, and Theodoret did not share a coherent doctrinal system. The effect of recent studies, though, has been to minimize the Antiochene "school."[75] Diodore and Theodore did have influence in Syria; in the 430s seventy-five bishops risked exile to defend them.[76] Perhaps the deconstruction of the school of Antioch has gone too far.

At this stage Theodoret's account comes in handy; for his *HE* envisions a different kind of school. It does not present a doctrinal abstraction or an autonomous institution. It describes a loose educational circle, led by Diodore and then Theodore, which formed part of the larger partisan effort. What we know of early Antiochene doctrine fits within the context that Theodoret provides. Not only do these teachings reflect the culture of late-fourth-century Antioch; they seem custom-made to reinforce the participants' friendships and enmities.

At the widest level, Antiochene teaching fit well with the mix of doctrinal parties that Theodoret highlighted in Syria during the later fourth century. By the 360s Christians had been openly feuding about the Trinity for half a century. The fluidity of prior debates (of which Meletius, Flavian, and Diodore had partaken)[77] was passing; positions were becoming better articulated. In the Nicene party the Cappadocian fathers offered their vocabulary of *hypostases* and *ousiai*, for which they slowly won support. (Meletius, in fact, embraced their terminology early on and, as Theodoret noted, well before Paulinus).[78] The Cappadocian vocabulary scarcely ended the controversy, but for Nicenes it drew clearer lines between orthodoxy and heresy. Yet settling one question opened others. Nicenes had to deal with inconsistent past authorities. The third-century scholar Origen, for instance, had faced prior controversy, but the new terminology sharpened concerns about his orthodoxy. More pressing than Origen, though, was the Nicenes' basic evidentiary problem: *ousia* and *hypostasis* had no scriptural precedent. In fact, biblical quotations could more easily undercut the Nicene position than defend it. Homoians hit upon this, chanting gospel lines, such as "My Father is greater than I" (John

14:28). Nicenes labeled the Homoians as "Arian," but they still had to meet these challenges with a public response.

In the 360s Diodore took up the defense of Nicaea against the Homoians. The fragments attributed to him show that he traced out an immense doctrinal project: the creation of harmony between Scripture, Cappadocian terminology, and Nicaea's supporting authors. This task involved cross-referencing, lexical analysis, etymological research, and narrative summation, all familiar activities to former students of sophists. It was as part of this project that Diodore employed those tropes associated with the school of Antioch. When it came to describing Christ, he spoke of two "voices," a human and a divine, to which passages of Scripture might refer.[79] Initially he called the two aspects by the biblical epithets, "Son of David" and "Son of God,"[80] or the "Word" (logos) and the "flesh"(sarx).[81] His students abandoned "sons" and "logos-sarx" in favor of "natures," but they still stressed the distinction between divinity and humanity.[82] Inspiration for this terminology has been variously located, but whatever the roots, the proximate cause was public controversy. By assigning some scriptural lines to the human and some to the divine, Diodore found an answer to the Homoians' taunts.

It was exegetical tropes, however, that seem to have marked Diodore's firmest response. By building up from the "literal" to the "historical," he aimed to approach the *hypothesis* of biblical texts—their moral and narrative significance.[83] Diodore's rejection of certain tropes as "allegory" was the natural extension of discerning what fell outside Scripture's underlying message. This approach may have proved too limiting for some contemporaries, but it gave Diodore a rhetorical edge. Homoians might claim the words of Scripture, but Diodore claimed a deeper connection to the narrative.

Diodore's doctrinal and exegetical tropes thus make sense as an effort to distinguish his party from its rivals, the Homoians. They similarly aimed for separation from another set of foes, the Anomoians. Theodoret informs us that Diodore had been particularly hostile to "dissimilar" formulas, even before joining Meletius's following.[84] Aetius and Eunomius lost episcopal sponsorship in Antioch in 360, but they maintained a Syrian following. This group developed its own style of doctrinal production, based on Scripture and on dialectical reasoning. By the 380s its members were challenging Nicenes such as Chrysostom to take up their favorite lines of argument.[85] Evidence suggests a general disdain for the Anomoians within the clergy, but the Anomoians' claim to exact reasoning caused problems for all the other clerical parties.

The Antiochenes' response to the Anomoians was as thorough as their response to the Homoians: they outdid their opponents' claims to systematic logic. Diodore was famous for his efforts to create a consistent language of theology, linking the words of Jesus, biblical narrative, and common parlance. Theodore extended this drive, even rejecting some of his teacher's favored terms. And yet, Diodore and

Theodore claimed to avoid un-scriptural speculation. This they did by displaying long years of scriptural learning, to contrast with the supposedly ill-grounded reasoning of Aetius and Eunomius.[86] In other words, they claimed superior *paideia*, like the sophists who had trained them. The assertion of deeper learning was more rhetorical than substantive. Nonetheless, the Antiochenes took it seriously. They seem to have levied this claim against Paulinus, whom Theodoret, at least, viewed as a simpleton.[87] They may also have levied it against Nicenes in Egypt. Antiochenes worried about Alexandria-style allegory partly because it opened scriptural interpretation to any logician's schemes.

By the 380s, it was not Homoians or Anomoians who most troubled Diodore and Theodore; it was the (Nicene) followers of Apollinarius. Son of a grammarian turned priest in Laodicea, Apollinarius distinguished himself by writing dialogues in defense of the Christian faith. By all accounts he had a fondness for Neoplatonic philosophers. Yet it was apparently Apollinarius's friendship to the Nicene hero Athanasius that inspired the bishop of Laodicea to excommunicate him in the 360s.[88] By Sozomen's reckoning, Apollinarius began crafting his defense of Nicene doctrine at this time,[89] contemporary with Diodore's efforts. Indeed, he responded to many of the same opponents. Apollinarius's doctrinal solutions differed from Diodore's. His Christology asserted that God the Word had united with Jesus's humanity by taking the place of the "mind" (Greek: *nous*). Yet much like Diodore, he sought a quick response to rhetorical challenges. He thus compiled a set of reduced formulas to signal orthodoxy, such as "one nature of the divine incarnate Word."[90] Until the mid 370s Apollinarius and Diodore seem to have tolerated each other. Then a rivalry developed, resulting in the ordination of Vitalis. Apollinarius was condemned and deposed in 381, in part at the urging of Meletius. According to Theodoret, however, Apollinarius claimed secret followers for at least another forty years, infiltrating the Nicene church with their hidden "unsoundness."[91]

The Antiochene response to Apollinarius was more than a mere rhetorical targeting. Diodore and Theodore turned Apollinarians into their favorite *bête noire*. Like the Cappadocians, Theodore took aim at the "incomplete humanity" of Apollinarius's Christ. But he was also troubled by the phrase "one nature."[92] His "two natures" was probably a response to the Laodicean bishop's formulation. By the early fifth century, Apollinarius's formulas had receded from the discourse; it was enough to label someone as Apollinarian. A follower of Theodore's, Alexander of Hierapolis, later recalled how he and several colleagues threatened to resign unless suspected Apollinarians were excluded from the clergy.[93] In a sense, nothing came to mark Antiochene inclusion more than the exclusion of "Apollinarians."

The doctrinal tropes of Diodore's circle can thus be seen as a response to the rivalries that formed around them during the 360s and 370s. Theodoret suggested that his forebears were more concerned with Homoians, Anomoians, and Apollinarians than they were with Egyptians. His suggestion makes sense given the Antiochenes' social circumstances. Meletius's following needed to distinguish itself from opponents and build a sense of certainty. So Diodore provided socio-doctrinal cues to mark out orthodoxy, first in contrast to Anomoians and Homoians, and then in opposition to Apollinarius. It was the need for sequential triangulation that in part led clerics to assemble the most familiar Antiochene doctrines.

And yet, early Antiochene teaching (insofar as we can discern it) did more than trace out the boundaries of orthodoxy. It also affirmed the friendships and patronage ties which, according to Theodoret, formed Meletius's network. As the Trinitarian feuds developed in the 360s and 370s, all parties organized alliances. Nicenes across the empire communicated and, in some cases, coordinated efforts. Yet building such alliances was not easy. Not only did clerics compete for authority, they also faced the prospect of doctrinal disharmony. Where some Nicenes favored "eternal generation of the Son," for instance, others preferred God's "begetting before all time."[94] The more clerics scrutinized one another's teachings, the more they risked disagreement. To avoid these dangers Nicenes tended to seek general formulas on which they could agree: the equal trinity, or later one *ousia* in three *hypostases*. But this broad alliance depended on distance. For closer cooperation clerics needed more specific terms of agreement. According to Theodoret, Meletius's following included preachers, teachers, lay leaders, and noted ascetics. Whatever Diodore taught would have to meet their general approval.

Diodore's teachings appear custom-made to affirm the social attachments that, according to Theodoret, were developing around him. One such affirmation involved the collaboration of preachers and teachers. According to Theodoret, Diodore worked in the background, providing "scriptural thoughts," to support Flavian's public presentations. In fact, Diodore's efforts could help greatly. His commentaries formed sourcebooks of quotations and observations, geared to counter the Homoians and other foes. Flavian could turn to these commentaries to craft stirring sermons and dramatic demonstrations. Meanwhile, the continuing public confrontation spurred on Diodore's research. Doctrinal production could thus resonate with Flavian's and Diodore's relations.

Another affirmation concerned the collaboration with ascetics. According to Theodoret, Flavian and Diodore worked with Acacius's monastic friends, benefiting from their reputation for miracles. Again Diodore's teachings supported these cooperative ventures. Not only did he offer his own ascetic instruction in conjunction with scriptural training.[95] He also provided Acacius a way to recruit monastic help. Miracles "attested even by the enemies of truth"[96] had long been cited as evidence of God's favor. But Diodore and his students were able to explain the powers of ascetics by presenting them as types of the prophets or Christ. Thus Julian Saba could "strengthen the proclamation of truth," directly through his deeds.[97] The glory of Julian's following then reflected back on the *asketerion*. According to

Chrysostom, it was the "simpler life" that attracted Libanius's pupils to Diodore's foundation in the first place.[98] Doctrinal production could thus also resonate with relations between ascetics and doctrinal masters.

Theodoret's narrative offers a consistent perspective on the social dynamics of early Antiochene doctrine. By Theodoret's account, Antiochene exegesis and theology coalesced inside a clique of partisans: a group of ascetics, clerics, and laymen discovering its alliances and its enmities. Resonating with preaching and ascetic behavior, Antiochene doctrine affirmed these new relationships. Conversely, the relationships fostered the Antiochene doctrinal project. It is not clear how far Diodore's teachings were shared, even within Meletius's coalition. Most likely, his doctrinal tropes spread in a graduated fashion, more densely among star pupils than among nonlocal allies. Whether doctrine proceeded canvassing or vice versa, Theodoret does not say. He sheds little light on the doctrines' cultural roots. But before Meletius's partisans achieved episcopal rank, some were shaping Antiochene cues for their network, including dyophysite Christology, typological asceticism, monastic education, and anti-Arian (or anti-Apollinarian) taunting.

"CONFORMING TO HIS *POLITEIA*": MONASTIC RECRUITMENT

A striking feature of Theodoret's account is the extent to which he traced a continuous chain of episcopal recruitment. Theodoret relished naming bishops like Elpidius of Laodicea, who "conformed to [Meletius's] way of life (*politeian*) more fully than wax does to the type of a seal ring." He noted their orderly successions: how Elpidius "succeeded the great Pelagius," just as "the divine Marcellus was followed by the illustrious Agapetus," a disciple of the ascetic Marcian.[99] These were minor characters in his *HE*, but Theodoret included them, along with dozens of new prelates linked to Meletius's offspring. Such order in succession was rare in the fourth century. Any recruitment scheme signaled an innovation. But the most surprising part of this account was the supposed involvement of a (volatile) ascetic scene. Monks could make fine bishops. But for reliable recruitment, the monastic community had to be organized, instructed, and transformed. If Meletius's party staged coups, this would be a revolution.

The reshaping of Syrian asceticism has been recognized as a key shift in Christian culture. In the fourth century Aramaic-speaking Christians already had a full tradition of self-deprivation, self-transformation, and self-control. Some ascetics lived within the larger church community. "Single ones" (Syriac: *ihidaye*) and "covenanters" (Syriac: *bnay/bnath qyama*) reaped praise from the clergy for their celibacy, their poverty, and their liturgical roles. A few even became bishops. Other ascetics separated from the main community. Also called "single ones," they wandered and preached in imitation of the apostles.[100] Between 350 and 425, ascet-icism in Syria spread and diversified. Some "single ones" remained in towns. Oth-ers (like Julian Saba) took to remote wanderings or various forms of seclusion.[101] Most famous was the new extreme, theatrical asceticism. Theodoret spoke of men donning iron underwear or sleeping in leaky wooden boxes.[102] Then there were the confrontational ascetics, decamping to pagan shrines in search of martyr-dom.[103] Big numerical change came with communal asceticism. Ascetic masters collected disciples, while coenobitic monasteries formed in towns and villages.[104] But categories of ascetic life remained fluid.[105] By the 420s Syrian monasticism defied easy classification. It also defied cultural geography. It spread to Armenian and Arabic speakers. And it permeated the Greek-speaking world, such that "sin-gle ones" were equated to "monks" (Greek: *monachoi*).

Causes of this transformation are variously located, but one factor was the involvement of the clergy. While most innovations probably took place indepen-dently, Syrian bishops supported new forms of asceticism, with financing, public praise, advice, oversight, ordination, and coercion. Usually scholars have treated this involvement as part of a larger Mediterranean trend.[106] In fact, each region fostered its own pattern of relations between monks and clerics—much depended on the people involved.

Early links between Syrian clerics and ascetics usually had to do with educa-tion. For generations virgins and covenanters had served as moral examples in preaching. By the 360s early hermits (such as Julian Saba) were cast in a similar role.[107] Meanwhile, clerics began pushing ascetic practice as educationally useful. Diodore's *asketerion* was touted for its three-year curriculum of discipline and study (similar to a sophist's school). Soon hermits also attracted Christians seek-ing formal guidance. And by the 380s Chrysostom (a failed hermit) was advising congregants to take their children to the monks for moral instruction.[108] Cler-ics may have been responding to the ascetics' (competing) popularity, but they also appreciated the monks' teaching capacity. Both hermits and archimandrites offered a model way of life (Greek: *politeia*) from which followers could build a sense of self within a community.[109]

Meletius and his allies, however, sought more from the monks than moral guid-ance. According to Theodoret, they wanted *clerics* imprinted with Meletius's *polit-eia*. Initially, they found new bishops through Diodore's *asketerion*, while most ascetic allies seem to have filled supporting roles. As the party grew, however, the bishops had to expand recruitment. They needed a permanent schooling appa-ratus, including curricula and reliable faculty. They also needed some way to sift pupils and place candidates in clerical vacancies. At the same time, the partisans had to extend the loyalties that had brought them success. This meant socializing clerical recruits. It also meant maintaining the cooperation of monastic leaders, in case they had to mobilize.

It was for these reasons that Syrian bishops got involved in monastic organizing, which according to Theodoret took off after 390. Part of this effort took the form of new individual contacts. Flavian and Acacius, we are told, visited with leading hermits. Some failed to meet their doctrinal standards—especially the "Messalians."[110] Others (such as Marcian and Macedonius) were certified as orthodox and ordained. Theodoret claimed that they expected no new labor from these monk-clerics, but his examples show how the mere title changed expectations.[111] In any case, Theodoret traced each master's disciples, revealing multigenerational "monastic families"[112] (again, see figure 10). Another part of the organizing effort involved encouraging coenobites. The *HR* pointed to seven new monasteries linked to ascetic allies (the *HE* added an eighth, in Edessa), listing their archimandrites up to the author's own day. But Theodoret was interested in more than new hermits and new houses. He named six bishops who emerged from this monastic following.[113] Such bishops, we are told, continued ascetic lives, while other bishops praised ascetics and enriched the clerical-monastic alliance.

Theodoret's (filtered) picture of Syrian monasticism fits well with the regional trend of ascetic-clerical cooperation. It also makes sense of Antiochene doctrinal development, particularly the works of Theodore. Theodore's writings survive in fragments or later translations, which sometimes mutually disagree. What is clear is that he wrote on nearly every biblical and doctrinal topic, revising Diodore's teachings. His exegesis extended the "literal, historical" trope with new definitions and explanations. He developed a wider list of biblical types and clearer typological reasoning. He also refined Diodore's doctrinal conclusions, turning from "two sons" to dyophysitism. And he extended the doctrinal logic to Mary, suggesting the parallel appellations (*theotokos* and *anthropotokos*) that would bedevil Nestorius.[114] These were not isolated speculations; they constituted a nearly comprehensive exegetical and anti-heretical corpus. Theodore was explicit about his aim to educate Christians in divine learning, stage by stage.[115] His works may have been written for various immediate purposes, but they could all be used as teaching texts for new network members. Commentaries served as a basic public discourse, inculcating habits of Christian reading.[116] The *Catechetical Homilies* then helped initiates to learn basic formulas. More detailed works like (the fragmentary) *On the Incarnation* probably served confidants, later in their curriculum. Such a corpus would work well with a graduated network of clerical recruitment.

Theodoret's account also helps to make sense of another development in the Syrian clergy, the new interest in translation. Meletius's original partisans were Greek-speakers.[117] Neither Diodore nor Theodore wrote in any other language. But from the start they claimed Syriac-speaking ascetic allies. By the 410s these favorite ascetics had developed multilingual hermit circles and either mixed or parallel monasteries. Interestingly, it was around the same time that Antiochene clerics in Edessa (under Bishop Rabbula) started translating their doctrinal writings.[118] Edessa also hosted Armenian translations. Armenian sources describe how Sahak, *Katholikos* of Persian Armenia, sent agents there, led by Mashdotz, to acquire important Christian writings.[119] Theodore likely knew of these translation efforts. It was probably Mashdotz to whom he dedicated his *Against the Magi*.[120] Theodoret's account ignores these efforts. But multilingual monasteries provide a probable context for early translations. These groups would need not only rules and prayers, but also teaching texts, in multiple languages.

Perhaps most significantly, Theodoret's account helps to explain why the early Antiochenes may have taken such interest in monasteries. Recruitment, after all, is only one part of network building; members must create a sense of solidarity. This was hard enough in a local partisan following, let alone across a large region. Signals of shared orthodoxy must have helped. Everyone could join in the hostility to Arians and Apollinarians, while the inner circle of experts worked with more detailed formulas. Theodoret, however, returned repeatedly to the sharing of a *politeia*, a way of living. Monasticism was celebrated in the late fourth century for its "brotherhood" of shared habits and values.[121] It is understandable how clerics wanted to apply the same brotherhood to the clergy. Monastic origins would provide a common bond among Antiochene recruits. Praise of asceticism could enrich the exchange of cues among bishops, priests, hermits, and archimandrites, as well as their followers.

Theodoret's account thus helps to explain Antiochene involvement in the monastic community. Moreover, it makes sense of the continuity of the network. By the early fifth century, Meletius's partisans were linking up with hermits and archimandrites across the region. No doubt they hoped to gain from ascetics' holy reputations. But Theodoret suggests more practical purposes: to organize new partisans, to train new clerics, and to consecrate loyal bishops. Clerics did not control the monastic community; Theodoret may overstate their role. But certain developments, he suggests, were due to specific Syrian bishops, working to perpetuate the Antiochene network.

"DOCTOR OF THE WHOLE CHURCH": INFORMAL CLERICAL LEADERSHIP

Few concerns pervade Theodoret's *HE* as much as proper church leadership. Since the early fourth century, church historians had sought to highlight the virtues of their favorite leading bishops. Socrates celebrated Proclus of Constantinople, a genteel peacemaker. Sozomen took to Chrysostom, a rigorous reformer. Theodoret touted several, mostly Syrian figures: Eusebius the calm confessor, Meletius the patient party-builder, Flavian the courageous communicator, and Acacius the active ambassador, as well as Diodore the resourceful researcher and Theodore the doctor of orthodoxy.[122] The purpose of his portraits was more than hero veneration. Collectively they outlined a model for episcopal authority. The model contained standard elements: personal piety, good oratory, interpretive skill, ascetic discipline, generosity, and precise orthodoxy. But there were unusual features. Theodoret's favorites received mixed treatment from other historians. Half of his heroes held minor sees. Nearly all made a mark before taking episcopal office, some before becoming clerics. Most important, Theodoret's favorites showed a cooperative sensibility. His ideal was not one leading bishop, but an informal leading group. This perspective is surprising because it runs counter to trends in church governance. If Theodoret was correct, the Antiochenes maintained a distributed sort of authority from Meletius's day to his own.

One of scholars' favorite topics has been the development of episcopal hierarchy. Since at least the second century, each bishop had asserted control over his own see.[123] While bishops established a loose mutual oversight, autonomous prelates remained the norm. The fourth century, however, began a deepening of church hierarchy. The Council of Nicaea gave special status to the metropolitan of every province (except in Egypt and parts of North Africa). It assigned higher honors to three primates (Rome, Alexandria and Antioch), to which a later council (in 381) added a fourth (Constantinople).[124] Often scholars have treated the canons as grants of legal power. These statements, however, were deliberately vague. Councils claimed to be reaffirming traditional privileges, which varied between regions.[125] Fifth-century Christians still had to define what metropolitan status meant in practice. For primates even more was left to local tradition, or to the church leaders themselves.

In fourth-century Syria, most observers have found a broad distribution of clerical authority. Scholars have noted the rise of the bishop of Alexandria to directorship in Egypt.[126] The bishop of Antioch, by contrast, has seemed like a "first among equals."[127] Syrian metropolitans presided at provincial councils and consecrated new suffragans, but "irregular" ordinations were common. This looser hierarchy was recognized by the broader church. According to Socrates, the Council of Constantinople in 381 named two bishops (metropolitan Diodore of Tarsus and suffragan Pelagius of Laodicea) as superintendents of the East, all without "violating the rights of the see of Antioch."[128]

Theodoret's account suggests another factor in Syrian exceptionalism: the troubles of the original Antiochenes. The HE described multiple figures in roles of partisan leadership. Meletius claimed the highest office, but because of his exile he relied on agents and proxies. The three lieutenants then appear in complementary roles: Diodore as brain trust, Flavian as public agitant, and Acacius as universal liaison. Talent, devotion, and learning gave these partisans as much influence as any office did. And all of them needed the help of ascetics and other bishops (e.g., Eusebius of Samosata and Basil of Caesarea), not to mention the emperor, to take over the region's key sees. After Meletius's death, problems continued, as did cooperation. Flavian relied on Diodore and Acacius (his consecrators), as well as Nectarius of Constantinople. Again, it took the skills of multiple figures to maintain the network's influence. Theodoret paid honor to the bishop of Antioch and to metropolitans. But his narrative showed no Syrian bishop exerting coercive authority. What most of his leading figures claimed was centrality: connections to those inside and outside their network.

By the 410s and 420s, Antiochene bishops were more secure in their influence, but according to Theodoret, they remained interdependent. Bishops of Antioch were presented as solid (if imperfect) leaders. Neither Porphyrius, nor Alexander, nor Theodotus, however, ran the see for more than eight years. Acacius of Beroea lived on as the last original partisan, without a monopoly on authority. If Theodoret assigned anyone higher leadership it was Theodore. His writings won him the author's moniker "doctor of the whole church."[129] Still, the *HE* hints at (suffragan) Theodore's dependence on others. His commemoration, after all, appeared alongside that of Theodotus and Polychronius.

Thus Theodoret helps to explain the limited authority of Syrian metropolitans and primates. According to the *HE,* looser leadership was required for Meletius and his partisans, and remained essential for his successors. After two generations it could easily have become entrenched. Informal leadership may have older roots than Theodoret suggests. And it may not have been accepted by every Syrian bishop—his presentation omits some troubling episodes, as we shall see. Nevertheless, Theodoret suggests that the broader distribution of authority among Syrian bishops be seen as an Antiochene legacy.

"HIDEOUS DETAILS": EVALUATING THEODORET'S ACCOUNT

Theodoret's *HE* provides social context for the production of Antiochene doctrine, the reorganization of Syrian monks, and the distribution of episcopal authority. Like any narrative source, however, his account must be interpreted carefully, with an eye toward the author's situation. On the one hand, Theodoret was well-informed. He had contact with key figures and access to church archives, as well as personal experience. On the other hand, Theodoret wrote within a matrix of rhetorical aims. He wrote to encourage defenders of an embattled orthodoxy. It was sensible for him to celebrate Meletius's partisans, to recall their endurance of hardship, and to tout their solidarity. Theodoret and his friends had good reason to seek a supportive sense of heritage, or even to construct one. Thus before accepting Theodoret's representations, we must check them against other clerical sources for the late fourth and early fifth centuries.

The most obvious outside sources to check are the *Church Histories* of Socrates and Sozomen, who wrote about Syrian clerics with less investment than

Theodoret. We have already noted Socrates' and Sozomen's unflattering treatment of the machinations of Meletius's party. In their view, his partisans conspired to set Paulinus aside.[130] Acacius, in particular, was presented as ruthless and vindictive. To Socrates and especially Sozomen, Acacius was one of the main persecutors of John Chrysostom (more on this below).[131] Unlike Theodoret, Socrates and Sozomen were willing to find fault with these Syrian clerics. And they did not see Diodore and Theodore as lynchpins of Nicene triumph.

When it comes to social connections, however, Socrates and Sozomen generally confirm Theodoret. Socrates noted Diodore's ascetic and educational endeavors, and his recruitment of Theodore and Chrysostom.[132] Sozomen verified links between the main partisans, recalling how Diodore and Acacius worked on Flavian's behalf.[133] Neither Socrates nor Sozomen dealt continuously with Syrian clerics; Theodoret may have read their unflattering statements and wished to respond. Nonetheless, both church historians offer details that support Theodoret's depiction of a tight Antiochene partisan following.

Greater troubles for Theodoret's account come from direct clerical observers, and from one episode in particular: the controversy over John Chrysostom. Scholars have debated whether Chrysostom was "Antiochene" in his doctrinal thinking. Socially, however, he was clearly linked to the early partisans.[134] Theodoret recognized Chrysostom as a member of Meletius's following, a student of Diodore, and a friend to Theodore. He defended Chrysostom's actions as bishop of Constantinople, but he chose to omit the "hideous details."[135] Socrates and Sozomen had no such qualms, but they focused on Chrysostom's foes in Alexandria and Constantinople. It is mainly Palladius of Helenopolis, and Chrysostom himself, who reveal Syrian dimensions of the conflict that surrounded John's fall. Among the foes of Chrysostom Palladius included more Syrian bishops than Anatolians or Egyptians.[136] Other sources mention Acacius as Chrysostom's opponent, but Palladius made him an instigator of the controversy. Not only did he place Acacius and other Syrians at the Synod of the Oak in 403, which first deposed Chrysostom; he claimed that Acacius coordinated the colloquies of Easter 404, where John was finally exiled.[137] Palladius then noted the schism this inspired in Syria between Acacius's party and a "Johannite" faction. And he explained how Acacius and his allies rigged elections in Antioch to appoint their candidate, Porphyrius.[138] Palladius thus presents a Syrian clergy filled not with harmony but with factionalism. He even lists supporters of John who suffered for favoring the restoration of the exiled bishop.[139] Palladius's picture is partly affirmed by Chrysostom's letters written from exile. Here Chrysostom appealed to many bishops whom he counted as supporters, including Theodore.[140] We can see why Theodoret wanted to "throw a veil over the ill-deeds of men who share our faith."[141] Over an issue unrelated to doctrine, the followers of Meletius had torn their camaraderie apart.

Yet even this dark episode does not contradict Theodoret's basic representations of an Antiochene network; it merely complicates the picture. For the Syrian dimension of the Chrysostom affair looks like a contest for influence gone awry. As Flavian of Antioch grew frail, John Chrysostom and Acacius were two of several clerical figures with claims to his position of influence. If Palladius is accurate, Acacius used the controversy over John to build a following, which he employed to name his own candidates to open sees. Meanwhile, Theodore and the "Johannites" attempted to build their own faction. In chapter 2, we drew a network map with multiple figures of influence. Any such network might face divisive rivalries. In any case, the Syrian split over Chrysostom was eventually resolved. Bishops of Antioch restored John's name to the diptychs, and even Acacius assented.[142] Palladius saw Acacius's actions as a betrayal. But betrayal certainly plays a role in close-knit communities (see next chapter).

What most complicates Theodoret's story are stray notes about the loyalties of Syrian bishops. Theodoret's *HE* mentioned no opponents of his network in the Syrian clergy, apart from suspected Apollinarians. Yet his list of allies covers scarcely a sixth of the region's sees. Clearly the followers of Meletius did not completely take over the region. Some monastic groups (such as that of Alexander the Sleepless) resisted the bishops' oversight.[143] Theodoret acknowledged recruitment in monasteries or through ascetic relationships, but he said nothing about other modes of picking new clergymen. Yet his letters mention married bishops—even a twice-married bishop recruited by Acacius.[144] Almost all of Theodoret's examples of Syrian monk-bishops date to the 410s and 420s. Perhaps monastic recruitment was a more minor, later development than he suggested. Theodore's doctrinal influence beyond his inner circle may have been limited. His supporter-turned-critic, Rabbula of Edessa, complained that Theodore had doctrines he would only share with close confidants.[145] Even Theodore's admirers acknowledged that he sometimes had to retract controversial tropes when outsiders got wind of them.[146] Several letters recount contentions among the Antiochene leaders. The loose distribution of authority may have been an accident of competing claims rather than a shared tradition. Theodoret imagined a harmonious Nicene clergy from the 380s to the 420s. His actual predecessors must have seen things differently.

And yet, Theodoret's general picture cannot be dismissed. His narrative shows us glimpses of the early Antiochene network. Theodoret's prosopographic testimony remains largely uncontested. And the thicket of personal alliances that it presents finds confirmation across a spectrum of sources. The members of this network did not all share a single line of doctrinal thinking. But Theodoret suggests that they traded signals of friendship and shared orthodoxy, densely in a core group and more sparsely further afield. The late 420s furnish our earliest documents from the conciliar collections and a few personal letters. At this point we find the sort of Antiochene cues and connections discussed in chapters 1 and 2. At the start of the First Council of Ephesus (431), Antiochene clerical links stretched across Syria (see figure 11, in the next chapter). To build such an alliance need not require fifty years, but it would take some time. Theodoret's *Church History* offers one representation of the Antiochene heritage. His narrations were geared to inspire his contemporary allies. But they had to be plausible, to make sense of existing records. Theodoret's idealized picture of a clerical party was based, in all likelihood, on a real (i.e., intersubjective) cue-trading network. In any case, it was an Antiochene sense of heritage that grounded Theodoret and his associates during two decades of controversy. The contrast between the present (in the 430s and 440s) and the (partly constructed) past was all too obvious. The next chapter will turn from narrative analysis to documented micro-history, to follow the network through its "Nestorian" crisis and resulting transformation.

4

Ephesus and After

Leadership, Doctrinal Crisis, and
the Transformation of the Antiochene Network

Some time around 450 Nestorius, the empire's most infamous living "heretic," broke his silence with a memoir (known as the *Book of Heracleides*).[1] Nothing in two decades of controversy, he claims, had turned out right. Nestorius snipes first at his prosecutor. It was unconscionable that Cyril of Alexandria, "though he knew the faith, passed over it because of his enmity." In fact, Cyril "cast [Nestorius] out, wounded and naked" and on the basis of rumor convicted him. Nestorius does not blame the emperor, who had been supportive until twisted monks seduced him. He is less kind to fellow Syrians, who accepted a "deceptive peace" and left the faithful behind. This text suggests an image of Nestorius by the Oasis, preaching to a mirage crowd. "I endure all things for the ordering of the churches," he writes, "but all things have happened to the contrary."[2]

Nestorius's reminiscences brim with the bitterness of a failed church leader. Not one year passed from his consecration in Constantinople until clerics revolted against him. Nestorius had been selected in 428 because factions could not agree on a local candidate.[3] Dreaming of Chrysostom, courtiers turned to a learned Syrian ascetic known for stirring preaching. Nestorius arrived in Constantinople to find a dispute underway over how to address Mary.[4] It was an issue on which Theodore had written, so Nestorius and his carpetbaggers entered the fray. The result was a storm of protest.[5] Still, the controversy seemed local until Cyril of Alexandria weighed in.[6] With scattered arguments and a list of offensive sayings, he convinced Pope Celestine to condemn the bishop of the capital.[7] Then he composed *Twelve Anathemas against Nestorius* and in November 430 sent them across the empire (except, perhaps, to Syria).[8] At this point the dispute aligned with regional boundaries. Egyptians hung close to Cyril; in Nestorius they saw a denier of Christ's divinity. Syrian clerics (eventually) rallied behind Nestorius; in Cyril they saw a denier of God's impassibility. Both sides were exaggerating, but this controversy had wide ramifications. The argument caused a rupture between the clerics of Syria and those of Egypt. Just as importantly, it set the Syrian clergy against itself. And while Nestorius faced exile, his associates faced one another, seizing their chance to assert influence and somehow save their party.

This chapter examines the dispute over Nestorius from the perspective of the Antiochene network that supported and then abandoned him. Scholars have reveled in the chaos at Ephesus in 431, which (improbably) came to be called the Third Ecumenical Council.[9] Less discussed is how this episode became a crisis within the Syrian clergy. Through schism and negotiations the Antiochenes faced off over doctrinal precision, personal condemnation, leadership, and communal identity. The struggles allowed members to test their stature and reconfigure their loyalties. As we have noted, this is a well-documented episode. Cyril and his allies saved selected conciliar records; so did Count Irenaeus, the future bishop of Tyre.[10] Many of these documents are hard to sort chronologically. They can deceive modern readers looking for quick facts. Close analysis, though, allows the documents to be roughly sequenced and dated.[11] Unlike the narratives examined in the last chapter, they convey social information *outside* of Theodoret's editorial control.

Together the documents reveal a transformation of the Antiochene group, its leadership, and its sense of community. In the 420s, the Antiochene network probably remained informal, with a consensual leadership but an ill-defined periphery. Then came several unsettling deaths, just as confrontations were brewing. At the Council of Ephesus (in 431) the Antiochenes organized in opposition to Cyril. During the resulting schism, members competed to exercise influence. But it was negotiations to renew communion (432–433) that split the Antiochenes. For two more years members pushed for or against rejoining communion. After violence and failed mediation, a consensus reemerged, thanks in part to Theodoret. But the dispute had already altered relations. The crisis in Syria was not a mere addendum to wider theological feuding. It was a risky social process that reshaped the Antiochene community.

ANTIOCHENES BEFORE THE CRISIS:
SUCCESS AND UNCERTAINTY

The transformation of the Antiochene network began in the 420s, where Theodoret's *Church History* left off. In many ways, the Antiochenes looked successful, expanding within Syria and beyond. But success brought its own problems. Steady growth made the network looser and more dependent on leaders. When those leaders died, the bishops faced uncertainties over how to redistribute influence and redefine their ensemble. Every enduring group confronts transitions. For

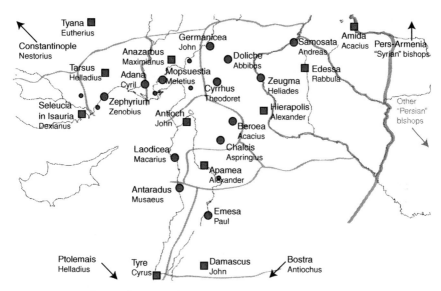

FIGURE 11. Map of Antiochene members, 430–431, noted in conciliar documents. Squares = metropolitan sees, large circles = major suffragan sees, small circles = minor suffragan sees, thin lines = approximate provincial boundaries, thick line = approximate frontier of Roman Empire.

the Antiochenes, transition coincided with doctrinal controversy—a crisis in the making.

Success for the Antiochenes came in the 420s with calm in regional clerical relations. The previous chapter outlined how Theodoret described the rise of the Antiochene network—its doctrinal cues, recruitment methods, and modes of leadership. As we noted, it is unclear how accurately he recalled these developments. By the 420s, however, the leading Antiochenes had clearly established the basic patterns that Theodoret described. Theodore's doctrinal works were accessible to core figures, with wider use of more ambiguous Antiochene cues.[12] Bishops of Antioch finally reconciled with the followers of Paulinus, as well as with former "Apollinarians."[13] Only minor disputes concerned the bishops, seemingly unrelated to grand old controversies.[14] Meanwhile, episcopal successions proceeded, with some recruits (such as Theodoret) coming out of the monasteries. No Syrian prelate claimed supreme authority, but four were held in high esteem: Theodore, Acacius, Theodotus of Antioch, and Polychronius of Apamea (Theodore's brother).[15] Whatever their prior disagreements, they seem to have built a web of mutual respect.

One sign of Antiochene success was the gradual growth of the network (again, see figure 11). Clearly the leading bishops continued to recruit in Syria. They also pushed for external expansion. To the north they courted the prelates of

Cappadocia. To the south, they canvassed Palestine.[16] Efforts proceeded on the desert frontier, with a new shrine to Saint Sergius at Rasapha.[17] Contacts deepened with Christians under Persian rule, especially in Armenia, where "Syrians" were invited to reeducate the clergy.[18] The grandest prize, of course, was Constantinople. When Nestorius was elected, Antiochenes were ready to take advantage. "Work with me to subdue the heretics," Nestorius was famously quoted, "and I will work with you [o emperor] to subdue the Persians."[19] Perhaps, in each case, he had Antiochene expansion in mind.

Steady growth had important social effects for the Antiochenes. In chapter 2, we noted a common impact of continued network growth: a modular scale-free topology. This basic pattern, we recall, features well-connected hubs and a loose periphery. The earliest conciliar documents and letters affirm this basic template and point to some case-specific implications. Most important, doctrinal involvement seems to have varied with one's place in the network. At the core sat writers and translators who surrounded Theodore and approved his doctrinal work.[20] Not every bishop joined this clique, but those who did formed an expert inner circle. On the periphery, we find a different scene. Parts of Syria and nearby regions had no experience of Antiochene teaching, not even its more ambiguous cues. Not surprisingly, bonds with outsiders employed general social signals. Here indoctrination and socialization would take time.

In fact, the growth and reshaping of the Antiochene network carried liabilities. For starters, expansion meant a coalition that was more peripheral and harder to oversee. The more Antiochenes sought distant allies, the more they risked differences in doctrine coming to light.[21] Even existing members might become harder to keep in line. Bishop Nestorius was too distant to join in customary consults or rituals. Quickly, such distance led to miscommunication.[22] Meanwhile, expansion raised the relative importance of core mediators and hubs. It also distinguished the highly Antiochene discourse surrounding these hubs from the vaguer interactions of the periphery. An expanding network could survive these liabilities, if it developed new social practices. Otherwise it could lose its sense of community.

At this moment of uneasy expansion the Antiochene network was struck by a wave of mortality. Theodore died in 428. Theodotus of Antioch passed away the next year, followed by Polychronius.[23] These deaths were hardly unexpected. But the loss of three leading bishops unsettled the distribution of authority. Acacius still presided in Beroea, but at age one hundred he was too feeble to play ambassador. Nestorius may have excited hopes for leadership, but his distance and clumsy touch soon removed him from consideration. Thus by 430 the network lay in the hands of less prominent figures, who had to rearrange the relational map.

But which Syrian bishops (besides Acacius) could assert leadership? The main candidates were occupants of high-ranking sees. The new primate, John of Antioch, held substantial sway. So did experienced metropolitans: John of Damascus, Maximianus of Anazarbus, Helladius of Tarsus, Rabbula of Edessa, and Alexander of Hierapolis, as well as Eutherius of Tyana (in nearby Cappadocia II). Yet this did not exhaust the list. Some bishops had important connections, such as Paul of Emesa (Acacius's latest protégé)[24] or Meletius of Mopsuestia (Theodore's successor). Some benefited from urban wealth and geographic centrality, including Aspringius of Chalcis and Macarius of Laodicea. Some hailed from famous monasteries, above all Helladius of Tarsus.[25] Some held recognized writing talent, such as Andreas and Rabbula. Theodoret counted as a candidate, for his connections, his asceticism and his learning. No prelate represented the presumed heir.

Just as the Antiochenes had started to rearrange themselves, they confronted the Nestorian controversy. At first, Cyril informed John of Antioch of Nestorius's most troubling quotations and asked for support. John consulted with Archelaus of Seleucia Pieria, Aspringius of Chalcis, Heliades of Zeugma, Meletius of Mopsuestia, Macarius of Laodicea, and Theodoret. Their response in late 430 was to ask Nestorius to retract offending statements, as Theodore had once done.[26] It was thus understandable that Cyril wrote to Acacius, asking him to free Constantinople from another troublesome bishop.[27] By January 431, however, Nestorius had informed John of Antioch about the *Twelve Anathemas*. Cyril and Pope Celestine had demanded Nestorius sign this text within ten days or face excommunication. The surprise of this text effectively started the regional division. The *Anathemas* declared that Christ was none other than God the Word, "made one in subject (*hypostasin*)" and "by nature (*physin*)."[28] They also proclaimed that the "Word of God suffered in the flesh." John labeled these statements "Apollinarian," invoking the Syrians' *bête noire*. He spoke with Acacius and enlisted Andreas and Theodoret to write refutations.[29] But the Antiochenes were already late. Theodoret and Andreas argued against the *Anathemas* along divergent lines.[30] Even Acacius replied to Cyril inconclusively.[31] No one presented a shared Syrian perspective.

Behind this hesitancy lay problems of leadership that stemmed from the shape of the network. Except for Acacius, the decision makers in the winter of 430/431 stood on shaky ground. No other would-be leader had yet won extra centrality. No other figure had set an agenda, because none had pushed a claim to authority. In May 431, bishops gathered in Antioch to prepare notes and start a land journey to Ephesus. Most of the would-be leaders came along (except Acacius and Andreas).[32] Whatever their plans, they were unready for what was to come.

CRISIS PRECIPITATED: ANTIOCHENES AT THE FIRST COUNCIL OF EPHESUS

Few events brought as much anticipation as the ecumenical council of 431, the first in fifty years. No attending bishops knew what to expect. Any gathering this broad and ritualized would have social ramifications. In the case of Ephesus, the result was a stark division in the clergy. Obviously the Antiochenes fought in Ephesus to defend their definition of orthodoxy. Deeper processes, however, were at work, reshaping the relational context. The breakdown of the council forced the Antiochenes to see their divergence from the rest of the Nicene clergy. In response, they turned their network into an organized faction. The loose periphery was now cut back to a firm social boundary. Meanwhile clashes created an environment where aspirant leaders could start to test their influence. Even as schism boosted Antiochene solidarity, it facilitated internal conflict.

The basic story of the First Council of Ephesus has been recounted many times, but let us review the details. The emperor called a gathering for Pentecost (June 7, 431). Cyril of Alexandria, though already facing imperial criticism, prepared to preside.[33] Nestorius came on time, but his Syrian supporters did not, and from the start Cyril's party treated him as the accused.[34] The imperial envoy Candidianus delayed proceedings so that the Syrian bishops might participate. On June 21, an advance Syrian party (including Theodoret, Alexander of Apamea, and Alexander of Hierapolis) promised the rapid arrival of their delegation.[35] Nevertheless, on June 22, Cyril and the host bishop, Memnon, began the council. Candidianus protested, along with Theodoret and sixty-eight other bishops.[36] Still the council condemned Nestorius's doctrine and demanded that he recant.[37] Candidianus ordered his troops to blockade the city, while Count Irenaeus lent bodyguards to protect Nestorius's dwelling.[38] Cyril's envoys summoned Nestorius but were turned away with a beating. So the council leaders declared Nestorius deposed.[39] On June 26, John of Antioch arrived with the Syrian delegation. After consulting with Theodoret, the Alexanders, Nestorius, Candidianus, and Irenaeus, he called a counter-council, the "real council" of Ephesus. John took testimony on Cyril's misbehavior. As many as fifty-eight attendees denounced Cyril as a violent heretic.[40] Within an hour, the counter-council deposed Cyril and Memnon and excommunicated around one hundred sixty collaborators.[41] Still the confrontation worsened. On the evening of June 27, the counter-council tried to storm the main church of Ephesus, probably to consecrate a new bishop. When Cyril's supporters blocked them, mutual accusations gave way to urban riots.[42] As Hiba of Edessa later reported, "Bishop went against bishop, congregation against congregation."[43]

In one week the Nicene clergy had turned a frustrating disagreement into a violent feud. Just as quickly the Antiochene social world was transformed. Before their arrival, the Syrian bishops had condemned Cyril's Anathemas but knew little of where they stood with other Nicenes. The gathering in Ephesus showed them the breadth of Cyril's coalition, including Roman Armenia, Cappadocia, and Palestine. The main Antiochene response was reflexive solidarity, expressed in angry acclamations. The Eastern bishops found extraregional allies. Initially, they had more metropolitans supporting them than Cyril did.[44] But Syria still supplied 60 percent of the counter-council attendees. This group had departed from Syria representing a diffuse network. Feuding in Ephesus turned it into a recognized party, with a director, an advisory council, and a clear membership.

From June to July confrontations in Ephesus continued. Cyril and Memnon held the main churches, from which they preached against Nestorius and his supporters.[45] John and Theodoret (among others) took to the streets but could not sway the crowds.[46] On July 10, papal legates arrived and sided with Cyril, who reconvened his council. He heard complaints against the Syrians, then excommunicated his opponents, now numbering just thirty-four.[47] In Ephesus the Antiochenes were obviously losing ground.

Local confrontations, however, were only part of the story. The bishops also competed to win sympathy in the capital. Cyril was first to get his synodical letters to Constantinople. Even before the Syrian delegation arrived in Ephesus, he had monastic allies demonstrating for him before the palace.[48] Meanwhile, Nestorius and some allies appealed to the emperor for a new council. And Candidianus sent a report, critical of Cyril.[49] Hearing these conflicting reports, Theodosius forbade the bishops to leave Ephesus and sent a new official (Palladius) to investigate.[50] After the counter-council and riot, more letters went to the capital. John and his allies sent synodicals, while Count Candidianus sent a second report.[51] Cyril countered with new letters and got Palladius to report more favorably for his side. The Antiochenes' best hope was Count Irenaeus, who went to Constantinople in late July.[52] Cyril may have claimed the support of monks and crowds. But the Antiochenes still expected their contacts to win the court to their side.

High hopes and contacts, however, were poorly supported by the Antiochenes' written appeals. Their bold denunciations made sense in open letters to the laity. By decrying Cyril's "tyranny," and his reliance on "Egyptian sailors," and "Asian farm-boys,"[53] Antiochenes rallied their supporters. But stridency was less likely to sway prefects and generals. Demands for a hearing brought no reply.[54] Nothing, however, matched the Antiochenes' bombastic appeals to the emperor. Not only did they denounce Cyril's "civil war." They presumed to issue policy suggestions— proposing a new council with two bishops per province (to balance out Cyril's and Memnon's roughly ninety suffragans).[55] A direct appeal was always risky; it left no escape if the emperor said no. In this case, it also shows an ignorance of the webs of persuasion that constituted Theodosius's court.

Then came another Antiochene misstep: inaction. In late July the court sent a third envoy to Ephesus, John, count of the Sacred Largesses. With the parties refusing to speak, he announced an imperial judgment. Amazingly, the emperor had corresponded with Acacius of Beroea. On Acacius's advice he accepted *both* councils: Cyril and Memnon were to be deposed along with Nestorius.[56] It was probably the best the Syrian bishops could hope for—Irenaeus must have helped behind the scenes. But then, the Antiochenes hesitated. They lost sympathy pressing for Nestorius's release. Cyril, meanwhile, arranged monastic protests. He showered courtiers with gifts and exposed the "false reports" of Irenaeus.[57] Soon the Antiochene agents were sidelined.

So why did the Antiochenes make so shoddy an effort to sway the court? The evidence suggests that the leaders were focused on their own community. John of Antioch wrote on behalf of the whole counter-council. He relied on advice from the Alexanders, Helladius of Tarsus, and Theodoret. Simulated networks that stop growing usually tighten, reducing the importance of hubs. By late July, the Antiochenes had lost as many as twenty-three (non-Syrian) supporters. The easiest way for the leaders to maintain their status was to stand firm for the network. With stories of violence and "tyranny," John and his advisors stoked Antiochene solidarity.[58] The cost was an inability to tailor appeals.

In late August, the Antiochenes received yet another chance. The emperor invited eight petitioners from each side to speak to his consistory. Cyril and Memnon were kept under house arrest in Ephesus; Nestorius was sent back to his Antioch monastery.[59] But Theodosius wanted a theological agreement. Cyril's party chose delegates that revealed their geographical scope. Legates of the pope joined Anatolian and Libyan bishops, with Firmus of Caesarea (in Cappadocia) and Acacius of Melitene (in Roman Armenia) in the lead.[60] The Antiochenes anointed a familiar clique. John of Antioch, Aspringius of Chalcis, and Alexander of Hierapolis were picked, along with Paul of Emesa (to represent Acacius of Beroea). They were joined by three more Syrians—Macarius of Laodicea, John of Damascus, and Helladius of Ptolemais—and Himerius of (Anatolian) Nicomedia. Soon Alexander of Hierapolis pulled out, perhaps to avoid pressure to compromise. His place passed to Theodoret.[61] Since public disorder unsettled the capital, the meeting was moved to Chalcedon.[62] This change probably suited the Antiochenes, who were no doubt sick of hostile crowds.

Again, the Antiochenes failed to persuade. The delegations met in the imperial presence five times in September and October, their arguments framed by written briefs. In their opening petition the Antiochenes retained their bombast. They declared their hope in the emperor, who "after the power on high is the only savior of the world." But they echoed Nestorius on the cost of error: the loss of Christ's favor in Roman-Persian relations. The Antiochenes gave no ground and repeated that they were ready to lose their sees.[63] At the first oral arguments, the Antiochene delegates saw signs of success. As spokesman, Theodoret scored some stinging attacks against Cyril, while his opponent, Acacius of Melitene, seemed to have offended the emperor.[64] But the Antiochenes had been star-struck. With no settlement, Theodosius drifted toward Cyril's side.[65] He prepared to restore Cyril and Memnon and invited their delegates to consecrate a new bishop of Constan-

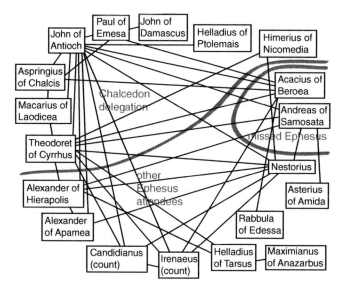

FIGURE 12. The Antiochene leadership core, 430–431, according to letters and conciliar documents. Links approximate evident or implied exchange of 2 or more Antiochene social cues (including at least one doctrinal cue) within 1 year of 431 (more links may have existed).

tinople (Maximianus). The remaining bishops he sent home.[66] Desperate, the Antiochenes tried more petitions. "You are not just their emperor," they pleaded, "but ours as well." Still, they denounced Cyril's crimes. "If Your Piety will not accept ... our doctrine from God," they added, "we shall shake off the dust of our feet and cry with the blessed Paul, 'We are all made pure from Your blood' (Acts 20:26)."[67] It is hard to see how the emperor *could* have received this argument favorably.

Again the Antiochenes' failure makes more sense when we examine the place of leaders in the community. The meeting in Chalcedon created a tense new environment. By separating leading bishops from followers, the emperor tried to over-awe them toward agreement. But the delegates were left in a difficult position. They had to keep clerical support in Ephesus and crowd support in Chalcedon, all while winning over the court. Meanwhile, the delegates had to work with one another (see figure 12). This mattered less for Cyril's representatives, who had his direct instructions. But the Antiochenes had settled neither their doctrinal judgments nor their disposition of influence. Again, their words were aimed at their own associates as much as at the court.

Party unity, however, was not the only motive for the eight Antiochene delegates. The meetings in Chalcedon created opportunities to test their leadership, especially for Theodoret. Before the council, he had been essentially a staff writer. Now he took a public role. He made the Antiochene case in person, and probably in writing. He helped to inform associates in Ephesus and back in Syria.[68] He even preached, deluging Cyril with invective from the Prophets.[69] Theodoret's proudest moment came in a conversation with the emperor, which he reported to his peers:

> The most pious emperor learned that a crowd clung to us, and meeting with us alone, he said, "I know that you are gathering illegally." Then I said, "Since you have given me the right to speak frankly (*parrhēsian*), listen with leniency. Is it just that heretics and excommunicates conduct church services, but that we who struggle for the faith ... cannot enter a church?" He said, "And what am I to do?" So I responded to him, "What your [officials] did in Ephesus ... It was fitting that you gave orders to the bishop of that place not to allow either them or us to gather until we made accord, in order that your just sentence may be known to all." And to these things he responded, "I cannot give orders to a bishop." So I replied, "Do not, then, give an order to us, and we may take a church and gather, and your Piety will know that numbers on our side are much above the numbers on theirs." ... We told him that our gathering held neither a reading of the Holy Scriptures nor an offering [of the Eucharist], but only prayers on behalf of the faith and his rule and speeches about piety. So he gave his approval. And the gatherings increased; everyone was pleased to hear our instruction.[70]

This episode hardly marks a moment of grand persuasion. Even this quotation suggests that the emperor was barely listening.[71] Still, Theodoret had represented his colleagues; he had boldly spoken to earthly authority. Records are sparser for the other delegates. John of Antioch delivered his own sermon.[72] The other six must have made their own efforts at leadership. Most likely they competed to show stridency.

All told, the meetings in Ephesus and Chalcedon brought a crisis for the Antiochene network. The primary loser was still Nestorius. Attempts to question his guilt elicited hissing in the consistory.[73] While allies would keep pushing the court to reconsider his fate,[74] by October he had been replaced. The rest of the Antiochenes kept their sees but faced excommunication by more than two hundred peers.[75] The Antiochenes also received a rough course in court relations. They saw how quickly foes could sideline their high-placed friends. Perhaps the most startling blow was to the Antiochenes' informal sense of community. For the first time they openly confronted their differences with other Nicenes. In their view Cyril must have "dogmatize[d] tyrannically instead of piously."[76] For they could not understand how so many bishops disagreed with their orthodoxy. The Antiochenes' first reaction was to reify community boundaries. At the same time, would-be leaders were starting to compete for influence. For the moment, these trends worked together, but competition, if not managed carefully, could tear any group apart.

SCHISM AND NEGOTIATION: THE ANTIOCHENE
COMMUNITY, 431-435

Antiochene bishops returned from Ephesus united by conflict. The next few years, however, presented new pressures, from distant bishops, from regional defectors, and from lay officials. The Antiochenes were forced by the imperial court to negotiate, and the more they rearranged their positions, the more they disagreed. On the surface these arguments concerned orthodoxy, but doctrine alone cannot explain all the internal hostility. What we see here is a leadership struggle—not just a contest for influence, but a clash of visions for the Antiochene community.

When the Syrian delegation first returned in November 431, they worked to secure their sense of unity. Already the bishops were worried about imperial coercion. So John of Antioch contacted military leaders to get a safety guarantee.[77] Just as worrisome were wavering (or absent) bishops. So John called regional councils in Tarsus and Antioch, which starkly condemned Cyril and his *Anathemas*.[78] Other leaders joined the effort. Theodoret sent to Constantinople and to Syrian monasteries theological tomes that left little room for compromise.[79] A boost of confidence came with the approval of Acacius of Beroea, who figured that Cyril succeeded by bribing the palace eunuch.[80] By the end of 431, Syria's churches echoed with anti-Cyril rhetoric. Calling him "the Egyptian," the Antiochenes asserted that they were the universal church.

To define their community after Ephesus, Antiochenes relied on the symbols of communion. For centuries celebrating the Eucharist had expressed Christian unity. The reading of "orthodox" names from the diptychs, a newer practice, extended these links across space and time.[81] The symbolic power of communion played a part in many conflicts. Its role was probably magnified in Syria, where everyone from Ephrem to Rabbula viewed the Eucharist as a type of Christ.[82] The breaking of communion had immediate consequences for the "Cyrillians" and the Antiochenes.[83] Communion, however, remained an ambiguous concept. Some asserted an absolutist ecclesiology. Communicants had to be doctrinally pure or they could transmit contagion.[84] Others took a more flexible perspective. Doctrinal unity, in their view, required discretion and trust.[85] Ecclesiological differences mattered little in late 431; vague symbols were enough to unite the network. But the differences led to divergent responses in the controversy.

By mid-432, the Antiochene communion faced mounting pressure to cave. One source of this pressure was canvassing by Cyril's allies. Juvenal of Jerusalem retained for Cyril the support of all Palestinian prelates. Firmus of Caesarea found less unity in Cappadocia, so he chased Eutherius of Tyana away and tried to replace him.[86] Acacius of Melitene conducted a larger operation in Roman and Persian Armenia. Eventually he turned the *Katholikos* Sahak into a friendly anti-Antiochene.[87] A greater source of pressure was defection within Syria. At this point Rabbula of Edessa revealed that he had abandoned his colleagues for Cyril's side. A spring council in Antioch tried to contain the damage, with little apparent success.[88] Then came pressure from the court. In late spring, Theodosius II determined that the schism was pointless. He empowered a new envoy, Aristolaus, to bring Cyril and John to a one-on-one negotiation. He even asked the famous ascetic Symeon Stylites to urge the Syrians to come.[89] John avoided this new conference, pleading weak health, but he could not ignore Aristolaus.[90] He called on his colleagues to start negotiations.

Negotiations proved frustrating for the Antiochenes, and divisive. By the summer of 432 the Syrian clerics were already behind the curve. Even before Aristolaus's visit, Cyril had begun writing Syrian bishops stating his desire for peace.[91] So John convened a consultation in Antioch. The group included familiar faces: Alexander of Hierapolis, Alexander of Apamea, Helladius of Tarsus, Paul of Emesa, Macarius of Laodicea, and Theodoret. Andreas, recovered from his illness, joined in. So did Acacius—the meeting may have been moved to Beroea to include him.[92] The group drafted six proposals to send to Egypt. Five listed specific dogmas and requisite actions; the sixth proposed that the Nicene Creed be the sole test of orthodoxy, along with Athanasius of Alexandria's *Letter to Epictetus*. Unimpressed with most of the proposals, Aristolaus urged the Antiochenes to send only the vague sixth. They agreed, but they refused to condemn Nestorius. And they insisted that Cyril condemn Apollinarius and foreswear his *Twelve Anathemas*.[93] Soon Aristolaus returned with a reply. Cyril agreed to work from the Nicene Creed, Athanasius's letter, and a few more supporting authors. He denounced Apollinarius, but he still demanded the condemnation of Nestorius and kept silent about the *Anathemas*.[94] This time, the Antiochenes had divergent reactions. Acacius and John saw hopeful signs. Alexander of Hierapolis was skeptical, and the others postponed judgment.[95] In the fall of 432, John met in Beroea with Paul of Emesa and Acacius, and gave more ground.[96] Alexander grew upset, as did Helladius of Tarsus and Eutherius of Tyana.[97] Through the fall rumors circulated that John had betrayed Nestorius, though even Alexander insisted the rumors were false.[98] Schism had kept most Antiochenes united. Negotiations now brought new fissures right within the core.

This dispute among Antiochenes was not merely a new clash of theology. Core members, in fact, preferred the same doctrinal tropes: "two natures, a difference between them, and a union without confusion."[99] So far Cyril had not provided sufficient detail to determine if he had set aside the *Anathemas,* and thus held an acceptable faith. To play along, Antiochenes had to negotiate with someone who condemned an orthodox colleague. They had to "condescend" to accept communion with him despite his reticence. The choice to cooperate or to protest

depended on the bishops' understanding of communion, and on how much confidence they had in their decision-making process.

During the fall and winter of 432/433, Antiochene positions on negotiations
grew less coherent. When Alexander first grew worried, he sent Acacius a list of
demands, which John called "the superminutiae of the minutiae of dialectic."[100]
Both backed by new supporters, the two men headed for a breach. Some Syrian
bishops tried to bridge the gap, most notably Theodoret. He agreed with John
that Cyril's statements could be seen as orthodox, so long as he condemned three
groups: "those who say Christ is purely man, those who divide ... Christ into two
sons, and those who deny His divinity." But he agreed with Alexander that he
could not accept the condemnation of Nestorius or the communion of those who
condemned him. By splitting these judgments, Theodoret established a middle
ground.[101] His statements, however, confused many colleagues. Rumors circulated
in Alexander's camp that *Theodoret* had betrayed Nestorius. Meanwhile, John
behaved as though he had won an endorsement.[102] In December 432, he sent Paul
of Emesa to Egypt with Aristolaus to finish negotiations. After a few meetings Paul
reported success. Not only had he outlined an agreement; he had embraced Cyril's
communion and joined him in preaching.[103] John reported the breakthrough, but
others waited for the full text to decide where they stood.

It was the final stages of agreement that brought the Antiochene crisis to a
head. The return of Paul of Emesa and Aristolaus in February 433 confirmed their
critics' fears. Paul had agreed to speak of a union between God the Word and a
human "temple." This formula could support two distinct natures, but it remained
ambiguous; it said nothing about the *Twelve Anathemas*.[104] Still, Paul would not
have sparked such hostility, had not he also agreed to condemn Nestorius and welcome Maximianus instead.[105] Moreover, Paul and Aristolaus were accompanied by
two clerics from Alexandria, with Cyril's letter declaring communion. They had
been instructed to give the letter to John only if he condemned Nestorius. If not,
Aristolaus was ready to report it to the emperor.[106] John endorsed the arrangement
and took communion. In April 433, he and Cyril published a *Formula of Reunion*.
The accord called Christ "consubstantial to the Father according to His divinity,
and consubstantial to us according to His humanity." It affirmed a "union of two
natures," without confusion. It distinguished scriptural passages tied to the divinity from those tied to the humanity.[107] The agreement fell just short of endorsing
"two natures in Christ." But it still said nothing directly about the *Twelve Anathemas*. And it condemned Nestorius and demanded communion with Maximianus of Constantinople, Cyril, and even Rabbula. Now the bishops of Syria openly
faced their choice.

The aftermath of John's agreement with Cyril reveals how deep the disputes
among Antiochenes went. In mid-433, bishops met province by province. Syria

I, most of Phoenicia I and II, Arabia, and Mesopotamia sided with John. They accepted the *Formula,* condemned Nestorius, and embraced Cyril's communion.[108] Osrhoene had already defected to Cyril; their agreement was assumed. In Syria II, Alexander of Apamea hesitated, but then led his suffragans to join John's communion.[109] Bishops of other provinces decided differently. Isauria and Cilicia I and II condemned "the Egyptian" and cut ties to those sharing his communion.[110] Euphratensis (except for Alexander of Hierapolis) issued no condemnations, but shared communion with the other protesters.[111] By fall, more than forty Syrian bishops had rejected the settlement, along with links to most Nicenes (see figure 13). Two years would pass before this split abated.

Thus the Antiochene network fractured into various clusters and two main parties. But why did this internal split take place? Theology offers an insufficient explanation, for the camps had similar preferences. What we see in this schism, I argue, is a struggle over network leadership. I do not mean that the bishops were merely fighting for influence. Rather the contenders, occupying various relational positions, tried to build their own coalitions. They did so by performing various roles of leadership, and by presenting visions for the community. We can see the basic social forms and the tenets of the two main camps. One side formed a diffuse network, within a broad communion that agreed to an ambiguous theology. The other built a tight faction, with communion limited to protect a pure orthodoxy. When it comes to personal behavior, however, we must look more closely. For each would-be leader held a distinct social vantage point, sought specific allies, and laid out his own vision for the Syrian clergy.

THE GODFATHER: ACACIUS OF BEROEA

The most imposing Syrian church leader during the Nestorian controversy had to be Acacius of Beroea. Alone Acacius claimed renown for eight decades of asceticism. Alone he inspired fear for the rivals he had destroyed. By the 430s Acacius's presence was surreal. Age and frailty limited his participation. Still, he remained irreplaceable to clerical relations. He guided both the dispute and the settlement with his string-pulling. He quietly reshaped the network with his claims to authority.

In terms of credentials Acacius stood by himself. Not only was he the oldest, most experienced Roman bishop; he had an unmatched record of Nicene devotion. Only Acacius had worked with Meletius's early partisans. Only he had learned from Julian Saba, the innovator of Syrian monasticism. Bishop since 379, Acacius had destroyed multiple opponents—Arians as well as Chrysostom and other Nicenes.[112] Bishops across the empire trod carefully around him. Acacius's frailty curtailed his travels and preaching. His impending death encouraged clerics to look past him. But five decades of recruitment had given him centrality and

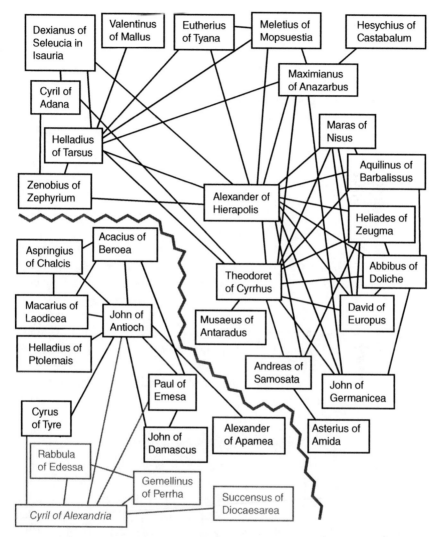

FIGURE 13. The Antiochene episcopal network in schism, 433–434, according to letters and conciliar documents. Links approximate evident or implied exchange of 2 or more Antiochene social cues (including at least one doctrinal cue), dated roughly to 433 or 434 (more links may have existed). Grey links = non-Antiochene.

influence over almost every other leader. Once he had competed for authority; now he had no serious rivals.

Acacius worked behind the scenes from the start to manage the Antiochene crisis. He used his reputation to mediate outside relationships. When Cyril asked him to help condemn Nestorius, he refused so politely that he still seemed sympathetic.[113] He also mediated by validating information. Colleagues trusted him to know how Cyril might "persuade" imperial courtiers. The emperor trusted him to know how to force a compromise. Thus Acacius gave breathing room to the Antiochenes at Ephesus and after, and in some sense gave shape to the initial schism.

During the negotiations for communion, Acacius had a larger impact. When Cyril sent pacific signals in 432, Acacius started inching colleagues toward a settlement. He encouraged John of Antioch to keep negotiating. He facilitated the choice of Paul of Emesa as envoy. The final settlement looks rather "Acacian," in that it abandoned an ally. In 433, sources on Acacius go silent. Perhaps he fell ill or died (though Theodoret recorded a later date for his passing). The mere name of Acacius, however, bolstered the communion agreement. No cleric chose to attack the godfather.

Acacius's deepest influence is visible in the way he reshaped the competition for influence. In a sense, Acacius did not join the contest. Other would-be leaders preferred to wait him out. At every stage, however, the centenarian bishop picked favorites and brought them together. And he urged key players to act without hesitating. Acacius left hints of his vision of leadership for his community. He shared it with Cyril via an augmented Pauline quotation: "If I choose to provide myself with authority, 'which God gave us for building up, not tearing down, I will not be ashamed' (II Corinthians 10.8)."[114] According to Acacius, it was individual authority that defended orthodoxy, not group stridency. Since the 380s Antiochenes had shared decision making. Under Acacius's influence, some bishops sought to direct the once informal community.

THE DEFECTOR: RABBULA OF EDESSA

Acacius played a key role in the crisis, but almost as prominent was Rabbula of Edessa. Rabbula came with his own credentials and following. He could have played a central part in schismatic governance or in negotiations. Instead, he defected and assaulted his former allies. Rabbula left the Antiochene group, but he did claim influence in the Syrian clergy, as a sectional leader in Cyril's party.

Rabbula possessed his own record of accomplishments. Born in Chalcis around 370, Rabbula received an elite education, in Greek as well as in Syriac. Disciple to the famous ascetic Abraham, he became a hermit, perhaps even a would-be martyr.[115] It was Acacius, however, who consecrated him bishop in 412.[116] Rabbula's doctrinal writings are not preserved from before the First Council of Ephesus. Others say that he was part of Theodore's fanclub.[117] In any case he specialized in Syriac translation—his *vita* credits him with correcting translations of Scripture.[118] All the while, he retained his ascetic habits and brought covenanters and monks under his authority. He may have won over more distant ascetics, including Barsauma, a famous anti-pagan zealot based near Perrha.[119] By 430, Rabbula was part of the Antiochene network, but also leader of his own fiefdom, dependent on his translations and his patronage.

Thus Rabbula was well placed to exercise influence. His about-face stunned the Antiochene community. He started preaching against Nestorius and even Theodore. Translations of their works were burned, and resistors chased into exile.[120] Meanwhile, he wrote to Cyril of a "widespread heresy infecting the whole East."[121] When Andreas observed the fleeing clerics, he was greeted with Rabbula's condemnation. Otherwise Rabbula chose not to announce his defection. Most of the network learned of it from Andreas, in early 432.[122] The Antiochenes tried to salvage Osrhoene province, but Rabbula retained support from his suffragans and from one bishop in Euphratensis.[123] Rabbula accepted the *Formula of Reunion*. He was eager to enforce its provisions. In late 433 or early 434 his posse (perhaps including Barsauma) chased Andreas out of Samosata; they may have consecrated a replacement.[124] Only Andreas's acceptance of communion (see below) halted this feuding.

Why, then, did Rabbula turn on his allies? The sources leave us guessing. In letters (all post defection), Rabbula presented himself as a consistent opponent of Nestorius and Theodore, then as Cyril's informant and enforcer. The *vita*, meanwhile, shows Rabbula zealous to correct all enemies of orthodoxy. It even claims that he went to Constantinople to preach against the new "heretics."[125] Neither his letters nor the *vita* mention Rabbula's Antiochene past. Only Irenaeus's document collection records his presence at the counter-council of Ephesus (and his support for its rulings).[126] Rabbula's new foes speculated about his motives in defecting. Hiba asserted that he nursed a "secret hatred" against Theodore, since Theodore had publicly rebuked him in a synod.[127] But neither piety nor pride makes for a sufficient explanation.

Rabbula's words and actions, however, do reveal his own vision of leadership within the clerical community. Like Acacius, Rabbula endorsed a model of decisive personal influence. "Whoever loves does not argue, but obeys," he wrote in a sermon; "he does not inquire, but believes."[128] Ascetic acts, patronage, and translation created a subnetwork dependent on one holy authority. By defecting, Rabbula showed control over present bishops as well as over Theodore and other past figures. He subordinated himself to Cyril doctrinally. Apparently, he could live with this limitation, as he commanded a Syrian section of the anti-Antiochene party.

Rabbula had mixed success in claiming authority. After 433 he remained an advance guard against the Antiochenes and kept pushing for a wider attack (see chapter 5). When Rabbula died in 436, he was succeeded by an Antiochene (Hiba), but some monks and clerics clung to Rabbula's memory. On the fringes of the Antiochene network, Rabbula's confrontational approach had lasting appeal.

THE DECIDER?: JOHN OF ANTIOCH
AND HIS BLUNDERS

Any examination of Antiochenes' leaders should consider the titular primate, John of Antioch. Institutionally, he remained a hub of the network. His voice initiated councils. His hand touched (almost) every letter to outside bishops or the court. At the same time, John relied on others' help, doctrinal, social, and even military. After he sent Paul of Emesa to finish negotiations, this help seemed more like dependence. Rabbula and Acacius exercised influence despite their limitations. John held default leadership and bungled it. Faced with local opponents, he turned to coercion to keep some control.

John of Antioch's leadership rested on an institutional base. While his personal background is unknown, support probably came from Acacius, who later vouched for him.[129] Still, the see of Antioch brought coffers, crowds, and connections. Early in his career (429–431), John benefited from these assets, which allowed him to gain centrality. His greatest social boost, though, came from the privileges of primacy. Bishops relied on him to conduct councils and to pen the results. These ritualized tasks made him a natural mediator in wider clerical relations.

At the same time, John of Antioch's authority faced important constraints. Some limits were institutional. With no tradition of directorship in Syria, he needed support from metropolitans and suffragans alike. Other limits were personal. With little doctrinal expertise, he needed constant advice, even whole theological phrases lifted from peers.[130] John had success representing an Antiochene consensus, at Ephesus and after. His colleagues supported him, so long as he offered agreed socio-doctrinal cues. He faced difficulties mainly when he tried to tweak social signals or redirect the community.

It was in 432 and 433 that John of Antioch encountered problems. From the start he had operated by calling small councils, a pattern he continued into negotiations. But as John consulted with Acacius, he narrowed the circle of participants. At the same time John tried to limit the spread of information. The circulation of hostile rumors in the fall of 432 was the result. John misread the local opposition. He expected Theodoret to be his "messenger of sweet things."[131] When colleagues expressed worry, he refused to renegotiate. John was not yet explicit in claiming regional directorship, but his actions demonstrated how he made decisions.

In fact, John's control was illusory. Most decisions were foisted upon him by Cyril or the imperial court. John started negotiating under pressure from Aristolaus. He continued guided by Acacius, with whom Cyril dealt directly.[132] To seal the deal, John turned to Paul of Emesa, known to be Acacius's man. While he sent instructions, he gave Paul the flexibility to "survey with [Cyril] what can be done to set the world right."[133] John first announced peace without having seen the details. When Paul returned with Aristolaus and two Alexandrian clerics, John could not easily reverse course. So he embraced communion, condemned Nestorius, and signed the *Formula*. The idea that a "remote" titular leader could dictate terms, however, offended many colleagues.

The reaction to John's assertion of authority came as negotiations concluded. At first, critics avoided direct attacks; they chose to blame Paul. Rumor had it that Paul had ignored his instructions and endorsed suspect documents—"support of the devil" in some eyes.[134] By April critics were rebuking John, for acting "as if his deeds were guaranteed by the Savior, as if He pronounced [them] in law."[135] By the summer, bishops in Cilicia, Isauria, and Euphratensis were blaming him for the whole operation. They did not call John a heretic. Still they refused his communion, for his tainted associates, his duplicity, and his condemnation of an orthodox man.[136]

It was John's response to criticism that most reflected his new claim to authority. First, he sought support from fellow primates, Cyril, Pope Xystus, and Maximianus of Constantinople.[137] Next he asked court officials to pressure the recalcitrant bishops. The emperor warned bishops to accept communion with all four primates or face deposition. And the generals Dionysius and Titus were ordered to get involved.[138] In 434 warnings gave way to interventions. Before Easter John went with an army contingent to replace Abbibus of Doliche and Aquilinus of Barbalissus, neighbors of Alexander of Hierapolis and Theodoret. Then John raised the pressure on Alexander. He removed the shrine of St. Sergius from Hierapolis's control, appointing a bishop of Rasapha. [139]All the while, he refused to stop riotous clerics from enforcing threats themselves.[140]

John's vision for his community emerges from his exercise of leadership. His authority rested on institutional rank, as well as on soldiers and courtiers. He preferred to persuade colleagues but was willing to coerce them. John chose not to reject Cyril's communion; he valued peace more than purity. "Now is neither a time of philosophers nor of martyrs," he wrote, "but of corruption for the whole world and disturbance for the church."[141] His network could only persist, in his view, as a jurisdiction of the church. Hence he could tolerate neither schism nor overt challenges to his authority.

Ultimately John could not compel all his colleagues. The more firmly he pushed for compliance, the more vociferously his opponents defied him. John kept the support of sixty Syrian bishops, the other primates and the court. By 434, though, he stood oddly alone. Acacius had fallen silent and Paul of Emesa (who might have shared the blame) took ill and died.[142] John continued to hold a position of leadership, but he had to contend with another kind of authority: the courage of the opposition.

CONFESSORS: ALEXANDER OF HIERAPOLIS
AND HIS FOLLOWING

Against John of Antioch stood clerics with an antithetical approach to leading their community. They touted bold self-sacrifice when John demanded deference; they set up social barriers when he sought open relations. John's foes came from diverse locations in the region and the network. By late 432 they had formed a cluster, led by Maximianus of Anazarbus, Meletius of Mopsuestia, Eutherius of Tyana, and above all Alexander of Hierapolis. These opponents to reunion shared some key judgments. Cyril they viewed as a duplicitous heretic, Nestorius as an ill-spoken but orthodox bishop. What most marked this group, however, was its pursuit of Antiochene purity. To guard the traditions of their mentors, these confessors were ready to endure what would come.

Leaders of the anti-communion camp based their effort on personal credentials. Little is known about the backgrounds of Maximianus, Meletius, or Eutherius. All three were skilled in Antiochene doctrine, having probably consulted directly with Theodore. Meletius served as John's advisor before the council of Ephesus, though less so during or after. Alexander is better known; his credentials rivaled almost anyone in the network. Like Acacius, he claimed long experience. A committed ascetic in the 390s, by 404 he was already running his large diocese. Alexander took pride in his diligent clerical oversight. His support of the cult of St. Sergius in Rasapha won him connections across the Middle East.[143] Still, his reputation rested on devotion to Antiochene doctrine. When some bishops joined communion with repentant Apollinarians circa 400–404, Alexander refused. Ready to lose his see, he won over his colleagues (including Flavian of Antioch and Acacius).[144] Alexander played a key role in Ephesus, assembling the anti-Cyril party before most Syrians arrived. He then knew when to "disappear," to avoid the trap of compromise.[145] As an expert Alexander expected to be consulted. He met often with confidants (especially Helladius of Tarsus, Andreas, and Theodoret) during negotiations. When John rejected his advice, he assembled his cluster and took a firmer stand.

Alexander's resistance movement began with limited actions and careful rhetoric. By December 432, he had distanced himself from a process that did not meet his standards. He did this not to reject John's doctrine, he said, but to "segregate his soul," from "the Egyptian."[146] He pointed out flaws in negotiation documents, which, to his eye, signaled forgery. He accused John of being deluded, and said he was "doubly scandalized" that John would condemn an orthodox man and his orthodox faith.[147] In Alexander's view, this behavior called for calm resistance. "Whether they set upon me exile or death, the precipice, fire or beasts," he declared, "with God strengthening me I shall endure everything rather than join communion with the likes of them."[148] Even before the peace agreement, Alexander was anticipating persecution.

Alexander presented a consistent leadership performance and a striking direction for his community. He valued the Antiochene network as a bastion of orthodoxy. Members (even Nestorius) were trusted to be defenders of the faith. Outsiders (like Cyril), however, had no such privilege. Their words had to be scrutinized. Alexander wanted no gaps between judgments of persons and judgments of doctrine. Communion had to be separated "from every heretical mixing."[149] Alexander had little interest in the ranks among bishops; anyone counted who stood firm. He led by example and took care to align his behavior, his company, and his conscience.

Alexander's performance as leader attracted a cluster of allies, which took on a life of its own. His circle featured old confidants (e.g., Helladius, Andreas, and Theodoret) willing to debate him. It also included new imitators (e.g., Maximianus, Meletius, and Eutherius) who magnified his rhetoric. It was Meletius of Mopsuestia who called Paul of Emesa a tool of the devil. Through a spy on John's staff he agitated Alexander with reportage.[150] It was Eutherius of Tyana who first called John tyrannical. He and Helladius drafted an appeal to the pope to share with Alexander.[151] These lieutenants influenced bishops in Isauria and Cilicia. "With Christ's cooperation," wrote the bishops of Cilicia II, "we will not endure welcoming Cyril into communion as if he were orthodox, nor [will we accept] those who join him, unless those heretical [*Twelve Anathemas*] are totally cast out, even if it is fitting for us to go together to the fire, the sword and the teeth of wild beasts."[152] In this new faction the confessor spirit, and the collaborative sense of leadership, held sway.

Alexander's leadership, however, confronted limits, as did his strict concept of a faithful community. Some of his followers were scared off by Rabbula's rioters or John's interventions. But even his suffragans were willing to tolerate Cyril, rejecting a bifurcated worldview.[153] Alexander soon distanced himself from his colleagues. He decried "the false empathy of those who seem to love us (really they hate us), the censures, affronts, mockeries, and reproaches of those who in these times changed themselves, [especially] the blandishments of our own."[154] Meanwhile he obsessed over the ideal of a confessor or martyr, "the proper life course of . . . an apostle."[155] Confessorship remained attractive for aspiring Christian leaders, especially in a clique of nominal equals. At the same time, it could be a social trap, isolating its exponents from the rest of the community.

By late 434 it was clear where Alexander was headed. He and his admirers clung to their pure communion. They forged a tight clique with a clear boundary and informal leadership. They cast themselves as confessors, with John as their persecutor, and they prepared for exile (and eventually divine vindication). Persecutor and resistor, however, were not the only available roles. By 434, there were other would-be leaders, pursuing backers with their own visions and plans.

FLIP-FLOPPERS: HELLADIUS OF TARSUS
AND ANDREAS OF SAMOSATA

As Syrian disputes intensified, several figures tried to bridge the social gaps. By the fall of 433, communion marked out at least two Syrian clerical networks, but individual bishops retained various points of view. A few, in fact, maintained relations with both camps: Alexander of Apamea, John of Germanicea, and Asterius of Amida, but especially Helladius of Tarsus, Andreas, and Theodoret. Each of these figures tried individually to mediate. Some members made overtures by renewing friendships or preserving cordiality. Others suggested a compromise on communion or the other issues at hand. Before Theodoret had any success, however, the would-be mediators failed repeatedly. Each of the five other figures returned to a side. For some reason their efforts signaled unreliability, rather than a reason to reunite the party.

From the start of internal Syrian conflicts there were bishops left in the middle ground. Most of them left no trace of their concerns, but in 432 and 433, even leading figures were torn. Alexander of Apamea had been involved in decision making since 430. The final negotiations gave him pause. He consulted with Alexander of Hierapolis, and then settled into John's camp.[156] No further attempts by him to mediate are known. Asterius of Amida showed less hesitation in supporting communion. Still, he apparently kept connections with the "schismatics" and protected clerics whom Rabbula had chased away.[157] No specific deal seems to have come from his hospitality. Perhaps Amida was too distant for easy diplomacy. A more likely mediator was John of Germanicea. Like Theodoret, he sought a nuanced position in negotiations. By mid-433 he sat in Alexander's camp but still reached for an accord. Unfortunately, bridging efforts made him suspect to Alexander. So he, too, rejoined John of Antioch's communion, sometime in 433 or 434.[158] None of these figures seems to have organized a new alliance. Each operated informally and independently. In each case, however, a cordial bishop found it impossible to maintain connections across the hostile divide.

Perhaps the most robust mediation effort belonged to Andreas of Samosata. Bishop for at least fifteen years, Andreas was known as an educated writer and master of Antiochene doctrine. He missed the Council of Ephesus because of illness. But he joined in subsequent councils (especially the response to Rabbula's defection) and he updated his pro-Antiochene work.[159] Andreas had a central position in the old network. He had the early trust of John of Antioch but was closest to Alexander of Hierapolis and Theodoret. He was thus well positioned to build a mediating coalition.

Andreas, however, failed to build that coalition, for he could not maintain consistent positions when pressured by his peers. At first, during the negotiations with Cyril, Andreas was drawn to the critics' camp. Alexander pointed out imprecision in Cyril's various doctrinal statements. Andreas called them "tricks of the devil." In fact, Andreas was terrified by Cyril's communion. He told Alexander about a recurring nightmare: "I was with your piety and certain other bishops, when you said to me that the heretic Apollinarius was alive." But when the pair went to argue with the aged heretic, they found him verbally blessing John of Antioch, holding everyone (including Alexander) by the hand, "on account of a 'condescension,' which he said had been compelled."[160] Not only did Andreas fear that Cyril, the new Apollinarius, was worming his way into the faith. He worried about the constancy of his colleagues, even of Alexander. But then Andreas conversed with Theodoret and changed his mind. Like Theodoret he determined that Cyril might be orthodox. He refused to condemn Nestorius, but he asked Alexander to "condescend" to negotiate.[161] After April 433, Andreas held to a centrist stance. With Theodoret's help he convinced other suffragans of Euphratensis to break communion with Cyril but condemn no one. Still he kept his links to Alexander, hoping for a middle ground. Andreas's mediation effort faltered when he came under personal threat. After fleeing from Rabbula's rioters in 433 or 434, he joined communion with Cyril and John. Andreas tried to explain to Alexander that communion was no big deal (as John had already said). He had condemned no Christians and professed only orthodoxy. Alexander told him to stop writing.[162] To Alexander, Andreas's (forced) acceptance of communion seemed inconsistent with a pure Antiochene community.

After Andreas, Helladius of Tarsus tried to find a middle ground. He was also an auspicious mediator, with long experience as a metropolitan, after three decades running an allied monastery.[163] Helladius had shared in decisions before and during the council of Ephesus. He hosted one of the councils that affirmed the schism when the delegation returned. He calmly endured threats from soldiers and rioters (unlike Andreas). After a brief exile he returned to his see, hosting Eutherius of Tyana (who was likewise forced to flee but could not return).[164] By 433, Helladius was firmly behind Alexander. And when he offered confessor-style rhetoric, he had the experience to back it up.[165] Meanwhile he remained a central figure in clerical-ascetic relations. That, plus his rank, gave his coalition-building efforts a starting base.

Helladius's mediation began small at an opportune moment. In April 434, Maximianus of Constantinople died. His successor, Proclus, was one of Nestorius's original hounders, but even as he denounced "Nestorianism" he sent conciliatory signals.[166] Helladius received an accession letter from Proclus and forwarded it to Meletius of Mopsuestia, Theodoret, and Alexander of Hierapolis. Patiently, he discussed whether to accept the new bishop's communion. He chose to do so.[167] Helladius still refused to condemn Nestorius, but he was willing to accept reality. No doubt he hoped to get John (and the court) to cease enforcing their threats. Even more important than his position was the way he reached it—openly and with due deliberation. Thus he acted in a fashion that seemed to endorse the values of both sides.

Helladius thus took one small compromise step, which was celebrated or tolerated in both camps. But his move seemed insufficient to Alexander and to John of Antioch, and the effort was never expanded. Helladius's open style of leadership gave way to passivity. When officials told Cilician bishops to join communion (or else), he sat to consider.[168] When Alexander ranted about John's crimes, he replied, "Useful are the words of your apostolic zeal."[169] Soon Helladius turned from his mediation efforts. He kept communion with Alexander until the fall of 434, when both he and his Cilician colleagues shifted course. By then, however, Helladius was taking his cues from others. It was hard for him to rebuild Antiochene unity because he refused to push his influence.

All of these would-be mediators proved unsuccessful at building a broad coalition. Their difficulties are hard to explain. All of them had contacts in both camps. All had sympathy for Alexander's motives and John of Antioch's predicament. Hence they sought ways to reestablish communion, in part or in full, while preserving a pure Antiochene orthodoxy. None won over Alexander or John. For Andreas the problem appears to be inconsistency; for Helladius, hesitancy. But deeper social factors were at work. None of these five mediators could claim the level of outside connections held by John of Antioch (let alone Acacius). None of them offered a leadership performance as coherent as Alexander's, or a new way to reaffirm the Antiochene community.

COALITION-BUILDER: THE FALL
AND RISE OF THEODORET

The final candidate for leadership was, of course, Theodoret, and he (eventually) had some success. We have noted Theodoret's personal assets: his elite connections, his asceticism, and his breadth and depth of learning. Such assets brought him a position as doctrinal advisor and then spokesman for the network. Scholars have tended to treat Theodoret as the leading Antiochene throughout the Nestorian conflict.[170] His doctrinal work, however, did not make him instantly influential. Until 432, his network centrality was no higher than several older colleagues'. Theodoret gathered influence by repeatedly playing mediator. Even so, his early attempts offended his peers. Only after several failed overtures did Theodoret find broad support, by offering a new rationale for redirecting the Antiochene party.

Theodoret's rise to influence grew out of his unsuccessful early mediation. He first tried to mediate during the negotiations of 432, by showing doctrinal "flexibility." Theodoret found Cyril orthodox, much as he did Nestorius. He could do this because his orthodoxy allowed for multiple levels of precision. Theodoret accepted the general terms that united all Nicenes. He then took a more "exacting" view of terms that resonated with Antiochene tradition. Thus Theodoret suggested his basic solution: to condemn "those who say Christ is purely a man, those who divide Christ into two sons, and those who deny His divinity."[171] It was this dual-level approach to orthodoxy that set the framework for the ambiguous *Formula of Reunion.*[172] Theodoret found little connection between orthodoxy and the mistreatment of Nestorius. So he separated the two issues. Yet Theodoret's cleverness failed to win over many colleagues. Forced to fend off nasty rumors, he could not prevent the breach between Alexander and John. In the summer of 433, Theodoret tried again to mediate. He restated his split judgments, to lay the groundwork for restoring communion. This time he won over his provincial colleagues (except for Alexander). Theodoret reassured his metropolitan of an essential solidarity. "I have already told Your Holiness that if they anathematize the dogma of Nestorius, I shall not join communion," he wrote, "If it pleases Your Holiness to insert this in our letter to Antioch, let it be done."[173] At the same time he tried to preserve cordial links with John, informing him of decisions, " by a personal friendly letter, not a synodical."[174] Nevertheless, Theodoret failed to prevent the souring of relations. After John's interventions, and riots in his own diocese, he joined Alexander in avoiding the bishop of Antioch, whom he now diminutively called "the Antiochene."[175] As of late 433 Theodoret had done no better as a mediator than John of Germanicea or Andreas.

It was in the spring of 434 that Theodoret found the standing for more successful mediation. He gained some ground for new outreach from his own (relative) consistency. From the fall of 432, he kept to the same judgment regarding Cyril's teaching, unlike many of his colleagues. Theodoret also benefited from his rhetorical caution. Not even at the height of hostilities did he condemn a regional colleague. Perhaps most important was his effort to find nontraditional allies. From at least the end of 431, he offered friendly letters to envoys and imperial enforcers, especially the general Titus.[176] He also made contact with another general (who has to be Anatolius). Promising continued loyalty (and taxes), he asked for protection for him and his brethren (that is, from other Roman soldiers).[177] This canvassing proved successful. Anatolius gave him the backing to quell riots and postpone interventions.[178] Thus the bishop of Cyrrhus raised his status with colleagues. The final catalyst, however, was not his outreach, but his receipt of a (non-episcopal) scolding. At the prompting of Titus, Theodoret was contacted by three famous hermits, Baradatus, Jacob of Cyrrhestica, and Symeon Stylites. "They filled me with a deep sadness, " he later recalled, "demanding of us many actions for the sake of peace, as if they held us guilty." In this case, it was Theodoret who was persuaded. He promised the hermits to meet with John, as well as with Alexander, to discuss terms.[179]

Gradually Theodoret unveiled a new effort at mediation. He began with proposals to John approved by Alexander. These called for the condemnation of Cyril's *Twelve Anathemas*, the removal of "false" local bishops, and the exoneration of Nestorius (Proclus was accepted).[180] John soon offended Alexander with condemnations of Nestorius. Theodoret chose to read between the lines: "he did not say 'we anathematize his doctrine,' but rather, 'whatever of his could be said or thought somehow alien to the apostolic doctrine.' "[181] Finally, Theodoret offered to accept communion with John, Cyril, and Proclus, so long as no condemnations were required and deposed bishops were restored. John responded favorably: he would forgive all who accepted his communion. By fall of 434 the two were reconciled; Theodoret said his conscience was satisfied.[182]

At the heart of Theodoret's mediation was a rationale for redirecting the Antiochene community. For three years he had joined Alexander in protecting a pure communion. Now contacts compelled him to look outside. "Our obstinacy, I see, sweetly profits for nothing," he declared, "but brings disturbances to the churches and surrenders congregations ... like raw meat to the hungry wolves." The wolves, in this case, were known heretics. And Theodoret worried about them more than Cyril's imprecision or Nestorius's honor. Theodoret admired confessors. But "excessive exactness," he feared, might bring "penalties from God, because we tend to what is ours and do not consider what is useful for the laity."[183] Theodoret still saw the Antiochenes as a bastion of orthodoxy, but he regarded the network as part of a larger community, relying on bishops for spiritual needs. One by one Theodoret addressed the holdout bishops. He praised their constancy but intoned Ecclesiastes: "a time for war and time for peace."[184] Thus he explained how his (familiar) compromise position was now proper for the Antiochenes.

This time Theodoret built a broad supporting coalition. First he won backing from Andreas and John of Germanicea, and then most of Euphratensis. Then he won over Maximianus of Anazarbus, and most bishops of Cilicia II. Helladius held out until he was (again) threatened with exile, but eventually he followed suffragans of Cilicia I and Isauria into communion. Helladius knew he was abandoning deposed holdouts. He wrote to Nestorius, "May Your Divine Love find your share on the day of judgment." Now he made clear his reason for changing course. "With those who [congregate] around the most God-friendly Theodoret, one may count us."[185]

Theodoret's "success" arose from a confluence of factors, only some of his own making. Theodoret did not launch the process of dispute resolution. Negotiations were demanded by the emperor and high imperial officials.[186] Even his last mediation effort was inspired by the three famous ascetics. Theodoret found no new formula for doctrinal compromise. His basic judgments were unchanged since 432; all he did was decouple communion from opinions about Nestorius. Yet Theodoret kept warm relations with nearly everyone from the old Antiochene network. He also won new allies in the army, who probably promised protection. Meanwhile Thodoret performed a role of informal leadership. Instead of threatening coercion or promising endurance, he presented himself as a tireless persuader. Perhaps Theodoret's biggest contribution was a new sense of purpose for the Antiochene community. He signaled bishops to look beyond their order of primacy, or their purity of orthodoxy, to the pastoral needs of the laity. His pastoral argument was hardly groundbreaking. But with the bishops tired of playing persecutors and confessors, the time was ripe for a coalition to support it.

CRISIS RESOLVED: THE NEW ANTIOCHENE NETWORK

So the "Nestorian controversy" concluded. After seven years, both the conflict and the participants had been transformed. It is hard to explain this whole episode as a doctrinal dispute. Nestorius's teachings did help to spark the schism between Syria and Egypt (along with the *Twelve Anathemas* against him). By the end he was a side issue, abandoned by his friends.[187] In Syria doctrine played one small part of a crisis, in which the Antiochene network turned on itself, to establish itself anew. As we have seen, this crisis involved a struggle for influence. Leaders offered contrasting performances, and competing directions for the Antiochene community.

In some sense, the crisis ended with the restoration of one communion of active Nicene bishops. By the spring of 435, Theodoret and John had the backing of most of the hundred and twenty Syrian prelates. Four holdouts (besides Nestorius) remained in the region: Eutherius of Tyana, Zenobius of Zephyrium, Meletius of Mopsuestia, and Alexander of Hierapolis.[188] Theodoret urged Alexander to relent. He promised to come in person and tried to win him more time. He even asked Nestorius to tell Alexander to abandon his own cause! But the confessor took no visitors and refused to budge.[189] Meletius, for his part, elaborately denounced Cyril, begging officials to do their worst. He kept agitating around Cilicia even after troops chased him from his town.[190] In April of 435, the court fully intervened. Theodosius exiled all who refused John's and Cyril's communion. Officials removed the Syrian holdouts (and eight bishops in other regions). Alexander was dragged out of his church by soldiers.[191] No doubt this pained the Antiochenes, but it could have been worse: more than thirty bishops narrowly avoided exile.

Theodoret's mediation, however, did more than end the threat of exile. It healed several social lacerations. Before his efforts the network looked to be falling apart. John's communion featured sixty Syrian bishops, including loyal partisans, failed mediators, and anti-Antiochenes. Alexander's communion featured about thirty prelates, committed to varying degrees. Theodoret rebuilt relations with John of Antioch and his backers (Aspringius of Chalcis, Macarius of Laodicea, John of Damascus, and possibly Acacius). He reconnected with earlier mediators and Alexander's former followers in Cilicia, Isauria, and Euphratensis. And, of course,

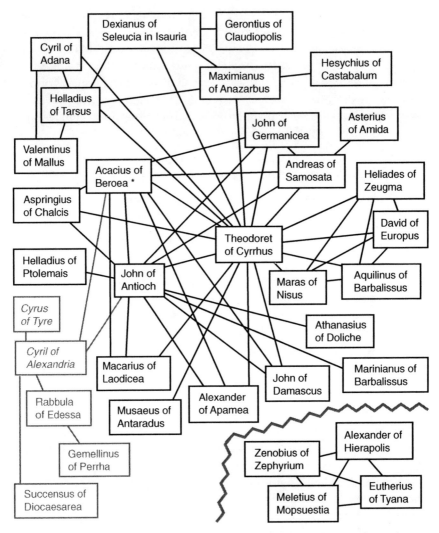

FIGURE 14. The Antiochene network after Theodoret's mediation, 435, according to letters and conciliar documents. Links approximate evident or implied exchange of 2 or more Antiochene social cues (including at least one doctrinal cue), dated from fall 434 to fall 436 (more links may have existed). Grey links = non-Antiochene.

he retained his protective government contacts. Without Theodoret the network might have survived, but his internal and external contacts were hard to replace (see figure 14).

Meanwhile, Theodoret's success established a new distribution of influence and a new sense of community. By 434 Syria hosted fifteen would-be leaders. At least eight had tried for grander influence, as string-pullers, defectors, directors, confessors, or mediators. The result had been nasty rivalries. Theodoret laid out the rationale for these leaders to cooperate. John saw the appeal of Theodoret's "concern for the laity." He granted the bishop of Cyrrhus wide latitude, "even if I am seen to be influenced by Your Charity."[192] Other bishops let themselves be persuaded, for they, too, were concerned for the congregations. Theodoret made no claim to higher rank or purity, or to formal authority. But he did show a way to be Antiochene *and* part of a wider church. Thus he built his coalition and became the most central figure of the network.

As Theodoret resolved the crisis, his network remained recognizably Antiochene. The same basic doctrinal tropes still united the membership. Theodore's expert pupils still populated the core. Bishops had endorsed an ambiguous *Formula of Reunion* and abandoned Nestorius. This barely affected their Christological preferences, as even the condemned "arch-heretic" admitted. Ascetic practices still excited Antiochene bishops. Monastic connections retained their role in socialization and recruitment. In chapter 2, we mapped Theodoret's network with its modular scale-free topology. This basic pattern was, in all likelihood, set before the controversy. Theodoret's "concern for the laity" essentially justified the old pattern of a tight core of experts and a diffuse periphery.

And yet, by 435, the Antiochene network had been transformed. Of the four old leaders, at least three had died. Fifteen new claimants had become five hubs (Acacius, John of Antioch, Andreas, Theodoret, and General Anatolius). Schism had temporarily imposed firm boundaries. A once diffuse network periphery had been reduced, segmented, and then reopened. It was the Nestorian crisis that shaped the social arrangement mapped in chapter 2. It was this crisis that created a new sense of Antiochene community. Thanks to the crisis Theodoret had the chance to guide his clerical party, to rebuild it during a truce, and to preserve it through more controversy.

5

—

Forging Community

Theodoret's Network and Its Fall

It was probably the summer of 448 when Theodoret received a key surveillance brief from his confidant, Basil of Seleucia in Isauria. For several months Theodoret had confronted shadowy opponents attacking Antiochene doctrine. Rumor had it that someone in Cilicia was preaching that God suffered—a red flag for altered allegiance. Theodoret had alerted the bishops of Cilicia,[1] but Basil was a more reliable spy. When Basil reported no sign of this heresy, Theodoret took joy at the "heartening news." Then he made a new request. Alexandria had sent a prelate to the capital to run an anti-Theodoret campaign. "Let your piety deign to show [this Egyptian] the proper goodwill, as usual," he said with a wink, "and to array against falsehood the truth."[2]

Over the next year Basil proved Theodoret's best ally, until his defection. For months he organized in the capital. In the fall he helped to condemn Eutyches, the Egyptians' monastic ally.[3] It was thus startling when, two or three months later, Basil ceased writing letters. "No one familiar with our affinity," Theodoret wrote, "would believe it." Theodoret exhorted him "not to follow a multitude into evil (Exodus 23:2)." But he knew that Basil had joined the accusers. "I have for all other reasons feared this tribunal [of the Lord]," Theodoret stated, "but amid the words spoken against me I have reasons for consolation from the thought of it."[4]

Theodoret's relationship with Basil captures both the achievement and the paradox of his term of leadership. After the Nestorian crisis Theodoret took the initiative. His writings suggest that he restored the Antiochene network. Theodoret's instructions to Basil seem to underscore his success. A core of followers carried out his plans. Theodoret's writings, however, hide seeds of opposition that were germinating. In 448 and 449 he watched his network disintegrate faster apparently than he could imagine.

This chapter sketches Theodoret's performance as Antiochene leader and puts it to the test. In the late 430s the Antiochene network faced several mini-crises, to which Theodoret responded. He reinforced core Antiochene relations. He expanded contacts with distant clerics and lay officials. He reached out to non-Greek speakers and monastic groups. At the same time, Theodoret offered a new sense of Antiochene identity. He interwove doctrine, history, and social experience in ways that validated his own performance as leader. Still, none of this guaranteed a successful community. In the "Eutychean" controversy (447–451), opponents attacked Antiochene traditions and overthrew the Antiochenes. It is difficult to tell if Theodoret's network was robust or illusory. It may well have been robust and yet more vulnerable than Theodoret could see.

LOOMING DISASTER: SYRIAN DOCTRINAL CONFRONTATIONS, 435–440

Theodoret's leadership started in the late 430s amid frustration. Antiochenes remained vulnerable, despite their agreements with Cyril of Alexandria and the imperial court. Cyril and his allies made new demands of Syrian clerics, to guarantee their orthodoxy. Each demand threatened Theodoret's bonds with peers and protectors and could have unraveled his network. This time, however, confrontations strengthened the Antiochene community. Such success is difficult to explain. But one factor was surely Theodoret's performance as leader.

The situation that greeted Theodoret and his reunited associates was unappealing. By 435 the Nestorian dispute had permeated clerical and monastic communities. Most Antiochene bishops had settled their internal arguments. Some had condemned Nestorius, while others had said nothing. But everyone (except the exiled holdouts) had rejoined communion.[5] The result was, more or less, the social arrangement mapped in chapter 2. Official reconciliations, however, did not end Cyril's suspicion toward the Syrian clergy. Nor did they quell the ill will between Antiochene loyalists and defectors. In Edessa, Rabbula's followers cohabited uneasily with his critics. Each group prepared translations and canvassed for allies.[6] In Antioch, at least seven priests and archimandrites enrolled as Cyril's *proxenoi*. They informed against John and his allies. A few even rejected his communion. John and his colleagues tried to enforce discipline, but with every attempt the priests or monks sent Cyril a new appeal.[7]

Dissension in Syria, in fact, incubated new controversy. By 435, dissident clerics and monks were reporting "Nestorianism" to Cyril,[8] who informed the court. So the emperor sent Aristolaus back to Syria. He ordered bishops either to condemn Nestorius explicitly or to join him in exile. Worse, the emperor told the bishops to send statements to Cyril for inspection.[9] Cyril wrote new treatises to sway wavering bishops. His reports to the court kept the Antiochenes under a cloud of suspicion.

Dissension combined with cross-cultural tensions to cause the Antiochenes deeper problems. When Rabbula defected in 432, he denounced Theodore of Mopsuestia as Nestorius's mentor.[10] In late 434, he renewed this attack. He compiled a list of Theodore's objectionable teachings, which he correlated to statements of Nestorius. He sent the list to Acacius of Melitene, who enlarged it into a whole anti-Theodore dossier.[11] The controversy expanded when the two anti-Antiochenes linked up with Sahak, the *katholikos* of Persian Armenia. Sahak was already feuding with "Syrian" clerics in Armenia. When the Sassanid court deposed him in 435, he sought allies across the Roman frontier.[12] With Acacius of Melitene's help he sent envoys to Constantinople, asking for a denunciation of the "Syrian heresy."[13] Bishop Proclus replied with his *Tome to the Armenians,* a middle ground Christological summary that condemned some older Antiochene positions but did not name Theodore as their author.[14] Rabbula and Acacius were not satisfied. When Rabbula died in 436, the Antiochenes recirculated translations of Theodore.[15] So Acacius turned to Cyril, who denounced "Nestorius's teacher" far and wide. By 438[16] Cyril and Proclus were collaborating with some imperial support. The court sent Syrians the *Tome* (to affirm) and Theodore's statements (to condemn). Again, Cyril denounced their "Nestorian" heresy.[17] The stakes were high. Theodore (unlike Nestorius) was "held foremost among those who came before us [in the East]."[18] To condemn him was to destroy a key source of Antiochene solidarity.[19]

Between rumors of Nestorianism and denunciations of Theodore, the Antiochenes faced another confrontation. But this time, the network responded with solidarity. First, the Antiochenes denounced Nestorius. Some (e.g., John of Antioch and Helladius of Tarsus) did so explicitly; others (e.g., John of Germanicea and Theodoret) equivocated.[20] Even so, they maintained mutual support, despite pressure from Cyril and his friends.[21] Then the Antiochenes dealt with the dispute over Theodore. They affirmed Proclus's *Tome* but refused to condemn their hero.[22] Cyril persisted with polemics,[23] but seventy-five Syrian bishops gathered to defy him, and to ask the emperor for peace.[24] By 440, Acacius of Melitene was gone. And the court granted the petition from the Syrian bishops.[25] Proclus insisted he meant to condemn no one but Nestorius. And Cyril dropped his campaign against the dead.[26]

Why, in the late 430s, could the Antiochenes now defend themselves? One reason seems to involve Theodoret. Scholars sometimes credit Proclus and Cyril with the moderation to end the dispute. Or they claim that the feud was quashed by Theodosius II's court.[27] These "moderates," however, and even the emperor, were responding to Syrian bishops, united by renewed Antiochene leadership. John of

Antioch played an important part in the effort, calling councils and managing correspondence. He was aided by translators, ambassadors, and coordinators. But Theodoret proved essential. Not only did he write (the now fragmentary) *In Defense of Diodore and Theodore*. He led a whole program of community building, which continued after the conflict subsided.

RECRUITING AND REROOTING: THEODORET'S NETWORKING PROGRAM

Theodoret's organizational efforts took many forms. One was social initiative. In chapter 2, we noted the segmented state of Antiochene social relations. As opponents probed for Antiochene weaknesses, Theodoret sought to reinforce and grow his network. On one front Theodoret crafted a new central clique, including familiar prelates and those newly ordained. At the same time, he canvassed bishops in Armenia, Anatolia, and Constantinople. Theodoret backed up his clerical network with new contacts at court. He also sought support from Syria's lay elite. It is difficult to measure these efforts, but we can follow the strategy. As Cyril tried to marginalize the Antiochene network, Theodoret worked to broaden and deepen its social roots.

Theodoret's earliest initiatives aimed at the old core network. One target was Andreas of Samosata. By 436, Andreas had restored an "intimate" link with Theodoret and was greeted as a familiar companion.[28] Another target was John of Germanicea. After 436 the two men collaborated doctrinally, even in pressing circumstances.[29] Theodoret reforged a bond with John of Antioch. Not only did the primate defend Theodoret against outside critics. He must have trusted Theodoret to guide his nephew Domnus, a monk in Palestine,[30] who in 441 became bishop of Antioch. Other core players in the Nestorian crisis disappear in later sources. Most passed away in the late 430s or early 440s. Theodoret's scale-free network could absorb these steady losses, so long as he recruited their replacements.

Not surprisingly, Theodoret's initiatives extended to bringing in new bishops and confidants. Sometimes Theodoret helped to replace existing allies, like Dexianus of Seleucia in Isauria (who died after 435). Little is known about the first successor, John. But next, Basil became Theodoret's incomparable (if temporary) friend.[31] Sometimes Theodoret recruited on less friendly ground. Paul of Emesa and Acacius of Beroea had troubled Theodoret during the controversy. In the mid 430s they were succeeded by Pompeianus and Theoctistus, who joined him in tighter bonds.[32] By the mid 440s Theodoret had enough support in Emesa to advance Uranius over a local rival.[33] The most important efforts, however, emerged in Osrhoene, which had been marginalized from the network. When Rabbula of Edessa died in 436, Theodoret's allies there elected Hiba, whom Rabbula had once mistreated.[34] While Hiba faced protests, he reconnected suffragan sees to the net-

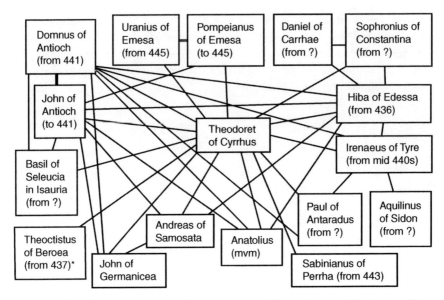

FIGURE 15. Theodoret's new inner circle, 435–448, according to letters and Syrian conciliar documents. Mvm = master of soldiers.
* Acacius of Beroea's death is here assumed to date to 437. See start of chapter 1.

work, often by ordaining his relatives.[35] Interventions then proceeded in Phoenicia I. There Theodoret and Domnus engineered the election of Paul of Antaradus over a local candidate.[36] When the bishop of Tyre died in the mid-440s, they consecrated Irenaeus, the familiar exiled count, who also recruited to fill vacancies.[37] Most of the new bishops proved close allies of Theodoret. Most became at least sectional hubs, restoring Antiochene influence to every Syrian province.

Beyond the episcopate, Theodoret worked to restore relations with lower clerics and monasteries, to bring the threat of riots to an end. This effort meant restoring clerical discipline. He toured his diocese in search of "heretics." He surveyed regional clerics for doctrinal precision and pastoral diligence.[38] Just as important was social maintenance. He tended to local hermits, including Symeon Stylites, Jacob of Cyrrhestica, and Baradatus.[39] He contacted affiliated monasteries, praising their leaders while looking for new ordinees.[40] None of these tasks was unusual for a bishop in his own diocese. Theodoret simply extended his oversight to a broader area.

Theodoret aimed further social efforts at clerics outside the region, where he tried to rebuild sympathy. One target was Constantinople. Since the early 430s Bishop Proclus had sometimes been inimical. Still Theodoret strove for a functional friendship. Doctrinally the two never fully aligned but could still cooperate.[41] Meanwhile, Theodoret courted Constantinople's clerics and monks, once so hostile to Nestorius. He connected with a few priests and visiting bishops, as well as the *oikonomoi*. And he sought sympathy from archimandrites, including Marcellus, head of the (once Syrian) "Sleepless" monks (Greek: *Akoimetoi*).[42] Another target was the Anatolian corridor leading to the capital. In a region of anti-Antiochenes, Theodoret approached younger bishops, like Eusebius of Ancyra.[43] At the least he hoped to find churchmen who could offer hospitality. Theodoret and his confidants sought out clerics in the Syrian-Armenian borderlands. Despite the growing anti-Antiochene sentiment, Hiba supplied allies with further translations.[44] When the Sassanid court launched an anti-Christian persecution in the mid-440s, Theodoret offered encouragement and advice.[45] He even nursed hopes of better relations with Cyril.[46] Theodoret knew he could not count on doctrinal agreement beyond his home region, so he sought cooperation, sympathy, and maybe new friends.

Finally, Theodoret looked beyond the clergy and monasteries to the political elite. The Nestorian crisis had already given him key allies. Irenaeus and Candidianus had lost imperial favor, but Anatolius grew in stature. Meanwhile, Theodoret turned to former foes. He sent letters to nearly every court figure except Theodosius—even to Empress Pulcheria.[47] Closer to home, he courted officials who had played minor roles in the dispute: the count of the East, provincial governors, former office-holders, and bureaucrats. Most of these officials had shown no sympathy for Antiochene doctrine. Theodoret had to relate on general terms (patronage, friendship, and pastoral care).[48] But even general relations could reduce the chance of doctrinal hostilities.

Theodoret's social efforts can be seen as responses to the assaults of his foes. Cyril sought to cast the Antiochene network as a vestige of Nestorianism. The more he presented the Antiochenes as regionally diminutive, the more he could paint his side as "universal."[49] Meanwhile, he looked for dissident Syrian clerics and archimandrites. If Syrian bishops distrusted their subordinates, they would have a hard time perpetuating their party. To protect his associates Theodoret needed to solidify his base. Surveillance of subordinates and recruitment of bishops kept Cyril's agents in check. At the same time, Theodoret had to reach beyond the Syrian clergy. Distant bishops and officials were less likely to condemn a familiar client or friend. A multi-front social strategy carried liabilities. The doctrinal tropes that brought network solidarity could prove troublesome in external relations, as we have seen. But well managed, these efforts countered hostile rhetoric and forestalled local opposition.

Ultimately Theodoret's greatest tool was the *perception* of social connectedness. It is not clear how much Theodoret won over churchmen or lay officials beyond his inner circle. His correspondence is one-sided and his list of contacts far from comprehensive. The best Theodoret could do was portray his efforts in letters. Showcasing his Antiochene attachments made Theodoret look like a good

representative, encouraging external contacts. Likewise, displaying external relationships made him look like a good social mediator, tightening his network
bonds. These virtual relationships, of course, had to be the right ones. For decades
the best way to prove orthodoxy was to have orthodox companions. It was no
accident that when Theodoret came under attack in 448, he began reading off
names of famous friends.[50]

PREACHING IN TONGUES: A NEW
MULTILINGUAL DYNAMIC

One mark of Theodoret's success was thus the accumulation of allies. Building
relations, however, was complicated in Syria by linguistic divides, as we saw in
chapter 1. After 436 Theodoret and his confidants remained eager to reach non-
Greek speakers. They expanded doctrinal translation in Syriac and Armenian.
They also encouraged education in Greek and celebrated the multiple Christian
languages. The translators still met resistance. By seeking cross-cultural communication, however, the Antiochenes laid the groundwork for a more multilingual
church community.

The Antiochenes' new multilingual efforts grew out of prior generations'
experience. Any clerical network that hoped to span Syria needed a multilingual
alliance. As we have noted, however, translation was trouble. New terminology
might be greeted hostilely. When successful it could still divide adherents from
their wider linguistic community. Translation might also clash with cultural ideology. Greek stereotypes still cast Aramaic and Armenian-speakers as simpletons.[51]
Early Antiochene translations ran afoul of these problems. Syriac and Armenian
versions of Theodore's work inspired fiery counterreactions, led by Rabbula and
Sahak respectively. Meanwhile, the translations scared paternalistic Greeks—
Nestorianism might infect the defenseless.[52] Linguistic difference did not create
the conflict over Theodore, but it intensified the dispute.

It was in the late 430s that the Antiochenes renewed efforts to bridge the linguistic divides, led by Hiba of Edessa. With Rabbula dead, Hiba again translated
works of Theodore into Syriac, and circulated some of this material. As Acacius
of Melitene spread around Greek lists of Theodore's "heresies," Hiba countered,
with Syriac lists of his orthodox teachings.[53] Beyond textual work, Hiba involved
himself in broader circles of education. There is little independent support for
the sixth-century accusation that he organized a pro-Antiochene "School of the
Persians." But he did deal with Armenian and Syriac teachers in Edessa, some of
whom may have collaborated as Antiochenes.[54]

Theodoret's multilingual involvements were less direct but important. So far
as we know, Theodoret wrote only in Greek, though he showed Aramaic knowledge.[55] But he must have heard of Hiba's activities and probably approved. Theo-

doret spread Antiochene knowledge in his own way. He urged students to master Greek sophistic learning before specialized doctrine.[56] His traditional approach did not undercut Hiba's labors; it might even create new expert translators. Theodoret intervened more directly regarding textual circulation. Older Syriac gospel texts, for instance, were replaced with "more accurate" renderings. More generally, he listened in on preachers, in Aramaic and Greek.[57] Perhaps Theodoret's largest contribution was rhetorical. His writings celebrated the multilingual nature of Syrian churches and monasteries. He praised Ephrem Syrus (Syriac writer *par excellence*), and advertised Greek versions of his writings.[58] While hardly the first Greek writer to mention a Syriac work, Theodoret made cross-linguistic contact into a virtue.

The multilingual efforts of Theodoret and Hiba bespeak a goal of broadening their network. In the early 430s connections were weak enough that Rabbula could command most of his subordinates to defect. Hiba and Theodoret worked to prevent such reversals. Translating and circulating texts spread specialized Antiochene knowledge. So did higher education. Censorship, meanwhile, removed alternative tropes. Theodoret and Hiba performed different tasks with a common goal. By broadening textual access and encouraging multilingual education, they could better integrate clerics of all tongues.

The new Antiochene multilingual programs met with divergent reactions. Some Syrian clerics were better integrated into the network. The seventy-five bishops who defended Theodore in 440 must have included men whose first language was Aramaic. Translation efforts probably aided connections across the Sassanid frontier, though the actual breadth of these links remains elusive.[59] Translations also enraged some opponents. In Armenia, Antiochene allies lost ground. Even in Osrhoene, Hiba offended local clerics, including bishop Uranius of Himerium (who spoke little Greek).[60] Meanwhile, Theodoret found objections to his push for sophistic learning. One cleric complained that he had been ordered to "expound on ... Plato and Aristotle," and to sign a creedal statement, before interpreting Scripture.[61] Neither Theodoret nor Hiba could quell fears that they were infecting a helpless East. Broader specialized knowledge may have cemented some bonds. But it disturbed ambiguities that helped to preserve a sense of shared orthodoxy.

Antiochene multilingual efforts yielded mixed results in the 430s and 440s but played an ongoing part in Theodoret's program. Hiba's translations continued. Texts circulated, allowing broad sharing of equivalent cues. Theodoret's advocacy of Greek education remained important, while relations with Syriac/Aramaic teachers deepened over time. Theodoret even tempered his sense of Greek superiority with encouragement of cultural exchange.[62] Again, perceptions mattered. Theodoret's network was harder to marginalize if it seemed to bridge linguistic lines. Theodoret and Hiba thus fostered a new dynamic in multilingual clerical relations, which would grow beyond their lifetimes.

BEFRIENDING THE FRIENDS OF GOD:
NEW ASCETIC RELATIONS

Theodoret's networking efforts stretched across linguistic boundaries. They particularly reached out to Syria's ascetics. Theodoret's prominence has rested heavily on his relations with famous hermits, publicized by his *History of the Friends of God* (a.k.a. *Historia religiosa* or *HR*). This text so enhanced his reputation that the sixth-century miaphysite Severus of Antioch tried to actively reclaim Symeon Stylites from his clutches.[63] The *Historia religiosa* includes a "historical" part on fourth-century ascetics, which we discussed in chapter 3. More than half of the *HR*, however, deals with Theodoret's contacts circa 440.[64] The *HR* can be imaginative, not least when the author discusses himself. Other texts by Theodoret, however, note his ascetic connections and provide context. The *HR* served as a rhetorical means to reinforce the Antiochene network. Not only did it claim holiness by association; it presented ascetics to clerics and lay elites in ways that bridged cultural divides.

One of Theodoret's plainest assertions in the *HR* was that he had befriended the friends of God. Writing about hermits and archimandrites, he touted his reciprocated companionship and exclusive access. He was the only bishop, he tells us, allowed into Marana's enclosure. He gave the Eucharist to Maris by special request. When Jacob of Cyrrhestica was deathly ill, Theodoret rescued him from the crowds. Naturally the holy man "immediately opened his eyes."[65] Throughout the text, Theodoret advises ascetics. He protects them from excesses and gives them the imprimatur of orthodoxy. Even when he depended on ascetics, he presents himself as chosen. It was a hermit, we are told, who enabled his birth.[66] Recent research has stressed the tendentious nature of Theodoret's assertions. He may exaggerate his intimacy with the ascetics. And he describes subjects using classical terms not shared by other Syrian sources.[67] In our skepticism, however, we should not lose sight of the social context. Letters and other documents reveal links to key monastic figures that were not pure invention.

In fact, Theodoret's letters provide a different perspective on his courting of the monastic community. In some ways the letters support the *HR*'s picture. Theodoret wrote to instruct monks in Antiochene orthodoxy. He wrote to ask for leading ascetics' personal attention and touted their cooperation.[68] Meanwhile, he visited ascetics locally and regionally. And he conducted oversight through an "exarch of the monasteries," not unlike Rabbula.[69] Theodoret's letters differ from the *HR* in their tone of mutuality. His doctrinal instruction was given as a service to "fellow mariners" on the ship of God.[70] Friendly letters stressed how much ascetics helped the author. "We are inactive and prone to laziness," he told one archimandrite, "and stand in great need of your prayers."[71] Most strikingly the letters reveal how ascetics influenced Theodoret. When Symeon, Jacob, and Baradatus pressed him to compromise in 434, they "afflicted [him] with a deep sadness," and he heeded their call.[72] This influence extended to less famous figures. Theodoret turned to one archimandrite to comment on new doctrinal writings.[73] And, of course, he sought to recruit new bishops from monasteries: Domnus of Antioch, Sabinianus of Perrha, and probably others.[74] Clearly he wanted to show his inclusion of worthy monks.

Theodoret's interactions with ascetics grew out of prior Antiochene experience. Theodoret's forebears had sought monastic help since the 360s. Doctrinal oversight and cooperation led to recruitment, as we saw in chapter 3. But not every relationship went smoothly. The diverse monastic movement had internal cultural clashes, and some groups (Messalians, Sleepless ones) ran into trouble with the urban clergy.[75] Then came the disputes of the 430s. Monastic leaders who once showed zeal against Jews and pagans (e.g., Barsauma) now did so against "Nestorians." By the mid 440s, Antiochenes were uncertain of their ascetic backing. So Theodoret wrote his letters, calling for closer alliances by stressing inclusion, doctrinal and otherwise.

It is in light of this social initiative that we must view Theodoret's hagiography, for the HR rhetorically reinforced his networking plans. The HR presented ascetics as part of an idealized community. While it reveled in their diverse self-deprivations, it emphasized their bonds across linguistic, geographic, and gender lines. Parts of the HR drew a lineage of mentorship from founding fathers (like Marcian and Julian Saba) to contemporaries. Other sections stressed the role of clerical ambassadors, who not only worked with monastic leaders, but also connected circles of disciples.[76] All of this served as an apologetic to outsiders. By displaying Syria's holy people, Theodoret lent support to their clerical associates. Indirectly he countered suspicions of heresy.[77] Just as important, the HR reinforced relationships within the Antiochene network. He featured cooperative ascetics, which made them more attractive to clerics. And he featured ascetic-minded clerics, which made them more attractive to the monks.

Most crucially, Theodoret approached ascetics with a common explanatory language. In letters, he praised ascetics for their "toils of virtue" in pursuit of "victory." The HR extended these metaphors. Monasteries become "exercise grounds (*palaistrai*)," and monks, "athletes of virtue."[78] Practices are justified by philosophic argument and biblical typology. Theodoret's explanations differ from those of Syriac writers. But his work had the goal of creating new social cues. By mixing sophistic language with regional practice, these signals could work across the cultural breadth of his network.

In his ascetic networking, Theodoret again relied on creating good impressions. It is difficult to measure his success at winning over monks. Some supported his doctrines and allies; others remained neutral or hostile. Theodoret's HR, however, circulated widely, in Greek and in Syriac.[79] His work presented a rich web of clerical-ascetic relations. Not only did this make the network look well rooted, it encouraged further bonding between himself, his colleagues, and his holy friends.

CRAFTING COHERENCE: DOCTRINE, HISTORY, LEADERSHIP, COMMUNITY

Theodoret's social initiatives thus proceeded on multiple fronts. In each case, new relationships coincided with rhetorical efforts to modify social cues. Besides canvassing, Theodoret worked culturally to *represent* his community. Between 436 and 450, he wrote half of his doctrinal works, most of his exegesis, and his *Church History* (as well as the *HR*). Generally this corpus has been carefully studied.[80] What has not always been recognized is how well these writings fit together within a social context. His exegesis and treatises offered a new doctrinal handbook, to give the Antiochenes a shared line of reasoning. His historical work provided a basic narrative to supply the Antiochenes with a renewed sense of community. When Theodoret achieved prominence in the mid-430s, his network was held together by scattered social signals. Over fifteen years of perpetual persuasion he outlined a coherent Antiochene identity.

Theodoret's effort to represent the Antiochenes centered on Christological doctrine. In 439 he wrote *In Defense of Diodore and Theodore*; in 447, the *Eranistes*. All along he reshaped the tropes of prior theologians to fit his situation. He began from a firm Antiochene base. He showed concern for "exact" terminology and emphasized the distinctness of God. He cited the soteriological role of Jesus' humanity, and defended "two natures in one Christ."[81] Theodoret avoided certain controversial Antiochene tropes, such as "assuming God" and "assumed man." Instead, he wrote of abstract natures, or the Cyrillian-sounding "divine Word" and "Word incarnate."[82] Theodoret gave advice for how to stay orthodox: Christological balance. Between the extremes of two sons and one nature sat his dyophysite position.[83] For him the *Formula of Reunion* captured this balance, if read correctly. Theodoret worked with Antiochene cues under a new sensibility.[84]

Theodoret also represented Antiochenes through exegesis. Between 436 and 450 he commented on nearly every corner of Scripture. Again, he retained an Antiochene foundation. He kept some of Theodore's emphasis on grammar, vocabulary, and narrative integrity.[85] He distinguished his exegesis, however, by his style of typology. While Theodore had limited types of Christ to a few symbols, Theodoret expanded the list by loosening the need for an exact match.[86] Theodoret, like his predecessor, read Scripture as having "literal" (Greek: *kata tēn lexin*), metaphorical, and typological meaning. Except with some texts (like the Song of Songs) he looked past the "literal" to a "spiritual" truth. This deeper search sometimes looks more like the work of Origen than the work of Theodore.[87] By expanding the use of types and accepting a spiritual subtext, Theodoret blurred the limitations that Theodore had once drawn.

Theodoret's doctrinal and exegetical presentation accorded well with his efforts to expand and reinforce his network. Traditional formulas and interpretive tropes affirmed core Antiochene alliances. His spiritual readings of Scripture spoke to a wider audience. The notion of doctrinal balance not only affirmed Antiochene orthodoxy; it made sense of the choice to endorse Proclus's *Tome* while resisting other formulations. Even Theodoret's literary stylings supported the renewed network. Outwardly the *Eranistes* was dialogue, a form used by philosophers and Christian writers, including Cyril, for doctrinal argument. But while many dialogues featured staid agreement, the *Eranistes* depicted a vital debate.[88] This simulated conversation affirmed the Antiochene practice of deliberations. It even indirectly blessed the schisms of the early 430s, because the argument had led to doctrinal balance. Theodoret's writings did more than modify old doctrinal tropes. They modeled and celebrated Antiochene theological discourse.

As Theodoret represented Antiochene doctrine, he also retold Antiochene history. His *Church History* was probably written in 449, during renewed controversy. From his hagiography and letters, however, it is clear that he had long pondered the Antiochene clerical heritage in light of his own experience. As noted in chapter 3, the *Church History* told heroic tales of Syria's Nicene bishops, especially Meletius of Antioch and his followers (Flavian, Diodore, Theodore, and Acacius). Theodoret's information seems accurate enough, but that did not prevent him from narrating in a pro-Antiochene fashion. We have already noted how Theodoret defended the honor of his forbears, while covering over troubling episodes. Understandably he celebrated Syrian heroes with his colleagues. At the same time Theodoret's narrative offered moral exemplars, men who resisted imperial pressure as they held to orthodoxy.[89] He probably hoped to edify his core allies, and maybe to draw in figures on the periphery. Theodoret's history served as a practical resource. It suggested ways to maintain solidarity, from public protests to regional recruitment. And, as we noted, his writings promoted the role of non-Greek speakers and ascetics in settling past controversies. Thus he aimed his moral models and practical advice toward a wider audience. The *Church History* used real people and events to create an idealized Antiochene heritage. By 449, and probably before, Theodoret was working on narratives in which he could find a place as part of the community.

Theodoret's teachings and stories were well suited to his social environment, but they did not sell themselves. The author had to support them with a performance of leadership. As a leading figure Theodoret had assets: his experience, his doctrinal acumen, his asceticism, and his record of mediation. Above all he had elite connections and centrality within his network. Rarely in his letters did Theodoret brag about his abilities.[90] Instead he left hints, by praising similar attributes in others.[91] Theodoret remained a suffragan ill positioned to command his colleagues. All he could do was display persistent persuasion: "Even if your religiosity persecuted, chased, and used invective against us," he told Alexander in 435, "I would not cease prostrating to beg at the feet of your holiness."[92] Theodoret was not always gentle. He threatened dissident clerics and probably had a colleague deposed.[93] In his writings, however, he hid any coercion behind a welcoming tone.

Theodoret's main performance of leadership lay in his writing. Through doctrinal and exegetical work Theodoret laid claim to Antiochene orthodoxy. His polished texts showed mastery of Scripture and dialectic. His prolific pen (more than one book per year) left little room for other voices of authority.[94] Through his historical narrative Theodoret linked himself to past mentors. He claimed the mantle of Theodore, for his doctrinal mastery, and the legacy of Acacius of Beroea for his mix of strictness (*akribeia*) and flexibility (*oikonomia*).[95] Whenever he wrote, Theodoret drew principles from his own experience. It should not surprise us that he praised mixing asceticism with clerical life, or seeking balanced doctrine. He was, after all, an ascetic turned bishop, who had brokered compromise. Theodoret wove himself into doctrinal discourse and church history. Thus he made his leadership seem natural.

Beyond self-affirmation, Theodoret's literary efforts outlined what it meant to be an Antiochene. His doctrinal syntheses resonated with his picture of Antiochene heritage. Both lent support to his social initiatives and backed up his claim to authority. By mixing communal narrative with personal performance, Theodoret supported his theology. He also supported his relationships and those of his allies. Narratives and authorial performances interlinked scattered social cues, and thus forged an Antiochene identity.

The coherence of Theodoret's writings, however, leads us into a dilemma. It is difficult to unravel Antiochene traditions from Theodoret's own concerns. Theodoret spoke for the Antiochene community, but his views may not have been widely shared. Though he tried to look inextricable, others may have been willing to dispense with him. The source of our trouble is Theodoret's control of the sources. Between 436 and 447, most extant social records come from his pen. After 447, the fuller mix of sources casts his network in a rather different light.

FRAGILE FELLOWSHIP: THE COLLAPSE
OF THEODORET'S NETWORK

From the vantage point of hostile outsiders, the Antiochene community proved more fragile than Theodoret's writings imply. From 447 clerics entered the "Eutychean" controversy. The network, which Theodoret presented as a coherent community, disintegrated at the hands of its adversaries, backed by the imperial court. The process is recorded in Theodoret's letters, but also in conciliar *acta* (from Ephesus in 449 and Chalcedon in 451). Some editors were sympathetic to Theodoret; others were hostile.[96] Together they reveal from multiple angles the undoing of Theodoret's efforts.

The dismemberment of Theodoret's network began from scattered wellsprings of hostility. The most obvious was Alexandria. By 440, Theodoret and Cyril had struck a truce. They had both endorsed the *Formula of Reunion* and Proclus's *Tome*. But they remained mutually suspicious. Cyril's death in 444 led to the succession of Dioscorus, and this former archdeacon under Cyril placed less value on his compromises. Dioscorus reconnected with Cyril's allies, including Juvenal of Jerusalem and the bishops of Cappadocia. He also approached Theodosius's court, where the loose support won by Cyril carried over to his successor.[97] It is not clear if Dioscorus had any offensive plans; he was simply managing an existing (anti-Antiochene) coalition.

Another source of hostility was Constantinople. Here the problem was not bishops (Proclus and, after 446, Flavian), but courtiers and monasteries. Eutyches may have been more a simple archimandrite than a scheming mastermind. But he did have allies in the monasteries and at least one at court (the eunuch Chrysaphius).[98] In fact, the court remained suspicious of Theodoret and his (known) networking activities. By 444 it had barred the bishop of Cyrrhus from meddling in church appeals hearings.[99] It would not take much to convince Theodosius that Theodoret meant trouble.

Extraregional hostilities thus awaited Theodoret. Further hostilities involved resentful clerics within Syria. The first troublesome figure was Athanasius of Perrha, a former bishop in Euphratensis. In 443 Athanasius had been accused of stealing church property. A council in Hierapolis was called to investigate. When Athanasius failed to appear, he was deposed. He appealed to Cyril and Proclus, who interceded with Domnus of Antioch. But the appeals hearing also sided against him.[100] Convinced (justifiably) that Theodoret had organized his downfall, Athanasius traveled to the capital and plotted revenge (see chapter 7 for details). Another source of opposition was clergymen from Osrhoene, loyal to the memory of Rabbula. In Edessa four priests (Samuel, Eulogius, Maras, and Cyrus) ran into trouble with Bishop Hiba. They found sanctuary nearby with Uranius of Himerium. In 445, the quartet petitioned Domnus, denouncing their bishop as a heretical tyrant. When Domnus let the matter drop, the four blamed Theodoret and sought new avenues of appeal.[101] The third party came from Phoenicia I: opponents of Irenaeus of Tyre. Before Irenaeus most of the province had been aligned with Cyril. The arrival of this reputed Nestorian must have inspired dissent, which grew as he appointed loyal Antiochenes (e.g., Aquilinus of Byblus). The dissenters assembled under Eustathius of Berytus. When their appeals went nowhere, they understood why.[102] Individually, these were local disputes, which did not always concern doctrine. But other dissenters existed: Cyril's old *proxenoi* (e.g., Maximus,

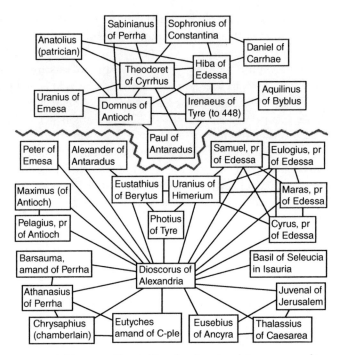

FIGURE 16. The opposition to Theodoret's network in 449, according to letters and conciliar records. amand = archimandrite, pr = priest.

Thalassius, and John) and Rabbula's rioters. By 447, a new Syrian clerical coalition was forming (see figure 16).

The spark of new conflict was apparently Theodoret's own writing. In 447, he published his *Eranistes,* as noted. This dialogue criticized some of Cyril's formulas ("out of two natures") and qualified others ("one nature incarnate"). Provocatively, it called these positions a heretical pastiche, held by simpletons.[103] Somewhere this argument touched a nerve. The opposition set forth to counter Theodoret's doctrines. This time, however, they made no direct demands, just back-channel accusations. Theodoret did not acknowledge the reach of his foes until he was already under threat.

From late 447 to early 448, Theodoret's network was repeatedly attacked; each time the imperial court got involved. First came a move against Irenaeus. In late 447, his local critics circulated accusations in the capital. The charges included Nestorianism, nepotism, tyranny, and escape from exile. But their firmest argument concerned episcopal eligibility: Irenaeus had been consecrated while married to his second wife, violating a (rarely observed) canon.[104] Theodoret defended

Irenaeus's rectitude, orthodoxy, and legitimacy. But Theodoret was unsure of the emperor's opinion, until March 448, when the court deposed Irenaeus and confined him.[105] Meanwhile, opponents started new attacks on Hiba. Imperial officials were presented with eighteen charges against him, ranging from embezzlement and nepotism to heresy. Pressed by the court, Domnus called a hearing for after Easter 448. Eleven bishops (including Theodoret) dismissed the financial charges (the other charges were not presented by the insecure plaintiffs).[106] So the quartet turned to Constantinople. By fall the court had vacated the tribunal's ruling.[107] It was a third assault, however, which caused the most worry. Theodoret was in Antioch in the spring of 448 when he read an edict against himself. Accusing him of conniving to disturb the orthodox, it confined him to his diocese. Theodoret tapped his contacts to learn what was going on.[108] Soon he understood. By summer Dioscorus was denouncing him and eight of his colleagues as heretics.[109] The accusations had become a conspiracy to destroy the Antiochenes, with the court ready to go along.

Between April 448 and May 449, Theodoret wrote repeatedly to bishops and courtiers, defending his behavior and teachings. At first, he touted his record of leadership: his asceticism, his benefaction, and his pursuit of heretics.[110] He denied wild doctrinal rumors and recited his (orthodox) reading list.[111] Later Theodoret produced some full doctrinal arguments. He denounced "one nature" and a "passable divinity."[112] To Disocorus, he made a (seemingly) unequivocal statement: "That I subscribed twice to the *Tomes* about Nestorius ... my own hands bear witness."[113] He also touted his friendship with Cyril and asked colleagues for *agapē*.[114] To make countermoves he enlisted Basil of Seleucia and Domnus of Antioch. From others he simply demanded a fair hearing, where he was sure he would prevail.[115]

Yet by the fall of 448, Theodoret found he was losing ground. Some contacts promised help, above all Anatolius. With the emperor's hostility now clear, most refused to reply. "I have already written two or three letters ... without a response," Theodoret wrote to the Consul Nomus. "Really, I do not know what offense I caused to your Magnificence."[116] Dioscorus sent what Domnus called "a letter that ought never have been written," threatening Theodoret and all his associates.[117] What probably hurt most was colleagues' passivity. Even Domnus merely pleaded with Dioscorus for a return to the *status quo ante*.[118] Theodoret must have realized that he was unlikely to find relief.

Elsewhere actions proceeded against Theodoret's confidants, again with imperial backing. In Tyre, Irenaeus privately worked on his *Tragedy*. The clerics of Phoenicia I feuded in writing and in the streets, even after Dioscorus consecrated a new metropolitan, Photius of Tyre.[119] Meanwhile, the court ordered a new tribunal for Hiba for February 449. For judges, they picked Eustathius of Berytus (enemy of Irenaeus) and Uranius of Himerium (critic of Hiba). As hosting judge they selected Photius of Tyre. Moved twice to avoid mob riots, the hearing took up all the charges against Hiba, and more against his nephew Daniel of Carrhae.[120] Daniel "resigned" as expected. But Hiba tried to negotiate. When he promised to condemn Nestorius, restore dissidents, and leave finances to the *oikonomoi*, the judges accepted his offer.[121] The imperial court, however, was unsatisfied. In March Hiba returned home to new riots and written clerical protests. Imperial officials imprisoned and effectively deposed him.[122] Thus Dioscorus and his court allies tore at weak links within Theodoret's network.

Theodoret's remaining defenders made one successful counterattack, when court backing seemed within reach. Antiochene supporters (including Basil of Seleucia) met in Constantinople and found a target in Eutyches the archimandrite. In November, he was accused of heresy before the Resident Synod. "Reluctantly," Bishop Flavian summoned him.[123] Pronouncing "one nature after the union," he was condemned by fifty-three bishops and archimandrites.[124] Theodoret responded quickly to the verdict. Domnus led a wintertime delegation to the capital, carrying pleas for the accused.[125] At last, it looked as if the court would show balance and reopen Syrian connections.

Yet this opening came to naught; the trial of Eutyches enabled Dioscorus to show the breadth of his doctrinal alliance. Eutyches may have looked theologically maladroit, but he still had clerical and monastic backers.[126] They claimed the tribunal had never heard the archimandrite's defense. Flavian sent a transcript to the consistory, which Eutyches' supporters called fraudulent.[127] In March, the court summoned an ecumenical council. But right away it signaled new leanings: Theodoret was forbidden to attend.[128] Meanwhile, the court vacated rulings against Eutyches, casting suspicion on the judges instead.[129] Back in Syria, Theodoret gave up on receiving a hearing. Basil stopped responding to letters. Irenaeus questioned Theodoret's doctrinal resolve; he sent his own agents to make the case. Domnus remained supportive, but given the court's obvious hostility, his expectations seemed naïve.[130] Theodoret was not only losing arguments in the palace; he was losing control of his association.

When the Second Council of Ephesus met in August 449, its judgments proved both farcical and telling. Domnus went to Ephesus with twenty-one other Syrian bishops. He then took ill and, after the first session, sat out the proceedings. Most other Syrians were sidelined under suspicion of heresy. Flavian of Constantinople was linked to "diabolical roots," and forbidden to speak.[131] But three Syrian collaborators were given prominent roles (Photius of Tyre, Eustathius of Berytus, and Basil of Seleucia), alongside the prime instigators (Juvenal of Jerusalem and Thalassius of Caesarea). The Syrian archimandrite Barsauma was given a vote to represent "orthodox monks."[132] The first session reviewed Eutyches's trial. After a select reading of the transcripts, attendees rehabilitated Eutyches and affirmed "one nature after the union." Next, suddenly Flavian was accused of augmenting the Nicene Creed. He could only scream "I appeal" to the papal legate before being dragged from the hall (he died en route to exile).[133] Scholars have pondered why so many bishops assented to these actions. Later reports described a threatening climate: attendees told to sign blank pages, cowering from soldiers wielding clubs.[134] But the extant *acta* preserve none of this. Dioscorus may have manipulated the records. But he had already declared his preferences and demonstrated imperial backing. The passivity of attending bishops may have been genuine.

In any case, the opening session was just a prelude to the main event: the gutting of Theodoret's network. First, witnesses reported the judgments and acclamations against Hiba. Amid murderous shouts the council condemned him and ordered his wealth seized.[135] Next, Daniel of Carrhae was excommunicated for immorality and embezzlement (he had already resigned).[136] Irenaeus was again condemned, along with his appointee Aquilinus.[137] Sophronius of Constantina was denounced for sorcery, his fate left up to a new metropolitan of Edessa.[138] Then came the attack on Theodoret. Syrian priests told stories of hidden meetings, where recruits were forced to read pagan philosophy and sign secret creeds. This was followed by a (generally accurate) synopsis of Theodoret's teaching. Dioscorus asked for his condemnation and all the Syrian attendees seem to have complied.[139] The council paused to reinstate bishops purportedly deposed by Theodoret.[140] Finally Domnus was himself indicted, as a collaborator in Theodoret's machinations.[141] These charges may seem absurd but they show an underlying logic. Dioscorus staged a pageant of Antiochene heresy and criminality. Through guilt by association, he neutralized the core Antiochene network.

As Dioscorus attacked the Antiochenes, he crafted a replacement network. Before the council he linked dissident Syrian clerics with distant sympathizers. By the summer of 449 he had two defectors and a new metropolitan.[142] In Ephesus Dioscorus showcased his new clerical allies (witnesses and plaintiffs). He found more new allies by replacing accused bishops with their local rivals. Major sees, however, he saved for his confidants. Constantinople went to Anatolius, Dioscorus's archdeacon. Antioch was given to Maximus, probably the priest who had served as Cyril's *proxenos*. By mid-450, most of Theodoret's inner circle was bound for exile (Theodoret to his old monastery in Nicertae). Those who remained largely acquiesced to the new setup (see figure 17). And Theodosius II expressed his support.[143]

Thus Dioscorus, with imperial backing, carried out a new ecclesiastical coup. Over eighteen months Theodoret's social and rhetorical efforts were undone. The anti-Antiochenes sequentially targeted Theodoret and his confidants. Some they accused and deposed, others they pressured to realign. In either case they mixed accusations of heresy with criminal charges, to reveal a dark conspiracy. The new coalition also targeted Antiochene social practices. Naming an archimandrite as voting representative altered Antiochene ascetic relations. Defending local

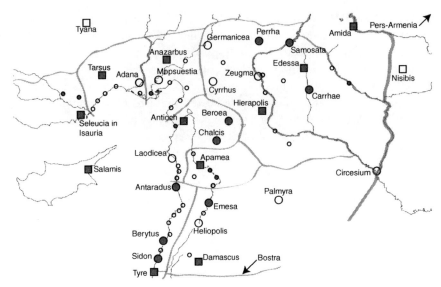

FIGURE 17. Map of Dioscorus's new Syrian network, 449–450, according to letters and conciliar records. Filled shapes = bishops in Dioscorus's coalition, empty shapes = dyophysite holdouts or unknown bishops.

candidates challenged Antiochene modes of recruitment. Obviously Dioscorus and his allies assaulted Antiochene doctrine. "Two natures after the incarnation" was declared Nestorian heresy. Books by Diodore, Theodore, Theodoret, and Hiba were ordered burned.[144] Even Antiochene patterns of informal leadership came under attack. The Second Council of Ephesus set up orderly patriarchates. Half of Syria now officially answered to Jerusalem and half to Antioch. Most of the old Antiochene periphery probably escaped direct harm. But as patriarchs applied a new orthodoxy, they had little choice but to comply. None of this was purely Dioscorus's doing. Repeatedly officials signaled the emperor's will. Dioscorus simply built his coalition and seized the opportunity to efface Theodoret's whole network.

AN AUTOPSY OF THE ANTIOCHENE NETWORK

The collapse of Theodoret's network complicates our understanding of his leadership and community. On the one hand, Theodoret's writings present a robust association with powerful allies, an informal leadership, and a developing sense of identity. On the other hand, conciliar records depict a doctrinal clique, surrounded by hostile clerics and monks and, when challenged, liable to crumble. There are several ways to interpret the contradictory sources. One could view Theodoret's network as robust until it was overthrown. One could also view the network as a representation, which proved illusory. There is, however, a more nuanced possibility, tied to the social patterns that this book has traced. Modular scale-free networks may be robust, but still be susceptible to collapse, all while limiting core members' perception of the peril.

The records of the Eutychean controversy shine a stark light on the network that Theodoret tried to forge. Sometimes the records support his picture of relations. Most of his intimate correspondents are confirmed as close allies, when they appear as Dioscorus' targets (or as featured defectors). But often the sources do not align. The *acta* reveal dissenting clerics, and local tensions, that Theodoret never acknowledged. In letters, Theodoret claimed to represent a broad, orthodox clergy. Dioscorus presented him as commanding a small heretical cabal. How far did Theodoret's teachings and attitudes extend to the rest of the Syrian clergy? By 450, few stood up on his behalf. Even before the controversy his support may have been weaker than he let on.

How then, should we view the Antiochene network and Theodoret's leadership? One approach would be to try to harmonize the contrasting sources. Theodoret's network could have been as robust and popular as he suggested, until opponents tore it apart. By 440, Theodoret had proven effective as a defender and mediator. His centrality within the network gave him standing to advance his program (recruitment, doctrine, heritage, and communal identity). Theodoret's texts remained popular long after his condemnation. It seems unlikely this following was invented out of whole cloth. Theodoret's influence may be gauged from what it took to get rid of him: a year of accusations, assaults on his subordinates, a highly controlled council, and hostile signals from the emperor. When Basil of Seleucia abandoned Theodoret, the abruptness of his decision indicates a network in the process of being conquered.

A second approach would be to treat the sources as social representations. Theodoret's network could have been an illusion of his pen, which dissolves when viewed through different writings. Theodoret presented himself as an accepted clerical leader. Beyond his inner circle, however, his contacts may have been unreliable. Lay officials ignored his pleas. Some monasteries embraced his opponents. His favorite ascetics never demonstrated on his behalf. Theodoret's multilingual efforts won him few allies in Armenia. Among Syriac writers it was Rabbula who claimed the most respect. Centuries later, even the Church of the East paid little attention to Theodoret (or Hiba).[145] Theodoret's leadership performance faced stark limits amid the deepening of the church hierarchy. By the 440s, patriarchs seemed useful both to courtiers (who had fewer prelates to worry about) and to clerics (who had clear lines of appeal). Theodoret had personal influence with Domnus, Hiba, and Basil. Records reveal little deference from other bishops. The number of Syrian supporters won over by Dioscorus suggests an Antiochene community that was rather hollow.

Between these two approaches, however, lies a more nuanced perspective, based on the relational patterns that this book has outlined. Theodoret's group could have seemed cohesive to its leaders but still be vulnerable to collapse. Throughout this book we have found a general Antiochene social pattern, a modular scale-free topology. Networks of this form are generally robust in computer simulations.[146] They survive the loss of random members (which in our case might mean by death or by defection). Modular, scale-free networks can be dissolved, however, if some force simultaneously removes most of the hubs. In 449 and 450, we see just such a force, led by Dioscorus and his imperial backers. The result was a cascade failure, which could occur even if Theodoret's relationships were intersubjectively "real."

In fact, Theodoret may not have understood his network's vulnerability; for the shape of social relations might have distorted his perception. In chapter 2, we mapped a tight Antiochene core surrounding five main hubs. We also mapped a segmented and spotty periphery. After 436, Theodoret worked to extend his network and maintain a tight inner circle, which reinforced this basic social arrangement. At the core, Theodoret was surrounded by Antiochene cues. It was feasible for him to assemble these signals into an Antiochene identity. Core allies probably shared enough of his stories and teachings to create the impression of a nascent community. Social experiences must have differed on the periphery. There Antiochene cues were rarer, emerging from a narrow central clique. Syrian dissidents must have felt out of the loop, and thus complained to Dioscorus. Hearing such complaints, he could easily imagine a heretical conspiracy.

This autopsy is, of course, premature. A year after the Second Council of Ephesus, Dioscorus's miaphysite order began to falter. First Pope Leo took up the cause of some victims of Ephesus (especially Flavian of Constantinople). A few courtiers may have been receptive.[147] Then in July 450, Theodosius II dropped dead. The new regime of Marcian and Pulcheria vacated conciliar rulings of the previous summer.[148] Theodoret and Hiba both returned to their sees. Other Syrian bishops hailed their return, including some defectors.[149] By the summer of 451 it was Dioscorus facing the threat of exile.

It is, in fact, easy to lose perspective in the study of church disputes. These conflicts were largely directed by a few hundred active participants. Doctrinal networks of lay patrons, clerics, and monks could crumble under pressure, especially from the imperial court. And then, beyond the church leadership lay the rest of late Roman society, whose relations with clerics are the focus of the next few chapters. As we shall see, the course of the Christological dispute depended significantly on that outside world.

PART II

Theodoret and Late Roman Networks of Patronage

6

Mediating Bishops

Patronage Roles and Relations
in the Fifth Century

There were times when the non-clerical world demanded a bishop's attention.

John of Antioch was just starting to push reluctant colleagues toward doctrinal compromise in 432, when he heard of the new trouble facing a neighboring bishop. Seleucia Pieria was a busy port town. That summer it endured some form of public violence. John did not record the details; perhaps, as in Tarsus, there had been a clerical riot. He thanked God that the local bishop was unharmed. Nevertheless, the clergy had offended the port's *augustalis,* and this midlevel bureaucrat[1] fined the see of Seleucia 8000 *solidi* (111 pounds of gold). John told colleagues of these new "sorrows." He asked for contributions.[2] Perhaps his critics would finally see why the schisms had to end.

With the punishment of his neighbor, John of Antioch confronted a common situation for bishops of the mid-fifth century: weakness in the face of political authority. Eight thousand *solidi* looked minor in the context of imperial expenditure. Wealthy senators would find it a bearable hardship. But if Seleucia's church assets were similar to Oxyrhynchus's, those coins represented a sizable portion of annual church funds.[3] Syrian bishops were not just doctrinal partisans, but local social leaders. They ran lawcourts and organized festivals. They funded monasteries, orphanages, charity doles, and civic amenities. An imperial penalty could disrupt these operations, not to mention clerical salaries. And that would undermine any bishop's authority.

Syrian bishops were part of a competition for status in Roman society that goes under the deceptively short label of patronage. Across the centuries great honors had gone to patrons who had saved cities from famines, financed temples, maintained city government, and protected towns from warriors and taxmen. Patronage relations relied on the exchange of favors and loyalties, physical benefits, and symbolic cues. Like doctrinal affinities they formed networks, except that patronage networks were more complicated, involving patrons, clients, agents, advocates, and friends. Patronage links facilitated communication and fostered community. Webs of patronage permeated Roman society, guiding expectations and imaginations. Cultural symbols came and went with the centuries, but patterns of patronage were long enduring.

Part II of this book examines the way Theodoret and his clerical associates participated in the patronage networks of late Roman society. Famously bishops supported dependents, such as widows and beggars. They lent aid to individuals and congregations. Yet bishops also dealt with figures of wealth and influence, sometimes trading favors, sometimes pleading for help. Theodoret's clerical network was bound by signals of friendship and shared orthodoxy. Outside the clergy, connections required different sorts of cues. Bishops were bound to clerical and ascetic allies, but patronage linked them to a still Christianizing Roman world. It pervaded the bishops' social experience and affected their theology. By the 440s patronage and doctrinal alliance were so interconnected that they lent new significance to clerical parties.

This chapter situates Theodoret's clerical network in the wider world of late Roman patronage. It examines the mediating roles that Theodoret and his colleagues sought vis-à-vis other elites, including local notables, educators, civil officials, military leaders, and "alternative" experts in religion. The evidence here comes predominantly from Theodoret, not his Antiochene allies. It comes from his personal letters, which give few hints as to how correspondents replied. For perspective, this chapter and the next will compare Theodoret's patronage efforts with those of several near contemporaries—bishops as well as other sorts of notables.

As we shall see, Theodoret and his clerical friends faced competition from patrons with greater resources and from networks with deeper roots. Still they managed to identify available, and desirable, social positions (though it is unclear how much they succeeded at fulfilling these roles). With most competing figures, Theodoret offered to trade favors and build connections. Only a few serious rivals were considered beyond the pale. Generally, the roles sketched out by Theodoret are similar to those sought by other (distant) bishops and non-clerical patrons (such as sophists). We do, however, see some special elements in Theodoret's clerical network, advantages that likely facilitated his relations and supported his cultural plans.

LATE ROMAN PATRONAGE: MODELS AND EVIDENCE

Few concepts find as much use in ancient social history as patronage. Decades of scholars have dubbed the Roman Empire a patronage society, especially communities of greater Syria. Syria, after all, hosted Libanius, whose speech *On Patrons* criticized soldiers for protecting villages with violence. Syria also hosted Theodoret, whose *Historia religiosa* praised holy men for protecting villages with prayers.[4] Libanius and Theodoret describe a familiar pattern: ordinary Romans winning favors from powerful figures by pledging their loyalty. These and other sources have led scholars to a model of Roman patronage, which they have used to explain the authority of emperors, landowners, holy men, and bishops.[5] Our conceptions of patronage can be enriched, however, if we employ the sociological concepts outlined in the introduction. As we have noted, patronage can be seen as a fluid transactional system, a relational web involving clients, patrons, and intermediaries. What defines these links as patronage relations is the exchange of favors and loyalties as social cues.[6] Participants in patronage may employ traditional symbols, such as public gifts or acclamations. They may add newer or narrower symbols. In any case, they must use these signals to perform the *roles* that they wish to assume.

The basic concept of patronage, of course, is well known to students of social history. By one common scholarly definition, patronage means personal, asymmetrical, non-monetary, reciprocal relationships of exchange.[7] This definition fits well within an Eastern Roman context. Ancient Greek boasted multiple terms for patronage. One is the protection (*prostasia*) that Libanius and Theodoret highlighted. Other rubrics included mediation (*mesiteia*), benefaction (*euergesia*), procurement (*proxenia*), solicitude (*prometheia*), and generosity (*philanthropia*). These terms described various activities: advocacy for individuals, settlement of disputes, improvement of cities, and defense of vulnerable communities. Varied terms and activities, however, do not obscure the consistency of Mediterranean patronage.[8] Many who have studied Roman patronage have crafted ideal types to measure real relations. More recently scholars have spoken of culturally constructed models of authority.[9] In either case, a basic template of patronage has remained central to Roman social history.

For historians, patronage conceptions play a key role in explaining the cohesion of Roman society. The Mediterranean world of the fifth century remained a diverse space and, as we have noted, Syria concentrated this diversity. The region held a varied landscape, supporting farmers, herders, city-dwellers, traders, and beduin. It also boasted a complicated political heritage.[10] Language provided one mark of diversity, with spoken and written Greek, Aramaic/Syriac, Armenian, Hebrew, Arabic, and Latin.[11] Religion added another, with multiple forms of Christian, Jewish, Magian, and pagan praxis. If any force could unite such a social patchwork, it had to be patronage. Relations between patrons and clients crossed social boundaries. Aramaic-speaking farmers might depend on Greek-speaking urban landowners, or German generals a thousand miles away.[12] These links fostered common expressions and expectations. Everywhere, clients were eager to promise loyalty; patrons, desirous "to supply communal and individual favors."[13] Patronage was so fundamental to late Roman society that it transcended political or religious ideology. It supplied the social logic by which other ideological discourses were offered and judged.[14]

And yet, to say patronage pervaded Roman society is only to scratch the surface of what it means. For starters, late Roman patronage was a dynamic interactive process inseparable from other social developments. From the fourth to the sixth century, Syria underwent a demographic expansion in marginal lands as well as in some cities. This expansion brought new resources, new vulnerabilities, and new possibilities for influence.[15] In this context, scholars have noted a "proliferation" of late Roman elite networks, with links further down the social hierarchy.[16] The writings of Theodoret and Libanius support this idea, showcasing soldiers who connected with scattered tenants, and ascetics who worked with distant villages. The result was an intensified competition among late Roman notables, a pursuit of stature through favor-trading. Famously bishops were gaining social authority in the fifth century, but they still constituted a small portion of the elite Romans who offered gifts in response to appeals.

Late Roman patronage was also a key force for cultural diversification and change. Patronage relations involved the sharing of symbols, not just material benefits. Ambitious patrons might use their funds to support their cultural preferences, with everything from baths and markets to basilicas and monasteries. Patronage relations also shaped group sensibilities. Clients and patrons bonded by finding cultural common ground. Scholars have noted the shift in late antiquity from benefits allotted to the local citizenry to charity destined for "the poor."[17] These were, in fact, two of many collective identities supported by some form of patronage. Naturally, patrons were in a position to influence the behaviors of their dependants. Libanius worried that soldiers were attracting peasants to violence through their protective services. Theodoret rejoiced that ascetics were drawing villages toward orthodoxy through their miracles.[18] In any case, patronage networks did more than supply necessities; they fostered various cultural communities.

Perhaps most important, late Roman patronage involved more than one sort of relationship. Most scholars have focused on overt dependence, such as between landlords and tenants or bishops and the poor.[19] In these vertical ties, clients appealed to patrons by showing their loyalty. Patrons then delivered favors that displayed their higher rank. Few patrons, however, controlled the resources to fulfill all requests. Most sought help from others.[20] As we have noted, Romans saw no firm boundary between friendship and patronage. "Friendship," wrote Firmus of Caesarea, "serves as the medium for business (*pragmasi*)."[21] Patronage interactions could get complicated, involving agents and middlemen, inside contacts and external brokers. These horizontal and diagonal links do not fit easily with "vertical" ideal types of relationships or cultural constructions of authority. But the full web of secondary connections was often required to communicate needs and promises, to distribute favors, and to inspire generosity.

The complexities of patronage thus require additions to the definitions used by prior historians. So do the relevant sources. Some of the richest evidence for ancient patronage comes from letters. But letters record only certain sorts of patronage. The stark dependency mentioned in laws, sermons, and papyri rarely appears in correspondence. Letters also cover only parts of the transaction process. Some feature appeals with no indication of the delivery of favors. Others recall favors without explaining the original request. Sometimes letters communicated directly between clients and patrons. More often, they involved mediators. And yet letters were essential to patronage activity. Unlike laws or sermons, the records requested actual favors and promised signs of loyalty.

There are, of course, many ways to deal with the social complexities of patronage and the available sources. This study seeks networks of patronage, by tracing the performance of social cues. We can look for traditional Roman favors, such as public amenities and discounted food, or traditional signals of loyalty, such as praise for the civic "savior" or the "generous giver." We can also look for specifically Christian favors, such as church buildings or charity, and Christian displays of loyalty, such as blessings or statements of faith.[22] We can even look for signals within smaller subcultures, such as the donatives and salutes of soldiers or the recommendations of sophists and students. Patronage networks cannot be delineated like clerical factions—the interactions are too fluid. We can, however, trace the sorts of favors requested by advocates in letters, and the kinds of loyal services promised in return. Together, these cues sketch the *roles* sought by letter-writers within the ever-shifting transactional web.

As in part I, our interest falls on the clerics of fifth-century Syria, and their place in the social fabric. The records for patronage, however, are narrower than those of doctrinal parties. A few historical and hagiographical references come from Syrian clerics of the mid-fifth century, but only Theodoret's personal correspondence furnishes multiple letters of appeal. This situation makes it hard to judge how much Theodoret and his colleagues sought the same roles. Luckily, Theodoret's letters are not *sui generis*. The mid-fourth century provides 1540 letters from Libanius, and 360 from Basil of Caesarea. The early fifth century adds 270 from the exiled John Chrysostom, and 150 from Synesius. Most helpful are the 46 letters of Firmus of Caesarea, one of Theodoret's main doctrinal foes. By comparing words and favors, we can begin to see what distinguished Theodoret's participation in patronage, or perhaps that of Syrian bishops.

Read carefully, Theodoret's letters showcase the openings for patronage relations, as pursued over three decades by one well-connected bishop. Some of these roles do fit ideal types of patronage. Some are familiar from cultural studies of episcopal authority. Many roles, however, are more ambiguous—and more collaborative.

The rest of this chapter will trace Theodoret's relations with various sorts of notable people, arranged to position him within the transactional web.

SYRIAN BISHOPS AND LOCAL NOTABLES

It was probably during the cleanup of a holiday meal that Theodoret reached a peak of annoyance with Maranas, a lawyer and notable of Cyrrhus.[23] "I do not know what I should call you, unfriendly [to me] or hater of our city," he declared, "but your lack of assistance in any of our festivals leads me to think that one of these must be true." Maranas had not only neglected to contribute to the festivities; he had failed to attend, "favoring [his] estates, oxen, and hoes," over "those who contend over possessions ... and require the balance of [his] judgment." Theodoret wrote to demand some civic pride. For it was not right that a wealthy professional should "diminish the city by his absence."[24]

No non-clerics consumed more of a bishop's energy than local notables like Maranas, the scions of privileged families that led Roman cities. For centuries these families had held a substantial portion of the land in nearly every locality. While poorer than senatorial houses, they outnumbered their superiors. And the wealthiest local notables controlled hundreds of scattered estates, or even whole villages. The best estimates of late Roman landholding come from early sixth-century Egyptian tax rolls. In Oxyrhynchus, at that time, the senatorial Apion family owed about 30 percent of the city's land taxes, a trio of local notable families, the next 40 percent. Church lands owed only 10 percent.[25] Local notables were not economic masters. Village sites in Syria suggest a large class of middling peasant proprietors.[26] But multiple estates and paying tenants were enough to confer a measure of political power. In the early empire, thousands of notable men had served on civic councils (Latin: curiae; Greek: boulai; Syriac: bule). Not only did these decurions implement imperial and local law; they wrote appeals for fellow residents and supplied both public and private benefaction.[27] Political shifts of the late empire altered the position of curial families. Councilmen faced financial burdens (e.g., fronting the city's taxes and keeping up its amenities), while the empire impinged on their public funds and stature. At the same time, local notable men tried to escape the burdens of the councils, pleading to imperial administrators for exemptions.[28] But local notables did not lose their wealth or influence. Civic power was concentrated in the hands of a few magnates (Latin: principales; Greek: proteuontes; Syriac: rawrbane). Some cities recovered funds and initiative through new magistracies (such as the pater civitatis, a financial official, and the defensor civitatis, a public tax advocate). Many local notables protected their wealth by achieving exempt status. All they had to do was win an imperial post, buy an "honor," work as a bureaucrat, get recognized as a physician or jurist, serve as a public educator, enlist in the army, or join the upper clergy.[29] Late Roman decurions whined about their poverty, but their protests should not be taken at face value.

Property and civic governance made local notables essential to any bishop's operations. The curial class controlled multiple times his resources and a treasury of old clients and friends. Local notables could use these resources to support the bishop and his projects. Or they could oppose a prelate whom they disliked.[30] Some bishops began as notables within their future sees. Others were recruited from the outside.[31] Theoretically, every bishop held lifetime tenure and a clerical staff (however loyal or disloyal). But if he wanted to leave a mark on his city, he needed a supportive local elite.

Luckily, bishops did have favors to give to curial families in return for their support; the bishops could play a role of coaching and coordination. Of course, bishops provided spiritual guidance. Theodoret sent notables notes of consolation, doctrinal instruction, and moral advice, as did Basil and other bishops.[32] But pastoral care was only the beginning. Local notables faced an array of obstacles and choices. They had to decide whether to seek power on local councils or pursue exemptions. Bishops hired some notables as clerics. They recruited physicians, orators, and lawyers, and helped them to secure tax breaks.[33] Bishops also helped notables to avoid burdens by guiding them through their range of options. Theodoret helped at least three decurions to evade their duties, either by winning honors or by looking poor. Like many colleagues, he recommended people for sophistic education, the path to teaching, law, and oratory.[34] Bishops could link up notables from distant locales. Theodoret not only introduced local lawyers and landowners; he also sought hospitality for curial refugees.[35] Bishops could even help the city councils. Theodoret worked with one *principalis* to defend Cyrrhus from charges of tax fraud. Firmus asked a governor to aggrandize his city (and council) by rearranging civic boundaries.[36] Local notables might outweigh the bishop in wealth and social roots, but they could benefit from his connections and advice.

Bishops could claim a special role of coaching for notable women. In much of the ancient Mediterranean, women faced constraints in their family lives. Greek and Syrian legal traditions limited women's control of family wealth (with the important exception of widows). Entrenched ideologies discouraged female participation in political and economic affairs.[37] Yet some notable women found ways to corral wealth or exercise public influence. Some assumed quasi-clerical positions. Others sponsored civic amenities or ascetic foundations.[38] Bishops provided notable women an important extrafamilial contact. Granted unusual intimacy, they could offer both moral and financial advice.[39] Theodoret sent most of his extant condolence letters to notable women, especially on the death of a husband. He asked at least two to become doctrinal allies and host a clerical delegation. Other bishops played similar roles in relation to wealthy women, most famously Chrysostom.[40] Widows and ascetics among these women may have been unusually independent, but it is unlikely that bishops would neglect the rest. By coaching wives and mothers, bishops could peek into notable family life.

The role of spiritual and worldly coach enabled bishops to ally with their cities' local notables, but some bishops had broader plans. Theodoret spent his own inheritance to build bridges, baths, stoas, and an aqueduct, as well as several shrines honoring "prophets and apostles."[41] He expected notables to contribute as well. Hiba of Edessa led a similar effort, erecting a new "Great" church of the Apostles and a *martyrium*, and coordinating donations across the elite.[42] Many bishops, of course, sponsored building projects, including Basil of Caesarea.[43] But Theodoret and his associates seem unusual for the scope of their projects and their stern expectations of notables' help.

In fact, Theodoret's projects were part of a larger cultural program to highlight Christian community. Part of this program involved new public festivals. Theodoret called a feast in Cyrrhus in honor of the prophets and apostles. This event probably featured multiple days of processions, fairs, and meals.[44] Adding festivities to the Christian calendar was scarcely a new practice. Meletius and Flavian of Antioch had elaborately honored the martyr Babylas. Firmus of Caesarea called his own saint's day festivities.[45] The mid-fifth century, however, marked a proliferation of local Syrian celebrations. Once Syrian towns had hosted pagan processions and feasts, which drew crowds and exhibited community.[46] Theodoret and his colleagues worked to replace these affairs with a Christian display. Again, they needed participation from the local elite.

Another part of the bishops' program involved private pastoral care. Theodoret wrote local notables words of consolation that stressed the basic Christian hopes for the afterlife. He also sent nearby notables moral rebukes, criticizing their support of un-Christian family practices. Theodoret solicited donations with similar Christian emphasis. Thus he urged notables to "hire the poor as advocates" before the "frightening tribunal" of heaven.[47] All the while he goaded figures like Maranas to attend church festivities. Theodoret was hardly unique in referring to Christian doctrines. His comments are often similar to Basil's.[48] But not every bishop was so insistently Christian in his writing. Firmus said more about the "white carriages and brass bedecked chariots [of the gods]" than Christ, even to clerical allies.[49] It seems, at least, that Theodoret pushed harder to raise civic notables' Christian commitment.

The efforts of Theodoret and local notables combined to form an intriguing dynamic, a dance of favor-exchange, resistance, and persuasion. Theodoret had plans to Christianize society but lacked the means to impose his will. So he offered local notables lessons and benefits to persuade them to help. Sometimes the process had an effect. Maranas may or may not have heeded Theodoret and attended the feast. But he did contribute a church structure, "built from [his] zeal-ous desire." Theodoret engaged in a similar dance with Aerius, a local sophist. This notable, having offended the bishop, restored good relations by reroofing a shrine.[50] Theodoret's give and take with notables has parallels, but his activities are distinguished by his programmatic persistence.

SYRIAN BISHOPS AND EDUCATIONAL NETWORKS

It must have been little surprise to the sophist Isocasius when a group of boys arrived holding another letter from Theodoret. "Again our bees run to your Attic meadows," the note said pithily. "By experience, they learn the useful part of the flowers. So let Your Education pour honey into them and teach them to weave honeycombs with skill." Theodoret had sent a batch of Cyrrhus's young elite to Antioch for a reputable education. Though Cyrrhus had its own sophists, the connections and skills of Isocasius outstripped what a small town could provide. Luckily the famous teacher had a long friendship with the bishop, despite their religious differences. Theodoret was upfront about his purposes; "I beg [Cyrrhus's students] to partake more of your solicitude; for I want our city to shine by your fruits."[51] He was less specific about the way his city might benefit. Perhaps some of these pupils would lend their oratory to the Nicene church.

Sophists like Isocasius were leading figures in late Roman academia, a profes-sional community with key similarities to the clergy. Like clerics, Roman edu-cators claimed a special status, marked by the title "Your Education" (Greek: *paideusis*). Like clerics they were arranged into ranks, from tutors to grammarians to rhetors/sophists and philosophers.[52] Once teachers had lived on tuition. By the fourth century they drew some funds from civic and imperial government. Mean-while, educators formed expansive patronage networks among students, alumni, and (sometimes) colleagues.[53] Philosophers, such as Hypatia and Themistius, bro-kered many bonds within the high elite. Sophists, such as Libanius, counted con-tacts throughout the administration and the curial class.[54] Educators lacked the institutional financing of clerics (though their own fortunes might compensate). But like clerics, teachers could use their position to rally funds from local notables or favors from those in power. The most successful led networks beyond the reach of all but a few bishops.[55]

What gave educators real influence, however, was their shared cultural pro-gram: protection of classical civilization. Philosophers, grammarians, and soph-ists might differ in their pedagogical tasks, but most late Roman educators valued both rhetoric and wisdom. Most saw themselves as tamers of the mind and body who preserved language and morality. Their *paideia* was presented as a gateway to the Roman elite.[56] There were doctrinal divisions among academics. Some treated Greek *paideia* as a matter of knowledge and decorum. Others viewed "Hellenism" as a cultic calling. Educators disagreed over preferred authors and traced different academic lineages.[57] And sophists contended bitterly for students and standing. But even Libanius's rivalries seem less factional than clerical relations—usually less was at stake. Non-rivals could cooperate effectively across the empire.[58] With robust internal networks and "non-Christian" cultural goals, classical educators could have become the bishops' antagonists.

Antagonism, however, was not the bishops' most evident response to purveyors of *paideia*. Position and cultural commitment made educators valuable allies in clerical patronage. Bishops relied on the fancy words of sophists to persuade officials. When one notable of Cyrrhus fell into tax arrears, Theodoret asked Isocasius to "sophistically write a tragedy of his poverty." Basil may also have asked a rhetor to help with advocacy.[59] Bishops also asked for the elegant words of sophists to win a wider public's generosity. Theodoret asked his sophist-friend Aerius to convince other well-off locals to host refugees.[60] Sophists could even prove useful in episcopal elections. The notion was at least plausible to Theodoret's foes, who accused him of hiring Isocasius to ensure that Domnus became bishop of Antioch.[61] Most crucially, bishops depended on sophists and grammarians for elite Greek education. Fifth-century clerics offered almost no general Greek schooling. Theodoret hired Greek orators to coach his clerics. And, of course, he sent young notables to absorb lessons from Isocasius. Again, this was not unusual. Basil probably sent pupils to Libanius. Firmus hired a sophist to coach his colleagues. In fact, Firmus presented "the perfume of Attic education" as a requisite for good bishops.[62] Antiochenes, however, seem especially dependent on classical educators. Diodore and Theodore had relied on sophistic training to interpret Scripture. Later clerics did the same—many favored terms (such as *akribeia*) come from the rhetorical classroom.[63]

At the same time, educators found allies in the clergy to protect themselves and their schools. Bishops could offer educators a means of recruitment. "If I had more sons, I would have sent you more disciples," Theodoret once told Isocasius, "So those I do have I send and deem worthy to share in Your Education."[64] Bishops could also help teachers deal with the Christian high elite. Educators were not alien at Theodosius's court. After all, Empress Eudocia was the daughter of a (pagan) sophist. But fifth-century sophists faced a more pious court culture; it was hagiography and biblical paraphrase to which Eudocia lent support.[65] Increasingly sophists had to prove their value to Christian society. By the 460s Isocasius could not frequent court circles without accepting baptism.[66] But bishops could offer sophists the cover of their company. Such protection probably helped Isocasius to stay pagan as long as he did.

Thus bishops and sophists could offer mutual help. In fact, they often built deeper relations. Like educators, most bishops came from the local notable class, with its accoutrements of culture. Theodoret lived as an ascetic, but he could still appreciate fine woodcarvings and Lesbos's famous wine.[67] Many other bishops had also had a sophistic education. Firmus paraded his *paideia*, with references to the "Sirens" and the "son of Sophroniscus" (i.e. Socrates). Theodoret was more reticent in his letters, but he could cite more obscure philosophers than almost anyone.[68] Both Theodoret and Firmus counted educators as companions, in a rather classical sense. As they traded benefits they relished the chance to "fulfill the laws of friendship by weaving praises of friends."[69]

The cordiality of these bishops toward educators is striking given the potential pitfalls. One such pitfall was latent cultural tension. The clergy and monasteries hosted exclusionists, who saw no need to look beyond the Bible.[70] Academia had its own exclusionists, who linked philosophy to pagan "theurgy."[71] Most of the time these culture warriors were probably a minor nuisance, but some tensions intruded. "If you say that the *Laws* [of Plato] do not hold sway in the present situation," Theodoret once declaimed to Aerius, "then go hear the Master of the universe legislating them!"[72]

Another source of trouble was educational alternatives. In the early empire sophists held a monopoly on elite learning. But by the fifth century there were alternative forms of pedagogy. One was secretarial instruction. Basic Greek and Latin education could segue into technical training in shorthand. Libanius complained about this shortcut. But the government hired notaries with respectable salaries, and in the 430s the emperor's notaries still held much influence.[73] Another alternative was legal education. The city of Berytus hosted aspirant jurists (Greek: *scholastikoi*), who after a short course in rhetoric turned to legal study (partly in Latin). Libanius also complained about the legal track, but he noted its worldly value. In the 430s the profession was booming, thanks to the compilation of the *Theodosian Code*.[74] A third choice, in Syria, was education in Syriac. Less information survives about such schooling—it is unclear if any towns had paid Syriac instructors. But Syriac written culture was flourishing. And in Edessa, at least, it was clerics who sponsored Syriac learning based on scriptural traditions.[75] Theodoret's writings show no interest in any form of learning besides rhetorical, philosophical *paideia*. But he knew notaries, *scholastikoi*, and clerics who wrote in Syriac.[76] He must have known the utility of the educational alternatives.

Despite old tensions and new options, Theodoret clung to the classical educators of his time. He engaged his favorite teachers in another dance of mutual benefit. In some sense, their difference in cultural missions aided friendship; for it enabled men of near social parity to share favors without rivalry. Some clerics kept their distance from Hellenism or supported the alternatives. Others stood with sophists arm-in-arm.

SYRIAN BISHOPS, IMPERIAL ADMINISTRATORS,
AND THE POLITICAL ELITE

At some point in the 430s or 440s, Theodoret received an inquiry from Florentius, six times prefect of the East. Florentius wanted to know about a certain priest, for some post. Theodoret responded with care. "In other situations I would not have the courage to address Your Greatness by letter, " he noted, "knowing, as I do, to measure my own humility and having seen the obvious extent of your power." But because the prefect, "adorned in faith and educated in divine matters," had already written to this "undistinguished man, nowhere of repute," Theodoret could bring himself forward, "as the prophet says, 'like a lamb dwelling together with the lion' (Isaiah 11:6)." Theodoret thanked Christ for this turn of fortune. As leader of "another [sort of] prefecture," he was ready to give advice. By the time he recommended the priest, he had spent fifteen lines excusing himself.[77] In the fifth century most Romans addressed the imperial government via communal shouting. Theodoret followed a different protocol. As a spiritual adviser, he offered useful information, while trying to limit his vulnerability.

However much local notables or sophists concerned Syrian bishops, they receded in importance beside the imperial power-elite. Traditionally the highest Roman rank had been the senatorial order. The early fifth-century senates (East and West) included more than 3000 officials, ex-officials, sons of existing senators, and other imperially favored wealthy men. Many Eastern senators looked like poor upstarts compared to their Western counterparts. But even middling ones surpassed most bishoprics in terms of their holdings. Senators had valuable privileges, from tax exemptions to judicial immunity.[78] Senatorial women faced social restrictions, but some commanded extraordinary resources, particularly when channeled into education or asceticism.[79]

Senatorial status, however, did not guarantee political influence; most senators were lucky to get two posts in a lifetime.[80] The primary center of power was the imperial court. Two dozen individuals repeatedly served as high officers (i.e., as prefect, consul, chamberlain, master of offices, count of the Sacred Largesses, or count of the Res privata). These officials were joined by relatives of the emperor, trusted secretaries, and top honorati (e.g., patricians) in the orbit of imperial power. Maintaining the highest rank, of course, depended on the emperor's favor. But such rank conferred sway over administrative networks beyond any official portfolio.[81] To all but a few bishops, senators were men of superior stature. True courtiers reminded any bishop of lions and lambs.

Bishops frequently needed help from the power-elite and made every effort to cultivate connections. Theodoret wrote thirty-six of his extant letters to the tiny group of regular courtiers (about 15 percent of the total). Firmus's letters show similar interest (17 percent), (though oddly not Basil's, 8 percent).[82] Bishops wrote to ask for friendship, or to verify their level of repute. But mostly they sent appeals. Theodoret pleaded for lower taxes, fair judgments, tax exemptions, and jobs for his clients and friends.[83] Basil and Firmus asked for everything from intervention in an inheritance dispute, to lower taxes, to redrawn provincial boundaries. Libanius requested even more benefits, especially for former students.[84] All of these patrons appealed to the same ranks of officials, regardless of any chain of command. But rarely did they address the emperor. For they appreciated the courtiers as mediators for less risky appeals.[85]

Luckily for bishops the court was not the only sphere of political authority. Beneath the top posts lay hundreds of lower officials and about 30,000 non-military employees.[86] First there were provincial governors (Latin: *praesides* or *consulares;* Greek: *archontes*),[87] the face of imperial authority. Governors ran lawcourts, organized taxation, distributed imperial edicts, and promised to keep order. But governors faced serious limits to their power. Some governorships went to senatorial scions, seeking a superior senatorial rank. Most passed to decurions, who thus became burden-exempt *honorati*. In either case, governors were usually assigned unfamiliar provinces. While empowered to torture malefactors, they needed local cooperation to accomplish basic tasks.[88] Then there were the agents and bureaucrats. Every governor and vicar employed secretaries and strongmen. The prefects and the master of offices had the largest staffs, including notaries, postmasters, imperial property managers, coin-minters, tax assessors, judicial clerks, palace-keepers, and special agents.[89] A few functionaries claimed direct imperial contact. Most were distant from imperial decisions. Still, even the lowest bureaucrat had access to key people and records, as well as job security beyond the governors' reach. Many maintained estates and connections in their hometowns. And Romans understood that virtually any level of functionary could "redirect" the implementation of policies.[90]

Episcopal dealings with lower officials and bureaucrats reflected their relative standing. With governors, the bishops gave the appearance of deference. They tried not to make lasting enemies but openly manipulated the temporary holders of the post. Theodoret urged governors to make no waves. "Those who limitlessly concern themselves with [the care of the rulers or the care of the ruled] do harm to each of them," he once told a *praeses*. "But those who mix activity with gentleness and blunt the force of action with generosity (*philanthrōpiai*) ... benefit [all concerned]."[91] Basil and Firmus praised governors more directly. Like Theodoret, however, they tended to presume cooperation, as did Libanius and Synesius.[92] Some bureaucrats actually garnered higher respect. Theodoret invited tax assessors to feasts and sent recommendations to quaestors and curators.[93] Basil, Libanius, and Synesius worked back channels with bureaucrats as readily as links to the office-holders themselves.[94]

These appeals to officials, of course, scarcely amounted to special influence. So bishops sought a firmer footing by serving as outside advisors. Bishops eagerly offered spiritual guidance. Theodoret consoled officials and bureaucrats, as he did local notables. He answered doctrinal questions, and he advised generosity in the sight of God.[95] Bishops were also eager to aid administrators in dealings with other administrators. High officials needed some way of evaluating subordinates. Governors and bureaucrats needed support to advance their careers.[96] Bishops strove to be helpful on both counts by making recommendations. Theodoret gave favorable reports to a quaestor about one governor, who "during the whole time of his rule, navigated wisely and caused the ship [of state] to be carried by favorable winds." He begged a former prefect to "send [this governor] again to us," for a second term.[97] Basil and Libanius offered similar reviews; Synesius did the reverse for a *praeses* with denunciations.[98] Not every bishop or sophist took so bold a stance, but they could always drop subtler cues.

Thus bishops furnished civil administrators with advice and intercession, both spiritual and mundane. Still, what distinguishes Theodoret (and perhaps his associates) was again the Christian program. By the 430s most high officials and governors were Christian, but many midlevel officials remained unaffiliated with a church. So Theodoret tried to bring them to baptism. He asked nearby governors to embrace the true faith so that he could praise them. He sent similar messages to bureaucrats, and even to a consul. The bishop was willing to deal with catechumens and non-Christians. A baptism, however, might lead to unique access, a chance to guide the powerful in their beliefs and benefactions.[99] Theodoret was hardly unique in offering basic Christian instruction. Chrysostom coordinated a mission to Phoenicia from exile. But Basil, Firmus and Synesius seem less interested.[100] Again, Theodoret seems quicker to link mundane social brokering with spiritual connections.

Theodoret's best hope for winning favors from the political system was to serve as both spiritual father and outside collaborator. To win influence a bishop had to convince officials that he could facilitate imperial business. At the same time he had to stand apart as a guide to divine authority. Results of imperial cooperation could be spotty. Syrian bishops were hardly the only political facilitators or the only spiritual fathers. But Theodoret still tried to dance with the officials and bureaucrats by offering his counsel.

SYRIAN BISHOPS AND THE ROMAN MILITARY

In 446 Theodoret approached the patrician Anatolius with yet another request. Philip, a *principalis* of Cyrrhus, had gone to Constantinople, seeking to lower the tax assessment of his city. Through him the bishop had appealed to a former consul, the prefect, and even an empress, with uncertain results. Anatolius, however, was very familiar; for more than a decade he had led the Eastern army (as *magister utriusque militiae*). "All the Easterners hold the same affection for you as sons do a father," Theodoret declared, "so why have you shown hate toward those who love you?" He was joking; Anatolius had been a strong doctrinal ally and a generous donor.[101] He just needed a playful reminder to come to Syria's aid. Yet he might have made all the difference; for generals like him held authority commensurate with the forces under their command.

No organization occupied as large a place in Roman society as the army. Military staff outnumbered the clergy; their resources dwarfed those of the church. Between in-kind taxation, coin payments, land grants, and supply contracts, the Roman army represented a redistributive force unparalleled in the premodern world.[102] Military power supported the imperial court, with an ideology of eternal victory and the threat of violence. It had deep effects in frontier regions such as Syria. From Armenia to Arabia were stationed frontier troops (*limitanei* and auxiliaries). Augmented by the mobile armies, they marked the densest concentration of soldiers in the empire.[103] The soldiers' presence in Syria knew no clear bounds. After Julian's disastrous invasion of Persia in 363, the frontier had been fixed near a tributary of the Khabur River, arbitrarily dividing the east-west axis of settlement. Cities of Mesopotamia and Osrhoene (such as Amida, Edessa, Constantina, and Carrhae) became military focal points. But soldiers billeted all along routes of supply and communication, by the Euphrates and Tigris rivers, and westward to Antioch.[104] Officially the soldiers stood ready to battle Persian forces, which they did during two short wars (421–422 and 440–441).[105] At other times, they were called to attack bandits, quell urban riots, or enforce doctrinal compromise. In more mundane fashion, the soldiers recruited, traveled, and traded. They contracted to protect people and served as lenders of last resort.[106] Nor were regular soldiers the only armed presence. We also hear of private mercenaries and "Arab" tribal allies, not to mention Persian soldiers and federates.[107] And yet, despite its ubiquity, the military remained a distinct subculture, a "total institution" with its own (religious) customs and laws.[108] Most important, it had its own leadership. Frontier commanders (*duces* and *phylarchae*) held job security beyond the reach of governors. So did mobile unit commanders (*comites rei militaris*).[109] And then there were the top brass, the masters of soldiers and counts of the Domestici. Anatolius commanded Syria's armies for sixteen years; he and four others (Titus, Fl. Dionysius, Areobindus, and Zeno) nearly monopolized the Eastern generalships. Not only did the generals claim institutional wealth and loyalties; they became true power brokers, from the frontier to the emperorship itself.[110]

It is thus no surprise that bishops sought military contacts, especially among the generals. Masters of soldiers received the same sorts of requests as civilian courtiers. Areobindus, who owned land near Cyrrhus, found Theodoret pleading for the lenient treatment of tenants. Anatolius was asked to finance church building programs across the region.[111] Bishops' appeals to generals resembled their letters to civil administrators. Again, they could offer spiritual guidance or facilitate government business. But the institutional power of the military raised the stakes. As Theodoret learned in the 430s, bishops had to befriend generals or face ongoing hostility.[112]

With ordinary soldiers, bishops faced a more complicated situation—unfamiliar concerns. A few bishops had the background to do military strategy. Synesius advised officers in Cyrenaica on tactics and organization.[113] A few more were drafted as ambassadors. Many fulfilled the Christian command to ransom war captives. One reportedly took his charge so seriously that he ransomed Persians as well as Romans.[114] Others crafted cultural links to the soldiery. Alexander of Hierapolis built his shrine at Rasapha to honor Sergius, a soldier-martyr. By the 430s his complex was receiving pilgrims, including Roman, Arab, and Persian soldiers.[115] In each case, bishops forged direct links with soldiers though favors and symbolic gestures.

Not every bishop, however, could readily connect with the army. Theodoret's letters reveal tenuous links to the common soldiery. Theodoret dealt with soldiers who served as loan sharks. He interceded for a troubled soldier, accused of abandoning his duties. He sought indirect links through ascetics and chaplains.[116] Theodoret valued troop support. One of his longest "doctrinal" letters was sent to the soldiers at a critical moment of controversy.[117] Still Theodoret seems removed from the army scene. So do Basil and Firmus (and Libanius, to a lesser extent).[118] The cultural gap between soldiers and urban clerics could hinder social connections.

Syrian bishops' dealings with the military were both essential and frustrating. Frequently the bishops needed the influence of generals. They needed promises of security up and down the chain of command. Theodoret's relations with Anatolius were essential to the survival of the Antiochene network in the 430s. Later these links may have sprung Theodoret from exile.[119] But trading patronage with the self-reliant soldiers was harder than it was with civil administrators. Some bishops had more success than others at building military connections.

SYRIAN BISHOPS AND THE RELIGIOUS ALTERNATIVES

In his *Historia religiosa*, Theodoret described a campaign of his to defend orthodoxy, aided by Jacob, the famous local ascetic. Once Cyrrhus's territory had reportedly been a den of Marcionites, heretics who "tried to make war invisibly by using magic spells and cooperating with evil demons." Theodoret had tried to preach against the Marcionites, with little success. Then Jacob lent a hand. Before Theodoret approached the main Marcionite village, he asked the ascetic if God would support him. Jacob responded by relating a vision: "As I began my [usual] course of hymns in the part [of the countryside] where those villages (*choria*) lie, I saw a fiery serpent creeping from west to east, bearing itself through the middle of the air. I dispatched three prayers, and I saw it again, bent into a circle, its tail conjoined to its head. I again made prayers, eight of them, and watched it be sliced in two and vanish into smoke." The next morning Theodoret traveled to the village, where a "Marcionite company" stood against his "apostolic phalanx. ... By the third hour [the Marcionites] had circled up and thought only of guarding their own ... By the eighth hour they had dispersed, allowing us into the village." Theodoret examined the deserted dwellings and found a cult object, the bronze head of a serpent.[120] And he understood what had happened. Theodoret "won" the visible contest, but only because Jacob had defeated the Marcionites in spiritual combat.

Theodoret's story highlights another set of patronage options beyond the clergy: alternative religious networks. Despite six decades of imperial support for the Nicenes, the Roman world retained a variety of religious leaders credited with otherworldly powers. Generally scholarship has portrayed the early fifth century as the last critical stage in "Nicenization" and "Christianization." Egyptian papyri and Anatolian funerary markers suggest an outwardly Christian majority. Inscriptions on the Syrian Limestone Massif declare that "One God has conquered."[121] Church histories of the era describe violent acts against pagans, Jews, and heretics, in Syria and elsewhere. Clerical writings are filled with hostile rhetoric, marking the heterodox as deluded and damned.[122] And yet, changes in Syria were less straightforward than the stories or rhetoric suggest. Alternative religion continued outside of episcopal oversight. Alternative religious experts maintained translocal connections, hosting visitors, trading texts, distributing favors, and making appeals. It is not always clear what content passed along these networks; Theodoret's labels must be greeted with caution. But when it came to spiritual patronage, the bishops faced some competition.

The largest collection of alternative religious figures went under the label of "pagan" (Latin: *paganus;* Greek: *Hellenes;* Syriac: *hanpa*). In fact, none of these appellations adequately describes non-biblical religion. Before the fourth century Syria had hosted a heterogeneous mix of cults. Greek language served as a medium for combining diverse practices. Traditional religion was usually organized locally by priestly families. Certain towns had achieved fame for their pagan devotion, notably Heliopolis and Carrhae.[123] Yet centuries of imperial rule had also fostered broader religious organizations. Syria hosted some "Magi." These Mazdaeans (perhaps already Zoroastrians) maintained priestly lineages, protected by Roman-Persian treaties.[124] By the fourth century Syria also hosted theurgists, the philosophic group associated with Iamblichus and Emperor Julian. These "Hellenes" fused Neoplatonic doctrines with polytheistic ritual. They treated literary oracles as Holy Scripture and traced a "golden chain" of philosophers from

Pythagoras and Plato to themselves.[125] Not all "pagans" followed the theurgists. Not all Mazdaeans followed an Iranian hierarchy. But bishops worried about these organizations. Both had important backers (sophists or Persian courtiers). Both offered universalizing theologies.[126] Both had the potential to link cults in numerous towns and villages, keeping clerics on the margins.

Another set of alternative religious experts fell under the label of Jews, although here, too, the terminology proves inadequate. For centuries, self-described Jews had spanned the Greek- and Aramaic-speaking world. Imperial law defined a semi-autonomous community, led by a patriarch in Palestine and (eventually) an exilarch in Babylonia. But these two patrons oversaw contested religious terrain.[127] Judges, synagogue-heads, teachers, healers, and philosophers competed for influence, offering different visions of Jewish community. In the fifth century most Jewish leaders were localized; Antioch's Jews looked primarily to a council of *archisynagogoi*. Some children of Israel were isolated from the rest—such as the Samaritans of Central Palestine.[128] Others were building translocal connections. Amoraic sages led the conversations of Talmud and Midrash. They crafted traditions of moral formation and traced a lineage of "true teachers of Torah." Initially, rabbinic influence went no further than Southern Syria and Palestine; its extent in the fifth century is unclear. But the *amoraim* were expanding their reach among Jews and their resistance to Christian discourse.[129] Bishops worried about Jewish leaders' influence and social proximity. Traditional polemics contrasted the "new chosen people" with the "crucifying Jews." But with similar holidays, shared texts, and common languages, the groups were hard to pull apart.[130]

Both pagans and Jews worried bishops; larger concerns surrounded heterodox Christians. Syria abounded in doctrinal variation. According to Nicene sources, the region hosted Arians, Eunomians, Apollinarians, Messalians, Tatianites, Bardaisanians, Marcionites, and Manichees, even in the fifth century. These labels were, of course, polemically constructed. It is unclear whether they reflected active doctrinal parties.[131] But sources do reveal opponents of the Nicene order. Some clung to condemned teachers. Others merely behaved in a way that roused clerical suspicion. Heterodox traditions persisted on private land, protected by sympathetic owners and easygoing officials. They thrived in villages large enough to set their own orthodoxy.[132] In fact, the cultural landscape of Syria encouraged doctrinal diversity. The patchwork of climate and language partly isolated some communities. Traveling preachers supported parallel religious networks, and would for centuries to come.[133]

By the fifth century Nicenes had found standard ways to deal with alternative religious networks. One approach was direct persecution. Since the mid-fourth century bishops had urged the government to legally disfavor their competitors. They pushed for edicts against temple construction and pagan sacrifice (in the 380s and 390s and beyond). They won rulings that limited Jewish building and dissolved the Jewish patriarchate (circa 429). And they lobbied for anti-heresy laws, which denied certain labeled groups the right to control imperial property or inherit private property (in the 380s and 390s and again in the 420s).[134] Some bishops backed violence against their religious foes. They organized the destruction of temples, such as in Apamea (circa 388) and Edessa (in the 410s). Some supported confrontational monks, who occupied old cult sites or "sought martyrdom" at active pagan shrines. A number of bishops backed attacks on synagogues, such as in Callinicum (circa 390) and Edessa (again in the 410s). Many worked to force heretics from their churches, by law and by popular rioting.[135] Scholars have noted the rarity of serious violence and the limits of legal enforcement. All the same, they have recognized the symbolic power of persecution. Both laws and violence visibly degraded the social status of religious outsiders, marking them as societal impurities.[136]

Another approach to religious competition was polemical rhetoric. For centuries bishops had penned arguments against pagans and Magi. Clerics, such as Chrysostom, used a traditional polemic against the Jews, which portrayed them as God-killers and hypocrites, all while countering Jewish readings of Scripture. And countless churchmen argued against heretics with stereotyping and scriptural quotation. Scholars have doubted if stock images and quotations converted many people. They have not dismissed the importance of polemic. Traditional arguments helped clerics to construct their own notions of orthodoxy, and build (semi-stable) identities.[137]

Fifth-century bishops thus inherited methods for confronting "erroneous" religion. But social competition demanded finesse. Theodoret apparently avoided violent confrontations with Jews and pagans. He did attack heretics, mainly to seize cult objects and books. When other clerics did violence, Theodoret made cautious judgments. He criticized a bishop who destroyed a Magian fire-temple, then lauded the same bishop for refusing to rebuild it. He praised a Roman bishop who dismantled pagan temples, but only with imperial permission and the troops to keep public peace.[138] Theodoret fully joined in polemical rhetoric. He reproduced some standard arguments against "Hellenes," Magians, Jews, and a catalog full of heretics. But his arguments went beyond stock images to resemble classroom instruction. Theodoret's *Treatment of Hellenic Maladies* presented classical culture as one route to Christianity. It obliquely attacked theurgic doctrine by arguing that Chrstianity made for better philosophy. Theodoret's preaching also challenged alternative worship by pointing out signs of the providence of (one) God.[139] Theodoret's anti-Jewish work treated the Torah as a temporary stop on the way to Christianity. It contrasted Jewish readings of prophecy with "proper" Christian interpretation. Theodoret's attacks on heresy were more pointed. But his catalog spent less time demonizing the heterodox than it did categorizing their errors and suggesting replies.[140] While Theodoret borrowed tropes from predecessors, his caution and didacticism marked a shift away from traditional religious polemic.[141]

Theodoret's didactic works formed part of his drive to oppose the religious alternatives. But even as he wrote polemics he sought to curtail the social networks of his rivals. Theodoret's letters reveal no direct contacts with non-Nicene religious experts. He once mentioned a "Marcionite priest," but the label seems dubious. Theodoret tried to convert pagan notables, but only those whom he already knew.[142] Theodoret's letters show efforts to ostracize rivals. He asked one notable not to mention "Hermes, the Muses, and the heretical Eunomius." He told two others to avoid a religious suspect.[143] Theodoret may have avoided non-Christian leaders and "heresiarchs." More likely, he knew local leaders by face and name. Conspicuous silence had been a prime rabbinic method of sidelining Christians.[144] Theodoret applied the same tactic against his rivals.

Actually, it was not heterodox leaders that most concerned bishops, but the wavering. It is difficult to scrutinize the tenets of suspected heretics or the practices of Jews. It is hard to judge what portion of Syrians owed allegiance to traditional gods. Our labels do not account for the compromises and dissonances to which all belief is subject. Private churches abounded on rural estates. Remote villages might go months without clerical contact. Monks kept their own networks of discipleship and doctrine.[145] Bishops worked to expand their clerical networks. But they faced physical and cultural obstacles, not to mention foes *within* the Nicene community.

Theodoret's arguments against pagans, Jews, and heretics were important because they helped to attract the uncommitted. His polemics were unlikely to win over a theurgist, a rabbi, or a heresiarch. But they could appeal to someone already willing to convert. Not only did the texts distinguish error from orthodoxy. They also presented narrative scripts, by which converts could enact their conversion and explain it after the fact. Heresiology was particularly important in local villages, where Theodoret found worrisome rigorist practices. By labeling such behaviors "Manichean" or "Marcionite," he could make episcopal oversight appear necessary.

Theodoret's polemics were also significant because they created a framework for cooperating with potential rivals within the Nicene fold. Theodoret faced hostility from episcopal foes, such as Cyril. But the two men could agree on how to oppose Jews and polytheists. Hence the mutual respect that Theodoret claimed that they achieved by comparing their anti-pagan writings.[146] Theodoret was unsure of the doctrinal loyalty of some leading monastics, including Jacob. But both he and Jacob were opposed to Marcionites. Not only could the bishop benefit from ascetics' prayers; he could also better oversee the countryside with the new set of eyes and ears.

Theodoret's approach to religious competitors fits within the spectrum of approaches taken by his peers. On one end were social accommodationists. Synesius conversed with leading non-Christians, even on doctrinal matters. He also courted the goodwill of local monks.[147] On the other end were enforcers. Cyril and Rabbula attacked pagans and Jews, as well as perceived heretics, to display Christian superiority. They sponsored confrontational monks (like Barsauma) and proclaimed their own authority.[148] Theodoret followed a middle course. He endorsed only limited violence. "Not even the divine apostle [Paul] destroyed altars," he wrote, "but convicted [pagans] by his arguments." But he did censor and ostracize, to clip opposing social webs. He spoke of spiritual "combat," shared with other Nicene figures of authority.[149] In general, he reinforced social boundaries, which rhetoric and violence had already created.

CLERICAL NETWORKS AND MEDIATING BISHOPS

By this point it should be clear what a complicated situation bishops confronted outside of the clergy. Late Roman society hosted many sorts of would-be patrons: local families with more wealth and deeper roots, sophists with powerful pupils, officials with legal and fiscal powers, army men with coercive capabilities, and religious experts with durable followings. Bishops lacked the resources to overpower these rivals. But through letters and other rhetorical performances, they could make themselves hard to ignore. The bishops could seek openings with other notables for cooperation and mutual benefit. Or they could work to marginalize their rivals and redefine the social bounds. When it came to building patronage networks, bishops held key assets. Institutional supports gave them the standing to offer favors and write appeals. Existing dependents lent credibility to their gestures and words. Theodoret and his associates had some added advantages. Doctrinal alliance could facilitate cooperation of even the most mundane forms. But assets and openings were merely an entry pass to a competitive elite social world.

The letter collections of Theodoret and his counterparts reveal the bishops' social possibilities. They showcase the roles that bishops could assume within the favor-trading elite. With local notables, Theodoret played a moral and financial advisor. Other bishops tried their own forms of coaching. With academics Theodoret acted as recruiter and sponsor. Others might support different avenues of learning or follow this lead. To high officials, Theodoret offered spiritual and practical help. Other bishops *hoped* for such contacts. To military leaders Theodoret offered support. Some bishops gave the army a more direct helping hand. Most Roman elites were willing to work with bishops. Only non-Nicene religious experts were excluded *prima facie*. Theodoret avoided the violence of some clerics toward pagans and Jews; heretics he attacked in limited fashion. Either way, he tried to isolate religious rivals, partly to connect with the wavering. None of these roles gave bishops a position of dominance. But it might confer more social influence to have something to offer as part of the favor-exchange.

When bishops sought roles of patronage, they held some institutional advantages. Bishops controlled enough financing to initiate projects. They led a clerical labor force that could convey distributions and appeals. Bishops had special legal protections—they could not be taken to criminal court without the concurrence of their colleagues.[150] Bishops held a rhetorical platform as public as any sophist—and only bishops could back their words with sacramental symbols of their authority.[151] Symbols and assets did not prevent all displays of resistance by clerics or lay congregants. Nevertheless, even the title of bishop made for an advantage, for a bishop could always offer spiritual benefits—when pleading with potentates he never went empty-handed.

Bishops also claimed an advantage from their reliable clientele. Bishops had "responsibility," according to the *Apostolic Constitutions,* for widows and orphans (including children with living mothers). They were expected to give financial support, instruction, judicial protection, and other services.[152] Bishops were also supposed to sponsor ascetics: from *kanonikai* and "covenanters" to hermits and whole monasteries.[153] Bishops are known for links to "the poor." Sermons and saints' lives called up images of beggars, but this category might include marginal renters, landowners, clerics, and even ascetics.[154] All of these groups received material aid. Theodoret offered refugee women his protection, poor laborers his advocacy, and orphan girls his marital advice.[155] Such dependents might seem powerless, but they allowed a bishop to play his protective role. Thus they created the socio-cultural context for wider patronage operations.[156]

Institutional assets and reliable clients supported nearly every bishop in patronage operations. Further advantages accrued to members of clerical parties. Theodoret's Antiochene links were doctrinal friendships, but they readily deepened to support other cooperative ventures. Correspondence within Theodoret's network enabled bishops to coordinate patronage activities. Regular communication extended the distribution of favors across the region. Priests, deacons, and monks were available to help to the bishop with his patronage transactions. So were other bishops.[157]Thus Theodoret reached for a wider audience, and thus he surrounded people of influence with choruses of appeal. Of course, many bishops used their doctrinal connections for mundane business. Synesius relied on the bishop of Alexandria for a variety of services. Firmus shared with his doctrinal allies non-doctrinal appeals.[158] But Theodoret's letters reveal a particularly tight circle of patronage collaboration. His main helpers—Domnus, Andreas, Hiba, Irenaeus, and Anatolius—all belonged to the core Antiochene network.

There are, in fact, many aspects of Theodoret's patronage activity that could be linked to his doctrinal network. Theodoret's building projects required resources from across the region. His new festivals needed agents to spread the word. Antio-chene associates could assist by preaching generosity—the closer the coordina-tion, the more effective the message. Theodoret's broad relations complimented his partisan network. His work with hermits and monasteries solidified the "holy association" begun by his predecessors. His connections to generals, governors, and sophists robed doctrinal relations in a coat of cordiality. Theodoret, as we have seen, took a programmatic approach to benefaction, to encourage Chris-tian community. This program, however, would have been difficult without the Antiochene network. Its rhetorical sophistication enabled the courting of multiple audiences. Its informal community sustained cultural confidence in the face of a faintly Christian world.

Theodoret's letters reveal one bishop's efforts to find openings, tap networks, and join the exchange of favors and loyalties. There was, however, more than one way to be a bishop-patron. Theodoret assumed one set of roles and pushed one program. Some clerics followed suit. Theodoret's closest allies only appear as patrons in hostile, unreliable sources, but their alleged crimes are telling. Hiba was attacked for diverting too much money to public building projects; Domnus, for his ties to pagan sophists. Both Hiba and Domnus were treated as Theodoret's co-conspirators—and their "crimes" seem to echo his pursuits and preferences.[159] Other Syrian bishops, however, cut a different profile. Consider Rabbula. The *Life of Rabbula* may be even less reliable as a source, but the "saint's virtues" are also telling. He avoids large building projects in favor of charity for the destitute. He seeks no ties to sophists or pagans, but violently confronts all enemies of the faith. Like Theodoret he gets help from clerics and ascetics, but by issuing stern commands.[160] The real Rabbula may not have acted so boldly. Nevertheless, he inspired followers to imagine a different mode of patronage.

Ultimately, no institution, no program, and no supportive crowd guaranteed a bishop success at playing a (mediating) patron. Fifth-century bishops faced an array of would-be clients and other would-be patrons. Clerical networks like The-odoret's allowed for the pooling of resources and the chorusing of appeals. Suc-cess, however, required more than an opening with the right allies. As we shall see in the next chapter, it demanded thorough social strategies, and careful personal performances.

7

The Irreplaceable Theodoret

Patronage Performance and Social Strategy

At some point amid the doctrinal feuding of 434, Theodoret accepted a (non-doctrinal) request from a friend. Palladius, a philosopher, had legally contracted for a soldier to protect him. But "barbarians," had "tossed this [soldier] to the denouncers," probably to try him for desertion. Theodoret penned two letters to deal with the situation. First, he wrote to Titus, the general overseeing the proceedings. "Justice has many enemies," Theodoret noted, "but injustice yields if the lovers of justice join the contest." The bishop praised the fairness of his military correspondent as he asked for an "unbribed decision." He encouraged the general to sympathize with the defendant.[1] Meanwhile, Theodoret wrote Palladius about the case. After musing on the wretchedness of this life, he pointed to a source of solace, "the instructions of God." The bishop quoted Thucydides that "one must bear courageously what comes from one's enemies." But such words, he said, were "cheap casings," which Palladius would recognize if he studied Christian truth.[2] As a bishop, Theodoret was well placed to mediate patronage. To the soldier and philosopher he offered both spiritual guidance and judicial advocacy. These letters cannot tell us if Theodoret's client won his case, but they reveal methods and strategies employed on his behalf. Through these letters Theodoret had to cast a good light on his clients, his contacts, and himself. Even in this simple scenario he had to manage several relationships and to pursue multiple goals.

This chapter looks at the process of mediating patronage: the methods by which Theodoret sought favors, established relationships, and created community. As we noted in the introduction, Theodoret's written appeals can be treated as social performances. Theodoret employed various theatrical techniques to present himself and his clients to selected audiences. He tried to win readers' sympathy for his clients. To this end, he offered symbolic phrases and references that demonstrated common ground. At the same time, he tried to make favors look feasible and necessary. This he did with cues that distanced him from the audience and then invited actions to restore rapport. Theodoret had to coordinate some large coalitions, and to manage relationships for the long term. He also had to deal with the chance of failure—a negative audience response. Theodoret's patronage letters are hardly *sui generis,* but when compared to other late Roman collections, they feature some distinctive performance techniques.

Theodoret performed to win clients immediate favors, but he also aimed at long-term social goals, above all elite inclusion. Theodoret's patronage might seem unrelated to his doctrinal contentions. In fact, the two pursuits were intertwined. During the Nestorian controversy, he augmented his elite network. He courted neutral officials and onetime opponents as potential benefactors. During the Eutychean dispute, he lost many contacts, as foes challenged his theology and his behavior as a patron. His performances were insufficient defense against a hostile imperial court. Theodoret took advantage of an imperial transition to restore his social standing. By then, however, he was cast less as the patronage advocate than as the confessor, a more isolating role.

PATRONAGE EXCHANGE AND PATRONAGE "PERFORMANCE": TWO CASE STUDIES FROM THEODORET'S LETTERS

Theodoret's letters have long served as a source for social history. Scholars have used the collection to investigate imperial administration, taxation, rural economic conditions, the fate of cities, and the development of the church.[3] And they have scanned the letters for evidence of patronage exchange. Recent scholars have cautioned against positivist interpretations of patronage letters.[4] Few, however, have looked closely at the social interactions revealed in written appeals. One way to explore these interactions is to treat them as performances, to use theatrical metaphors to illuminate the appeals process. Theatrical terms are an imperfect fit for written communication. They do, however, work well with the notion of networks, for advocates like Theodoret performed in order to pursue their larger social goals.

To explore the methodological issues raised by written appeals, consider two case studies. Twice in his extant collection Theodoret took up a larger patronage project, which required many coordinated appeals. The first project involved the settlement of refugees. In 439, Vandal forces completed their capture of Proconsular Africa. Many elite Romans fled for safer ground. By 443, some of these refugees had reached Syria. And Theodoret offered to help. He sent fleeing clerics to stay with his colleagues. He helped an orphan girl to search for her kin.[5] He apparently gave one case special attention. The decurion Celestiacus had exhausted all his funds dragging his family to Cyrrhus, before asking help from God. "And I was struck with fear," wrote the bishop, "for as is said in Scripture: I do not know what tomorrow may bring" (Proverbs 27:1).[6]

The case of Celestiacus (and other refugees) is intriguing for several reasons. It demonstrates the slight impact of Western Roman problems on the Eastern Empire. It reveals the significance of social rank across the Mediterranean. Theodoret's appeals show us people who might sympathize with an impoverished notable family, including bishops, sophists, decurions, and *honorati*. Above all, these letters showcase the rhetorical skills of Theodoret. For in various recommendations, he turned a desperate decurion into a philosopher, a devout Christian, and a paragon of gentility.[7]

Theodoret's second large patronage project concerned taxation. Between 445 and 447, the government was scheduled to perform the indiction census, the reassessment of each city's taxable assets (Latin: *iugatio*) that took place every fifteen years.[8] After the previous census (430–432) the decurions of Cyrrhus had complained, along with those of other towns, that tax demands were unfair. In 435 the complaint was answered with a "visitation" (Greek: *epopsia;* Latin: *peraequatio*). The investigators would not lower Cyrrhus's total assessment, but reportedly they agreed to redistribute the burden between free holdings and imperial lands.[9] Now, in the mid 440s, accounts would be reexamined, and potential disaster loomed. Someone in the capital was denouncing the decurions of Cyrrhus for falsifying their records. The perpetrator, we hear, was a deposed bishop, probably Athanasius of Perrha.[10] If the bureaucrats believed this "enemy of Cyrrhus," the town might be penalized. In 445 and 446, Theodoret met with local civic leaders to craft a response. They contacted allies and sent at least twelve letters. "Some [taxpayers] are living as beggars, while others run away," Theodoret pleaded. "The shape of the city is reduced to one man, and he will not hold out, unless a remedy is applied."[11]

The case of Cyrrhus's taxes has drawn attention from scholars. Theodoret's appeals constitute the best literary evidence for tax assessment in the fifth century. They paint a picture of economic trouble. Scholars have challenged this dark financial portrait.[12] Still, this episode reveals intriguing facets of late Roman society, including the cooperation of clerics and *curiales,* the influence of officials and ex-officials, and the intersection of church affairs with imperial bureaucracy. Again the letters showcase the rhetoric of Theodoret, for the bishop knew when to cite numbers, when to decry injustice, when to recall past favors, and when to mention holy friends.[13]

These episodes represent the best-documented patronage efforts of Theodoret's career, but both dossiers have limitations as sources. The letters do not enumerate refugees in Syria or measure their condition. They present a partial account of Cyrrhus's taxable assets (in both senses of the term).[14] Theodoret never tells us who, if anyone, hosted Celestiacus. He never clearly states if Cyrrhus had to pay penalties. Occasionally Libanius's collection hints at his success.[15] Theodoret never records if favors were fully exchanged. The letters tell us more about late Roman culture. As Theodoret wrote, he used various tropes to construct social authority—to build a model of the proper patron. Theodoret's rhetorical constructions, however, vary greatly depending on who was involved. Theodoret's letters produce limited general information, because they are socially embedded; they were designed to send certain signals to specific people.

One way to account for the social facets of these appeals is to approach them as performances. Following recent sociologists, we may use theatrical metaphors to illuminate the transactional process.[16] Whenever Theodoret wrote appeals, he assumed a stage persona. He directed an ensemble of clients and mediators. These "players" then tried to connect with an intended audience and inspire it to respond. Theodoret employed existing cultural elements as scripts in his performances. His troupe, however, usually had to improvise based on how audiences received them. Now any link in a social network, we have noted, may be viewed as a performance. Appeals for refugees, taxpayers, or criminal defendants are simply dramatic examples. Theatrical analogies do not capture every aspect of the patronage process. But they work well within a network-based perspective on society.[17] For appeals are not just about winning favors; they are about forging relationships and building communities.

Theodoret's letters offer glimpses of a bishop using his office to stage appeals. They provide limited insight into the level of taxation or the plight of refugees. Rather they show us how an advocate made local taxpayers look sympathetic to administrators and refugees look appealing to hosts. Perhaps most importantly, the letters show us how Theodoret cast himself as a mediator and made himself look irreplaceable. As we shall see, this effort had implications for Theodoret's doctrinal pursuits and his social stature.

DEMONSTRATING COMMON GROUND

Requests for patronage are almost always plays for sympathy. And sympathy usually begins from a sense of common ground. Advocates must find connections between their clients and their contacts and present their clients accordingly. Theodoret had many ways to build a feeling of commonality. He might appeal to shared culture or religion. He might turn to mutual knowledge or experience. He could play to local pride or even Roman identity. Each time, Theodoret had to display the right terms and symbols to hide differences, and to bind participants as a single, if temporary, community.

Theodoret began his approach to performing appeals by accepting some realities of the late Roman social hierarchy. Most of the time, Theodoret wrote appeals to wealthy, educated audiences. So he discussed common features of elite Roman life (such as the role of pedagogues as familial enforcers).[18] He also endorsed elite social perspectives; peasants, he wrote, were a "divine gift" to their landlords, a chance to show nobility.[19] Theodoret wrote in the tones of panegyric, which Romans used to signal social status. He praised sophists for their "Attic" language and officials for their "gentleness."[20] He even turned praises into a source of common ground. To an *honoratus* he once recommended an orator who "pleases me all the more for being a warm lover of Your Magnificence. I contend with him in proclaiming your deeds and by my praises I am the conqueror."[21] Omnipresent in Theodoret's appeals were references to the role of patron. Theodoret knew that his contacts were "zealous to provide ... favors."[22] All of these phrases pointed to the Roman social hierarchy, which served as a basic common ground.

Beyond the social context, Theodoret appealed to his audience by displaying cultural commonality. Not surprisingly, he often turned to Christian faith. Shared faith was a powerful motivator for generosity in the Christianizing Roman east. It presented an opening to rare audiences. "Since you ... illuminate the purple by your faith," he once wrote to Empress Pulcheria, "we are so bold as to write you a letter."[23] Evoking shared religion, however, was complicated, even dangerous. It could inspire grand favors and enduring loyalties or remind people of cultural conflict.

Sometimes Theodoret pointed to shared Christian teachings, a risky approach. Theodoret signaled doctrinal agreement with known allies. He mentioned "exact (*akribēs*) knowledge of divine matters" when he asked Anatolius to help with Cyrrhus's taxes.[24] In semi-public writings, however, his words had to remain ambiguous. Outside his doctrinal party, even basic symbols were problematic; some powerful people still did not share the Nicene Creed.[25] All he could discuss in these situations was "providence," "God's mercy," or other generalities.[26] Theodoret also sought common ground in Christian moral teachings. Yet here, too, he faced challenges. Some Christians heeded tenets to give generously, while others hoarded wealth. Some "converted" to asceticism, while others sneered at monks. When Theodoret dealt with other clerics, he could point to requisites of office, such as the command to welcome visitors.[27] When he dealt with other ascetics, he could point to their shared "toils of virtue."[28] But most of Theodoret's clients were neither monks nor clerics. So, again, he wrote ambiguously. He cited "philosophy" instead of asceticism. He spoke of exchanging "impiety" for "the wealth of faith."[29] Anything more specific would highlight differences rather than commonalities.

For a safer source of common ground, Theodoret turned to Christian Scripture. A well-chosen Biblical allusion could signal shared learning without causing offense.[30] Theodoret could interweave countless quotations. One letter to an Armenian bishop went from Paul's praises of pastor Timothy (I Corinthians 4:17) to Jacob's care of his flocks (Genesis 31:38) to Ezekiel's attack on "bad shepherds"

(Ezekiel 34:2) to Jesus's parable of the talents (Matthew 25:26–27), and so on for page after page.[31] But his appeals were usually simpler. He asked correspondents to show to visitors "the kindliness of Abraham" (Genesis 18:1–15).[32] He quoted obvious passages—"When one limb suffers, all limbs suffer with it" (I Corinthians 12:26)—to remind landowners and peasants what they shared.[33] Even the words of Scripture had to be fitted to the audience.

Appeals based on Christian faith thus required careful scripting, lest they prove troublesome.[34] So perhaps just as often, Theodoret turned to shared classical culture. For centuries the East Roman elite had treasured pre-Christian Greek literature. Pagans, Jews, and Christians studied with grammarians and sophists to maintain social standing. Whenever Theodoret dealt with pagans he turned to this corpus of learning.[35] Even with many clerics, he returned to pre-Christian *paideia*.[36] Theodoret cited the classics to showcase his learnedness, but also to signal shared values, such as humanity and self-control. Reliance on classical culture, however, brought its own dilemmas. Greek learning meant different things in different situations.

Sometimes Theodoret performed shared *paideia* through displays of literary knowledge. The right classical allusion could inspire generosity as readily as the Bible. Of course, not every Greek knew the same canon. Theodoret could plumb the depths of philosophy, as he did in his *Treatment of Hellenic Maladies*.[37] His appeals were usually simpler. To Palladius the philosopher, he offered a Thucydides-style lament about the "shamelessness" of the present age (*Historiae* 2.53), then an unmarked quotation from Demosthenes, to "endure magnanimously whatever the god gives you" (*De corona* 97).[38] If Theodoret chose a philosophic reference for an appeal, it was almost always Plato.[39] More commonly, Theodoret turned to epic and tragedy. To one local official he referred to Euripides; fortune, he said, "has not wished to stay with the same people, but hastens to pass to others" (*Troades* 1204–6). And he asked one notable for the "Hospitality of Alcinous" (*Odyssey* 7),[40] which nearly any Greek-speaker could understand.

At other times, Theodoret performed shared *paideia* through refined Greek language. This meant Attic grammar and rhetoric, which Roman educators taught as a mark of self-control. It also meant stock metaphors, which served as reminders for elite behavioral codes.[41] Theodoret's appeals featured *polysyndeton* (emphasis via multiple adjectives), *paronomasia* (the naming of objects by their attributes), and other rhetorical figures. They included familiar comparisons to athletics, seafaring, and medicine.[42] But not all linguistic tricks guaranteed a commonality of values. Some learned audiences expected a high style. Firmus met such expectations when he returned a borrowed hunting dog (named Helen) with a panegyric to canine beauty.[43] Others expected the direct style of Libanius, which featured compelling visual scenes.[44] Theodoret produced highly rhetorical sentences, when friends might expect them. Usually, to inspire generosity, he followed the direct visual style. Thus he vividly related the "tragic saga" of decurions and refugees.[45]

Christian faith and classical culture were rich sources of common ground. But some audiences required an additional approach, which recognized "broader" bonds of community. One such approach was to appeal to civic identity. Since the early empire, eastern Roman elites had championed the splendor and virtue of their home cities.[46] Theodoret rallied notables of Cyrrhus to show some local pride and not to "diminish the city."[47] He appealed to residents of other towns by encouraging municipal competition. "If our city, which has but a few poor inhabitants, consoles the [refugees] who have arrived here," he wrote to a nearby bishop, "how much more fitting it is for Beroea, raised in piety, to do so!"[48] Another approach was to appeal to Roman identity. By the fourth century, nearly all imperial residents were citizens and potentially full Romans.[49] Theodoret appealed to "shared" Roman history. When recommending refugees from North Africa, he recounted the last time Carthage had been conquered (in 146 B.C. by the Roman Republic).[50] Theodoret also acknowledged the importance of Roman political boundaries. When he spoke of "Syrians," "Cilicians," or "Easterners," he was not spouting separatism but affirming governmental jurisdictions (and the authority of those who drew them).[51] Theodoret celebrated Roman virtues, which he contrasted with the Persians' supposedly scandalous ways.[52] He also used well-worn Roman stereotypes of freeborn citizens and slaves.[53] These appeals to Roman or civic identity might seem hopelessly broad, like appealing to common humanity, but they were multivalent enough to reinforce both classical culture and Christian faith. And they were vague enough to work where culture or faith might offend.

Neither *paideia,* nor Christian faith, neither local pride, nor Roman identity, could guarantee connections between clients and contacts. Every appeal required a fresh performance, suited to the audience and the situation. Sometimes the resulting piece was straightforward. Such was the case when Theodoret wrote the sophist Aerius to recommend refugees. He compared the fleeing Africans to Athenians imprisoned in Sicily in the 410s B.C. (Thucydides, *Historiae* 7.82–87). He described "tempests" and "shipwrecks" and again asked for the "hospitality of Alcinous."[54] His request was simple; his contact's preferences, familiar. So he went with classical allusions.

Other situations required more elaborate displays of commonality. Such was the case when Theodoret pleaded for a taxpayer to Constantine, the former prefect. He started with vaguely Christian philosophy. "The God of the Universe established the nature of humans by his Word (*logōi*)," he wrote. "Because of this, human nature figures out what it needs of its own accord." Then he praised *paideia*, which, if used selectively, augmented nature with "admirable art-pieces of virtue." Theodoret compared philosophers and writers to bees. He praised the prefect for his "rationality" (*logon*), which allowed him to swim the sea of passions and navigate a political life. To introduce his client, Theodoret offered this rhetorical flourish: "I beg that you take joy in your solicitude for the illustrious and most amazing Dionysius, who holds a position of leadership against his will, cohabiting with poverty, maintaining a modest and wise way of life, pressed for funds which he could not give over even if he were to become a slave instead of a free man." He offered no details but claimed that the "tragic tale" would move anyone to sympathy, especially a compassionate former prefect. By the end, he had interwoven philosophy with Christian theology. He had linked the troubles of political leadership to the burdens of servitude.[55] The favor he asked was probably annoying. So he bathed his request in shared experience, status, *paideia,* and faith.

Performances of common ground thus required considerable tailoring. They also required clever ambiguity. Theodoret had to choose the right elements of shared culture and experience. The sense of commonality had to be specific enough to create sympathy but vague enough to hide cultural differences. Sometimes Theodoret could simply state all the memberships shared by his clients and contacts. Mostly, he relied on symbols open to multiple interpretations. When he wrote about "mimicking the bee," he might mean a full Attic education, or the selective learning once advised by Basil.[56] When he mentioned "philosophy" he might mean asceticism or intellectual debate. The right ambiguity could bridge divides. The refugee Celestiacus was neither a master of *paideia* nor a committed cleric. But Theodoret could still commend him to sophists for his noble virtue, and to bishops for his "wealth of faith."[57]

Ultimately, every demonstration of common ground was an attempt to define a sense of community. Allusions and rhetoric were useless unless they bound performers to audience members. Theodoret did build on social similarities, but the challenge was to encourage moral identification. Luckily, Theodoret was there to demonstrate the right course. He performed the commonality that he was seeking, by writing.

MARKING SOCIAL DISTANCE

Theodoret's performance of appeals displayed common ground, but shared culture or experience was rarely enough to get audiences to respond. A mediator like Theodoret was only needed when something separated the generous from the needy. Advocates, therefore, had to point out the differences that necessitated their involvement. And they had to position themselves as honest brokers, who shared enough with clients, and enough with would-be patrons, to bridge the divide. Theodoret found many ways to stage social and cultural divisions. He used these techniques to position himself as a concerned outsider. He used the same techniques to create rhetorical foils—divisions that would be overcome if the audience properly responded.

Theodoret began most appeals by distinguishing his clients, usually by describing their plight. When advocating for peasants, for instance, he emphasized the disparity between them and their landlords. Some tenant farmers may have been nearly self-sufficient, but in appeals they were cast as perpetual suppliants. They were also presented collectively, without names.[58] When advocating for notables, Theodoret stressed their descent into deprivation. Refugees "who once decorated [Carthage's] famous *curia*," he wrote, "now wander all over the world, getting from the hands of strangers the means of survival." Taxpaying estates near Cyrrhus were now supposedly "abandoned by their owners."[59] Appeals, it seems, required casting clients in lowly roles.

Theodoret appeals also set his clients apart by showing what they had to offer. Theodoret recommended refugees as props for preaching. "Some people [God] punishes," Theodoret wrote to a colleague, "others He teaches by the punishments of [those who have suffered]"—a lesson suitable for any Christian congregation.[60] He also promised less tangible benefits. It was "the poor," he said, who made good "advocates" before the "frightful [heavenly] tribunal."[61]

Theodoret stressed such distinctions to make patronage relations seem necessary and profitable. This was mostly a prelude, however, to his casting himself in the role of trustworthy mediator. This role required a sense of connection to clients and contacts. It also required a sense of separation from the interests of either side. Thoeodoret showed himself ready for this role by highlighting his episcopal office. In some appeals, he directly noted how "God ordered that ... [he] shepherd souls."[62] In others, he chose an indirect tack. When he castigated a former bishop for actions "unworthy of manual laborers," "slaves" or (ironically) "stage actors," he revealed by contrast his own professional virtue.[63] Sometimes Theodoret suggested that his appeals required a bishop like himself. The holy man Jacob of Cyrrhestica, we are told, wanted to defend the taxpayers, but he "holds silence in such regard that he cannot be convinced to write."[64] In other words, Jacob needed a trusted spokesperson, namely the bishop of Cyrrhus.

Theodoret also distinguished himself by displaying his learnedness and his strict lifestyle. He never bragged about his education, but he revealed his scriptural skills in allusion-rich sermons and occasionally in appeals.[65] He displayed his classical learning even more rarely.[66] Occasionally he spoke of "poets, orators, and philosophers," although he swore that "the sacred writings suffice."[67] Theodoret hinted at his ascetic lifestyle by denigrating the present world. But he rarely made direct mention of his personal regimen (he did so more often when fending off charges of heresy).[68] For him, the role of bishop required a humble persona. So personal qualifications had to be demonstrated indirectly.

Marking social distance thus helped to set the scene within Theodoret's appeals. The same basic techniques supported his most distinctive tactic: the staging of foils. By foils, I mean performance elements that create a temporary distance, but which are then used to inspire renewed commonality in the longer term. Like many advocates, Theodoret presented vice, or vicious people, as foils, evoking the morality that most people supposedly shared. By decrying the "hatred" and "lies" of his foe in the tax-fraud case, he signaled the rectitude of nearly everyone else.[69] More surprisingly, Theodoret often distanced himself from his actual target audience, in order to invite them to join in a deeper connection. Consider his reply to a notable who had sent a gift of wine from Lesbos. Theodoret praised the "clarity of [the wine's] appearance," in accord with elite conventions. But then he redirected. "For me, this wine is totally useless if indeed, as you say, it makes the drinker long-lived; for I am no lover of long life," he wrote, "since the waves of this life are numerous and troublesome."[70] Thus high-class finery served as a foil for a Stoic mindset, which he hoped his correspondent would embrace.

Theodoret staged various foils in his appeals. Sometimes he used classical culture as a foil for encouraging Christian faith. When recommending refugees to a sophist, he celebrated *paideia,* then shifted to the mystery "which words cannot fathom, nor the mind comprehend."[71] At other times Theodoret used customs of panegyric as a foil for building faith. Hoping to baptize the courtier Zeno, he praised the general's mix of "courage, gentleness, and softness," which amounted to a "wealth of virtue." But this, he wrote, paled in comparison to the "garb that is indescribable and divine."[72] Theodoret's rhetorical pieces could be obvious. Appealing for Cyrrhus's taxpayers, he jokingly asked Anatolius, "Why have you shown hate to those that love you?" before shifting back to panegyric.[73] Or his pieces could be almost satirical, such as when a governor wanted to attend a festival and Theodoret hoped to keep him away. "The Hideous She-Monster (*mormō*) is a fright to children, as are the pedagogues and teachers to young boys," Theodoret began, "the biggest fear for high-born men is the judge ... and the collection of dues. Yet the fear of these ... is doubled for those in poverty." Normally a bishop would labor mightily, he said, "so that you may partake of the festive assembly, decorate the city [with your presence] and play chorus-leader." But the citizens were afraid of the governor's "mask of authority" (*archēs prosōpeion*). Besides, he wrote, "even in being absent, you will be associated with the festive assembly, honoring the apostles and prophets by your rest and truce."[74] Here elite experiences served as a foil for shared faith. Thus Theodoret protected his congregants by writing a disinvitation.

Foils were not unique to Theodoret,[75] but they were important to his appeals because they created a moral tension that the audience was empowered to resolve. Theodoret created tension when he described the sufferings of refugees. He added to it when he shamed clerics for their lackluster charity, or when he told sophists to "prove the utility of fancy words."[76] Theodoret created tension when he noted the deprivations of taxpayers. He augmented it by describing their informant as a hate-filled denouncer. In each case, Theodoret offered his audience a way to relieve the tension. By defending taxpayers, they could align themselves with the forces of righteousness. By helping refugees, they could share in divine mercy.

Displays of distance were as central to Theodoret's social performance as displays of commonality. An effective mediator had to do more than find some shared virtue. He had to position himself to bridge social gaps and to motivate people to reach across divides. Different situations called for different acts of repositioning. Sometimes Theodoret distanced himself from the audience while embracing his clients. Sometimes, he separated from clients while embracing the audience. Other advocates had their own formulas for signaling distance and commonality.[77] Theodoret usually sought a balance, sharing just enough with clients and with providers to mediate between them.

DIRECTING ENSEMBLES

Advocates performed complicated maneuvers to motivate generosity. But appeals were never solo performances. Nearly every late Roman letter involved letter-bearers and observers. Large-scale appeals featured agents performing before multiple audiences. Somehow advocates had to direct these ensembles of performers and texts. Theodoret took up this task when defending taxpayers and when pleading for refugees, as well as in simpler scenarios. Each situation called for its own directorial approach.

When preparing appeals, Theodoret's first consideration had to be the coalition of participants. Each problem afflicted specific clients, seeking help from some set of patrons. In every situation, Theodoret considered whom to employ as agents and brokers, before which audiences. He also decided which opposing forces had to be overcome. For every appeal Theodoret chose envoys to fit with the message and its intended recipients. But it was Theodoret's grand appeals that demanded the most stage-direction. His approaches to the two extant cases differed as sharply as the problems themselves.

With refugees, Theodoret faced a straightforward, if difficult, situation. Letters record five parties who asked him for assistance: two bishops, a young woman, a notable layman, and the household of Celestiacus. The parties' needs varied from clerical employment to familial reunion. But all sought hospitality and new elite connections. Refugee relief did not require a particular provider. Indifference was the only opposing force. Indifference, however, might be enough to hinder help.

To aid the refugees, Theodoret assembled a cast of advocates, each with a target demographic. For starters, he drew in bishops from his doctrinal party, including Domnus of Antioch (*ep.* S 31), Hiba of Edessa (*ep.* S 52), and Irenaeus of Tyre (*ep.* S 35).[78] He also tapped a miaphysite bishop (Eusebius of Ancyra, *ep.* P 22), who had already sent a refugee to Syria.[79] Theodoret relied on his colleagues' preaching to

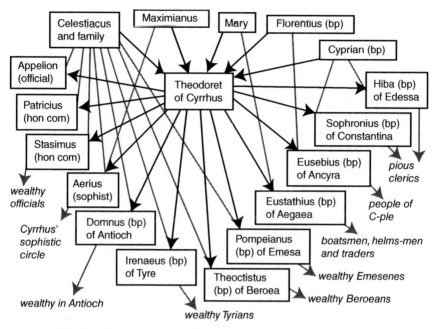

FIGURE 18. Theodoret's patronage ensemble: African refugees, 442–444, according to his letters. Black arrows = direct appeals, grey arrows/lines = indirect links/appeals, bp = bishop, hon com = honorary count.

motivate local notables. He relied on their connections to facilitate travel. Most of all he relied on their geographical scatter to maximize his audience. In addition to bishops, Theodoret tapped an official and two *honorati*. Their status gave them access to "those in wealth and office," even those who avoided sermons.[80] He also tapped the sophist Aerius (*epp.* P 23, S 30), whose eloquent circle might reach people uninterested in the faith. No precise sequence is apparent in these letters. None was required. The goal of this troupe was to reach the widest set of potential hosts across the segments of late Roman society.[81]

With Cyrrhus's tax woes, Theodoret faced a more complicated situation. As we noted, Cyrrhus had had its assessment last adjusted in 435. The city council sought to confirm this assessment with the administration. Constantinopolitan bureaucrats kept records of assessments (the *praefectiani* for free holdings, the *palatini* for imperial lands). Their "field agents" (*tractatores* and *rationales*) inspected accounts that were in arrears. Any of these men could influence the calculations, as could their superiors, the prefect of the East and the count of the *Res privata*.[82] The emperor could impose his will, if he was paying attention. In fact, any courtier could influence the process. Somehow Theodoret had to find out which figures were influential and win them over via agents and letters. Meanwhile, Cyrrhus faced an active opponent, who claimed that the city council had falsified its assessment. Somehow Theodoret had to neutralize this "denouncer." Thus Cyrrhus needed many advocates and supporters, and a coordinated plan.

To protect Cyrrhus's taxpayers Theodoret progressively built his coalition with a sequence of appeals that can be reconstructed.[83] Theodoret and his local allies began in mid-445 by dealing with the central bureaucracy. Having heard something of the problem, the city sent Philip the *principalis* to Constantinople, to the offices of the prefecture and the *Res privata*. Theodoret paved the way with a recommendation to Bishop Proclus. Once in the capital, Philip probably learned in detail about the accusations. But his meeting with the bureaucrats was clearly insufficient to counter them. He reported to Theodoret, who asked the count of the East to delay extra collections (*ep.* P 17). Later in 445, Theodoret began a second act before an audience of higher authorities. He asked the help of Jacob of Cyrrhestica, the "friend of God," whose name he dropped repeatedly.[84] Then he sent a new envoy to the capital to meet with Philip (and Proclus, *ep.* P 20). They delivered letters to Constantine, the prefect of the East (*ep.* S 42), and Empress Pulcheria (*ep.* S 43). They also hired a lawyer (Peter) to speak on Cyrrhus's behalf.[85] These appeals had more success. Cyrrhus was to be assessed by the old formula; Philip's entourage came home.

The antagonist, however, continued to accuse Cyrrhus of tax fraud. He made enough headway at court that Theodoret had to initiate a third act. Philip returned to Constantinople in the summer of 446, to reengage with Peter (*ep.* S 46) and Proclus (*ep.* S 47). And he delivered new appeals to courtiers, including Senator, the prefect during the last reassessment (*ep.* S 44), and Anatolius, the familiar general (*ep.* S 45). The final outcome is not known, but at each point in the drama Theodoret had a plan. Each wave of appeals built on the last. Each employed the existing cast while reaching for new members. Each targeted a new audience of decision-makers, surrounding them with advocates and texts. The goal was to inspire favorable talk, from the bureaucrats up to the courtiers, which could hold the accusations at bay.[86]

Theodoret worked hard to stage-manage patronage troupes such as these. But even when he did simpler appeals for clients, he had to deal with the larger social context. First, he had to fit with prior interactions with his audience. Consider his appeals to Areobindus, the wealthy general who owned estates near Cyrrhus. Tenants of Areobindus had trouble paying the rent (in this case, olive oil) when harvests were poor. They repeatedly asked Theodoret to plead for reductions. One time, Theodoret fulfilled this request with a standard appeal; the "divine gift of peasant laborers" had given the landlord a chance to show his generosity.[87] When he wrote a second appeal, he began similarly. Again, the bishop said, God made poverty as a "means of usefulness;" he had given further "opportunities to the

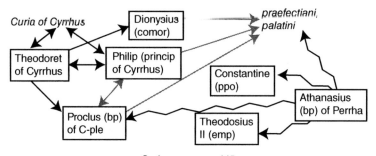

Spring–summer 445

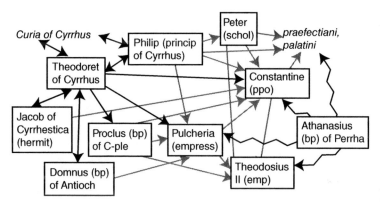

Summer–fall 445

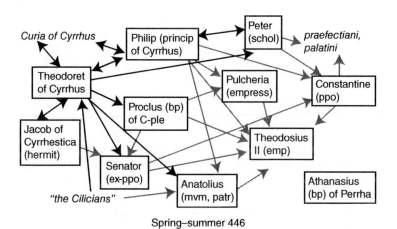

Spring–summer 446

FIGURE 19. Theodoret's patronage ensemble: Cyrrhus's taxes, 445–446, according to his letters. bp = bishop, comor=count of the East, emp = emperor, patr = patrician, ppo = praetorian prefect of the East, princip = principalis, schol = scholasticus.

well-off for showing generosity." But this time the performance included more symbolism. Instead of oil the peasants brought a "suppliant's olive branch," the bishop's letter. Areobindus could then turn a bad harvest into "spiritual abundance."[88] Thus Theodoret played off prior patronage to create an expanded storyline. And he built a connection progressively across multiple appeals.[89]

Beyond individual relationships, Theodoret had to consider the wider community of mediators and patrons. Theodoret's partners in advocacy were interlinked. Consider Eurycianus the tribune. In 434, Eurycianus delivered letters from Titus the general, warning Theodoret that schismatic bishops might be deposed. Later he received a consolation letter from Theodoret.[90] Like Theodoret, he was friendly with the sophist Isocasius, who once sent him to Cyrrhus in search of a good woodcarver. He probably also knew Philip the *principalis* through either the sophist or the bishop (or both).[91] Theodoret included men like these in his ensembles, and he had to consider the interconnections.[92] After all, anything he wrote or said could be passed around.

In fact, Theodoret had to consider not just people, but texts—the way letters presented his associates and himself. Most appeals were publicized. Not only were they read aloud;[93] if granted they were commemorated in ceremony and perhaps in stone.[94] Appeals could also be reused for new purposes. Thus Theodoret wrote for Palladius and his hired soldier, then used the same text to encourage Palladius's faith.[95] Appeals, like all letters, were collected. Clients assembled multiple appeals to deepen their sense of protection.[96] Advocates assembled appeals, probably to display their record as mediators.

Whenever Theodoret directed ensembles, he sought to represent his clients and contacts as part of an attractive, face-to-face community. His letters introduced clients and contacts, agents and brokers, friends and providers. The written texts introduced supporters who could not participate directly. If Theodoret succeeded, his appeals would follow one another to create decades-long sagas of favor and loyalty.

MANAGING THE RISK OF FAILURE

Theodoret's appeals were ambitious productions. Each was a gamble that contacts would respond to the right advocates at the right time. Friendships and patronage links could endure a few misconnections, but repeated performance failures endangered these bonds. "Do not ask for great things," Synesius once opined; "Either you may wound another or you may be wounded."[97] Every time Theodoret performed appeals, he tried to minimize the risk of refusal. Or he tried to lessen the consequences. He managed expectations in appeals by claiming inferiority. He excused ambitious requests by claiming a spiritual motive. He avoided risky tactics and sometimes refused to get involved. Thus Theodoret worked to maintain social links even when his requests failed.

Theodoret's prime method for dealing with the chance of failure was to stress his own inferiority. He declared his lack of stature to the political elite. "If I sent a letter to Your Greatness with no imposing necessity," he wrote to one prefect, "I would have likely been found guilty of presumption;" for then he would seem "ignorant of the magnitude of your authority."[98] Theodoret also stressed his lowliness to near-equals. Writing to sophists, he called himself inarticulate. Writing to archimandrites he dubbed himself "lazy." Even his own subordinate clerics he called "friends."[99] This practice of written self-deprecation was common among Christian ascetics.[100] But in the Roman elite it was far from universal. Bishop Firmus approached some courtiers as their *philos*. Libanius even rebuked some officials who were not proving helpful.[101] But Theodoret saw the value of playing down his capacities. By declaring his weakness, Theodoret accentuated the stature of his audience. He gave those providers a clear role to play while stressing their agency. Theodoret also minimized the chance of conflict. With near-equals he reduced the sense of rivalry. With superiors he reduced the appearance of presumption. All of this helped to preserve relations with contacts, so that he could appeal again without risking offense.

Theodoret's second method for dealing with failure was to stress his unassailable Christian motives. Sometimes he explained his advocacy as a pious duty. "After God ordered that, despite my unworthiness, I shepherd souls," he began one appeal, "I often must take care of things that are troublesome for me but advantageous for my sins."[102] His message was clear: making unlikely requests was part of the clerical life. Sometimes Theodoret claimed that appeals were really acts of pastoral care. His contacts, he hoped, would show "generosity," because they "longed to receive the same from God."[103] He knew that many appeals would get no immediate audience response, but if done for higher purposes, these performances were not really failures.

A third method for limiting dangers was to avoid risky settings for appeals. Theodoret preferred contacts whom he already knew. A doctrinal ally (such as Domnus or Anatolius) could always be asked to help with refugee settlement, taxes, or legal cases. But even a onetime opponent (such as Eusebius of Ancyra or Titus the general) was better than a stranger.[104] Theodoret also preferred familiar institutional scenes. He knew the habits of the clergy and the civil bureaucracy. He was less familiar with military life. This may be why he defended Palladius's soldier at Titus's tribunal, rather than that of a lower officer.[105] Theodoret sent his appeals in Greek, even to speakers of Latin or Syriac. He left the risk of translation to his recipients. Perhaps most striking, Theodoret chose to avoid the emperor. Once he had directly "persuaded" Theodosius II. Yet none of his later extant letters addressed the Augustus.[106] To petition the emperor was to risk a final denial, and that might endanger his entire patronage network.

Finally, Theodoret could avoid the risk of failure by refusing to perform appeals. Refusal was hardly his declared preference, but there were some unsupportable causes and unsupportable people. Theodoret's letters include one outright refusal, when Apelles, a Constantinople lawyer, asked for help for a friend. "I am not ignorant of human nature, nor do I bear humanity, of which I have great need, with an ill grace," Theodoret began. "Indeed, I know to provide for friends when they ask it, since I wish to receive [help] when I need it." But this request went out of bounds: "I wish to ask and be asked for things that do not cause great outrage." Theodoret never specified what was objectionable. Maybe Apelles' friend was heterodox (the letter calls him an "instrument of the opposing power.") Theodoret was upset, to "suffer the reputation that [he] heard insensitively."[107] But reticence and refusal might have protected everyone involved.

In dealing with the dangers of failed performances, Theodoret sought to preserve relationships. Even when refusing Apelles, he emphasized the goodwill between them. Theodoret's bonds with clients and many friends relied on a record of favor distribution. Protecting these relationships meant projecting that record into the future. The best outcome for advocacy was usually a successful transaction. But the loss of an appeal need not spell disaster, so long as his performances promised favors to come.

STRATEGIES OF INCLUSION: THE BUILDING OF A PATRONAGE NETWORK

Theodoret's letters thus showcase methods that he employed to perform patronage appeals. For each situation, he selected a mix of tactics to secure favors (or the hope of favors at a later time). Patronage, however, meant more than momentary theatrics. Viewed together, Theodoret's letters reveal deeper social strategies. We have seen how Theodoret worked in the 430s and 440s to grow and solidify his doctrinal alliance. During the same decades, he tried to assemble a patronage network. He sought to accumulate clients, to build elite relationships, and to achieve a sense of inclusion. The appeals examined so far in this chapter appear unrelated to theological debate, but patronage performances were, in fact, linked to the Christological conflict. It was the dispute over Nestorius that gave Theodoret the chance to perform grand appeals. And it was Theodoret's patronage performance that supported his leadership of the Antiochenes.

Theodoret's social strategies aimed to accumulate relationships, and patronage performances proved essential in this regard. In chapter 1, we saw some of the ways in which Theodoret fostered friendships with fellow clerics. Outside the clergy, his friendly links extended to people who shared his curial background, his ascetic habits, his learning, or his faith. Theodoret's appeals may or may not have won clients material favors. Either way, they allowed him to cooperate with all sorts of locals: priests, monks, professionals, *curiales,* notable women, bureaucrats, soldiers, and *honorati.* They also enabled him to interact with elites that otherwise might be inaccessible: senators, generals, courtiers, empresses, clerical foes, and unfamiliar colleagues. Both locally and across the elite, appeals provided the chance to promise mutual benefit.

Beyond the accumulation of relationships, Theodoret's strategies aimed to achieve a sense of social inclusion. Once again, patronage performances proved essential. We have noted how late Roman Syria was segmented socially and culturally. We have seen how Theodoret connected with multiple subcultures and social spheres. But he was not satisfied with serving as the link to outsiders. He strove to give disparate people a sense of connectedness, and patronage provided the opportunity. In his appeals he cast clients alongside advocates and one another and represented them favorably to elite audiences. He showcased differences of geography, culture, and social rank, and then invited audiences to bridge those gaps. The crucial aspect of these performances remained the role of mediator. Inevitably Theodoret presented himself as the man who could bring together officials with subjects, landlords with tenants, academics with clerics, (former) pagans with Christians, and everyone within the church.[108] Naturally, Theodoret was concerned with his own place in the community. Relations with clients mattered to Theodoret. But these letters were less about extracting loyalty from clients than about auditioning for an elite circle of friends.

Theodoret assembled patronage contacts throughout his career, in a fashion that at first seems unconnected with doctrinal debate. A closer look, however, reveals links between Theodoret's patronage activity and the Christological dispute. We have seen how Theodoret bonded with his clerical associates via friendship and doctrinal affinity. We have also seen how doctrinal allies were drafted as fellow mediators of patronage.[109] Such cooperation was probably old news in 430. It was never limited just to those within the Antiochene fold. But the process of schism and reconciliation seems to have encouraged Antiochenes to share in efforts at appeal.[110] In any case, the Nestorian controversy did boost Theodoret's connections with figures of real power: not just allies but also former foes. Theodoret probably already knew Anatolius from Antioch. But protection arrangements after the First Council of Ephesus cemented this relationship.[111] Theodoret may or may not have known Dometianus the quaestor, Eurycianus the tribune, Antiochus the prefect, and Titus the general before they acted to oppose the Antiochenes. By 434, all were receiving his recommendations, reading his judicial briefs, asking his advice, or serving as his envoys.[112] Travels to Ephesus and Chalcedon in 431 introduced Theodoret to courtiers such as Senator, Florentius, and Taurus. All later received the bishop's appeals.[113] Proclus the layman had denounced Nestorius, but as bishop he became Theodoret's perennial partner. Even Empress Pulcheria, who had shown hostility to Nestorius, was courted for the financial support of allied monasteries[114] and the protection of taxpayers. It is not clear how much Theodoret served as a high-level advocate before the First Council of Ephesus; few of his letters from the 420s remain. Still, controversy clearly taught Theodoret more about the power elite. It seems unlikely that he could have hoped for favors from all these contacts without the Nestorian conflict.

However Theodoret found his elite contacts, his letters suggest that he achieved a certain kind of success. In this case success meant not a vast record of favors delivered, but a compelling, multi-front performance. Clients had to believe that Theodoret held close connections to people who could secure benefits. Elite audiences had to be persuaded that he managed a broad clientele. Partners in patronage had to be convinced of both his base of clients and his list of friends. And everyone had to trust that he was mediating responsibly, to the benefit of all involved. Theodoret's role as Antiochene leader was part of this dynamic. Clerical leadership enhanced his quest for patronage contacts by projecting a picture of broad social support. Patronage contacts enhanced his claim to clerical leadership, by projecting a picture of elite access. We have noted how Theodoret won protection during the Nestorian crisis. We have also noted how he led the Antiochenes to defend the name of Theodore in the face of opposition. Patronage links may have contributed to Theodoret's capacity to maintain the Antiochenes' protection, and loyalty, right up to 448. Thus he could make headway with all his social strategies, so long as he played mediator and seemed irreplaceable.

STRATEGIES OF PERSEVERANCE: PATRONAGE AND THE EUTYCHEAN CONTROVERSY

Theodoret's patronage appeals were both singular performance pieces and part of a larger strategy: to act his way to the heart of multiple social networks. Playing advocate, however, did not work in every circumstance, amid doctrinal conflict. Theodoret gained stature as both a clerical leader and a mediator of patronage during the dispute over Nestorius. The next confrontation went differently. The Eutychean controversy forced Theodoret to defend both his record of patronage and his orthodoxy. He could not maintain his social position in the face of accusations and a hostile court. Theodoret took advantage of the imperial transition to restore some contacts. But it is unclear how much he rebuilt, once he had been forced to play roles other than mediator.

The accusations that Theodoret and his allies faced in 448 and 449 provide a vivid illustration of how intertwined the role of clerical leader was with that of patronage mediator. In chapter 5, we noted the list of Theodoret's foes during the Eutychean controversy. Some of these figures had already challenged doctrines of the Antiochenes. Others held unknown theological views but were somehow side-lined by Theodoret's network. One such foe was Athanasius of Perrha, probably the cleric who accused Cyrrhus of tax fraud.[115] Theodoret and his allies were eventually fingered as Nestorian heretics, as we have seen. But that is not how opponents began their attacks. First, Irenaeus of Tyre was accused of mismanagement, personal impropriety, and defiance of imperial authority. Then Hiba was charged with gross nepotism and misappropriation of finances to fancy buildings rather than the worthy poor. In the spring of 448, Theodoret was accused of neglecting his flock while conspiring to tyrannize other dioceses.[116] All three, in other words, were being labeled as irresponsible patrons.

Before Theodoret knew of any doctrinal attacks, he defended his reputation as a patron. "When did we ever act offensively about anything to His Serenity [the emperor], or the high officials?" he asked Anatolius. "When were we ever obnoxious to the many illustrious landowners here?" Rather, the bishop claimed, he had "lavishly spent much of [his] church revenues on public works, building stoas and baths, repairing bridges and caring for the common needs."[117] Writing to Nomus the Consul, Theodoret further described his career. "Before I was bishop, I lived in a monastery, and then I was consecrated against my will; in my twenty-five years as bishop," he wrote, "I was neither brought to trial by anyone, nor did I accuse anyone. Not one of my pious clergymen ever approached a court." Meanwhile, Theodoret asserted his value as a collaborator. "No one informs you of the size of the dangers," he declared—no one except for him.[118]

As Theodoret defended his reputation and then his teachings, he used performance techniques that served him in appeals. By late 448 he had written apologies to most of his (known) patronage contacts, from prefects and patricians to archimandrites and bishops. Each time, he sought common ground. To Anatolius he sent reminders of the long mutual record of protection and loyalty.[119] With less familiar courtiers, he appealed to fairness: "If someone persists in accusing me of teaching something alien," he wrote, "let him argue it to my face."[120] Theodoret tried to position himself as a "prominent teacher of evangelic dogmas."[121] He touted his willingness to hold communion with accusers and to mediate secondary disputes. Theodoret built his coalition carefully. First he consulted with close allies, such as Domnus of Antioch.[122] From mid- to late 448 he wrote to familiar courtiers including Anatolius (epp. S 79, 92), Eutrechius (epp. S 80, 91), Nomus (epp. S 81, 96), Taurus (epp. S 88, 93), Antiochus (ep. S 105), Florentius (ep. S 89), and Senator (ep. S 93).[123] He hired a lawyer (Eusebius) to present oral arguments.[124] And he sent Basil of Seleucia to the capital to survey the clerical scene (ep. S 85). In the winter of 448–449 he and Domnus coordinated their embassy to the court, with the help of Basil, Flavian of Constantinople, Anatolius, several lower clerics, and several notable women.[125] Their aim was to surround the court with an unignorable chorus of appeals. Theodoret tried to avoid causing offense;

he spoke of the "boundaries" that he would never violate except out of despera-
tion. He showed self-deprecation and defended his motives. "We have been guilty
of many other sins," he told a prefect, but "right up to today we have kept the apostolic faith untainted."[126] His best argument was probably that of Basil of Caesarea:
innocence by association. "I think your Piety is well aware that Cyril of blessed
memory often wrote to me," he wrote to Dioscorus, recalling the kindnesses that
they had traded.[127] Thus Theodoret acted as his own advocate to maintain inclusion in the circle of orthodox friends.

Theodoret's appeals performance, however, confronted the limitations of his
situation, under rhetorical assault and facing court hostility. For starters, his
efforts were limited by his physical circumstance, relegated to the territory of
Cyrrhus. Opponents denounced him in person in the capital; he could respond
only in writing. Opponents mixed nefarious rumors with exaggerated doctrinal
accusations. All he could do was deny the "slanders of his denouncers"—the sort
of denials that might actually sustain suspicions.[128] The bishop's foes also isolated
Theodoret from most of his patronage contacts. By late 448, he was shocked to
have his letters go unanswered. He could not even get the urban prefect Eutrechius to share intelligence or to announce that the bishop was protesting accusations.[129] The reason for this silent treatment was the now obvious anti-Theodoret
leanings of the imperial court.[130] No clever performance could win much public
sympathy once the emperor had signaled his displeasure.

Meanwhile Theodoret was forced to change his whole mode of performance.
As foes denounced his heresy to receptive imperial audiences, Theodoret left the
role of advocate for that of confessor. Before the council in 449, he started truth-
telling to his remaining allies. He warned Domnus of the synod's impending
doom. He wrote snidely to Anatolius about the "most righteous judges at Ephesus," and declared himself ready for exile.[131] Once condemned, Theodoret deepened his prophetic performance. With loyal allies he traded denunciations of the
church's "general apostasy." He reveled in shared suffering and promised secret
refutations.[132] When lay notables wrote in sympathy, he responded bluntly. "In no
great length of time, those who dared these deeds will pay the penalty," he wrote to
Maranas the lawyer, "For the Lord of the Universe governs all things with a weight
and a measure."[133] As Theodoret prepared for exile, he wrapped up old patronage
operations. Professionals, whom the bishop had enticed to Cyrrhus, joined him in
leaving town.[134] The bishop had not lost all of his elite favor. With Anatolius's help,
he successfully asked to be exiled to Nicertae.[135] But even in this appeal Theodoret
was not begging for mercy; he was waiting for divine vindication.

In late 449, Theodoret put his performance skills to work on one more *apologia*, to Pope Leo and his coterie. First, Theodoret wrote a long appeal directly to
Leo. "If Paul ... ran to the great Peter to get from him a solution to the problems
of those in Antioch who were arguing about living according to the [Jewish] Law

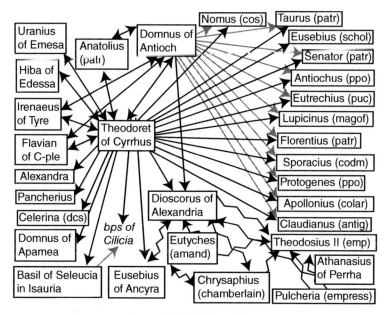

Stage 1: Early 448–mid 449

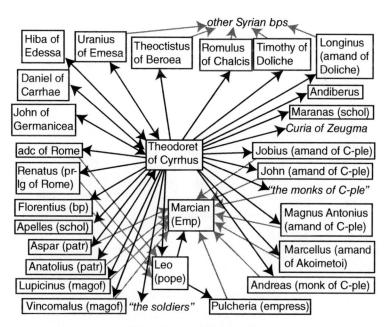

Stage 2: Late 449–late 450

FIGURE 20. Theodoret's self-defense ensemble, 448–451, according to his letters. adc = archdeacon, amand = archimandrite, cos = consul, codm = count of the Domestici, colar = count of the sacred largesses, emp = emperor, magof = master of offices, patr = patrician, ppo = praetorian prefect of the East, pr-lg = priest-legate, puc = urban prefect of C-ple, schol = scholasticus.

(Galatians 2.11–14)," he began, " all the more do we, humble and small, run to your apostolic see to get a remedy for the church's wounds." With this clever twist on Scripture, he signaled both shared Christian knowledge and deference to Leo's authority.[136] Theodoret proceeded in panegyric style, praising the "exactnesss" of Leo's doctrines. Naturally, he professed full agreement, on Christology and on the scandalous recent council. When Theodoret turned to himself, he chose not to play up his sufferings. Rather he stressed his diligence as a manager of eight hundred churches, a hunter of heresies, an ascetic, and a benefactor. If Leo wanted doctrinal details, Theodoret offered his full library of writings.[137] At the same time, Theodoret appealed beyond the pope. He wrote to Bishop Florentius, probably a confidant of Leo's, requesting help in defending justice. He also wrote to Renatus, the papal legate disrespected by the recent council. This letter explicitly endorsed Roman primacy as it again recalled the author's past patronage.[138] Theodoret asked the archdeacon of Rome to "kindle the zeal" of the pope. And he sent all these notes with a special entourage: two of his country-bishops and a liaison to Cyrrhus's monasteries.[139] Thus he surrounded Leo with living examples of his conscientiousness and with reinforcing second-hand messages. The most striking feature of these appeals, however, was Theodoret's actual request. "I supplicate and beg your Holiness to help me," he wrote to Leo, "as I appeal to your just and righteous tribunal. Above all I beg to learn from you whether or not I should be satisfied with my unjust deposition."[140] This time, he (nearly) suppressed his "confessing." He promised loyalty, like a client accepting subordination.

It is not clear from extant letters how far Pope Leo supported Theodoret,[141] But even before the death of Theodosius II, something was shifting behind the scenes. Leo made contact with the empresses Galla Placidia and Pulcheria by early 450.[142] When Marcian secured the emperorship in August, Theodoret found that he had court allies. Anatolius's partiality was surely no secret. More surprising was the support of Aspar the patrician and Vincomalus the master of offices, since neither had been considered Theodoret's friend.[143] In September 450, the new emperor started reversing sentences of exile. From Nicertae, Theodoret launched new appeals. To monks of the capital, he sent a public letter, detailing his Christology. To monastic allies, such as the *Akoimetoi,* he sent full doctrinal dossiers. He even responded to a group of soldiers with quotable arguments.[144] Meanwhile, Theodoret approached colleagues who had abandoned him. He offered his forgiveness (whether or not it had been requested).[145] He thanked the emperor and empress through several intermediaries.[146] But he hoped not to rely *only* on imperial favor. His aim was to reestablish a network, which could affirm his restoration.

Theodoret did rebuild some support among clerics, monks, and courtiers. By this point, however, his claim to social leadership had been transformed. Theodoret had high-placed contacts, to whom he was now beholden. His social debts made it harder to make grand requests without seeming presumptuous. Theodoret had old clerical allies, from whom he was now separated. His presence reminded many bishops of their own uncomfortable decisions. Theodoret retained a base of clients. Some clerics, monks, and laypeople now treated him as an exemplar of resolute faith.[147] Such veneration enhanced Theodoret's claim to holiness, but it also limited his social versatility. The more he played a confessor, the harder it was for him to tailor his performance of appeals. It is unclear how much Theodoret served as an advocate in the 450s, given the lack of extant letters. In any case, he faced new obstacles in performing grand appeals.

In the Eutychean controversy, we thus see an equally significant link between doctrinal conflict and patronage performance. Doctrinal foes attacked not just Theodoret's Christology, but also his career as a patron. They understood that his mediation of (non-doctrinal) favors was one key to his influence, doctrinal and otherwise. Theodoret defended all aspects of his career with a strategy of perseverance. He reached the right contacts, at a fortuitous moment, to save his episcopacy—except now he may have been typecast as the confessor, rather than the flexible mediator.

Ultimately, Theodoret's performances of patronage were inseparable from his performances of Antiochene leadership. His doctrinal influence rose or fell based on his ability to trade favors. His patronage appeals rose or fell based on his acceptance as a voice of orthodoxy. So important was patronage to Theodoret and his allies that it even affected their expressions of theology, to which the final chapter shall now turn.

Patronage, Human and Divine

The Social Dynamics
of Theodoret's Christology

In the fall of 444, Dioscorus of Alexandria received a remarkable letter from a (temporarily tolerated) Syrian colleague. This papyrus was certainly expected. Dioscorus had written an accession letter, a public statement of faith, to which colleagues usually responded in cordial tones. So Theodoret wrote back with a panegyric. He praised Dioscorus's "humble mindset," (*tou phronēmatos metrion*), which he naturally associated with the example of Christ. But offering his own doctrinal statement, Theodoret took an intriguing turn:

> For though by nature (*physei*) God is … most high, by in-human-ating himself (*anthrōpēsas*) he took hold for himself of the meek and lowly mindset (*phronēma*). Therefore, sir, since you are watchful of Him, you see neither the crowd of those subject to your authority nor the height of your thrones; you notice only the nature (*physin*) and rapid changes of [this] life, following, as you do, the divine laws, the keeping of which procures (*proxenei*) the kingdom of heaven.[1]

These two sentences brought together a startling array of theological concepts. First the passage expressed his Christology. God, he claimed, had assumed a humble (human) element distinguishable from his divinity. The term "mindset" in this context was unobjectionable, even to a miaphysite. But by later adding the word "nature" Theodoret subtly signaled his preferences. Then the passage analyzed Dioscorus's own behavior. Just like God, the Alexandrian bishop had assumed a lowly state of mind, distinct from the glory of his see. Finally, the statement made a claim about salvation. For by his behavior Dioscorus was revealing how to win God's favor, and others could follow his lead. It is not known how this letter was received in Alexandria, but we could understand if the recipient was annoyed. Not only did the letter hint at a (hated) two-nature Christology; it implied that Dioscorus's own behavior demonstrated such teachings.

Theodoret's letter could be dismissed as crafty rhetoric, but it actually reveals something significant about ancient theology. Theodoret connected his understanding of Christ to human behavioral ideals. This may seem unremarkable. Christian theologians used stranger analogies– everything from architecture to politics, and bodily functions to milk.[2] But Theodoret went beyond a clever analogy. His expressions rested on deep metaphors and basic narratives. "Condescension" (*synkatabasis*) was not just a part of the Christ myth, but a behavior that leaders could imitate. "To procure" (*proxenein*) was not just a soteriological concept, but also a term for patronage.[3] Thus Theodoret used God as a behavioral example for bishops, and he relied on social categories to explain transcendent truth.

This final chapter explores a theme that has shadowed this book: the links between Antiochenes' doctrines and their social relations. We have seen the partial overlap of Theodoret's patronage network with his doctrinal party. We have also seen how his doctrinal influence boosted his patronage, and how his patronage supported his doctrinal leadership. Now, let us consider a more conceptual overlap, at the level of language and cognition. For patronage interactions seem to have influenced Theodoret's actual theology. Like other ancient writers, Theodoret drew comparisons between divinity and normal human leadership. He linked his model of a good bishop to the apostles and Christ. In the *Eranistes,* Theodoret presented Christ as a mediator between God and humanity, whose effectiveness required that he have two full natures, human and divine. He spoke of salvation as the perfection of human nature, procured by Christ and distributed, via his "friends," to all of humanity. While his doctrinal formulas were drawn from Antiochene tradition, his interpretations of these formulas show parallels to his own performance as a mediator of patronage. In the manner of cognitive linguists, we could say that Theodoret was explaining Antiochene theology using deep metaphors culled from social experience.

Cognitive-linguistic explanations of this sort are inherently speculative, especially in a historical context. But the correlation between Theodoret's Christology and his patronage follows a larger pattern observed throughout this book: resonance between religious doctrine and social interaction. The Antiochene network fostered such resonance in many forms, with important consequences for the people involved. At the core of Theodoret's party we have seen the sharing of Antiochene doctrinal culture. We have also seen the sharing of intimate friendship and patronage performance. Here resonance between culture and social interactions, I argue, reinforced theological certainty and a sense of Antiochene community. Theodoret and his allies worked to extend this reinforced orthodoxy to clients, contacts, and peripheral colleagues. Outside the Antiochene core, however, the traditions did not necessarily match with social experience. For Cyril and Dioscorus the result was revulsion, and the drive to build their miaphysite network. If this argument is correct, it leads to a new explanation for the ardor of this religious controversy. Essentially, in the natures dispute, we see two clerical networks that, for core members, fostered different experiences of faith and community and could not be easily combined.

GENEROSITY FROM ON HIGH: PATRONAGE AND ANCIENT THEOLOGY

Bishops of the fifth century knew that they were supposed to be more than overseers. According to the *Apostolic Constitutions,* a bishop was "the minister of the Word, the keeper of knowledge, the mediator between God and you [the laity] in His worship services, the teacher of piety—indeed, after God, he is the father!"[4] This text was one of many to tout episcopal authority by linking bishops to the divine. And this link concerned more than ritual or orthodoxy. For Theodoret and others, it had a lot to do with patronage. People of the Mediterranean had long compared human patronage with divine activity, in doctrinal works, in narratives, and in everyday language. Theodoret played off this tradition. Not only did he mix theological and social terms; he typologically linked the saints, and Christ, to mediating bishops like himself.

The connection between human patronage and divinity was found across the ancient Mediterranean, embedded in everyday language. For centuries the same Greek terms were used to describe gods and human patrons. Both gods and patrons were called "protectors" (*prostatai*), or "benefactors" (*euergetai*). Both were praised for their "favor" (*charis*), or their "generosity" (*philanthrōpia*).[5] Christians like Theodoret often noted the differences between God and humanity, but they still described both God and patrons with the same words.[6] If anything, they added to the conceptual overlap. Thus the idea of "condescension" (*synkatabasis*)—the leader becoming like a servant—could be applied by Theodoret both to a bishop-patron and to God.

The linguistic link between patronage and divinity was then enshrined in formal doctrines. Throughout the Hellenistic and Roman periods, philosophers asked how the distant, perfect gods could do anything for humanity. Their answer was to posit human-divine mediators. Some such mediators were forces in the unseen world, such as heroes and *daimones*. Others were divinely inspired humans, true philosophers and prophets, for example. Neoplatonists variously ranked the mediators and explained the mediation process.[7] But all of these figures were described as advocates or as dispensers of "grace," by people using familiar social vocabulary. By the fifth century, Christians had their own lists of mediators, including angels, prophets, apostles, martyrs, dead ascetics, and living holy men. Theodoret discussed such mediators in his *Treatment of Hellenic Maladies*. Bishops could also be seen as divine mediators, as advocates for the faithful and distributors of blessing. Naturally, Theodoret drew on this notion in his appeals.[8]

Perhaps the most potent link between human patronage and divinity was narrative typology. Heroic stories provided prototypes to which people and experiences were compared. Classical writers had long juxtaposed their lives with those of Homeric characters and famous philosophers. By the fifth century Christians took typology to a new level. Not only did they compare their lives to biblical characters. They presented those characters, and later holy people, as "types" of a single reality.[9] Theodoret sought many biblical types by which to measure Christian leaders. His favorite was Paul, "the most perfect" apostle. Not only was Paul "an excellent physician," with remedies suited to each patient. He was adaptable, "a Jew to the Jews," a gentile to the gentiles. "For it was to be useful to the masses that he employed the masks of the actor," wrote Theodoret, "not to take up the life of the flatterer, nor to contrive a harmful gain, but to effect a benefit for those whom he was teaching."[10] In other words, Theodoret saw Paul as a precursor to the patronage-performing bishop.

For Christians, not surprisingly, the links between patronage and theology were concentrated in discussions about Jesus Christ. It was Christ whom they termed their savior and protector. It was he who embodied God's *synkatabasis* ("condescension"), and *oikonomia* ("dispensation," or "flexibility"). It was Christ who played the main role in human-divine mediation. "There is one God and one mediator (*mesitēs*) between God and humanity," read the Epistle to Timothy, "the man Jesus Christ who gave himself as a ransom for all" (Timothy 2:5–6). How and what Christ mediated was left to future exegetes, including Theodoret.[11] Of course, Jesus was presented as a moral exemplar, especially for the clergy. "O Bishops, this Jesus, our Savior, Emperor, Lord, and God, you must hold as a pattern (*skopon*)," read the *Apostolic Constitutions,* "You must imitate him in being meek, quiet, compassionate, merciful, peaceable, free from anger,"[12] and so on. More importantly Jesus was presented as the best example of a responsible patron. To Theodoret he was the ultimate "procurer" (*proxenos*) of benefit for humanity.[13]

Thus Christians deepened the old conceptual connection between patronage and theology. But what are we to make of this "inextricable link between theological language and its social context?"[14] Over the last century anthropologists have bound divinity to social relations in numerous ways.[15] Scholars of late antiquity have tied Christian theology to familial structure, gender relations, and political ideology, as well as to patronage.[16] Divinity is *not* a direct reflection of social constructs. Both Christian and non-Christian theologians recognized a gap between divinity and humanity, which rendered God foreign to human experience.[17] Even sophisticated theologians, however, relied on language with social connotations. They depended on widely-held assumptions about rulership (divine or human),

friendship (with God or humans), patronage (from God or humans), and mediation (between people or between humans and God). Narrative typology, in particular, encouraged the mixing of ideas about social relations and about God.
Christians were told to model themselves on the divine, not vice versa. "A type
does not have all the characteristics of the reality,"[18] Theodoret explained. But in
the realm of associative thinking, it was nearly impossible not to reverse directions. Believers of all stripes came to envision God as an (aggrandized) version of
themselves.

The network approach of this book shows another way to view links between
theology and social relations: God can be treated as part of a perceptual or rep-
resentational network. Cognitive research has bound religious experience to the
same neural systems that manage social interaction (see above, introduction).
Humans perceive relationships not just with acquaintances, but also with unseen
forces (from disembodied spirits to forebears to contemporaries whom they have
never met). Theology is essentially the formal representation of these extended
social perceptions.[19] We have seen how doctrinal tropes bound together Theodoret and his allies. We have seen how these same relationships were augmented
by performances of patronage. Given the social and conceptual overlaps, it would
hardly be surprising if doctrine influenced patronage performance, and vice versa.

"MEDIATION" CHRISTOLOGY
IN THEODORET'S *ERANISTES*

Two natures in one person (*prosōpon*) of Christ after the union—so professed
Theodoret and (some of) his allies before the Council of Chalcedon. Theodore of
Mopsuestia had outlined this terminology.[20] Theodoret then made it the basis of
further teachings. Theodoret wrote on Christology in polemics, apologetics, and
exegesis, as well as in treatises like *On the Incarnation of the Lord*.[21] Scholars have
often treated him as a mere mouthpiece for Antiochene tradition,[22] but Theodoret
proved innovative in how he reframed Antiochene language. It was the *Eranistes*
(published in 447)[23] that allowed Theodoret to champion his take on orthodoxy
on multiple fronts. This text defended "two natures" by explaining how Christ
needed them to mediate between God and humanity.

The *Eranistes* marked Theodoret's boldest foray into Christology, in terms of
doctrinal argument and literary performance. The literary innovations of the
Eranistes are striking. The text intermixed three different genres used to defend
doctrine. The largest part is a dialogue, in which *Eranistes* ("collector of [hereti-
cal] rags") argues with *Orthodoxos* ("correct thinker").[24] Other Christian theologians had, of course, employed this philosophic genre, from Justin Martyr to Cyril
of Alexandria. Most presented either a circle of disciples who deferred to their
teacher, or a stylized adversary who rarely interrupted.[25] The *Eranistes,* however,

simulated an active debate over terminology and scriptural explication.[26] The tension of this scene was enhanced by the use of theatrical-style speaking cues (e.g., ERANISTES: No, I do not; ORTHODOXOS: Yes, you do).[27] Woven into the dialogue was a more traditional form of doctrinal defense, supportive *florilegia*. Theodoret's protagonist marshals helpful quotations from dozens of church fathers.[28] The text never solely relies on argument from tradition, but each "conclusion" is backed by a chorus of agreement from shared Nicene heroes.[29] The text concludes with yet another type of defense, dialectic syllogism. The three scenes of dialog and three *florilegia* are followed by the author's epitome of his argument. Theodoret stated his aim, to foster an accessible debate: "I beg those who may happen on [this book] to stand apart from every preconception and conduct a trial of the truth." The dramatic style invited readers into the argument, which prepared them for formal logic and surrounded them with friendly voices of authority. The effect, he hoped, would be to "make it utterly clear that the apostolic message is preserved by us."[30]

Theodoret's boldness, however, went beyond literary style to the arguments.[31] For the *Eranistes* reopened a festering controversy. Since 433 (for some, or 435, for the rest), bishops of the Mediterranean had subscribed to the ambiguous *Formula of Reunion*. It spoke of Christ as a union "of two natures ... consubstantial with God the Father according to his divinity, and consubstantial with us according to his humanity."[32] Disputants interpreted these phrases to support various formulas, including "one nature incarnate" and "two natures." But official agreements (like Proclus's *Tome*) retained the *Formula*'s ambiguity. So did some of Theodoret's exegesis.[33] The *Eranistes* broke from this pattern. Not only did it affirm "two natures" after the union. It criticized some formulas of Cyril (now deceased), as a gateway to several heresies.[34]

The main arguments of the *Eranistes* centered on a triad of traditional Antiochene tenets. First, Theodoret argued that since God is the creator, he is by nature immutable. Consequently He only "became flesh" (John 1:14) in the sense that He assumed a distinguishable human nature.[35] Second, Theodoret argued that the human and divine natures of Christ were not intermingled. Both the human nature and the divine nature remained intact, in his view, so that the entirety of human nature could be saved.[36] Third, Theodoret tried to prove that God was impassible. Because of the distinction between the natures, only the human aspect of Christ suffered, and by its suffering it perfected all humanity.[37] Each of these claims had been raised by Theodore, and Theodoret drew (selectively) from his mentor.[38] Indeed, behind the claims lay the Antiochene assumption that the Creator and the created were separated by a permanent ontological divide.

Yet Theodoret's doctrinal presentation went beyond traditional terms and assumptions. As we have noted, Antiochene doctrine never constituted a single system. Theologians who accepted "two natures" still had to explain the meaning and purpose of such terminology. Theodore had described a "cooperating" (*syner-geia*) of the two natures, bound together by God's highest "good grace" (*eudokia*). He had chosen these words to fit together several scriptural referents, while stressing the simultaneous activity of both Christ's humanity and His divinity.[39] Theodoret, however, was writing in response to the Nestorian controversy. Opponents had cast suspicion on *synergeia* and *eudokia* as leading to the worship of "two sons." He thus needed a more unitive way to describe Christ, which nonetheless required two distinct natures. So he scanned Scripture and prior theological works, and he looked for persuasive ways to explain.

Theodoret's best-studied contrast with his opponents concerns his understanding of "nature." Traditionally, "nature" (Greek: *physis*), like "substance" (Greek: *ousia*), had signified a set of innate qualities, attributed either to an individual subject, or to a whole category.[40] For Theodoret, nature (and substance) came to mean something more tailored: a *self-consistent* bundle of attributes, applicable *in its entirety* to a genus and each of its exemplars.[41] To possess a given nature, by this definition, was to claim membership in a community, by sharing in its key characteristics. Divine nature thus featured such traits as immutability, impassibility, invisibility, unfathomability, incorporeality, and immortality. It applied to all members of the Trinity.[42] Human nature, by contrast, was characterized by mutability, passibility, reasonability, and (since the expulsion from Eden) mortality. This nature applied to all people, body and soul united.[43] For Cyril, and many other theologians, the union of natures signified the sharing of attributes (*idiomatōn*), the mysterious process which enabled God to make real contact with humanity.[44] Theodoret, however, could not abide the "nonsensical" idea that one nature might contain opposing attributes. He would not accept that an immutable nature could change.[45] It was feasible to him that a single person (*prosōpon*) could bring together opposing traits. Humans, he explained, were already composites of body and soul, each a smaller-scale "nature" with its own attributes. So Christ could also be a composite. For Theodoret, in other words, Christ was a full member of two genera at the same time.[46]

Another well-scrutinized distinction between Theodoret and his opponents concerns what force accomplished salvation in Christ. Cyril presented salvation as an act of divine Grace, the divinization of humanity. The active force was thus simply God (or more precisely, the Word). God had lowered himself, in Cyril's view, to undergo incarnation, suffering, and resurrection, "according to the flesh." Christ's humanity served as the "instrument" (*organon*), by which God did His divinizing.[47] Theodoret started from a different premise: that humanity could not be divinized, only made "incorruptible and immortal." God had, indeed, lowered Himself, in his view—merely by uniting with human nature in Christ.[48] Thereafter God was still the main active force, but not the only factor. Christ, in his view, did the work of salvation *using both his natures*. His divine nature did wonders and powered the resurrection, while His human nature withstood temptation and suffering. Theodoret could not imagine a single divine force accomplishing everything unaided. "To deny the [human] nature is to deny the sufferings [of Christ]," he stated, "and to deny the sufferings is to do away with salvation."[49]

Scholarly discussions of natures and salvific forces, however, have tended to overlook a key part of Theodoret's argument: Christ's existence as a mediator between humanity and the divine. That Christ was such a mediator was a common idea, as we have seen. Cyril, for instance, admitted that the mediator was "composed of a humanity like ours," as well as "the Son that emerged from God." Yet he insisted that the mediator was "God by nature, albeit not separated from the flesh."[50] In the *Eranistes* Theodoret concurred with Cyril, "The name mediator indicates both the Divinity and the humanity [of Christ]." For Theodoret, however, the mediator had to be a two-nature entity. "[Christ] is called mediator because he does not exist as God alone; for how, if he had nothing of ours, could he have mediated between us and God?"[51] Much has been made by patristic scholars of the question of "subjects"—of who really acted or experienced action as Christ. Scholars have agreed that Cyril taught a Christology in which God the Word was the sole subject.[52] They have debated whether Theodoret also taught one subject (with a different vocabulary), or posited two subjects (human and divine), or showed either evolving ideas or inconsistency.[53] This debate, however, rests on the assumption that a "real" subject must be an exclusive, indivisible identity.[54] Theodoret argued to the contrary. For him, Christ was one subject, a mediator with two identities. It was only because of these two unconfounded natures, he claimed, that Christ could mediate effectively.

Theodoret thus turned to mediation to explain how two natures were united and why two natures were required. He used the same ideas to explain the link between ordinary believers, holy people, and Christ. After the description of Christ's mediation, Theodoret's antagonist offers an objection: "But was not Moses called a mediator (Galatians 3:19), even though he was a mere man?" This leads the debate to the crucial topic of typology. Moses, says Orthodoxos, "was a type of the reality." The protagonist explains that Scripture sometimes labels types by the attributes of the reality. Hence Moses, while not divine by nature, "was called a god to fulfill the type."[55] The dialogue mentions several other figures who share in Christ's status by becoming his type. It then explains how holy people will be rendered incorruptible, by sharing in (some of) the reality of Christ. Theodoret acknowledged symbolic types, from the Eucharist to sacrificial goats. He used these types to show that Scripture testified to both natures of Christ.[56] But it was behavioral types that most interested him. After all, as he wrote to Dioscorus, it was the keeping of divine laws that allowed one to partake of heaven.

It is easy to miss the significance of mediation in the *Eranistes*. Theodoret does not return to the term, as he does to "nature," or "type-reality."[57] But mediation holds together his central argument about a two-nature Christ, and his logic for how holy people were associated with Christ. It is possible to view Theodoret's reasoning as a product of Antiochene definitions and assumptions. Consider, however, a broader perspective. We have noted how doctrinal reasoning cannot be truly autonomous; it must operate through the socio-cultural systems of language. As we shall see, Theodoret's doctrinal expressions have some intriguing, if latent, associations.

SOCIAL REFERENTS IN THEODORET'S CHRISTOLOGY: METAPHORS AND NARRATIVES OF MEDIATION

The Christological argument in the *Eranistes* seems to be linked to the author's social interactions. Theodoret set out to write about theology, not about his social life. But his discussion of Christ as mediator and savior may be associated, at a cognitive-linguistic level, with his own role in ordinary patronage. Such a claim may look like a stretch. Indeed, it is always speculative to probe words for latent connotations. Still, scholars have noted how mere connotations can have profound social impact, when linked to basic metaphors and shared narratives. Patronage mediation, I suggest, provided a deep metaphor for Theodoret's explanation of Christology. Patronage networks furnished a frame for Theodoret's notion of salvation. Meanwhile, Christology and soteriology set out a narrative template for enacting key relationships. Theodoret, it seems, thought with Christ about patronage and with patronage about Christ.

Theodoret's Christology is usually read as a precise teaching. From a wider vantage point, however, it can be seen as a metaphorical construct: Christ as mediator of divine patronage. As we have noted, in the *Eranistes,* Christ is identified with two categories of beings, divinity and humanity. Christ demonstrates divine identity by his transcendent words and miraculous deeds. He reveals his human identity by his earthly desires and bodily needs.[58] For Theodoret, these identities represent two natures. They also explain how Christ mediated God's favors for humanity. Through his connection with God the Father, Christ wins the favors of salvation, incorruptibility, and immortality. Through a commonality with ordinary humans, he models the behaviors that God demanded as signs of their loyalty. We have seen how Theodoret called Christ the "procurer" of divine grace. Here, while defending dyophysitism, he trod similarly, turning Christ into the ultimate patronage connection.

Theodoret's notion of salvation can similarly be seen, in a wider light, as a gift of divine patronage distributed through Christ's network. As we have noted, in the *Eranistes,* salvation is defined as the perfection of humanity. Christ risen represents the "firstfruits" of this salvation, which will then, he says, pass to all who believe in him.[59] There is, however another category relevant to Theodoret:

Christ's coalition of helpers. This group includes prophets, who predict his arrival, apostles (and their successors) who report his deeds and teachings, martyrs who display the pinnacle of loyalty, and ascetics who display human perfectibility. These "friends of God" form a neat network of those linked to Christ as types of his reality. Thus they partly share in his titles and powers,[60] which they use to extend salvation as they extend the faith.

The notion of Christ as a mediator of salvation is hardly unusual, as we have seen. What is intriguing about Theodoret's Christology is how it seems to parallel his own patronage performances. Just like his Christ, Theodoret displayed multiple identities as he reached out to various audiences by showcasing common ground. As Christ positioned himself to win people divine favor, so Theodoret positioned himself to get people hospitality and lower taxes. Theodoret, of course, built his own coalitions. Like Jesus he claimed high contacts, supportive allies, loyal clients, and grand plans. It is doubtful Theodoret worried about Christ's risk of failure. But he did present Christ choosing to show weakness, as Theodoret showed weakness in appeals. When Theodoret described Christ as a dyophysite mediator, his Christ looks like a favor-trading bishop writ large.

Thus with Theodoret we see a specific instance of social conceptions overlapping religious doctrine. But what does this really mean? In the *Eranistes,* Theodoret was arguing theology. He was not making a coded statement about patronage. The text almost always used traditional terms and analogies. References to social experience are either inadvertent or implied. Moreover, theology never merely echoes social structure. Most theologians sought a God who was distant from human indignities. There is, in other words, no *exclusive* link between dyophysitism and any one mode of social performance.

And yet, the parallels between theology and social roles hold significance; for they may reveal the presence of latent social metaphors. Cognitive linguists point to deep metaphorical constructs ("frames") as the foundation of commonsense reasoning. Ideology, they claim, is usually explained in relation to a basic cultural category—such as "the body" or "the family"—in some variation.[61] Few social experiences were more common for Theodoret than mediating favors and appeals. His Christological argument, I suggest, employs social mediation as a deep metaphor, a basis for theological common sense. This social metaphor elicited no direct comment in the *Eranistes,* but elsewhere Theodoret was more explicit. "Just as the person wanting to reconcile two people fighting with each other puts himself in the middle and, taking one by the right hand and the other by the left, brings them together in friendship (*philia*)," he wrote in his *Commentary* on Timothy, "in this case, by uniting humanity to the divine nature [Christ] effected a pure and indissoluble peace."[62] Theodoret knew that Christ could be one subject, a mediator sharing in two identities. He knew this, I suggest, because he joined with various clients and contacts by performing his own multiple identities.

The parallels between Christology and patronage hold another significance; they may reveal the use of theological stories to affirm acts of cooperation. As we noted in the introduction, sociologists have stressed the capacity of basic narratives to motivate social action. Ideological language drives people to act in concert when it reinforces a story in which the speaker and audience find their place.[63] Theodoret's soteriology recalls the basic Christ myth—his ministry, death, resurrection, and salvation of the faithful. More specifically, it presents a narrative framework in which Christ works with his network of "types" to procure the perfection of humanity. The basic Christ narrative held meaning for many late antique Christians. Theodoret's version, however, carved out a special place for his closest associates and himself. For them to collaborate in patronage was more than a matter of friendship; it could be seen as the imitation of Christ.

Theodoret's *Eranistes* can be seen as a technical theological treatise. It can also be seen as a work of religious ideology, in which the author thinks with Christ about social relations and thinks with social relations about Christ. In this work, Theodoret did not publicly showcase social referents to his Christology. But explicit mention of these tropes was not required. According to cognitive linguists, the power of deep metaphors and narratives lies in their latency. If someone like Theodoret holds a deep metaphor or a basic narrative, a few symbolic phrases would activate it.[64] The result would be a strong ideological identification, in which the participants would view a myth as "our own story" or a theological argument as "common sense."

RESONANCE: ANTIOCHENE
SOCIO-DOCTRINAL DYNAMICS

Looking for deep metaphors and sharable narratives, we may thus find a dynamic link between Theodoret's dyophysite doctrine and his role in late Roman patronage. But how much does this (admittedly speculative) connection really matter for bishop patrons or Antiochenes? It is difficult to determine how far Theodoret's Christological perspective was accepted. Even his confidants had varied takes on dyophysitism.[65] It is impossible, moreover, to prove communal sharing of latent metaphors and narratives in a historical context. These speculations, however, hold significance because they are part of a larger pattern: resonance between Antiochene religious traditions and social relations. In this book we have observed how some clerics relied on doctrinal and emotional cues to define their connections. We have also seen how the Antiochene network developed its social and cultural patterns and arrived at consensual leadership. We have noted how Theodoret wove doctrinal idioms, historical narratives, and leadership performances into a sense of Antiochene community. Now we have explored how patronage interactions were bound up with Antiochene doctrine, in terms of social strategizing and, perhaps, theological discourse. These socio-cultural links have important implications. They constitute a set of processes by which certain religious traditions reinforced specific relationships, and certain relational patterns reinforced particular teachings. This socio-cultural dynamic, I argue, pervaded the core of the Antiochene network, where it fostered doctrinal certainty and communal identity.

The concept of resonance requires some explanation, for it does not appear often in social or cultural history. Resonance describes a condition in various network systems, when signals transmitted by a network align with network architecture, causing the signal to be magnified. Socio-cultural resonance refers to an analogous condition, when cultural traditions affirm social patterns, which in turn reaffirm those cultural traditions. Resonance in a social network might take many forms. It might involve the tightening of bonds from repeated use of varied social cues.[66] It might involve the historical development of cues in tandem with certain patterns and customs. Resonance could emerge from the creation of communal narratives, which validate cultural symbols and existing social arrangements. And resonance could come from the use of common social patterns as ideological frames.[67] Socio-cultural resonance may be temporary; both cultural tropes and social patterns are always shifting. For as long as it operates, however, such resonance has a palpable impact, fostering a sense of community. Throughout this book we have followed the core of the Antiochene network, centered on a dozen (or so) cooperating bishops. Written records from this core group show numerous instances of resonance between cultural elements and social interactions.

One sort of resonance can be found in the mix of social signals shared by core Antiochenes. In chapters 1 and 2, we noted a set of cues that Theodoret and his associates used to mark out their clerical network. Emotional terms, such as *philia* and *agapē*, were combined with doctrinal watchwords, such as *akribeia* and *synkatabasis*, to indicate key attachments. For the closest allies, this set of cues was augmented by more elaborate signals of intimacy and affection. Councils and visits turned shared doctrine into rituals of shared orthodoxy. Epistolary customs showcased these clerical bonds in a concentrated form. Tracing the exchange of these signals led us to a basic network map, which revealed, among other things, a dense thicket of core Antiochene bonds. In the last two chapters we added another source of clerical connection, shared patronage performances. Trading favors and joining advocacy ensembles provided a further demonstration of friendship. Patronage networks were not a precise match for doctrinal party links, but Theodoret's closest doctrinal allies were also frequent partners in patronage. The result, among *core* Antiochenes, was a thoroughly mixed social discourse, and a web of dense, multiplex relations. This served to magnify the socio-doctrinal signals and reinforce the network.

Another sort of resonance can be seen in the development of Antiochene patterns and traditions, particularly the establishment of agreed leadership. In chapter 3 we looked for the roots of the Antiochene network by contextualizing Theodoret's works of history. We followed his tale of a small Nicene circle devoted to Bishop Meletius, which built alliances, found enemies, taught theology, and preached, until it had taken over most of Syria's important bishoprics. Theodoret's story is sometimes tendentious, but it reveals diachronic social patterns that withstand comparative scrutiny. From Theodoret we thus have a partial account of the rise of the Antiochene party, as a network with a tight core and a loose periphery. We also have an account of the shaping of Antiochene traditions, including doctrinal idioms, ascetic involvements, and informal modes of leadership. In chapter 4 we followed the operation of this network during the Nestorian controversy. We observed the party transform itself, through external conflict and internal feuding. The struggles among Antiochenes did concern doctrine, but they also involved a competition for leadership. When Theodoret successfully mediated disputes, he won a position of centrality and influence. These struggles were risky, and not every member emerged unscathed. The whole process, however, reaffirmed Antiochene traditions, under Theodoret's influence, and reinforced the core network.

A third form of resonance is visible in Theodoret's efforts to interweave Antiochene doctrine with communal narratives and leadership performances. In chapter 5, we noted Theodoret's networking drive, as he reached out to distant bishops, Syrian recruits, non-Greek-speaking clerics, lay notables, and monastic leaders. This initiative was supported by his hagiographical work, which depicted some Syrian ascetics as holy, friendly to bishops, and comprehensible to the educated class. It was also supported by Theodoret's doctrinal work, which reestablished a "dual level" notion of orthodoxy—useful for connecting with Antiochene experts and the broader Nicene clergy. By 449 Theodoret was supporting his efforts with narratives of (Antiochene-centered) church history. He was also interweaving all of these elements with his own performance as a coalition-building leader. All of these cultural products served to idealize Antiochene social arrangements and to foster a sense of community. As we have noted, it is unclear how far Theodoret succeeded in inspiring his colleagues. For those who were receptive, however, Theodoret's tenets and stories supplied a ready-made partisan identity.

A fourth form of resonance is observable in Theodoret's social strategies as he pursued patronage and defended dyophysite doctrine. In chapter 6 we surveyed the patronage roles sought by bishops such as Theodoret in relation to various late Roman elites. We noted both the limitations that bishops faced and the advantages that they gained, especially if they joined a clerical network. In chapter 7, we followed Theodoret's performances as a mediator of patronage. We also traced his larger social strategy, to accumulate contacts and win a sense of inclusion. We saw how Theodoret's doctrinal involvements helped him to find patronage connections, which then protected him and his doctrinal network. We also saw how his opponents attacked his doctrinal network, in part by undercutting his performance as a patron. Much of Thodoret's advocacy work involved matters far removed from doctrinal disputation. But clearly both he and his opponents interwove their various social and doctrinal strategies.

Now we may add a fifth layer of resonance: metaphorical and narrative links between Theodoret's patronage performance and his Christology. Theodoret's version of dyophysite doctrine relies on the concept of mediation, which seems to refer to his own experience mediating favors and appeals. As we have noted, this sort of cognitive-linguistic analysis is speculative, even regarding a single theologian. It is always difficult to know how far a group shares theology. We can, however, note the potential social impact of sharing deep metaphors and basic narratives. Those who mediated patronage had a "commonsense" way to understand Theodoret's dyophysitism. Those who followed his retelling of salvation could view appeals performances as the imitation of Christ. Whenever Antiochene bishops spoke of theology they could think of shared advocacy. Whenever they joined in advocacy, they could think of their shared faith.

Individually, these instances of resonance may seem like curiosities. Collectively, they trace out a larger pattern: the interlacing of Antiochene traditions and social bonds within a mutually reinforcing dynamic. Antiochene doctrinal tropes served as signals of more than partisan alliance. These expressions developed as part of a set of socio-cultural practices. Antiochene doctrinal expressions were incorporated into leaders' efforts to weave a sense of communal identity. They helped to drive a search for the elite protection that patronage relations promised to provide. They may have drawn metaphorically on patronage relations and cast such relations as holy. By the 440s Antiochene doctrinal cues stood for a whole matrix of cultural tropes and social practices. Terms like *synkatabasis, akribeia,* and *oikonomia* connoted everything from theological learning to proper lifestyle, from good clerical management to skill as a patronage advocate. Terms such as these thus became more than signals of existing social attachments. They could inspire collaboration on ideological as well as on practical matters.

It was thus socio-cultural resonance that enabled Theodoret and some of his associates to solidify their sense of orthodoxy and their community. The reinforcing of core relationships produced a chorus of dyophysite agreement that inspired religious certainty. The mixing of patronage, friendship, and shared faith inspired the narratives and personal performances that could foster group solidarity. Resonance helps to explain why Theodoret and his closest allies seem so invested in patronage. Their performance as advocates not only secured protectors, it may have echoed their dearest theological conceptions. Resonance also helps to explain why Theodoret and some allies maintained "two natures" even when threatened with exile. This teaching not only marked relationships; it symbolized a whole complex of social life and religious community.

REVULSION: ANTI-ANTIOCHENE
SOCIO-DOCTRINAL DYNAMICS

Socio-doctrinal resonance, in my view, inspired Antiochene solidarity in the 430s and 440s at the core of Theodoret's network. But what resonates temporarily for one group of people may have different effects in another social context. Doctrinal certainty and social commitment do not always reach peripheral figures. Some combinations of doctrine and social experience have a dissonant, rather than a resonant, effect. We have seen how the core Antiochene clerics lost their wider web of contacts. Theodoret's peripheral associates did not stand firm for his doctrines, his leadership, or his vision of community.[68] Perhaps they did not feel included in his soteriological narrative or find much sense in his Christological reasoning. Meanwhile, Cyril and his allies had their own clerical alliance cemented by miaphysite doctrinal cues, and by patronage operations, which overlapped with their clerical party. They may have used their own social metaphors for Christology (though here the evidence is too thin to do more than speculate). In any case, given their visceral hostility to dyophysitism, they probably experienced their own socio-doctrinal resonance. By 449, this miaphysite network had extended even into Syria, by offering those alienated by the Antiochenes a new alternative.

Antiochene doctrine, I hold, resonated with the social relations of Theodoret and his core allies, but on the periphery of the network, such resonance was less likely. Peripheral figures shared fewer Antiochene social cues. They were, by definition, more distant from the choices of leaders. They probably felt less included in narratives about clerical forbears and less invested in partisan doctrinal goals. Theodoret and his close allies performed constantly as advocates and enacted some ambitious appeals. Most clerics could not manage mediation on such a scale. Some lacked the connections or the performance skills. Others held different ideas about how a bishop should play patron.[69] In any case, clerics who did not share Theodoret's patronage experiences would not share the same metaphorical frames, which produce ideological common sense. Nor would they be attached to his retelling of myths, which motivate collective action. Whatever resonance existed at the core of his network could dissipate in different circumstances.

The larger problem for the Antiochene network came from its opponents. As we have seen, these foes developed their own socio-doctrinal network, led by Cyril and then Dioscorus.[70] This opposition network has fewer extant records, but it clearly employed emotional signals. It also had its own doctrinal cues, such as "hypostatic union," "one incarnate nature of the divine Word," God "suffering in the flesh" and God's "divinization" of humanity.[71] As with the Antiochenes, it is telling how the friendships of famous Cyrillians aligned with doctrinal affinities.[72] Cyrillian doctrine built off the work of honored forebears such as Athanasius—though not without modifications.[73] Cyril's alliance was, of course, centered in

Egypt. In part it rested on an institutional hierarchy, with the primate supported by suffragans and monasteries.[74] From 429, Cyril reached out to clerics and monks in other regions. He helped to establish network satellites: one in Cappadocia led by Firmus of Caesarea, one in Roman Armenia led by Acacius of Melitene, one in Palestine led by Juvenal of Jerusalem, and Rabbula's circle in Osrhoene (to name a few). Alexandria, however, remained the center of the Cyrillian network, with its bishop as the clear leader and the irreplaceable hub.[75]

Parallel to this doctrinal alliance, Cyril led his own network of patronage. Less evidence survives for his network than for Theodoret's, but what remains reveals a contrast. Bishops of Alexandria used their authority to deliver grand favors. The wealth of their see allowed for direct distributions on a scale that Theodoret could never match.[76] Institutional support for the bishop of Alexandria allowed him to challenge certain prefects and (on occasion) to prevail.[77] Cyril advocated for individuals and communities. We have only his appeals for clerics,[78] but lay notables and common crowds must have turned to him for help. Cyril's authority did not give him a free hand. In Egypt he had to deal with pressure from local bishops, lower clergy, lay confraternities, and monastic leaders.[79] In other regions satellite leaders had essentially distinct patronage operations.[80] Nevertheless, patronage efforts that involved the bishop of Alexandria featured a stark display of his authority, which Theodoret, in his letter to Dioscorus, acknowledged.[81]

When Cyril explained his Christology, his words also seem to parallel his social performances. Cyril, we recall, presented a single-subject Christ, in which God was the sole director. The humanity of Christ was cast as an "instrument" of God.[82] With this explanation Cyril may well have been metaphorically referencing his own social experience. For him, God acted like the primate of Alexandria, with Christ's humanity playing the subordinate role. Cyril's God did not act alone. Holy people served as symbols of the divinization of humanity. This seems to parallel the patronage operations that Cyril and his successor directed. Again, this sort of analysis is speculative. There were many ways to explain miaphysite Christology, which did not necessarily require identical deep metaphors.[83] The clerics who (eventually) touted Cyril as a paragon of orthodoxy may or may not have worked from the same frames. Still, Cyril and the Egyptians had Christological formulas, which they regarded as self-evidently orthodox. Perhaps their commonsense theology came out of their own performances of patronage.

Before the First Council of Ephesus, Cyril and his Egyptians already had some cultural tropes and social practices that could resonate. It was, however, the reaction to dyophysite formulations that established the wider Cyrillian network. Famously Cyril responded to Nestorius with revulsion. The terminological parsing that was central to Antiochene discourse elicited in Cyril a visceral hostility.[84] Theodoret was practiced at doctrinal reticence. Yet he did eventually attack the divine-subject Christology that Egyptians saw as common sense. As we have noted, it was Syrian dissenters who laid the groundwork for overthrowing Theodoret. Some were hostile to Theodoret's behavior as a leader; some to his teachings. The dissenters may not have shared much social context with Dioscorus and his Egyptians. Once alienated from Theodoret's circle, however, these Syrians were removed from most Antiochene resonance. So they embraced the teachings and metaphors of a distant figure of authority.

By 448, Antiochene doctrine had inspired two starkly different reactions. Among some clerics, mostly in Syria, it met with approval, as a reasonable view of salvation and Christ. Among other clerics, in Egypt and elsewhere (including Syria), it caused revulsion, as a heresy and an affront to Christ. This divergence stems from two distinct threads of Nicene theology. But it may also stem from the differences in social context. Traditions that were resonant with one pattern of social interaction (at the core of the Antiochene network) proved dissonant with social arrangements in some other situations.

DIFFERENTIATION: PARTISAN NETWORKS AND THE CHRISTOLOGICAL DISPUTE

Socio-doctrinal resonance thus helps to explain the divergent reactions that greeted Theodoret's doctrinal work. More generally, it helps to explain the acrimony of the Christological dispute, within the clergy and beyond. As we have seen, the 430s and 440s featured an active socio-doctrinal network based in Syria and a wider network centered in Egypt. Each of these networks boasted a core of clerics with a shared sense of orthodoxy. Each counted critical allies in distant bishoprics, in selected monasteries, and at the imperial court. Each sought supporters based on doctrinal agreement, patronage cooperation, or both at once. On the periphery these networks were not mutually exclusive.[85] They always claimed to represent the same Nicene church. Neither network held as much influence as other social webs, such as the army or the imperial bureaucracy. From the cores of these two networks, however, the Christian world looked increasingly bifurcated. Through each episode of conflict, doctrinal arguments grew more intertwined with the social performances of clerical leaders. It was probably this link between doctrine and social conduct that extended religious divisions beyond the clergy to much of late Roman society. By 449 the conflict was more than a mismatch of Christologies. It was a clash of socio-cultural communities.

Throughout the natures dispute, we see two parties combining doctrinal causes with social pursuits. Both the Antiochenes and the Cyrillians were regionally centered. Both shared localized church customs and face-to-face contact. It is hardly surprising to find friendships and patronage ties overlapping with regional clerical groups. More surprising is how patronage and friendship intruded upon doctrinal confrontations. In chapter 7 we saw how, in 448, Theodoret and his allies were accused both of heresy and of misconduct as patrons. The whole Christological dispute, in fact, was marked by doctrinal differences that inspired denunciations of leading clerics' behavior, and feuding over patronage and social status that inspired doctrinal hostilities.

The first round of partisan conflict involved doctrinal hostilities that launched a confrontation about proper leadership. Before 428, the Antiochenes had constituted a quietly developing network. The "Cyrillian" party did not really exist yet, except as the "patriarchate" of Alexandria and, perhaps, a vague legacy of Athanasius's influence.[86] Nestorius's statements about Mary first revealed to Cyril and many clerics the Antiochenes' exacting terminology. Cyril and his new allies then accused Nestorius of heresy, while Nestorius's supporters in Syria responded in kind.[87] Once at Ephesus, however, the argument expanded to include the proper conduct of episcopal leadership. Nestorius's support from civil (and military) officials clearly offended the leaders of the "main" council. They accused him of tyranny and conspiracy.[88] Cyril's control of the council offended Nestorius and the counter-council attendees. They accused the Alexandrian bishop of "dogmatizing tyrannically instead of piously."[89] Violent confrontations only confirmed each party's fears that the other was led by dangerous men. When both sides appealed to the court, their arguments reflected divergent notions of clerical leadership. The Antiochenes claimed to represent the spirit of collaboration among learned clerics and lawful administrators. The Cyrillians claimed to represent all Christians under one legitimate (generous, gift-giving) religious authority.[90]

As conflict gave way to negotiations, leaders in each network continued to mix doctrinal argument with disputation over proper leadership. In late 432, Theodoret judged that Cyril was potentially orthodox. He accepted an ambiguity soon enshrined in the *Formula of Reunion*. Nevertheless, he rejected Cyril's "tyrannizing" and refused Cyril's communion for two more years.[91] By late 434, Theodoret had mediated an end to the schisms within Syria (apart from a few holdouts). He thus achieved informal leadership and expanded his patronage connections. His influence, however, became one of Cyril's prime targets. Cyril challenged the bishop of Cyrrhus, not just as a crypto-Nestorian, but as an insult to the see of Antioch and its rightful authority.[92] It took displays of Antiochene unity (in support of Theodore) for Cyril and his imperial backers to relent. As we have seen, it was probably Theodoret's influence that led to this display of Antiochene unity.[93] It was no doubt his court connections that helped to keep the truce that followed.

The second round of conflict also mixed Christological argument with social confrontation, as we have already seen. Theodoret reignited the Christological feud with his *Eranistes*. But as we noted, the first accusations involved patronage, especially expenditures and extraclerical connections.[94] The Second Council of Ephesus portrayed the Antiochenes as a heretical conspiracy to subvert monasteries and ensnare the laity.[95] The result was exile for Theodoret and some associates, and the virtual dissolution of their party. The leaders of the Second Council of Ephesus then faced their own criticism. Pope Leo and others accused Dioscorus of heresy and leading a "den of thieves" (Latin: *latrocinium*). The tables were turned with the death of the Emperor Theodosius II. By the fall of 451 it was Dioscorus's turn to face exile, labeled as a heretic and a tyrant.[96]

Through twenty-three years, doctrinal and social confrontations thus went hand in hand. In part this dynamic had to do with standard patterns of rhetoric. The old Roman stereotype of the tyrannical administrator could be used to demonize a suspected heretic. The ideal of the conscientious patron could be used to defend a claim to orthodoxy.[97] Rhetorical tropes, however, only work if they are plausible, and that requires a certain socio-cultural context. Resonance, of the sort discussed in this chapter, provided such a context. Among the core members of each clerical network, doctrine and social leadership would inevitably seem interwoven. Whatever challenged Theodoret's doctrine or social leadership would seem to threaten his entire socio-doctrinal effort. And whatever bolstered his teachings or influence would seem to reaffirm his community.

By the late 440s the core Cyrillian and Antiochene networks had fostered clerical cultures so different that to many participants they appeared irreconcilable. If doctrine were the only problem, the parties might have reached a new accord. Compromise formulas abounded, including the *Formula of Reunion* and Proclus's *Tome to the Armenians*. Even at Chalcedon in 451, delegates made ambiguous suggestions that followed the old agreements.[98] But compromise formulas such as these ran up against the certainty at the core of each network, a certainty that was largely a social product. In the 440s Theodoret surrounded himself with doctrinal allies, and so did Dioscorus. Each man drew visions of the past and future that celebrated his alliances. Each may have crafted Christological explanations based metaphorically on social experience. Doctrinal accords could always be reinterpreted. They could not, however, resolve a discrepancy in social roles between the patronizing patriarch (of Alexandria) and the mediating (Syrian) bishop. Each network leader witnessed the other attacking symbols at the heart of his communal identity. Each claimed the other was assaulting a commonsense truth. It is difficult to determine how widely doctrinal certainty was shared within each network, but the core of each party remained committed after many allies had abandoned its cause.

The acrimony of clerical divisions, of course, raises another question: why would people other than committed partisans care so much about Christ's natures? Perhaps some did not, but plenty of monks, lower clerics, officials, soldiers, notables, and ordinary laypeople followed a party in the conflict. Scholars have suggested various explanations, from civic and congregational loyalties, to divisions among linguistic groups; from the link between Christology and liturgical performances to the involvement of monks widely considered holy.[99]

The argument of this book suggests another explanation for wider doctrinal partisanship: the interconnections between doctrine and social relations. Doctrinal expertise was largely confined to clerics and learned monks. A few hundred partisans incubated Christological teachings. Bonds of friendship and patronage, however, situated party experts within late Roman society. Bishops served as teachers, liturgical leaders, pastoral caregivers, legal arbitrators, charity distributors, community organizers, and voices of appeal. For lay Christians, choosing a doctrinal side meant more than congregational devotion. Pronouncing doctrinal formulas was a convenient way to respond to a bishop's favors, with an unmistakable display of loyalty. And yet, these pronouncements were not just part of some crude quid pro quo. As we have seen, the theological formulas stood for a whole resonating complex of traditions and relationships. Not only did they secure real benefits; they promised a sense of religious certainty, and of inclusion among the truly orthodox.[100] Neither the Antiochenes nor their opponents had the means to compel belief in a given theology. But they did have something powerful to offer: inclusion within a supportive network of faith.

The natures dispute of the 430s and 440s thus features more than divergent doctrines; it presents a clash of socio-cultural experiences and nascent communities. On the periphery of each network it was possible to accept old compromises. But within the core of each network, the compromises were insufficient. Leadership customs, history, patronage, and doctrine reinforced one another. Encircling relationships gave leaders the sense that they had deep support, while limiting their contact with other perspectives. Neither Theodoret's network nor that of his opponents formed institutions in the 430s and 440s (separate churches were a later creation). Both parties sought to control the same Nicene clerical hierarchy. Both were soon transformed by the upheavals that they initiated, as we shall see.[101] But even temporary socio-doctrinal resonance had profound consequences. Our sources reveal the intensity of the Christological conflict for a few hundred active participants. It is the development of socio-doctrinal networks that created this intensity, and spread it to a wider slice of late Roman society.

Epilogue

The Council of Chalcedon
and the Antiochene Legacy

And so this book ends where it began, with the Council of Chalcedon, a moment of reckoning for the Antiochene network. The gathering in 451 did not end Theodoret's career. One letter and a heresy catalog reveal his further efforts to claim influence.[1] Nor did the council end the conflicts over Christology, which raged for three centuries. The meeting in Chalcedon, however, redrew clerical relations throughout the Eastern Mediterranean. The social dynamics of Chalcedon are too complicated to be fully covered in this volume. Here we shall merely glance at the positioning of known Antiochenes in relation to the council. On the one hand, the council accepted at least two forms of dyophysitism, which met the approval of most Antiochenes. It directly blessed Theodoret, returning him and some allies to their sees. On the other hand, the synod rearranged most of Theodoret's social project. The Antiochenes were split up and subsumed within larger networks, leaving a fragmented but important legacy.

The Council of Chalcedon interests historians and theologians for a number of reasons. Greatest attention has fallen on three elements: its processes, its theological judgments, and its administrative rulings. Most obviously, Chalcedon set new conciliar practices. Virtually all bishops were invited to the council and allowed to express grievances, but the proceedings would be tightly organized by imperial lay officials. It was these lay commissioners who arranged for the delegates to condemn Dioscorus. It was they who screened doctrinal statements and selected the authors of all rulings.[2] Famously the council reframed heresy and orthodoxy. Nestorianism and Eutycheanism were condemned as opposite heresies. Cyril, Flavian of Constantinople, and Pope Leo were treated as touchstones of true faith. The verbal differences that separated these authors (and their supporters) were elided when the bishops shouted "Leo and Cyril teach the same."[3] Finally, Chalcedon reorganized the clerical hierarchy. Most monasteries were officially subjected to the oversight of local bishops.[4] Suffragans were more often subordinated to the authority of metropolitans. And nearly all bishops were placed under five patriarchs, who were now assigned clear jurisdictions.[5] The procedures and rulings of the council inspired immediate hostility, especially in monasteries. Juvenal of Jerusalem was chased away by murderous rioting monks (some apparently allied with Empress Eudocia).[6] The new patriarch of Alexandria was greeted by riots, until thousands of soldiers intervened.[7] Scholars who have examined the council rulings have offered elaborate (and divergent) analyses. Few have looked closely at the central role of the Antiochenes, and the thoroughly conflicted effect on their socio-doctrinal legacy.[8]

In many ways the Council of Chalcedon vindicated Theodoret and his teachings. Not only did the commissioners declare Theodoret and some allies orthodox; they guided theological discussions to a statement that looks Antiochene. It was just minutes into the first session when Theodoret entered. Amid threatening shouts the commissioners insisted that he be seated. The only obvious cost to him came a few days later: the public condemnation of Nestorius.[9] Theodoret coordinated with Hiba, John of Germanicea, and a few other core Antiochenes. Critically, these partisans retained the support of General Anatolius, the prime council organizer, along with other commissioners.[10] Theodoret played little role in drafting the council's (suppressed) first statement of faith, but he and his allies pushed for revisions.[11] The result was a sort of dyophysite formula: "one (*hypostasis* of) Christ made known in two natures." The delegates acclaimed this phrase as Cyril's teaching (once prompted by the lay commissioners).[12] The formula did not fully match Theodoret's preferences, but it was acceptable with interpretive tweaking. That tweaking came in the form of Pope Leo's *Tome*, now labeled as orthodox. By the end of the council Theodoret was treating this *Tome* as an official statement of faith. Thus he defended the council to skeptical allies as an embrace of Antiochene teachings.[13]

And yet, the council of Chalcedon was not a complete triumph for Theodoret's network. It reshaped some parts of the Antiochene socio-doctrinal dynamic. For starters, the council altered Antiochene patterns of relations within the clergy. Theodoret and his clerical allies had fostered a broad informal network, centered on bishops. See-based primacy mattered, but so did centrality, experience, and expertise. The new canons on metropolitans and patriarchs cut at these leadership traditions. Bishops could have resisted these rulings; throughout the controversy they kept building doctrinal networks. But now they had to contend with a more centralized vision of regional authority, and beyond that a broader institutional frame. In any case, Theodoret and his core allies owed their jobs to the council: they were in no position to dismiss its decrees.

The Council of Chalcedon also hindered traditional Antiochene relations between clerics and monasteries. Theodoret's network had maintained interdependent links with a few favorite monastic houses. The rest were pushed aside or ignored. The new canons on monastic subordination posited a more comprehensive dynamic. Clerics and monks could have ignored this ruling. In future decades some monasteries would grow in their attachment to particular parties of bishops. Just like clerics, however, monks now confronted clearer marks of hierarchy within a larger institutional system. Again, Theodoret and his associates were too dependent on the council to object.

Finally, the council exacerbated divisions within the Syrian episcopate. Partly the divisions came from the council's limited restoration of core Antiochenes. Some bishops, like Domnus, were called orthodox but urged to retire. Others, like Irenaeus, were treated as heretics (somewhat arbitrarily). These exiles formed a small shadow network of true believers, who seem to have resented Theodoret's latest compromises.[14] Partly the divisions had to do with sudden doctrinal reversals. Many bishops, such as Basil of Seleucia, had switched from the Antiochenes, to the miaphysites, to the Chalcedonian settlement within just two years. Basil parsed his words carefully each time; others were less precise. Either way, the shifts strained relations with congregants and fellow clerics, both those who had held fast and those who had floated with the tide.[15] A larger chasm in the Syrian clergy divided old Antiochenes from newer bishops, appointed by Dioscorus and his lieutenants. Maximus of Antioch and Photius of Tyre may have forsworn their Egyptian mentor.[16] They still held their own alliances and owed little to the Antiochenes. Tense divisions were nothing new to Syrian clerics. Theodoret may have again tried to mediate, to maintain a firmly dyophysite network. But this time it would be more difficult to corral clerics or speak for the entire Roman East.

The Council of Chalcedon rearranged Antiochene socio-doctrinal dynamics by placing dyophysite doctrine in a new social context. Theodoret had tried to give coherence to his network, with historical narratives, leadership, and (perhaps) social referents for Christology. The result was greater theological certainty and, temporarily, greater solidarity.[17] The council recognized neither the social patterns, nor the social metaphors that, I suggest, informed Antiochene theology. The result was a fracturing of the network. Some core members were forced into the shadows, others were absorbed into the Chalcedonian coalition. Many were no doubt confused and caught in between.

It thus may be understandable how, over the next four decades, the dyophysite coalition lost its hold on Syria. In 457, Emperor Marcian died, and supporters of Chalcedon faced a major test. A cabal of Egyptian monks and bishops seized the moment to consecrate Timothy the Cat as an anti-Chalcedonian patriarch of Alexandria. A few weeks later the old pro-Chalcedonian patriarch was lynched in the streets.[18] Leo, the new emperor, called for an episcopal plebiscite on recent events and councils. Most responding bishops opposed Timothy and affirmed Chalcedon, but Syrian bishops were no longer driving the cause.[19] In 458, Hiba of Edessa died, to be succeeded by Nonnus, his onetime replacement (449–451). Invoking the memory of Rabbula, Nonnus led the bishops of Osrhoene to reject Chalcedon.[20] The 470s saw the return of competing episcopal claimants in Antioch and other towns.[21] And the 480s marked a tipping point. Emperor Zeno backed an "Edict of Oneness" (*Henotikon*), which avoided explicit dyophysitism. The anti-Chalcedonian Peter the Fuller agreed to this compromise and won support as patriarch of Antioch. Several Syrian dyophysites assembled in opposition to Peter. But they were soon ousted, accused of backing a failed imperial usurper.[22] After 485 the churches of Euphratensis were led by Philoxenus, a Syriac-writing miaphysite. Some Syrian socio-doctrinal traditions were clearly contiguous. But when Philoxenus dealt with other clerics, he deemphasized "exactness" (Syriac: *hatitutha;* Greek: *akribeia*) and stressed "flexibility" (Syriac *mdabranutha;* Greek: *oikonomia*). Theodoret's favorite symbolic formula had been reversed.[23]

The long-term outcome of the Christological dispute was the forming of separate churches. The old miaphysite network struggled. But eventually it grew into an anti-Chalcedonian communion, linking Egyptians with Ethiopians and Armenians as well as with many Syrians.[24] The old dyophysite network was split and subsumed into two larger groupings. Some joined Justinian's Neo-Chalcedonian community. The cost, in this case, was to condemn Theodore of Mopsuestia and other parts of the Antiochene heritage.[25] A few committed dyophysites ended up within the Church of the East. Somehow the scattered Antiochene links to Persian Mesopotamia inspired a growing devotion there to Theodore's teachings.[26] By 486, the Church of the East had doctrinally differentiated from its Roman counterpart. By the late sixth century, Roman clerics had begun to form parallel Chalcedonian and miaphysite hierarchies.[27] Some scholars have tried to explain this outcome by contrasting supposedly popular Cyrillians in the 430s and 440s to supposedly isolated Antiochenes.[28] We should be wary of such teleological reasoning. Theodoret's network appears as robust and well connected as the opposition. His patronage might have won him deeper (doctrinal) support if his core group had not been attacked so systematically. In any case, it was the Council of Chalcedon that framed the new confrontations and new socio-doctrinal possibilities.

The Council of Chalcedon thus left Theodoret's network with a fragmented, but important legacy. His network, which had ignited the dispute, made a scattered impact within larger institutions. Theodoret's efforts were not fully celebrated by any of the three churches. Miaphysite churches treated him as a dangerous heretic. The Church of the East barely remembered him. Chalcedonian churches preserved most of his works, with the warning not to trust everything he said.[29] Under the surface, however, Theodoret's network had already reshaped the experience of clerical community. Theodoret and his foes set parameters for ongoing debates. Later clerics would build their theology from Cyril's or Theodoret's formulations (aware or unaware of their influences). More important, these networks made doctrine part of a larger socio-cultural dynamic. Theodoret's network was temporary. It was often overshadowed by other centers of influence. But Theodoret's party was followed by new socio-doctrinal networks, with grander organizing plans. Theodoret and his people demonstrated the solidarity made possible by interweaving patronage, friendship, and faith.

NOTES

INTRODUCTION

1. Price and Gaddis, *Acts of Chalcedon,* 3:193–203, estimate the number of voting delegates at 370, including those represented by proxy.

2. *Acta concilii Chalcedonensis* session 1 (*ACO* II.1.1: 70).

3. For more on these famous episodes, see chapters 4–5.

4. On the seating arrangement, see Price and Gaddis, *Acts of Chalcedon,* 1:42–43. On the geographical terms "Syria" and "the East," see later in this chapter.

5. See Cyril of Alexandria, *Ep. ad Succensum episc. Diocaesareae,* sec. 2–3 (CPG #5346, *ACO* I.1.6: 158–59). The term miaphysite is now preferred because "monophysite" served as an inconsistent label of heresy. In this study miaphysite refers not just to those tarred as heretics, but to anyone who preferred to discuss "one nature" in Christ.

6. See Theodore of Mopsuestia, *Homiliae catecheticae* 3 (Mingana: 141, tr. Mingana: 37). In this book, "Antiochene" always refers to this doctrinal party; for the sake of clarity it is never herein used as a geographical label.

7. For a full discussion of these Trinitarian debates, see Hanson, *Search,* esp. chaps. 10–12. For a summary, see J. N. D. Kelly, *Early Christian Doctrines,* 240–69.

8. Sullivan, *Christology of Theodore,* 162; Greer, *Theodore,* 48–49; Norris, *Manhood and Christ,* 207–9.

9. On the Antiochenes' exegetical focus, see Greer, *Theodore: Exegete and Theologian.* Wilken, "Tradition, Exegesis."

10. On Cyril of Alexandria's pursuit of a direct, if mysterious, statement that Christ was God and yet human, see McGuckin, *St. Cyril,* esp. 175–89. See also Gavrilyuk, *Suffering of the Impassible God,* chap. 6.

11. Nestorius, *Liber Heraclidis* (tr. Hodgson and Driver, 98–101); Eusebius of Dorylaeum, *Contestatio* (CPG #5940, *ACO* I.1.1: 101–2).

12. For Cyril's attack on Nestorius, see his *Ep. ad Caelestinum papam* (CPG #5310, *ACO* I.1.5: 10–12); *Commonitorium ad Posidonium diaconum* (CPG #5311, *ACO* I.1.7: 171–72); *Ep. ad Nestorium (una cum synodo Alexandrina)* (CPG #5317, *ACO* I.1.1: 33–42). For Syrian replies, see Theodoret, *Impugnatio xii anathematismorum Cyrilli* (CPG #6214, *ACO* I.1.6: 108–44); Andreas, *Impugnatio xii anathematismorum Cyrilli Alexandrini* (CPG #6373, *ACO* I.1.7: 33–65).

13. Theodosius II, *Sacra ad Cyrillum Alex. et ad singulos metropolitas* (CPG #8652, *ACO* I.1.1: 114–16). On the council, see Hiba of Edessa, *Ep. ad Marim Persam* (CPG #6500, *ACO* II.1.3: 33). On the colloquy in Chalcedon, see John of Antioch et al., *Contestio secunda ad Theodosium et Valentinianum imp. aug.* (CPG #6330: *ACO* I.1.7: 75).

14. On the protests, see Theodoret, *Commonitorium ad Alexandrum Hierapolitanum* (CPG #6243, *ACO* I.4: 87); John of Antioch, *Ep. ad clerum populumque Tarsensem* (CPG #6348, *ACO* I.4: 90); *Ep. ad Alexandrum Hierapolitanum* (CPG #6303, *ACO* I.4: 113); Cyril, *Commonitorium ad Maximum diac. Antioch.* (CPG #5357, *CVatGr 1431*: 21).

15. Theodosius II, *Sacra ad Iohannem Antiochenum* (CPG #8810, *ACO* I.1.4: 3–5); *Sacra ad Symeonem Stylitem* (CPG #8811, *ACO* I.1.4: 5). For threats against holdouts, see Theodosius II, *Sacra a Iohanne Antiocheno impetrata contra Alexandrum, Helladium, Maximianum et Theodoretum* (CPG #6423, *ACO* I.4: 166–67).

16. On opponents of the *Formula of Reunion,* see chapter 4.

17. On suspicions of Theodoret, see Cyril, *Ep. ad Acacium Melitenum* (CPG #5369, *CVatGr 1431*:15–16), and see chapter 5. On divisions in Syria, see Rabbula of Edessa, *Ep. ad Cyrillum Alexandrinum* (CPG #6494, *ACO* IV.1: 89).

18. For Theodoret's new dyophysite apology, see his *Eranistes* (see below, chapter 8). The point at which Eutyches first faced criticism is not clear; see Bevan and Gray, "Trial of Eutyches." For the accusations against Theodoret and his allies, see Theodoret, *ep.* S 110 (SC 111:38–42); *Acta concilii Chalcedonensis* session 11 (*ACO* II.1.3: 24–26); Dioscorus, *Ep. ad Domnum Antiochenum* (CPG #5456; Flemming: 132–39; tr. Perry: 327–38).

19. For the trial of Eutyches, see *Acta concilii Chalcedonensis,* session 1 (*ACO* II.1.1: 100–147). For Theodosius II's doctrinal shift, see session 1 (*ACO* II.1.1: 150–78).

20. For the rehabilitation of Eutyches, see *Acta concilii Chalcedonensis* session 1 (*ACO* II.1.1: 141, 182–86). For the condemnation of Theodoret and his allies, see session 1 (*ACO* II.1.1: 191–96) and *Syriac Acts of the Second Council of Ephesus* (Flemming: 60–128; tr. Perry: 134–318). Flavian died in custody; see Chadwick, "Death of Flavian."

21. Marcian, *Ep. ad Leonem papam* (*ACO* II.1.1: 18); *Acta concilii Chalcedonensis* session 1 (*ACO* II.1.1: 70).

22. For praise of Cyril, see *Acta concilii Chalcedonensis* session "3," 5 (*ACO* II.1.2: 80–81, 126–29). For the new dyophysite formula, see session 5 (*ACO* II.1.2: 129). On Eutyches and Dioscorus, see session "2," 5 (*ACO* II.1.2: 8–29, 124–27).

23. Zacharias Rhetor, *HE* 3.3 (CSCO SS 38:155–57); Evagrius Scholasticus, *HE* 2.5 (Fontes Christiani 57: 226–32).

24. For more on the (later) formation of three separate churches, see Frend, *Monophysite Movement,* chap. 6; Moeller, "Chalcédonisme;" Gray, *Defense of Chalcedon,* esp. chap. 6; Brock, "Church of the East." See Epilogue.

25. On the landscape, climate, and settlement of Syria, see Tchalenko, *Villages antiques,* esp. chaps. 1–3; Downey, *History of Antioch,* chap. 1; Tate, *Campagnes de Syrie,* esp. chap. 4; Millar, *Roman Near East,* esp. chaps. 7–12; Casana, "Archaeological Landscape."

26. On the urban population of Syria, see Liebeschuetz, *Decline,* 54–74, 169. On the large, unplanned villages in Syria, see Wickham, *Framing the Early Middle Ages,* 442–59.

27. On the expansion of agricultural villages in Syria, see Tchalenko, *Villages antiques,* esp. 44–45, 75–91; Tate, *Campagnes de Syrie,* esp. 184–88, 257–58, 303–31; and Wickham, *Framing the Early Middle Ages,* 442–59. On settlement expansion in the vicinity of Antioch, see Casana, "Archaeological Landscape."

28. On the status of senatorial elites, local notables, and middling freeholders, see Heather, "Senates and Senators;" Liebeschuetz, *Decline,* chap. 3; and Wickham, *Framing the Early Middle Ages,* 158–68, 239–51, 442–59.

29. On Roman political structures, see Jones, *LRE,* esp. chaps. 11–14, 16, 19. On the imperial administration, see also C. Kelly, *Ruling the Roman Empire,* chaps. 1–2. On municipal administration, see also Petit, *La vie municipale;* Laniado, *Notables municipaux;* Liebeschuetz, *Antioch,* chaps. 4–5; *Decline,* chaps. 3, 5. On the coherence of the Eastern Roman government, see Millar, *Greek Roman Empire,* chaps. 1–3.

30. On Sassanid Persia, see Howard-Johnson, "Great Powers in Late Antiquity." On the Eastern army, see Treadgold, *Byzantium and its Army,* esp. 43–59, 87–93; Isaac, *Limits of Empire,* esp. chaps. 3–4, 6. On imperial attention in Syria, see Millar, *Greek Roman Empire,* 69–76. On limited warfare, see Greatrex, "Two Fifth-Century Wars." Raiding Isaurians and distant Huns fostered worries; see Millar, *Greek Roman Empire,* chap. 2.

31. On the demographic history of Syria, see Millar, *Roman Near East,* chaps. 1–4. Major spoken languages were Greek, Aramaic/Syriac, Armenian, Arabic, and Hebrew. See Millar, "Ethnic identity" and *Greek Roman Empire,* chap. 3; Brock, "Greek and Syriac;" Garsoïan, *L'église arménienne,* esp. intro, chap. 1.

32. On Hellenistic influence in western Syria, see Millar, *Roman Near East,* chaps. 7–8.

33. On the impact of local rule in Syria, see Millar, *Roman Near East,* chaps. 1–5. On Syriac written culture, see Millar, "Ethnic Identity," but also Brock, "Greek and Syriac." On early Armenian writings, see Garsoïan, *L'église arménienne,* 67–70.

34. See Bowersock, *Hellenism,* esp. chap 2.

35. On Magians in Syria, see Basil *ep.* 258 (LCL 4:45–47). On Manichees, see Lieu, *Manichaeism.* On pagan theurgists' presence, see Bowersock, *Hellenism,* 31–33. On Jews' presence, see Meeks and Wilken, *Jews and Christians in Antioch;* Hezser, *Rabbinic Movement,* esp. 162–63; Gafni, *Land, Center and Diaspora.*

36. See Trombley, *Hellenic Religion and Christianization,* esp. chaps. 8, 10.

37. On urban congregations, see Maxwell, *Christianization and Communication,* esp. chap. 3. On the rarity of village clerics in Syria, see Trombley, *Hellenic Religion and Christianization,* chaps. 8, 10; "Christian demography." On wandering rural preachers, see Brown, "Town, Village and Holy Man;" Caner, *Wandering Begging Monks,* chap. 2.

38. On the development of the monastic movement in Syria, see chapter 3.

39. On Greek-Syriac cultural differences, see Stewart, *Working the Earth of the Heart,* chap. 5; Harvey, "Sense of a Stylite." On Syrian theological diversity, see Murray, *Symbols of Church and Kingdom,* 6–7; Griffith, "Ephrem the Deacon."

40. See Rapp, *Holy Bishops*, chap. 6.

41. See chapter 6.

42. All knowledge of Theodoret's early life comes from his *HR* 9.4–15, 12.4, 13.16–17 (SC 234:412–34, 464–66, 502–8) and his *epp.* S 79–81 (SC 98:182–98), S 113, 116 (SC 111:56–66, 68–72). A wide reading list is clear from his *Graecarum affectionum curatio*.

43. See chapters 5–7. On Theodoret's upbringing, see Leroy-Molinghen, "Naissance et enfance." On his bilingualism, see Millar, "Theodoret." On his death, see Azéma, "Date de la mort."

44. On the record-keeping practices of church councils, see Lim, *Public Disputation*, 217–30; Sillett, "Culture of Controversy," chap. 1; Millar, *Greek Roman Empire*, 235–42.

45. See *ACO* I.1–4. On the transmission of *acta* from the First Council of Ephesus, see Galtier, "Le centenaire d'Éphese;" Devreesse, "Les actes du concile d'Éphese;" and Sillett, "Culture of Controversy," chap. 1.

46. For the two half-transcripts from Ephesus in 449, see *ACO* II.1.1 (tr. Price and Gaddis, *Acts of Chalcedon*, vol. 1) and Flemming (tr. Perry).

47. See *ACO* II.1–5 (tr. Price and Gaddis, *Acts of Chalcedon*).

48. On these topics in Theodoret's letters, with comparisons, see chapters 1, 6, and 7.

49. This number does not include those letters of Pope Leo I and Emperor Theodosius II (and his officials) that dealt with unrelated topics.

50. Irenaeus of Tyre collected nearly 150 letters while in exile (435–443, or after 448) as part of a larger set of conciliar documents geared to show how the pure dyophysite teaching was betrayed by Christian leaders. His work, the *Tragoedia*, was then found in the mid-sixth century by Rusticus, a deacon of Rome, who translated large portions in order to write a point-by-point refutation. Only this edited translation survives, as the *Collectio Casiniensis*. For more on the textual history, see Schwartz, in *ACO* I.4 vii–xx.

51. Theodoret's letters present a peculiar textual transmission history. One of the two surviving textual traditions, *Collectio Patmensis* (first published by Sakkelion in 1885), features 52 letters from a single manuscript. The other, *Collectio Sirmondiana* (first published by Sirmond in 1642) , features 146 letters from numerous manuscripts, but it repeats only five entries from *Patmensis*. These represent a small fraction of the more than 500 letters reportedly available in medieval Constantinople (see Nikephoros Kallistos, *Historia* 14.54, *PG* 146:1257). On the textual history of Theodoret's letters, see Azéma, *Théodoret Correspondance* (SC 40:66–72; SC 98:9–18).

52. The letters of Firmus survive in one tenth-century manuscript. For more on the textual history, see Calvet-Sebasti and Gatier, *Firmus de Césarée, Lettres*, 8–18.

53. For a summary of evidentiary issues, see Millar, *Greek Roman Empire*, Appendix A.

54. On the limits of letters as evidence, see Mullett, *Theophylact*, 42–44.

55. On the major studies of these works, see esp. chapters 3, 5, 8.

56. For lists of Theodoret's exegesis, see Guinot, *L'éxegèse de Théodoret*, 41–64. On Theodore's corpus, see Greer, *Theodore: Exegete and Theologian;* Zaharopoulos, *Theodore on the Bible*.

57. Most important are the works of Socrates, Sozomen, Philostorgius, and Theodoret.

58. The era also produced the *Historia lausiaca* and *Dialogus de vita Ioannis Chrysostomi* by Palladius of Helenopolis, the anonymous *Vita Barsaumae*, and the anonymous *Vita Alexandri acoemetae*. On the major studies of these works, see chapters 3–5.

59. On archaeological finds in and near Antioch, see Dobbins, "Houses;" Kondoleon, "Mosaics;" J. Russell, "Household Furnishings;" and Vermeule, "Sculptures." See also Liebeschuetz, *Decline,* 54–74; Casana, "Archaeological landscape," 117–20. On the remains of Cyrrhus, see Frezouls, "L'exploration archéologique de Cyrrhus" and "Recherches historiques et archéologiques." For surveys of rural Syria, see Tchalenko, *Villages antiques;* Tate, *Campagnes de Syrie;* and Casana, "Archeological Landscape." On relevant Syrian inscriptions, see Trombley, "Christian Demography."

60. Noted by Millar, *Greek Roman Empire,* 236.

61. Notable studies include Schwartz, *Konzilstudien;* Devreesse, *Essai sur Théodore;* Richard, "L'évolution doctrinale;" Sullivan, *Christology of Theodore;* D. Wallace-Hadrill, *Christian Antioch;* Grillmeier, *Christ;* J.N.D. Kelly, *Early Christian Doctrines;* Norris, *Manhood and Christ;* Young, *From Nicaea to Chalcedon;* McGuckin, *St. Cyril;* O'Keefe, "Kenosis or Impassibility;" Fairbairn, *Grace and Christology;* Clayton, *Christology of Theodoret.*

62. On church-state institutional politics, see Jones, *LRE,* 874–94, 933–37; Rapp, *Holy Bishops,* esp. chap. 8; Millar, *Greek Roman Empire,* chaps. 4–6; Norton, *Episcopal Elections.* On church resources, see Jones, *LRE,* 894–910; Wipszycka, *Ressources;* Rapp, *Holy Bishops,* esp. chap. 7. On clerics' social background, see Jones, *LRE,* 920–29; Rapp, *Holy Bishops,* esp. chap. 6. On relations with local communities, see Garnsey and Woolf, "Patronage of the Rural Poor;" Tompkins, "Relations;" Van Dam, *Becoming Christian,* 25–45; Mayer, "Patronage, Pastoral Care;" Rapp, *Holy Bishops,* esp. chap. 9.

63. E.g., Brown, *Power and Persuasion,* chaps. 2–3 and *Poverty and Leadership;* Sterk, *Renouncing the World;* Maxwell, *Christianization and Communication;* Gaddis, "No Crime;" Rapp, *Holy Bishops;* Harvey, "Sense of a Stylite" and "The Stylite's Liturgy."

64. On Theodoret's doctrine and exegesis, see esp. Guinot, *L'exegèse de Théodoret;* Clayton, *Christology of Theodoret;* Leppin, "Zum kirchenpolitischen Kontext." On his social relations, see esp. Canivet, *Monachisme syrien;* Tompkins, "Relations." On his cultural endeavors, see Urbainczyk, *Theodoret;* but also Krueger, *Writing and Holiness;* Sillett, "Culture of Controversy;" and Papadoyannakis, "Christian Therapeia."

65. See, e.g., McGuckin, *St. Cyril* (which dismisses criticism of Cyril's ambition for power) and Rapp, *Holy Bishops* (which does not explore bishops' doctrinal authority).

66. Examples of interdisciplinary work include Young, *Biblical Exegesis;* Wessel, *Cyril of Alexandria;* Lim, *Public Disputation;* Brown, *Poverty and Leadership;* Gaddis, "No Crime;" Millar, *Greek Roman Empire;* and Sillett, "Culture of Controversy."

67. E.g., Geertz, "Religion as a Cultural System;" Douglas, *Natural Symbols.* For a cognitivist's critique of Geertz's definition, see Pyysiäinen, *How Religion Works,* chap. 3.

68. E.g., Foucault, *Archaeology,* chap. 3, or, regarding late Roman religion, Boyarin, *Border Lines.* For critiques of post-structuralism, see Douglas, *How Institutions Think,* 45–53, 69–90; Ramachandran, *Tour of Human Consciousness,* chap. 4, esp. 80–82.

69. See Boyer, *Naturalness of Religious Ideas,* esp. chaps. 1, 4, 6; Guthrie, *Faces in the Clouds;* Pyysiäinen, *How Religion Works.* For a critique of cognitivist perspectives, see Laidlaw, "Problems with the Cognitive Science of Religion."

70. Polletta, "Contending Stories." See also Somers, "Narrative Constitution of Identity," esp. 616–35; H. White, "Value of Narrativity."

71. Lakoff, *Moral Politics,* esp. chaps. 1–6.

72. Bourdieu, *Outline*, esp. chaps. 2, 4; Alexander "Cultural Pragmatics." See also Goffman, *Forms of Talk*, introduction. Regarding late Roman religion, see Burrus, "In the Theatre of this Life."

73. Sociologists Rodney Stark and William Bainbridge applied network concepts to several religious movements (e.g., "Networks of Faith: Interpersonal Bonds").

74. E.g., Boissevain, *Friends of Friends*, chaps. 2–3, 5. Similar selection methods were used by historians E. Clark (*Origenist Controversy*, chap. 1) and Mullett (*Theophylact*, part 1).

75. For early work on communication as a trading of symbolic cues, see Blumer, *Symbolic Interactionism.* For an updated perspective, see J. Alexander, "Cultural Pragmatics."

76. There are, in fact, several sorts of centrality measured by network analysts. The type of centrality discussed herein is "closeness centrality," which involves measuring the sum of distances (number of links) between a given node and all other nodes in the network. See Wasserman and Faust, *Social Network Analysis*, 184–87.

77. On the methods of network analysis, see Scott, *Social Network Analysis;* Wasserman and Faust, *Social Network Analysis.* For the popularizing of some of these terms, see Shils, *Center and Periphery.*

78. On friendship, see Boissevain, *Friends of Friends*, chap. 5. For a broader survey, see Eisenstadt and Roniger, *Patrons, Clients and Friends*, chaps. 1–2. On patronage, see Boissevain, chap. 6. For a cross-cultural survey, see Eisenstadt and Roniger, chap. 4.

79. See Boissevain, *Friends of Friends*, chaps. 5–7.

80. McLean, *Art of the Network*, chap. 1, frames these issues differently. In his view, people perform roles "aspirationally," based on the positions that they wish to assume.

81. Barabási, *Linked*, esp. 86–92, 226–38. Modular refers to the tendency of people to form cliques by bonding with friends of friends. "Scale-free" is a descriptive term tied to the tendency of people to prefer to attach to the well-connected. If these assumptions are modeled, they produce relational systems in which the number of people (N) who possess a certain number of links (k) has a power-law relationship to that number of links (or $N(k) = ak^{-\gamma}$, with a and γ as constants). See also Watts, *Six Degrees*, chaps. 3–4, 8.

82. Barabási, *Linked*, 109–22. Watts, *Six Degrees*, 188–94.

83. E. Clark, *Origenist Controversy* did network analysis to give context for the "cultural construction" of doctrine. Hezser, *Rabbinic Movement*, linked network structures to the patterns of discourse in rabbinic literature. Mullett, *Theophylact*, used network maps to explore the way letters convey a sense of the authorial self.

84. Ruffini, *Social Networks in Byzantine Egypt.* See esp. his introduction.

85. Paul McLean has also combined network theory and "performative" sociology to study patronage in renaissance Florence (*Art of the Network*, esp. chap. 1).

CHAPTER 1. TRACES OF A NETWORK: FRIENDSHIP, DOCTRINE, AND CLERICAL COMMUNICATION, 423–451

1. Acacius was ordained in 379, and Theodoret (*HR* 2.9, SC 234:214–16) claimed that he served for fifty-eight years. Some scholars (e.g., McGuckin, *St. Cyril*, 110–13) date his death to 433, since none of his letters survive thereafter.

2. E.g., Balai, who wrote five Syriac *madrashe* in Acacius's honor (Overbeck: 259–69).

3. Theodoret, *HR* 2.9 (SC 234:214–16).

4. On Acacius as Theodoret's mentor, see Theodoret, *ep.* S 75 (SC 98:106–62), On Acacius as Rabbula of Edessa's mentor, see *Chronicon Edessenum* year 723 = A.D. 412, CSCO SS 1.4:6).

5. See chapters 3–4.

6. *Philia* actually carries a broader range of meanings than just "friendship." For a discussion of *philos* and its derivatives, see Konstan, *Friendship*, esp. 53–92.

7. Some observers have scrutinized concepts like *philia* and *agapē* and found incompatible terminologies (e.g., Kierkegaard, *Works of Love*, 280–82, 288–91). Others point to the ready combination of such terms (e.g., C. White, *Christian Friendship*, chaps. 3–5).

8. Some claim letters were too formulaic for honest emotions (e.g., Jones, *LRE*, 1009). Others find them reliably genuine (e.g., Van Dam, *Families and Friends*, esp. 129–38).

9. Direct commands of *agapē* to fellow humans: *Constitutiones apostolorum*, 1.2, 2.3, 2.20, 2.25, 2.28, 2.49 (SC 320:109, 148, 196–98, 228, 244, 294); 3.19, 4.12, 6.23, 6.29 (SC 329:162, 190–92, 368–70, 386–88); 7.2, 7.5 (SC 336:26, 34). On the dating of this text, see Metzger, *Les constitutions apostoliques*, 14–24, 54–62.

10. *Agapē*: E.g., Theodoret, *ep.* P 1, P 15, P 30, P 43 (SC 40:74, 86–87, 96, 106–8), S 2, S 24, S 56, S 62, S 75 (SC 98:20–22, 80–82, 132, 140–42. 160–62). Fatherly affection: *epp.* P 28, P 32, P 45 (SC 40:95, 98, 109–11). For more on *agapē* as a preferred term in Christian correspondence, see Konstan, *Friendship*, 149–61, 173.

11. E.g., Theodoret, *epp.* P 1–2, P 4, P 15, P 22, P 41, P 43, P 49 (SC 40:74–75, 77, 86, 92–94, 105, 106–8, 119), S 4, S 11, S 25, S 38–39, S 49–50, S 54–55, S 60, S 74, S 77–78 (SC 98:30, 38–40, 82–84, 102–4, 124–26, 132, 136–38, 160, 166–82).

12. See Teeter, "Christian Letters of Recommendation."

13. John Chrysostom, *De sacerdotio* 2.1–2, 6.5–7 (SC 272:100–106, 320–30).

14. Bishops: *Constitutiones apostolorum* 2.25 (SC 320:230–32); priests and deacons: 2.26–32 (SC 320:236–52); bishop like God, deacon like prophet: 2.30 (SC 320:248).

15. Plato, *Lysis*, esp. 221b–d.

16. Aristotle, *Ethica Nicomachea*, esp. 8.iii.6, 8.vi.7, 8.xiv.1 (ed. Burnet, 1156b, 1158b, 1163a–b). See Konstan, *Friendship*, chap. 2.

17. (Pseudo-) Demetrius, *De elocutione* 223–240 (LCL: Aristotle, *The Poetics*, 438–448). See also Malherbe, *Ancient Epistolary Theorists*.

18. Synesius of Cyrene, *ep.* 51 (ed. Garzya, 90–91) to Theotimus (poet in Constantinople).

19. See Børtnes, "Eros Transformed," and Lim, *Public Disputation*, 37–44.

20. On the overlap of friendship and patronage, see Saller, "Patronage and Friendship," 57–60; Johnson and Dandekker, "Patronage: Relation and System," 231–32.

21. E.g., Theodoret, *HR* 31.17, 21 (SC 257:300, 314).

22. With priests and archimandrites, Theodoret often employed the vocative *theophilestate*, indicating their friendship with both him and God (*epp.* S 19, S 50, S 62 [SC 98:66, 126, 142]). For the unequal friendships (or more often father-son bonds) that Theodoret claimed with those above him in rank, see chapter 7.

23. E.g., Synesius, *ep.* 138 (Garzya, 240–41). See C. White, *Christian Friendship*, 56, 100–108.

24. Firmus used *philia* or *philos* in *epp.* 3–5, 8–10, 14, 20–21, 25–26, 29, 32, 34, 37–39 (SC 350:72–78, 86–92, 102, 118–20, 128–30, 136, 144, 148, 154–58). He used *agapē* only in *ep.* 11 (SC 350:94).

25. Theodoret, *ep.* S 75 (SC 98:160–62).

26. Theodoret, *ep.* S 75 (SC 98:162).

27. On this theme, see Burrus, "'In the Theatre of this Life.'"

28. Diodore, *Commentarii in Psalmos,* preface (CCG 6:1–2); *Quaestiones in Octateuchem* (frag) (Schäublin, "Diodor von Tarsus," in *Theologische Realenzyklopädie* 8:764–65). Theodore of Mopsuestia, *Commentarii in Psalmos,* 35 prologue (ST 93:194).

29. Diodore, *Commentarii in Psalmos,* preface (CCG 6:1–2). See also his fragment of *Quaestiones in Octateuchem,* noted by Schäublin, "Diodor von Tarsus," 764–65.

30. Diodore, *Fragmenta in Epistulam ad Romanos,* Rom 5.13–14, 9.1 (in Staab, *Paulus-kommentare,* 83, 97). Theodore, *Commentarii in Psalmos* 77.8b (ST 93:520); *Commentarii in XII prophetas minores,* Jonah, prologue (repeatedly), Micah 4.1 (repeatedly) (170–72, 207). On typology in Theodoret, see Guinot, *L'éxegèse de Théodoret,* esp. 304–19. On typology in Theodore, see Greer, *Theodore, Exegete and Theologian,* esp. 93–111; and esp. McLeod, "Christological Ramifications."

31. The terminology shifted. Diodore used "Son of David," and "Son of God" (see R. Abramowski, "Der Theologische Nachlass des Diodor," esp. 26–33). Theodore spoke of "knowing the natures of both" (*Homiliae catecheticae* 8, ed. Mingana: 200; tr. Mingana: 84), though he used other formulations and (in Syriac translations) preferred "God the Word who assumed," (*alaha melltha haw de-nsav*) and "man who was assumed," (*barnash haw de-ethnsev*) (*Homiliae catecheticae* 8, ed. Mingana: 198; tr. Mingana: 82). Nestorius professed "two natural *prosōpa*" united as a "common *prosōpon* of the divinity and the humanity" or a "*prosōpon* of union" (*Liber Heraclidis,* tr. Driver and Hodgson, 149, 160–61); see also R. Chestnut, "Two prosopa." Theodoret kept to "two natures in one *prosōpon,*" at least after 433 (Richard, "La lettre de Théodoret"). See Clayton, *Christology of Theodoret,* chaps. 4–5; Gray, "Theodoret on the 'one hypostasis.'"

32. Key efforts to interpret "Antiochene" doctrine include Sullivan, *Christology of Theodore;* Norris, *Manhood and Christ;* Grillmeier, *Christ in Christian Tradition;* Greer, *Theodore, Exegete and Theologian;* Lampe and Woolcombe, *Essays on Typology;* Young, *Biblical Exegesis;* Fairbairn, *Grace and Christology,* chaps. 1, 2, 7. Efforts to seek cultural roots include Vööbus, *School of Nisibis,* 21–22; D. Wallace-Hadrill, *Christian Antioch,* chap. 5; H. J. W. Drijvers, "Early Forms of Antiochene Christology;" Greer, *Theodore: Exegete and Theologian;* Young, *Biblical Exegesis;* Schäublin, *Untersuchungen,* esp. 34–42, 55–65. For more on this scholarship, see Schor, "Theodoret on the School of Antioch."

33. Grillmeier, *Christ,* 2:334, calls Antiochene teachings barely coherent. Guinot, *L'éxegèse de Théodoret,* 627–28, notes the fluidity of "Antiochene" and "Alexandrian" tropes. Young, *Biblical Exegesis,* chaps. 7–9, stresses the similarity of Antiochene and Alexandrian exegesis. O'Keefe, "'A Letter that Killeth,'" argues that Antiochene doctrine appealed only to a sophistic elite. Kalantzis, *Theodore: Commentary on John,* intro., finds a divergence between Antiochene Greek works and Syriac versions. E. Clark, *Reading Renunciation,* chaps. 1–2, questions the notion of a doctrinal school.

34. On inexpressible theology, see Cyril of Alexandria (in *Acta concilii Ephesini; ACO* I.1.1: 56), John Chrysostom, *De incomprehensibili dei natura homiliae* 1.705–7 (SC 28:90–100); Creed of 325 Council of Antioch (J.N.D. Kelly, *Early Christian Creeds*, 209–10). See also P.S. Russell, "Ephraim on the Utility of Language;" McGuckin, *St. Cyril*, 175; MacMullen, *Voting about God*, 36–38. For an effort to look behind ambiguities in language, see Fairbairn, "Puzzle of Theodoret's Christology."

35. For an example of theological gesticulation (Meletius of Antioch's hand signals), see Theodoret, *HE* 2.31 (GCS 5:172–73). See chapter 3.

36. At the start of their doctrinal negotiations, John of Antioch and Cyril of Alexandria agreed on Athanasius as a paragon of orthodoxy (see John of Antioch, *Propositiones Cyrillo Alexandrino missae* [CPG #6308, ACO I.1.4: 146]).

37. Theodoret, *Epp.* S 81–82 (SC 98:192, 198, 202–4), S 113 (SC 111:58–62); *Eranistes* prologue (ed. Ettlinger, 61–62). See similar condemnations (usually of Arius) by Basil, *epp.* 69–70, 90–92 (LCL 2:44, 48, 126, 130, 136), 188 (a fuller list), 242 (LCL 3:10, 432).

38. On these key terms, which are all credited to Diodore of Tarsus, see Hill, *Diodore, Commentary on the Psalms*, xvii–xxiv.

39. On Theodoret's "types" and "realities," see Guinot, *L'exégèse de Théodoret*, 304–19.

40. Theodoret spoke of two natures in one person repeatedly in his *Eranistes, De incarnatione Domini* and his *Impugnatio xii anathematismorum Cyrilli* (*ACO* I.1.6: 108–44). Theodoret's defense of some of Theodore's other formulas can be seen in the fragmentary *Pro Diodoro et Theodoro*. For others' use of the same basic formulas in treatises, albeit with widely varied interpretations, see Andreas of Samosata, *Impugnatio xii anathematismorum Cyrilli* (*ACO* I.1.7: 33–65); Hiba of Edessa, *Ep. ad Marim Persam* (CPG #6500, ACO II.1.3: 32–33); Nestorius, *Ep. ad Cyrillum Alexandrinum ii* (CPG #5669, ACO I.1.1: 29–32).

41. Theodoret, *Ep. ad Iohannem Antiochenum* (CPG #6266, ACO I.1.7: 164).

42. John of Antioch, *Ep. ad Nestorium* (CPG #6316, ACO I.1.1: 93–96).

43. E.g., Theodoret, *Ep. ad Iohannem Antiochenum* (CPG #6266, ACO I.1.7: 164). Two more letters, *Epp. ad Alexandrum Hierapolitanum* (CPG #6250, 6251, ACO I.4: 172, 174), while preserved only in Latin translation, furnish *acribia*, a transliteration from Greek. See also Hill, *Thodoret, Commentary on the Letters of St. Paul*, 14.

44. John of Antioch et al., *Acta et sententia synodi Orientalium* (CPG #6352, ACO I.1.5: 121).

45. Condescension: Theodoret, *Ep. ad Alexandrum Hierapolitanum* (CPG #6253, ACO 1.4: 188); Andreas of Samosata, *Ep. ad Alexandrum Hierapolitanum* (CPG #6376, ACO I.4: 102). Both are Latin translations, but the terms match consistently. See also John of Antioch, *Ep. ad Alexandrum Hierapolitanum* (CPG #6303, ACO I.4: 112–13); Andreas, *Ep. ad Alexandrum Hierapolitanum* (CPG #6380, ACO I.4: 136).

46. Theodoret *ep.* S 16 to Irenaeus of Tyre (SC 98:56–62). Similar sentiments appear in John of Antioch, *Ep. ad Cyrillum episc. Alexandriae* (CPG #6312, ACO I.5: 310).

47. Irenaeus of Tyre scolded Theodoret for such reticence (Theodoret, *ep.* S 16, SC 98:58–60).

48. Chrysostom was praised in Theodoret's sermons (*Sermones quinque in Iohannem Chrysostomum*, CPG #6225, fragments from Photius, *Bibliotheca*, PG 104:229–36). For Acacius, see Theodoret *ep.* S 75 (SC 98:160–62). On the feud between Acacius and John, see

chapter 3. For a sample of conflicting opinions on how to label Chrysostom's theology and exegesis, see Grillmeier, *Christ*, 418–21; Lawrenz, *Christology of John Chrysostom*; Fairbairn, *Grace and Christology*, 204–11.

49. E.g., *Codex Theodosianus* 16.5.12–13.

50. E.g., Theodore, *Contra Apollinarium* (fragments, in Swete, *Theodore of Mopsuestia, Minor Epistles of St. Paul*, 312–22). Theodoret, *Ep. ad Iohannem Antiochenum* (CPG #6264, ACO I.1.6: 107–8) and *HE* 5.40 (GCS 5:348); Andreas of Samosata, *Ep. ad Alexandrum Hierapolitanum* (CPG #6375, ACO I.4: 100–101); Alexander of Hierapolis, *Ep. ad Theodoretum episc. Cyri* (CPG #6416, ACO I.4: 187). John of Antioch led his allies at Ephesus in 431 to declare Cyril's teachings in accord with Arius, Eunomius, and Apollinarius (*Acta et sententia synodi Orientalium*, CPG #6352, ACO I.1.5: 122).

51. See chapter 8.

52. See the convincing argument of Millar, *Greek Roman Empire*, chap. 3.

53. Theodoret spoke some form of Aramaic (*HR* 21.15, [SC 257:94]). His reading skills in Syriac are unclear. For a detailed investigation of Theodoret's languages, see Millar, "Theodoret."

54. On the distribution of Syrian languages, see Millar, *Greek Roman Empire*, chap. 3; and "Theodoret." For a more expansive view of the place of Syriac, see Brock, "Greek and Syriac." For Armenian, see Garsoïan, *L'église arménienne*, esp. intro, chap. 1.

55. Brock, "Greek into Syriac;" Garsoïan, *L'église arménienne*, 67–70; Winkler, "Obscure Chapter," 87–90.

56. For Ephrem, see Brock, "From Antagonism to Assimilation." For Theodoret, see Urbainczyk, "The Devil Spoke Syriac," and *Theodoret*, 72–79.

57. J. Payne Smith, *Compendious Syriac Dictionary*, 538.

58. Brock, "History of Syriac Translation" and "Aspects of Translation Technique."

59. See Brock, "Some Aspects of Greek Words in Syriac."

60. *Ousia* was usually rendered into Syriac as *ithaya*, *hypostasis* as *qnoma*. See J. Payne Smith, *Compendious Syriac Dictionary*, 15, 509–10. See Brock, "Christology of the Church of the East in the Synods," esp. 130–31.

61. Brock, "Greek into Syriac," 3–4 (420–419, reverse pagination) and "History of Syriac Translation."

62. See J. Payne Smith, *Compendious Syriac Dictionary*, 213, 464, 510. For person as *qnoma*, see Theodoret of Mopsuestia, *Contra Apollinarium* (fragment in a miaphysite florilegium, PO 13:188). For person as *partsopa* see *Homiliae catecheticae* 7 (Mingana: 195). See esp. Brock, "Christology of the Church of the East." Terminological shifts had taken place by the 480s in Edessa and Nisibis (see *Pronouncement of the Council of Seleucia-Ctesiphon in 486*, tr. Brock "Christology of the Church of the East in the Synods," 133–34).

63. See J. Payne Smith, *Compendious Syriac Dictionary*, 623. For an example, see Theodore of Mopsuestia, *Commentarius in evangelem Iohannis Apostoli* (Syriac version): 1.35, 4.1–3, 4.54 (CSCO SS 62–63:48, 85, 97).

64. Conflict erupted when lines from Diodore and Theodore were "discovered" in Syriac (ca. 432) and Armenian (436–438), then re-collected in Greek. See chapters 4–5.

65. J. Payne Smith, *Compendious Syriac Dictionary*, 163. For examples, see Theodore of Mopsuestia, *Homiliae catecheticae* 1, 5, 6, 7 (Mingana 117, 160, 179, 195); *Commentarius in*

evangelem Iohannis Apostoli (Syriac version) preface, 1.19, 1.35, 3.3?, 4 17 (CSCO SS 62 63:11, 19, 48, 82, 90).

66. J. Payne Smith, *Compendious Syriac Dictionary*, 252. For examples, see Theodore of Mopsuestia, *Homiliae Catecheticae* 1, 5, 6, 7 (Mingana: 118, 161–64, 179, 186–93). For Philoxenus's use of this term, see Michelson, "Practice Leads to Theory," chap. 1.

67. The "Antiochenes" were not unique in celebrating Syriac-speaking heroes. Sozomen said more about Ephrem than Theodoret did (see Millar, "Theodoret," 121).

68. Theodore as "Herald of truth": Hiba of Edessa, *Ep. ad Marim Persam* (CPG #6500, ACO II.1.3: 33, now in Greek, originally Syriac). Acacius as "noble brother in Christ" and monastic: *Vita Rabbulae* (Overbeck: 158–59, tr. Doran, *Stewards of the Poor*, 68).

69. Mani: Theodore of Mopsuestia, *Homiliae Catecheticae* 5 (Mingana: 164). Marcion: *Homiliae catecheticae* 5 (Mingana: 164). Arius and Eunomius: *Homiliae catecheticae* 1, 3, 5 (Mingana: 124, 146, 165); *Commentarius in evangelem Iohannis Apostoli* (Syriac version), preface (CSCO SS 62–63:3). Apollinarius: *Contra Apollinarium* (PO 13:188); Hiba, *Ep. ad Marim Persam* (CPG #6500, ACO II.1.3: 32–33), now in Greek, but originally in Syriac. All of these "heretics," except Apollinarius, had been denounced by Ephrem Syrus in the 360s (e.g., *Second Discourse to Hypatius*, tr. Mitchell, *St. Ephrem's Prose Refutations*, xxix–l). All were also denounced by Rabbula's miaphysite allies in the *Vita Rabbulae* (Overbeck: 192–94; tr. Doran, *Stewards of the Poor*, 92–93). On Rabbula's early anti-heretical work, see Blum, *Rabbula*: 94–106.

70. Again, see *Pronouncement of the Council of Seleucia-Ctesiphon in 486*, tr. Brock, "Christology of the Church of the East in the Synods," 133–34.

71. Both Rabbula and Hiba of Edessa gained prominence via Syriac translation efforts; Mashdotz did so via Armenian translations. On Rabbula and Hiba, see Brock "Greek into Syriac;" J. W. Drijvers, "Protonike Legend and Bishop Rabbula;" and Garsoïan, "Acace de Mélitène." On Mashdotz, see Garsoïan, "Acace de Mélitène," 74–75.

72. See previous note.

73. Some passages from Theodore of Mopsuestia were first translated in the 430s and 440s by his critics, such as Rabbula of Edessa; others, around the same time, by his backers, such as Hiba. New translation drives by supporters took place in the 460s–470s in Edessa, and in the 490s in Nisibis, as well as by both critics and supporters in the 530s–550s in Constantinople, during the so-called Three-Chapters controversy (see epilogue).

74. On the textual history of Latin *acta*, see Sillett, "Culture of Controversy," chap. 1.

75. E.g., Theodoret, *Ep. ad Alexandrum Hierapolitanum* (CPG #6250, ACO I.4: 172); John of Antioch, *Ep. ad Theodoretum episc. Cyri* (CPG #6321, ACO I.4: 124); Helladius of Tarsus, *Ep. ad Nestorium* (CPG #6441, ACO I.4: 205). Transliteration remained a choice—sometimes Rusticus chose otherwise (e.g., *Acta et sententia synodi Orientalium*, CPG #6352, where Greek *akribēn*, ACO I.1.5: 121, became Latin *integram*, ACO I.4: 35).

76. Theodoret, *ep.* P 15 (SC 40:86–87).

77. Theodoret has reversed the message of II Corinthians 6, where Paul was actually rebuking his addressees for their limited sense of love.

78. Theodoret, *epp.* P 20 (SC 40:92), S 47 (SC 98:122–24), both dated to 446. Other letters imply contacts in 434, 435, 438, 443, and 445–446, at a minimum.

79. Theodoret, *ep.* P 49 (SC 40:119).

80. Self-deprecation in Christian writing was a commonplace, but still meaningful, gesture. See Krueger, *Writing and Holiness,* chap. 5.

81. See Mullett, *Theophylact,* 176–78, noting "wordplay" as one of three "tests of intimacy" in Theophylact's letters.

82. Basil of Seleucia sided with Dioscorus of Alexandria at the Second Council of Ephesus (449), agreeing to Theodoret's deposition. See chapter 5.

83. E.g., Theodoret, *ep.* P 14 (SC 40:86).

84. New intimacy with praise of Irenaeus's virtues: Theodoret, *ep.* S 35 (SC 98:96), probably dated to 443. Brotherhood in passing: *ep.* S 3 (SC 98:22–30), dated to 447–448.

85. E.g., Theodoret, *ep.* S 48 (SC 98:124), taking a familiar tone with Eustathius of Berytus, who by 449 was leaning miaphysite (though in prior years he may have been viewed as an ally). See also Theodoret's letters to the pagan sophist Isocasius (see chapter 6).

86. Theodoret expressed pain when former allies like Basil of Seleucia responded with obvious formulas to his letters of self-defense (see Theodoret, *ep.* S 102 [SC 111:20–22]).

87. *Council of Nicaea,* canon 5 (Joannou, *Discipline,* 1:27–28), *Constitutiones apostolorum* 8.47 canon 37 (SC 336:286).

88. Records showcase eight councils in Syria I, two councils in Cilicia I, two councils in Cilicia II, and four in Euphratensis. See chapter 4.

89. On rituals as semi-improvised performances, see Tambiah, "Performative Approach to Ritual;" Turner, "Images and Reflections;" Schechner, *Performance Theory,* chap. 4.

90. John of Antioch, in *Acta et sententia synodi Orientalium* (CPG #6352, ACO I.1.5: 121–22).

91. The trial of Athanasius of Perrha held in Antioch in 445 (*Acta concilii Chalcedonensis* session 15, ACO II.1.3: 69–81) reveals the order of primacy at work in a regional council.

92. On ritualized councils, see Lim, *Public Disputation,* 217–30; Mendels, *Media Revolution.* For a defense of the democratic element of councils see MacMullen, *Voting about God,* chaps. 2, 7. For a defense of the dialogic element, see Cooper and Dal Santo, "Boethius."

93. See, for instance, the trial of Athanasius of Perrha (*Acta concilii Chalcedonensis* session 15, ACO II.1.3: 69–81) in which all bishops follow one set of talking points.

94. *Constitutiones apostolorum* 2.56 (SC 320:308).

95. Theodoret was debarred by imperial edict from speaking at the trial of Athanasius of Perrha, but he sat among the judges and influenced proceedings (see *Acta concilii Chalcedonensis* session 14:158, ACO II.1.3: 83). See chapter 4. On nonattendance at councils, see MacMullen, *Voting about God,* 98–99.

96. In order to avoid a display of disagreement at a provincial council in 433, bishops of Euphratensis negotiated beforehand who would attend. Ultimately the metropolitan, Alexander, who disagreed with the majority, chose not to attend (Theodoret, *Ep. ad Alexandrum Hierapolitanum,* CPG #6248, ACO I.4: 135); Alexander of Hierapolis, *Ep. ad Theodoretum episc. Cyri,* CPG #6412, ACO I.4: 135–36). See chapter 4.

97. Consider, again, the statement of John of Antioch at the Counter-Council of Ephesus in 431, concerning exactness of doctrine, or hostility to the "heretic" Apollinarius (*Acta et sententia Synodi Orientalium,* CPG #6352, ACO I.1.5: 11.

98. For visits to Antioch, see Theodoret, *ep.* S 81 (SC 98:194–96), which recalled "only" five or six meetings, and *Ep. ad Himerium Nicomedensem* (CPG #6263, ACO

I.4: 107–8) which mentioned regular visits to Antioch just to collect mail. For via
Its to other sees, see Theodoret, *epp.* P 45 (SC 40:109–11, to a village in Antioch's terri-
tory), S 75 (SC 98:162, to Beroea), S 102 (SC 111:20, location unclear), *Ep.* ad Aca-
cium Beroeensem (CPG #6241, *ACO* I.4: 101, to Beroea), *Ep.* ad Alexandrum
Hierapolitanum (CPG #6245, *ACO* I.4: 108–9, to Hierapolis and Beroea), *Ep.* ad
Alexandrum Hierapolitanum (CPG #6248, *ACO* I.4: 135, to Zeugma), *Ep.* Ad Mocimum
oeconomum ecclesiae Hierapolitanae (CPG #6269, *ACO* I.4: 182, to Hierapolis), *Ep.* ad
Nestorium (CPG #6271, *ACO* I.4: 189, to Germanicea).

99. Theodoret *ep.* S 81 (SC 98:194–96) to Nomus the Consul.

100. Kouri-Sarkis, "Réception d'un évêque syrien," 159–62. Kouri-Sarkis (138–42)
locates the text in Euphratensis and dates it between the mid-fifth and early sixth
centuries.

101. Preaching by visiting bishops is recommended by the *Constitutiones apostolorum*
2.58 (SC 320:320–22). Theodoret and Domnus of Antioch reportedly shared preaching (*Syriac Acts of the Second Synod of Ephesus*, Flemming: 134; tr. Perry: 330–31).

102. On clerical meal hosting, see *Constitutiones apostolorum* 2.28 (SC 350:244–46).

103. Theodoret, *ep.* P 45 (SC 40:110).

104. In 435 Alexander of Hierapolis denied Theodoret's request to allow him to visit (*Ep.*
ad Theodoretum episc. Cyri, CPG #6416, *ACO* I.4: 186–87). Theodoret's visit with John of
Antioch in 434 marked a clear step toward reconciliation (Theodoret, *Epp.* ad Alexandrum
Hierapolitanum, CPG #6249–51, *ACO* I.4: 170–74).

105. On Roman letter-writing practices, see Stowers, *Letter-writing;* Stirewalt, *Ancient
Epistolography;* Trapp, *Greek and Latin Letters;* Dineen, *Titles of Address.*

106. Theodoret, *Ep.* ad Theosebium episc. Cii (CPG #6272, *ACO* I.4: 126).

107. Theodoret, *ep.* S 87 (SC 98:232) to Domnus of Apamea.

108. Consider Theodoret's letters to Hiba of Edessa (his close ally), which expressed his
desire to write, limited by lack of a courier (see Theodoret, *ep.* S 133, SC 111:126).

109. Theodoret, *epp.* S 4–6, S 25, S 38, S 54–56, S 63–64, S 72 (SC 98:30–32, 80, 102, 132,
142–44, 156–58). The only study I have found is Brok, "À propos des lettres festales."

110. Cyril of Alexandria, *Ep.* festalis 1 (A.D. 413, SC 372:142–87), ranged from anti-
Jewish polemic to appropriate fasting to a defense of his succession. *Ep.* festalis 17 (A.D. 429,
SC 434:254–94) was devoted to arguing against Nestorius. On the genre of festal letters in
Egypt, see Evieux, *Cyrille d'Alexandrie, Lettres festales,* 1:73–118.

111. Salvation: Theodoret, *ep.* S 5 (SC 98:30). Spiritual blessing: *ep.* S 6 (SC 98:32).

112. Theodoret, *ep.* S 72 (SC 98:158). On the genre, see Brok, "Lettres festales."

113. Christian clergy were hardly the only ones to expect holiday greetings. See, for
instance, Libanius, *ep.* F128, written for the Saturnalia and the Kalends of January.

114. Theodoret (*ep.* P 32, SC 40:98) once wrote to thank Theodotus of Antioch for cooperative efforts in a legal case, even though he had already offered thanks in person.

115. Theodoret, *ep.* P 1 (SC 40:74).

116. On the difficulty of obtaining envoys, see Van Dam, *Families and Friends,*
133–34.

117. On Byzantine letter collection and editing practices, see Mullett, *Theophylact,*
42–44.

118. Synesius, *ep.* 123 (Garzya, 211): "Reading your letters of the last two years, I poured upon them a great volume of tears." On letter collecting, see Bradbury, *Selected Letters of Libanius*, 20–21.

119. Alexander of Hierapolis (*Ep. ad Theodoretum episc. Cyri* , CPG #6416, ACO I.4: 186–87) noted five letters in his collection from a certain priest, "two ... in which the letter [of Cyril] is called orthodox and three ... in which [the author] calls it heretical."

120. Synesius, *ep.* 105 (Garzya, 235–41) to his brother Euoptius.

121. Cyril and Rabbula did public readings of letters (Cyril, *Ep. ad Rabbulam Edessenum*, CPG #5374, in Overbeck: 227–28). Alexander of Hierapolis forwarded other clerics' letters (*Ep. ad Theodoretum episc. Cyri*, CPG #6415, ACO I.4: 174–75).

122. On the public reading of letters, see Constable, *Letters and Letter Collections*, 11–12; Trapp, *Greek and Latin Letters*, 17; and Bradbury, *Selected Letters of Libanius*, 19–20.

123. Wagner ("Chapter in Byzantine Epistolography," 160–61) noted the "tyranny of the rhetorical tradition." Constable, *Letters and Letter Collections*, 16–20, allowed for more flexibility. Van Dam, *Families and Friends*, chap. 8, suggests that rhetorical formulas could serve as pathways for emotional expression rather than as barriers.

124. Maximianus of Anazarbus, *Ep. ad Alexandrum Hierapolitanum* (CPG #6450, ACO I.4: 140).

125. For a direct accusation, see, Meletius of Mopsuestia, *Ep. ad Alexandrum Hierapolitanum* (CPG #6455, ACO I.4: 129). For hiding of names, see Theodoret, *epp.* S 42, S 84 (SC 98:106–8, 220) and S 109 (SC 111:34–36).

126. Consider Eutherius of Tyana, *Ep. ad Alexandrum Hierapolitanum* (CPG #6150, ACO I.4: 213–21), a long doctrinal letter. The document remained to be collected by Irenaeus alongside short notes of information and friendship.

127. Alexander of Hierapolis (*Ep. ad Andream Samosatenum,* CPG #6398, ACO I.4: 138) broke with Andreas by asking for no more letters. Theodoret worried about his standing with Helladius, who had "written one sole letter of recommendation [to Theodoret] all summer" (*Ep. ad Helladium episc. Tarsi,* CPG #6261, ACO I.4: 141).

128. Theodoret, *ep.* P 15 (SC 40:87) to Proclus (on Naucratian the tribune).

129. Theodoret, *ep.* P 41 (SC 40:105) to Andreas of Samosata (on Damian the priest).

130. Theodoret, *ep.* P 15 (SC 40:86–87). For a detailed study of recommendations, see Kim, *Form and Structure of the Familiar Greek Letter of Recommendation.*

131. *Constitutiones apostolorum* 2.58 (SC 320:320–22).

132. Andreas's priest Damian preached in Cyrrhus while Theodoret was ill (Theodoret, *ep.* P 41, SC 40:105).

133. Theodoret used two of his priests to recruit the orator Athanasius (Theodoret, *epp.* S 19–20, SC 98:66–68).

134. On envoys' oral communication, see Mullett, *Theophylact,* 36–37. Basil, *ep.* 94 (LCL 2:152) called unaugmented written notes "soulless letters." Liebeschuetz, *Antioch,* 18–22, notes how Libanius evaded the accusations of treason that bedeviled other notables of Antioch in the 350s by writing letters with no damaging details.

135. Theodoret, *ep.* S 24 (SC 98:82) to Andreas of Samosata.

136. Negotiations after the council of Ephesus relied on Aristolaus, the emperor's tribune (John of Antioch, *Propositiones Cyrillo Alexandrino missae,* CPG #6308, ACO I.1.7:

146). Sensitive exchanges also involved Bishop Paul of Emesa (John of Antioch, *Ep. ad Cyrillum Alexandrinum,* CPG #6309, *ACO* I.1.7: 151).

137. Synesius *ep.* 55 (Garzya, 95).

138. Theodoret, *ep.* S 62 (SC 98:140–42). Libanius made a similar request when former student Hyperechius sent important news via envoys (Libanius, *ep.* F777).

139. Theodoret, *ep.* 41 (SC 40:105).

140. For a different view of envoys (as conveyors of "presence") see Stirewalt, *Ancient Greek Epistolography,* 4–5.

141. Meletius of Mopsuestia, *Ep. ad Alexandrum Hierapolitanum* (CPG #6455, *ACO* I.4: 129), blamed Paul of Emesa for the results of doctrinal negotiations in the winter of 433.

142. Theodoret, *ep.* P 45 (SC 40:110–11) to Theodotus of Antioch.

143. On *proxenoi* in classical Greece, see Davies, *Democracy,* 69.

144. Agents of Rabbula and Gemellinus of Perrha chased Andreas of Samosata from his see (Andreas, *Ep. ad Alexandrum Hierapolitanum,* CPG #6380, *ACO* I.4: 136). At least six clerics in Antioch reported to Cyril of Alexandria (Cyril, *Ep. ad Anastasium, Alexandrum, Martinianum, Iohannem, Paregorium presb. et Maximum diac. ceterosque monachos Orientales,* CPG #5355, *ACO* I.1.4: 49–61).

145. Theodoret, *ep.* S 75 (SC 98:160–62), shows his knowledge about Beroea's clerics. His *Ep. ad Alexandrum Hierapolitanum* (CPG #6243, *ACO* I.4: 87) notes intelligence on feuding in Cappadocia. Meletius of Mopsuestia (*Ep. ad Maximianum episc. Anazarbi,* CPG #6462, *ACO* I.4: 155) revealed his spying on the Quaestor Dometianus.

146. There is no evidence that similarities between Western Christological expressions and those of Syrians had any basis in partisan cooperation until 449. See chapters 5, 7.

147. Theodoret, *ep.* S 112 (SC 111:54) to Domnus of Antioch. Just one other letter makes similar statements: *Ep. ad Alexandrum Hierapolitanum* (CPG #6243, *ACO* I.1.7: 79–80).

CHAPTER 2. SHAPE OF A NETWORK:
ANTIOCHENE RELATIONAL PATTERNS

1. On ties to John of Antioch, Alexander of Hierapolis and Theodoret, see Andreas, *Ep. ad Alexandrum Hierapolis* (CPG #6375, *ACO* I.4: 100); *Ep. ad Theodoretum episc. Cyri* (CPG #6383, *ACO* I.4: 102).

2. Andreas's split with John of Antioch: Theodoret, *Ep. ad Iohannem Antiochenum* (CPG #6266, *ACO* I.4: 131–32). His split with Theodoret and Alexander of Hierapolis: Maximianus of Anazarbus, *Ep. ad Alexandrum episc. Hierapolis* (CPG #6450, *ACO* I.4: 140–41). Rabbula's effort to oust him: Andreas, *Ep. ad Alexandrum Hierapolitanum* (CPG #6380, *ACO* I.4: 136–37).

3. Andreas, *Ep. ad Alexandrum Hierapolitanum* (CPG #6380, *ACO* I.4: 137). New links to Theodoret came a bit later (see Theodoret, *epp.* P 41 (SC 40:105), S 24 (SC 98:80–82).

4. Refusal of contact: Alexander of Hierapolis, *Ep. ad Andream Samosatenum* (CPG #6398, *ACO* I.4: 138). Andreas's begging: Andreas, *Ep. ad Alexandrum Hierapolitanum* (CPG #6381, *ACO* I.4: 137–38). On Alexander's exile, see Irenaeus, *Quanti a sanctis ecclesiis exierunt nolentes suam conscientiam vulnerare* (CPG #6431, *ACO* I.4: 203–4).

5. See *Acta concilii Ephesini*, esp. session 1 (*ACO* I.1.2: 3–7, 55–64). *Acta et Sententia synodi Orientalium* (CPG #6352, *ACO* I.1.5: 119–24, I.4: 37–38).

6. Acts of the Second Council of Ephesus, *Acta concilii Chalcedonensis* session 1 (*ACO* II.1.1: 78–82).

7. The fullest list of bishops is the official subscriptions to the Chalcedonian confession: *Acta concilii Chalcedonensis* session 6 (*ACO* II.1.2: 141–55). Only about eighty-three Syrian bishops personally attended the council (listed by province by Dionysius Exiguus, *ACO* II.2.2: 65–77). See Price and Gaddis, *Acts of Chalcedon*, vol. 3 appendix 2.

8. The other sees either sent no one to councils before Chalcedon or were not yet separate church dioceses.

9. The other bishop-author of an extant personal collection, Firmus of Caesarea, did not use the Antiochene set of social cues.

10. Before 443: Theodoret, *epp.* P 2, P 22 to Eusebius of Ancyra (SC 40:74, 92–94), P 15 to Proclus of Constantinople (SC 40:86–87), S 83 to Dioscorus of Alexandria (SC 98:214–16). After 443: *epp.* S 77–78 (SC 98:166–180) and S 113, S 118 (SC 111:46, 74).

11. E.g., John of Antioch, *Ep. ad Xystum, Cyrillum et Maximianum (una cum synodo Antiochena)* (CPG #6335, *ACO* I.1.4: 33).

12. Additional data come from commemoration in histories, hagiographies and sermons.

13. On the modular scale-free topology, see Barabási, *Linked*, 79–92, 227–38; Watts, *Six Degrees*, chaps. 3–4, 8. See above, Introduction, esp. figure 1.

14. The scale of the clergy can be seen in conciliar records. In early 449, 66 clerics (1 country bishop, 15 priests, 39 deacons, and 11 subdeacons) signed a statement supporting bishop Hiba (*Acta concilii Chalcedonensis* session 11, *ACO* II.1.3: 35–37). In mid 449, 38 clerics (20 priests, 11 deacons, 8 subdeacons) petitioned for his removal, including about 20 who signed the other petition (*Syriac Acts of the Second Council of Ephesus*, Flemming: 22; tr. Doran, *Stewards of the Poor*, 151–55). On the extent of the clergy, see Brown, *Poverty and Leadership*, 48–49.

15. On roles assigned to each clerical rank, see *Constitutiones Apostolorum* 2.1–63, 3.9–11, 3.16–20 (SC 320:144–338, SC 329:142–46, 154–64). On roles for monks and *bnay/bnath qyama* ("covenanters"), see Rabbula, *Praecepta ad sacerdotes et regulares* and *Monita ad coenobitas* (CPG #6490–92; Vööbus, *Syriac and Arabic Documents*, 34–50, 27–33).

16. Theodoret, *ep.* S 51 (SC 98:126–28), thanking the priest for recruiting bishop Thomas.

17. Theodoret, *Ep. ad Mocimum oeconomum eccl. Hierapolitanae* (CPG #6269, *ACO* I.4: 182).

18. For examples, see chapter 1.

19. Theodoret, *ep.* P 43 (SC 40:106–7) involved the monk Agianus in matchmaking; *ep.* P 20 (SC 40:92) touted the support of the hermit Jacob for a tax appeal.

20. See Theodoret, *Ep. ad Alexandrum Hierapolitanum* (CPG #6249, *ACO* I.4: 170–71).

21. Theodoret, *ep.* S 75 (SC 98:160–62). Other communal letters include *Ep. ad eos qui in Euphratesia et Osrhoena regione, Syria, Phoenicia et Cilicia vitam monasticam degunt*, CPG #6276, *PG* 83:1416–33) and (much later) *ep.* S 146 (SC 111:172–200), as well as conciliar letters probably drafted by Theodoret (*Ep. synodi Orientalium ad clerum populumque Antiochenum* [CPG #6339, *ACO* I.4: 57–58]; *Ep. synodi Orientalium ad clerum CPolitanum* [CPG #6341, *ACO* I.1.5: 127]).

22. Theodoret, *ep.* P 41 (SC 40:105) to Andreas of Samosata, about the priest Damian.

23. The aforementioned Agianus (Theodoret, *ep.* P 43 [SC 40:106–8]).

24. See Maxwell, *Christianization and Communication,* esp. chaps. 4, 6.

25. Note of consolation to a Cyrrhus resident: Theodoret, *ep.* S 14 (SC 98:46–52). Moral rebuke to notables of other towns: *epp.* P 8–9 (SC 40:79–82).

26. Consider Maranas the *scholasticus,* whom Theodoret rebuked for avoiding Cyrrhus (*ep.* P 34, SC 40:99–100), then thanked for donating a shrine (*ep.* S 67, SC 98:148).

27. One possible local notable involvement I have not included. The (pagan) sophist Isocasius was accused of helping to get Domnus chosen as bishop of Antioch. The accusation is believable but never verified. See chapter 6.

28. E.g., Theodoret, *ep.* P 36 (SC 40:100–101).

29. E.g., Theodoret, *ep.* P 47 (SC 40:111–17).

30. The emperor sent Aristolaus, a tribune, to deal with disputes in 432 (Theodosius II, *Sacra ad Iohannem Antiochenum,* CPG #8810, ACO I.1.4: 3–5).

31. Theodoret, *Ep. ad Himerium Nicomedensem* (CPG #6263, ACO I.4: 107–8).

32. *Constitutiones apostolorum* 2.1–63 (SC 320:144–338), 3.9–11, 3.16–20 (SC 329: 142–46, 154–64).

33. For commands mixed with declarations of friendship, see Theodoret *epp.* S 19 (SC 98:66) and S 61 (SC 98:138–40), to priests, or *ep.* P 50 (SC 40:119–20) to a layman.

34. Council of Nicaea, canon 6 (Joannou, *Discpline,* 1:28–29).

35. On models of primacy region by region, see Norton, *Episcopal Elections,* chap. 5.

36. For the bishop of Antioch's chairing of councils, see chapter 1. For examples of his role in consecration, from Theodoret's *HE,* see chapter 3.

37. See chapter 4.

38. Domnus of Antioch, *Ep. ad Flavianum CPolitanum* (Syriac, Flemming: 118–22; tr. Perry: 298–306). Elsewhere the letter is credited to Theodoret (*ep.* S 86, SC 98:226–32, esp. 230). Azéma suggests that Theodoret drafted the letter for Domnus.

39. Council of Nicaea, canons 4–5 (Joannou, *Discpline,* 1:26–28). Theodoret, *Ep. ad magistrum militum [Anatolium]* (CPG #6254, ACO I.4: 161). Generally on metropolitan status in the Roman East, see Norton, *Episcopal Elections,* chaps. 5, 7.

40. Theodoret, *Ep. ad Alexandrum Hierapolitanum* (CPG #6248, ACO I.4: 135).

41. *Consitutiones apostolorum* 8.47 canon 34 (SC 336:284).

42. Theodosius II, *Sacra ad concilium Ephesinum* (ACO I.1.3: 31–32).

43. For a full list, see chapter 4.

44. Jerome, *De viris illustribus,* measured accomplishment by the size of a writer's corpus.

45. For more on the ascetic and pragmatic components of episcopal authority, see Rapp, *Holy Bishops,* chaps. 1–4.

46. E.g., John of Antioch, *Ep. ad Cyrillum Alexandrinum* (CPG #6312, ACO I.5: 313–14), where John refused to abandon his support of Theodoret.

47. John of Antioch, *Ep. ad Theodoretum episc. Cyri* (CPG #6322, ACO I.4: 153–54), stated that he was eager to cooperate "even if I seem to be influenced by Your Charity."

48. E.g., *Acta et sententia synodi Orientalium* (CPG #6352, ACO I.1.5: 119).

49. The count of seventy-five is from Pelagius, *In defensione Trium capitulorum* (Devreesse: 15). Barhadbeshabba of Arbaya, *HE* 29 (Nau, 572) counted eighty.

50. Andreas and Acacius missed the First Council of Ephesus for health reasons. See chapter 4.

51. On Rabbula and his suffragans, see John of Antioch, *Ep. ad episcopos Osrhoenae contra Rabbulam episc. Edessae (una cum synodo Antiochena)* (CPG #6347, ACO I.4: 87). On the later defection of Uranius of Himerium, see *Syriac Acts of the Second Council of Ephesus* (Flemming: 38–40, 52, 58–60; tr. Perry: 95–96, 121–22, 132–33).

52. On the monks and clerics who reported to Alexandria, see Cyril, *Ep. ad Anastasium, Alexandrum, Martinianum, Iohannem, Paregorium presb. et Maximum diac. ceterosque monachos Orientales* (CPG #5355, ACO I.1.4: 49–61).

53. See Irenaeus's summary of what became of exiles (*Quanti a sanctis ecclesiis exierunt nolentes suam conscientiam vulnerare,* CPG #6431, ACO I.4: 203).

54. Theodoret and Helladius of Tarsus continued to write Nestorius, but constantly apologized for their neglectfulness (Theodoret, *Epp. ad Nestorium,* CPG #6270–71, ACO I.4: 149–50, 189; Helladius, *Ep. ad Nestorium,* CPG #6441, ACO I.4: 205). Alexander simply refused to correspond (see the start of this chapter).

55. For more on these alternative religious networks, see chapter 6.

56. For more on the possibility of Theodoret's social misperceptions, see chapter 5.

57. Network theorists are divided as to whether modular scale-free networks tend to grow more successfully or whether growing networks tend to become modular and scale-free (Barabási, *Linked,* 88–107; Watts, *Six Degrees,* esp. 108–29).

58. Barabási, *Linked,* 96–107.

59. All these simulations assume that members still seek new relationships with other existing members. On situations in which the scale-free topology no longer approximates real networks, see Watts, *Six Degrees,* chap. 4.

CHAPTER 3. ROOTS OF A NETWORK: THEODORET ON THE ANTIOCHENE CLERICAL HERITAGE

1. See Theodoret, *ep.* S 79 (SC 98:184).

2. Theodoret, *ep.* S 112 (SC 111:48).

3. Chesnut, "Date of Composition," dated the *HE* between 442 and August 449. While accurate, this underplays the likelihood that Theodoret responded to Socrates or Sozomen. See Leppin, "Church Historians I," and see later in this chapter, note 6.

4. For Socrates' dates, see Chesnut, *First Christian Histories,* 174–77; Urbainczyk, *Socrates,* 20–23. For Sozomen's dates, see Roueché, "Theodosius II," 130–32.

5. On the authorship of the Greek version of Rufinus's *HE,* see Amidon, *Church History of Rufinus,* xiii–xviii. On non-Nicene sources used by Philostorgius, see Parmentier, *Theodoret Kirchengeschichte,* lxxxviii.

6. Theodoret, *HE* 1.1 (GCS 5:4; tr. Jackson, *NPNF II* 3:33). Many scholars assumed that Theodoret responded to Socrates or Sozomen. Chesnut, "Date of composition," argued that he wrote independently. Parmentier, *Theodoret Kirchengeschichte,* lxxxiii–xcviii, suggested that Theodoret drew passages from Socrates or Sozomen (see also Leppin, "Church Historians I"). Theodoret could have responded to Rufinus or to Philostorgius's sources. But he seems to shadow Socrates' or Sozomen's narrative and to respond to criticism of Syrians

(see Socrates, *HE* 5.5, 5.8 [GCS 1:276–77, 279–81]; Theodoret, *HE* 5.3, 5.23 [GCS 5: 279 82, 321–24]. It seems unlikely that the well-connected Theodoret was ignorant of Socrates' semi-official history.

7. For Theodoret, Eustathius of Antioch's endurance rivaled Athanasius's; Marcellus of Apamea's temple destructions matched Theophilus's (*HE* 1.8, 5.21–22 [GCS 5:33–38, 317–21]).

8. Theodoret, *HE* 2.18 (GCS 5:137–38); Socrates, *HE* 2.40–41 (GCS 1:171–78).

9. Theodoret, *HE* 2.31–32, 4.14–18 (GCS 5:170–74, 233–42).

10. The split arose between supporters of Pelagius and those of Apollinarius (Theodoret, *HE* 5.3–4 [GCS 5: 279–84]). On Apollinarius, see later in this chapter.

11. Theodoret, *HE* 2.32, 4.14–15 (GCS 5:173–74, 233–35). Eusebius's second replacement, we are told, chose a more violent approach.

12. Theodoret, *HE* 2.31 (GCS 5:170–71), named Eusebius of Samosata as Meletius's sponsor. On the compromise, see Spoerl, "The Schism at Antioch," 101–20.

13. Socrates, *HE* 2.44 (GCS 1:181–82), and Sozomen, *HE* 4.28 (GCS 4:184–86). Both claimed that Meletius preferred moral preaching to doctrinal argument.

14. Theodoret, *HE* 2.31 (GCS 5:170–71) related a tale in which Meletius met George of Laodicea (Homoian) and Acacius of Caesarea (Anomoian) in a speaking contest before Constantius II. After the others spoke, Meletius began to declare his support for Nicaea. When asked for clarification, he raised three fingers, then one—the homoousion trinity! Sozomen, *HE* 4.28 (GCS 4:184–86), claimed that the hand signals came during a sermon, because a Homoian archdeacon had put a hand over Meletius's mouth.

15. According to Epiphanius, *Panarion,* 73.28.1 (Holl, 3:302), Meletius's main booster was Acacius of Caesarea, who also backed Eunomius. Socrates, *HE* 2.44 (GCS 1:181–82), and Philostorgius, *HE* 5.1 (Bidez, 66–67), claimed that Meletius had earlier signed the Creed of Seleucia (359), which foreswore the term *ousia.*

16. For Paulinus's Eustathian past, see Theodoret, *HE* 3.4 (GCS 5:179–80), and Hanson, "The Fate of Eustathius of Antioch." For his consecration (by Lucifer of Cagliari), see Theodoret, *HE* 3.4 (GCS 5:179–80), and Devreesse, *Le Patriarcat d'Antioche,* 21–24.

17. Theodoret, *HE* 5.4 (GCS 5:282–83).

18. See Downey, *History of Antioch,* 410–13.

19. Socrates, *HE* 5.5 (GCS 1:276), said that Paulinus stayed because of his "eminent piety."

20. Basil of Caesarea, *epp.* 67–69, 92, 156 (LCL 2:32–46, 132–44, 384–90) and 258 (LCL 4:34–46).

21. Sozomen, *HE* 4.13, 28 (GCS 4:155–56, 184–86); Theodoret, *HE* 2.31 (GCS 5:170–73).

22. Rufinus of Aquileia, *HE* 10.28 (Schwartz and Mommsen, 990–91).

23. Theodoret's first mention of the see of Alexandria noted its supremacy stretching over "not only Egypt, but the adjacent regions of Libya and Thebaid as well" (*HE* 1.2 [GCS 5:6]). No parallel description of Antioch was included.

24. Canons from Nicaea required three bishops from the province to serve as consecrators (Council of Nicaea, canon 4 [Joannou, *Discipline* 1:26]). Other quasi-normative sources allow for two (e.g., *Constitutiones apostolorum* 3.20 [SC 329:164]; 8.47 canon 1 [SC 336:274]). On consecration practices, see Norton, *Episcopal Elections,* esp. 19–33.

25. Theodoret, *HE* 4.25 (GCS 5:263–64).

26. Philostorgius, *HE* 9.14, 9.19 (Bidez, 120, 125).

27. Athanasius and the Western bishops favored Paulinus, despite Basil's attempts to convince them otherwise (Basil of Caesarea, *ep.* 66–70, 92 [LCL 2:26–52, 132–44]).

28. Theodoret, *HE* 2.24 (GCS 5:154–55).

29. Theodoret, *HE* 2.24 (GCS 5:154–55). Such chanting was doubtless older.

30. Theodoret, *HE* 2.24 (GCS 5:154–55).

31. Basil of Caesarea encountered Diodore in Armenia while visiting the exiled Meletius (*ep.* 99 [LCL 2:178]). It is unclear whether he was there permanently. Theodoret only noted that he was "dialoguing ... abroad" (Theodoret, *HE* 4.25 [GCS 5:263–64]).

32. Theodoret, *HE* 5.3 (GCS 5:279–82), offered a later example of Flavian's skills, when he out-argued other Nicenes in 380 to claim the support of Theodosius I's court.

33. Diodore's school apparently survived his leaving (Socrates, *HE* 6.3 [GCS 1:313–15]).

34. Theodoret, *HR* 8.8 (SC 234:388–92).

35. Theodoret, *HR* 2.17–20 (SC 234:234–40).

36. Theodoret, *HE* 4.27–28 (GCS 5:267–69).

37. Sozomen, *HE* 7.28 (GCS 4:344–45).

38. Theodoret, *HE* 4.28 (GCS 5:268–69). Acacius trained with Asterius, a pupil of Julian Saba. (See *HR* 2.16 [SC 234:230–32]).

39. Theodoret, *HR* 2.16 (SC 234:230–32).

40. Theodoret, *HE* 4.29 (GCS 5:269–70), merely suggested the association. Ephrem's hymns in the 360s did shift toward Nicene positions (see Griffith, "Ephrem the Deacon"). On Ephrem's reputation in Greek as a monk, see Griffith, "Images of Ephrem," 9–13.

41. Socrates, *HE* 5.2 (GCS 1:275–76).

42. Theodoret, *HE* 5.6 (GCS 5:285–86).

43. Theodoret, *HE* 5.3 (GCS 5:279–81).

44. Socrates, *HE* 5.5 (GCS 1:276–77); Sozomen, *HE* 7.11 (GCS 4:314); Theodoret, *HE* 5.3 (GCS 5:281–82).

45. Socrates, *HE* 3.7, 3.9 (GCS 1:197–99, 203–4); Sozomen, *HE* 7.11 (GCS 4:314).

46. Theodoret, *HE* 5.3 (GCS 5:281–82).

47. Socrates, *HE* 5.5 (GCS 1:276–77).

48. Most noteworthy, besides the Council of Constantinople (381), was the multi-regional council of Antioch, in 379, mentioned in the synodical of the follow-up council in Constantinople, preserved by Theodoret, *HE* 5.9 (GCS 5:293).

49. Theodoret, *HE* 5.4 (GCS 5:282–84).

50. Meletius's death was marked at the council by Gregory of Nyssa, *Oratio funebris in Meletium episcopum* (CPG #3180; ed. Spira, 441–57).

51. On the departure of Gregory, see Sozomen, *HE* 7.7 (GCS 4:308–10). For speculation about Gregory's plans, see Devreesse, *Patriarcat d'Antioche,* 35–36.

52. Sozomen, *HE* 7.8–9 (GCS 4:310–13), noted Nectarius's links to Diodore and other Cilicians. Nectarius hailed from Tarsus, and Diodore had reportedly been instrumental in getting him listed as a candidate in Constantinople. As bishop, we are told, he took advice from Cyriacus of Adana and employed several Cilician clerics.

53. Sozomen, *HE* 7.8–11 (GCS 4:310–14); he barely mentions Nectarius's role. See Ambrose, *ep.* M 13 (= *Extra collectionem* 9, CSEL 82.3:201–4).

54. See Devreesse, *Patriarcat d'Antioche*, 35–38.

55. Theodoret, *HE* 5.9 (GCS 5:289–95), preserved the synodical from this new meeting without explaining the context of Paulinus's complaint.

56. Theodoret, *HE* 5.23 (GCS 5:322).

57. Sozomen, *HE* 8.3 (GCS 4:352–53).

58. Theodoret, *HE* 5.23 (GCS 5:321–24).

59. Theodoret, *HE* 5.35 (GCS 5:337–38).

60. Socrates, *HE* 6.3 (GCS 1:313–14); Sozomen, *HE* 8.2 (GCS 4:350–52); Theodoret, *HE* 5.27 (GCS 5:328–29).

61. Theodoret, *HE* 5.27 (GCS 5:328–29).

62. Consider Marcian, who hosted bishops (Theodoret, *HR* 3.11 [SC 234:266–68]) and Macedonius, who helped Flavian to win forgiveness for Antioch after the Statues Riot in 387 (Theodoret, *HE* 5.20 [GCS 5:315–16]; *HR* 13.7 [SC 234:486–90]; on this episode, see Brown, *Power and Persuasion*, 105–9).

63. Theodoret identified as members Maximus of Seleucia (Isauria), Theodore of Mopsuestia, John Chrysostom, Elpidius of Laodicea, Marcellus and Agapetus of Apamea (all *HE* 5.27 [GCS 5:328–29]), Helladius of Tarsus (*HR* 10.9 [SC 234:450–52]), Polychronius of Apamea (*HE* 5.40 [GCS 5:347–48]), Porphyrius and Alexander of Antioch (both *HE* 5.35 [GCS 5:337–38]), and Theodotus of Antioch (*HE* 5.38 [GCS 5:342]).

64. Theodoret, *HE* 4.25 (GCS 5:263–64).

65. Theodoret, *HE* 5.40 (GCS 5:347–48).

66. See chapter 1.

67. For attempts to identify an Antiochene doctrinal system, see Sullivan, *Christology of Theodore*, 162; Norris, *Manhood and Christ*, 207–9; Grillmeier, *Christ*, part 1 sec. 1; J. N. D. Kelly, *Early Christian Doctrines*, 301–9; Greer, *Theodore: Exegete and Theologian*, 48–49. For efforts to find an exegetical method, see Lampe and Woolcombe, *Essays on Typology*, but also Nassif, "Spiritual Exegesis."

68. Most scholars (e.g., Grillmeier, *Christ*, part 2, chaps. 3–5; J. N. D. Kelly, *Early Christian Doctrines*, chaps. 11–12) recognized an inconsistency in Antiochene terminology. Devreese, *Essai sur Théodore*, part 2, questioned the authenticity of many Antiochene works. On Antiochene "tendencies" see Sellers, *Council of Chalcedon*, sec. II chap. 2.

69. E.g., Barjeau, *L'école éxegetique d'Antioche*, chaps. 1–3. For plausible predecessors (e.g., Eustathius, Lucian of Antioch) see Schäublin, "Diodor von Tarsus," 763–66.

70. Aristotelian philosophy: Vööbus, *School of Nisibis*, 21–22. Platonic philosophy: D. Wallace-Hadrill, *Christian Antioch*, esp. chap. 5. Jewish-style reading: Greer, *Theodore: Exegete and Theologian*, 86–90, 110–11. Syriac reading: H. J. W. Drijvers, "Early Forms of Antiochene Christology."

71. Guinot, *L'éxegèse de Théodoret*, 627–28. Young, *Biblical Exegesis*, chaps. 7–9.

72. Young, *Biblical Exegesis*, chaps. 7–9 and O'Keefe, "Kenosis or Impassibility," both note that the Antiochenes were all worried about keeping the "narrative integrity" of Scripture. Fairbairn, *Grace and Christology*, 200–216, instead emphasizes internal theological disagreements among the so-called Antiochenes.

73. Young, *Biblical Exegesis*, chaps. 7–9; O'Keefe, "'A Letter that Killeth.'"

74. E.g., Kalantzis, *Theodore: Commentary on John*, introduction, esp. 28.

75. Esp. O'Keefe, "'A Letter that Killeth;'" Clark, *Reading Renunciation*, chaps. 1–2; Fairbairn, *Grace and Christology*, esp. 211–16.

76. See chapter 5.

77. Theodoret, *HE* 2.31 (GCS 5:170–73) explained Meletius's doctrinal reticence as clever timing. As to Diodore and Flavian, even Theodoret noted that they originally split from Leontius out of hostility to Anomoians, not Homoians (*HE* 2.24, GCS 5:154–55).

78. On this "Neo-Nicene" tradition, see Bergjan, *Theodoret und der Neunizänismus*. Theodoret, *HE* 5.3 (GCS 5:280–81), described the issues at stake as factions met in Antioch in 380: "At the time ... Paulinus affirmed that he was of the party of Damasus... The divine Meletius kept silent and put up with their discord. But Flavian ... said to Paulinus 'If, dear sir, you accept the communion of Damasus [and Gregory], show us clearly your agreement with his dogmas; for while he confesses one *ousia* of the trinity, he preaches three *hypostases* outright. You deny the trinity of the *hypostases.*'"

79. Scholars have recognized the anti-Arian context of Diodore's teaching. Sullivan, *Christology of Theodore*, 162, described it as a response to the major premise of Arian logic: the sufferings of a *homoousion* Christ would mean that God suffered as well. Greer, *Theodore: Exegete and Theologian*, chaps. 3–4, agreed but focused on soteriology, specifically the quest for human perfection. Norris, *Manhood and Christ*, 207–9, acknowledged the anti-Arian mission of Diodore, but for Theodore, he stressed the anti-Apollinarian polemic.

80. Diodore of Tarsus, *Fragmenta dogmatica* 19, 42 (in R. Abramowski, "Der theologische Nachlass des Diodor," 36–39, 56).

81. For a thorough discussion of "word-flesh" Christology, see Grillmeier, *Christ*, part II, sec. 1. For Diodore's use of *logos-sarx*, see Diodore, *Fragmenta dogmatica* IX (in R. Abramowski, "Der theologische Nachlass des Diodor," 62).

82. Judging by Syriac translations, Theodore seems to have used "natures" as genera, and their specific forms as "assuming Word" and "assumed man" (*Homiliae catacheticae* 8, Mingana, 197–200; tr. Mingana, 82–84). Kalantzis, *Theodore Commentary on John*, esp. 28–29, has questioned this. But Nestorius's "two *prosōpa* in one *prosōpon* of union" seems an outgrowth of these formulas (see McGuckin, *St. Cyril*, 140–45).

83. On the search for the *hypothesis* of biblical texts, see Schäublin, *Untersuchungen*, 83–84 (regarding Theodore).

84. Theodoret, *HE* 2.24 (GCS 5:153–55).

85. This situation is discussed fully by Lim, *Public Disputation*, esp. 112–38, 173–80.

86. See Lim, *Public Disputation*, 112–38.

87. Theodoret, *HE* 5.3 (GCS 5:280–81).

88. Sozomen, *HE* 6.25 (GCS 4:270–72).

89. Sozomen, *HE* 6.25 (GCS 4:270–72).

90. Apollinarius, *Ep. ad Dionysium* (*Fragmenta dogmatica*, ed. Lietzmann, 256–57). See Grillmeier, *Christ*, 221–30, who saw *physis* as signifying for Apollinarius one "self-determining being," and J.N.D. Kelly, *Early Christian Doctrines*, 289–95, who stressed Apollinarius's concern that Christ not have opposed wills. See also Spoerl, "Apollinarian Christology."

91. Theodoret, *HE* 5.3, 5.38 (GCS 5:280–82, 342). For more on Theodoret's views on Apollinarius, see Guinot, "Presence d'Apollinaire."

92. Theodore, *Homiliae catecheticae* 5 (Mingana, 164-73; tr. Mingana, 54-62). Theodoret was troubled primarily by the "one nature" formulation (*HE* 5.3 [GCS 5:279-80]).

93. Alexander of Hierapolis, *Ep. ad Theodoretum episc. Cyri* (CPG #6416, ACO I.4: 187).

94. On this distinction ("eternal generation" favored by Cyril of Jerusalem, "begotten before all time" favored by Hilary of Poitiers) see Hanson, *Search*, esp. 398-99, 482.

95. Socrates, *HE* 6.3 (GCS 1:313-14). Theodoret only hinted at this element (*HE* 5.40, GCS 5: 347-48). On the *asketerion's* pedagogy, see Leconte, "L'asceterium de Diodore."

96. Theodoret, *HE* 4.27 (GCS 5:267).

97. Theodoret, *HE* 4.27 (GCS 5:267).

98. John Chrysostom, *Epp. ad Theodorum lapsum*, 1.1 (SC 117:86); Chrysostom also recalled Diodore's scriptural assignments in *Laus Diodori* 3-4 (*PG* 52:763-66).

99. Theodoret, *HE* 5.27 (GCS 5:328-29).

100. Vööbus, *History of Asceticism*, part II, chaps. 1-5, surveyed fourth-century ascetics using works of "Ephrem Syrus" now considered spurious (Brock, "Brief Guide to Ephrem"). Murray, *Symbols of Church and Kingdom*, 12-17, distinguished *ihidaye* (apostolic figures) from *bnay qyama* (special clerical disciples). Griffith, "Monks, Singles," described *bnay qyama* and *ihidaye* as overlapping categories. On former *ihidaya/bar qyama* Jacob of Nisibis, see Theodoret *HR* 1 (SC 234:160-92, esp. 164, 176, 188-92); Ephrem Syrus, *Carmina Nisibena* 13 (CSCO SS 92:34-36); Bundy, "Jacob of Nisibis." On wandering Syrian ascetics of the third century, see Caner, *Wandering, Begging Monks*, chap. 2.

101. See Theodoret *HR* 2 (SC 234:194-244); Ephrem Syrus, *Hymns on Julian Saba* (CSCO SS 140: 37-85; 141: 42-87). See also Griffith, "Julian Saba."

102. Theodoret *HR* 10.2 (SC 234:450-52), 27.2 (SC 257:218-20).

103. See Gaddis, "No Crime," 155-68.

104. Sozomen *HE* 6.33 (GCS 4:289) suggested Egyptian influence. Vööbus, *History of Asceticism*, chap. 5, posited a separate Syrian coenobitic tradition based on works once attributed to Ephrem. Tchalenko (*Villages antiques*, 19) and Price (*History of the Monks of Syria*, xix-xx) distinguished a Syrian coenobitic tradition based on architectural forms.

105. See Canivet, *Monachisme syrien*, 209-11.

106. Most studies of this topic focus on other regions: Brakke, *Athanasius*, esp. 17-49, 80-97, 111-34; Elm, *Virgins of God*, chaps. 5-6; Sterk, *Renouncing the World*, chaps. 3, 7, 8.

107. E.g., Ephrem Syrus, *Hymns on Julian Saba* (CSCO SS 140:37-85; 141:42-87).

108. John Chrysostom, *Adversus oppugnatores vitae monasticae* 3.11-12 (*PG* 47:366-71).

109. See Rousseau, "Identity of the Ascetic Master;" and "Ascetics as Mediators." See also Festugière, *Antioche*, chap. 5; Canivet, *Monachisme syrien*, 273-77.

110. Theodoret, *HE* 4.11 (GCS 5:229-31). On the Messalian controversy, see Stewart, *Working the Earth of the Heart*, chap. 2; Caner, *Wandering, Begging Monks*, chap. 3.

111. Marcian: Theodoret, *HR* 3.11 (SC 234:266-68). Macedonius: *HR* 13.4 (SC 234:480-82). In each case, visiting bishops sought to ordain the ascetic.

112. On "monastic" families, see Canivet, *Le monachisme syrien*, chap. 7.

113. Theodoret's *HR* listed Acacius of Beroea (*HR* 2.9 [SC 234:214-16]), Agapetus of Apamea (HR 3.5 [SC 234:254-56]), Helladius of Tarsus (*HR* 10.9 [SC 234:450-52]), Abraham of Carrhae (*HR* 17.5 [SC 257:40-42]), and Aphthonius of Zeugma (*HR* 5.8 [SC 234:340-42]). He also mentioned himself (*HR* 4.10 [SC 234:312-16]). Understandably, he ignored three

others, Nestorius (from a monastery in Antioch), Rabbula of Edessa, and Eusebius of Constantina (both disciples of the ascetic Abraham; see *Vita Rabbulae*, Overbeck: 167; tr. Doran, *Stewards of the Poor*, 72–73).

114. Theodore of Mopsuestia, *De Incarnatione* 15 (in *Theodore of Mopsuestia, Minor Epistles of St. Paul*, ed. Swete, 2:310).

115. Theodore of Mopsuestia, *Homiliae Catecheticae* 2 (Mingana, 128–29; tr. Mingana, 27–28) highlights the progressive instruction provided by God, culminating in the theology of his age. On this theme, see Wickert, *Studien zu den Pauluskommentaren Theodors von Mopsuestia*, 89–101; and Becker, *Fear of God*, 117–19.

116. The pursuit of a wider public audience may explain the less overt dyophysite presentation in the Greek version of Theodore's *Commentary on John* (see Kalantzis, *Theodore: Commentary on John*, 27–29).

117. Based on his geographical origins, Meletius may have spoken Armenian as well.

118. On the translation efforts of Rabbula, see Vööbus, *School of Nisibis*, 14–21; Baarda, "The Gospel Text in the Biography of Rabbula;" J. W. Drijvers, "The Protonike Legend," and Doran, *Stewards of the Poor*, 54–57.

119. See Garsoïan, "Acace de Mélitène."

120. The extant text reads "Mastoubius." See Photius, *Bibliotheca* 81 (ed. Henry, 1:187). See also Garsoïan, *L'église arménienne*, 69–70.

121. E.g., Basil of Caesarea, *Ep.* 22 (LCL 1:128–40), which treats the monastic life as the pinnacle of Christian brotherhood.

122. Eusebius: Theodoret *HE* 4.14 (GCS 5:233–34). Meletius: *HE* 2.31 (GCS 5:170–72). Flavian: *HE* 4.25, 5.3, 5.23 (GCS 5:263–64, 281–82, 321–24). Acacius: *HE* 4.27 (GCS 5:267). Diodore: *HE* 4.25 (GCS 5:263–64), 5.40 (GCS 5:347–48). Theodore: *HE* 5.40 (GCS 5:347–48).

123. See, e.g., Ignatius of Antioch, *Ep. ad Ephesinos* 4 (Lightfoot, 2.2:4–42).

124. Council of Nicaea, canon 6 (Joannou, *Discipline*, 1:28). Council of Constantinople, canon 3 (Joannou, *Discipline*, 1:47–48). For more on the *de iure* authority of metropolitans and primates, see Norton, *Episcopal Elections*, chaps. 5–7.

125. Council of Nicaea, canon 4 (Joannou, *Discipline*, 1:26).

126. On authority in the Egyptian church, see Wipszycka, "La chiesa nell' Egitto."

127. This description belongs to Price and Gaddis, *Acts of Chalcedon*, 1:13.

128. Socrates, *HE* 5.8 (GCS 1:281).

129. Theodoret, *HE* 5.40 (GCS 5:347–48).

130. Sozomen, *HE* 7.11 (GCS 4:314).

131. Socrates, *HE* 6.18 (GCS 1:341–42); Sozomen, *HE* 8.20 (GCS 4:376–77).

132. Socrates, *HE* 6.3 (GCS 1:313–15).

133. Sozomen, *HE.* 7.11 (GCS 4:314).

134. On Chrysostom's doctrinal thinking, see Grillmeier, *Christ*, 418–21; Fairbairn, *Grace and Christology*, 204–11, both of whom stress his affinity with Athanasius and Cyril. See also Lawrenz, *Christology of John Chrysostom*, who sees an Antiochene thread.

135. Theodoret, *HE* 5.34 (GCS 5:336).

136. Palladius, *De vita Sancti Iohannis Chrysostomi* 4, 6 (SC 341:92–96, 126–36).

137. Palladius, *De vita Sancti Iohannis Chrysostomi* 8–9 (SC 341:162–64, 186–98).

138. Palladius, *De vita Sancti Iohannis Chrysostomi* 16 (SC 341:304–18).

139. Palladius, *De vita Sancti Iohannis Chrysostomi* 20 (SC 341:394–406), listed thirty-one allies of Chrysostom who suffered or struggled on his behalf.

140. E.g., John Chrysostom, *Ep.* 85–90 to bishops of Palestine (*PG* 52:653–55), 108–112 to bishops of Cilicia, including Theodore (*PG* 52:667–69), and 25, 114, 131, 138, 142, 230 to Elpidius of Laodicea, probably John's closest ally (*PG* 52:626, 669–71, 690, 695, 696–97, 737). On the letters of appeal, see Delmaire, " 'Lettres d'exil' de Jean Chrysostome," 76–86. John's known allies are noted in his prosopography (103–75).

141. Theodoret, *HE* 5.34 (GCS 5:336).

142. Atticus of Constantinople, *Ep. ad Cyrillum Alexandrinum*, sec. 3–4 (CPG #5652, *CVatGr 1431:* 23–24). Alexander (bishop 413–421) reinstated John's name. Acacius was clearly involved (Cyril, *Ep. ad Atticum CPolitanum,* sec. 10, CPG #5376, in *CVatGr 1431:* 25–28).

143. On Alexander the Sleepless's struggle with Theodotus of Antioch, see *Vita Alexandri acoemetae* 38–42 (*PO* 6:687–91); and Caner, *Wandering, Begging Monks,* chap. 4.

144. Theodoret, *ep.* S 110 (SC 111:40), mentioned Diogenes of Seleucobelus who was ordained by Acacius while married to a second wife in the 410s.

145. Rabbula of Edessa, *Ep. ad Cyrillum Alexandrinum* (CPG #6494, Overbeck: 225).

146. John of Antioch, *Ep. ad Nestorium* (CPG #6316, *ACO* I.1.1: 93–94).

CHAPTER 4. EPHESUS AND AFTER: LEADERSHIP, DOCTRINAL CRISIS, AND THE TRANSFORMATION OF THE ANTIOCHENE NETWORK

1. The *Liber Heraclidis* has interpolations, e.g., part 1 (tr. Hodgson and Driver, 7–86). See L. Abramowski, *Untersuchungen zum Liber Heraclidis;* Bebis, "Apology of Nestorius."

2. Cyril's enmity: Nestorius, *Liber Heraclidis* 1.3 (tr. Hodgson and Driver, 101). "Wounded and naked": *Liber Heraclidis* 1.3, 2.1 (tr. Hodgson and Driver, 121, 186, 265). Twisted monks: *Liber Heraclidis* 2.1 (tr. Hodgson and Driver, 273–81). "Peace in appearance": *Liber Heraclidis* 2.1 (tr. Hodgson and Driver, 289–93). "I endure all things …": *Liber Heraclidis* 2.1 (tr. Hodgson and Driver, 331).

3. Socrates, *HE* 7.29 (GCS 1:377–78).

4. See Sillett, "Culture of Controversy," 8.

5. Nestorius, *Liber Heraclidis* (tr. Hodgson and Driver, 98–101).

6. Cyril got involved in early 430 (Cyril, *Ep. ad Nestorium* [CPG #5304, *ACO* I.1.1: 25–28]). Even Eusebius, the loudest protester, was then a local layman (Eusebius of Dorylaeum, *Contestatio* [CPG #5940, *ACO* I.1.1: 101–2]).

7. Cyril of Alexandria, *Ep. ad Caelestine papam* (CPG #5310, *ACO* I.1.5: 10–12); *Commonitorium ad Posidonium diaconum* (CPG #5311, *ACO* I.1.7: 171–72); *Libri v contra Nestorium* (CPG #5217, *ACO* I.1.6: 13–106). Pope Celestine, *Ep. ad Cyrillum Alexandrinum* (CPG #5312, *ACO* I.1.1: 75–77).

8. Cyril of Alexandria, *Explanatio xii capitulorum* (CPG #5223, *ACO* I.1.5: 15–25) includes both the *Anathemas* and the author's later explanations. Initially the *Anathemas* were sent with *Ep. ad Nestorium (una cum Synodo Alexandrina)* (CPG #5317, *ACO* I.1.1: 33–42). On their distribution, see Evieux, "André de Samosate," 257.

9. Notable studies of the chaotic council include Hefele, *History of Councils*, book 9; Schwartz, *ACO I*; Galtier, "Le centenaire d'Éphèse;" Devreesse, "Les actes du concile d'Éphèse;" Person, *Mode of Theological Decision Making*, chap. 5; Gregory, *Vox Populi*, chap. 4; McGuckin, *St. Cyril*, chap. 1; Lim, *Public Disputation*, chap. 7; Sillett, "Culture of Controversy," chaps. 1–2; MacMullen, *Voting About God*; Wessel, *Cyril*, chaps. 3–6.

10. On the textual history of the Casiniensis collection, part 2 (Rusticus's sixth-century translation of Irenaeus's *Tragoedia*), see Galtier, "Le centenaire d'Éphèse." On the Vaticana, Atheniensis, and Palatina collections see Galtier; Devreesse, "Les actes du concile d'Éphèse." For a synopsis, see Sillett, "Culture of Controversy."

11. Attempts to date and sequence the letters include Schwartz, *Konzilstudien*, 30–46; *ACO* I.4; Devreesse, "Après le concile d'Éphèse," 271–92; and *Essai sur Théodore*, 125–51; Diepen, "La christologie des amis de Nestorius," 30–45; L. Abramowski, "Der Streit um Diodor und Theodor;" Sellers, *Council of Chalcedon*, 12–25; and Evieux, "André de Samosate." This chapter offers a new reconstruction, noting disagreements with prior dating. See Constas, *Proclus*, 79–127, for another viable interpretation.

12. For the core support of Theodore, see John of Antioch, *Ep. ad Nestorium* (CPG #6316, *ACO* I.1.1: 93–96; *pace* Fairbairn, "Allies or Merely Friends"). For more ambiguous cues of attachment from the 420s, see Theodoret, *epp.* P 32, P 45 (SC 40:98, 109–11) to Theodotus of Antioch (the only two of his letters securely dated to the 420s). Note also Hiba of Edessa's later recollections in his *Ep. ad Marim Persam* (*ACO* I II.1.3: 33–34).

13. For reconciliation with "Paulinians," see Atticus of Constantinople, *Ep. ad Cyrillum Alexandrinum*, sec. 5 (CPG #5652, *CVatGr 1431*: 23–24). For reconciliation with suspected Apollinarians, see Theodoret, *HE* 5.38 (GCS 5:342).

14. Theodotus of Antioch targeted Alexander the Sleepless, a Syrian monastic leader who had fled to Constantinople (Caner, *Wandering, Begging Monks*, 130–39).

15. Theodoret expressed his admiration and showed deference to all four.

16. In Cappadocia, the Antiochenes linked up with Eutherius of Tyana and tried to recruit Firmus of Caesarea (see John of Antioch, *Ep. ad Firmum Caesariensem*, CPG #6313, *ACO* I.4: 7). In Palestine, Juvenal of Jerusalem had to counter Antiochene canvassing (see John of Antioch et al., *Contestatio prima ad Theodosium et Valentinianum imp. aug.* [CPG #6350, *ACO* I.1.7: 72]).

17. On St. Sergius and Rasapha, see E. Fowden, *The Barbarian Plain*, esp. chap. 1.

18. On "Syrian" clerics in Armenia, see Winkler, "An Obscure Chapter," 94–109; and Garsoïan, *L'église Arménienne*, 66–76. Antiochene contacts with Persian Mesopotamia are difficult to locate precisely until the 480s. See Epilogue.

19. Quoted by Socrates, *HE* 7.29 (GCS 1:377).

20. See Hiba of Edessa, *Ep. ad Marim Persam* (CPG #6500, *ACO* II.1.3: 33).

21. Such discoveries occurred wherever the network expanded. See later in this chapter.

22. Nestorius's first extant letter exchange with Syrian colleagues reveals just such an episode of doubt and misinformation. See later in this section.

23. All three deaths were noted by Theodoret, *HE* 5.40 (GCS 5:347–48).

24. Acacius of Beroea, *Ep. ad Alexandrum episc. Hierapolis* (CPG #6478, *ACO* I.1.7: 147).

25. Theodoret, *HR* 10.9 (SC 234:450–52).

26. John of Antioch, *Ep. ad Nestorium* (CPG #6316, *ACO* I.1.1; 93–96) This letter concerned public relations strategy; it does not show a serious theological difference between him and Nestorius, who did ultimately accept some notion of the "double birth." (An observation I owe to Patrick Gray from an unpublished paper; *pace* Fairbairn, *Grace and Christology*, 211–16, and "Allies or Merely Friends").

27. Cyril of Alexandria, *Ep. ad Acacium Beroeensem* (CPG #5314, *ACO* I.1.1: 98–99).

28. Pope Celestine et al., *Ep. ad Nestorium (sententia synodi Romanae)* (CPG #8639, *ACO* I.1.1: 77–83) stated the timeline. Cyril et al., *Ep. ad Nestorium (una cum synodo Alexandrina)* (CPG #5317, *ACO* I.1.1: 33–34, 42) linked it to the *Twelve Anathemas*. For the *Anathemas*, see Cyril, *Explanatio xii capitulorum*, esp. 2, 5, 12 (CPG #5223, *ACO* I.1.5: 15–25).

29. Theodoret, *Impugnatio xii anathematismorum Cyrilli* (CPG #6214, *ACO* I.1.6: 108–44); Andreas, *Impugnatio xii anathematismorum Cyrilli Alexandrini* (CPG #6373, *ACO* I.1.7: 33–65). See also Acacius of Beroea, *Ep. ad Cyrillum Alexandriae* (CPG #6479, *ACO* I.1.1: 99–100).

30. Andreas argued against Cyril's supposed denial of the reality of Christ's humanity. Theodoret tried to refute Cyril's theopaschite notions and declarations of "one nature." See Grillmeier, *Christ*, 419–30; McGuckin, *St. Cyril*, 47–48.

31. Acacius of Beroea, *Ep. ad Cyrillum Alexandriae* (CPG #6479, *ACO* I.1.1: 99–100).

32. Acacius was too feeble, Andreas too ill. See later in this chapter.

33. Theodosius II, *Sacra ad Cyrillum Alex. et ad singulos metropolitas* (CPG #8652, *ACO* I.1.1: 114–16), suggests that the emperor wanted Cyril rebuked.

34. Nestorius, *Liber Heraclidis* (tr. Hodgson and Driver, 265–67, 281–83).

35. The two Alexanders carried a message from John of Antioch (*Ep. ad Cyrillum episc. Alexandriae*, CPG #6307, *ACO* I.1.1: 119, with a verbal addendum). Cyril took it to mean that he should start immediately (*Ep. ad Comarium Potamonem et Dalmatium archimandritam et Timothium et Eulogium presb.* [CPG #5323, *ACO* I.1.2: 66–68]).

36. *Contestatio directa Cyrillo et his qui cum eo convenerunt* (CPG #8669, *ACO* I.4: 27–30); sixty-eight signatories were present, one (Bosphorius of Gangra) signed by proxy. Only thirty-seven (at most) held firm a week later (*Acta synodi Orientalium*, Latin, *ACO* I.4: 37–38). See Vogt, "Unterschiedliches Konzilverständnis der Cyrillianer," 430–31.

37. *Acta concilii Epheseni*, session 1 (*ACO* I.1.2: 7–39).

38. Count Candidianus, *Contestio directa Cyrillo et his qui cum eo fuerant congregati* (CPG #8687, *ACO* I.4: 31–32). See also Cyril of Alexandria, *Relatio ad imperatores de Nestorii depositione*, sec. 4 (CPG #8684, *ACO* I.1.3: 4).

39. *Nestorium depositio ad eum missa a concilio* (CPG #8676, *ACO* I.1.2: 64).

40. The Latin *acta* (preserved by Irenaeus, *ACO* I.4: 37–38) record fifty-three signatures. A related letter (*ACO* I.4: 45–46) adds five more names. The Greek version (preserved by Cyril's allies, *ACO* I.1.5: 122–24) names only forty-three. The missing names include Cyrus of Tyre, Rabbula of Edessa, and Theophanius of Philadelphia, which may have been expunged to save the reputations of defectors.

41. *Acta et sententia synodi Orientalium* (CPG #6352, *ACO* I.1.5: 119–24). *Acta concilii Ephesini*, session 1 (*ACO* I.1.2: 54–64) lists 155 delegates supporting Cyril. Later letters and sessions list as many as 197 signatories, but some of these were defectors and others were

added by proxy or after the fact. See Vogt, "Unterschiedliches Konzilverständnis der Cyrillianer," 431–35; Crabbe, "Invitation List to the Council of Ephesus."

42. See John of Antioch et al., *Ep. synodi Orientali ad Theodosium et Valentinianum imp. aug.* (CPG #6324, *ACO* I.1.5: 125–26); Nestorius, *Liber Heraclidis* (tr. Hodgson and Driver, 266–67); Cyril of Alexandria et al., *Relatio Cyrillianorum ad Theodosium et Valentinianum imperatores*, sec. 5 (CPG #8697, *ACO* I.1.3: 10–13). On the Antiochenes' goal of naming a new bishop, see McGuckin, *St. Cyril*, 94–95.

43. Hiba of Edessa, *Ep. ad Marim Persam* (CPG #6500, *ACO* II.1.3: 33).

44. See Vogt, "Unterschiedliches Konzilverständnis der Cyrillianer," 448–51.

45. For the sermons of Cyril, Memnon, and their allies, see *ACO* I.1.2: 70–104. Nestorius acknowledged their effectiveness (*Liber Heraclidis*, tr. Hodgson and Driver, 270–71).

46. The Antiochene street sermons were described by Cyril's party as "threatening words against the orthodox faith" (*Acta concilii Epheseni, ACO* I.1.3: 16–17).

47. *Acta concilii Epheseni*, session 5–6 (*ACO* I.1.3: 15–25; I.1.7: 84–117). Again, several names may have been removed later.

48. *Episcoporum Constantinopoli consistentium commonitorium* (CPG #6891, *ACO* I.1.2: 65–66); Nestorius, *Liber Heraclidis* (tr. Hodgson and Driver, 271–73). See also T. Gregory, *Vox Populi*, 108–113.

49. For Nestorius's first appeal, see his *Ep. ad Imperatorem Theodosium* (CPG #5672, *ACO* I.1.5: 13–15). For Candidianus's initial brief report, see his *Contestatio alia post synodum* (CPG #8688, *ACO* I.4: 33).

50. Theodosius II, *Sacra ad synodum per Palladium* (CPG #8696, *ACO* I.1.3: 9–10).

51. John of Antioch et al., *Ep. ad Theodosium et Valentinianum imp. aug.* (CPG #6323, *ACO* I.1.5: 124).

52. Irenaeus's role as spokesman is mentioned by John of Antioch et al., *Ep. ad Theodosium et Valentinianum imp. aug.* (CPG #6326, *ACO* I.1.5: 131).

53. John of Antioch et al., *Ep. ad senatum CPolitanum* (CPG #6342, *ACO* I.1.5: 127–28).

54. John of Antioch et al., *Ep ad. Praefectum praetorio et magistrum militiae; Ep. ad Praepositum et Scholasticium eunuchum* (CPG #6337–38, *ACO* I.1.5: 132–33).

55. John of Antioch et al., *Ep. ad Theodosium et Valentinianum imp. aug.* (CPG #6324, *ACO* I.1.5: 125–26).

56. Theodosius II, *Sacra directa per Iohannem comitem concilio* (CPG #8723, *ACO* I.1.3: 31–32). On the reading of this *sacra*, see John, Count of Sacred Largesses, *Relatio ad Imperatorem Theodosium* (CPG #8724, *ACO* I.1.7: 67).

57. See Cyril, *Ep. ad Comarium Potomon episc. et Dalmatium archimandritam et Timotheum et Eulogium presb.* (CPG #5323, *ACO* I.1.2: 66–68); *Ep. ad Theopemptum Potamonem et Danielem episc.* (CPG #5328, *ACO* I.1.3: 50–51). See also Cyril's synodical letters (CPG #8730–32, *ACO* I.1.3: 49–53, I.3: 178). For Cyril's gifts, see *Breve directorum ad mandatorios C Polim missos* (CPG #5396, *ACO* I.4: 224–25).

58. John of Antioch et al., *Ep. ad Senatum CPolitanum* (CPG #6342, *ACO* I.1.5: 127–28).

59. Antiochus (Chuzon) the Prefect, *Ep. ad Nestorium* (CPG #8748, *ACO* I.1.7: 71).

60. Cyril of Alexandria et al., *Mandatum episcopis CPolim directis* (CPG #8740, *ACO* I.1.3: 33–36).

61. *Mandatum synodi Orientalium episcopis CPolim directis* (CPG #8742, *ACO* I.1.3. 36–39).

62. John of Antioch and the delegates, *Ep. ad episcopos Orientales Ephesi degentes* (CPG #6349, *ACO* I.1.7: 76–77).

63. John of Antioch and the delegates, *Contestio prima ad Theodosium et Valentinianum imp. aug.*, sec. 2–3 (CPG #6329: *ACO* I.1.7: 72).

64. Theodoret reported his limited success (*Ep. ad Alexandrum episc. Hierapolis* [CPG #6242, *ACO* I.1.7: 79–80]). Acacius of Melitene asserted that the Divinity could change, which reportedly caused the emperor to drop his cloak (John of Antioch and the delegates, *Ep. ad episcopos Orientales Ephesi degentes* [CPG #6350, *ACO* I.1.7: 77]).

65. By the time Theodoret reported to Alexander, he saw "no hope" that courtiers would back "two natures" (*Ep. ad Alexandrum episc. Hierapolis* [CPG #6242, *ACO* I.1.7: 80]).

66. John of Antioch and the delegates, *Contestio secunda ad Theodosium et Valentinianum imp. aug.* (CPG #6330, *ACO* I.1.7: 75).

67. John of Antioch and the delegates, *Contestatio tertia ad Theodosium et Valentinianum imp. aug.* (CPG #6331, *ACO* I.1.7: 75–76).

68. E.g., Theodoret, *Ep ad Andream Samosatenum* (CPG #6255, *ACO* I.4: 59–60); *Ep. ad Alexandrum Hierapolitanum* (CPG #6242, *ACO* I.1.7: 80).

69. Theodoret, *Sermo in Chalcedone habitus* (CPG #6228, *ACO* I.1.7: 82–83).

70. Theodoret, *Ep. ad Alexandrum Hierapolitanum* (CPG #6242, *ACO* I.1.7: 80).

71. This observation I owe to Ray Van Dam.

72. For John's sermon, see *ACO* I.4: 79.

73. Theodoret, *Ep. ad Alexandrum Hierapolitanum* (CPG #6242, *ACO* I.1.7: 79).

74. On these efforts, see Holum, *Theodosian Empresses,* 179–81.

75. This count includes the signatories to Nestorius's condemnation (*ACO* I.1.7: 111–17) and absent supporters.

76. John of Antioch, *Ep. ad Rufum episc. Thessalonicae* (CPG #6319, *ACO* I.1.3: 42).

77. John reportedly wrote to Appinianus, a *dux* of Mesopotamia (see Alexander of Hierapolis, *Ep. ad Iohannem Antiochenum* [CPG #6403, *ACO* I.4: 163–64]).

78. John of Antioch et al., *Ep. ad Theodosium et Valentinianum imp aug. (una cum synodo Antiochena)* (CPG #6332, *ACO* I.4: 80–81). The Latin calls Cyril's *Anathemas "nefas."*

79. Theodoret, *Ep. ad eos qui in Euphratesia et Osrhoena regione, Syria, Phoenicia et Cilicia vitam monasticam degunt* (CPG #6276, *PG* 83:1416–33); *Ep. ad populum CPolitanum* (CPG #6273, *ACO* I.4: 81–85).

80. Acacius of Beroea, *Ep. ad Alexandrum episc. Hierapolis* (CPG #6477, *ACO* I.4: 85). He did cite some evidence, a list of gifts to Scholasticius the eunuch.

81. On the symbols of communion that united Syrian Christians, see Taft, "One Bread, One Body." See also Tsirpanlis, "Structure of the Church." On the late origins of the diptychs, see Paverd, "Anaphoral intercessions."

82. See Blum, *Rabbula,* 111–31; Doran, *Stewards of the Poor,* 50–51, 62–64; Chadwick, "Eucharist and Christology."

83. John of Antioch, *Ep. ad Antiochum praefectum praetorium* (CPG #6306, *ACO* I.4: 79–80), reported ill treatment while traveling through Ancyra and Cappadocian Caesarea.

84. See Alexander of Hierapolis, *Epp. ad Theodoretum episc. Cyri* (CPG #6410, 6416; *ACO* I.4: 130, 187).

85. John of Antioch, *Ep. ad Alexandrum Hierapolitanum* (CPG #6303, *ACO* I.4: 112–13).

86. Juvenal's activities from late 431 until the late 430s are not recorded in surviving sources, but neither are any defections. Juvenal must have capitalized on his prior efforts at episcopal recruitment (Honigmann, "Juvenal," esp. 215–25). On the efforts of Firmus of Caesarea, see Theodoret, *Commonitorium ad Alexandrum Hierapolitanum* (CPG #6243, *ACO* I.4: 87). Van Dam, *Kingdom of Snow*, 36, links this episode to urban rivalry.

87. For Acacius's general collaboration see Cyril of Alexandria, *Ep. ad Acacium episc. Melitenae* (CPG #5340, *ACO* I.1.4: 20–31). For Acacius's connections to Pers-Armenia, see Acacius of Melitene, *Ep. ad sanctum Sahak Armenorum patriarcham* and *Ep. ad Armenos* (CPG #5794–5795; Latin tr. Richard, "Acace de Mélitène").

88. John of Antioch et al., *Ep. ad episcopos Osrhoenae contra Rabbulam episc. Edessae (una cum synoda Antiochena)* (CPG #6347, *ACO* I.4: 87). No further friendly contacts are attested between bishops of Osrhoene and the Antiochene "schismatics." Blum, *Rabbula*, 152–65, argues that Rabbula defected before 431, based on Rabbula's sermon against Nestorius (which he dates to 429) and the letter to Andreas (which he dates to early 431). But Irenaeus's *acta* list Rabbula as signing at the counter-council. We must either doubt the accuracy of Irenaeus or redate Rabbula's writings to 431/432. See Vogt, "Unterschiedliches Konzilverständnis der Cyrillianer," 444–45; see later in this chapter.

89. Theodosius II, *Sacra ad Iohannem Antiochenum* (CPG #8810, *ACO* I.1.4: 3–5); *Sacra ad Symeonem Stylitem* (CPG #8811, *ACO* I.1.4: 5–6).

90. John of Antioch, *Ep. ad Alexandrum Hierapolitanum* (CPG #6302, *ACO* I.4: 91).

91. These letters were mentioned by Acacius of Beroea, *Ep. ad Maximianum episc. CPolis* (CPG #6480, *ACO* I.1.7: 161–62).

92. The move of the Antioch meeting to Beroea could be inferred from the title: "A proposal made by Acacius from (*para*) John of Antioch and those with [John] ..." (John of Antioch et al., *Propositiones Cyrillo Alexandrino missae* [CPG #6308, *ACO* I.1.7: 146]). Evieux, however, "André de Samosate," 279–80, posited just one meeting in Antioch.

93. On the six proposals, see Alexander of Hierapolis, *Ep. ad Andream Samosatenum* (CPG #6394, *ACO* I.4: 99–100). For the one approved proposal, see John of Antioch et al., *Propositiones Cyrillo Alexandrino missae* (CPG #6308, *ACO* I.1.7: 146).

94. Cyril, *Ep. ad Acacium Beroeensem* (CPG #5333, *ACO* I.1.7: 147–50).

95. On John's and Acacius's hope, see John of Antioch, *Ep. ad Alexandrum Hierapolitanum* (CPG #6303, *ACO* I.4: 112–13); see also Theodoret, *Ep. ad Alexandrum Hierapolitanum* (CPG #6245, *ACO* I.4: 108–9). Alexander's skepticism: Alexander of Hierapolis, *Ep. ad Helladium episc. Tarsi* (CPG #6401, *ACO* I.4: 105–6). Waiting: Helladius of Tarsus, *Ep. ad Alexandrum episc. Hierapolis* (CPG #6345, *ACO* I.4: 105).

96. On the new meeting, see John of Antioch, *Epp. ad Alexandrum Hierapolitanum* (CPG #6303–4, *ACO* I.4: 112–14). Theodoret may have missed the meeting because of illness (Theodoret, *Ep. ad Acacium Beroeensem* [CPG #6241, *ACO* I.4: 101]).

97. Eutherius of Tyana, *Ep. ad Helladium Tarsensem* (CPG #6151, *ACO* I.4: 111–12). On Alexander's reaction, see John of Antioch, *Ep. ad Alexandrum Hierapolitanum* (*ACO* I.4: 113–14).

98. Alexander of Hierapolis et al., *Ep. ad Helladium episc. Tarsi* (CPG #6400, *ACO* I.4: 93).

99. Theodoret, *Ep. ad Iohannem Antiochenum* (CPG #6266, *ACO* I.1.7: 164).

100. John of Antioch, *Ep. ad Alexandrum Hierapolitanum* (CPG #6303, *ACO* I.4: 112).

101. Theodoret, *Ep. ad Andream Samosatenum* (CPG #6256, *ACO* I.4: 102). Theodoret's subtlety in splitting the judgments of doctrine and of persons is noted by Pásztori-Kupán, *Theodoret*, 15–17.

102. For the rumors that Theodoret had betrayed Nestorius, see Theodoret, *Ep. ad Helladium episc. Tarsi* (CPG #6260, *ACO* I.4: 106–7). For John's assumptions, see his later letter: John of Antioch, *Ep. ad Theodoretum episc. Cyri* (CPG #6321, *ACO* I.4: 124).

103. Paul of Emesa featured aspects of the agreement in his sermons in Alexandria: *Homilia i-ii de nativitate Alexandria habita* (CPG #6365-6366, *ACO* I.1.4: 9–14). Here, amid mostly ambiguous Scriptural formulas, he made quick mention of "two natures."

104. The focus on the humanity as "temple" is mentioned by Hiba of Edessa, *Ep. ad Marim Persam* (CPG #6500, *ACO* II.1.3: 32–34).

105. Paul of Emesa, *Libellus Cyrillo Alexandrino oblatus* (CPG #6368, *ACO* I.1.4: 6–7).

106. The plan was reported by Cyril of Alexandria, *Ep. ad Theognostum et Charmosynum presbyteros et Leontium diaconum* (CPG #5337, *ACO* I.1.7: 154).

107. John of Antioch, *Ep. ad Cyrillum Alexandrinum de pace* (CPG #6310, *ACO* I.1.4: 7–9); Cyril, *Ep. ad Iohannem Antiochenum de pace* (CPG #5339, *ACO* I.1.4: 15–20). This letter (sometimes called *Laetentur coeli*) served as the official *Formula* text.

108. No opponent of Cyril is attested from these provinces, except Musaeus of Aradus (see Cyril *Ep. ad Mosaeum episc. Aradi et Antaradi* [CPG #5365, *ACO* I.4: 231]).

109. Alexander of Apamea, *Ep. ad Alexandrum Hier.* (CPG #6390, *ACO* I.4: 159).

110. Maximianus of Anazarbus et al., *Sententia synodi an. 433 Anazarbi habitae* (CPG #6453, *ACO* I.4: 142–43); Helladius of Tarsus, *Ep. ad Alexandrum episc. Hierapolis* (CPG #6437, *ACO* I.4: 143). Isauria later returned to communion along with Cilicia II (Meletius of Mopsuestia, *Ep. ad Alexandrum episc. Hierapolis*, CPG #6458, *ACO* I.4: 191).

111. Theodoret, *Ep. ad Iohannem Antiochenum* (CPG #6266, *ACO* I.4: 131–32; the Greek version, *ACO* I.1.7: 163–64, is incomplete and misleading).

112. For more on the background of Acacius, see chapter 3.

113. See Acacius of Beroea, *Ep. ad Cyrillum Alexandriae* (CPG #6479, *ACO* I.1.1: 99–100).

114. Acacius of Beroea, *Ep. ad Cyrillum Alexandriae* (CPG #6479, *ACO* I.1.1: 100).

115. *Vita Rabbulae* (Overbeck: 160–62, 167–70; tr. Doran, *Stewards of the Poor*, 69–70, 74–75). Peeters, "La vie de Rabboula;" and Blum, *Rabbula*, 14–106, largely endorse this *vita*.

116. *Chronicon Edessenum* year 723 (= A.D. 412, CSCO SS 1.4:6). See Peeters, "La vie de Rabboula," 163–66.

117. Blum, *Rabbula*, 142–49, analyzed Rabbula's early doctrinal work, though he posited an evolution rather than an about-face. Doran, *Stewards of the Poor*, 58–62, plays down Rabbula's Antiochene affiliation. Hiba and Irenaeus do not (accurately or not).

118. *Vita Rabbulae* (Overbeck: 172; tr. Doran, *Stewards of the Poor*, 76–77). Burkitt, "Christian Church in the East," 501-2 argued that Rabbula penned the *Peshitta*. Vööbus,

Researches on the Circulation of the Peshitta, challenged this notion. Doran, *Stewards of the Poor*, 55–57, clarifies that the Syriac *hlaf*, "alter" could indicate textual corrections.

119. See Honigmann, *Le couvent de Barsauma*, 29–33.

120. Andreas, *Ep. ad Alexandrum Hierapolitanum* (CPG #6374, ACO I.4: 86–87); Hiba of Edessa, *Ep. ad Marim Persam* (CPG #6500, ACO II.1.3: 33–34).

121. Rabbula, *Ep. ad Cyrillum Alexandrinum* (CPG #6494, ACO IV.1: 89).

122. Rabbula, *Ep. ad Andream Samosatenum* (CPG #6495, Overbeck: 222–23). This exchange might date to 431, especially if Rabbula missed Ephesus (Blum, *Rabbula*, 152). If he attended, it must date to 432 (Evieux, "André de Samosate," 276–78). See also Vogt, "Unterschiedliches Konzilverständnis der Cyrillianer," 444–45.

123. John of Antioch et al., *Ep. ad episcopos Osrhoenae contra Rabbulam episc. Edessae (una cum synoda Antiochena)* (CPG #6347, ACO I.4: 87). Rabbula retained the support of Gemellinus of Perrha, who later helped him harass Andreas (see Andreas of Samosata, *Ep. ad Alexandrum Hierapolitanum*, CPG #6380, ACO I.4: 136–37).

124. Andreas of Samosata, *Ep. ad Alexandrum Hierapolitanum* (CPG #6380, ACO I.4: 136–37). A temporary replacement for Andreas, Zacharias, is mentioned only by the tendentious *Vita Barsaumae*. See Honigmann, *Le couvent de Barsauma*, 27–31.

125. *Vita Rabbulae* (Overbeck: 198; tr. Doran, *Stewards of the Poor*, 97–98). The same manuscript preserves the sermon Rabbula supposedly delivered in Constantinople (Overbeck: 239–44). The work might have been written a few years later in Edessa.

126. Blum, *Rabbula*, 152, 160–65, concluded that Rabbula could not have attended the First Council of Ephesus, since he was supposedly blind (see Theodore Lector, a.k.a. Theodore Anagnostes, *HE* 2.40, GCS 3:153). But this late, fragmentary source only notes "blindness" in passing, as a gloss upon the "illness" mentioned in Rabbula, *Ep. ad Andream Samosatenum* (CPG #6495, Overbeck: 222, datable either to 431 or to 432).

127. Hiba of Edessa, *Ep. ad Marim Persam* (CPG #6500, ACO II.1.3: 33). Barhadbeshabba, *Cause of the Foundation of the Schools* (PO 6:380–81) claimed that Theodore had publicly contradicted Rabbula when the latter tried to justify beating his clergy.

128. Rabbula, *Homilia Constantinopoli habita* (CPG #6496, Overbeck: 240; tr. Doran, *Stewards of the Poor*, 59). See especially the analysis of Blum, *Rabbula*, 133–37.

129. Acacius of Beroea, *Ep. ad Cyrillum Alexandrinum* (CPG #6479, ACO I.1.1: 99–100).

130. John needed the help of his colleagues to discern the "Apollinarian" implications of some of Cyril's formulations (e.g., his claim that the natures did not mix because "one is the Divinity and the other the body;" see John of Antioch, *Ep. ad Alexandrum Hierapolitanum* [CPG #6303, ACO I.4: 113]). Even the *Formula of Reunion* relied heavily on Theodoret's writings. (See J. N. D. Kelly, *Early Christian Doctrines*, 328–29.)

131. John of Antioch, *Ep. ad Theodoretum episc. Cyri* (CPG #6321, ACO I.4: 124).

132. Cyril, *Ep. ad Acacium Beroeensem* (CPG #5392, ACO I.1.7: 140–42).

133. John of Antioch, *Ep. ad Cyrillum Alexandrinum*, sec. 5 (CPG #6309, ACO I.1.7: 152).

134. Meletius of Mopsuestia, *Ep. ad Alexandrum episc. Hierapolis* (CPG #6455, ACO I.4: 129). For this quotation, see the later *Ep. ad Alexandrum episc. Hierapolis* (CPG #6456, ACO I.4: 176). Irenaeus asserted that Paul never gave Cyril John of Antioch's proposals, citing Cyril, *Ep. ad Rabbulam Edessenum* (CPG #5334, ACO I.4: 140–41).

135. Eutherius, *Ep. ad Alexandrum Hierapolitanum*, sec. 2 (CPG #6150, ACO I.4: 214).

136. Helladius of Tarsus, *Ep. ad Alexandrum Hierapolitanum* (CPG #6437, ACO I.4: 143–44). Alexander of Hierapolis, *Ep. ad Iohannem Antiochenum* (CPG #6403, ACO I.4: 163–64). Maximianus of Anazarbus et al., *Sententia synodi an. 433 Anazarbi habitae* (CPG #6453, ACO I.4: 142–43).

137. John of Antioch et al., *Ep. ad Xystum, Cyrillum et Maximianum (una cum synodo Antiochena)* (CPG #6335, ACO I.1.4: 33), affirmed communion with the other primates. His *Ep. ad Xystum episc. Romae* (CPG #6336, ACO I.1.7: 158–60) appealed for support.

138. Theodosius II, *Sacra a Iohanne Antiocheno impetrata contra Alexandrum, Helladium, Maximianum et Theodoretum* (CPG #6423, ACO I.4: 166–67). Dionysius the Master of Soldiers, *Rescriptum ad Titum comitem* (CPG #6424, ACO I.4: 168–69).

139. Theodoret, *Ep. ad magistrum militum (Anatolium)* (CPG #6254, ACO I.4: 160). Abbibus of Doliche, *Libellus ad Alexandrum episc. Hierapolis, Theodoretum episc. Cyri, Maram et Davidem episcopi, Acylinum episc. Barbalissi* (CPG #6388, ACO I.4: 162). Alexander of Hierapolis, *Ep. ad Acylinum episc. Barbalissi* (CPG #6393, ACO I.4: 176). Alexander et al., *Ep. ad Pulcheriam aliasque Augustas* (CPG #6408, ACO I.4: 162–63).

140. Andreas, *Ep. ad Alexandrum Hierapolitanum* (CPG #6380, ACO I.4: 136–37).

141. John of Antioch, *Ep. ad Alexandrum Hierapolitanum* (CPG #6303, ACO I.4: 112–13).

142. John of Antioch, *Ep. ad Maximianum episc. CPolis* (CPG #6315, ACO I.1.7: 160).

143. On Alexander of Hierapolis's "40 years of mourning sins," see his *Ep. ad Acacium Beroeensem* (CPG #6392, ACO I.4: 98). On his ordination and diligence, see his *Epp. ad Theodoretum episc. Cyri* (CPG #6416–17, ACO I.4: 186–89). On his sponsorship of Sergiopolis/Rasapha, see Fowden, *The Barbarian Plain*, esp. chap. 1.

144. Alexander of Hierapolis, *Ep. ad Theodoretum episc. Cyri* (CPG #6416, ACO I.4: 187).

145. Alexander departed from Ephesus in 431 as soon as he could. See the third section of this chapter.

146. Alexander of Hierapolis, *Ep. ad Theodoretum episc. Cyri* (CPG #6410, ACO I.4: 130).

147. Alexander of Hierapolis, *Ep. ad Theodoretum episc. Cyri* (CPG #6412, ACO I.4: 136).

148. Alexander of Hierapolis, *Ep. ad Andream Samosatenum* (CPG #6396, ACO I.4: 129).

149. Alexander of Hierapolis, *Ep. ad Iohannem Germaniciae* (CPG #6405, ACO I.4: 138).

150. Meletius of Mopsuestia, *Epp. ad Alexandrum Hierapolitanum* (CPG #6455–56, ACO I.4: 129–30, 176–77). Meletius performed a similar service for Helladius of Tarsus and Maximianus of Anazarbus (Meletius, *Ep. ad Helladium episc Tarsi* [CPG #6461, ACO I.4: 169–70; *Ep. ad Maximianum episc. Anazarbi* [CPG #6462, ACO I.4: 155]).

151. Eutherius and Helladius, *Ep. ad Xystum episc. Romae* (CPG #6148, ACO I.4: 145–48). This letter was sent as a draft to Alexander (see Eutherius, *Ep. ad Alexandrum Hierapolitanum et Theodoretum* [CPG #6149, ACO I.4: 144–45]).

152. Maximianus of Anazarbus et al., *Sententia synodi an. 433 Anazarbi habitae* (CPG #6453, ACO I.4: 142–43). Similar statements came from Cilicia I, where Helladius of Tarsus acknowledged the influence of Meletius and his priest envoy Olippius (Helladius, *Ep. ad Alexandrum episc. Hierapolis* [CPG #6437, ACO I.4: 143]).

153. Theodoret, *Ep. ad Alexandrum Hierapolitanum* (CPG #6247, ACO I.4: 134).

154. Alexander of Hierapolis, *Ep. ad Helladium episc. Tarsi* (CPG #6402, ACO I.4: 185).

155. Alexander of Hierapolis, *Ep. ad Acacium Beroeensem* (CPG #6392, ACO I.4: 98).

156. Alexander of Apamea, *Ep. ad Alexandrum Hier.* (CPG #6390, ACO I.4: 159).

157. Andreas probably took refuge in Mesopotamia province from rioting clerics (see his *Ep. ad Alexandrum Hierapolitanum* [CPG #6380, ACO I.4: 136–37]).

158. See Alexander of Hierapolis, *Ep. ad Iohannem Germaniciae* (CPG #6405, ACO I.4: 138–39); Maximianus of Anazarbus, *Ep. ad Alexandrum episc. Hierapolis* (CPG #6450, ACO I.4: 140–41).

159. E.g., Andreas, *Ep. ad Rabbulam* (CPG #6384, in Pericoli-Ridolfini, "Lettera di Andrea": 153–69), if Evieux's dating is correct (see the fourth section of this chapter).

160. Andreas of Samosata, *Ep. ad Alexandrum Hierapolis* (CPG #6375, ACO I.4: 100).

161. Andreas of Samosata, *Ep. ad Alexandrum Hierapolis* (CPG #6376, ACO I.4: 102–3).

162. Alexander of Hierapolis, *Ep. ad Andream Samosatenum* (CPG #6398, ACO I.4: 138).

163. Theodoret, *HR* 10.9 (SC 234:450–52).

164. John of Antioch, *Ep. ad clerum populumque Tarsensem* (CPG #6348, ACO I.4: 90). On Eutherius's expulsion by Firmus of Caesarea, see Theodoret, *Ep. ad Alexandrum Hierapolitanum* (CPG #6243, ACO I.4 :87).

165. Helladius of Tarsus, *Ep. ad Alexandrum episc. Hierapolis* (CPG #6437, ACO I.4: 143–44).

166. The portion of the synodical preserved by Irenaeus hardly seems conciliatory, calling local supporters of Nestorius "seditious" (Alexander of Hierapolis, *Ep. ad Theodoretum episc. Cyri* [CPG #6414, ACO I.4: 173]). Constas, *Proclus*, 86–88, took this as a sign of Proclus's hostility toward the Antiochenes. But the rest of the letter must have been friendlier or Helladius would not have accepted it (see next note).

167. Helladius of Tarsus, *Ep. ad Meletium Mopsuestiae* (CPG #6440, ACO I.4: 169), asked for advice about accepting Proclus. The response from Meletius (*Ep. ad Helladium episcopum Tarsi* [CPG #6461, ACO I.4: 169–70]) was to reject Proclus. Helladius's decision to conditionally accept Proclus is recounted in Theodoret, *Ep. ad Alexandrum Hieropolitanum* (CPG #6250, ACO I.4: 172–73).

168. Helladius of Tarsus, *Ep. ad Meletium Mopsuestiae* (CPG #6440, ACO I.4: 169).

169. Helladius of Tarsus, *Ep. ad Alexandrum Hierapolitanum* (CPG #6439, ACO I.4: 183).

170. E.g., J.N.D. Kelly, *Early Christian Doctrines*, 325–29; Grillmeier, *Christ*, part 2, chap. 1.

171. Theodoret, *Ep. ad Andream Samosatenum* (CPG #6256, ACO I.4: 102).

172. There is no evidence that Theodoret drafted the *Formula of Reunion*, but his work surely guided John of Antioch (see J.N.D. Kelly, *Early Christian Doctrines*, 328; McGuckin, *St. Cyril*, 113–16).

173. Theodoret, *Ep. ad Alexandrum Hierapolitanum* (CPG #6248, ACO I.4: 135).

174. Theodoret, *Ep. ad Iohannem Antiochenum* (CPG #6266, ACO I.4: 132).

175. Theodoret, *Ep. ad Meletium episc. Neocaesareae* (CPG #6268, ACO I.4: 157).

176. Theodoret, *epp.* P 6, P 11 (SC 40:78–79, 83). He also courted Eurycianus the tribune (*ep.* P 47, SC 40:111–17), and Dometianus the quaestor (*Ep.* P 40, SC 40:104).

177. Theodoret, *Ep. ad Magistrum Militum [Anatolium]* (CPG #6254, ACO I.4: 160). Azéma's argument that the recipient was probably Dionysius, because the letter assumes past contacts (see *Theodoret Correspondance*, SC 429:37–39), is not persuasive; it ignores Anatolius's roots in Antioch and his later relationship with Theodoret.

178. The success of Theodoret's appeal can be deduced from Titus's long delay in even threatening to enforce imperial orders, from the fall of 433 to the summer of 434.

179. Theodoret, *Ep. ad Alexandrum Hierapolitanum* (CPG #6249, ACO I.4: 170–71).

180. Alexander of Hierapolis, *Ep. ad Theodoretum episc. Cyri* (CPG #6413, ACO I.4: 171).

181. Theodoret, *Ep. ad Alexandrum Hierapolitanum* (CPG #6250, ACO I.4: 172).

182. Theodoret, *Ep. ad Cyrillum episc. Adanae* (CPG #6258, ACO I.4: 181).

183. Theodoret, *Ep. ad Alexandrum Hierapolitanum* (CPG #6251, ACO I.4: 174).

184. Theodoret, *Ep. ad Cyrillum episc. Adanae* (CPG #6258, ACO I.4: 181).

185. Helladius of Tarsus, *Ep. ad Nestorium* (CPG #6441, ACO I.4: 205).

186. Devreese, "Après le concile d'Éphèse," and Holum, *Theodosian Empresses*, 182–83, rightly stress the importance to this settlement of pressure from the imperial court.

187. By mid-435, some Syrian bishops had condemned Nestorius; others (Theodoret, Helladius, and Maximianus) had joined communion without condemning him. A year later, the court would compel (almost) every Syrian bishop to condemn Nestorius explicitly (see Theodosius II, *Codex Theodosianus* 16.5.66).

188. Abbibus of Doliche had died of an illness. Theodoret, *Ep. ad magistrum militum [Anatolium]* (CPG #6254, ACO I.4: 160).

189. Theodoret, *Ep. ad Alexandrum Hierapolitanum* (CPG #6252, ACO I.4: 186); *Ep. ad Nestorium* (CPG #6271: ACO I.4: 189). Alexander of Hierapolis, *Ep. ad Theodoretum episc. Cyri* (CPG #6416, ACO I.4: 186–87).

190. Denunciations: Meletius of Mopsuestia, *Ep. ad Maximianum episc. Anazarbi* (CPG #6463, ACO I.4: 178); *Ep. ad Titum comitem domesticorum* (CPG #6465, ACO I.4: 192–95). For Meletius's continued agitations, see John of Antioch, *Ep. ad Theodosium et Valentinianum imperatores augustos* (CPG #6334, ACO I.4: 196).

191. Theodosius II's first decree, which exiled Nestorius and whoever refused communion (ACO I.1.3: 67), should not be confused with a second decree (ACO I.1.3: 68, I.4: 204, *Codex Theodosianus* 16.5.66), which exiled those who refused to condemn Nestorius. Irenaeus noted the fates of exiles (*Quanti a sanctis ecclesiis exierunt nolentes suam conscientiam vulnerare* [CPG #6431, ACO I.4: 203–4]), listing four bishops of Syria removed for refusing communion and one (Aquilinus of Barbalissus) for refusing to condemn Nestorius, as well as eleven from other regions (including Nestorius and Eutherius). Irenaeus was also exiled (see Theodosius II, *Sacra de exsilio Irenaei* [CPG #6474, ACO I.4: 203]). For Alexander's ousting see Libianus, governor of Euphratensis, *Relationes ad vicarium Titum (aut comiti Orientis)* (CPG #6429–30, ACO I.4:200–202). Dating these decrees has proven troublesome. Texts note that the first decree was enforced in Hierapolis on April 15, and that the second was written on August 3. No years are recorded. Schwartz (*CVatGr 1431:92*) persuasively argued that the second edict dates to August 436, to fit with Aristolaus's travels. The first edict, however, makes more sense in April 435 (see Devreese, *Essai sur Théodore*, 133–34)—the court had threatened exile since the spring of 434, and probably would not wait more than a year.

192. John of Antioch, *Ep. ad Theodoretum episc. Cyri* (CPG #6322, ACO I.4: 153–54). Dating of this letter is uncertain—perhaps 434 (as implied here) or perhaps 433, before John and Theodoret parted ways. Neither option deeply alters our narrative.

CHAPTER 5. FORGING COMMUNITY: THEODORET'S NETWORK AND ITS FALL

1. Theodoret, *ep.* S 84 (SC 98:220–22).

2. Theodoret, *ep.* S 85 (SC 98:222–24). Basil is portrayed more negatively in *Vita et mirabilia sanctae Theclae*, miracle 12 (ed. Dagron, *Vie et miracles*, 316–22).

3. For the trial of Eutyches, at which Basil served as a jurist, see *Acta concilii Chalcedonensis* session 1 (*ACO* II.1.7: 147–77). See later in this chapter.

4. Theodoret, *ep.* S 102 (SC 111:20–22).

5. For explicit condemnations of Nestorius, see Helladius of Tarsus, *Ep. ad Theodosium et Valentinianum imp. aug.* (CPG #6442, ACO I.4: 204–5) and the account of Meletius of Mopsuestia, *Ep. ad Alexandrum episc. Hierapolis* (CPG #6459, ACO I.4: 196–97). No such condemnations were made in Euphratensis until 436. See chapter 4.

6. See the *libellus* of Leontius and Abelius: *Ep. episcoporum et presbytorum Magnae Armeniae ad Proclum* (CPG #5898; tr. Constas, *Proclus*, 102–3).

7. On Maximus's rejection of John's communion, see Cyril, *Commonitorium ad Maximum diac. Antioch.* (CPG #5357, CVatGr 1431, 21). For other appeals, see his *Ep. ad Maximum, Iohannem et Thalassium, presb. et archimandritos* (CPG #5364, ACO I.4: 229); *Ep. ad Mosaeum episc. Antaradi* (CPG #5365, ACO I.4: 231).

8. Cyril, *Commonitorium ad Maximum diac. Antioch.* (CPG #5357, CVatGr 1431, 21).

9. For the edict, see *ACO* I.1.3: 68, I.4: 204, *Codex Theodosianus* 16.5.66. For Cyril's and Aristolaus's roles, see Cyril, *Ep. ad Aristolaum tribunum* (CPG #5359, ACO I.4: 206).

10. Rabbula of Edessa, *Ep. ad Cyrillum Alexandrinum* (CPG #6494, ACO IV.1: 89).

11. Rabbula's and Acacius of Melitene's roles in distributing hostile *florilegia* of Theodore's works were best delineated by Devreesse, *Essai sur Théodore*, 134–42.

12. The conflict in Persian Armenia appears in contradictory Armenian sources. See Winkler, "Obscure Chapter;" Garsoïan, *L'église arménienne*, 45–134; and Constas, *Proclus*, 92–96. For Sahak's link to Acacius and Rabbula, see Acacius of Melitene, *Ep. ad sanctum Sahak Armenorum patriarcham* and *Ep. ad Armenos* (CPG #5794–95, Latin tr. Richard, "Acace de Mélitène," *Opera Minora* vol. 2 #50: 394–400).

13. Sahak, *Ep. ad Proclum* (CPG #5899; Armenian: Ismireantz, *Liber epistularum*, 9–13; French tr. Tallon, *Livre des lettres*, 72–77). See also Leontius and Abelius, *Ep. episcoporum et presbyterorum Magnae Armeniae ad Proclum* (CPG #5898; Bedjan, *Livre d'Héraclide*, 594–96; tr. Constas, *Proclus*, 102–3).

14. Proclus, *Tomus ad Armenianos* (CPG #5897, ACO IV.2: 187–95). Winkler, "Obscure Chapter," 126–35, regards the anti-Theodore *florilegia* and arguments as a later addition. Constas, *Proclus*, 102–12, reaffirms the anti-Theodore aims of Proclus's work.

15. Proclus, *Ep. ad Iohannem Antiochenum* (CPG #5900, ACO IV.1: 140–43). See also Winkler, "Obscure Chapter," 143–51.

16. Hereafter, the dating and course of the dispute over Theodore is unclear. Scholars have reconstructed it variously. See Schwartz, *Konzilstudien*, 18–53; *CVatGr 1431*, 92; Devreesse, "Après le Concile d'Éphèse;" *Essai sur Théodore*, 125–53; Richard, "Acace de Mélitène;" "Proclus;" L. Abramowski, "Der Streit um Diodor und Theodor," 252–87. My dating is largely based on Abramowski, augmented by Constas, *Proclus*, 115–24.

17. Cyril, *Ep. ad Acacium Melitenum* (CPG #5369, *CVatGr 1431*, 15–16); John of Antioch et al., *Ep. ad Cyrillum Alexandrinum* (CPG #6312, *ACO* I.5: 310–11).

18. John of Antioch et al., *Ep. ad Cyrillum Alexandrinum* (CPG #6312, *ACO* I.5: 313–14).

19. Sillett, "Culture of Controversy," 50–53, argues that Cyril sought to undercut the Antiochene party by attacking its heritage.

20. Helladius of Tarsus et al., *Ep. ad Theodosium et Valentinianum imp. aug.* (CPG #6442, *ACO* I.4: 204–5); John of Antioch et al., *Ep. ad Proclum episc. CPolis* (CPG #6317, *ACO* I.4: 208–10). Theodoret and John of Germanicea were rumored to have avoided condemning Nestorius (see Cyril, *Ep. ad Iohannem Antiochenum* [CPG #5363, *CVatGr 1431*, 15]; *Acta concilii Chalcedonensis* sessions 5, 9 [*ACO* II.1.2: 123, II.1.3: 9–10]).

21. Cyril of Alexandria, *Ep. ad Iohannem Antiochenum* (CPG #5363, *CVatGr 1431*, 15).

22. The end of this dispute remains obscure; it apparently involved two Antiochene councils. For the first meeting (in August 438), see John of Antioch, *Ep. ad Cyrillum Alexandrinum* (CPG #6312, *ACO* I.5: 310–14). Generally, see Richard, "Proclus," 303–8.

23. E.g., Cyril, *Contra Diodorum et Theodorum* (CPG #5229, *PG* 76:1437–52). On the dating of Cyril's polemics (438–439), see Devreesse, *Essai sur Théodore*, 152–59.

24. This second council held in Antioch (dateable to 439 or 440), is noted by Pelagius, *In defensione trium capitulorum* sec. 3 (ed. Devreesse, 15), which counted attendees, and by Barhadbeshabba of Arbaya, *HE* 29 (*PO* 9:573–78), which preserves a synodical letter.

25. Theodosius II, quoted in Facundus, *Defensio trium capitulorum* (SC 484:44).

26. Cyril of Alexandria, *Ep. ad Iohannem Antiochenum* sec. 5 (CPG #5391, *ACO* I.5: 314–15). Proclus of Constantinople, *Ep. ad Iohannem Antiochenum* (in Pelagius, *In defensione trium capitulorum* sec. 3; ed. Devreesse, 24–25).

27. E.g., Schwartz, *Konzilstudien*, 35; Sellers, *Chalcedon*, 28; Winkler, "Obscure Chapter," 164. Constas, *Proclus*, 122–23, suggests that Cyril relented to avoid encouraging the ecumenical pretensions of the bishop of Constantinople.

28. Theodoret, *ep.* P 41 (SC 40:105) and *ep.* S 24 (SC 98:80–82) to Andreas use techniques for evoking intimacy outlined in chapter 1, particularly jocularity.

29. Theodoret dedicated his *Explanatio in Canticum canticorum* to John of Germanicea (*PG* 81:28). Theodoret, *ep.* S 125 (SC 111:92–98) recalled his consistent support.

30. On Domnus as a monk in Palestine, see Cyril of Scythopolis, *Vita Euthymii* 16, 20 (TU 49.2:25–27, 32–33). On Domnus's links to Theodoret (darkly interpreted), see *Syriac Acts of the Second Council of Ephesus* (Flemming: 126; tr. Perry: 314–15).

31. Basil's consecration dates between 444 and 448. Dagron, *Vie et miracles*, 17–18, suggests not long before 448, based on *Vita et mirabilia sanctae Theclae*, miracles 12, 44 (ed. Dagron, *Vie et miracles*: 316–22, 402–6).

32. See Theodoret, *ep.* S 32 (SC 98:92–94) and *ep.* S 36 (SC 98:98–100).

33. Uranius's election was contested by a certain Peter, who later presented his case in the *Syriac Acts of the Second Council of Ephesus* (Flemming: 124; tr. Perry: 311). During the

Eutychean dispute, Theodoret worried that Uranius had turned on him, but was then reassured by a warm letter exchange (see Theodoret, *epp.* S 122–123 [SC 111:84–90]).

34. Hiba's background has been subject to wide speculation. The idea that Hiba headed a "School of the Persians" has no reliable support (see Becker, *Fear of God,* chap. 2). What is clear is what Hiba claimed in his *Ep. ad Marim Persam* (CPG #6500, *ACO* II.1.3: 33–34), that he went to Ephesus in 431 as a cleric and suffered Rabbula's "tyranny."

35. On protests against Hiba, see Proclus, *Ep. ad Iohannem Antiochenum* (CPG #5900, *ACO* IV.1: 140–43). Hiba consecrated his cousin Sophronius of Constantina and his nephew Daniel of Carrhae before 444 (Trial of Athanasius of Perrha, *Acta concilii Chalcedonensis* session 14, [*ACO* II.1.3: 69]).

36. So Athanasius of Perrha alleged, noting Pompeianus of Emesa as the third consecrator (*Syriac Acts of the Second Council of Ephesus* [Flemming: 126–27; tr. Perry: 315–17]).

37. Irenaeus ordained Aquilinus of Byblus, who was deposed at Ephesus in 449 (*Syriac Acts of the Second Council of Ephesus* [Flemming: 76–78; tr. Perry: 182–86]).

38. For Theodoret's heresy hunting, see his *ep.* S 81 (SC 98:192–94) and *HR* 21.15–18 (SC 257:92–98). For his extended oversight, see *ep.* S 75 (SC 98:160–62).

39. Theodoret, *epp.* S 28, S 42 (SC 98: 86, 112), *HR* 21.5–29, 26.14–19, 27.4 (SC 257:76–114, 192–200, 222).

40. Theodoret, *ep.* S 132 (SC 111:122–24) to Longinus, archimandrite of Doliche; *epp.* S 128–130 (SC 111:106–10), to other archimandrites. For a link to Nicertae see his *Ep. ad Alexandrum Hieropolitanum* (CPG #6244, *ACO* I.4: 104) and his *ep.* S 119 (SC 111:80).

41. Theodoret, *epp.* P 15, P 20 (SC 40: 86–87, 92); S 47 (SC 98:122–24). Despite all the struggles, neither man directly criticized the other. Proclus respected the Syrians by moving Chrysostom's remains to the capital (see Constas, *Proclus,* 114–15).

42. Theodoret, *epp.* S 142–43 (SC 111:152–58). On the *Akoimetoi* monks' shift from target to Antiochene ally, see Caner, *Wandering, Begging Monks,* chap. 4.

43. E.g., Theodoret, *ep.* P 2 (SC 40:74–75).

44. Proclus, *Ep. ad Iohannem Antiochenum* (CPG #5900, *ACO* IV.1: 140–43).

45. Theodoret, *epp.* S 77–78 (SC 98:166–82).

46. Theodoret, *ep.* S 83 (SC 98:216) recalled cordial exchanges with Cyril.

47. Theodoret's prominent contacts included Anatolius (*ep.* S 45 [SC 98:118–20]), but also Titus, count of the Domestici (*ep.* P 6 [SC 40:78–79]), Dometianus the Quaestor (*ep.* P 40 [SC 40:104]) and the Patrician Areobindus (*ep.* P 18 [SC 40:89–90]). On Pulcheria, see *ep.* S 43 (SC 98:112–14). See chapter 7.

48. See chapters 6 and 7.

49. See Sillett, "Culture of Controversy," chaps. 2–3, who argues that Cyril sought to marginalize the Antiochenes with an "Orientalizing" rhetoric.

50. See later in this chapter. For more examples, see chapter 1.

51. On Theodoret's association of Syriac with simplicity, see *HR* 8.2 (SC 234:376–78), 17.9 (SC 257:46); and Urbainczyk, *Theodoret,* 72–79. In fact, the cultural awareness of Syriac writers such as Ephrem could be quite rich; see Brock, *Luminous Eye,* 7–9; and Possekel, *Philosophic Concepts.*

52. Even the Syriac master Rabbula played off this idea in his *Ep. ad Cyrillum Alexandrinum* (CPG #6494, *ACO* IV.1: 89; Syriac: Overbeck, 225).

53. Proclus, *Ep. ad Iohannem Antiochenum* (CPG #5900, *ACO* IV.1:140-43).

54. The *Syriac Acts of the Second Council of Ephesus* (Flemming: 24; tr. Perry: 66-67) mention opposition in "the schools of Armenians, Persians, and Syrians," which implies some involvement with ethnic circles of learning. On the fictions and possible facts regarding the "School of the Persians" in Edessa, see Becker, *Fear of God*, chaps. 2-3.

55. See Guinot, *L'éxegèse de Théodoret*, 183-97; Millar, "Theodoret," esp. 121-23.

56. Theodoret constantly recommended students to nearby sophists (*epp.* P 7, P 27-28, P 44 [SC 40:79, 94-95, 108]). See chapter 6.

57. For Theodoret's concerns about the Syriac *Diatesseron* version of the gospels, see Theodoret, *Haereticarum fabularum compendium* 1.20 (*PG* 83:372A). See also Tompkins, "Relations," 248-52; Millar, "Theodoret," 119-20.

58. Theodoret, *HE* 4.29 (GCS 5:269-70). Theodoret was hardly the biggest proponent of Ephrem Syrus in a Greek context, but his mention of Ephrem's *works* was one of many ways he rhetorically featured Syriac Christian writing. See Millar, "Theodoret," 121-25.

59. The only evidence, besides the unremarkable presence of "Persians" in Edessa, is Hiba, *Ep. ad Marim Persam* (CPG #6500, *ACO* II.1.3: 33), which may refer to a bishop of Ctesiphon or an archimandrite near Constantinople. See Becker, *Fear of God*, 47-51.

60. Trial of Hiba, *Acta concilii Chalcedonensis*, session 10 (*ACO* II.1.3: 20).

61. *Syriac Acts of the Second Council of Ephesus* (Flemming: 86-88; tr. Perry: 212-13).

62. See Urbainczyk, *Theodoret*, 72-79.

63. Severus of Antioch, *Homilia 30 de Symeone Stylita* (*PO* 36:608; tr. Briere and Graffin, 609).

64. On the dating of the *HR* to 440, see Price, *History of the Monks of Syria*, xiv-xv. Other scholars have preferred 444 (e.g., Leppin, "Zum kirchenpolitische Kontext").

65. Marana: Theodoret *HR* 29.5 (SC 257:236); Maris: *HR* 20.4 (SC 257:66-68); Jacob: *HR* 21.7-10 (SC 257:80-84).

66. Peter the Galatian: Theodoret, *HR* 9.7-8 (SC 234:418-22).

67. On Theodoret's claim to holiness, see Urbainczyk, *Theodoret*, 130-42; Krueger, *Writing and Holiness*, chaps. 2-3. On his divergence from other (mainly Syriac) hagiographers, see Harvey, "Sense of a Stylite."

68. Theodoret, *epp.* S 28, S 42 (SC 98:86, 112).

69. Monastic exarch Alypius served as Theodoret's envoy to the pope in 449 (see his *ep.* S 113 (SC 111:66). On Rabbula's monastic involvements, see chapter 3.

70. Theodoret, *Ep. ad eos qui in Euphratesia et Osrhoena regione, Syria, Phoenicia et Cilicia vitam monasticam degunt* (CPG #6276, PG 83:1415).

71. Theodoret, *ep.* S 50 (SC 98:126). *Ep.* S 129 (SC 111:108) made similar statements.

72. Theodoret, *Ep. ad Alexandrum Hierapolitanum* (CPG #6249, ACO I.4: 170-71).

73. Theodoret, *ep.* P 4 (SC 40:77) to Agathon the archimandrite.

74. On Domnus, see above, this chapter. On Sabinianus, see his *Ep. ad Valentinianum et Marcianum imp. aug.* (in *Acta concilii Chalcedonensis* session 14, ACO II.1.3: 58).

75. On cultural clashes among monks, see Caner, *Wandering, Begging Monks*, chaps. 3-4.

76. Theodoret notes several ambassadors, such as Acacius of Beroea (*HR* 2.9, 2.16-18, 3.11, 4.7, 21.10 [SC 234:214-16, 230-38, 266-68, 304-8; SC 257:82-84]), Flavian of Antioch

(*HR* 3.11, 13.4 [SC 234:266–68, 480–82]), Theodotus of Antioch (*HR* 27.3 [SC 257:220]), Agapetus of Apamea (*HR* 3.4–5 [SC 234:252–54]), and others (but not Rabbula).

77. Leppin, "Zum kirchenpolitischen Kontext," makes this point, modifying the claim of Peeters, *Tréfonds oriental,* 96–101, that Theodoret was courting the monks themselves.

78. Theodoret, *epp.* P 4 (SC 40:77), S 28 (SC 98:86). *HR* 2.3, 2.9 (SC 234:200, 214–16), 18.1, 22.2, 26.4 (SC 257:52–54, 126, 164).

79. On the wide circulation of the *HR,* in Greek and Syriac, see Canivet and Leroy-Molinghen, *Histoire des moines de Syrie* (SC 234), 57–63.

80. See Introduction.

81. All these concerns show prominently in the *Eranistes.* See chapter 8.

82. On Theodoret's avoidance of "assuming God" and "assumed man" see Clayton, *Christology of Theodoret,* 169–207. "[Divine] Word" and "word incarnate": Theodoret, *Interpretatio in xiv epistulas sancti Pauli,* Philippians 2:6–11 (PG 82:569–73).

83. Theodoret, *Eranistes* dial. 2 (ed. Ettlinger, 118–19) compares orthodoxy to medicine—i.e., the balancing of humors. On the notion of doctrinal balance in the *Haereticarum fabularum compendium,* see Sillett "Culture of Controversy," chap. 6.

84. This idea of balance marked a shift in how Theodoret defended his orthodoxy after 432 (*pace* Clayton, *Christology of Theodoret,* chaps. 3–5, who stresses Theodoret's consistency, and Fairbairn, "Puzzle of Theodoret's Christology," who sees inconsistency). For the details of this debate, see chapter 8.

85. On Theodoret's direct debt to Theodore, see Guinot, *L'éxegèse de Théodoret,* 71–75.

86. On Theodore's few types, see Greer, *Theodore,* chaps. 5–6, and Zaharopoulos, *Theodore,* 130–36 (but see the terminological caveats of Young, *Biblical Exegesis,* chaps. 8–9). For Theodoret's use of types, see Guinot, *L'éxegèse de Théodoret,* 233–35, 308–22.

87. Guinot, *L'éxegèse de Théodoret,* 253–317, esp. 263–72. See also Trakatellis, "Theodoret's Commentary on Isaiah."

88. On the dating of the *Eranistes,* see Richard, "L'évolution doctrinale," 470. On traditional and new uses of dialogue in late antiquity, see König, "Sympotic Dialog;" but also Lim, "Christians, Dialogues and Patterns of Sociability." For the example of Cyril's dialogues see *De incarnatione unigeniti, Quod unus sit Christus* (both SC 97). On literary innovation in the *Eranistes,* see Lim, "Theodoret and the Speakers in Greek Dialogues." On the tense debate presentation, see Young, *From Nicaea to Chalcedon,* 280–82.

89. E.g., Eusebius of Samosata (Theodoret, *HE* 2.32 [GCS 5:173–74]); and Pope Liberius (*HE* 2.16 [GCS 5:131–36]; see Laing, "Theodoret and the Ideal Monarch," 180–82).

90. Theodoret only boasted of his asceticism, benefaction, and doctrinal expertise when others challenged them. See later in this chapter and chapter 7.

91. E.g., Theodoret, *ep.* S 24 (SC 98:82) to Andreas called him "a wise physician … who arrives on his own in the presence of those who need treatment." *Ep.* S 35 (SC 98:96) to Irenaeus of Tyre praised him for "generosity and contempt of wealth."

92. Theodoret, *Ep. ad Alexandrum Hierapolitanum* (CPG #6252, *ACO* I.4: 186).

93. For the case of Athanasius of Perrha, see later in this chapter.

94. On the dating of Theodoret's corpus, see Richard, "L'évolution doctrinale," and Guinot, *L'éxegèse de Théodoret,* 42–65.

95. Theodoret, *HR* 2.9 (SC 234:214–16).

96. The anonymous ancient editors of Theodoret's letters are mostly supportive (though Irenaeus did showcase Theodoret's inconstancy). The original records of the Second Council of Ephesus, preserved only in Syriac, were hostile. The interests of the editors of the *Acts of the Council of Chalcedon* (working for Anatolius of Constantinople and Emperor Marcian) are more complicated. See Schwartz, *ACO* II.1.1: v–viii, II.1.2: v–viiii, II.3: vii–xiii. For a summary, see Price and Gaddis, *Acts of Chalcedon* 1:75–85.

97. Dioscorus's court contacts have been the subject of speculation. Sellers, *Council of Chalcedon,* 30–37, suggests Chrysaphius the eunuch, Eutyches the archimandrite, and Empress Eudocia. In any case, some sort of transactional conspiracy is implied by Theodoret, *ep.* S 146 (SC 111:174). For Dioscorus's collaboration with Juvenal of Jerusalem and Thalassius of Caesarea in Cappadocia, see Theodosius II, *Sacra ad Dioscorum Alexandrinum,* in *Acta concilii Chalcedonensis* session 1 (*ACO* II.1.1: 74).

98. Accounts of Eutyches's influence fill the *Acts of Chalcedon,* but they seem exaggerated to create a scapegoat. See Bevan and Gray, "Trial of Eutyches." Eutyches did claim some affinity with Cyril from the early 430s (see *Acta concilii Chalcedonensis* session 1, *ACO* II.1.1: 90–91). His only well attested court contact was Chrysaphius (Evagrius Scholasticus, *HE* 2.2, *Fontes Christiani* 57:200–202), though Bevan and Gray express doubts here as well.

99. Theodoret was forbidden from sitting as a judge in the appeals trial of Athanasius of Perrha (*Acta concilii Chalcedonensis* session 15 [*ACO* II.1.3: 82]).

100. For Athanasius's appeals to Cyril and Proclus, see Cyril, *Ep. ad Domnum Antiochenum* (CPG #5377, *ACO* II.1.3: 66–67) and Proclus, *Ep. ad Domnum Antiochenum* (CPG #5910, *ACO* II.1.3: 67–68). For the deposition of Athanasius, see the transcript of his trial, *Acta concilii Chalcedonensis* session 15 (*ACO* II.1.3: 77–81).

101. See *Acta concilii Chalcedonensis* session 11 (*ACO* II.1.3: 29–30). For the quartet's view of Theodoret as mastermind, see *Syriac Acts of the Second Council of Ephesus* (Flemming: 58; tr. Perry: 129).

102. On Aquilinus of Byblus, see *Syriac Acts of the Second Council of Ephesus* (Flemming: 76–78; tr. Perry: 182–86). On Eustathius and other foes of Irenaeus, see *Syriac Acts* (Flemming: 74–76; tr. Perry: 171–77), and Theodoret, *ep.* S 48 (SC 98:124).

103. Theodoret, *Eranistes* prologue (ed. Ettlinger, 61–62). "*Eranistes*" personifies this pastiche throughout the dialog; on natures, see esp. dial. 2 (ed. Ettlinger, 132–34).

104. For the charges against Irenaeus, see Theodoret, *ep.* S 110 (SC 111:38–42).

105. The imperial law behind this action was *Codex Iustinianus* I.1.3 (ed. Krueger, 8–9), dated to February, but arriving later. Theodoret, *ep.* S 110 (SC 111:38–42) reported earlier rumors that Irenaeus had the favor of some courtiers.

106. See Trial of Hiba, *Acta concilii Chalcedonensis* session 11 (*ACO* II.1.3: 20–21). For the full list of charges against Hiba, see session 11 (*ACO* II.1.3: 24–26). For the dismissal of charges in Antioch (and the accusers' reasons for avoiding doctrinal accusations), see *Syriac Acts of the Second Council of Ephesus* (Flemming: 58–59; tr. Perry: 128–131) and Trial of Hiba, *Acta concilii Chalcedonensis,* session 11 (*ACO* II.1.3: 21–23).

107. Theodosius II, *Mandata ad Damascum tribunum et notarium* (Oct. 26, 448), in *Acta concilii Chalcedonensis,* session 11 (*ACO* II.1.3: 19).

108. Theodoret, *epp.* S 79–81 (SC 98:182–98).

109. Dioscorus, *Ep. ad Domnum Antiochenum* (CPG #5456, Flemming: 132–39; tr. Perry: 327–38). Besides Hiba and Irenaeus, accusations came against Daniel of Carrhae, Sophronius of Constantina, John of Theodosiopolis, Aquinus of Byblus, Sabinianus of Perrha, and Uranius of Emesa. See later in this chapter.

110. Theodoret, *epp.* S 79–81 (SC 98:182–98).

111. Theodoret, *ep.* S 89 (SC 98:236–38): "Ignatius and Eusathius [of Antioch], Athanasius [of Alexandria], Basil [of Caesarea], Gregory [of Nazianzus], and John [Chrysostom]."

112. E.g., Theodoret, *ep.* S 85 (SC 98:222–24).

113. Theodoret, *ep.* S 83 (SC 98:218).

114. Friendship with Cyril: Theodoret, *ep.* S 83 (SC 98:216) to Dioscorus. *Agapē: ep.* S 84 (SC 98:220–22) to the bishops of Cilicia.

115. E.g., Theodoret, *ep.* S 89 (SC 98:238).

116. Theodoret, *ep.* S 96 (SC 111:10) to Nomus the Consul. Formulaic letters often complain of no reply, but the insistent tone here suggests that Theodoret was surprised.

117. Theodoret, *ep.* S 86 (SC 98:228) via Domnus to Flavian of Constantinople.

118. See Domnus of Antioch, *Epp. ad Dioscorum Alexandrinum* (CPG #6509–10, Flemming: 138–41, 144–47; the first letter tr. Perry: 339–43).

119. Violence was reported by Theodoret, *ep.* S 80, S 87 (SC 98:188–90, 232–34). On Photius, see *Syriac Acts of the Second Council of Ephesus* (Flemming: 72–74; tr. Perry: 172–73).

120. For parameters of the meeting, see Theodosius II, *Mandata ad Damascum tribunum et notarium* (Oct. 26, 448), in *Acta concilii Chalcedonensis,* session 11 (*ACO* II.1.3: 19). A second associate was also named: John of Theodosiopolis. For the trial, see the discontinuous *Acta concilii Chalcedonensis,* session 11 (*ACO* II.1.3: 16–42). For a cogent account, see Price and Gaddis, *Acts of Chalcedon,* 2: 265–70.

121. For Daniel's resignation, see *Syriac Acts of the Second Council of Ephesus* (Flemming: 68; tr. Perry: 157–58; Doran, 138). For Hiba's plea bargain, see *Acta concilii Chalcedonensis* session 10 (*ACO* II.1.3: 14–16). Doran, *Stewards of the Poor,* 117–18, argues that the judges compromised out of caution, since the court had yet to weigh in on the fate of Eutyches. Perhaps Photius was willing to work with either side, as Anatolius of Constantinople and Maximus of Antioch would do in 450 (see Epilogue).

122. For the third tribunal of Hiba, conducted by Chaereas, governor of Osrhoene, see *Syriac Acts of the Second Council of Ephesus* (Flemming: 34–54; tr. Perry: 87–123; tr. Doran, 139–82). For the deposition, see *Syriac Acts* (tr. Perry: 10–13).

123. For Eusebius's accusations, see *Acta concilii Chalcedonensis,* session 1 (*ACO* II.1.1: 101, 103, 113, 123–37). For Flavian's reluctance, see session 1 (*ACO* II.1.1: 130–31). Scholars have suggested that Eusebius manipulated Flavian (Sellers, *Chalcedon,* 56–60; Gregory, *Vox Populi,* 129–34). Bevan and Gray ("Trial of Eutyches") see both Flavian and Eusebius as part of a brief imperial effort to make an example of Eutyches.

124. Trial of Eutyches, *Acta concilii Chalcedonensis,* session 1 (*ACO* II.1.1: 143–47).

125. Theodoret, *epp.* S 92–95 (SC 98:242–48). The delegation also carried *epp.* S 96, S 99–101, S 103–106, S 109 (SC 111:10–12, 16–18, 22–30, 34–38).

126. Eusebius of Doryleaum noted Eutyches's influence with other monks (*Acta concilii Chalcedonensis,* session 1, *ACO* II.1.1: 132–33). Thalassius of Ceasarea and Eusebius of Ancyra joined in supporting Eutyches at the April 449 hearing (*ACO* II.1.1: 150–53).

127. April 449 Hearing, *Acta concilii Chalcedonensis* session 1, *ACO* II.1.1: 177–79).

128. Theodosius II (and Valentinian III), *Sacra ad Dioscorum Alexandrinum* (*Acta con cilii Chalcedonensis* session 1 [*ACO* II.1.1: 68–69], Syriac vers. [Flemming: 5; tr. Perry: 8–9]).

129. April 449 Hearing, *Acta concilii Chalcedonensis* session 1 [*ACO* II.1.1: 150–79]).

130. Theodoret, *ep.* S 16 (SC 98:56–62) to Irenaeus; *ep.* S 112 (SC 111:46–56) to Domnus.

131. Theodosius II, *Sacra ad Concilium Ephesinum, Acta concilii Chalcedonensis* session 1 (*ACO* II.1.1: 73). On Flavian's near silence (effectively required), see Acts of the Second Council of Ephesus, *Acta concilii Chalcedonensis* session 1 (*ACO* II.1.1: 181).

132. On Photius, Eustathius and Basil, see *Syriac Acts of the Second Council of Ephesus* (Flemming: 62–64, 70–78, 110–12, 150; tr. Perry: 137–41, 159–86, 255–58, 362–63). On Barsauma's vote, see Theodosius II, *Sacra ad Dioscorum Alexandrinum* and *Sacra ad Barsaumam archimandritum, Acta concilii Chalcedonensis* session 1 (*ACO* II.1.1: 71).

133. On the rehabilitation of Eutyches, see *Acta concilii Chalcedonensis* session 1 (*ACO* II.1.1: 141, 182–86). On the condemnation of Flavian, see session 1 (*ACO* II.1.1: 191–96). The Syriac version offers fuller charges (tr. Perry: 430–31). On the physical abuse of Flavian, see Flavian, *Ep. ad Leonem papam* (CPG #5935, *ACO* II.1.1: 38–40). On the death of Flavian, see Chadwick, "Exile and Death of Flavian."

134. *Acta concilii Chalcedonensis* session 1 (*ACO* II.1.1: 75, 88). See Gaddis, "No Crime," 297–309.

135. *Syriac Acts of the Second Council of Ephesus* (Flemming: 60–68; tr. Perry: 134–45).

136. *Syriac Acts of the Second Council of Ephesus* (Flemming: 68–72; tr. Perry: 155–65).

137. *Syriac Acts of the Second Council of Ephesus* (Flemming: 72–78; tr. Perry: 171–86).

138. *Syriac Acts of the Second Council of Ephesus* (Flemming: 80–84; tr. Perry: 189–99).

139. *Syriac Acts of the Second Council of Ephesus* (Flemming: 84–110; tr. Perry: 207–74).

140. Peter of Emesa and Athanasius of Perrha (implied by Theodoret, *epp.* S 123, S 127 [SC 111:88–90, 104–6]).

141. *Syriac Acts of the Second Council of Ephesus* (Flemming: 114–28; tr. Perry: 288–363).

142. Basil (see earlier in this chapter), Domnus of Apamea (Theodoret, *ep.* S 87 [SC 98:232–34]), and Photius of Tyre (see earlier in this section).

143. Theodosius II, *Sacra ad Dioscorum Alex.* (Flemming: 150–52; tr. Perry: 364–67).

144. Dioscorus et al., *Ep. synodicalis concilii Epheseni* (Flemming: 154–58; tr. Perry: 373–75).

145. Barhadbeshabba of Arbaya, *HE*, said nothing about either Hiba or Theodoret.

146. See Introduction and chapter 2.

147. Pope Leo I, *epp.* 43, 44, 45, 49 (*ACO* II.4: 26–27, 19–21, 23, 24), sent October 449.

148. Marcian, *Ep. ad Leonem papam* (CPL #1656, *ACO* II.3.1: 18) dated November 450.

149. *Acta concilii Chalcedonensis* session 1 (*ACO* II.1.1: 70).

CHAPTER 6. MEDIATING BISHOPS: PATRONAGE ROLES
AND RELATIONS IN THE FIFTH CENTURY

1. On the duties of *augustales* within the prefects' bureaucracy, see Jones, *LRE*, 587–88.

2. John of Antioch, *Ep. ad Alexandrum Hierapolitanum* (CPG #6303, *ACO* I.4: 113).

3. Early sixth-century papyri indicate that the see of Oxyrynchus owed about 10 percent of the cities' taxes, while the Apion estate owed about 30 percent. *P. Oxy. 16.1918* records the

gross monetary income for the Apionic estates at 20,010 *solidi*, with 6,917 *solidi* paid in gold taxes. Thus we might estimate Oxyrhynchus's episcopal land revenue at 5,000–8,000 *solidi* (see Wipszycka, *Les ressources,* 48–50; Ruffini, *Social Networks in Byzantine Egypt,* 101–5). Donations would augment these funds, but the order of magnitude is still similar to the *augustalis*'s fine. For more on aristocratic fortunes, see Wickham, *Framing the Early Middle Ages,* esp. 158–68, 239–40, 242–51.

4. Libanius, *Or.* 47 (*Selected Works,* LCL 2:500–34); Theodoret, *HR* 17.2–4 (SC 257: 36–40). See Brown, *Power and Persuasion,* chap. 2; "Rise and Function of the Holy Man."

5. For an example of consistent use of one model, see nearly all the papers in A. Wallace-Hadrill, ed., *Patronage in Ancient Society.* See also Saller, *Personal Patronage.* For a more sophisticated model, see Moxnes, "Patron-Client Relations."

6. See Introduction.

7. Boissevain, *Friends of Friends,* chap. 6. For more detailed definitions, see Blok, "Variations in Patronage;" Eisenstadt and Roniger, *Patrons, Clients and Friends,* 48–49.

8. On "Mediterranean" patronage, see Boissevain, *Friends of Friends,* esp. chap. 1, 4–5; Gellner, "Patrons and Clients."

9. E.g., Brown, *Power and Persuasion,* chaps. 2–3; *Poverty and Leadership,* chap. 2; Rapp, *Holy Bishops,* esp. chaps. 1–4.

10. On the complicated political history of Syria, and the uneven effects of Roman rule, see Millar, *Roman Near East,* chaps. 1–4.

11. On the distribution of spoken languages, see Brock, "Greek and Syriac," but also Millar, "Ethnic Identity," and *Greek Roman Empire,* 13–21, 94–99, 107–16; Garsoïan, *L'église arménienne,* chap. 1.

12. For this example, see Theodoret, *ep.* P 18 (SC 40:89–90). See next chapter.

13. Theodoret, *ep.* P 33 (SC 40: 98–99). Synesius, *ep.* 119 (Garzya, 204) wrote similarly.

14. See Veyne, *Bread and Circuses,* 5–18.

15. On the expansion of settlement in Syria, see Tchalenko, *Villages antiques,* 44–45, 75–91; Tate, *Campagnes de Syrie,* 184–88, 257–58, 303–31. On urban growth due to political reorganization, see Jones, *LRE,* 563–66, 586–96, 601–6; Isaac, *Limits of Empire,* 282–303, 331–32, 372–79. New opportunities for influence undergirded what Brown called the Syrian "crisis of leadership" ("Rise and Function of the Holy Man," 85).

16. Matthews, "Proliferation of Elites;" Brown, *Poverty and Leadership,* 81–86. C. Kelly, *Ruling the Later Roman Empire,* 180.

17. Brown, *Poverty and Leadership,* chaps. 1–2; Patlagean, *Pauvreté économique,* chaps. 1–2.

18. Libanius *Or.* 47.4–6, 10 (*Selected Works,* LCL 2:502–4, 508–10); Theodoret, *HR* 17.4 (SC 257:38–40).

19. E.g., Garnsey and Woolf, "Patronage of the Rural Poor;" Brown, *Poverty and Leadership,* chap. 2.

20. On "social brokering" in general, see Boissevain, *Friends of Friends,* chap. 6; Blok "Variations in Patronage." For the Roman context, see Moxnes, "Patron-Client Relations," 248–49; and Liebeschuetz, *Antioch,* 196–99.

21. Firmus, *ep.* 26 (SC 350:130).

22. On the honors for city benefactors, see Veyne, *Bread and Circuses*, 122–30. On appeals to common faith, see Van Dam, *Roman Revolution of Constantine*, chap. 6. Theodoret used all of these idioms in his appeals (see chapter 7).

23. In this book, "local notable" refers to the *curiales*, professionals, and *honorati* of every Roman city.

24. Theodoret, *ep.* P 34 (SC 40:99–100).

25. See Wipsycka, *Les ressources*, 48–49. For estimates of landholdings in Egypt, see Bagnall, *Egypt in Late Antiquity*, 148–53, 289–93. For a broad survey of elite landholding, see Wickham, *Framing the Early Middle Ages*, chaps. 4, 7–8.

26. On the middling landowners of Syria, some of whom built multi-room houses on the Limestone Massif, see Tate, *Campagnes de Syrie*, 15–188, 257–65. Wickham, *Framing the Early Middle Ages*, 442–59, affirms this general picture, while suggesting that local notables held larger estates closer to urban centers than the limestone villages.

27. See Petit, *La vie municipale*, chaps. 1–3; Jones, *LRE*, esp. 724–40; Liebeschuetz, *Antioch*, 101–9, 133–35, 167–74; Veyne, *Bread and Circuses*, 83–156. See esp. Garnsey, *Famine and Food Supply*, 74–79.

28. On curial burdens, see Jones, *LRE*, 734–40. On the quest for exemptions, see Jones *LRE*, 740–52; Liebeschuetz, *Antioch*, 175–80; Laniado, *Notables municipaux*, chaps. 1, 4.

29. On *principales*, see Petit, *La vie municipale*, 85–88; Jones, *LRE*, 731, 761–62; Liebeschuetz, *Antioch*, 171–85. Liebeschuetz, *Decline*, 110–20, notes that by the 490s, *proteuontes* meant wealthy notables in general, on or off the council. In the 430s and 440s, it still seems connected to curial service. On the *pater civitatis, defensor civitatis,* and other local magistracies, see Jones, *LRE*, 726–27, 758–59; Liebeschuetz, *Antioch*, 167–70, 205–6; Harries, *Law and Empire*, 55; Laniado, *Notables municipaux*, 92–94. For more on burden-exempt classes, see Jones, *LRE*, 740–52.

30. Basil put it succinctly: "The management of the churches is for those who have been entrusted with its protection (*prostasian*), but they are strengthened by the [leading] laymen" (*ep.* 230, LCL 3:356). *Curiales* joined with clerics in the protests against Hiba. See *Syriac Acts of the Second Council of Ephesus* (Flemming: 37; tr. Doran, 146).

31. See chapter 3.

32. E.g., Theodoret *epp.* S 15, S 18, S 21 (SC 98:54–56, 64–66, 68–78), P 8–9 (SC 40: 79–82). Basil *epp.* 5, 56 (LCL 1:32–38, 350–52), 160 (LCL 2:398–410), 228 (LCL 3:348–50). By contrast, Firmus's extant letters offer only friendship, and Chrysostom's mainly offer thanks for help lent to him during his exile.

33. Theodoret, *epp.* S 19–20 (SC 98:66–68), S 46 (SC 98:120–22), S 114–15 (SC 111:68). Compare to Basil, *ep.* 36 (LCL 1:190–92); Firmus, *epp.* 7–8, 13 (SC 350:84–86, 100).

34. Avoidance of burdens: Theodoret, *epp.* P 33, P 44, P 52 (SC 40:98–99, 108–9, 120–21). See also Basil, *ep.* 84 (LCL 2:102–8). Compare Libanius's efforts to defend the tax immunity of his associate Eusebius (*epp.* F904–909). Education: see later in this chapter.

35. Theodoret, *epp.* S 29–36 (SC 98:88–100).

36. Theodoret, *epp.* S 42–47 (SC 98: 106–24); Firmus *ep.* 16 (SC 350:106). See similar advocacy work by Basil, *epp.* 74–76 (LCL 2: 66–82).

37. See G. Clark, *Women in Late Antiquity*, esp. chaps. 1–2, 4.

38. On female civic benefactors, see Fantham, "Aemellia Pudentilla;" Fantham, Foley et al., *Women in the Classical World*, chap. 13, esp. 360–68; Connor, *Women of Byzantium*, chap. 5. On Theodoret's mother as sponsor of ascetics, see his *HR* 9.4–9, 9.14–15 (SC 234:412–424, 430–34).

39. Tellingly, Rabbula pushed rules that forbade other male clerics or monks from contact with women (*Vita Rabbulae*, Overbeck: 176–77; tr. Doran, 79–80).

40. Theodoret, *epp.* S 7–8, S 14, S 69 (SC 98:32–36, 46–52, 150–52); Basil, *epp.* 6, (LCL 1:38–44), 105, 107, 174 (LCL 2:198–200, 202–4, 452–56), 269, 283 (LCL 4:134–40, 170–72). John Chrysostom, *epp.* 1–18, 32–34, 39–40, 43, 52, 57, 76, 94, 98–99, 103–6, 117, 120, 133, 178–79, 185, 192, 219, 227, 229, 231–32, 242 (PG 52:549–623, 628–30, 631–32, 633, 634–35, 637, 640–41, 649, 657–59, 660–61, 662–65, 672–73, 674–75, 691–92, 713, 716, 719, 731–32, 736, 737, 737–39, 746–48). On Chrysostom's pastoral care for women, see Mayer, "Patronage, pastoral care." See also Tilley, "No Friendly Letters."

41. On his civic projects, see Theodoret, *epp.* S 79, S 81 (SC 98:186, 196). On the new church, see his *ep.* P 36 (SC 40:101).

42. *Chronicon Edessenum* years 746, 749, 753 (= A.D. 435, 438, 442; CSCO SS 1.4:7). Hiba's prime partner was Anatolius, but other links are implied. Tellingly, Hiba's *martyrium* honored St. Sergius, to whom Alexander of Hierapolis had dedicated the Rasapha shrine. See Doran, *Stewards of the Poor*, 115–16.

43. On Basil's *Basileias*, see his *ep.* 94 (LCL 2:148–52), Sozomen *HE* 6.34 (GCS 4:291); Van Dam, *Kingdom of Snow*, 50–52, and *Families and Friends*, 79–80; and Brown, *Poverty and Leadership*, 34–40.

44. See Theodoret, *ep.* P 36 (SC 40:100–101).

45. Firmus, *ep.* 15 (SC 350:104). On Babylas, see Shepardson, "Controlling Contested Places," esp. 492–98.

46. On the traditional pagan feasts in Antioch, see Liebeschuetz, *Antioch*, 230–31.

47. Theodoret, *ep.* P 3 (SC 40:75–77) to Theodotus the (honorary) Count.

48. E.g., Basil, *ep.* 5 (LCL 1:32–38), which resembles Theodoret's letters of consolation; *ep.* 160 (LCL 2:398–400), which resembles Theodoret's moral rebuke, *ep.* P 8 (SC 40:79–81).

49. Firmus, *ep.* 19 (SC 350:114) to Acacius of Melitene.

50. Theodoret *ep.* S 67 (SC 98:148) to Maranas; *ep.* S 66 (SC 98:146–48) to Aerius.

51. Theodoret, *ep.* P 27 (SC 40:94–95).

52. On Roman education generally, see Marrou, *History of Education*, esp. 96, 112, 150–75. On grammarians, see Kaster, *Guardians of Language*, esp. chaps. 1–2, 6. On sophistic education, see Cribiore, *School of Libanius*, 24–37, 137–72. On the deepening hierarchy among educators, see Lim, *Public Disputation*, 65–69.

53. On the steep educational fees in second and third century Athens, see Watts, *City and School*, 28–30. On municipal funding for *some* sophists, see Marrou, *History of Education*, 299–313. On sophists' networks, see Petit, *Étudiants de Libanius*, but also Cribiore, *School of Libanius*, chap. 3; Watts, *City and School*, chap. 3; Bradbury, "Libanius's Letters." On the narrower network of theurgic philosophers, see Eunapius, *Vitae philosophorum et sophistarum*; Watts, *City and School*, esp. chaps. 4, 8; Penella, *Greek Philosophers and Sophists*, esp. 31–34, 135–45.

54. For Hypatia's contacts, see Synesius, *epp.* 10, 15–16, 46, 81, 154 (Garzya, 30–31, 35–37, 86, 146–47, 271–77, all to Hypatia); 136–46 (Garzya, 237–58, to a fellow pupil). See also Watts, *City and School*, 192–203. On Themistius's influence, see Vanderspoel, *Themistius and the Imperial Court*, esp. chaps. 3–4, 7–9. On Libanius's network, see previous note and next section.

55. On sophists' wealth, see Liebeschuetz, *Antioch*, 40–52; Cribiore, *School of Libanius*, 182–91. On the patronage activities of Libanius, see Liebeschuetz, *Antioch*, esp. 192–203.

56. On the broader mission of classical *paideia*, see Kaster, *Guardians of Language*, esp. chaps. 1–2; Brown, *Power and Persuasion*, esp. chap. 2.

57. On Themistius's and Libanius's non-cultic Hellenism, see Brown, *Authority and the Sacred*, 36–40; *Power and Persuasion*, 68–70. On the "theurgic" approach of Iamblichus and Proclus, see Penella, *Greek Philosophers and Sophists*, 135–44; Watts, *City and School*, 19–21, 100–110. On educational lineage see Cox Miller, "Collective Biography."

58. On rivalries among sophists, see Libanius, *Autobiographia* (*Or.* 1) 38, 43–44, 86, 98–99, 109, 113–15, 186–87 (*Autobiography*, LCL 1:98, 104–6, 150–52, 162–64, 174, 178–80, 250–52). See also Lim, *Public Disputation*, chap. 2; Watts, *City and School*, 35–38, 42–45, 50–63; Cribiore, *School of Libanius*, 42–82, 180–82, 191–96. For cooperation between distant educators, consider the "friendship" of shared appeals Libanius claimed with Themistius (e.g., *epp.* F40, F62, F66, F70, F86, F99, F112, F241, F252, F434, F476, F793, F1186). See also Cribiore, *School of Libanius*, 60–66, 91–94, 107–110. For some of Libanius's other cooperative relations with sophists, see *epp.* F458, F1230.

59. Theodoret, *ep.* P 52 (SC 40:121). Basil, *ep.* 310 (LCL 4:246–48), does not record the name of the addressee, but he is called "your eloquence."

60. Theodoret *ep.* S 30 (SC 98:88–90) asked Aerius to persuade wealthy locals to host a refugee decurion from Carthage.

61. *Syriac Acts of the Second Council of Ephesus* (Flemming: 126; tr. Perry: 314–15), noted by Brown, *Power and Persuasion*, 132.

62. Basil, *epp.* 335–360 (LCL 4:284–330); Libanius *epp.* F501, F647. Many scholars have treated these letters as spurious, but Cribiore, *School of Libanius*, 101–4, notes that some are likely genuine. Firmus, *epp.* 13, 30 (SC 350:100, 138–40). Consider also Synesius, *ep.* 96 (Garzya, 163–64), which presented the office of bishop as a way to further philosophy.

63. On the sophistic elements of Diodore and Theodore's work, see chapter 3. On the use of *akribeia* by sophists, see Cribiore, *School of Libanius*, 202.

64. Theodoret, *ep.* P 28 (SC 40:95).

65. On Eudocia's background and literary sponsorship, see Holum, *Theodosian Empresses*, 111–29, 185–90, but also Alan Cameron, "Empress and the Poet," 270–87.

66. See John of Nikiu, *Chronicon* 88.7–11 (tr. Charles, 109–110) and the *Chronicon Paschale* A.D. 467 (Dindorf, 595–96), noted by Brown, *Power and Persuasion*, 132–33.

67. Woodcarving: Theodoret, *ep.* P 38 (SC 40:102–3). Wine: *ep.* S 13 (SC 98:44).

68. Sirens and Sophroniscus: Firmus, *ep.* 2 (SC 350:68–70). On Theodoret's obscure references in his *Curatio*, see Papadoyannakis, "Christian *Therapeia*," esp. 104–6.

69. Theodoret, *ep.* P 31 (SC 40:97).

70. Even the learned Rufinus of Aquileia decried Jerome's continued references to pre-Christian literature (Rufinus, *Apologia contra Hieronymum* 2.6–8 [CCL 20:87–90]).

71. On theurgic academics in Athens and Alexandria, see Trombley, *Hellenic Religion and Christianization*, 1:292–324, 2:1–20; and esp. Watts, *City and School*, chaps. 4–5, 7–8.

72. Theodoret, *ep.* P 50 (SC 40:120).

73. On notaries, see Libanius, *Or.* 62 (Foerster, 4:346–83). See also Kaster, *Guardians of Language*, 47–48, 55–56; Liebeschuetz, *Antioch*, 242–44; Festugière, *Antioche*, 410–12; Cribiore, *School of Libanius*, 207. On the influence of one notary, see chapter 4.

74. On legal education in Berytus, see Hall, *Roman Berytus*, 202–13; and Cribiore, *School of Libanius*, 208–10. For Libanius's recommendations of students en route to law school, see *epp.* F87, F553, F652–653, F1171, F1336, F1431. On jurists' role in drafting the *Theodosian Code*, see Harries, *Law and Empire*, 35–64.

75. Segal, *Edessa*, 149–52, envisioned city-funded schooling in Syriac and higher learning at "The School of the Syrians." This was challenged by Millar, "Ethnic Identity," 165–67 and Becker, *Fear of God*, chaps. 2–3. Still clerics in Edessa sponsored Syriac writing (see above, chapter 5). Jerome hired a tutor for spoken Aramaic (Jerome, *ep.* 7.2; Valero 1:96).

76. Theodoret befriended the notary Eurycianus (*epp.* P 38, P 47 [SC 40:103–4, 111–17]) and several *scholastikoi*, including Apelles (*epp.* P 51 [SC 40:120], S 115 [SC 111:68]), who may have worked on the *Theodosian Code* (*PLRE II* "Apelles 2," and Tompkins, "Relations," 89). On Theodoret's associations with Syriac learning, see chapter 5.

77. Theodoret, *ep.* P 5 (SC 40:77–78), which resembles Basil, *ep.* 111 (LCL 2:212).

78. On the admission and privileges of senators, see Jones, *LRE*, 525–545; Heather "Senates." On senators' wealth, see Jones, *LRE*, 554–57; Wipszycka, *Les ressources*, 48–49; Wickham, *Framing the Early Middle Ages*, chap. 4, esp. 155–68, 239–51.

79. On senatorial women, see G. Clark, *Women in Late Antiquity*, esp. chap. 4. On ascetic elite women see E. Clark, "Women and Asceticism."

80. See Jones, *LRE*, 383.

81. On the top senators, see Jones, *LRE*, 527–34. On repeat office-holders, see Heather "Senates," 190–95. In theory, administrative hierarchies were sharply defined, but lines of authority were frequently altered or ignored (see C. Kelly, *Ruling the Later Roman Empire*, esp. chaps. 1–2). Hence Theodoret's scattershot appeals for Cyrrhus's taxpayers (see chapter 7).

82. Basil dealt with a theologically hostile court. Nonetheless, Métivier, *Cappadoce*, 207–9, suggests that Basil had some protection from the prefect Modestus.

83. E.g., Theodoret, *epp.* P 17, P 19, P 33 (SC 40:88–89, 90–91, 98–99); S 23, S 42–44 (SC 98:80, 106–18).

84. E.g., Firmus, *epp.* 16–17, 30 (SC 350:106–10, 138–40); Basil, *epp.* 32 (LCL 1:178–84, regarding Caesarius's will), 74–76 (LCL 2:66–82, regarding provincial boundaries), 104 (LCL 2:194–96), 110 (LCL 2:210–12, regarding taxes), 111, 177, 180 (LCL 2:212, 460–62, 466), 274, 279–81, 303 (LCL 4:152–54, 164–68, 234–36, all recommendations); Libanius, *epp.* F37, F61, F64, F72, F97, F101, F196–97, F205, F251, F276–77, F361, F366–67, F409, F440–41, F503–4, F550–59, F563, F804, F840, F846, F852, F857–58, F886–87, F904–909, F922–24, F926–930, F932, F936–37, F959–60, F1051, F1148, F1173, F1224, F1259, F1365, F1367–68, F1443, F1459 (most of which are recommendations). Libanius still worried about his relations with courtiers (see *epp.* F529, F990, F1021).

85. Libanius appealed to Caesar Julian (e.g., *ep.* F369). But Libanius had briefly taught Julian, and his relationship cooled when Julian was Augustus (see *epp.* F610, F760).

86. Heather, "Senates," 202–5.

87. The governors of Syria I, Cilicia I, Phoenicia I, Palestine I, and Cyprus were called *consulares* and had a superior status. See Jones, *LRE*, 106–7, 142–44, 1458–59.

88. On the tenure and distant postings of governors, see Jones, *LRE*, 381. On seeking governorships for exemptions, see Libanius, *Or.* 49.3–5 (*Selected Works*, LCL 2:462–66); Liebeschuetz, *Antioch*, 175–91.

89. For a survey of bureaucratic positions, see Jones, *LRE*, 366–410, and esp. 563–606. On the organization of the *praefectiani*, see C. Kelly, *Ruling the Roman Empire*, chaps. 1–2.

90. On the perquisites and tenure of bureaucrats, see Jones, *LRE*, 566, 572, 576, 579, 584–86, 591–92, 601–6; C. Kelly, *Ruling the Later Roman Empire*, chap. 2. On record-keeping, see C. Kelly, 117–20. On bureaucrats' lands and curial connections, see C. Kelly, 145–52. On the perception of bureaucratic influence, see S. Mitchell, *Anatolia*, 2:80.

91. Theodoret, *ep.* P 37 (SC 40:101–102). Compare to Libanius, *ep.* F1351.

92. Appeals to governors: Firmus, *epp.* 12, 26 (SC 350:96–98, 130); Basil, *epp.* 84, 86 (LCL 2:102–8, 112–14), 306 (LCL 4:238–40); Libanius, *epp.* F95, F149–50, F156, F158–59, F166, F170, F175, F192, F217, F250, F275, F285, F287, F298, F317, F560, F625, F629, F636, F646, F715, F722, F743, F763, F767, F790, F819–820, F834–835, F838, F994, F1168–1170, F1180, F1208, F1251, F1253, F1273, F1351, F1360, F1364, F1381, F1392, F1406, F1422, F1460, F1464. Most of these were recommendations or judicial briefs. Larger requests tended to involve high officials (e.g., Libanius, *epp.* F308, F617).

93. Theodoret, *epp.* S 72 (SC 98:156–58), P 40, P 46 (SC 40:104, 111). *Curatores* were local officials, but appointed by governors (see Laniado, *Notables municipaux*, 99–101).

94. Basil, *epp.* 33 (LCL 1:184), 83, 142–44 (LCL 2:100–102, 344–48), 225 (LCL 3:320–24), 286 (LCL 4:176–78); Libanius, *epp.* F83, F210, F215, F911, F1454; Synesius, *epp.* 39, 59, 61, 73, 95, 110, 116 (Garzya, 50–51, 98–99, 100–102, 130–33, 157–63, 195–97, 201). See also S. Mitchell, *Anatolia* 2:80.

95. Consolation: Theodoret, *epp.* P 47 (SC 40:111–17), S 18, S 58 (SC 98:64–66, 134–36). Consultations: *epp.* P 5 (SC 40: 77–78), S 59, S 76 (SC 98:136, 162–66). Generosity: *ep.* P 3 (SC 40:75–77).

96. See insightful comments of Liebeschuetz, *Antioch*, 192–95.

97. Theodoret, *ep.* P 39–40 (SC 40:103–4).

98. Basil *epp.* 77, 96 (LCL 2:82–84, 156–60), 147–49 (LCL 2:352–60), advocated for a former governor in judicial trouble. Synesius, *epp.* 41–42 (Garzya, 52–75), denounced Andronicus to clerics. For Libanius, see *epp.* F163, F308, F459, F1221, F1296.

99. Appeals for conversion or baptism: Theodoret, *epp.* S 71 (SC 98:154–58) to Zeno the Consul, S 37 (SC 98:100–102) to Salustius the Governor of Euphratensis. Theodoret still conducted patronage with the pagan Salustius (Günther, *Theodoret und die Kämfe*, 10).

100. On Chrysostom's mission to Phoenicia, see his *epp.* 53–54, 123, 126, 221 (PG 52:637–39, 676–78, 685–87, 732–33). See also J. N. D. Kelly, *Goldenmouth*, 264. No such letters from Firmus or Synesius survive. Basil's extant letters of conversion went to local notables (e.g., *epp.* 277–78 [LCL 4:156–62]).

101. Theodoret, *ep.* S 45 (SC 98:118). For the date, see Tompkins, "Problems of Dating," 183–95. On the support of Anatolius, see chapters 4 and 5 and earlier in this chapter.

102. On army organization, see Jones, *LRE,* 608–9, 640–49; Treadgold, *Byzantium and its Army:* 87–93. On troop numbers, see Jones, *LRE:* 679–86, Treadgold, *Byzantium and its Army:* 43–59. On the economic impact of the army, see Whittaker, *Frontiers,* esp. chap. 4.

103. On the army in Syria, see Isaac, *Limits of Empire,* esp. chaps. 3–4, 6.

104. On the border, see Jones, *LRE,* esp. 1446, 1450, 1458–60 and maps 2, 4. Whittaker, *Frontiers,* chap. 1, doubted that Roman politicians perceived an exact border (see also his "Where are the Frontiers Now?"). This has been challenged by Potter, "Emperors, Their Borders." On billeting, see Jones, *LRE,* 630–32. On new military routes and centers, see *Vita Alexandri acoemetae* 33 (*PO* 6:683–84).

105. On fifth-century Roman-Persian wars, see Socrates *HE* 7.18–20 (GCS 1:363–68), *Chronicon Arbelae* 16 (CSCO SS 199:67; tr. Kawerau, 91); Marcellinus Comes, *Chronicon* A.D. 441 (ed. Mommsen, Croke, 17). See also Greatrex and Lieu, *Roman Eastern Frontier,* 2:36–45; Schrier, "Syriac Evidence for the Roman-Persian War, 421–22;" Holum, "Pulcheria's Crusade;" Greatrex, "Two Fifth-Century Wars."

106. On riot management, see Isaac, *Limits of Empire,* chap. 2. On "bandits" see Hopwood, "Bandits, Elites and Rural Order." For soldier's lending and protection, see Libanius *Or.* 47 (*Selected Works,* LCL 2:500–534); *Vita Alexandri acoemetae* 33 (*PO* 6:683–84).

107. On private forces (e.g., Synesius's corps, *ep.* 125 [Garzya, 213–14]), see Jones, *LRE,* 665–67; Liebeschuetz, *Barbarians and Bishops,* chap. 4. On Arab *foederati,* see Jones, *LRE,* 611–13, 663–68; Greatrex, *Rome and Persia at War,* 24–31. On Persian forces, see Howard-Johnson, "Great Powers in Late Antiquity," 169–80; Greatrex, *Rome and Persia at War,* 52–59.

108. On Roman army courts, see Jones, *LRE,* 487–89; Brennan, "Last of the Romans," 191–203; Pollard, "Roman Army as 'Total Institution.'" The distinct religion of soldiers included Mithraism (Turcan, *Mithra,* 37–41; Winter, "Mithraism and Christianity"), and, later, some Gothic "Arianism." See Socrates, *HE* 4.33, 6.6 (GCS 1:269, 317–22).

109. On military commanders and their job security, see Jones, *LRE,* 380–81.

110. On the careers of Anatolius, Areobindus, Dionysius, Titus, and Zeno, see *PLRE II:* 84, 145, 364–65, 1123, 1199. On top generals as power brokers, see Jones, *LRE,* 342–44, 352–53. Anatolius conducted the negotiations that ended the Roman-Persian War of 440–441 (see Greatrex, "Fifth-Century Wars," 2–9). Later, General Aspar largely orchestrated the accession of Marcian (see Burgess, "Accession of Marcian," esp. 62–68).

111. Areobindus: Theodoret, *ep.* P 18 (SC 40:88–90). Anatolius: Evagrius Scholasticus, *HE* 1.18 (FC 57:174–76).

112. See chapter 4. Basil also sought protection (*epp.* 152–53 [LCL 2:374–76]). Compare to Libanius's deeper army involvements, *epp.* F866–868, F925, F972, F1057.

113. Synesius, *ep.* 77–78 (Garzya, 136–38) advised Anysius the *dux* to keep the *Unnigardae* corps mobile. *Ep.* 94 (Garzya, 156–57) related efforts to reorganize regional troops.

114. Ambassadors included Moses, bishop to Mavia's "Saracens" (Socrates, *HE* 4.36, [GCS 1:270–71]; Sozomen, *HE* 6.38 [GCS 4:297–300]; Theodoret, *HE* 4.23 [GCS 5:260–62]); and Marutha of Martyropolis, who befriended King Yazdgird (Socrates, *HE* 7.8 [GCS 1:353–

54]). Acacius of Amida ransomed Persian prisoners after the war of 421–422 (see Socrates, *HE* 7.21 [GCS 1:367–68]).

115. For a late fifth-century version of Sergius's story, see *Passio antiquior sanctorum Sergii et Bacchi* (AB 14:373–95). On the search for a real Sergius, see E. K. Fowden, *Barbarian Plain*, 7–17; on the archaeology of Rasapha, 17–30; on the appeal of Sergius to Roman, Arab, and Persian warriors, chaps. 4–5.

116. Theodoret, *ep.* P 37 (SC 40:102), mentions loans from soldiers. *Ep.* P 11 (SC 40:83) interceded with a general for a soldier employed by a friend (compare to Basil, *ep.* 112 [LCL 2:214–20]). Theodoret, *ep.* P 2 (SC 40:75), recommended Agapetus, an army chaplain. *HR* 21.12 (SC 257:88) links Jacob of Cyrrhestica to someone doing "army exaction."

117. Theodoret, *ep.* S 145 (SC 111:162–72).

118. Basil's letters reveal virtually no connection to soldiers. Firmus appealed to keep an army away from Caesarea during a famine, but his letter went to the governor (see Firmus, *ep.* 12 [SC 350:96–98]). Libanius's letters (like Theodoret's) include personal appeals for a few soldiers (see Libanius, *epp.* F233, F1464). The sophist also conversed with soldiers to make sense of events in the Persian War of 363 (*ep.* F1220).

119. On Theodoret's protection by Anatolius in 434, see above, chapter 4. On Theodoret's salvation from exile, see chapter 7.

120. Theodoret, *HR* 21.15–18 (SC 257:92–98).

121. See Mitchell, *Anatolia*, 2:56–64; Trombley, *Hellenic Religion and Christianization*, 2:251–313. See also MacMullen, *Christianizing the Roman Empire*, chaps. 9–10; *Christianity and Paganism*, chap. 1.

122. Rufinus, *HE* 11.22–29 (ed. Schwartz and Mommsen, 1025–35); Socrates, *HE* 5.16, 7.15 (GCS 1:289–90, 360–61); Sozomen, *HE* 7.15, 7.20 (GCS 4:319–22, 332–33); Theodoret, *HE* 5.21–22 (GCS 5:317–20). On these violent episodes, see Thelamon, *Païens et Chrétiens*, part 2, chaps. 2–4; Brown, *Authority and the Sacred*, esp. chaps. 1–2; Gaddis, "No Crime," 177–79. On polemical rhetoric, see Wilken, *Chrysostom and the Jews*, chaps. 4–5; Taylor, *Anti-Judaism*; Boyarin, *Border Lines*, esp. intro., chaps. 1, 6, 8.

123. On Greek as a medium for cultic combination, see Bowersock, *Hellenism*, chap. 2. On families who ran the cult of Atargatis in Hierapolis, see Lucian of Samosata, *De dea Syriana* 42–43, 50 (ed. Lightfoot, 274, 276). On the pagan cities of Heliopolis and Carrhae, see Theodoret, *HR* 17.5 (SC 257:40–42), *Vita Rabbulae* (Overbeck: 169–70; tr. Doran, 74) and Trombley, *Hellenic Religion and Christianization*, vol. 2, esp. chap. 10.

124. On the Magian presence in Cappadocia and Syria, see Basil *ep.* 258 (LCL 4:45–47). On the Magi's protected status, see *Chronicon Arbelae* 16 (CSCO SS 199:67; tr. Kawerau, 91) and Schrier, "Syriac Evidence for the Roman-Persian War, 421–22," 82–85.

125. On Neoplatonic theurgy, see Shaw, *Theurgy and the Soul*; Clarke, *Iamblichus' De Mysteriis*, esp. chap. 2. On Syria as a center of theurgy, see Bowersock, *Hellenism*, 31–33. On the *Chaldean Oracles* as scripture, see Athanassiadi, "Chaldean Oracles," 149–52, 175–82. On the "golden chain," see Eunapius, *Vitae philosophorum et sophistarum*, preface; and Penella, *Greek Philosophers and Sophists*, 31–34.

126. On Zoroastrian theology, see Nigosian, *Zoroastrian Faith*, chap. 4 (what fifth-century Magians taught is unclear). On theurgic theology, see Shaw, *Theurgy and the Soul*, chaps. 12–17, 21; Bowersock, *Hellenism*, 13–28, 32–33, 44–47, 56–57.

127. On the legal status of Jews, see *Codex Theodosianus*, 16.8.1–16.9.5. On the patriarch as Jewish patron-in-chief, see Libanius, *epp.* F914, F973–74, F1251; *Codex Theodosianus* 16.8.22 (which in 415 declared Patriarch Gamaliel V an honorary prefect); Hezser, *Rabbinic Movement*, 221–39, 288–97; Gafni, *Land, Center and Diaspora*, 100–102.

128. On the variety of Jewish leaders, see Janowitz, "Rabbis and their Opponents" and "Rethinking Jewish Identity." On the *archisynagogoi* in Antioch, see Meeks and Wilken, *Jews and Christians in Antioch*, esp. 6–10; Rajak and Noy, "*Archisynagogoi.*" On the Samaritans in fifth-century Palestine, see Crown, *The Samaritans*, chap. 4.

129. On the recruitment and pedagogy of the amoraic rabbis, see Hezser, *Rabbinic Movement*, esp. part 2, chaps. 3–6. On their lineage, see Strack and Stemberger, *Introduction to the Talmud*, chap. 7; but also Hezser, part 1, chaps. 1–2. On their geography, see Hezser, esp. 162–63. On their resistance to Christian discourse, see Boyarin, *Border Lines*, esp. chaps. 3, 6, 8.

130. E.g., Aphrahat, *Demonstrationes* 1.11 (Parisot: 25; tr. Valavanolickal, 31–32). John Chrysostom, *Adversus oppugnatores vitae monasticae* 1.1 (*PG* 47:319–20). On the traditionalism of this polemic, see Simon, *Verus Israel*, 214–15; Gager, *Origins of Anti-Semitism*, 158; Taylor, *Anti-Judaism*, esp. chap 4. On the social proximity of Jews and Christians, see Meeks and Wilken, *Jews and Christians in Antioch*, 19–36; and Boyarin, *Dying for God*, intro, chap. 1.

131. For these "heresies," see Theodoret, *Haereticarum fabularum compendium*. On the rhetorical construction of heresy, see Le Boulluec, *Notion d'hérésie*, esp. chaps. 1.2, 2.4, 3.2, 6.2–3, 6.6; and Boyarin, *Border Lines*, esp. chaps. 1–2. For efforts to find real heretics, see, e.g., Tardieu, "Marcionisme;" Canivet, "Théodoret et le messalianisme;" Lieu, "Self-Identity of Manichaeans."

132. On private heterodoxy, see Maier, "Religious Dissent," 49–54. For Manichees seeking protection, see Libanius, *ep.* F1253. On large villages, see Dagron, "Entre village et cité."

133. On the diversity of Syrian sects, see Murray, *Symbols of Church and Kingdom*, 6–7; Griffith, "Ephraem the Deacon," 37. On preachers, see Caner, *Wandering, Begging Monks*, 50–77.

134. Anti-pagan edicts: *Codex Theodosianus* 16.10.7–25. Anti-Jewish edicts: 16.8.27, 16.8.29. Anti-heresy edicts: 16.5.7–8, 16.5.13, 16.5.17, 16.5.34, 16.5.65.

135. Pagan temple destructions: Sozomen, *HE* 7.15 (GCS 4:319–22); Theodoret, *HE* 5.21–22 (GCS 5:317–21); *Vita Rabbulae* (Overbeck: 192–95; tr. Doran, 92–94). Monastic confrontation: *Vita Rabbulae* (Overbeck: 169–70; Doran, 74–75), *Vita Barsaumae* 1, 26 (in ed. Nau, "Resumé de monographies syriaques," 18: 273–74, 385–87, 19:120–24). See also Gaddis, "No Crime," chaps. 2, 5. Synagogue destruction: Ambrose, *ep.* M 40 (= new # 74, CSEL 82.3:58–63); *Chronicon Edessenum* year 723 (= A.D. 412, CSCO SS 1.4:6). Anti-heresy laws and riots: *Codex Theodosianus* 16.5.6; Socrates *HE* 5.8–10, 5.13 (GCS 1:279–85, 287a); Sozomen *HE* 8.8 (GCS 4:360–61).

136. On the rarity of violence, see Brown, *Authority and the Sacred*, chap. 2; but also Gaddis, "No Crime," 3–25, 155–58.

137. Recent studies in this vein include Frede, "Origen's Treatise *Against Celsus*," and "Eusebius's Apologetic Writings;" Papadoyannakis, "Christian *Therapeia*," and "Defining Orthodoxy in Pseudo-Justin;" Wilken, *Chrysostom and the Jews;* Taylor, *Anti-Judaism;*

Jacobs, *Remains of the Jews,* esp. 200–208; Averil Cameron, "How to Read Heresiology;" Boyarin, *Border Lines,* King, "Social and Theological Effects of Heresiological Discourse;" Arnal, "Doxa, Heresy and Self-Construction."

138. Fire temple destroyed: Theodoret, *HE* 5.39 (GCS 5:342–43)—Theodoret notes how this sparked a full persecution. Peaceful temple destructions: *HE* 5.21–22 (GCS 5:317–21).

139. On Theodoret's anti-pagan *Graecarum affectionum curatio,* see Papadoyannakis, "Christian *Therapeia,*" esp. 39–40. For Theodoret's pro-monotheistic preaching, see *De providentia orationes x,* esp. Or. 1–2 (*PG* 83:556–88). Theodoret's polemic *Against the Magi* (mentioned in *ep.* S 113 [SC 111:64]) is no longer extant.

140. Theodoret's anti-Jewish arguments survive as exegetical disputes, such as *Eranistes* dial. 1 (Ettlinger, 81–82), which criticized Jews' linking of Psalm 86 to Solomon and Zerubabbel, as opposed to Christ. On Theodoret's anti-Jewish tropes, see Guinot, *L'exegèse de Théodoret,* 484–521; McCollough, "Theodoret as Biblical Interpreter." For Theodoret's suggested arguments against heretics, see *Haereticarum fabularum compendium* (e.g., *PG* 83:381). See also Sillett, "Culture of Controversy," chap. 6; Guinot, *L'exegèse de Théodoret,* 539–53.

141. Compare Theodoret's treatment of Cerdo and Marcion in *Hareticarum fabularum compendium* 1.24 (*PG* 83:373–76) to Epiphanius, *Panarion* 42.1–10. While borrowing some organizational ideas, Theodoret removes the hostile narrative of origins and clarifies (and corrects) the account of Marcionite doctrine. Similar didacticism pervaded Theodoret's *Curatio* (see Papadoyannakis, "Christian *Therapeia,*" esp. conclusion).

142. Marcionite priest: Theodoret, *Haereticarum fabularum compendium* (*PG* 83:376). The label may have arisen because the bishop saw this "priest" wash in his own saliva. Conversion of pagans (or at least baptism of catechumens): e.g., Theodoret, *ep.* S 71 (SC 98:154–56) to Zeno the Consul.

143. Hermes: Theodoret, *ep.* P 13 (SC 40:85). Avoidance: *epp.* P 50–51 (SC 40:119–20).

144. On the rabbinic labeling of (some) Christians as *minim* (heretics), see Herford, *Christianity in Talmud,* 103–65, but also Janowitz, "Rethinking Jewish identity."

145. On compromises, consider the Syrian "pagans'" and "Christians'" worshiping of angels (see Bowersock, *Hellenism,* 19–20). Consider also pagan and Christian instances of pillar-dwelling (Frankfurter, "Stylites and Phallobates"). On the slow rural spread of clerics, see Trombley, *Hellenic Religion and Christianization,* chaps. 8, 10.

146. Theodoret, *ep.* S 83 (SC 98:216).

147. Synesius, *epp.* 10, 16, 81 (Garzya, 30, 36–37, 146–47) to Hypatia; *ep.* 147 (258–59) to John (a new monk).

148. On Cyril's anti-pagan and anti-Jewish attacks, see McGuckin, *St. Cyril,* 8–15; Haas, *Alexandria in Late Antiquity,* esp. 121–27, 169–71, 295–316. On Rabbula's destruction of temples and synagogues, see *Chronicon Edessenum* 723 (= A.D. 412, CSCO SS 1.4:6). See also Gaddis, "No Crime," 260–68. Doran, *Stewards of the Poor,* 51–54. On Barsauma, see *Vita Barsaumae* 1, 26 (ed. Nau, "Resumé de monographies syriaques," 18:273–74, 385–87, 19:120–24). On the dubious nature of this *vita,* see Gaddis, "No Crime," 188–90. On the likely links between Rabbula and Barsauma, see chapter 5. On ascetics and the Alexandrian patriarch, see McGuckin, *St. Cyril,* 3–4. On Rabbula's attempted control of ascetics, see Rabbula, *Canones monasticae* (Vööbus, 27–33).

149. Paul's arguments: Theodoret, *HE* 5.39 (GCS 5:343–47). Spiritual combat: *HR* 21.18 (SC 257:98).

150. For bishops' legal privileges, see *Codex Theodosianus* 16.2.12; Jones, *LRE*, 491–92.

151. See, for instance, *Constitutiones apostolorum* 2.26, 2.57 (SC 320:236–40, 310–20).

152. *Constitutiones apostolorum* 3.1–5, 3.8, 4.1–3 (SC 329: 120–30, 140–42, 170–74).

153. See Brakke, *Athanasius*, esp. chaps. 1–2; Sterk, *Renouncing the World*, esp. chaps. 2–3.

154. See Brown, *Poverty and Leadership*, 17–26, 45–55.

155. Theodoret, *epp.* S 70 (SC 98:152–54), P 18, P 43 (SC 40:89–90, 106–8).

156. Theodoret, *epp.* P 43 (SC 40:106–7), S 70 (SC 98:152–54).

157. E.g., Theodoret, *epp.* P 43 (SC 40: 106–8), S 19–20, S 24, S 31–32, S 35–36, S 51–53, S 70 (SC 98:66–68, 80–82, 90–94, 96–100, 126–30, 152–54).

158. Synesius, *epp.* 9, 66–69, 76, 80, 90 (Garzya, 29–30, 105–125, 135, 145–46, 152–53). Firmus, *epp.* 19, 22, 35, 42 (SC 350:114–16, 122, 150, 164). Basil's collection includes almost no appeals to Nicene colleagues not about clerical conflicts.

159. *Syriac Acts of the Second Council of Ephesus* (tr. Perry: 129–31, 288–97). For a somewhat different perspective, see Gaddis, *"No Crime,"* 301–9.

160. *Vita Rabbulae* (Overbeck: 176–81, 200–205; tr. Doran, 79–83, 99–102). See Harvey, "The Holy and the Poor," 51; Gaddis, *"No Crime,"* 260–68; Doran, *Stewards of the Poor*, 57–58, 118–19, 130–31. See also J. W. Drijvers, "Man of God of Edessa."

CHAPTER 7. THE IRREPLACEABLE THEODORET: PATRONAGE PERFORMANCE AND SOCIAL STRATEGY

1. Theodoret, *ep.* P 11 (SC 40:83).

2. Theodoret, *ep.* P 12 (SC 40:83–84).

3. All of these topics interested Jones (*LRE*, 172, 355, 385, 542, 854, 952–55).

4. See Mullett, *Theophylact*, chaps. 1, 6. In this case, see Tompkins, "Relations," 112–13.

5. Clerics: Theodoret, *epp.* P 22 (SC 40:92–94), S 52–53 (SC 98:128–30). Orphan girl: *ep.* S 70 (SC 98:152–54). On Vandal conquest, see Theodoret, *ep.* S 29 (SC 98:86–88).

6. Theodoret *ep.* S 29 (SC 98:86–88).

7. Celestiacus as philosopher: Theodoret, *ep.* S 29 (SC 98:88–90); as devout Christian: *ep.* S 31 (SC 98:92–94); as paragon of gentility: *ep.* S 35 (SC 98:96–98).

8. On the indiction process (including the census), see Jones, *LRE*, 449–62, but on *iugatio* (the assessment of taxable land assets set for each city) and *capitatio* (the charge for each household), see Grey, "Revisiting the Problem of *Agri Deserti*."

9. On Cyrrhus's taxes, see Tompkins, "Relations," 96–123; "Problems of Dating," 176–95, but esp. Gascou, "KLEROI APOROI."

10. Athanasius goes unnamed but is the only bishop whose removal from office (detailed in *Acta concilii Chalcedonensis* session 15, *ACO* II.1.3: 63–83) fits with descriptions in Theodoret, *epp.* S 42–47 (SC 98:106–24).

11. Theodoret, *ep.* S 43 (SC 98:112–14).

12. See Garnsey and Whittaker, "Rural Life," esp. 281–85.

13. Numbers: Theodoret, *ep.* S 42 (SC 98:106–12). Injustice: *ep.* P 20 (SC 40:92). Past favors: *ep.* S 45 (SC 98:118–20). Holy friends: *epp.* P 20 (SC 40:92), S 42–44 (SC 98:106–18).

14. Theodoret cites statistics for Cyrrhus's assessment (*ep.* S 42 [SC 98:106–12]), but they may have been selected to support his agenda.

15. For signals of Libanius's success, see *epp.* F142, F651, F732, F1259, F1354.

16. See esp. Goffman, *Forms of Talk,* introduction; J. Alexander, "Cultural Pragmatics;" Eyerman, "Performing Opposition." For an application of performative sociology to historical situations, see McLean, *Art of the Network.*

17. Again, see McLean, *Art of the Network.*

18. Theodoret, *ep.* P 36 (SC 40:100); compare to Libanius, *ep.* F1188.

19. Theodoret, *ep.* P 18 (SC 40:89–90).

20. "Attic": Theodoret, *epp.* P 7, 27, 31 (SC 40:79, 94, 97); compare to Firmus *epp.* 27, 30 (SC 350:132, 138), Basil, *ep.* 20 (LCL 1:122–24). "Gentleness": Theodoret, *epp.* P 19, P 37 (SC 40:90–91, 102); compare to Basil, *epp.* 63, 110 (LCL 2:18, 210), Libanius *ep.* F351.

21. Theodoret, *ep.* S 22 (SC 98:78) to Count Ulpianus. Compare to Libanius, *ep.* F510.

22. Theodoret, *ep.* P 33 (SC 40:98–99). Compare to Firmus, *epp.* 25–26, 33 (SC 350.128–30, 146); Synesius, *epp.* 29, 35 (Garzya, 44, 48); Basil, *ep.* 84 (LCL 2.112–14); Libanius *ep.* F559.

23. Theodoret, *ep.* S 43 (SC 98:112–14).

24. Theodoret, *ep.* S 45 (SC 98:118).

25. Aspar the general held Homoian theological preferences; see Zacharias Rhetor *HE* 4.7 (CSCO SS 38:179; tr. Brooks, CSCO SS 41:124) and *PLRE II:* 164.

26. Theodoret, *epp.* S 29, S 31 (SC 98:88, 92).

27. E.g., Theodoret, *epp.* P 22 (SC 40:93), S 51 (SC98:126–28). On the welcoming of visitors, see *Constitutiones apostolorum* 2.58 (SC 320:320–22).

28. Theodoret, *ep.* S 28 (SC 98:86). Basil, by contrast, wrote of "renunciation of the world" (e.g., *ep.* 23, LCL 1:142).

29. Philosophy: Theodoret, *ep.* S 29 (SC 98:86–88). Wealth of faith: *ep.* S 31 (SC 98:90).

30. On allusion and typology in Christian moral discourse, see Young, *Biblical Exegesis,* esp. chaps. 11–12. See also Rousseau, "Identity of the Ascetic Master."

31. Theodoret, *ep.* S 78 (SC 98:176–82).

32. Theodoret, *ep.* S 29 (SC 98:88).

33. Theodoret, *ep.* P 18 (SC 40:89).

34. Compare to Libanius's relatively straightforward appeals to shared "pagan" faith sent to Modestus (e.g., *epp.* F220, F617).

35. See Calvet-Sebasti, "Comment écrire à un païen."

36. Firmus turned to classical *paideia* in nearly every letter to bishops.

37. On Theodoret's obscure references, see Azéma, "Citations d'auteurs et allusions profanes," 5–13; Papadoyannakis, "Christian *Therapeia,*" 19, 93–107.

38. Theodoret, *ep.* P 12 (SC 40:83–85). Compare to references to Thucydides in Libanius, *ep.* F1404, or the unmarked allusion to Herodotus in *ep.* F1266.

39. References to Plato: Theodoret, *epp.* P 50 (SC 40:120), S 21 (SC 98:70–72). Compare to Libanius, *ep.* F220, and Synesius's regular allusions to nearly every Platonic work.

40. Euripides: Theodoret, *ep.* S 33 (SC 98:94–96). Alcinous: *epp.* P 23 (SC 40:94), S 30 (SC 98:88). See similar tragic references in Basil, *epp.* 9 (LCL 1:98), 63 (LCL 2:19); and

Libanius, *ep.* F625. See similar references to Odysseus and Alcinous in Firmus, *ep.* 35 (SC 350:150, to another bishop) and Basil, *ep.* 74 (LCL 2:68).

41. On the moral significance of Attic grammar, Kaster, *Guardians of Language,* chaps. 1–2. On metaphorical reasoning, see Lakoff, "Contemporary Theory of Metaphor."

42. *Polysyndeton:* e.g.,Theodoret, *epp.* P15 (SC 40:86–87), S 29 (SC 98:86–88). *Paronomasia: epp.* S14, S 42 (SC 98:46, 110) (both noted by Spadavecchia, "Rhetorical Tradition," 250). On Theodoret's stock metaphors see Spadavecchia, esp. 251; Wagner, "Chapter in Byzantine Epistolography," esp. 169–70. Athletics: Theodoret *ep.* S 71 (SC 98:156). Seafaring: *ep.* P 30 (SC 40:96). Medicine: *epp.* P 7 (SC 40:79), S 43 (SC 98:114). Compare to Basil, *epp.* 34 (LCL 1:86–88), 150, 164–65 (LCL 2:360–70, 424, 430).

43. Firmus, *epp.* 44–45 (SC 350:168–74). Eunapius criticized sophists who avoided the flamboyant style (see Penella, *Greek Philosophers and Sophists,* esp. 107–8).

44. On Libanius's approach to rhetoric, see Schouler, *La tradition hellénique,* 139–221; Cribiore, *School of Libanius,* 154–55. He could do high style if required (e.g., *ep.* F578).

45. High rhetoric: Theodoret, *epp.* P 19 (SC 40: 90–91), S 13 (SC 98:44). Tragic: *epp.* P 19 (SC 40:90–91), S 29, S 33, S 70 (SC 98:86–88, 94, 96, 152–54).

46. For ancient advice on local pride, see Plutarch, *Praecepta de administrando civitatis,* esp. 10–20 (*Plutarch's Moralia* [LCL 10:190–252]).

47. Theodoret, *ep.* P 34 (SC 40:100).

48. Theodoret, *ep.* S 32 (SC 98:92–94). Compare to Basil, *ep.* 96 (LCL 2:156–60). Also compare to Synesius's patriotism for the Pentapolis *(epp.* 52, 69, 78; Garzya, 91–93, 125, 136–38), more rarely for Cyrene *(ep.* 119; Garzya, 204–5).

49. On the spread of Roman political identity, see Ando, *Imperial Ideology,* esp. chaps. 4, 9.

50. Theodoret, *ep.* S 29 (SC 98:86). Synesius (e.g., *ep.* 51; Garzya, 90–91) culled historical references mostly from classical Greece. Sometimes this ex-courtier oddly distinguished himself from "the Romans" (e.g., *ep.* 100; Garzya, 168–69).

51. E.g., Theodoret, *ep.* S 45 (SC 98:118). On the lack of separatism, see Millar, *Roman Near East,* 505–16; "Ethnic Identity;" Mitchell, "Ethnicity, Acculturation," esp. 117–19.

52. Theodoret *ep.* P 8 (SC 40:80).

53. Theodoret, *ep.* P 19 (SC 40:91).

54. Theodoret, *ep.* P 23 (SC 40:94).

55. Theodoret, *ep.* P 19 (SC 40:90–91).

56. E.g., Theodoret, *ep.* P 27 (SC 40:94–95). For Basil's advice on selective learning (and bees), see his *Ad iuvenes* (LCL 4:378–434, esp. 390–92).

57. See earlier in this section.

58. Theodoret, *epp.* P 18 (SC 40:89–90), S 23 (SC 98:80).

59. Refugees: Theodoret, *ep.* S 29 (SC 98:86–88). Taxpaying estates: *ep.* S 43 (SC 98:112–14). Compare to Basil, *epp.* 74, 84 (LCL 2:80–82, 100–108).

60. Theodoret, *ep.* S 32 (SC 98:92).

61. Theodoret, *ep.* P 3 (SC 40:76).

62. Theodoret *ep.* P 18 (SC 40:89–90). Compare to Synesius, *ep.* 96 (Garzya, 163–64).

63. Laborers: Theodoret, *ep.* S 42 (SC 98.108); slaves: *ep.* S 47 (SC 98:122); actors: *ep.* S 44 (SC 98:116).

64. Theodoret, *ep.* S 42 (SC 98:110–12).

65. Sermons: e.g., Theodoret, *Sermo habita in Chalcedone 431* (*ACO*: I.4: 77–79). Appeals: *epp.* S 77–78 (SC 98:166–82).

66. On Theodoret's learning, see Papadoyannakis, "Christian *Therapeia*," esp. chap. 5.

67. Theodoret, *ep.* S 21 (SC 98:74).

68. Asceticism (explicitly): Theodoret, *ep.* P 18 (SC 40:89). Asceticism (obliquely): *ep.* S 13 (SC 98:44). Compare to direct references by Basil, *ep.* 117 (LCL 2:236–38). For Theodoret's ascetic defense against charges of heresy, see later in this chapter.

69. Theodoret, *epp.* S 42–45, S 47 (SC 98:106–20, 122–24).

70. Theodoret, *ep.* S 13 (SC 98:44).

71. Theodoret, *ep.* S 30 (SC 98:88–90).

72. Theodoret, *ep.* S 71 (SC 98:154–56).

73. Theodoret, *ep.* S 45 (SC 98:118).

74. Theodoret, *ep.* P 36 (SC 40:100–101). This disinvitation appears *sui generis*.

75. Basil, *ep.* 94 (LCL 2:148–52), which defended his *Basileias* to a governor, used shared Christian faith as a foil for greater reputation.

76. Theodoret, ep. S 30 (SC 98:88–90).

77. Firmus almost never marked his distance based on his office. Consider his *ep.* 32 (SC 350:144) to the layman Ekdicus, and *ep.* 38 (SC 350:156) to the Bishop Volusianus, which use the same anecdote about Alexander the Great and his treasury of friends. Libanius usually cited "eloquence" as common ground, but almost always he reminded his correspondents of his educational rank (e.g., *epp.* F255, F535).

78. Theodoret also sent refugees to Theoctistus of Beroea (*ep.* S 32 [SC 98:92–94]), Pompeianus of Emesa (*ep.* S 36 [SC 98:98–100]), Sophronius of Constantina (*ep.* S 53 [SC 98:130–32]), and Eustathius of Aegaea (*ep.* S 70 [SC 98:154]).

79. The refugee bishop sent to Hiba and Sophronius of Constantina had come via Ancyra with Eusebius's recommendation (Theodoret, *ep.* S 52 [SC 98:130]).

80. Stasimus the count and *defensor* (*ep.* S 33 [SC 98:94–96]) and Patricius the count (*ep.* S 34 [SC 98:96–98]). For this quotation, see *ep.* S 33 (SC 98:94).

81. Compare Theodoret's coalition management to Libanius's seeking funds and beasts for games sponsored by cousins and friends (e.g., *epp.* F544–45, F586–87, F598).

82. On the *praefectiani*, see Jones *LRE*, 449–58, but also C. Kelly, *Ruling the Later Roman Empire*, chaps. 1–2; on the *palatini* (or *privatiani*), see Jones *LRE*, 412–14, but also Tompkins, "Relations." 106–10.

83. Tompkins, "Problem of Dating," analyzed the timing of these letters. My sequence and dating follows his work, with two modifications. First, *ep.* P 20 to Proclus must have been sent concurrently with *ep.* S 42 to Constantine the prefect (summer or fall of 445). Both had to be carried by an unnamed envoy, while Philip was already in the capital, since both mention Jacob of Cyrrhestica, who had not been involved when Philip first set out. Second, *ep.* S 43 to Pulcheria could have been sent with Philip on his original visit or with this later envoy. The later carrier is more likely, since Pulcheria would have made more sense as an advocate among courtiers than among bureaucrats.

84. Theodoret mentions Jacob's support in *epp.* P 20 (SC 40:92) to Proclus, S 42 (SC 98:112) to Constantine, and S 44 (SC 98: 116–18) to Senator.

85. Peter's prior work is implied by Theodoret, *ep.* S 46 (SC 98:120–22).

86. Compare Theodoret's tax ensemble to Libanius's efforts to convince the official Datianus not to punish Antioch after his property was looted (Libanius, *epp.* F1173, F1184–87, F1259). See helpful analysis of Bradbury, *Selected Letters of Libanius*, 80–81.

87. Theodoret, *ep.* P 18 (SC 40:89–90).

88. Theodoret, *ep.* S 23 (SC 98:80).

89. Compare to Libanius's long-term cultivation of Spectatus (*epp.* F74, F98, F352, F365). See helpful analysis of Bradbury, *Selected Letters of Libanius*, 32–37.

90. Theodoret, *ep.* P 47. For Eurycianus's role in the Nestorian controversy, see Theodoret, *Ep. ad Alexandrum Hierapolitanum* (CPG #6249, ACO I.4: 170–71).

91. Theodoret, *ep.* P 38 (SC 40:101–2). On Philip, see Theodoret, *ep.* P 44 (SC 40:108).

92. Compare to Libanius's tangled relations with the family of Spectatus (see Bradbury, *Selected Letters of Libanius*, 38–47).

93. See Trapp, *Greek and Latin Letters*, 17.

94. Consider inscriptions at Hispellum (Italy) and Orcistus (Galatia), preserving petitions to Emperor Constantine (see Van Dam, *Roman Revolution of Constantine*, chaps. 1, 5).

95. Theodoret, *epp.* P 11–12 (SC 40:83–84).

96. Theodoret, *ep.* S 70 (SC 98:154), reported that a refugee hoped to accumulate several recommendations from bishops to accentuate her level of support while traveling.

97. Synesius, *ep.* 64 (Garzya, 104).

98. Theodoret, *ep.* S 42 (SC 98:106–8). Compare to Basil, *epp.* 104, 111–112 (LCL 2:194–96, 212–14).

99. Inarticulate: Theodoret, *ep.* S 2 (SC 98:20–22); lazy: *ep.* S 50 (SC 98:126); subordinates as friends: *ep.* P 29 (SC 40:95). Compare to Basil *epp.* 97, 123 (LCL 2:160–62, 254–56). Libanius, Synesius, and Firmus rarely denigrated themselves this way.

100. See Krueger, *Writing and Holiness*, chap. 5.

101. E.g., Firmus, *epp.* 20–21 (SC 350:118–20) to Lausus (an official) and Plinthas (a former consul!); Libanius, *ep.* F253. Still, Libanius did sometimes plead moral or rhetorical weakness (e.g., *epp.* F123, F558).

102. Theodoret, *ep.* P 18 (SC 40:89–90).

103. Theodoret, *ep.* P 18 (SC 40:89–90).

104. Titus: Theodoret, *ep.* P 11 (SC 40:83). Eusebius: *ep.* P 22 (SC 40:92–94). On the lack of expectation that strangers would be helpful, see Theodoret, *epp.* S 140–41 (SC 111:148–52), and see later in this chapter.

105. Theodoret, *ep.* P 11 (SC 40:83).

106. On Theodoret's encounter with Theodosius II, see chapter 4. Compare to Libanius's contact with Julian (e.g., *epp.* F369, F610, F760; see chapter 6).

107. Theodoret, *ep.* P 51 (SC 40:120).

108. Officials and subjects: Theodoret, *epp.* P 36–37 (SC 40:100–102). Landlords and tenants: *epp.* P 18 (SC 40:89–90), S 23 (SC 98:80). Academics and clerics: *epp.* P 12, P 50 (SC 40:83, 120). Pagans and Christians: *epp.* S 37, S 71 (SC 98:100–102, 154–58).

109. Clerical allies who helped with appeals include Irenaeus of Tyre, Pompeianus of Emesa, Theoctistus of Beroea, Domnus of Antioch, Hiba of Edessa, Sophronius of Constantina, Eustathius of Aegaea, and Basil of Seleucia. See earlier in this chapter.

110. It is tantalizing, though not conclusive, that all the dateable examples of Antio-chenes' sharing in Theodoret's patronage appeals date from 434 onward.

111. Theodoret, *Ep. ad magistrum militum [Anatolium]* (CPG #6254, ACO I.4: 60–61).

112. On Dometianus and Eurycianus's role in the controversy, and Titus's threats, see Theodoret, *Ep. ad Alexandrum Hierapolitanum* (CPG #6249, ACO I.4: 170–71); Meletius of Mopsuestia, *Ep. ad Maximianum episc. Anazarbi* (CPG #6462, ACO I.4: 155). On Antiochus Chuzon's role, see *PLRE II*, "Antiochus Chuzon 2," 103. For appeals to these men, see Theodoret, *epp.* P 11, P 33, P 38–40 (SC 40:83, 98, 102–4).

113. On the careers of these courtiers, see *PLRE II*, "Fl. Taurus 4" (105–7), "Fl. Florentius 7" (478–80), "Fl. Senator 4" (990–91). For appeals to these men, see Theodoret, *epp.* P 5 (SC 40:77), S 44, S 88–89, S 93 (SC 98:116, 244–46, 244).

114. On Pulcheria's support for the *Akoimetoi*, see Caner, *Wandering, Begging Monks*, 126–28.

115. See earlier in this chapter.

116. For charges against Irenaeus, see Theodoret, *ep.* S 110 (SC 111:38–42). For charges against Hiba, see *Acta concilii Chalcedonensis* session 11 (ACO II.1.3: 24–26). See also Doran, *Stewards of the Poor*, part 3, introduction. For more details, see chapter 5. Theodoret reported the initial (non-doctrinal) accusations in *epp.* S 80–81 (SC 98:188–98). Charges of "two sons" first appear in *ep.* 82 (SC 98:200).

117. Theodoret, *ep.* S 79 (SC 98:182–88).

118. Theodoret, *ep.* S 81 (SC 98:192–98).

119. Theodoret, *ep.* S 79 (SC 98:182–88).

120. Theodoret, *ep.* S 88 (SC 98:234–36).

121. Theodoret, *ep.* S 81 (SC 98:194).

122. Theodoret *ep.* S 110 (SC 111:38–42). See also *ep.* S 86 (SC 98:226–32), which was apparently sent to Domnus as a draft letter to Flavian of Constantinople and then reused.

123. Theodoret also sent appeals to Lupicinus the master of offices (*ep.* S 90), Proto-genes the prefect (*ep.* S 94), Sporacius the count (*ep.* S 97), Claudianus the shorthand (*ep.* S 99), and Apollonius the count (*ep.* S 103).

124. On the hiring of Eusebius the *scholasticus*, see Theodoret, *ep.* S 21 (SC 98:68–78).

125. For requests to Flavian and Anatolius to facilitate the embassy, see Theodoret, *epp.* S 92 (SC 98:236–38), S 104 (SC 111:24–30). Participants include *oikonomoi* Eulogius and Abraham, priests Theodotus and Acacius (Theodoret, *epp.* S 105–108 [SC 111:30–32]), Cel-erina the deaconess and Alexandra (*epp.* S 100–101 [SC 111:16–20]).

126. Boundaries: Theodoret, *ep.* S 88 (SC 98:234). Guilty of sins: *ep.* S 89 (SC 98:236).

127. Theodoret, *ep.* S 83 (SC 98:204–18, esp. 214).

128. Theodoret, *ep.* S 89 (SC 98:236–38).

129. Theodoret, *ep.* S 80 (SC 98:188–90).

130. For an intriguing take on the court's shift against Theodoret, see Bevan and Gray, "Trial of Eutyches."

131. Theodoret *epp.* S 112, S 119 (SC 111:46–56, 76–82).

132. Theodoret *epp.* S 125 (SC 111:92–96), S 131, S 133–134 (SC 111:110–22, 224–28).

133. Theodoret, *ep.* S 124 (SC 111:90–92).

134. Theodoret, *epp.* S 114–15 (SC 111:68). For the suggestion that these physicians left Cyrrhus out of loyalty to Theodoret, see Tompkins, "Relations," 88–93.

135. See Theodoret, *ep.* S 119 (SC 111:80).

136. Theodoret *ep.* S 113 (SC 111:56–58). Theodoret altered the meaning of Galatians 2:11–14. In this passage, Paul reports how he and Barnabas came to terms with "the Pillars of Jerusalem," led by James. He then points out his conflict with Peter in Antioch, after Peter refused to eat with the gentile Christians. By focusing on Peter as Paul's problem-solver (instead of Paul's problem), Theodoret could make this story fit with the popes' (relatively new) claim to authority, as the successors of the lead apostle.

137. Theodoret, *ep.* S 113 (SC 111: 58–66).

138. Theodoret, *epp.* S 116–117 (SC 111:68–74). It is not clear which bishop Florentius fits.

139. Theodoret, *epp.* S 117–118 (SC 111:74–76).

140. Theodoret, *ep.* S 113 (SC 111:64).

141. Scholars have questioned the authenticity of Leo's reply to Theodoret's letter: Pope Leo, *ep.* 120 (*PL* 54:1046–55); see Silva-Tarouca, *S. Leonis Magni,* part 2, xxxiv–xxxviii. If genuine, this letter was sent after the Council of Chalcedon. Leo's other statements about restoring deposed bishops were categorical. Theodoret was uncertain enough of Pope Leo's support that he wrote Leo's envoy to the court, Abundius of Como, with more evidence of his orthodoxy (and that of Hiba and Aquilinus of Byblus). See *Ep. ad Abundium Comensem* (CPG #6277, *PG* 83:1492–94).

142. The influence of Pulcheria has been noted (e.g., Goubert, "Sainte Pulchérie;" Holum, *Theodosian Empresses,* chaps. 5–7). It is difficult to determine her precise role.

143. Theodoret, *epp.* S 140–141 (SC 111:148–52).

144. Monks in the capital: Theodoret, *ep.* S 146 (SC 111:172–200); see also *epp.* S 138, S 144 (SC 111:138–42, 158–62). *Akoimetoi: epp.* S 142–143 (SC 111:152–58). Soldiers: *ep.* S 145 (SC 111:162–72).

145. E.g., Theodoret, *ep.* S 136 (SC 111:132–36) to Romulus of Chalcis.

146. Theodoret, *epp.* S 139–141 (SC 111:142–52).

147. Theodoret's letters suggest such support from Maranas the *scholasticus,* the *curiales* of Zeugma, Sabinianus of Perrha, Jobius the archimandrite, Candidus the archimandrite, Antonius the priest, Timothy of Doliche, Longinus the archimandrite of Doliche, Hiba, and John of Germanicea (see Theodoret, *epp.* S 124–134 ([SC 111:90–128]).

CHAPTER 8. PATRONAGE, HUMAN AND DIVINE: THE SOCIAL DYNAMICS OF THEODORET'S CHRISTOLOGY

1. Theodoret, *ep.* S 60 (SC 98:136–38), playing off Philippians 2:5–7: "Let the same mind be in you as was in Christ Jesus, who, though he was in the form of God, did not view equality with God as something to be exploited, but emptied himself, taking the form of a slave ..." (tr. NRSV).

2. Theology from architecture: Aphrahat, *Demonstrationes* 1.2–1.4 (Parisot, 5–13). Theology from politics: Amphilochius of Iconium (according to Theodoret, *HE* 5.16 [GCS 5:305–6]) and Eusebius of Caesarea (see Van Dam, *Roman Revolution of Constantine,* chaps.

9–12). Theology from bodily functions: Aetius, as quoted by Theodore of Mopsuestia in his *Contra Eunomium* (Vaggione, "Some Neglected Fragments of Theodore," 413–19; see Van Dam, *Becoming Christian*, 11–12). Theology from milk: Demophilus of Constantinople (quoted by Philostorgius, *HE* 9.14; Bidez, 121; see Hanson, *Search*, 117, 591–98).

3. See Lampe, *Patristic Greek Lexicon*, 1159.

4. *Constitutiones apostolorum* 2.26.4 (SC 320:236–38).

5. Gods as *prostatai*: Sophocles, *Trachiniae* 209; Emp. Julian (quoted by Cyril, *Contra Iulianum imperatorem* 4 [*PG* 76:717]); Clement of Rome, *Ep. i ad Corinthos* 36 (ed. Lightfoot, 2:111). Gods as *euergetai*: Plato, *Cratylus* 403e; Clement of Rome, *Ep. i ad Corinthos* 20.11 (ed. Lightfoot, 2:74–75); Hippolytus of Rome, *Refutatio omnium heresium* 1 preface (ed. Marcovich, 55). Divine *charis*: Aeschylus, *Agamemnon* 182; Hippolytus of Rome, *Refutatio* 1 preface (ed. Marcovich, 55). Divine *philanthropia*: Plato, *Symposium* 189c; Clement of Alexandria, *Protrepticus* 10 (SC 2:159). See Veyne, *Bread and Circuses*, 101–14, 310–15; Brown, *Poverty and Leadership*, 3–6, 10–11.

6. E.g., Theodoret, *epp.* P 17–18, P 33, P 37 (SC 40:89–90, 98–99, 101–2), S 23, S 30, S 34, S 42, S 44 (SC 98:80, 88–90, 96, 110–12, 116–18).

7. On mediators, see Plutarch *De defectu oraculorum* 10–15 (*Moralia*, LCL 5:376–94). On mediators in Neoplatonism, see Rodriguez Moreno, "Les héros comme METAXY l'homme et la divinité," 91–100; Shaw, *Theurgy and the Soul*, esp. chaps. 12–15.

8. Theodoret, *Graecarum affectionum curatio* 3.87–99 (SC 57.1:196–99, on angels), 8.1–11, 51–70 (SC 57.2:310–14, 328–35, on martyrs), 12.8–10 (SC 57.2:420–21 on ascetics as God's friends). On Theodoret's treatment of mediation, see Papadoyannakis, "Christian Therapeia," esp. chap. 3. For the mediating role of the bishop in Theodoret's appeals, see, e.g., *epp.* P 32 (SC 40:98), S 32, S 36, S 60 (SC 98:92–94, 98–100, 136–38).

9. See Young, *Biblical Exegesis*, 99, 151–56, 175–213; Brown, *Poverty and Leadership*, 70–73; Krueger, "Typological Figuration." For an older patristic perspective, see Lampe and Woolcombe, *Essays on Typology*, esp. chap. 2.

10. Paul as "most perfect": Theodoret, *Eranistes* dial. 2 (Ettlinger: 131). Paul as "excellent physician": Theodoret, *Interpretatio in xiv epistulas sancti Pauli*, Romans 3 (*PG* 82:80). Paul as a "Jew to the Jews," using theatrical "masks": *ep.* S 3 (SC 98:24).

11. Theodoret, *Interpretatio xiv epistulas sancti Pauli* Timothy 2:5–6 (*PG* 82:797–800). For the specific interpretation, which was reused in his *Eranistes*, see next section.

12. *Constitutiones apostolorum* 2.24.7 (SC 320:226). For similar links in Syriac Christian culture, see Murray, *Symbols of Church and Kingdom*, chap. 5.

13. Theodoret, *Interpretatio in xiv epistulas sancti Pauli*, Ephesians 2 (*PG* 82:521). John Chrysostom, *Homiliae in Romanos* 10.1 (*PG* 60:475), also called Christ a *proxenos*.

14. To borrow a phrase from Charles Bobertz, "Patronage Networks," 23.

15. For two notable examples, see Durkheim, *Elementary Forms*; Douglas, *Natural Symbols*. See Introduction.

16. Theology from familial structure: Van Dam, *Families and Friends*, chaps. 4, 7. Theology as gender ideology: Burrus, *Begotten, Not Made*. Theology from political discourse: Van Dam, *Roman Revolution of Constantine*, chaps. 9–12. Early Christian theology and patronage: Theissen and Kohl, *Social Reality and the Early Christians*; Moxnes, "Patron-Client Relations."

17. E.g., Plutarch, *De defectu oraculorum* 10–15 (*Moralia*, LCL 5:376–94). Iamblichus, *De mysteriis* (see Shaw, *Theurgy and the Soul*, esp. chaps. 15–17). Christians and Jews could build their notions of a human-divine gap from (for example) Isaiah 55:8–9: "My thoughts are not your thoughts, nor are your ways my ways… But as the heavens are higher than the earth, so are my ways higher than your ways, and my thoughts than your thoughts." (tr. NSRV). On the ontological gap in Antiochene works, see chapter 3.

18. Theodoret, *Eranistes*, dial. 2 (Ettlinger, 122).

19. Pyysiäinen, *How Religion Works*, esp. chaps. 3, 6–7.

20. Theodoret, *Eranistes*, syllogisms (Ettlinger, 257). On Theodore's use of the components of this formula, see chapters 1 and 3.

21. Theodoret's prior Christological arguments include *Graecarum affectionum curatio* 6.74–92 (SC 57.1:281–87),the *Expositio rectae fidei*, the *De incarnatione Domini*, the *Reprehensio xii anathematismorum*, the *Ep. ad eos qui in Euphratesia et Osrhoena regione, Syria, Phoenicia et Cilicia vitam monasticam degunt* (CPG #6276), the (fragmentary) *Pentalogus*, and the (fragmentary) *Pro Diodoro et Theodoro*, as well as Commentaries on Isaiah and the Pauline Epistles. These works are dated by Richard, "L'évolution doctrinale" and analyzed by Clayton, *Christology of Theodoret*, chaps. 3–4.

22. E.g., J. N. D. Kelly, *Early Christian Doctrines*, 325; Sellers, *Council of Chalcedon*, 158–61. Grillmeier, *Christ*, 419–27, generally avoided this shortcut. Clayton, *Christology of Theodoret*, explicitly defends his calling Theodoret the "last Antiochene" (Clayton, 2). Fairbairn, "Puzzle of Theodoret's Christology," doubts his representative status.

23. On the *Eranistes*' date, see Richard, "L'évolution doctrinale." The extant text contains an interpolation, perhaps by Theodoret himself, which quotes Pope Leo's *Tome*.

24. For Theodoret's explanation of the names, see *Eranistes*, preface (Ettlinger, 61–62).

25. Justin Martyr, *Dialogus cum Tryphone* features a quiet adversary. Cyril of Alexandria, *De incarnatione unigeniti* and *Quod unus sit Christus* feature deferential disciples. On the origins of dialog as a genre modeling philosophic "negotiation of debate," see Ford, "Beginnings of Dialogue." On the varied aims of dialogue, see Long, "Plato's Dialogues." On Christian use of dialogue, see König, "Sympotic Dialogue;" Lim, "Christians, Dialogues and Patterns of Sociability."

26. Young, *From Nicaea to Chalcedon*, 280–82, makes a similar observation.

27. On this non-traditional stylistic choice, see *Eranistes*, preface (Ettlinger, 62). On roots of this theatrical notation, see Lim, "Theodoret of Cyrus and the Speakers."

28. See Saltet, "Les sources de l'*Éranistes*," but also Ettlinger, *Theodoret of Cyrus Eranistes*, 23–35 and Clayton, *Christology of Theodoret*, 216–20.

29. Lim, "Christians, Dialogues and Patterns of Sociability," 165–66, stresses Theodoret's pursuit of clarity, rather than affability, via this chorus of agreement.

30. Theodoret, *Eranistes*, preface (Ettlinger, 62).

31. *Pace* Saltet, "Les sources de l'*Éranistes*."

32. Cyril of Alexandria, *Ep. ad Iohannem Antiochenum de pace* (CPG #5339, ACO I.1.4: 15–20). See chapter 4.

33. See Constas, *Proclus*, esp. 101–12; Grillmeier, *Christ* 1:521. For Theodoret's "moderate" Christology in his exegesis, see Guinot, *L'exégèse de Théodoret*, 598–627. For a contrasting interpretation, see Clayton, *Christology of Theodoret*, 179–207.

34. For oblique critiques of Cyril's formulas, see Theodoret, *Franistes,* preface, dial. 1, 2 (Ettlinger, 61, 80–82, 133–34, 143–44).

35. Theodoret, *Eranistes,* dial. 1 (Ettlinger, 63–111, summarized 254–57).

36. Theodoret, *Eranistes,* dial. 2 (Ettlinger, 112–88, summarized 257–61).

37. Theodoret, *Eranistes,* dial. 3 (Ettlinger, 189–253, summarized 261–65).

38. E.g., Theodore of Mopsuestia, *Homiliae catecheticae* 8 (Mingana, 201–4, 207; tr. Mingana, 85–87, 89). Theodoret chose not to cite Theodore but found supportive lines from Athanasius, the Cappadocian Fathers, Chrysostom, and Cyril of Alexandria.

39. Theodore of Mopsuestia, *De incarnatione* frag. 7 (Swete, *Theodore of Mopsuestia, Minor Epistles of St. Paul,* 2:294–97). The scriptural referents were John 2:19–20 (where Jesus compares his body to a temple), and then the series of Old Testament descriptions of God's presence in the temple. Fairbairn, *Grace and Christology,* chap. 2, takes Theodore to mean that Christ was primarily a human being to whom was given special divine grace. But in the *Catechetical Homilies,* at least, Theodore parallels the salvific deeds of the "assuming word" with those of the "assumed man." See later in this section.

40. Both the individual and collective senses of *physis* drew in part on Aristotle (e.g., *De partibus animalium* 639–41). McGuckin, *St. Cyril,* 136–41, chronicles shifts of meaning for *physis* and related terms. Theodoret knew that meanings had shifted (*Eranistes,* dial. 1; Ettlinger, 64–66).

41. Theodoret, *Eranistes* dial. 2 (Ettlinger, 135). See Clayton, *Christology of Theodoret,* esp. 98–99, 221.

42. Immutability: Theodoret, *Eranistes* dial. 1 (Ettlinger, 65–66). Impassability: dial. 2 (148), dial. 3 (189–93). Invisibility, unfathomability: dial. 1 (72). Incorporeality: dial 1 (65). Immortality: dial. 1 (72). Theodoret later adds "goodness, righteousness, truth, …, infinity, and eternity" (dial. 3 [197]). For applicability to the Trinity, see dial. 1 (65).

43. Human mutability: Theodoret, *Eranistes* dial. 1 (Ettlinger, 67). Passibility: dial. 2 (148–49). Reasonability: dial. 1 (69). Potential mortality: dial. 1 (66). Theodoret excludes "sin" from human nature, ascribing it to "bad will" (dial. 1 [69]). On the requirement to possess both body and soul to have a full human nature, see dial. 2 (118–19).

44. For more on Christ's *communicatio idiomatum,* see J. N. D. Kelly, *Early Christian Doctrines,* 298–301, 322, 326; McGuckin, *St. Cyril,* 190–93.

45. Theodoret, *Eranistes* dial. 2 (Ettlinger, 135–36). Cyril linguistically waved away this problem by saying that God changed and suffered "economically," or "according to the flesh" (see McGuckin, *St. Cyril,* 201–5, 216–22).

46. On human nature as a composite of body and soul, see Theodoret, *Eranistes* dial. 1 (Ettlinger, 114). To prove that Christ always possessed full divinity and full humanity, Theodoret tried the Ciceronian technique of *exceptio probat regulum.* He treated the biblical phrase "according to the flesh" as an indication of Christ's human nature. Wherever the phrase was not mentioned in relation to Christ, he read in "according to the divinity" (*Eranistes* dial. 1 [Ettlinger, 87–88]).

47. E.g, Cyril of Alexandria, *De incarnatione unigeniti* 691–92 (SC 97:230–32). Fairbairn, *Grace and Christology,* chap. 3, argues that this notion of salvation as God giving of Himself led necessarily to his single-divine-subject Christology.

48. Theodoret, *Eranistes* dial. 2 (Ettlinger, 148). Dial 3 (205–7) elaborates on the point.

49. Theodoret, *Eranistes* dial. 2 (Ettlinger, 120). This line of argument echoes what Theodoret had written twenty-five years earlier in the *Graecarum affectionum curatio* 6.77–80 (SC 57.1:282–83). See Clayton, *Christology of Theodoret*, 80–82.

50. E.g., Cyril of Alexandria, *De incarnatione unigeniti* 688, 709 (SC 97:220–22, 286).

51. Theodoret, *Eranistes* dial. 2 (Ettlinger, 122). Theodoret made the same basic point a few years earlier in his exegesis. See next section.

52. See Gavrilyuk, *Suffering of the Impassible God*, chap 6; Fairbairn, *Grace and Christology*, chap. 3. Fairbairn's contention that Theodore, by contrast, treated Christ primarily as a human subject underplays Theodore's discussions of the power of Christ's divinity (e.g., *Homiliae catecheticae* 4–5 [Mingana: 156–65; tr. Mingana, 48–55]).

53. The scholarly literature here is voluminous; here are a few examples. Arguing that Theodoret had a one-subject Christology: Sellers, *Chalcedon*, 171–75; Young, *From Nicaea to Chalcedon*, 275–77; Guinot, *L'exégèse de Théodoret*, chap. 7. Arguing that he had a two-subject Christology: O'Keefe, "Kenosis or Impassibility," esp. 364–65; Clayton, *Christology of Theodoret*. Arguing that Theodoret evolved in his doctrine toward one-subject Christology: Richard, "L'évolution doctrinale;" Grillmeier, *Christ*, 419–26. Arguing that Theodoret's doctrine always featured inconsistencies: Fairbairn, "Puzzle of Theodoret's Christology."

54. Fairbairn, *Grace and Christology*, expresses this idea most explicitly.

55. Theodoret, *Eranistes* dial. 2 (Ettlinger, 122).

56. Eucharist: Theodoret, *Eranistes* dial. 2: (Ettlinger, 150–52). Goats: dial. 3 (210–11). Theodoret notes that there were two goats, only one of which was killed, to indicate the two natures and what happened to each of them.

57. This may be why Clayton passes over "mediation" with little comment (*Christology of Theodoret*, 202, 231), while most other scholars ignore the term (though Young, *From Nicaea to Chalcedon*, 275, accords a generalized importance to mediation).

58. Divine powers: Theodoret, *Eranistes* dial. 1 (Ettlinger, 73–74). Human needs: dial. 2 (145–46).

59. Theodoret, *Eranistes* dial. 3 (Ettlinger, 204–5).

60. On the prophets, apostles, martyrs, and ascetics as types of Christ, see Theodoret, *Graecarum affectionum curatio* 3.87–99, 8.1–9, 8.12–28, 12.8 (SC 57.1:196–99, 310–13, 314–19, 420), and (more briefly) *Eranistes*, dial. 2 (Ettlinger, 122–26), dial. 3 (210–12).

61. On deep metaphors in cognition, see Lakoff, "Contemporary Theory of Metaphor," esp. 244–49; Lakoff and Johnson, *Philosophy in the Flesh*, part 1.

62. Theodoret, *Interpretatio in xiv epistulas sancti Pauli*, Timothy (PG 82:799–800).

63. On the importance of underlying communal narratives, see Somers, "Narrative Constitution of Identity," and Polletta, "Contending Stories."

64. See Lakoff and Johnson, *Philosophy in the Flesh*, esp. chap. 2.

65. At the trial of Eutyches in 448, Basil of Seleucia offered the formula "one Christ, made known in two natures, even after the incarnation" (*Acta concilii Chalcedonensis* session 1, *ACO* II.1.1: 117; noted by Sellers, *Chalcedon*, 105–9). This statement, while acceptable to Theodoret, differed from his "two natures in Christ." See Epilogue.

66. This suggestion is similar to the power of "multiplex" relations to magnify conflict, noted by Clark, *Origenist Controversy*, chap. 1.

67. On the social impact of narrative and metaphor, see Introduction.

68. See chapters 5 and 7.

69. For instance, admirers of Rabbula. See chapter 6.

70. See chapters 4 and 5.

71. On these key Cyrillian phrases, see McGuckin, *St. Cyril*, 200–216.

72. See Firmus, *epp.* 19, 22, 35, 37, 38, 44–45 (SC 350:114–16, 122, 150, 154, 156, 168–74). Cyril, *Epp. ad Acacium episc. Melitenae* (CPG #5340, *ACO* 1.1.4: 20; CPG #5369, *CVatGr* 1431: 15–16) ; *Ep. ad Acacium episc. Scythopolis* (CPG #5341, *ACO* I.1.4: 40–41); *Ep. ad Domnum Antiochenum* (CPG #5377, *ACO* II.1.3: 66).

73. On Cyril's conceptual affinity to Athanasius, see J. N. D. Kelly, *Early Christian Doctrines*, 317–23; McGuckin, *St. Cyril*, esp. 175–83. Grillmeier, *Christ*, part 3 chap. 3, emphasized Cyril's modifications. See also Norris, "Christological models;" Meunier, *Le Christ de Cyrille*. Beeley, "Cyril and Gregory," by contrast, stresses Gregory of Nazianzus as Cyril's primary influence.

74. On the see of Alexandria's control, see Wipszycka, "La chiesa nell' Egitto," 143–44.

75. For details, see chapters 4 and 5.

76. On the bishop of Alexandria's resources and expenditures, see Wipszycka, *Les ressources*, 34–56, 110–20; Haas, *Alexandria*, 249–58.

77. On Cyril's conflict with Orestes the prefect, see Socrates, *HE* 7.13–15 (GCS 1: 357–61).

78. Cyril wrote appeals for dissident priests in Syria (e.g., *Ep. ad Iohannem Antiochenum* [CPG #5390, *ACO* I.1.7: 153–54]), and for Athanasius of Perrha *(Ep. ad Domnum Antiochenum* [CPG #5377, *ACO* II.1.3: 66–67]).

79. On suffragan bishops in Egypt, see Wipszycka, "La chiesa nell' Egitto." On the role of lower clerics, see "Ordres mineurs." On confraternities, see "Confrèries;" Haas, *Alexandria*, 235–41. On the influence of monastic leaders with certain clerics, see Wipszycka, "Monachisme egyptien," 305–28. On the critical views of the clergy from one monastic leader, see Evieux, *Isidore de Péluse*, 206–39.

80. Firmus cooperated with Acacius of Melitene and Cyril (see *epp.* 19, 35, 37 [SC 350:114–16, 150, 154]) but most of his extant appeals involved proximate colleagues.

81. See the start of this chapter.

82. Cyril of Alexandria, *De incarnatione unigeniti* 691–92 (Durand, 230–32).

83. On Cyril's evolving Christology, see Grillmeier, *Christ*, part 3 chap. 3. McGuckin, *St. Cyril*, 175–77, stresses Cyril's thematic consistency but notes his adaptability when it came to specific language. On variations in miaphysite Christology, see R. Chesnut, *Three Monophysite Christologies*, esp. 111–12, 141–43.

84. See Cyril, *Ep. ad Caelestinum papam* (CPG #5310, *ACO* 1.1.5: 10–12). See also Chadwick, "Eucharist and Christology."

85. Both, for instance, worked well with Proclus of Constantinople, Eurycianus the tribune, and Symeon Stylites. See chapters 4 and 5.

86. Cyril's debt to Athanasius's Christological works is clear. But the Antiochenes also claimed Athanasius, especially his *Letter to Epictetus*. See Beeley, "Cyril and Gregory."

87. See chapter 4.

88. Cyril of Alexandria et al., *Relatio Cyrillianorum ad Theodosium et Valentinianum imperatores* (CPG #8697, *ACO* I.1.3: 10–13). See also Gaddis, *"No Crime,"* 284–85.

89. John of Antioch et al., *Ep. ad Rufum episc. Thessalonicae* (CPG #6319, ACO I.1.3: 41–42).

90. See John of Antioch et al., *Contestatio prima ad Theodosium et Valentinianum imp. Aug.* (CPG #6329, ACO I.1.7: 72); *Relatio synodi Cyrillianorum ad imperatores per legatos* (CPG #8741, ACO I.1.3: 65–66).

91. E.g., Theodoret, *Ep. ad Helladium episc. Tarsi* (CPG #6260, ACO I.4: 106–7).

92. Cyril of Alexandria, *Ep. ad Iohannem Antiochenum* (CPG #5363, CVatGr 1431: 15).

93. See chapter 5.

94. See chapter 7.

95. See chapter 5.

96. Dioscorus was accused of heresy and tyrannical behavior (by Eusebius of Dorylaeum). He was deposed when he failed to appear at his trial, with imperial officials preventing him from attending (*Acta concilii Chalcedonensis* session "2" (ACO II.1.2: 8–9, 28–29).

97. On the stereotype of tyrannical administrators, see Gaddis, "*No Crime*," 268–82.

98. At Chalcedon many bishops declared their preference for "a union of two natures." The suppressed first statement of faith probably reflected this (*Acta concilii Chalcedonensis*, session 5 [ACO II.1.2: 123–24]). See Sellers, *Chalcedon*, 116–17.

99. Civic and congregational loyalties: e.g., T. Gregory, *Vox Populi*, conclusion. Linguistic divisions: e.g., Woodward, *Christianity and Nationalism* (discredited, see Jones, "Were Heresies National or Social Movements?"). Liturgical factors: e.g., Chadwick, "Eucharist and Christology;" Davidson, "Staging the Church." Monks' involvement: e.g., Bacht, "Die Role des orientalischen Monchtums;" Frend, *Monophysite Movement*, esp. 136–42.

100. This may help to explain why some clerics and laypeople rioted in reaction to bishops who repeatedly switched positions in the natures dispute (e.g., Basil of Seleucia; see Epilogue). Such shifts caused dissonance in place of the promise of resonance.

101. On the formation of separate churches, see Frend, *Monophysite Movement*, chap. 6; Moeller, "Chalcédonisme;" Gray, *Defense of Chalcedon*, esp. chap. 6; Brock, "Church of the East in the Sassanian Empire." See also Epilogue.

EPILOGUE: THE COUNCIL OF CHALCEDON AND THE ANTIOCHENE LEGACY

1. Theodoret, *Ep. ad Iohannem Aegaeatem* (CPG #6278, PO 13:190–91); *Haereticarum fabularum compendium*, dated by Cope, "Heresiological Method of Theodoret," 45–53.

2. *Acta concilii Chalcedonensis* session 1, "2", 5 (ACO II.1.1: 195, II.1.2: 10–12, 124–27). On the role of the lay commissioners, see Sellers, *Chalcedon*, 108–9, Price and Gaddis, *Acts of Chalcedon* 1:41–43; but also Bevan and Gray, "Trial of Eutyches."

3. *Acta concilii Chalcedonensis* session "3", 5 (ACO II.1.2: 80–83, 126–30).

4. *Acta concilii Chalcedonensis*, canon 4, 7, 8 (ACO II.2.2: 55–56).

5. The "pentarchy," introduced at Ephesus in 449, was amended at Chalcedon (*Acta concilii Chalcedonensis* session 8, and canon "28," [ACO II.1.3: 5–7, 86–99]). Rulings also clarified the powers of metropolitans, e.g., to approve elections and call provincial councils (canon 6, 12, 19, 25 [ACO II.2.2: 34–40]). On the titles and jurisdictional authority of patriarchs, see Wuyts, "Le 28e canon de Chalcédoine," and Honigmann, "Juvenal of Jerusalem," esp. 222–23, 231–32, 245–47, 271–75.

6. On the violence in Palestine from 451 to 453, see Zacharias Rhetor, *HE* 3.3, (CSCO SS 38:155–57); and Honigmann, "Juvenal of Jerusalem," 247–54.

7. See Evagrius Scholasticus, *HE* 2.5 (FC 57: 226–30).

8. On the doctrinal rulings at Chalcedon, see Sellers, *Chalcedon,* part 2 chap. 1; Galtier, "Saint Cyrille d'Alexandrie et saint Léon;" Ortiz de Urbina, "Das Glaubensymbol von Chalkedon." See also Gray, *Defense of Chalcedon,* chap. 1 (he has since revised his views) and Price and Gaddis, *Acts of Chalcedon,* 1:56–75. On patriarchates, see Martin, "Twenty-Eighth Canon of Chalcedon;" Honigmann, "Juvenal of Jerusalem." On the monastic rulings, see Ueding, "Die Kanones von Chalkedon;" Caner, *Wandering, Begging Monks,* 206–8, 236–41; Gaddis, *"No Crime,"* chap. 8. On conciliar procedures, see Goemans, "Chalkedon als 'Allgemeines Konzil;'" Lim, *Public Disputation,* chap. 7; Price and Gaddis, *Acts of Chalcedon,* 41–45, 75–76; MacMullen, *Voting about God.*

9. For Theodoret's condemnation of Nestorius, see *Acta concilii Chalcedonensis* session 9 (*ACO* II.1.3: 9).

10. Theodoret won support from Anatolius, Aspar, Vincomalus (*epp.* S 139–141 [SC 111:142–52]), and Sporacius (*Haereticum fabularum compendium* preface [*PG* 83:336]).

11. John of Germanicea objected to the ambiguity of "of two natures." He was shouted down, but papal legates took up his point, and the commissioners responded (*Acta concilii Chalcedonensis,* session 5 [*ACO* II.1.2: 123–24]). Most scholars (e.g., Sellers, *Chalcedon,* 117–19) have stressed only the papal legates' role here.

12. *Acta concilii Chalcedonensis* session 5 (*ACO* II.1.2: 129–30).

13. See Theodoret, *Ep. ad Iohannem Aegaeatem* (CPG #6278, *PO* 13:190–91); see also Gray, "Theodoret on the 'One Hypostasis.'"

14. One aim of Irenaeus's *Tragoedia* may have been to celebrate the firm Alexander of Hierapolis, in contrast to the compromising Theodoret. See chapter 4.

15. Basil of Seleucia faced criticism among Isaurian clerics for his flip-flopping (see John Rufus, *Plerophoria* 21 [*PO* 8:43–47]). See also Frend, *Monophysite Movement,* 150. On Basil's carefully worded statements, see Van Parys, "L'évolution de la doctrine christologique de Basil de Séleucie."

16. *Acta concilii Chalcedonensis,* session "3" (*ACO* II.1.2: 34–35).

17. See chapter 8.

18. Evagrius Scholasticus, *HE* 2.8–9 (FC 57:238–46), blames the murder of Patriarch Proterius on a mob of Timothy's supporters, but he also reports Zacharias Rhetor's claim that the killer was a lone soldier.

19. For the results of the imperial "poll," see Emperor Leo I, *Codex Encyclicus* (*ACO* II.5: 22–98). Responses from Euphratensis, Cilicia II, and Arabia are missing. The rest of the Syrian bishops supported Chalcedon and condemned Timothy, except for the Isaurian bishops, who equivocated. Nothing suggests that Syrian bishops influenced this plan.

20. On Nonnus, see Barhadbeshabba of Arbaya, *HE* 31 (*PO* 9:603), which incorrectly claims that this bishop of Edessa was named Qura (i.e. Cyrus).

21. See Evagrius Scholasticus, *HE* 3.5, 3.10–13, 3.17 (FC 57:342–46, 354–58, 368–72).

22. The text of the *Henotikon* is preserved in Evagrius Scholasticus, *HE* 3.14 (FC 57:358–64). This compromise condemned Eutyches, but made no mention of Chalcedon. Troublingly, it endorsed Cyril's *Twelve Anathemas,* which the Antiochenes had opposed. For the expulsion of Callendio of Antioch and nine other dyophysite bishops (who hailed from

Cyrrhus, Tarsus, Mopsuestia, and other formerly Antiochene locales), see Evagrius Scholasticus, *HE* 3.16 (FC 57:366–68); Theophanes Confessor, *Chronographia* year 5982 (489–90 A.D.) (De Boor: 133–34).

23. See Michelson, "Practice Leads to Theory," chap. 1, esp. 40–47. Philoxenus also worked to challenge Antiochene translation efforts, particularly to undercut the influence of Theodore's works in Syriac (see Michelson, chap. 3).

24. See Frend, *Monophysite Movement*, chap. 6.

25. For more on "Neo-Chalcedonianism," see Moeller, "Chalcédonisme;" Gray, *Defense of Chalcedon*, esp. chap. 6.

26. The earliest links between the Antiochenes in Roman Syria and those in Persia are difficult to locate. Van Esbroek, "Who is Mari," challenged the traditional Persian identity of the recipient of Hiba's famously troublesome letter (CPG #6500). Becker, *Fear of God*, chaps. 2–3, notes how little is known about the "School of the Persians" in Edessa, which Barhadbeshabba credits with spreading Theodore's teachings. The only other suggested link is Marutha, a friend of Chrysostom's who counseled Persian kings and bishops (see Socrates, *HE* 6.15, 7.8 [GCS 1:337, 353–54]) and helped to organize the Synod of Seleucia-Ctesiphon in 410 (Brock, "Christology of the Church of the East in the Synods," 126). His Christological preferences are never specified.

27. On the "Antiochene" shift in Persian Christian theology, see *Pronouncement of the Council of Seleucia-Ctesiphon in 486* (tr. Brock, "Christology of the Church of the East in the Synods," 133–34). See also de Vries, "Die syrisch-nestorianische Haltung," but esp. Brock, "Church of the East." On the formation of parallel hierarchies, see Honigmann, *Évêques et évêqués monophysites*, esp. part 2; Van Roey, "Les débuts de l'Église jacobite;" and Frend, *Monophysite Movement*, chaps. 6–7.

28. E.g., Frend, *Monophysite Movement*, 20, 136–42. For a similar point, see Fairbairn, *Grace and Christology*, 222.

29. For a miaphysite view of Theodoret, see Severus of Antioch, *Homilia 30 de Symeone Stylita* (*PO* 36:608; French tr. Briere and Graffin, 609). For a Persian Christian who ignored Theodoret, see Barhadbeshabba of Arbaya, *HE*. For Chalcedonian ambivalence toward Theodoret, see *Acta concilii oecumenicae Cpolis ii* (*ACO* IV.1: 130–36) and Gray, *Defense of Chalcedon*, 64–70, 122–24.

BIBLIOGRAPHY

ANCIENT TEXTS AND TRANSLATIONS

This list includes documents used for network analysis in chapters 1 and 2 but not otherwise cited.

Acta concilii Chalcedonensis. Text (Greek and Latin): *ACO* II.1–2; translation: *The Acts of the Council of Chalcedon*, 3 vols., translated by R. M. Price and J. M. Gaddis (Liverpool, 2005).

Acta concilii Ephesini. Text (Greek): *ACO* I.1.2: 3–64, I.1.3: 15–26, 53–63, I.1.7: 84–117.

Acta concilii oecumenicae CPolis ii. Text (Latin): *ACO* IV.1.

Acta et sententia synodi Orientalium (CPG #6352). Text (Greek): *ACO* I.1.5: 119–24; text (Latin translation of Rusticus): *ACO* I.4: 33–38.

Canons of the Catholic Church. Text: *Discipline generale antique*, 2 vols., edited by P. P. Joannou (Rome: 1962); translation: *NPNF II* vol. 7.

Chronicon Edessenum. Text (Syriac): *Chronica Minora*, CSCO SS 1.4, edited by I. Guidi; translated by E. Brooks and T. Chabot, 1–13 (textus), translation (Latin) 1–11 (verso),(Paris, 1903).

Chronicon Paschale. Text (Greek): *Chronicon Paschale*, edited by L.Dindorf and B. Niebuhr (Bonn, 1832); translation: *Chronicon Paschale 284–628 AD*, translated by M. and M. Whitby (Liverpool, 1989).

Codex Iustinianus. Text (Latin and Greek): *Codex Iustinianus*, edited by P. M. Krueger (Berlin, 1877); translation: *The Civil Law*, vol. 12, *The Code of Justinian*, edited by S. P. Scott (Cincinatti, 1932).

Codex Theodosianus. Text (Latin): *Theodosiani libri 16 cum Constitutionibus Sirmondianis et Leges novellae ad Theodosianum pertinentes*, edited by T. Mommsen and P. M. Meyer (Berlin, 1962); translation: *The Theodosian code and novels, and the Sirmondian constitutions*, translated by C. Pharr (Princeton, 1952).

Constitutiones apostolorum. Text (Greek) and translation (French): *Les constitutions apostoliques,* 3 vols., edited by M. Metzger (Paris, 1985).

Doctrina Addai. Text (Syriac) and translation: *Malpanuta d-Addai Sliha: The Doctrine of Addai the Apostle,* edited and translated by G. Phillips (London, 1876).

Episcoporum Constantinopoli consistentium commonitorium (CPG #6891). Text (Greek): *ACO* I.1.2: 65–66.

Mandatum synodi Orientalium episcopis Cpolim directis (CPG #8742). Text (Greek): *ACO* I.1.3: 36–39.

Passio antiquior sanctorum Sergii et Bacchi. Text (Greek): edited by J. van den Gheyn, *AB* 14 (1895): 373–95.

Pronouncement of the Council of Seleucia-Ctesiphon in 486. Text (Syriac): *Synodicon Orientale,* edited by J. B. Chabot, 54–55 (Paris, 1902); translation: in S. P. Brock, "The Christology of the Church of the East in the Synods of the Fifth to Early Seventh Centuries," in *Aksum-Thyateira: A Festschrift for Archbishop Methodios,* edited by G. Dragas, 133–34 (London, 1985).

Syriac Acts of the Second Council of Ephesus. Text (Syriac) and translation: edited by Flemming and translated by Perry. Partial retranslation: *Stewards of the Poor: The Man of God, Rabbula, and Hiba in Fifth-Century Edessa,* translated by R. Doran, 133–88 (Kalamazoo, 2006).

Vita Alexandri acoemetae. Text (Greek): *Vie d'Alexandre l'acémète,* edited by E. de Stoop, *PO* 6, 659–701 (Paris, 1911); translation: *Life of Alexander Akoimetos,* translated by D. Caner, *Wandering, Begging Monks: Spiritual Authority and the Promotion of Monasticism in Late Antiquity,* 249–80 (Berkeley, 2002).

Vita Barsaumae. Text (Syriac) and translation (French): edited and translated by F. Nau, "Résumé de monographies syriaques," *Revue de l'Orient chrétien* 18 (1913): 270–76; 19 (1914): 378–89.

Vita et mirabilia sanctae Theclae. Text (Greek) and translation (French): *Vie et miracles de sainte Thècle,* edited and translated by G. Dagron. (Brussels, 1978).

Vita Rabbulae. Text: Overbeck, pp. 159–209; translation: "The Heroic Deeds of Mar Rabbula," in *Stewards of the Poor: The Man of God, Rabbula, and Hiba in Fifth-Century Edessa,* translated by R. Doran, 65–107 (Kalamazoo, 2006).

Abibus, bishop of Doliche. *Libellus ad Alexandrum episc. Hierapolis, Theodoretum episc. Cyri, Maram et Davidem episc., Aquilinum episc. Barbalissi* (CPG #6388, Casiniensis #222); text (Latin): *ACO* I.4: 162.

Acacius, bishop of Beroea. *Confessio fidei* (CPG #6481, Casiniensis #312); text (Latin): *ACO* I.4: 243–45.

———. *Ep. ad Alexandrum episc. Hierapolis* (CPG #6477, Casiniensis #130); text (Latin): *ACO* I.4: 85–86.

———. *Ep. ad Alexandrum episc. Hierapolis* (CPG #6478); text (Greek): *ACO* I.1.7: 146–47.

———. *Ep. ad Cyrillum episc. Alexandriae* (CPG #6479); text (Greek): *ACO* I.1.1: 99–100; translation: *St. Cyril of Alexandria, Letters 1–50,* translated by J. McEnerney (Washington, 1987): 75–77.

————. *Ep. ad Cyrillum Alexandrinum (fragmenta)* (CPG #6482); text (Syriac): *Severi Antio cheni liber contra impium Grammaticum,* edited by J. Lebon (Louvain, 1952): 10–11.

————. *Ep. ad Maximianum episc. Constantinopolis* (CPG #6480); text (Greek): *ACO* I.1.7: 161–62.

Acacius, bishop of Melitene. *Ep. ad Armenos* (CPG #5795); text (Armenian): *Liber epistularum (armeniace),* edited by J. Ismireantz (Tiflis, 1901): 15; translation (Latin): M. Richard, "Acace de Mélitène, Proclus de Constantinople et la grande Arménie," *Opera Minora,* vol. 2 #50, translated by M. Richard (Louvain, 1977): 398–400.

————. *Ep. ad Cyrillum Alexandrinum* (CPG #5793, Casiniensis #172); text (Latin): *ACO* I.4: 118–19, and 232 (alternate version).

————. *Ep. ad sanctum Sahak Armenorum patriarcham* (CPG #5794); text (Armenian): *Liber epistularum (armeniace),* edited by J. Ismireantz (Tiflis, 1901): 14–15; translation (Latin): M. Richard, "Acace de Mélitène, Proclus de Constantinople et la grande Arménie," *Opera Minora,* vol. 2 #50, translated by M. Richard (Louvain, 1977): 394–96.

————. *Sermo Ephesi habitus* (CPG #5792); text (Greek): *ACO* I.1.2: 90–92.

Aeschylus, *Agamemnon;* text (Greek) and translation: *Aeschylus,* edited and translated by H. W. Smyth. LCL (Cambridge, MA, 1960): 6–151.

Alexander, bishop of Apamea. *Ep. ad Alexandrum Hierapolitanum* (CPG #6390, Casiniensis #220); text: *ACO* I.4: 159.

Alexander, bishop of Hierapolis. *Ep. ad Acacium Beroeensem* (CPG #6392, Casiniensis #146); text (Latin): *ACO* I.4: 98–99.

————. *Ep. ad Andream episc. Samosatorum* (CPG #6394, Casiniensis #147); text (Latin): *ACO* I.4: 99–100.

————. *Ep. ad Andream episc. Samosatorum* (CPG #6395, Casiniensis #153); text (Latin): *ACO* I.4: 103.

————. *Ep. ad Andream episc. Samosatorum* (CPG #6396, Casiniensis #181); text (Latin): *ACO* I.4: 129–30.

————. *Ep. ad Andream episc. Samosatorum* (CPG #6397, Casiniensis #190); text (Latin): *ACO* I.4: 137.

————. *Ep. ad Andream episc. Samosatorum* (CPG #6398, Casiniensis #192); text (Latin): *ACO* I.4:138.

————. *Ep. ad Aquilinum episc. Barbalissi* (CPG #6393, Casiniensis #242); text (Latin): *ACO* I.4: 176.

————. *Ep. ad Dionysium magistrum militiae Orientis* (CPG #6399, Casiniensis #271); text (Latin): *ACO* I.4: 199–200.

————. *Ep. ad Helladium episc. Tarsi* (CPG #6400, Casiniensis #143); text (Latin): *ACO* I.4: 93.

————. *Ep. ad Helladium episc. Tarsi* (CPG #6401, Casiniensis #158); text (Latin): *ACO* I.4: 105–6.

————. *Ep. ad Helladium episc. Tarsi* (CPG #6402, Casiniensis #253); text (Latin): *ACO* I.4: 184–86.

————. *Ep. ad Iohannem Antiochenum et Theodoretum* (CPG #6419); text (Syriac): "The Letters of Symeon the Stylite," edited by C. Torrey. *Journal of the American Oriental Society* 20 (1899): 271–72.

——. *Ep. ad Iohannem episc. Antiochiae* (CPG #6403, Casiniensis #224); text (Latin): *ACO* I.4: 163–64.

——. *Ep. ad Iohannem Germaniciae* (CPG #6405, Casiniensis #193); text (Latin): *ACO* I.4: 138–39.

——. *Ep. ad magistrianum qui litteras Iohannis Antiocheni attulerat* (CPG #6404, Casiniensis #215); text (Latin): *ACO* I.4: 156.

——. *Ep. ad Meletium episc. Mopsuestiae* (CPG #6406, Casiniensis #244); text (Latin): *ACO* I.4: 177.

——. *Ep. ad Meletium episc. Mopsuestiae* (CPG #6407, Casiniensis #267); text (Latin): *ACO* I.4: 197–98.

——. *Ep. ad Theodoretum episc. Cyri* (CPG #6409, Casiniensis #154); text (Latin): *ACO* I.4: 103–4.

——. *Ep. ad Theodoretum episc. Cyri* (CPG #6410, Casiniensis #182); text (Latin): *ACO* I.4: 130–31.

——. *Ep. ad Theodoretum episc. Cyri* (CPG #6411, Casiniensis #184); text (Latin): *ACO* I.4: 133–34.

——. *Ep. ad Theodoretum episc. Cyri* (CPG #6412, Casiniensis #188); text (Latin): *ACO* I.4: 135–36.

——. *Ep. ad Theodoretum episc. Cyri* (CPG #6413, Casiniensis #235); text (Latin): *ACO* I.4: 171.

——. *Ep. ad Theodoretum episc. Cyri* (CPG #6414, Casiniensis #237); text (Latin): *ACO* I.4: 173.

——. *Ep. ad Theodoretum episc. Cyri* (CPG #6415, Casiniensis #240); text (Latin): *ACO* I.4: 174–75.

——. *Ep. ad Theodoretum episc. Cyri* (CPG #6416, Casiniensis #255); text (Latin): *ACO* I.4: 186–87.

——. *Ex ep. ad Theodoretum episc. Cyri (fragmenta)* (CPG #6417, Casiniensis #257); text (Latin): *ACO* I.4: 188–89.

Alexander, bishop of Hierapolis, Theodoret, bishop of Cyrrhus, et al. *Ep. ad episc. Syriae et Ciliciae i ac ii et Cappadociae ii* (CPG #6418, Casiniensis #217); text (Latin): *ACO* I.4: 157–58.

——. *Ep. ad Pulcheriam aliasque augustas* (CPG #6408, Casiniensis #223); text (Latin): *ACO* I.4: 162–63.

Ambrose, bishop of Milan. *Epistulae;* text (Latin): *Sancti Ambrosii Opera Pars X* (CSEL 82.3), edited by M. Zelzer (Vindobona, 1982); translation: *Letters / Saint Ambrose*, translated by M. Beyenka (New York, 1984).

Anatolius, bishop of Constantinople. *Ep. ad Leonem papam (fragmentum)* (CPG #5956); text (Greek): *ACO* II.4: xlv–xlvi.

Anatolius, bishop of Constantinople and Council of Chalcedon, (451). *Ep. ad Leonem papam* (CPG #5957); text (Greek): *ACO* II.1.3: 116–18.

——. *Ep. ad Leonem papam* (CPG #5958); text (Greek): *ACO* II.4: 52–54.

——. *Ep. ad Leonem papam* (CPG #5959); text (Latin): *ACO* II.4: 168–69.

Andreas, bishop of Samosata. *Ep. ad Alexandrum Hierapolitanum* (CPG #6374, Casiniensis #132); text (Latin): *ACO* I.4: 86–87.

——. *Ep. ad Alexandrum Hierapolitanum* (CPG #6375, Casiniensis #148); text (Latin): *ACO* I.4: 100–101.

——. *Ep. ad Alexandrum Hierapolitanum* (CPG #6376, Casiniensis #152); text (Latin): *ACO* I.4: 102–3.

——. *Ep. ad Alexandrum Hierapolitanum* (CPG #6377, Casiniensis #171); text (Latin): *ACO* I.4: 117–18.

——. *Ep. ad Alexandrum Hierapolitanum* (CPG #6378, Casiniensis #178); text (Latin): *ACO* I.4: 127.

——. *Ep. ad Alexandrum Hierapolitanum* (CPG #6379, Casiniensis #186); text (Latin): *ACO* I.4: 134–35.

——. *Ep. ad Alexandrum Hierapolitanum* (CPG #6381, Casiniensis #191); text (Latin): *ACO* I.4: 137–38.

——. *Ep. ad oeconomos Alexandri Hierapolitani* (CPG #6382, Casiniensis #194); text (Latin): *ACO* I.4: 139.

——. *Ep. ad Rabbulam episc. Edessae* (CPG #6384); text (Syriac): "Lettera di Andrea di Samosata a Rabbula di Edessa," edited by F. Pericoli-Ridolfini. *Revista degli studi orientali* 28 (1953): 153–69.

——. *Ep. ad Theodoretum episc. Cyri* (CPG #6383, Casiniensis #151); text (Latin): *ACO* I.4: 102.

——. *Impugnatio xii anathematismorum Cyrilli Alexandrini* (CPG #6373); text (Greek): *ACO* I.1.7: 33–65.

Antiochus (Chuzon), praetorian prefect. *Ep. ad Nestorium* (CPG #8748); text (Greek): *ACO* I.1.7: 71.

Aphrahat "the Persian Sage." *Demonstrationes;* text (Syriac): *Aphraatis sapientis persae Demonstrationes,* edited by J. Parisot, Patrologia Syriaca 1.1 (Paris 1894); translation: *Aphrahat Demonstrations,* translated by K. Valavanolickal (Kerala, India, 2005).

Apollinarius, bishop of Laodicea. *Fragmenta dogmatica;* text (Greek): *Apollinaris von Laodicea und seine Schule,* edited by H. Lietzmann (Tübingen, 1904).

Aristotle. *De partibus animalium;* text (Greek) and translation: *Parts of Animals, Movement of Animals, Progression of Animals,* translated by A. L. Peck and E. S. Foerster, LCL (Cambridge, MA, 1937).

——. *Ethica Nicomachea;* text (Greek): *The Ethics of Aristotle,* edited by J. Burnet (New York, 1973); translation: *Aristotle, Nicomachean Ethics,* translated by T. Irwin (Indianapolis, 1985).

Atticus, bishop of Constantinople. *Ep. ad Cyrillum Alexandrinum* (CPG #5652); text (Greek): *CVatGr 1431:* 23–24; translation: *St. Cyril of Alexandria. Letters 51–110,* translated by J. McEnerney (Washington, 1987): 83–85.

Balai. *Five Madrashe in Honor of the Departed Holy Bishop Acacius of Beroea;* text (Syriac): Overbeck: 259–69.

Barhadbeshabba. *Causa fundationis scholarum;* text (Syriac): *Cause de la fondation des écoles,* edited by A. Scher, *Patrologia Orientalis* 4 (Paris, 1908); translation: *Sources for the Study of the School of Nisibis,* translated by A. Becker (Liverpool, 2008): 86–160.

Barhadbeshabba, of Arbaya. *Historia ecclesiastica;* text (Syriac) and translation (French): *La second partie de l'histoire ecclésiastique,* edited and translated by F. Nau, *PO* 9 (Paris,

1913): 576–636; partial translation: *Sources for the Study of the School of Nisibis*, translated by A. Becker (Liverpool, 2008): 47–85.

Basil, bishop of Caesarea. *Ad iuvenes*; text (Greek) and translation: *Basil of Caesarea, Letters and To Young Men on How They Might Profit from Pagan Literature*, edited and translated by R. J. Deferrari and M. McGuire, LCL vol. 4 (Cambridge, MA, 1970): 378–435.

———. *Epistulae*; text (Greek) and translation: *Saint Basil: The Letters*, 4 vols., translated by R. J. Deferrari, LCL (Cambridge, MA, 1950).

———. *Prologus v (sermo asceticus)*; text (Greek): *PG* 31:881–88; translation: *Ascetical Works*, translated by M. Wagner (New York, 1950): 217–28.

Candidianus, count of the Domestici. *Contestatio alia post synodum* (CPG #8688, Casiniensis #85); text (Latin): *ACO* I.4: 33.

Celestine, pope. *Ep. ad Cyrillum Alexandrinum* (CPG #5312); text (Greek): *ACO* I.1.1: 75–77; translation: *St. Cyril of Alexandria: Letters 1–50*, translated by J. McEnerney (Washington, 1987): 67–70.

Clement, pope. *Epistula i ad Corinthos*; text (Greek) and translation: in *The Apostolic Fathers, Clement, Ignatius and Polycarp*, J. B. Lightfoot ed. and trans. (Grand Rapids, MI, 1981) 1.2: 5–188 (text), 271–305 (translation).

Clement of Alexandria. *Protrepticus*; text (Greek) and translation (French): *Le protreptique*, C. Mondésert and M. A. Plassart ed. and trans. (Paris 1949).

Cyril, bishop of Alexandria. *Apologia xii anathematismorum contra Theodoretum* (CPG #5222); text (Greek): *ACO* I.1.6: 110–46.

———. *Apologia xii capitulorum contra Orientales* (CPG #5221); text (Greek): *ACO* I.1.7: 33–65.

———. *Breve directorum ad mandatarios Constantinopolim missos* (CPG #5396, Casiniensis #294); text (Latin): *ACO* I.4: 224–25; translation: *St. Cyril of Alexandria. Letters 51–110*, translated by J. McEnerney (Washington, 1987): 70–71.

———. *Commonitorium ad Eulogium presbyterum* (CPG #5344); text (Greek): *ACO* I.1.4: 35–37; translation: *St. Cyril of Alexandria: Letters 1–50*, translated by J. McEnerney (Washington, 1987): 186–89.

———. *Commonitorium ad Maximum diac. Antiochenum* (CPG #5357); text (Greek): *CVatGr 1431*: 21–22; translation: *St. Cyril of Alexandria: Letters 51–110*, translated by J. McEnerney (Washington, 1987): 39–40.

———. *Commonitorium ad Posidonium diaconum* (CPG #5311); text (Greek): *ACO* I.1.7: 171–72; translation: *St. Cyril of Alexandria: Letters 1–50*, translated by J. McEnerney (Washington, 1987): 65–66.

———. *Contra Iulianum imperatorem* (CPG #5233); text (Greek): *PG* 76:504–1064.

———. *De incarnatione unigeniti* (CPG #5227); text (Greek) and translation (French): *Deux dialogues christologiques*, edited and translated by G. de Durand (Paris, 1964): 188–301.

———. *Ep. ad Acacium Beroeensem* (CPG #5314); text (Greek): *ACO* I.1.1: 98–99; translation: *St. Cyril of Alexandria: Letters 1–50*, translated by J. McEnerney (Washington, 1987): 73–74.

———. *Ep. ad Acacium Beroeensem* (CPG #5333); text (Greek): *ACO* I.1.7: 147–50; trans lation: *St. Cyril of Alexandria: Letters 1–50*, translated by J. McEnerney (Washington, 1987): 128–35.

———. *Ep. ad Acacium Beroeensem* (CPG #5392); text (Greek): *ACO* I.1.7: 140–42; translation: *St. Cyril of Alexandria: Letters 51–110*, translated by J. McEnerney (Washington, 1987): 141–44.

———. *Ep. ad Acacium Melitenum* (CPG #5340); text (Greek): *ACO* I.1.4: 20–31; translation: *St. Cyril of Alexandria: Letters 1–50*, translated by J. McEnerney (Washington, 1987): 153–67.

———. *Ep. ad Acacium Melitenum* (CPG #5368, Casiniensis #303); text (Latin): *ACO* I.4: 231–32; translation: *St. Cyril of Alexandria: Letters 51–110*, translated by J. McEnerney (Washington, 1987): 65.

———. *Ep. ad Acacium Melitenum* (CPG #5369); text (Greek): *CVatGr 1431*: 15–16; translation: *St. Cyril of Alexandria: Letters 51–110*, translated by J. McEnerney (Washington, 1987): 66–67.

———. *Ep. ad Amphilochium episc. Sidae* (CPG #5382); text (Greek): *CVatGr 1431*: 20; translation: *St. Cyril of Alexandria: Letters 51–110*, translated by J. McEnerney (Washington, 1987): 107–8.

———. *Ep. ad Anastasium, Alexandrum, Martinianum, Iohannem, Paregorium presb. et Maximum diac. ceterosque monachos Orientales* (CPG #5355); text (Greek): *ACO* I.1.4: 49–61; translation: *St. Cyril of Alexandria: Letters 51–110*, translated by J. McEnerney (Washington, 1987): 15–36.

———. *Ep. ad apocrisarios Constantinopoli constitutos* (CPG #5309); text (Greek): *ACO* I.1.1: 110–12; translation: *St. Cyril of Alexandria: Letters 1–50*, translated by J. McEnerney (Washington, 1987): 55–59.

———. *Ep. ad Aristolaum tribunum* (CPG #5359, Casiniensis #283); text (Latin): *ACO* I.4: 206; translation: *St. Cyril of Alexandria: Letters 51–110*, translated by J. McEnerney (Washington, 1987): 43–44.

———. *Ep. ad Aristolaum tribunum* (CPG #5360, Casiniensis #300); text (Latin): *ACO* I.4: 230; translation: *St. Cyril of Alexandria: Letters 51–110*, translated by J. McEnerney (Washington, 1987): 45–47.

———. *Ep. ad Atticum Constantinopolitanum* (CPG #5376); text (Greek): *CVatGr 1431*: 25–28; translation: *St. Cyril of Alexandria: Letters 51–110*, translated by J. McEnerney (Washington, 1987): 86–91.

———. *Ep. ad Caelestinum papam* (CPG #5310); text (Greek): *ACO* I.1.5: 10–12; translation: *St. Cyril of Alexandria: Letters 1–50*, translated by J. McEnerney (Washington, 1987): 60–64.

———. *Ep. ad clerum populumque Alexandrinum* (CPG #5320); text (Greek): *ACO* I.1.1: 116; translation: *St. Cyril of Alexandria: Letters 1–50*, translated by J. McEnerney (Washington, 1987): 98–99.

———. *Ep. ad clerum populumque Alexandrinum* (CPG #5321); text (Greek): *ACO* I.1.1: 117; translation: *St. Cyril of Alexandria: Letters 1–50*, translated by J. McEnerney (Washington, 1987): 100–101.

——. *Ep. ad clerum populumque Alexandrinum* (CPG #5324); text (Greek): *ACO* I.1.1: 117–18; translation: *St. Cyril of Alexandria: Letters 1–50,* translated by J. McEnerney (Washington, 1987): 107.

——. *Ep. ad clerum populumque Alexandrinum* (CPG #5325); text (Greek): *ACO* I.1.1: 118–19; translation: *St. Cyril of Alexandria: Letters 1–50,* translated by J. McEnerney (Washington, 1987): 108–9.

——. *Ep. ad clerum populumque Constantinopolitanum* (CPG #5327); text (Greek): *ACO* I.1.3: 45–46; translation: *St. Cyril of Alexandria: Letters 1–50,* translated by J. McEnerney (Washington, 1987): 112–14.

——. *Ep. ad Comarium et Potamonem episcopos et Dalmatium archimandritam et Timotheum et Euglogium presbyteros* (CPG #5323); text (Greek): *ACO* I.1.2: 66–68; translation: *St. Cyril of Alexandria: Letters 1–50,* translated by J. McEnerney (Washington, 1987): 103–6.

——. *Ep. ad Domnum episc. Antiochiae* (CPG #5377); text (Greek): *ACO* II.1.3: 66–67; translation: *St. Cyril of Alexandria: Letters 51–110,* translated by J. McEnerney (Washington, 1987): 92–93.

——. *Ep. ad Dynatus episc. Nicopolis* (CPG #5348); text (Greek): *ACO* I.1.4: 31–32; translation: *St. Cyril of Alexandria: Letters 1–50,* translated by J. McEnerney (Washington, 1987): 207–9.

——. *Ep. ad episcopos qui sunt in Libya et Pentapoli* (CPG #5379); text (Greek): *Fonti* II: 281–84; translation: *St. Cyril of Alexandria: Letters 51–110,* translated by J. McEnerney (Washington, 1987): 97–98.

——. *Ep. ad Euoptium episc. Ptolemaidis* (CPG #5384); text (Greek): *ACO* I.1.6: 110–11; translation: *St. Cyril of Alexandria: Letters 51–110,* translated by J. McEnerney (Washington, 1987): 113–15.

——. *Ep. ad Eusebium presb. Antiochenum* (CPG #5354); text (Greek): *ACO* I.1.7: 164–65; translation: *St. Cyril of Alexandria: Letters 51–110,* translated by J. McEnerney (Washington, 1987): 12–14.

——. *Ep. ad Gennadium presb. et archimandritam* (CPG #5356); text (Greek): *CVatGr 1431*: 17; translation: *St. Cyril of Alexandria: Letters 51–110,* translated by J. McEnerney (Washington, 1987): 37–38.

——. *Ep. ad Iohannem Antiochenum* (CPG #5313); text (Greek): *ACO* I.1.1: 92–93; translation: *St. Cyril of Alexandria: Letters 1–50,* translated by J. McEnerney (Washington, 1987): 71–72.

——. *Ep. ad Iohannem Antiochenum* (CPG #5361, Casiniensis #284); text (Latin): *ACO* I.4: 207; translation: *St. Cyril of Alexandria: Letters 51–110,* translated by J. McEnerney (Washington, 1987): 48–49.

——. *Ep. ad Iohannem Antiochenum* (CPG #5362, Casiniensis #298); text (Latin): *ACO* I.4: 228–29; translation: *St. Cyril of Alexandria: Letters 51–110,* translated by J. McEnerney (Washington, 1987): 50.

——. *Ep. ad Iohannem Antiochenum* (CPG #5363); text (Greek): *CVatGr 1431*: 15; translation: *St. Cyril of Alexandria: Letters 51–110,* translated by J. McEnerney (Washington, 1987): 51.

———. *Ep. ad Iohannem Antiochenum* (CPG #5389); text (Greek): *ACO* I.1.7: 153; transla tion. *St. Cyril of Alexandria: Letters 51–110,* translated by J. McEnerney (Washington, 1987): 132.

———. *Ep. ad Iohannem Antiochenum* (CPG #5390); text (Greek): *ACO* I.1.7: 153–54; translation: *St. Cyril of Alexandria: Letters 51–110,* translated by J. McEnerney (Washington, 1987): 133–34.

———. *Ep. ad Iohannem Antiochenum de pace* (a.k.a. *Laetentur coeli*) (CPG #5339); text (Greek): *ACO* I.1.4: 15–20; translation: *St. Cyril of Alexandria: Letters 1–50,* translated by J. McEnerney (Washington, 1987): 147–52.

———. *Ep. ad Iohannem Antiochenum et synodum Antiochenum* (CPG #5367); text (Greek): *ACO* I.1.4: 37–39; translation: *St. Cyril of Alexandria: Letters 51–110,* translated by J. McEnerney (Washington, 1987): 61–64.

——— *Ep. ad Iohannem Antiochenum pro Theodoro* (CPG #5391); text (Latin): *ACO* I.5: 314–15; translation: *St. Cyril of Alexandria: Letters 51–110,* translated by J. McEnerney (Washington, 1987): 135–37.

———. *Ep. ad Iuvenalem et ceteros concilii legatos Constantinopolim missos* (CPG #5332); text (Greek): *ACO* I.1.7: 137; translation: *St. Cyril of Alexandria: Letters 1–50,* translated by J. McEnerney (Washington, 1987): 126–27.

———. *Ep. ad Iuvenalem Hierosolymitanum* (CPG #5316); text (Greek): *ACO* I.1.1: 96–98; translation: *St. Cyril of Alexandria: Letters 1–50,* translated by J. McEnerney (Washington, 1987): 78–79.

———. *Ep. ad Lamponem presb. Alexandrinum* (CPG #5370); text (Greek): *CVatGr 1431:* 16–17; translation: *St. Cyril of Alexandria: Letters 51–110,* translated by J. McEnerney (Washington, 1987): 68–69.

———. *Ep. ad Maximianum Constantinopolitanum* (CPG #5331); text (Greek): *ACO* I.1.3: 72; translation: *St. Cyril of Alexandria: Letters 1–50,* translated by J. McEnerney (Washington, 1987): 121–25.

———. *Ep. ad Maximianum Constantinopolitanum* (CPG #5349); text (Greek): *ACO* I.1.4: 34; translation: *St. Cyril of Alexandria: Letters 1–50,* translated by J. McEnerney (Washington, 1987): 210–11.

———. *Ep. ad Maximum diac. Antiochenum* (CPG #5358); text (Greek): *CVatGr 1431:* 20–21; translation: *St. Cyril of Alexandria: Letters 51–110,* translated by J. McEnerney (Washington, 1987): 41–42.

———. *Ep. ad Maximum, Iohannem, Thalassium presb. et archimandritas* (CPG #5364, Casiniensis #299); text (Latin): *ACO* I.4: 229; translation: *St. Cyril of Alexandria: Letters 51–110,* translated by J. McEnerney (Washington, 1987): 52–53.

———. *Ep. ad Monachos Aegypti* (CPG #5301); text (Greek): *ACO* I.1.1: 10–23; translation: *St. Cyril of Alexandria: Letters 1–50,* translated by J. McEnerney (Washington, 1987): 13–32.

———. *Ep. ad monachos Constantinopolitanos (fragmentum)* (CPG #5399); text (Greek): *CVatGr 1431:* 34; translation: *St. Cyril of Alexandria: Letters 51–110,* translated by J. McEnerney (Washington, 1987): 156.

———. *Ep. ad monachos de fide* (CPG #5400); text (Syriac): "An unknown letter of Cyril of Alexandria," edited by R.Y. Ebied and L.R. Wickham, *JTS* ns. 22 (1971): 420–34; translation: *St. Cyril of Alexandria: Letters 51–110*, translated by J. McEnerney (Washington, 1987): 157–59.

———. *Ep. ad Mosaeum episc. Aradi et Antaradi* (CPG #5365, Casiniensis #302); text (Latin): *ACO* I.4: 231; translation: *St. Cyril of Alexandria: Letters 51–110*, translated by J. McEnerney (Washington, 1987): 54.

———. *Ep. ad Nestorium* (CPG #5302); text (Greek): *ACO* I.1.1: 23–25; translation: *St. Cyril of Alexandria: Letters 1–50*, translated by J. McEnerney (Washington, 1987): 34–37.

———. *Ep. ad Nestorium* (CPG #5304); text (Greek): *ACO* I.1.1: 25–28; translation: *St. Cyril of Alexandria: Letters 1–50*, translated by J. McEnerney (Washington, 1987): 38–42.

———. *Ep. ad Nestorium* (CPG #5306); text (Greek): *PG* 77, 57–60; translation: *St. Cyril of Alexandria, Letters 1–50*, translated by J. McEnerney (Washington, 1987): 49–50.

———. *Ep. ad patres monachorum* (CPG #5326); text (Greek): *ACO* I.1.2: 69–70; translation: *St. Cyril of Alexandria: Letters 1–50*, translated by J. McEnerney (Washington, 1987): 110–11.

———. *Ep. ad Proclum Constantinopolitanum* (CPG #5372); text (Greek): *CVatGr 1431*: 17–19; translation: *St. Cyril of Alexandria: Letters 51–110*, translated by J. McEnerney (Washington, 1987): 72–74.

———. *Ep. ad quendam Nestorii studiosum* (CPG #5308); text (Greek): *ACO* I.1.1: 108; translation: *St. Cyril of Alexandria: Letters 1–50*, translated by J. McEnerney (Washington, 1987): 53–54.

———. *Ep. ad Rabbulam Edessenum* (CPG #5334); text (Latin): *ACO* I.4: 140; translation: *St. Cyril of Alexandria: Letters 1–50*, translated by J. McEnerney (Washington, 1987): 136–37.

———. *Ep. ad Rabbula Edessenum* (CPG #5374); text (Syriac): Overbeck: 226–29.

———. *Ep. ad Rabbulam Edessenum* (CPG #5401); text (Syriac): edited by I. Guidi, *Atti della R. Accademia dei Lincei* 2: 545–47; translation: *St. Cyril of Alexandria: Letters 51–110*, translated by J. McEnerney (Washington, 1987): 160–63.

———. *Ep. ad Rufum Thessalonicensem* (CPG #5342); text (Greek): *CVatGr 1431*: 19; translation: *St. Cyril of Alexandria: Letters 1–50*, translated by J. McEnerney (Washington, 1987): 183.

———. *Ep. ad Rufum Thessalonicensem* (CPG #5343); text (Greek): *CVatGr 1431*: 19–20; translation: *St. Cyril of Alexandria: Letters 1–50*, translated by J. McEnerney (Washington, 1987): 184–85.

———. *Ep. ad Succensum episc. Diocaesareae* (CPG #5345); text (Greek): *ACO* I.1.6: 151–57; translation: *St. Cyril of Alexandria: Letters 1–50*, translated by J. McEnerney (Washington, 1987): 190–97.

———. *Ep. ad Succensum episc. Diocaesareae* (CPG #5346); text (Greek): *ACO* I.1.6: 157–62; translation: *St. Cyril of Alexandria: Letters 1–50*, translated by J. McEnerney (Washington, 1987): 198–204.

———. *Ep. ad Theodosium imperatorem* (CPG #5371, Casiniensis #288); text (Latin): *ACO* I.4: 210–11; translation: *St. Cyril of Alexandria: Letters 51–110*, translated by J. McEnerney (Washington, 1987): 70–71.

———. *Ep. ad Theognostum et Charmosynum presbyteros et Leontium diaconum* (CPG #5337); text (Greek): *ACO* I.1.7: 154; translation: *St. Cyril of Alexandria: Letters 1–50,* translated by J. McEnerney (Washington, 1987): 142–43.

———. *Ep. ad Theopemptum, Potamonem et Danielem episcopos* (CPG #5328); text (Greek): *ACO* I.1.3: 50–51; translation: *St. Cyril of Alexandria: Letters 1–50,* translated by J. McEnerney (Washington, 1987): 115–16.

———. *Ep. ad Valerianum episc. Iconii* (CPG #5350); text (Greek): *ACO* I.1.3: 90–101; translation: *St. Cyril of Alexandria: Letters 1–50,* translated by J. McEnerney (Washington, 1987): 212–27.

———. *Ep. ad vituperatores* (CPG #5307); text (Greek): *ACO* I.1.1: 109; translation: *St. Cyril of Alexandria: Letters 1–50,* translated by J. McEnerney (Washington, 1987): 51–52.

———. *Ep. ad Xystum episc. Romae (fragmenta)* (CPG #5353); text (Greek): *PG* 77:285–88; translation: *St. Cyril of Alexandria: Letters 51–110.* translated by J. McEnerney (Washington, 1987): 11.

———. *Ep. canonica ad Domnum episc. Antiochiae* (CPG #5378); text (Greek): *Fonti* II: 276–81; translation: *St. Cyril of Alexandria: Letters 51–110,* translated by J. McEnerney (Washington, 1987): 94–96.

———. *Epistulae festales;* text (Greek) and translation (French): *Lettres festales / Cyril d'Alexandrie,* edited and translated by P. Evieux (Paris, 1991).

———. *Explanatio xii capitulorum* (CPG #5223); text: *ACO* I.1.5: 15–25.

———. *Libri v contra Nestorium* (CPG #5217); text (Greek): *ACO* I.1.6: 13–106.

———. *Quod unus sit Christus* (CPG #5228); text (Greek) and translation (French): *Deux dialogues christologiques,* edited and translated by G. de Durand (Paris, 1964): 302–514.

———. *Relatio ad imperatores de Nestorii depositione* (CPG #8684); text (Greek): *ACO* I.1.3: 3–5.

Cyril, bishop of Alexandria and the Council of Alexandria. *Ep. ad clerum populumque Constantinopolitanum* (CPG #5318); text (Greek): *ACO* I.1.1: 113–14; translation: *St. Cyril of Alexandria: Letters 1–50,* translated by J. McEnerney (Washington, 1987): 93–95.

———. *Ep. ad monachos Constantinopolitanos* (CPG #5319); text (Greek): *ACO* I.1.5: 12–13; translation: *St. Cyril of Alexandria: Letters 1–50,* translated by J. McEnerney (Washington, 1987): 96–97.

———. *Ep. ad Nestorium* (CPG #5317); text (Greek): *ACO* I.1.1: 33–42; translation: *St. Cyril of Alexandria: Letters 1–50,* translated by J. McEnerney (Washington, 1987): 80–92.

Cyril, bishop of Alexandria and the First Council of Ephesus. *Mandatum episcopis CPolim directis* (CPG #8740); text (Greek): *ACO* I.1.3: 33–36.

———. *Relatio Cyrillianorum ad Theodosium et Valentinianum imperatores* (CPG #8697); text (Greek): *ACO* I.1.3: 10–13.

———. *Relatio synodi Cyrillianorum ad imperatores per legatos* (CPG #8741); text (Greek): *ACO* I.1.3: 65–66.

Cyril, bishop of Alexandria and Memnon, bishop of Ephesus. *Libellus ad concilium Ephesinum* (CPG #5395); text (Greek): *ACO* I.1.3: 16–17; translation: *St. Cyril of Alexandria: Letters 1–50,* translated by J. McEnerney (Washington, 1987): 148–50.

Cyril, bishop of Scythopolis. *Vita Euthymii;* text (Greek): *Kyrillos von Skythopolis,* edited by
    E. Schwartz, TU 49.2 (Leipzig, 1939): 5–85; translation: *Lives of the Monks of Palestine,*
    translated by R. M. Price (Kalamazoo, 1991): 1–92.

Demetrius, (Pseudo-). *De elocutione;* text (Greek) and translation: *Aristotle: The poet-
    ics. "Longinus": On the sublime. Demetrius: On style,* translated by W. R. Roberts, LCL
    (Cambridge, MA, 1939).

Demosthenes. *De corona;* text (Greek) and translation: *Orationes xviii–xix, De corona, De
    falsa legatione,* translated by C. A. Vince and J. H. Vince, LCL (Cambridge, MA, 1926).

Diodore, bishop of Tarsus. *Fragmenta dogmatica contra Synousiastas* (CPG #3820); text
    (Greek): L. Abramowski, ed., "Der theologische Nachlass des Diodor von Tarsus,"
    Zeitschrift für die Neutestamentliche Wissenschaft und die Kunde der Alteren Kirche 42
    (1949): 19–69.

Dionysius, master of soldiers for the East. *Ep. ad Alexandrum episc. Hierapolis* (CPG #6427,
    Casiniensis #270); text (Latin): *ACO* I.4: 199.

———. *Ep. ad iudicem secundae Ciliciae* (CPG #6467, Casiniensis #268); text (Latin): *ACO*
    I.4: 198.

———. *Ep. ad unumquemque episcoporum* (CPG #6425, Casiniensis #231); text (Latin):
    ACO I.4: 169.

———. *Rescriptum ad comitem et vicarium Titum* (CPG #6424, Casiniensis #230); text
    (Latin): *ACO* I.4: 168–69.

Dioscorus, bishop of Alexandria. *Ep. ad Domnum Antiochenum* (CPG #5456); text (Syriac):
    Flemming: 132–39; translation: Perry: 327–38.

———. *Ep. ad Domnum Antiochenum* (CPG #5457); text (Syriac): Flemming: 140–43: trans-
    lation: Perry: 344–51.

———. *Ep. ad Solitarios in Henadon (fragmentum)* (CPG #5454); text (Syriac): (unpublished
    manuscript); translation: Perry: 392–94.

Dioscorus and the Second Council of Ephesus. *Ep. synodicalis concilii Epheseni;* text (Syr-
    iac): Flemming: 154–58; translation: Perry: 373–75.

Domnus, bishop of Antioch. *Ep. ad Flavianum episc. CPolis* = Theodoret, *ep.* S 86.

———. *Ep. ad Theodosium imperatorem* (CPG #6508); text (Latin): *Facundi ecclesiae Herm-
    ianensis opera omnia,* edited by J. Clement and R. vander Plaetse (Turnholt, 1974):
    244–45.

———. *Ep. i ad Dioscorum Alexandrinum* (CPG #6509); text (Syriac): Flemming, 138–41;
    translation: Perry: 339–43.

———. *Ep. ii ad Dioscorum Alexandrinum* (CPG #6510); text (Syriac): Flemming: 144–47.

———. *Fragmenta e sermonibus* (CPG #6511); text (Syriac): Flemming: 118–19.

Dorotheus, bishop of Marcianopolis. *Ep. ad Alexandrum episc. Hierapolis et Theodoretum
    episc. Cyri* (CPG #5782, Casiniensis #225); text (Latin): *ACO* I.4: 164–65.

———. *Ep. ad Iohannem Antiochenum* (CPG #5783, Casiniensis #167); text (Latin): *ACO*
    I.4: 114.

———. *Ep. ad Iohannem Antiochenum* (CPG #5784, Casiniensis #203); text (Latin): *ACO*
    I.4: 144.

Ephesus, Counter-council of. *Ep. ad episcopos Orientales in Constantinopoli (Chalce done);*
    text (Greek): *ACO* I.1.7: 77–79 (Latin signatures: *ACO* I.4: 66–67).

Ephrem Syrus, deacon of Nisibis and Edessa. *Carmina Nisibena;* text (Syriac) and translation (German): CSCO SS 92, edited and translated by E. Beck (Louvain, 1961).

———. *Hymns on Julian Saba;* text (Syriac) and translation (German): CSCO SS 140–41
edited and translated by E. Beck (Louvain, 1972): 37–85 (140), 42–87 (141).

———. *Second Discourse to Hypatius;* text (Syriac): Overbeck: 59–74; translation: *St. Ephraim's
Prose Refutations,* edited and translated by C. W. Mitchell (Oxford, 1912): xxix–l.

———. *Sermones de fide;* text (Syriac) and translation (German): CSCO SS 212, 288, edited
and translated by E. Beck (Louvain, 1961).

Epiphanius, bishop of Salamis. *Panarion;* text (Greek): *Epiphanius Ancoratus und Panarion,*
3 vols., edited by K. Holl (Leipzig, 1933); translation: *The Panarion of Epiphanius of Salamis,* 2 vols., translated by F. Williams (Leiden, 1987, 1994).

Eunapius, of Sardis. *Vitae philosophorum et sophistarum;* text (Greek) and translation: *Phi-
lostratus and Eunapius: The Lives of the Sophists,* translated by W. C. Wright, LCL (Cambridge, MA, 1968).

Eusebius, bishop of Dorylaeum. *Contestatio* (CPG #5940); text (Greek): *ACO* I.1.1: 101–2.

———. *Ep. ad imperatores* (CPG #5942); text (Greek): *ACO* II.1.1: 66–67.

———. *Libellus ad concilium Chalcedonense* (CPG #5943); text (Greek): *ACO* II.1.2: 8–9.

———. *Libellus ad Flavianum episc. Constantinopolis et synodum* (CPG #5941); text (Greek):
ACO II.1.1: 100–101.

———. *Libellus appellationis ad Leonem papam* (CPG #5944); text (Latin): *ACO* II.2.1: 79–81.

Eutherius, bishop of Tyana. *Ep. ad Alexandrum Hierapolitanum* (CPG #6150, Casiniensis
#291); text (Latin): *ACO* I.4: 213–21.

———. *Ep. ad Alexandrum Hierapolitanum et Theodoretum* (CPG #6149, Casiniensis #204);
text (Latin): *ACO* I.4: 144–45.

———. *Ep. ad Helladium Tarsensem* (CPG #6151, Casiniensis #163); text (Latin): *ACO* I.4:
111–12.

———. *Ep. ad Iohannem Antiochenum* (CPG #6152, Casiniensis #162); text (Latin): *ACO*
I.4: 109–11.

Eutherius, bishop of Tyana and Helladius, bishop of Tarsus. *Ep. ad Xystum episc. Romae*
(CPG #6148, Casiniensis #205); text (Latin): *ACO* I.4: 145–48.

Eutyches, archimandrite of Constantinople. *Ep. ad imperatores* (CPG #5946); text (Greek):
ACO II.1.1: 152–53.

———. *Ep. ad imperatores* (CPG #5947); text (Greek): *ACO* II.1.1: 177–78.

———. *Libellus appellationis ad Leonem papam* (CPG #5948); text (Latin): *ACO* II.2.1: 33–34.

———. *Libellus quem dedit Flaviano vel synodo* (CPG #5949); text (Latin): *ACO* II.2.1: 34–35.

Evagrius Scholasticus. *Historia ecclesiastica;* text (Greek): *Evagrius Scholasticus Kirchengeschichte,* edited by A. Hübner, Fontes Christiani 57 (Turnhout, 2007); translation: *Ecclesiastical History of Evagrius Scholasticus,* translated by M. Whitby (Liverpool, 2000).

Facundus, bishop of Hermiane. *Defensio trium capitulorum;* text and translation (French):
Facundus d'Hermiane, Défense des Trois Chapitres (à Justinien), 5 vols., edited by J. Clément and R. Vander Plaetse, translated by A. Fraïsse-Bétoulières, SC 471, 478, 479, 484,
499 (Paris, 2003, 2004, 2006).

Firmus, bishop of Caesarea. *Epistulae* (CPG #6120); text (Greek) and translation (French):
Lettres / Firmus de Césarée, edited and translated by M. Calvet-Sebasti (Paris, 1989).

Flavian, bishop of Constantinople. *Damnatio* (CPG #5932); text (Greek): *ACO* II.1.1: 145–47.

———. *Ep. ad Eutychen* (CPG #5930); text (Greek): *ACO* II.1.1: 126.

———. *Ep. ad Eutychen* (CPG #5931); text (Greek): *ACO* II.1.1: 129.

———. *Ep. ad Leonem papam* (CPG #5933); text (Greek): *ACO* II.1.1: 36–37.

———. *Ep. ad Leonem papam* (CPG #5935); text (Greek): *ACO* II.1.1: 38–40.

———. *Ep. ad Theodosium imperatorem* (CPG #5934); text (Greek): *ACO* II.1.1: 35–36.

———. *Libellus appellationis ad Leonem papam* (CPG #5936); text (Latin): *ACO* II.2.1: 77–79.

Gregory, bishop of Nyssa. *Oratio funebris in Meletium episcopum* (CPG #3180); text (Greek): *Gregorii Nysseni opera, vol. IX Sermones*, edited by A. Spira (Leiden, 1967): 441–57; translation: *Funeral Oration on Meletius* translated by W. Moore and H. Wilson *NPNF II* 5:513–17.

Helladius, bishop of Tarsus. *Ep. ad Alexandrum episc. Hierapolis* (CPG #6435, Casiniensis #157); text (Latin): *ACO* I.4: 105.

———. *Ep. ad Alexandrum episc. Hierapolis* (CPG #6436, Casiniensis #199); text (Latin): *ACO* I.4: 142.

———. *Ep. ad Alexandrum episc. Hierapolis* (CPG #6437, Casiniensis #202); text (Latin): *ACO* I.4: 143–44.

———. *Ep. ad Alexandrum episc. Hierapolis* (CPG #6439, Casiniensis #252); text (Latin): *ACO* I.4: 183.

———. *Ep. ad Meletium episc. Mopsuestiae* (CPG #6440, Casiniensis #232); text (Latin): *ACO* I.4: 169.

———. *Ep. ad Nestorium* (CPG #6441, Casiniensis #282); text (Latin): *ACO* I.4: 205.

———. *Ep. ad Theodosium et Valentinianum imperatores augustos* (CPG #6442, Casiniensis #281); text (Latin): *ACO* I.4:204–5.

Helladius, bishop of Tarsus, Cyril, bishop of Adana, Zenobius, bishop of Zephyrium and Matronianus, bishop. *Ep. ad Alexandrum episc. Hierapolis, Theodoretum, Heliadem, Abibum, Maram, Davidem et Aquilinum* (CPG #6438, Casiniensis #218); text (Latin): *ACO* I.4: 158–9.

Hermogenes, bishop of Flavias, Meletius, bishop of Mopsuestia, Hesychius, bishop of Castabalum and Heliodorus, bishop. *Ep. ad Alexandrum episc. Hierapolis, Theodoretum, Heliadem, Abibum, Maram, Davidem, Aquilinum* (CPG #6445, Casiniensis #219); text (Latin): *ACO* I.4: 159.

Hesychius, bishop of Castabalum. *Ep. ad Meletium episc. Mopsuestiae* (CPG #6447, Casiniensis #245); text (Latin): *ACO* I.4: 177.

Hiba (a.k.a. Ibas), bishop of Edessa. *Ep. ad Marim Persam* (CPG #6500); text (Greek): *ACO* II.1.3: 32–34.

Hippolytus of Rome. *Refutatio omnium haeresium;* text (Greek): edited by M. Marcovich (Berlin, 1986).

Ignatius, bishop of Antioch. *Ep. ad Ephesinos;* text (Greek) and translation: *The Apostolic Fathers*, edited and translated by J. B. Lightfoot (Grand Rapids, MI, 1981) 2.2:20–89 (text), 543–50 (translation).

Irenaeus, count, then bishop of Tyre. *Ep. ad episcopos Orientales* (CPG #6471); text (Greek): *ACO* I.1.5: 135–36.

———. *Quanti a sanctis ecclesiis exierunt nolentes suam conscientiam vulnerare* (CPG #6431, Casiniensis #279); text (Latin): (part of *Tragoedia*), *ACO* I.4: 203–4.

———. *Tragoedia;* text (Latin): portions preserved in Rusticus, *Synodico adversus Irenaei Tragoediam, ACO* I.3–4.

Isidore, praetorian prefect of the East. *Praeceptum de exsilio Irenaei et Photii* (CPG #6475, Casiniensis #278); text (Latin): *ACO* I.4: 203.

Jerome. *De viris illustribus;* text (Latin): *Hieronymus liber De viris inlustribus; Gennadius liber De viris inlustribus,* E.C. Richardson ed. (Leipzig, 1896); translation: *Jerome and Gennadius, On Illustrious Men,* translated by E.C. Richardson, *NPNF II,* 3:359–384.

———. *Epistulae;* text (Latin): *Epistolario, ediccion bilingue,* edited by J. Valero (Madrid, 1993).

John, bishop of Aegaea. *Ep. ad Theodoretum (fragmenta)* (CPG #6160); text (Syriac): *Documents pour servir à l'histoire de l'Eglise nestorienne,* edited by F. Nau *PO* 13 (Paris, 1919): 188–89.

John, bishop of Antioch. *Commonitorium ad clerum populumque Hierapolitanum* (CPG #6345, Casiniensis #276); text (Latin): *ACO* I.4: 202.

———. *Ep. ad Acacium Beroeensem* (CPG #6301, Casiniensis #107); text (Latin): *ACO* I.4: 58–59.

———. *Ep. ad Alexandrum Hierapolitanum* (CPG #6302, Casiniensis #139); text (Latin): *ACO* I.4: 91.

———. *Ep. ad Alexandrum Hierapolitanum* (CPG #6303, Casiniensis #165); text (Latin): *ACO* I.4: 112–13.

———. *Ep. ad Alexandrum Hierapolitanum* (CPG #6304, Casiniensis #166); text (Latin): *ACO* I.4: 113–14.

———. *Ep. ad Alexandrum Hierapolitanum* (CPG #6305, Casiniensis #214); text (Latin): *ACO* I.4: 156.

———. *Ep. ad Antiochum praefectum praetorio* (CPG #6306, Casiniensis #127); text (Latin): *ACO* I.4: 79–80.

———. *Ep. ad clerum populumque Tarsensem* (CPG #6348, Casiniensis #138); text (Latin): *ACO* I.4: 90.

———. *Ep. ad Cyrillum Alexandrinum* (CPG #6307); text (Greek): *ACO* I.1.1: 119; translation: *St. Cyril of Alexandria: Letters 1–50,* translated by J. McEnerney (Washington, 1987): 102.

———. *Ep. ad Cyrillum Alexandrinum* (CPG #6309); text (Greek): *ACO* I.1.7: 151–52.

———. *Ep. ad Cyrillum Alexandrinum* (CPG #6311); text (Greek): *ACO* I.1.7: 155.

———. *Ep. ad Cyrillum Alexandrinum de pace* (CPG #6310); text (Greek): *ACO* I.1.4: 7–9; translation: *St. Cyril of Alexandria: Letters 1–50,* translated by J. McEnerney (Washington, 1987): 144–46.

———. *Ep. ad Firmum Caesariensem* (CPG #6313, Casiniensis #79); text (Latin): *ACO* I.4: 7.

———. *Ep. ad Helladium Tarsensem* (CPG #6314, Casiniensis #137); text (Latin): *ACO* I.4: 90.

———. *Ep. ad Maximianum episc. Constantinopolis* (CPG #6315); text (Greek): *ACO* I.1.7:160–61.

———. *Ep. ad Nestorium* (CPG #6316); text (Greek): *ACO* I.1.1: 93–96.

———. *Ep. ad omnes episcopos Orientis* (CPG #6346); text (Greek): *ACO* I.1.7: 156–57.

———. *Ep. ad Proclum episc. Constantinopolis (fragmentum)* (CPG #6356); text (Latin): *Facundi episc. ecclesiae Hermianensis opera omnia*, edited by J. M. Clément, J. M. and R. vander Plaetse (Turnholt, 1974): 6.

———. *Ep. ad Rufum episc. Thessalonicae* (CPG #6319); text (Greek): *ACO* I.1.3: 39–42; translation: (Theodoret), *ep.* CLXX, translated by B. Jackson, *NPNF II* 3:342–44.

———. *Ep. ad Taurum praefectum praetorio* (CPG #6320, Casiniensis #211); text (Latin): *ACO* I.4: 154.

———. *Ep. ad Theodoretum episc. Cyri* (CPG #6321, Casiniensis #174); text (Latin): *ACO* I.4: 124–25.

———. *Ep. ad Theodoretum episc. Cyri* (CPG #6322, Casiniensis #210); text (Latin): *ACO* I.4: 153–54.

———. *Ep. ad Theodosium et Valentinianum imperatores augustos* (CPG #6334, Casiniensis #265); text (Latin): *ACO* I.4: 196.

———. *Ep. ad Theodosium et Valentinianum imperatores augustos (per Aristolaum tribunum)* (CPG #6333); text (Greek): *ACO* I.1.7: 157.

———. *Ep. ad Theodosium imperatorem (fragmentum)* (CPG #6358); text (Latin): *Pelagii diaconi ecclesiae Romae. In defensione trium capitulorum*, edited by R. Devreesse (Rome, 1932): 18–19.

———. *Ep. ad Xystum episc. Romae* (CPG #6336); text (Greek): *ACO* I.1.7: 158–60.

———. *Fragmentum epistulae ad Cilicum patres* (CPG #6340); text (Latin): *ACO* I.4: 213.

———. *Propositiones Cyrillo Alexandrino missae* (CPG #6308); text (Greek): *ACO* I.1.7: 146.

———. *Sermo Chalcedone habitus* (CPG #6355); text (Greek): *ACO* I.1.7: 84.

John, bishop of Antioch and the Council of Antioch. *Ep. ad episcopos Osrhoenae contra Rabbulam episc. Edessae* (CPG #6347, Casiniensis #133); text (Latin): *ACO* I.4: 87.

———. *Ep. ad Theodosium et Valentinianum imperatores augustos* (CPG #6332, Casiniensis #128); text (Latin): *ACO* I.4: 80–81.

———. *Ep. ad Xystum, Cyrillum et Maximianum* (CPG #6335); text (Greek): *ACO* I.1.4: 33; translation: *St. Cyril of Alexandria: Letters 1–50*, translated by J. McEnerney (Washington, 1987): 138–39.

John, bishop of Antioch and the Council of Antioch, 438. *Ep. totius synodi orientalis (fragmenta)* (CPG #6357); text (Latin): *ACO* I.4: 208, and *Pelagii diaconi ecclesiae Romanae. In defensione trium capitulorum*, edited by R. Devreesse (Rome, 1932): 15–17.

John, bishop of Antioch and the Council of Antioch, bishops of Syria I (437). *Ep. ad Proclum episc. Constantinopolis* (CPG #6317, Casiniensis #287); text (Latin): *ACO* I.4: 208–10.

John, bishop of Antioch and the Council of Antioch, bishops of the East (438). *Ep. ad Cyrillum Alexandrinum* (CPG #6312); text (Latin): *ACO* I.5: 310–15; translation: *St. Cyril of Alexandria: Letters 51–110*, translated by J. McEnerney (Washington, 1987): 55–60.

John, bishop of Antioch and the Counter-council of Ephesus. *Ep. ad clerum Constantinopolitanum* (CPG #6341); text (Greek): *ACO* I.1.5: 127.

———. *Ep. ad clerum populumque Antiochenum* (CPG #6339, Casiniensis #106); text (Latin): *ACO* I.4: 57–58.

———. *Ep. ad clerum populumque Hierapolitanum* (CPG #6344, Casiniensis #96); text (Latin): *ACO* I.4: 44–46.

———. *Ep. ad episcopos excommunicatos* (CPG #6354); text (Greek): *ACO* I.1.5: 124.

——. *Ep. ad populum Constantinopolitanum* (CPG #6343); text (Greek): *ACO* I.1.5: 128–29.

——. *Ep. ad praefectum praetorio et magistrum militiae* (CPG #6337); text (Greek): *ACO* I.1.5: 132–33.

——. *Ep. ad praepositum et Scholasticium eunuchum* (CPG #6338); text (Greek): *ACO* I.1.5: 133.

——. *Ep. ad Pulcheriam et Eudociam augustas* (CPG #6318); text (Greek): *ACO* I.1.5: 131–32; translation: (Theodoret), *ep.* CLIII, translated by B. Jackson, *NPNF II* 3:333–34.

——. *Ep. ad senatum Constantinopolitanum* (CPG #6342); text (Greek): *ACO* I.1.5: 127–28.

——. *Ep. ad Theodosium et Valentinianum imperatores augustos* (CPG #6323); text (Greek): *ACO* I.1.5: 124–25; translation: (Theodoret), *ep.* CLII, translated by B. Jackson, *NPNF II* 3:333.

——. *Ep. ad Theodosium et Valentinianum imperatores augustos* (CPG #6324); text (Greek): *ACO* I.1.5: 125–27.

——. *Ep. ad Theodosium et Valentinianum imperatores augustos* (CPG #6325); text (Greek): *ACO* I.1.5: 129–31; translation: (Theodoret), *ep.* CLVII, translated by B. Jackson, *NPNF II* 3:334–35.

——. *Ep. ad Theodosium et Valentinianum imperatores augustos* (CPG #6326); text (Greek): *ACO* I.1.5: 131; translation: (Theodoret), *ep.* CLVIII, translated by B. Jackson, *NPNF II* 3:335.

——. *Ep. ad Theodosium et Valentinianum imperatores augustos* (CPG #6327); text (Greek): *ACO* I.1.5: 133–35.

——. *Ep. ad Theodosium et Valentinianum imperatores augustos* (CPG #6328); text (Greek): *ACO* I.1.7: 69–70.

——. *Expositio fidei synodi Orientalium* (CPG #6353); text (Greek): *ACO* I.1.3: 38–39.

——. *Sententia synodi Orientalium* (CPG #6352); text (Greek): *ACO* I.1.5: 122–24.

John, bishop of Antioch, Theodoret, bishop of Cyrrhus, and the Counter-council protest delegation. *Contestio prima ad Theodosium et Valentinianum imperatores augustos* (CPG #6329); text (Greek): *ACO* I.1.7: 72–73; translation: (Theodoret), *ep.* CLXVI, translated by B. Jackson, *NPNF II* 3:337–39.

——. *Contestio secunda ad Theodosium et Valentinianum imperatores augustos* (CPG #6330); text (Greek): *ACO* I.1.7: 74–75; translation: (Theodoret), *ep.* CLXVII, translated by B. Jackson, *NPNF II* 3:339–40.

——. *Contestio tertia ad Theodosium et Valentinianum imperatores augustos* (CPG #6331); text (Greek): *ACO* I.1.7: 75–76; translation: (Theodoret), *ep.* CLXVIII, translated by B. Jackson, *NPNF II* 3:340–41.

——. *Ep. ad episcopos Orientales Ephesi degentes* (CPG #6349); text (Greek): *ACO* I.1.7: 76–77; translation: (Theodoret), *ep.* CLXIII, translated by B. Jackson, *NPNF II* 3:336.

——. *Ep. ad episcopos Orientales Ephesi degentes* (CPG #6350); text (Greek): *ACO* I.1.7: 77; translation: (Theodoret), *ep.* CLXIV, translated by B. Jackson, *NPNF II* 3:336–37.

——. *Ep. ad episcopos Orientales Ephesi degentes* (CPG #6351); text (Greek): *ACO* I.1.7: 81; translation: (Theodoret), *ep.* CLXV, translated by B. Jackson, *NPNF II* 3:337.

John, bishop of Nikiu. *Chronicon;* text (Ethiopic): unavailable; translation: *The Chronicle of John, Bishop of Nikiu,* translated by R. H. Charles (Merchantville, NJ, 2007).

John Chrysostom, bishop of Constantinople. *Ad Theodorum lapsum libri i-ii* (CPG #4305); text (Greek): *A Théodore, par Jean Chrysostom,* edited by J. Dumortier (Paris, 1966); translation: *An Exhortation to Theodore after His Fall,* translated by W. Stephens, *NPNF I* 9:91–116.

———. *Adversus oppugnatores vitae monasticae libri i-iii* (CPG #4307); text (Greek): *PG* 47:319–86; translation: *A Comparison between a King and a Monk / Against the Opponents of the Monastic Life, Two Treatises by John Chrysostom,* translated by D. G. Hunter (Lewiston, NY, 1988): 77–176.

———. *De incomprehensibili dei natura homiliae 1–5;* text (Greek): *Sur l'incomprehensibilité de Dieu,* edited by R. Flacelière (Paris, 1950); translation: *On the Incomprehensible Nature of God,* translated by P. Harkins (Washington, 1984).

———. *De sacerdotio libri i–vi* (CPG #4316); text (Greek): *De sacerdotio of St. John Chrysostom,* edited by J. Nairn, (Cambridge, 1906); translation: *Six Books on the Priesthood,* translated by G. Neville (Crestwood, NY, 2002).

———. *Ep. ad Olympiadem* (CPG #4405a); text (Greek): *Lettres à Olympias,* edited by A.-M. Malingrey (Paris, 1947); translation: *Letters of St. Chrysostom to Olympias,* translated by W. Stephens, *NPNF I* 9:285–304.

———. *Epistulae* (CPG #4405); text (Greek): *PG* 52:549–748.

———. *Homiliae in Romanos;* text (Greek): *PG* 60:391–682; translation: *NPNF I* 11.

———. *Laus Diodori episcopi* (CPG #4406); text (Greek): *PG* 52:761–66.

Leo I, emperor. *Codex Encyclicus;* text (Greek): *ACO* II.5: 22–98.

Leo I, pope. *Epistulae;* text (Latin): *PL* 54:593–1218; translation: *Letters and Sermons of Leo the Great,* translated by C. L. Feltoe, *NPNF II* 12:1–114.

Leontius, priest of Armenia and Abelius, priest of Armenia. *Ep. episcoporum et presbyterorum Magnae Armeniae ad Proclum* (CPG #5898); text (Syriac): *Nestorius: Le livre d'Héraclide de Damas,* edited by P. Bedjan (Paris, 1910): 594–96; translation (French): *L'église arménienne et le grand schisme d'Orient,* translated by N. Garsoïan (Louvain, 1999): 91–92.

Libanius of Antioch. *Autobiographia;* text (Greek) and translation: *Libanius: Autobiography and Selected Letters,* vol. 1, edited and translated by A. F. Norman, LCL (Cambridge, MA, 1977): 52–337.

———. *Epistulae;* text (Greek): *Libanii opera,* edited by R. Foerster (Leipzig, 1903–1927), vol. 10–11; partial translations: *Autobiography and Selected Letters,* translated by A. F. Norman, LCL (Cambridge, MA, 1992); *Selected Letters of Libanius from the Ager of Constantius and Julian,* translated by S. Bradbury (Liverpool, 2004); *The School of Libanius in Late Antique Antioch,* Appendix 1, translated by R. Cribiore (Princeton, 2007).

———. *Orationes;* text (Greek): *Libanii Opera,* edited by R. Foerster (Leipzig, 1903–27), vol. 1–4; partial text (Greek) and translation: *Libanius: Selected Orations,* 2 vols., edited and translated by A. F. Norman, LCL (Cambridge, MA, 1977).

Libianus, judge of Euphratensis. *Relatio ad vicarium Titum* (CPG #6429, Casiniensis #273); text (Latin): *ACO* I.4: 200–201.

———. *Relatio secunda ad comiti Orientis (Titum)* (CPG #6430, Casiniensis #274); text (Latin): *ACO* I.4: 201.

Lucian of Samosata. *De dea Syriana;* text (Greek) and translation· *On the Syrian Goddess,* J. L. Lightfoot ed. and trans. (Oxford, 2003).

Marcellinus Comes. *Chronicon;* text (Latin) and translation: *The Chronicle of Marcellinus,* edited by T. Mommsen, translated by B. Croke (Sydney, 1995).

Marcian, Emperor. *Ep. ad Leonem Papam;* text (Greek): *ACO* II.3.1: 18.

Maximianus, bishop of Anazarbus. *Ep. ad Alexandrum episc. Hierapolis* (CPG #6449, Casiniensis #156); text (Latin): *ACO* I.4: 104–5.

———. *Ep. ad Alexandrum episc. Hierapolis* (CPG #6450, Casiniensis #197); text (Latin): *ACO* I.4: 140–41.

———. *Ep. ad Alexandrum episc. Hierapolis* (CPG #6451, Casiniensis #200); text (Latin): *ACO* I.4: 142.

Maximianus, bishop of Anazarbus and Council of Anazarbus, 433. *Ep. syn. ad Iohannem Antiochenum* (CPG #6453, Casiniensis #201); text (Latin): *ACO* I.4: 142–43.

Maximianus, bishop of Anazarbus and Council of Cilicia II. *Ep. synodica ad Iohannem Antiochenum* (CPG #6452, Casiniensis #247); text (Latin): *ACO* I.4: 179–80.

Meletius, bishop of Antioch. *Homilia in Prov 13:22* (CPG #3417); text (Greek): *Epiphanius, Werke III,* edited by K. Holl (Leipzig, 1933): 303–8.

Meletius, bishop of Mopsuestia. *Ep. ad Alexandrum episc. Hierapolis* (CPG #6455, Casiniensis #180); text (Latin): *ACO* I.4: 129.

———. *Ep. ad Alexandrum episc. Hierapolis* (CPG #6456, Casiniensis #243); text (Latin): *ACO* I.4: 176–77.

———. *Ep. ad Alexandrum episc. Hierapolis* (CPG #6457, Casiniensis #251); text (Latin): *ACO* I.4: 182–83.

———. *Ep. ad Alexandrum episc. Hierapolis* (CPG #6458, Casiniensis #259); text (Latin): *ACO* I.4: 190–91.

———. *Ep. ad Alexandrum episc. Hierapolis* (CPG #6459, Casiniensis #266); text (Latin): *ACO* I.4: 196–97.

———. *Ep. ad Alexandrum episc. Hierapolis, Theodoretum, Abibum, Heliadem, Maram, Davidem, Aquilinum episc.* (CPG #6460, Casiniensis #207); text (Latin): *ACO* I.4: 149.

———. *Ep. ad Helladium episc. Tarsi* (CPG #6461, Casiniensis #233); text (Latin): *ACO* I.4: 169–70.

———. *Ep. ad Maximianum episc. Anazarbi* (CPG #6462, Casiniensis #212); text (Latin): *ACO* I.4: 155.

———. *Ep. ad Maximianum episc. Anazarbi* (CPG #6463, Casiniensis #246); text (Latin): *ACO* I.4: 178–79.

———. *Ep. ad Neoterium comitem* (CPG #6464, Casiniensis #229); text (Latin): *ACO* I.4:167–68.

———. *Ep. ad Titum comitem domesticorum* (CPG #6465, Casiniensis #263); text (Latin): *ACO* I.4: 192–95.

Memnon, bishop of Ephesus. *Ep. ad clerum Constantinopolitanum* (CPG #5790); text (Greek): *ACO* I.1.3: 46–47.

Nestorius, bishop of Constantinople. *Ep. ad Alexandrum Hierapolitanum (fragmenta)* (CPG #5675); text (Greek): *ACO* IV.1: 179.

——. *Ep. ad Alexandrum Mabbugensem (Hierapolitanum) (fragmenta)* (CPG #5681); text (Syriac): *Contra grammaticum,* edited by J. Lebon, CSCO SS 112, 227.

——. *Ep. ad Antiochum praefectum praetorio* (CPG #5674); text (Greek): *ACO* I.1.7: 71.

——. *Ep. ad Caelestinum papam i* (CPG #5665); text (Latin): *ACO* I.2: 12–14.

——. *Ep. ad Caelestinum papam ii* (CPG #5667); text (Latin): *ACO* I.2: 14–15.

——. *Ep. ad Caelestinum papam iii* (CPG #5670); text (Latin): *ACO* I.5: 182.

——. *Ep. ad Cyrillum Alexandrinum i* (CPG #5666); text (Greek): *ACO* I.1.1: 25; translation: *St. Cyril of Alexandria: Letters 1–50,* translated by J. McEnerney (Washington, 1987): 37.

——. *Ep. ad Cyrillum Alexandrinum ii* (CPG #5669); text (Greek): *ACO* I.1.1: 29–32; translation: *St. Cyril of Alexandria: Letters 1–50,* translated by J. McEnerney (Washington, 1987): 43–48.

——. *Ep. ad hyparchum (Antiochum) (fragmentum)* (CPG #5682); text (Syriac) and translation (Latin): *PO* 9 (in Barhadbeshabba of Arbaya, *Historia ecclesiastica*), edited and translated by F. Nau (Paris, 1913), 555–56.

——. *Ep. ad imperatorem Theodosium* (CPG #5672); text (Greek): *ACO* I.1.5: 13–15.

——. *Ep. ad Iohannem Antiochenum* (CPG #5671); text (Latin): *ACO* I.4: 4–6.

——. *Ep. ad Scholasticium eunuchum* (CPG #5673); text (Latin): *ACO* I.4: 51–53.

——. *Ep. ad Theodoretum* (CPG #5676, Casiniensis #209); text: *ACO* I.4: 150–53.

——. *Ep. i ad praesidem Thebaidis (fragmenta)* (CPG #5677); text (Greek): *Evagrius: The Ecclesiastical History,* edited by J. Bidez and L. Parmentier (Amsterdam, 1964): 14–15.

——. *Ep. ii ad praesidem Thebaidis (fragmentum)* (CPG #5678); text (Greek): *Evagrius: The Ecclesiastical History,* edited by J. Bidez and L. Parmentier (Amsterdam, 1964): 15–16.

——. *Ep. ii ad Theodoretum (fragmentum)* (CPG #5679, Casiniensis #209); text (Syriac): *Nestoriana,* edited by F. Loofs, I.4:201–2.

——. *Liber Heraclidis* (CPG #5751); text (Syriac): *Le livre d'Héraclide de Damas,* edited by P. Bedjan (Paris, 1910); translation: *Nestorius: The Bazaar of Heracleides,* translated by L. Hodgson and G. Driver (Oxford, 1925).

Nikephoros Kallistos. *Historia ecclesiastica;* text (Greek): *PG* 145–46.

Palladius, bishop of Helenopolis, then bishop of Aspuna. *Dialogus de vita Iohannis Chrysostomi* (CPG #6037); text (Greek): *Palladios—Dialogue sur la vie de Jean Chrysostome,* SC 341–342 (Paris, 1988); translation: *Dialogue on the Life of St. John Chrysostom,* translated by R. T. Meyer (New York, 1985).

——. *Historia lausiaca* (CPG #6036); text (Greek): *The Lausiac History of Palladius,* edited by C. Butler (Cambridge, 1904); translation: *Lausiac History / Palladius,* translated by R. T. Meyer (Westminster, MD, 1965).

Paul, bishop of Emesa. *Ep. ad Anatolium magistrum militiae* (CPG #6369, Casiniensis #195); text (Latin): *ACO* I.4: 139–40.

——. *Homilia i de nativitate Alexandriae habita* (CPG #6365); text (Greek): *ACO* I.1.4: 9–11.

——. *Homilia ii de nativitate Alexandriae habita* (CPG #6366); text (Greek): *ACO* I.1.4: 11–14

——. *Homilia de pace Alexandriae habita* (CPG #6367); text (Greek): *ACO* I.1.7: 173–74.

———. *Libellus Cyrillo Alexandrino oblatus* (CPG #6368); text (Greek)· *ACO* I.1.4: 6 7; translation: *St. Cyril of Alexandria: Letters 1–50*, translated by J. McEnerney (Washington, 1987): 140–41.

Pelagius I, pope. *In defensione trium capitulorum* (CPL #1703); text (Latin): *Pelagi Diaconi in defensione trium capitulorum*, edited by R. Devreese (Rome, 1932).

Philostorgius. *Historia ecclesiastica*; text (Greek): *Kirchengeschichte. Mit dem Leben des Lucian von Antiochien und den Fragmenten eines arianischen Historiographen*, edited by J. Bidez (Berlin, 1972); translation: *Philostorgius Church History*, translated by P. R. Amidon (Atlanta, 2007).

Photius, patriarch of Constantinople. *Bibliotheca*; partial text and translation (French): *Bibliothèque*, 4 vols., R. Henry ed. and trans. (Paris, 1959); remaining text: *PG* 101–4.

Plato, *Cratylus*; text (Greek): *Platonis opera*, edited by J. Burnet (Oxford, 1990) 1:383–440; translation: *Plato, Cratylus, Parmenides, Greater Hippias, Lesser Hippias*, translated by H. N. Fowler, LCL (Cambridge, MA, 1939): 6–191.

———. *Lysis*; text (Greek): *Platonis opera*, edited by J. Burnet (Oxford, 1990) 3:203–23; translation: *Plato, Lysis, Symposium, Gorgias*, translated by W. R. M. Lamb, LCL 3 (Cambridge, MA, 1925): 7–71.

———. *Symposium*; text (Greek) and translation: *Plato, Lysis, Symposium, Gorgias*, translated by W. R. M. Lamb, LCL 3 (Cambridge, MA, 1925): 80–245.

Plutarch of Caeronea. *Moralia*; text (Greek) and translation: *Plutarch's Moralia*, 16 vols., translated by F. C. Babbitt, LCL (Cambridge, MA, 1949–76).

Proclus, bishop of Constantinople. *Ep. ad Domnum Antiochenum (Ep. 13)* (CPG #5910); text (Greek): *ACO* II.1.3: 67–68.

———. *Ep. ad Iohannem Antiochenum (Ep. 3)* (CPG #5900); text (Latin): *ACO* IV.1: 140–43.

———. *Ep. ad Iohannem Antiochenum (Ep. 10, fragmentum)* (CPG #5907); text (Latin): *Diaconi Pelagii In defensione Trium Capitulorum*, edited by R. Devreesse (Paris, 1932): 24.

———. *Ep. synodica (fragmentum)* (CPG #5914, Casiniensis #238); text (Latin): *ACO* I.4: 173–74.

———. *Homilia i. De laudibus sanctae Mariae* (CPG #5800); text (Greek): *ACO.* I.1.1: 103–7; translation: N. Constas, *Proclus of Constantinople and the Cult of the Virgin in Late Antiquity* (Leiden, 2003): 136–56.

———. *Homilia ii. De incarnatione* (CPG #5801); text (Greek) and translation: N. Constas, *Proclus of Constantinople and the Cult of the Virgin in Late Antiquity* (Leiden, 2003): 163–92.

———. *Tomus ad Armenios (Ep. 2)* (CPG #5897); text (Greek): *ACO* IV.2: 187–95.

"The Quaestor." *Ep. ad Helladium episc. Tarsi* (CPG #6443, Casiniensis #213); text (Latin): *ACO* I.4: 155–56.

Rabbula, bishop of Edessa. *Canones* (CPG #6492); text (Syriac): A. Vööbus, *Syriac and Arabic Documents Regarding Legislation Relative to Syriac Asceticism*, A. Vööbus ed. and trans. (Stockholm, 1960): 78–86.

———. *Ep. ad Andream Samosatenum* (CPG #6495); text (Syriac): Overbeck: 222–23.

———. *Ep. ad Cyrillum Alexandrinum (fragmenta)* (CPG #6494); text (Syriac): Overbeck: 225.

———. *Ep. ad Gemellinum episc. Perrhae* (CPG #6493); text (Syriac): Overbeck, 231–38.

———. *Homilia Constantinopoli habita* (CPG #6496); text (Syriac): Overbeck: 239–44.

———. *Monita ad coenobitas* (CPG #6491); text (Syriac) and translation: A. Vööbus, *Syriac and Arabic Documents regarding Legislation relative to Syriac Asceticism* (Stockholm, 1960): 24–33.

———. *Praecepta ad sacerdotes et regulares* (CPG #6490); text (Syriac) and translation: *Syriac and Arabic Documents regarding Legislation relative to Syriac Asceticism*, A. Vööbus ed. and trans. (Stockholm, 1960): 34–50.

Rheginus, bishop of Constantia in Cyprus, Zeno, bishop, and Evagrius, bishop. *Libellus ad concilium Ephesinum* (CPG #6485); text (Greek): *ACO* I.1.7: 118–19.

Rufinus, Tyrannius, of Aquileia. *Apologia contra Hieronymum;* text (Latin): *Tyrannii Rufini Opera*, edited by M. Simonetti, CCSL 20 (Turnhout, 1961): 29–123; translation: *The Apology of Rufinus*, translated by W. H. Fremantle, *NPNF II* 3:434–82.

———. *Historia ecclesiastica;* text (Latin): *Eusebius Werke 2.2, Die Kirchengeschichte*, edited by E. Schwartz and T. Mommsen (Leipzig, 1908); translation: *The Church History of Rufinus of Aquileia*, translated by P. Amidon (Oxford, 1997).

Rufus, John. *Plerophoria;* text (Syriac) and translation (French): *Plerophories: témoinages et révélations contre le concile de Chalcédoine, Patrologia Orientalis* 8 edition, translated by F. Nau (Paris, 1912).

Sabinianus, bishop of Perrha. *Ep. ad Valentinianum et Marcianum imperatores augustos;* text (Greek): in *Acta concilii Chalcedonensis* session 14, *ACO* II.1.3: 58; translation: *The Acts of the Council of Chalcedon*, translated by R. M. Price and J. M. Gaddis (Liverpool, 2005), 3:38–39.

Sahak, katholikos of Persian Armenia. *Ep. ad Acacium Melitenum* (CPG #5796); text (Armenian): *Liber epistularum*, edited by J. Ismireantz (Tiflis, 1901): 16–18; translation (Latin): "Acace de Mélitène, Proclus de Constantinople et la Grande Arménie" in *Opera Minora* 2: sec. #50, translated by M. Richard (Louvain, 1977): 396–98.

———. *Ep. ad Proclum* (CPG #5899); text (Armenian): *Liber epistularum (armeniace)*, edited by J. Ismireantz (Tiflis, 1901): 9–13; translation (French): *Le livre des lettres*, translated by M. Tallon (Beirut, 1955): 72–77.

Severus, bishop of Antioch. *Homilia 30, De Symeone Stylita;* text (Syriac) and translation (French): *Les homélies cathédrales de Sévère d'Antioche, PO* 36, edited and translated by M. Briere and F. Graffin (Turnhout, 1971): 608–39.

Socrates (Scholasticus). *Historia ecclesiastica;* text (Greek): *Kirchengeschichte / Socrates*, edited by G. C. Hansen, GCS 1 (Berlin, 1995); translation: *Church History*, translated by A. C. Zenos, *NPNF II* 2:1–178.

Sophocles. *Trachiniae;* text (Greek) and translation: *Sophocles, Antigone, The Women of Trachis, Philoctetes, Oedipus at Colonus*, edited and translated by H. Lloyd-Jones, LCL 2 (Cambridge, MA, 1994): 129–251.

Sozomen. *Historia ecclesiastica;* text (Greek): *Sozomenus Kirchengeschichte*, edited by J. Bidez and G. C. Hansen, GCS 4 (Berlin, 1960); translation: *Church History*, translated by C. D. Hartranft, *NPNF II* 2:179–427.

Synesius, of Cyrene, bishop of Ptolemais. *Epistulae* (CPG #5640); text (Greek): *Synesii Cyrensis Epistolae*, edited by A. Garzya (Rome, 1979); translation: *The Letters of Synesius of Cyrene*, translated by A. Fitzgerald (Oxford, 1926).

Theodore, bishop of Mopsuestia. *Comentarii in Prophetas minores* (CPG #3834); text (Greek): *PG* 66:124–632.

———. *Commentarius in evangelem Iohannis apostoli;* text (Syriac) and translation (Latin): CSCO SS 62–63, edited and translated by J. M. Vosté (Louvain, 1940).

———. *Contra Apollinarium* (CPG #3857); text (Latin): in *Theodore of Mopsuestia, Commentary on the Minor Epistles of Saint Paul,* edited by H. B. Swete (Cambridge, 1969) 2: 312–22. Syriac fragment: ed. Nau, *PO* 13: 188.

———. *Contra Eunomium (fragmenta)* (CPG #3859); text: in *Theodore of Mopsuestia, Commentary on the Minor Epistles of Saint Paul,* edited by H. B. Swete (Cambridge, 1969) 2: 322–23; in R. P. Vaggione, "Some Neglected Fragments of Theodore of Mopsuestia's Contra Eunomium," *JTS* ns. 31(2) (1980): 405–70.

———. *Contra Magos* (fragmentum Syriacum); text and translation: in *Commentaire du Livre d'Abba Isaie (logoi i–xv) par Dadisho Qatraya,* edited and translated by R. Draguet, CSCO SS 144–45:208–9 (text), 212 (translation).

———. *De incarnatione* (CPG #3856); text (Latin): in *Theodore of Mopsuestia, Commentary on the Minor Epistles of Saint Paul,* edited by H. B. Swete (Cambridge, 1969) 2: 290–312.

———. *Expositio in psalmos* (CPG #3833); text (Latin): *Le commentaire de Théodore de Mopsueste sur les Psaumes,* edited by R. Devreesse (Paris, 1939).

———. *Homiliae catecheticae (Liber ad baptizandos)* (CPG #3852); text (Syriac) and translation: *Commentary of Theodore of Mopsuestia on the Nicene Creed, Commentary of Theodore of Mopsuestia on the Lord's Prayer and on the Sacraments of Baptism and the Eucharist,* edited and translated by A. Mingana (Cambridge, 1932–33).

Theodore Lector, a.k.a. Theodore Anagnostes. *Historia ecclesiastica* (fragmenta); text (Greek): *Theodoros Anagnostes Kirchengeschichte,* edited by G. C. Hansen, GCS 3 (Berlin, 1995).

Theodoret, bishop of Cyrrhus. *Commonitorium ad Alexandrum Hierapolitanum* (CPG #6243, Casiniensis #134, *ep.* C 7); text (Latin): *ACO* I.4: 87; text and translation (French): translated by Y. Azéma, SC 429:156–59.

———. *De incarnatione domini* (CPG #6216); text (Greek): *PG* 75:1420–77; translation: I. Pásztori-Kupán, *Theodoret of Cyrus,* The Early Church Fathers (New York, 2006): 138–71.

———. *De providentia orationes x* (CPG #6211); text (Greek): *PG* 83:556–773; translation: *On Divine Providence,* translated by T. Halton (New York, 1988).

———. *Ep. ad Abundium episc. Comensem* (CPG #6277); text (Greek): *PG* 83:1492–94; translation: *ep.* CLXXXI, translated by B. Jackson, *NPNF II* 3:347–48.

———. *Ep. ad Acacium Beroeensem* (CPG #6241, Casiniensis #149, *ep.* C 9); text (Latin): *ACO* I.4: 101–2; text and translation (French): translated by Y. Azéma, SC 429:164–69.

———. *Ep. ad Alexandrum Hierapolitanum* (CPG #6242, *ep.* C 3a); text (Greek): *ACO* I.1.7: 79–80; translation: *ep.* CLXIX, translated by B. Jackson, *NPNF II* 3:341–42; text and translation (French): translated by Y. Azéma, SC 429:80–89.

———. *Ep. ad Alexandrum Hierapolitanum* (CPG #6244, Casiniensis #155, *ep.* C 11a); text (Latin): *ACO* I.4: 104; text and translation (French): translated by Y. Azéma, SC 429:176–79.

————. *Ep. ad Alexandrum Hierapolitanum* (CPG #6245, Casiniensis #161, *ep.* C 14); text (Latin): *ACO* I.4: 108–9; text and translation (French): translated by Y. Azéma, SC 429:196–99.

————. *Ep. ad Alexandrum Hierapolitanum* (CPG #6246, Casiniensis #170, *ep.* C 15); text (Latin): *ACO* I.4: 117; text and translation (French): translated by Y. Azéma, SC 429:200–201.

————. *Ep. ad Alexandrum Hierapolitanum* (CPG #6247, Casiniensis #185, *ep.* C 19); text (Latin): *ACO* I.4: 134; text and translation (French): translated by Y. Azéma, SC 429:224–27.

————. *Ep. ad Alexandrum Hierapolitanum* (CPG #6248, Casiniensis #187, *ep.* C 20a); text (Latin): *ACO* I.4: 135; text and translation (French): translated by Y. Azéma, SC 429:228–31.

————. *Ep. ad Alexandrum Hierapolitanum* (CPG #6249, Casiniensis #234, *ep.* C 27); text (Latin): *ACO* I.4: 170–71; text and translation (French): translated by Y. Azéma, SC 429:282–85.

————. *Ep. ad Alexandrum Hierapolitanum* (CPG #6250, Casiniensis #236, *ep.* C 28a); text (Latin): *ACO* I.4: 172–73; text and translation (French): translated by Y. Azéma, SC 429:286–89.

————. *Ep. ad Alexandrum Hierapolitanum* (CPG #6251, Casiniensis #239, *ep.* C 29); text (Latin): *ACO* I.4: 174; text and translation (French): translated by Y. Azéma, SC 429:294–97.

————. *Ep. ad Alexandrum Hierapolitanum* (CPG #6252, Casiniensis #254, *ep.* C 33); text (Latin): *ACO* I.4: 186; text and translation (French): translated by Y. Azéma, SC 429:310–13.

————. *Ep. ad Alexandrum Hierapolitanum* (CPG #6253, Casiniensis #256, *ep.* C 34); text (Latin): *ACO* I.4: 187–88; text and translation (French): translated by Y. Azéma, SC 429:314–17.

————. *Ep. ad magistrum militum* [Anatolium] (CPG #6254, Casiniensis #221, *ep.* C 25); text (Latin): *ACO* I.4: 160–61; text and translation (French): translated by Y. Azéma, SC 429:264–77.

————. *Ep. ad Andream Samosatenum* (CPG #6255, Casiniensis #108, ep. C 2a); text (Latin): *ACO* I.4: 59–60; text and translation (French): translated by Y. Azéma, SC 429:72–75.

————. *Ep. ad Andream Samosatenum* (CPG #6256, Casiniensis #150, *ep.* C 10a); text (Latin): *ACO* I.4: 102; text and translation (French): translated by Y. Azéma, SC 429:170–75.

————. *Ep. ad Candidianum comitem domesticorum* (CPG #6257, Casiniensis #131, *ep.* C 6); text (Latin): *ACO* I.4: 86; text and translation (French): translated by Y. Azéma, SC 429:152–55.

————. *Ep. ad Cyrillum Adanensem* (CPG #6258, Casiniensis #249, *ep.* C 31); text (Latin): *ACO* I.4: 181; text and translation (French): translated by Y. Azéma, SC 429:304–7.

————. *Ep. ad Dorotheum episc. Marcianopolis* (CPG #6259, Casiniensis #226, *ep.* C 26); text (Latin): *ACO* I.4: 165; text and translation (French): translated by Y. Azéma, SC 429:278–81.

————. *Ep. ad eos qui in Euphratesia et Osrhoena regione, Syria, Phoenicia et Cilicia vitam monasticam degunt* (CPG #6276, *ep.* C 4); text (Greek): *PG* 83:1416–33; translation:

Ep. CLI, *NPNF II* 3:325–32; text and translation (French): translated by Y. Azéma, SC 429:96 129.

———. *Ep. ad Helladium episc. Tarsi* (CPG #6260, Casiniensis #159, *ep.* C 12); text (Latin): *ACO* I.4: 106–7; text and translation (French): translated by Y. Azéma, SC 429:182–85.

———. *Ep. ad Helladium episc. Tarsi* (CPG #6261, Casiniensis #198, *ep.* C 22); text (Latin): *ACO* I.4: 141–42; text and translation (French): translated by Y. Azéma, SC 429:242–49.

———. *Ep. ad Helladium episc. Tarsi* (CPG #6262, Casiniensis #248, *ep.* C 30); text (Latin): *ACO* I.4: 180; text and translation (French): translated by Y. Azéma, SC 429:298–303.

———. *Ep. ad Himerium Nicomediensem* (CPG #6263, Casiniensis #160, *ep.* C 13b); text (Latin): *ACO* I.4: 107–8; partial translation (only the final paragraph is translated): *ep.* CLXXIV, translated by B. Jackson, *NPNF II* 3:345; text and translation (French): translated by Y Azéma, SC 429:192–95.

———. *Ep. ad Iohannem Aegaeatem (fragmenta)* (CPG #6278); text (Syriac): *Documents pour servir à l'histoire de l'Église nestorienne, II, PO* 13, edited by F. Nau (Paris, 1919): 190–91.

———. *Ep. ad Iohannem Antiochenum* (CPG #6264, *ep.* C 1a); text (Greek): *ACO* I.1.6: 107–8; text and translation (French): translated by Y. Azéma, SC 429:62–67.

———. *Ep. ad Iohannem Antiochenum* (CPG #6265, Casiniensis #175, *ep.* C 16); text (Latin): *ACO* I.4: 125–26; text and translation (French): translated by Y. Azéma, SC 429:202–7.

———. *Ep. ad Iohannem Antiochenum* (CPG #6266, Casiniensis #183, *ep.* C 21a–b); partial text (Greek, *ep.* C 21a): *ACO* I.1.7: 163–64; partial translation: *ep.* CLXXI, translated by B. Jackson, *NPNF II* 3:344; partial text and translation (French): translated by Y. Azéma, SC 429:234–37; whole text (Latin, *ep.* C 21b) *ACO* I.4: 131–32; whole text and translation (French): translated by Y. Azéma, SC 429:236–41.

———. *Ep. ad Iohannem Antiochenum* (CPG #6267, Casiniensis #261, *ep.* C 36); text (Latin): *ACO* I.4: 191–92; text and translation (French): translated by Y. Azéma, SC 429:322–27.

———. *Ep. ad Meletium episc. Neocaesareae* (CPG #6268, Casiniensis #216, *ep.* C 24); text (Latin): *ACO* I.4: 157; text and translation (French): translated by Y. Azéma, SC 429:260–63.

———. *Ep. ad Mocimum oeconomum ecclesiae Hierapolitanae* (CPG #6269, Casiniensis #250, *ep.* C 32); text (Latin): *ACO* I.4: 182; text and translation (French): translated by Y. Azéma, SC 429:308–9.

———. *Ep. ad Nestorium* (CPG #6270, Casiniensis #208, *ep.* C 23a); text (Latin): *ACO* I.4: 149–50; translation: *ep.* CLXXII, translated by B. Jackson, *NPNF II* 3:344–45; text and translation (French): translated by Y. Azéma, SC 429:250–53.

———. *Ep. ad Nestorium* (CPG #6271, Casiniensis #258, *ep.* C 35); text (Latin): *ACO* I.4:1 89; text and translation (French): translated by Y. Azéma, SC 429:318–21.

———. *Ep. ad populum Constantinopolitanum* (CPG #6273, Casiniensis #129, *ep.* C 5); text (Latin): *ACO* I.4: 81–85; text and translation (French): translated by Y. Azéma, SC 429:130–51.

———. *Ep. ad populum Constantinopolitanum* (CPG #6274, Casiniensis #136, *ep.* C 8); text (Latin): *ACO* I.4: 89; text and translation (French): translated by Y. Azéma, SC 429:160–63.

————. *Ep. ad populum Constantinopolitanum* (CPG #6275, Casiniensis #227, *ep.* C 18a); text (Latin): *ACO* I.4: 165–66; text and translation (French): translated by Y. Azéma, SC 429:214–21.

————. *Ep. ad Theosebium episc. Cii* (CPG #6272, Casiniensis #176, ep. C 17); text (Latin): *ACO* I.4: 126–27; text and translation (French): translated by Y. Azéma, SC 429:208–13.

————. *Epistulae, collectio Patmensis* (CPG #6239); text (Greek) and translation (French): *Correspondance, vol. 1,* edited and translated by Y. Azéma, SC 40 (Paris, 1955).

————. *Epistulae, collectio Sirmondiana* (CPG #6240); text (Greek): *Correspondance, vols.* 2–3, edited and translated by Y. Azéma, SC 98, 111 (Paris, 1964–1965); translation: *Letters,* translated by B. Jackson, *NPNF II* 3: 250–324.

————. *Eranistes* (CPG #6217); text (Greek): *Eranistes,* edited by G. H. Ettlinger (Oxford, 1975); translation: *Eranistes,* translated by B. Jackson, *NPNF II* 3:160–249.

————. *Explanatio in canticum canticorum* (CPG #6203); text (Greek): *PG* 81:28–213; translation: *Commentary on the Song of Songs/ Theodoret of Cyrus,* translated by R. C. Hill (Brisbane, 2001).

————. *Graecarum affectionum curatio* (CPG #6210); text (Greek) and translation (French): *Thérapeutique des maladies helleniques,* edited and translated by P. Canivet (Paris, 1958).

————. *Haereticum fabularum compendium* (CPG #6223); text (Greek): *PG* 83:336–556; translation: G. M. Cope, "An Analysis of the Heresiological Method of Theodoret of Cyrus in the 'Haereticarum Fabularum Compendium,'" (PhD Diss., Catholic University of America, Washington, D.C., 1990).

————. *Historia ecclesiastica* (CPG #6222); text (Greek): *Kirchengeschichte,* edited by L. Parmentier, L. and F. Scheidweiler, GCS 5 (Berlin, 1954); translation: *Church History,* translated by B. Jackson, *NPNF II* 3:33–159.

————. *Historia religiosa* (CPG #6221); text (Greek): *L'histoire des moines de Syrie,* edited and translated by P. Canivet and A. Leroy-Molinghen (Paris, 1977); translation: *A History of the Monks of Syria,* translated by R. M. Price (Kalamazoo, MI, 1985).

————. *Impugnatio xii anathematismorum Cyrilli* (CPG #6214); text (Greek): *ACO* I.1.6: 108–44; translation: I. Pásztori-Kupán, *Theodoret of Cyrus,* The Early Church Fathers (New York, 2006): 173–87.

————. *Interpretatio in psalmos* (CPG #6202); text (Greek): *PG* 80:857–1997; translation: *Theodoret of Cyrus: Commentary on the Psalms,* translated by R. C. Hill (Washington, D.C., 2000).

————. *Interpretatio in xiv epistulas sancti Pauli* (CPG #6209); text (Greek): *PG* 82:36–877; translation: *Commentary on the Letters of Saint Paul,* translated by R. C. Hill (Brookline, MA, 2001-2).

————. *Pro Diodoro et Theodoro (fragmenta)* (CPG #6220); text (Latin): *ACO* IV.1: 94–95.

————. *Quod unicus filius sit dominus noster Iesus Christus* (CPG #6219); text (Greek): *PG* 83:1433–41.

————. *Sermo in Chalcedone habitus* (CPG #6228); text (Latin): *ACO* I.4: 77–79.

————. *Sermones quinque in Iohannem Chrysostomum* (CPG #6225); text (fragmentary): Photius, *Bibliotheca, PG* 104:229–36.

Theodosius II, Emperor. *Imp. sacra de exsilio Irenaei* (CPG #6474, Casiniensis #277); text (Latin): *ACO* I.4: 203.

———. *Mandata ad Damascum tribunum et notarium* (Oct. 26, 448); text (Greek): in *Acta concilii Chalcedonensis*, session 11, *ACO* II.1.3: 19; translation: *The Acts of the Council of Chalcedon*, translated by R. M. Price and J. M. Gaddis (Liverpool, 2005), 3:6–7.

———. *Sacra a Iohanne Antiocheno impetrata contra Alexandrum, Helladium, Maximianum et Theodoretum* (CPG #6423); text: *ACO* I.4: 166–67.

———. *Sacra a Iohanne Antiocheno impetrata contra Alexandrum Hierapolitanum, Helladium Tarsensem, Maximianum Anazarbenum et Theodoretum* (CPG #6423, Casiniensis #228); text (Latin): *ACO* I.4: 166–67.

———. *Sacra ad concilium Ephesinum;* text (Greek): *ACO* I.1.3: 31–32.

———. *Sacra ad Cyrillum Alex. et ad singulos metropolitas* (CPG #8652); text (Greek): *ACO* I.1.1: 114–16.

———. *Sacra ad Dioscorum Alex.;* text (Syriac): Flemming: 150–52; translation: Perry: 364–67.

———. *Sacra ad Dioscorum Alexandrinum;* text (Greek): in *Acta concilii Chalcedonensis* session 1, *ACO* II.1.1: 74; translation: *The Acts of the Council of Chalcedon*, translated by R. M. Price and J. M. Gaddis (Liverpool, 2005), 1: 136–37.

———. *Sacra ad Iohannem Antiochenum* (CPG #8810); text: *ACO* I.1.4: 3–5.

———. *Sacra ad Symeonem Stylitem* (CPG #8811); text; *ACO* I.1.4: 5.

Theodosius II, Emperor, and Valentinian III, Emperor. *Ep. ad Iohannem Antiochenum* (CPG #5909, Casiniensis #310); text (Latin): *ACO* I.4: 241.

———. *Sacra ad Dioscorum Alexandrinum;* text (Greek): in *Acta concilii Chalcedonensis* session 1 (*ACO* II.1.1: 68–69); translation: *The Acts of the Council of Chalcedon*, translated by R. M. Price and J. M. Gaddis (Liverpool, 2005), 1:132–34; text (Syriac): Flemming: 5; translation: Perry: 8–9.

Theophanes Confessor. *Chrongraphia;* text (Greek): edited by C. De Boor, Corpus Scriptores Historiae Byzantinae (Leipzig, 1883–1885); translation: *The Chronide of Theophanes Confessor: Byzantine and Near Eastern History*, A.D. 284–813, translated by C. Mango, R. Scott, and G. Greatrex (Oxford, 1997).

Thucydides. *Historiae;* text (Greek) and translation: *History of the Peloponnesian War*, translated by C. F. Smith, LCL (Cambridge, MA, 1952).

Titus, count of the Domestici. *Ep. ad Alexandrum episc. Hierapolis* (CPG #6426, Casiniensis #269); text (Latin): *ACO* I.4: 198–99.

———. *Ep. ad Meletium* (CPG #6466, Casiniensis #262); text (Latin): *ACO* I.4:192.

———. *Praeceptum ad Libianum Euphratesiae iudicem* (CPG #6428, Casiniensis #272); text (Latin): *ACO* I.4: 200.

Zachariah, rhetor, bishop of Mitylene. *Historia Ecclesiastica;* text (Syriac) and translation: *Historia ecclesiastica Zachariae rhetori*, CSCO SS 38–39, translated by E. W. Brooks, CSCO SS 41–42 (Louvain, 1953).

Zachariah, bishop of Mitylene (Pseudo-). *Chronicon;* text: unavailable; translation: *The Syriac chronicle known as that of Zachariah of Mitylene*, translated by F. Hamilton and E. W. Brooks (New York, 1979).

Zenobius, bishop of Zephyrium. *Ep. ad Alexandrum episc. Hierapolis* (CPG #6470, Casiniensis #264); text (Latin): *ACO* I.4: 195.

MODERN SCHOLARLY WORKS

Abramowski, L. "Histoire de la recherche sur Nestorius et le nestorianisme." *Istina* 40:1 (1995): 44–55.

———. "Der Streit um Diodor und Theodor zwischen den beiden ephesinischen Konzilien." *Zeitschrift für Kirchengeschichte* 67 (1956): 252–87.

———. "Zur Theologie Theodors von Mopsuestia." *Zeitschrift für Kirchengeschichte* 72 (1961): 263–93.

———. *Untersuchungen zum Liber Heraclidis des Nestorius.* Louvain, 1963.

Abramowski, R. "Der theologische Nachlass des Diodor von Tarsus." *Zeitschrift fur die neutestamentliche Wissenschaft* 42 (1949): 19–69.

Adnes, A., and P. Canivet. "Guérisons miraculeuses et exorcismes dans l'*Histoire philothée* de Théodoret de Cyr." *Revue de l'Histoire des Religions* 171:1 (1967): 53–82.

Alexander, J. C. "Cultural Pragmatics: Social Performance between Ritual and Strategy." In *Social Performance: Symbolic Action, Cultural Pragmatics, and Ritual,* edited by J. C. Alexander, B. Giesen, and J. L. Mast, 29–90. Cambridge, 2006.

Allen, P. "Zacharias Scholasticus and the *Historia Ecclesiastica* of Evagrius Scholasticus." *JTS* ns. 31:2 (1980): 471–88.

Amidon, P. *The Church History of Rufinus of Aquileia.* Oxford, 1997.

———. "Paulinus's Subscription to the *Tomus ad Antiochenos*." *JTS* ns. 53:1 (2002): 53–74.

Anderson, B. *Imagined Communities: Reflections on the Origin and Spread of Nationalism.* London, 1983.

Ando, C. *Imperial Ideology and Provincial Loyalty in the Roman Empire.* Berkeley: 2000.

Arnal, W. E. "Doxa, Heresy, and Self-Construction: The Pauline *Ekklesiai* and the Boundaries of Urban Identities." In *Heresy and Identity in Late Antiquity,* edited by E. Iricinischi and H. M. Zellentin, 50–101. Tübingen, 2008.

Ashby, G. W. "The Hermeneutic Approach of Theodoret of Cyrrhus to the Old Testament." *Studia Patristica* 15:1 (1984): 131–35.

———. "Theodoret of Cyrrhus on Marriage." *Theology* 72 (1969): 482–91.

Athanassiadi, P. "The Chaldean Oracles: Theology and Theurgy." In *Pagan Monotheism in Late Antiquity,* edited by P. Athanassiadi and M. Frede, 149–83. Oxford, 1999.

Azéma, Y. "Citations d'auteurs et allusions profanes dans la Correspondance de Théodoret." In *Uberlieferungsgeschichtliche Untersuchungen,* edited by F. Paschke, 5–13. Berlin,1981.

———. "Sur la chronologie de trois lettres de Theodoret de Cyr." *Revue d'études grecques* 67 (1954): 82–94.

———. "Sur la date de la mort de Théodoret de Cyr." *Pallas* 31 (1984): 137–55.

———. *Théodoret Correspondance,* 4 vols. Paris, 1955, 1964, 1965, 1984.

Baarda, T. "The Gospel Text in the Biography of Rabbula." *Vigiliae Christianae* 14 (1960): 102–27.

Bacht, H. "Die Rolle des orientalischen Mönchtums in die kirchenpolitischen Auseinandersetzungen um Chalkedon (431–519)." In *Das Konzil von Chalkedon: Geschichte und Gegenwart,* edited by A. Grillmeier and H. Bacht, vol. 2:193–314. Würzburg, 1951.

Bagnall, R. *Egypt in Late Antiquity.* Princeton, 1993.

Barabási, A. L. *Linked: How Everything is Connected to Everything Else and What it Means for Business, Science, and Everyday Life.* New York, 2003.

Barjeau, J. P. *L'école exegetique d'Antioche*. Paris, 1898.

Barnes, T. D. *Athanasius and Constantius: Theology and Politics in the Constantinian Empire*. Cambridge, MA, 1993.

———. "Synesius in Constantinople." *Greek, Roman, and Byzantine Studies* 27 (1986): 93–112.

Barrett, J. L. "Gods." In *Religion, Anthropology and Cognitive Science*, edited by H. Whitehouse and J. Laidlaw, 179–207. Durham, NC, 2007.

Barry, W. "Roof Tiles and Urban Violence in the Ancient World." *Greek, Roman, and Byzantine Studies* 37 (1996): 55–74.

Bebis, G. S. "The 'Apology' of Nestorius: A New Evaluation [The Bazaar of Heracleides]." *Studia Patristica* 11 (1972): 107–112.

Becker, A. *Fear of God and the Beginning of Wisdom: The School of Nisibis and Christian Scholastic Culture in Late Antique Mesopotamia*. Philadelphia, 2006.

Beeley, C. A. "Cyril of Alexandria and Gregory Nazianzen: Tradition and Complexity in Patristic Theology." *JECS* 17.3 (2009): 381–419.

Bell, C. *Ritual Theory, Ritual Practice*. Oxford, 1992.

Bergjan, S. P. *Theodoret von Cyrus und der Neunizänismus: Aspekte der Altkirchlichen Trinitatslehre*. Berlin, 1994.

Bevan, G. A., and P. T. R. Gray. "The Trial of Eutyches: A New Interpretation." *Byzantinische Zeitschrift* 101:2 (2009): 617–57.

Blasi, A. "Early Christian Culture as Interaction." In *Handbook of Early Christianity: Social Science Approaches*, edited by A. Blasi, J. Duhaime, and P. Turcotte, 291–308. Walnut Creek, CA, 2002.

Blok, A. "Variations in Patronage." *Sociologische Gids* 16 (1970): 365–78.

Blum, G. G. *Rabbula von Edessa: Der Christ, der Bischof, der Theologe*. Louvain, 1969.

Blumer, H. *Symbolic Interactionism: Perspective and Method*. Englewood Cliffs, NJ, 1969.

Bobertz, C. A. "Patronage Networks and the Study of Ancient Christianity." *Studia Patristica* 24 (1993): 20–27.

Boissevain, J. *Friends of Friends: Networks, Manipulators, and Coalitions*. Oxford, 1974.

Børtnes, J. "Eros Transformed: Same-Sex Love and Divine Desire." In *Greek Biography and Panegyric in Late Antiquity*, edited by T. Hägg and P. Rousseau, 180–93. Berkeley, 2000.

Bourdieu, P. *Outline of a Theory of Practice*. Translated by R. Nice. Cambridge, 1977.

Bowersock, G. *Hellenism in Late Antiquity*. Ann Arbor, 1990.

———. "The Syriac *Life of Rabbula* and Syrian Hellenism." In *Greek Biography and Panegyric in Late Antiquity*, edited by T. Hägg and P. Rousseau, 255–71. Berkeley, 2000.

Boyarin, D. *Border Lines: The Partition of Judaeo-Christianity*. Philadelphia, 2004.

———. *Dying for God: Martyrdom and the Making of Christianity and Judaism*. Stanford, 1999.

Boyer, P. *The Naturalness of Religious Ideas: A Cognitive Theory of Religion*. Berkeley, 1994.

Bradbury, S. "Libanius's Letters as Evidence for Travel and Epistolary Networks among Greek Elites in the the Fourth Century." In *Travel, Communication, and Geography in Late Antiquity*, edited by L. Ellis and F. Kidner, 73–80. Burlington, VT, 2004.

———. *Selected Letters of Libanius from the Age of Constantius and Julian*. Liverpool, 2004.

Brakke, D. *Athanasius and the Politics of Asceticism*. Oxford, 1995.

Braund, D. "Function and Disfunction: Personal Patronage in Roman Imperialism." In *Patronage in Ancient Society*, edited by A. Wallace-Hadrill, 137–52. New York, 1989.

Bregman, J. *Synesius of Cyrene, Philosopher-bishop.* Berkeley, 1982.

Brennan, P. "The Last of the Romans: Roman Identity and the Roman Army in the Late Roman Near East." *Mediterranean Archaeology* 11 (1998): 191–203.

Brock, S. P. "Aspects of Translation Technique in Antiquity." *Greek, Roman and Byzantine Studies* 20 (1979): 69–87.

———. "A Brief Guide to the Main Editions and Translations of the Works of St. Ephrem." *The Harp* 3:1 (1990): 7–25.

———. "Christians in the Sassanid Empire: A Case of Divided Loyalties." In *Religion and National Identity: Studies in Church History XVIII,* edited by S. Mews, 1–19. Oxford, 1982.

———. "The Christology of the Church of the East." In *Traditions and Heritage of the Christian East,* edited by D. Afinogenov and A. Muraviev, 159–79. Moscow, 1996.

———. "The Christology of the Church of the East in the Synods of the Fifth to Early Seventh Centuries." In *Aksum-Thyateira: A Festschrift for Archbishop Methodios,* edited by G. Dragas, 125–42. London, 1985.

———. "The Church of the East in the Sassanian Empire up to the Sixth Century and its Absence from the Councils in the Roman Empire." *Syriac Dialogue* 1 (1994): 69–86.

———. "Early Syrian Asceticism." *Numen* 20 (1973): 1–19.

———. "From Antagonism to Assimilation: Syriac Attitudes to Greek Learning." In *East of Byzantium: Syria and Armenia in the Formative Period,* edited by N. Garsoïan, T. Matthews, et al., 17–34. Washington, D.C., 1982.

———. "From Ephrem to Romanos." *Studia Patristica* 20 (1989): 139–51.

———. "Greek and Syriac in Late Antique Syria." In *Literacy and Power in the Ancient World,* edited by A. K. Bowman and G. Wolf, 149–60. Cambridge, 1994.

———. "Greek into Syriac and Syriac into Greek." *Journal of the Syriac Academy* 3 (1977): 1–17 (422–406, reverse pagination).

———. *The Luminous Eye: The Spiritual World of Saint Ephrem.* Kalamazoo, MI, 1992.

———. "Some Aspects of Greek Words in Syriac." In *Synkretismus im syrisch-persischen Kulturgebiet,* edited by A. Dietrich, 80–108. Göttingen, 1975.

———. "Towards a History of Syriac Translation Technique." *Orientalia Christiana Analecta* 221 (1983): 1–14.

Brok, M. F. A. "À propos des lettres festales." *Vigiliae Christianae* 5:2 (1951): 101–10.

Brown, P. *Authority and the Sacred: Aspects of the Christianization of the Roman World.* Cambridge, 1995.

———. *Poverty and Leadership in the Later Roman Empire.* Waltham, MA, 2002.

———. *Power and Persuasion in Late Antiquity: Towards a Christian Empire.* Madison, 1992.

———. "The Rise and Function of the Holy Man in Late Antiquity." *Journal of Roman Studies* 61 (1971): 80–101.

———. "The Saint as Exemplar in Late Antiquity." *Representations* 2 (1983): 1–21.

———. "The Study of Elites in Late Antiquity." *Arethusa* 33:3 (2000): 315–45.

———. "Town, Village and Holy Man: The Case of Syria." In *Society and the Holy in Late Antiquity,* 153–65. Berkeley, 1981.

Bundy, D. "Jacob of Nisibis as a Model for the Episcopacy." *Le Museon* 104 (1991): 235–50.

———. "Language and Knowledge of God in Ephrem the Syrian." *Patristic and Byzantine Review* 5:2 (1986): 91–103.

Burgess, R. W. "The Accession of Marcian in the Light of Chalcedonian Apologetic and Monophysite Polemic." *Byzantinische Zeitschrift* 86/87 (1993/4): 47–68.

Burkitt, F. C. "The Christian Church in the East." In *The Cambridge Ancient History.* Vol. XII, *Imperial Crisis and Recovery,* edited by S. A. Cook, F. E. Adcock, et al., 476–514. Cambridge, 1956.

Burrus, V. *Begotten, Not Made: Conceiving Manhood in Late Antiquity.* Stanford, 2000.

———. " 'In the Theatre of this Life': The Performance of Orthodoxy in Late Antiquity." In *The Limits of Ancient Christianity: Essays in Late Antique Thought and Culture in Honor of R. A. Markus,* edited by W. Kingshern and M. Vessey, 80–96. Ann Arbor, 1999.

Calvet-Sebasti, M. A. "Comment ecrire à un païen: l'exemple de Gregoire de Nazianze et de Théodoret de Cyr." In *Les apologistes chrétiens et la culture grecque,* edited by B. Pouderon and J. Doré, 369–81. Paris, 1998.

Calvet-Sebasti, M. A., and P. L. Gatier. *Firmus de Césarée, Lettres,* SC 350. Paris, 1989.

Camelot, T. "De Nestorius à Eutychès: l'opposition du deux christologies." In *Das Konzil von Chalkedon: Geschichte und Gegenwart,* edited by A. Grillmeier and H. Bacht,1:213–42. Würzburg, 1951.

Cameron, Alan. "The Empress and the Poet: Paganism and Politics at the Court of Theodosius II." In *Later Greek Literature,* edited by J. Winkler and G. Williams, 217–89. Cambridge, 1982.

Cameron, Averil. "How to Read Heresiology." In *The Cultural Turn in Late Ancient Studies,* edited by D. Martin and P. Cox Miller, 193–212. Durham, NC, 2005.

Caner, D. *Wandering, Begging Monks: Spiritual Authority and the Promotion of Monasticism in Late Antiquity.* Berkeley, 2002.

Canivet, P. "Catégories sociales et titulaire laïque et ecclésiastique dans l'*Histoire philothée* de Théodoret de Cyr." *Byzantion* 39 (1969): 209–50.

———. "Contributions archéologiques à l'histoire des moines de Syrie: à propos de l'*Histoire philothée* de Theodoret." *Studia Patristica* 13 (1975): 444–60.

———. *Histoire d'une entreprise apologètique au Ve siècle.* Paris, 1957.

———. *Le monachisme Syrien selon Théodoret de Cyr.* Paris, 1977.

———. "Théodoret et le messalianisme." *Revue Mabillon* 51 (1961): 26–34.

Canivet, P. and A. Leroy-Molinghen. *Théodoret de Cyr: histoire des moines de Syrie, histoire philothée.* Paris, 1977.

Casana, J. "The Archaeological Landscape of Late Roman Antioch." In *Culture and Society in Later Roman Antioch,* edited by I. Sandwell and J. Huskinson, 102–25. Oxford, 2004.

Cavallera, F. *Le schisme d'Antioche.* Paris, 1905.

Chadwick, H. "Bishops and Monks." *Studia Patristica* 24 (1993): 45–61.

———. "Eucharist and Christology in the Nestorian Controversy." *JTS* ns. 2 (1951): 145–64.

———. "The Exile and Death of Flavian of Constantinople: A Prologue to the Council of Chalcedon." *JTS* ns. 6 (1955): 17–34.

———. "The Role of the Christian Bishop in Ancient Society." In *The Role of the Christian Bishop in Ancient Society,* edited by H. Chadwick, 1–14. Berkeley, 1980.

Chesnut, G. F. "The Date of Composition of Theodoret's *Church History.*" *Vigiliae Christianae* 35 (1981): 245–52.

———. *The First Christian Histories: Eusebius, Socrates, Sozomen, Theodoret, and Evagrius.* Macon, GA, 1986.

———. *Three Monophysite Christologies.* Oxford, 1976.

———. "Two Prosopa in Nestorius's *Bazaar of Heracleides.*" *JTS* ns. 29 (1978): 392–409.

Chuvin, P. *A Chronicle of the Last Pagans.* Cambridge, MA, 1990.

Clark, E. *The Origenist Controversy: The Cultural Construction of an Early Christian Debate.* Princeton, 1992.

———. *Reading Renunciation: Asceticism and Scripture in Early Christianity.* Princeton, 1999.

———. "Women and Asceticism in Late Antiquity: The Refusal of Status and Gender." In *Asceticism,* edited by V. Wimbush and R. Valantasis, 33–48. Oxford, 1995.

Clark, G. *Women in Late Antiquity: Pagan and Christian Lifestyles.* Oxford, 1993.

Clarke, E. *Iamblichus' De mysteriis: A Manifesto of the Miraculous.* Burlington, 2001.

Clayton, P. B. *The Christology of Theodoret of Cyrus: Antiochene Christology from the Council of Ephesus (431) to the Council of Chalcedon (451).* Oxford, 2007.

Connor, C. *Women of Byzantium.* New Haven, CT, 2004.

Constable, G. *Letters and Letter Collections.* Typologie des sources du moyen âge occidental, vol. 17. Turnhout, 1976.

Constas, N. *Proclus of Constantinople and the Cult of the Virgin in Late Antiquity.* Leiden, 2003.

Cooper, K. and M. Dal Santo. "Boethius, Gregory the Great and the Christian 'Afterlife' of Classical Dialogue." In *The End of Dialogue in Late Antiquity,* edited by S. Goldhill, 173–89. Cambridge, 2008.

Cope, G. M. "An Analysis of the Heresiological Method of Theodoret of Cyrus in the *Haereticarum fabularum compendium.*" PhD Diss., Catholic University of America, 1990.

Cox, P. *Biography in Late Antiquity: A Quest for the Holy Man.* Berkeley, 1983.

Cox Miller, P. "Strategies of Representation in Collective Biography: Constructing the Subject as Holy." In *Greek Biography and Panegyric in Late Antiquity,* edited by T. Hägg and P. Rousseau, 209–54. Berkeley, 2000.

Crabbe, A. "The Invitation List to the Council of Ephesus and Metropolitan Hierarchy in the Fifth Century." *JTS* ns. 32.1 (1981): 369–400.

Craun, C. C. "Matronly Monks: Theodoret of Cyrrhus' Sexual Imagery in the *Historia religiosa.*" In *Holiness and Masculinity in the Middle Ages,* edited by P. H. Cullum and K. J. Lewis, 43–57. Cardiff, 2004.

Cribiore, R. *The School of Libanius in Late Antique Antioch.* Princeton, 2007.

Crown, A. D., ed. *The Samaritans.* Tübingen, 1989.

Cumont, F. *Études syriens.* Paris, 1917.

Dagron, G. "Entre village et cité: La bourgade rurale des 4e au 7e siècles en Orient." *Koinonia* 3 (1979): 29–52.

———. "Les moines et la ville: Le monachisme à Constantinople jusqu'au concile de Chalcédoine." *Travaux et mémoires* 4 (1970): 229–76.

———. "La vie ancienne de Saint Marcel l'Acémète." *AB* 86 (1968): 271–321.

Daley, B. "Position and Patronage in the Early Church: The Original Meaning of Primacy of Honor." *JTS* ns. 44:2 (1993): 529–53.

Davidson, I. "Staging the Church? Theology as Theater." *JECS* 8.3 (2000): 413–51.

Davies, J. K. *Democracy and Classical Greece*. Revised edition. Cambridge, MA, 1993.

Delmaire, R. "Jean Chrysostome et ses amis d'après le nouveau classement de sa correspondance." *Studia Patristica* 32 (1997): 501–13.

———. "Les 'lettres d'exil' de Jean Chrysostome: études de chronologie et prosopographie." *Recherches augustiniennes* 25 (1991): 71–180.

Dennis, G. "Gregory of Nazianzus and the Byzantine Letter." In *Diakonia: Studies in Honor of Robert T. Meyer*, edited by T. Halton and J. Williman, 3–13. Washington D.C., 1986.

Devreesse, R. "Les actes du concile d'Éphèse." *Revue des sciences philosophiques et théologiques* 18 (1929): 223–42.

———. "Après du concile d'Ephèse: le rétour des Orientaux a l'unité." *Échoes d'Orient* 30 (1931): 271–92.

———. *Essai sur Théodore de Mopsueste*. Vatican City, 1948.

———. *Le Patriarcat d'Antioche depuis la paix de l'église jusqu'à le conqête arabe*. Paris, 1945.

De Vries, W. "Die syrische-nestorianische Haltung zu Chalkedon." In *Das Konzil von Chalkedon: Geschichte und Gegenwart*, edited by A. Grillmeier and H. Bacht, 1:603–35. Würzburg, 1951.

Dewart, J. M. *The Theology of Grace of Theodore of Mopsuestia*. Washington, D.C., 1971.

Diepen, H. M. "La christologie des amis de Nestorius." In *Les trois chapitres au concile de Chalcédoine*, 30–45. Oosterhout, 1953.

Dineen, L. *Titles of Address in Greek Epistolography to 527 AD*. Washington, D.C., 1929.

Dobbins, J. J. "The Houses of Antioch." In *Antioch: The Lost Ancient City*, edited by C. Kondoleon, 51–61. Princeton, 2000.

Doran, R. *The Lives of Simeon Stylites*. Kalamazoo, MI, 1992.

Douglas, M. *How Institutions Think*. Syracuse, NY, 1986.

———. *Natural Symbols: Explorations in Cosmology*. 2nd edition. New York, 1996.

Downey, G. *A History of Antioch in Syria*. Princeton, 1961.

Drake, H. A. *Constantine and the Bishops: The Politics of Intolerance*. Baltimore, 2000.

Drijvers, H. J. W. "Early Forms of Antiochene Christology after Chalcedon." In *After Chalcedon: Studies in Theology and Church History offered to Albert van Roey*, edited by C. Laga, J. Munitiz, et al., 99–113. Louvain, 1985.

———. "East of Antioch: Forces and Structures in the Development of Early Syriac Theology." In *East of Antioch*, 1–27. Brookfield, 1984.

———. "Jews and Christians at Edessa." *Journal of Jewish Studies* 36:1 (1985): 88–102.

Drijvers, J. W. "The Man of God of Edessa, Bishop Rabbula, and the Urban Poor." *JECS* 4:2 (1996): 235–48.

———. "The Protonike Legend, *Doctrina Addai*, and Bishop Rabbula of Edessa." *Vigiliae Christianae* 51 (1997): 298–309.

Durkheim, E. *The Elementary Forms of the Religious Life*. Translated by J. W. Swain. New York, 1965.

Eisenstadt, S. N., and L. Roniger. *Patrons, Clients, and Friends: Interpersonal Relations and the Structure of Trust in Society*. Cambridge, 1984.

Elm, S. "The Dog that Did Not Bark: Doctrine and Patriarchal Authority in the Conflict between Theophilus of Alexandria and John Chrysostom of Constantinople." In *Christian Origins: Theology, Rhetoric, and Community*, edited by L. Ayres and G. Jones, 68–93. New York, 1998.

———. *Virgins of God: The Making of Asceticism in Late Antiquity.* Oxford, 1994.

Evieux, P. "André de Samosate: un adversaire de Cyrille d'Alexandrie durant la crise nestorienne." *Revue d'études byzantines* 32 (1974): 255–300.

———. *Isidore de Péluse.* Théologie historique 99. Paris 1995.

———. *Lettres festales, Cyril d'Alexandrie.* SC 372, 392, 434. Paris, 1991.

Eyerman, R. "Performing Opposition or, How Social Movements Move." In *Social Performance: Symbolic Action, Cultural Pragmatics, and Ritual,* edited by J. C. Alexander, B. Giesen and J. L. Mast, 193–217. Cambridge, 2006.

Fairbairn, D. "Allies or Merely Friends: John of Antioch and Nestorius in the Christological Controversy." *Journal of Ecclesiastical History* 58:3 (2007): 383–99.

———. *Grace and Christology in the Early Church.* Oxford, 2003.

———. "The Puzzle of Theodoret's Christology: A Modest Suggestion." *JTS* ns. 58:1 (2007): 100–133.

Fantham, E. "Aemellia Pudentilla: or the Wealthy Widow's Choice." In *Women in Antiquity: New Assessments,* edited by R. Hawley and B. Levick, 220–32. New York, 1995.

Fantham, E., H. P. Foley, et al. *Women in the Classical World: Image and Text.* Oxford, 1994.

Festugière, A. J. *Antioche païenne et chrétienne: Libanius, Chrysostome et les moines de Syrie.* Paris, 1959.

———. *Éphèse et Chalcédoine: actes de conciles.* Paris, 1982.

Ford, A. "The Beginnings of Dialogue: Socratic Discourses and Fourth Century Prose." In *The End of Dialogue in Late Antiquity,* edited by S. Goldhill, 29–44. Cambridge, 2008.

Foucault, M. *The Archaeology of Knowledge and the Discourse on Language.* Translated by A. M. Sheridan Smith. New York, 1972.

Fowden, E. K. *The Barbarian Plain: Saint Sergius between Rome and Iran.* Berkeley, 1999.

Fowden, G. "The Pagan Holy Man in Late Antique Society." *Journal of Hellenic Studies* 102 (1982): 33–59.

Frankfurter, D. "Stylites and Phallobates: Pillar Religions in Late Antique Syria." *Vigiliae Christianae* 44 (1990): 168–98.

Frede, M. "Eusebius's Apologetic Writings." In *Apologetics in the Roman Empire: Pagans, Jews, and Christians,* edited by M. Edwards, M. Goodman, and S. Price, 223–50. Oxford, 1999.

———. "Origen's Treatise Against Celsus." In *Apologetics in the Roman Empire: Pagans, Jews, and Christians,* edited by M. Edwards, M. Goodman, and S. Price, 131–56. Oxford, 1999.

Frend, W. H. C. *The Rise of the Monophysite Movement.* Cambridge, 1972.

Frezouls, E. "L'exploration archéologique de Cyrrhus." *Fouilles d'Apamée de Syrie* 7 (1969): 81–92.

———. "Recherches historiques et archéologiques sur la ville de Cyrrhus." *Annales archéologiques de Syrie* 4/5 (1955–1956): 89–121.

Gaddis, J. M. *"There is No Crime for Those Who Have Christ': Monastic Violence in the Christian Roman Empire.* Berkeley, 2005.

Gafni, I. *Land, Center and Diaspora: Jewish Constructs in Late Antiquity.* Sheffield, 1997.

Gager, J. *Kingdom and Community: The Social World of Early Christianity.* New York, 1975.

———. *The Origins of Anti-Semitism: Attitudes toward Judaism in Pagan and Christian Antiquity.* Oxford, 1985.

Galtier, P. "Le centenaire d'Éphèse: Les actes du concile—Rome et le Concile." *Recherches de sciences religieuses* 21 (1931): 169–99.

———. "Nestorius mal compris, mal traduit." *Gregorianum* 34 (1953): 427–33.

———. "Saint Cyrille d'Alexandrie et saint Léon le Grand à Chalcédoine." In *Das Konzil von Chalkedon: Geschichte und Gegenwart,* edited by A. Grillmeier and H. Bacht, 1:345–87. Würzburg, 1951.

———. "*L'unio secundum hypostasim* chez Saint Cyrille." *Gregorianum* 33 (1952): 351–98.

Garnsey, P. *Famine and Food Supply in the Graeco-Roman World: Responses to Risk and Crisis.* Cambridge, 1988.

Garnsey, P., and G. Woolf. "Patronage of the Rural Poor in the Roman World." In *Patronage in Ancient Society,* edited by A. Wallace-Hadrill, 153–167. New York, 1989.

Garnsey, P., and C. R. Whittaker. "Rural Life in the Later Roman Empire." *Cambridge Ancient History* XIII, 277–311. Cambridge, 2000.

Garsoïan, N. "Acace de Mélitène et la presence de dyophysites en Arménie au début du Ve siècle." *Res Orientales* 7 (1995): 74–75.

———. *L'église arménienne et le grand schisme d'Orient.* Louvain, 1999.

Gascou, J. "KLEROI APOROI: (Julien, Misopogôn, 370d–371b)." *Bulletin de l'Institut français d'archéologie orientale* 77 (1977): 235–55.

Gaspar, C. "Theodoret of Cyrrhus and the Glory of the Syrian Ascetics." *Archaeus* 4 (2000): 211–40.

Gavrilyuk, P. *The Suffering of the Impassible God: The Dialectics of Patristic Thought.* Oxford, 2004.

Geertz, C. "Religion as a Cultural System." In *Anthropological Approaches to the Study of Religion,* edited by M. Banton, 1–42. London, 1966.

Gellner, E. "Patrons and Clients." In *Patrons and Clients in Mediterranean Societies,* edited by E. Gellner and L. Waterbury, 1–6. London, 1977.

Goemans, M. "Chalkedon als 'Allgemeines Konzil.'" In *Das Konzil von Chalkedon: Geschichte und Gegenwart,* edited by A. Grillmeier and H. Bacht, 1:251–89. Würzburg, 1951.

Goffman, E. *Forms of Talk.* Philadelphia, 1981.

Goubert, P. "Le role de Sainte Pulchérie et de l'eunuque Chrysaphios." In *Das Konzil von Chalkedon: Geschichte und Gegenwart,* edited by A. Grillmeier and H. Bacht, 1:303–21. Würzburg, 1951.

Gray, P. T. R. *The Defense of Chalcedon in the East (451–533).* Leiden, 1979.

———. "Palestine and Justinian's Legislation on Non-Roman Religions." In *Law, Politics and Society in the Ancient Mediterranean,* edited by B. Halpern and D. Hobsen, 241–70. Sheffield, 1993.

———. "Theodoret on the 'One Hypostasis': An Antiochene Reading of Chalcedon." *Studia Patristica* 15:1 (1984): 301–5.

Greatrex, G. *Rome and Persia at War, 502–32.* Leeds, 1998.

———. "The Two Fifth-Century Wars between Rome and Persia." *Florilegium* 12 (1993): 1–14.

Greatrex, G. and S. Lieu, eds. *The Roman Eastern Frontier and the Persian Wars, Part II, A.D. 363–628.* New York, 2002.

Greer, R. A. *Theodore of Mopsuestia, Exegete and Theologian.* London, 1961.

———. "Use of Scripture in the Nestorian Controversy." *Scottish Journal of Theology* 20 (1967): 413–22.

Gregory, T. *Vox Populi: Violence and Popular Involvement in Religious Controversies.* Columbus, OH, 1979.

Grey, C. "Revisiting the Problem of *Agri Deserti* in the Late Roman Empire." *Journal of Roman Archaeology* 20 (2007): 362–82.

Griffith, S. "Asceticism in the Church of Syria." In *Asceticism,* edited by V. Wimbush and R. Valantasis, 220–45. Oxford, 1995.

———. "Ephraem, the Deacon of Edessa and the Church of the Empire." In *Diakonia: Studies in Honor of Robert T. Meyer,* edited by T. Halton and J. Williman, 22–52. Washington D.C., 1986.

———. "Images of Ephrem: The Syrian Holy Man and His Church." *Traditio* 45 (1989): 7–34.

———. "Julian Saba, 'Father of the Monks' of Syria." *JECS* 2:2 (1994): 185–216.

———. "Monks, 'Singles' and the 'Sons of the Covenant': Reflections on Syriac Ascetic Terminology." In *EULOGEMA: Studies in Honor of Robert Taft, S.J.,* edited by E. Carr, S. Parenti, et al., 141–60. Rome, 1993.

Grillmeier, A. *Christ in Christian Tradition.* London, 1965.

Guinot, J. N. "La christologie de Théodoret de Cyr dans son Commentaire sur le Cantique." *Vigiliae Christianae* 39 (1985): 256–72.

———. "Un évêque exégète: Théodoret de Cyr." In *Le Monde grec ancien et la Bible,* edited by C. Mondésert, 335–60. Paris, 1984.

———. *L'Exégèse de Théodoret de Cyr.* Paris, 1995.

———. "Présence d'Apollinaire dans l'oeuvre exégétique de Théodoret." *Studia Patristica* 19 (1989): 166–72.

———. "Qui est 'le Syrien' dans les commentaires de Théodoret de Cyr." *Studia Patristica* 25 (1993): 60–71.

———. "Les sources de l'exégèse de Théodoret de Cyr." *Studia Patristica* 25 (1993): 72–94.

Günther, K. *Theodoret von Cyrus und die Kämpfe in der orientalischen Kirche vom Tode Cyrills bis zur Einberufung des sogen. Räuber-Konzils.* Aschaffenburg, 1913.

Guthrie, S. *Faces in the Clouds: A New Theory of Religion.* Oxford, 1993.

Haas, C. *Alexandria in Late Antiquity: Topography and Social Conflict.* Baltimore, 1997.

Hall, L. J. *Roman Berytus: Beirut in Late Antiquity.* New York, 2004.

Hanson, R. P. C. "The Fate of Eustathius of Antioch." *Zeitschrift für Kirchengeschichte* 91:2 (1984): 171–79.

———. *The Search for the Christian Doctrine of God.* Edinburgh, 1988.

Harries, J. *Law and Empire in Late Antiquity.* Cambridge, 1999.

Harvey, S. A. "The Holy and the Poor: Models from Early Syriac Christianity." In *Through the Eye of a Needle: Judeo-Christian Roots of Social Welfare,* edited by E. Hanawalt and C. Lindberg, 43–66. Kirksville, MO, 1994.

———. "Olfactory Knowing: Signs of Smell in the Vitae of Symeon Stylites." In *After Bardaisan: Studies on Continuity and Change in Honor of Professor Han J. W. Drijvers,* edited by G. Reinink, 23–34. Louvain, 1999.

———. "The Sense of a Stylite: Perspectives of Symeon the Elder." *Vigiliae Christianae* 42:4 (1988): 376–94.

———. "The Stylite's Liturgy: Ritual and Religious Identity in Late Antiquity." *JECS* 6:2 (1998): 523–39.

Heather, P. "Senates and Senators." In *The Cambridge Ancient History*. Vol. 13, *The Late Empire, 337–425*, edited by Averil Cameron and P. Garnsey, 184–210. Cambridge, 1998.

Hefele, J. *A History of the Councils of the Church*. Edinburgh, 1972.

Herford, R. T. *Christianity in Talmud and Midrash*. Clifton, NJ, 1966.

Hezser, C. *The Social Structure of the Rabbinic Movement in Roman Palestine*. Tübingen, 1997.

Hill, R. C. *Commentary on the Letters of Saint Paul / Theodoret of Cyrus*. 2 vols. Brookline, MA, 2000.

———. *Diodore of Tarsus, Commentary on Psalms 1–51*. Atlanta, 2005.

———. "A Spiritual Director from Antioch." *Pacifica* 12 (1999): 181–91.

Holum, K. "Pulcheria's Crusade AD 421–22 and the Ideology of Imperial Victory." *Greek, Roman, and Byzantine Studies* 18 (1977): 153–72.

———. *Theodosian Empresses: Women and Imperial Dominion in Late Antiquity*. Berkeley, 1982.

Honigmann, E. *Le couvent de Barsauma et le patriarcat jacobite d'Antioche et de Syrie*. Louvain, 1954.

———. *Évêques et évêqués monophysites d'Asie antérieure au VI siècle*. CSCO Subsidia 2. Louvain, 1951.

———. "Juvenal of Jerusalem." *Dumbarton Oaks Papers* 5 (1950): 209–79.

———. "The patriarchate of Antioch: A revision of Le Quien and the *Notitia Antiochena*." *Traditio* 5 (1947): 135–61.

Hopwood, K. "Bandits, Elites and Rural Order." In *Patronage in Ancient Society*, edited by A. Wallace-Hadrill, 171–88. New York, 1989.

Howard-Johnson, J. D. "The Great Powers in Late Antiquity: A Comparison." In *The Byzantine and Early Islamic Near East: States, Resources, Armies*, Studies in Late Antiquity and Early Islam vol. 3, edited by Averil Cameron, 157–226. Princeton, 1995.

Humphries, M. *Communities of the Blessed: Social Environment and Religious Change in Northern Italy, AD 200–400*. Oxford, 1999.

Isaac, B. *Limits of Empire: The Roman Army in the East*. Oxford, 1990.

Jacobs, A. S. *Remains of the Jews: The Holy Land and Christian Empire in Late Antiquity*. Stanford, 2004.

Jankowiak, W. "Adoring the Father: Religion and Charisma in an American Polygamous Community." In *Explorations in Anthropology and Theology*, edited by F. A. Salamone and W. R. Adams, 157–74. Lanham, MD, 1997.

Janowitz, N. "Rabbis and Their Opponents: The Construction of the 'Min' in Rabbinic Anecdotes." *JECS* 6:4 (1998): 449–62.

———. "Rethinking Jewish identity in Late Antiquity." In *Ethnicity and Culture in Late Antiquity*, edited by S. Mitchell and G. Greatrex, 205–19. London, 2000.

Johnson, T., and C. Dandeker. "Patronage: Relation and System." In *Patronage in Ancient Society*, edited by A. Wallace-Hadrill, 219–34. New York, 1989.

Jones, A. H. M. *The Later Roman Empire: A Social, Economic and Administrative Survey*. 2 vols. Baltimore, 1986. (*LRE*)

————. "The Social Background of Pagan/Christian Struggles." In *The Conflict between Paganism and Christianity in the Fourth Century*, edited by A. Momigliano, 17–37. Oxford, 1964.

————. "Were Ancient Heresies National or Social Movements in Disguise?" *JTS* ns. 10 (1959): 280–98.

Jouassard, G. "Le cas de Nestorius." *Revue d'histoire ecclésiastique* 80:2 (1979): 346–48.

Kalantzis, G. *Theodore of Mopsuestia: Commentary on the Gospel of John*. Early Christian Studies 7. Strathfield, 2004.

Kaster, R. *Guardians of Language: The Grammarian and Society in Late Antiquity*. Berkeley, 1988.

Kearsley, R. "The Impact of Greek Concepts of God on the Christology of Cyril of Alexandria." *Tyndale Bulletin* 43 (1992): 307–9.

Kelly, C. *Ruling the Later Roman Empire*. Cambridge, MA, 2004.

Kelly, J. N. D. *Early Christian Creeds*. 3rd edition. London, 2006.

————. *Early Christian Doctrines*. Revised edition. New York, 1978.

————. *Goldenmouth: The Story of John Chrysostom*. Ithaca, NY, 1995.

Kennedy, D. "The Roman Army in the East." In *The Roman Army in the East*, edited by D. Kennedy, 9–24. Ann Arbor, 1996.

Khouri-Sarkis, E. "Réception d'un évêque syrien au VIe siècle." *L'Orient syrien* 2 (1998): 137–84.

Kierkegaard, S. *The Works of Love*. In *The Essential Kirkegaard*, edited by H. Hong and E. Hong, 277–310. Princeton, 2000.

Kim, C. H. *Form and Structure of the Familiar Greek Letter of Recommendation*. Missoula, MT, 1972.

King, K. L. "Social and Theological Effects of Heresiological Discourse." In *Heresy and Identity in Late Antiquity*, edited by E. Iricinischi and H. M. Zellentin, 28–49. Tübingen, 2008.

Kondoleon, C. "Mosaics of Antioch." In *Antioch: The Lost Ancient City*, edited by C. Kondoleon et al., 63–77 . Princeton, 2000.

Kondoleon, C. et al. *Antioch: The Lost Ancient City*. Catalog for the exhibition at the Worcester Museum of Art. Princeton, 2000.

König, J. "Sympotic Dialog in the First to Fifth Centuries CE." In *The End of Dialog in Antiquity*, edited by S. Goldhill, 85–113. Cambridge, 2008.

Konstan, D. *Friendship in the Classical World*. Cambridge, 1997.

————. "How to Praise a Friend: St. Gregory of Nazianzus' Funeral Oration for St. Basil the Great." In *Greek Biography and Panegyric in Late Antiquity*, edited by T. Hägg and P. Rousseau, 160–79. Berkeley, 2000.

Krueger, D. "Typological Figuration in Theodoret of Cyrrhus' *Religious History* and the Art of the Post-biblical Narrative." *JECS* 5:3 (1997): 393–419.

————. *Writing and Holiness: The Practice of Authorship in the Early Christian East*. Philadelphia, 2004.

————. "Writing as Devotion: Hagiographical Composition and the Cult of the Saints in Theodoret of Cyrrhus and Cyril of Scythopolis." *Church History* 66 (1997): 707–19.

Kyle, R. G. "Nestorius: The Partial Rehabilitation of a Heretic." *Journal of the Evangelical Theological Society* 32 (1989): 73–83.

Laidlaw, J. "A Well-Disposed Social Anthropologist's Problems with the 'Cognitive Science of Religion.'" In *Religion, Anthropology, and Cognitive Science*, edited by H. Whitehouse and J. Laidlaw, 211–46. Durham, NC, 2007.

Laing, S. D. "Theodoret of Cyrus and the Ideal Monarch." PhD Diss., Southern Baptist Theological Seminary, 2004.

Lakoff, G. "The Contemporary Theory of Metaphor." In *Metaphor and Thought,* edited by A. Ortony, 202–49. Cambridge, 1993.

———. *Moral Politics: How Liberals and Conservatives Think.* Chicago, 2002.

Lakoff, G., and M. Johnson. *Philosophy in the Flesh: The Embodied Mind and its Challenge to Western Thought.* New York, 1999.

Lamoreaux, J. C. "Episcopal Courts in Late Antiquity." *JECS* 3:2 (1995): 143–68.

Lampe, G. W. H. *A Patristic Greek Lexicon.* Oxford, 1961.

Lampe, G. W. H., and H. J. Woolcombe. *Essays on Typology.* London, 1957.

Laniado, A. *Recherches sur les notables municipaux dans l'Empire protobyzantin.* Travaux et mémoires du Centre de recherche d'histoire et civilisation de Byzance 13. Paris, 2002.

Lawrenz, M. *The Christology of John Chrysostom.* Lewiston, NY, 1996.

Le Boulluec, A. *La notion d'hérésie dans la littérature grecque IIe–IIIe siècles.* Paris, 1985.

Leconte, R. "L'asceterium de Diodore." In *Mélanges bibliques redigés en l'honneur d'André Robert,* edited by J. Trinquet, 531–37. Paris, 1957.

Leppin, H. "Church Historians I: Socrates, Sozomen, Theodoretus." In *Greek and Roman Historiography in Late Antiquity,* edited by G. Marasco, 219–54. Leiden, 2003.

———. *Vom Constantin dem Grossen zu Theodosius II: das christliche Kaisertum bei den Kirchenhistoriken Socrates, Sozomenus und Theodoret.* Göttingen, 1996.

———. "Zum kirchenpolitischen Kontext von Theodorets Mönchsgeschichte." *Klio* 78 (1996): 212–30.

Leroy-Molinghen, A. "Les Ages de la vie dans un passage de l'*Histoire philothée* de Théodoret de Cyr." In *Uberlieferungsgeschichtliche Untersuchungen,* edited by F. Paschke, 385–87. Berlin, 1981.

———. "À propos du texte de l'*Histoire philothée* de Théodoret de Cyr." In *Zetesis,* edited by E. de Strycker, 732–35. Antwerp, 1973.

———. "Naissance et enfance de Théodoret." In *L'enfant dans les civilisations orientales,* edited by A. Theodorides, 153–58. Louvain, 1980.

Liebaert, J. *La doctrine christologique de Cyrille d'Alexandrie avant la querelle nestorienne.* Lille, 1950.

———. "L'evolution de la christologie de saint Cyrille d'Alexandrie à partir de la controverse nestorienne." *Mélanges de Science Religieuse* 27 (1970): 27–48.

Liebeschuetz, J. H. W. G. *Antioch: City and Imperial Administration in the Later Roman Empire.* Oxford, 1972.

———. *Barbarians and Bishops: Army Church and State in the Age of Arcadius and Chrysostom.* Oxford, 1990.

———. *The Decline and Fall of the Roman City.* Oxford, 2001.

———. "Ecclesiastical Historians on Their Own Times." *Studia Patristica* 24 (1993): 151–63.

Lieu, S. *Manichaeism in the Later Roman Empire and Medieval China.* Tübingen, 1992.

———. "The Self-Identity of Manichaeans in the Roman East." *Mediterranean Archaeology* 11 (1998): 205–27.

Lim, R. "Christians, Dialogues and Patterns of Sociability in Late Antiquity." In *The End of Dialogue in Late Antiquity,* edited by S. Goldhill, 151–72. Cambridge, 2008.

———. *Public Disputation, Power, and Social Order in Late Antiquity.* Berkeley, 1995.

———. "Theodoret of Cyrus and the Speakers in the Greek Dialogues." *Journal of Hellenic Studies* 111 (1991): 181–82.

Long, A. "Plato's Dialogues and a Common Rationale for Dialogue Form." In *The End of Dialogue in Late Antiquity,* edited by S. Goldhill, 45–59. Cambridge, 2008.

Loofs, F. *Nestorius and His Place in the History of Christian Doctrine.* Cambridge, 1914.

MacDonald, M. "Some Reflections on Epigraphy and Ethnicity in the Roman Near East." *Mediterranean Archaeology* 11 (1998): 177–90.

MacMullen, R. *Christianity and Paganism in the Fourth to Eighth Centuries.* New Haven, 1997.

———. *Christianizing the Roman Empire (AD 100–400).* New Haven, 1984.

———. *Voting about God in Early Church Councils.* New Haven, CT, 2006.

Maier, H. O. "Religious Dissent, Heresy and Households in Late Antiquity." *Vigiliae Christianae* 49 (1996): 49–57.

Malherbe, A. J. *Ancient Epistolary Theorists.* Atlanta, 1988.

Mandac, M. "L'union christologique dans les oeuvres de Théodoret anterieures au concile d'Éphèse." *Ephemerides Theologicae Lovanienses* 1 (1971): 64–96.

Mariès, L. *Le Commentaire de Diodore de Tarse sur les Psaumes.* Paris, 1924.

Marrou, H. *A History of Education in Antiquity.* Translated by G. Lamb. New York, 1964.

Martin, T. O. "The Twenty-Eighth Canon of Chalcedon: A Background Note." In *Das Konzil von Chalkedon: Geschichte und Gegenwart,* edited by A. Grillmeier and H. Bacht, 2:433–58. Würzburg, 1951.

Matthews, J. "The Roman Empire and the Proliferation of Elites." *Arethusa* 33:3 (2000): 229–46.

Maxwell, J. L. *Christianization and Communication in Late Antiquity: John Chrysostom and his Congregation in Antioch.* Cambridge, 2006.

Mayer, W. "John Chrysostom: Extraordinary Preacher, Ordinary Audience." In *Preacher and Audience: Studies in Early Christian and Byzantine Homiletics,* edited by P. Allen and M. Cunningham, 105–37. Leiden, 1998.

———. "Patronage, Pastoral Care and the Role of the Bishop at Antioch." *Vigiliae Christianae* 55:1 (2001): 58–70.

McCollough, C. T. "A Christianity for an Age of Crisis: Theodoret of Cyrus' Commentary on Daniel." In *Religious Writings and Religious Systems.* ed. J. Neusner and E. S. Frerichs, 157–174. Atlanta, 1989.

———. "Theodoret of Cyrus as Biblical Interpreter and the Presence of Judaism in the Later Roman Empire." *Studia Patristica* 18:1 (1985): 327–34.

McGinn, B. "Asceticism and Mysticism in Late Antiquity and the Early Middle Ages." In *Asceticism,* edited by V. Wimbush and R. Valantasis, 58–74. Oxford, 1995.

McGuckin, J. A. "The Christology of Nestorius of Constantinople." *Patristic and Byzantine Review* 7:1 (1988): 2–3.

———. "The Concept of Orthodoxy in Ancient Christianity." *Patristic and Byzantine Review* 8:1 (1989): 5–24.

———. "Nestorius and the Political Factions of Fifth-Century Byzantium: Factors in his Personal Downfall." *Bulletin of the John Rylands University Library of Manchester* 78 (1996): 7–21.

———. *St. Cyril of Alexandria and the Christological Controversy*. New York, 2004.

McLean, P. D. *The Art of the Network: Strategic Interaction and Patronage in Renaissance Florence*. Durham, NC, 2007.

McLeod, F. "The Christological Ramifications of Theodore of Mopsuestia's Understanding of Baptism and the Eucharist." *JECS* 10:1 (2002): 38–63.

Meeks, W. *The First Urban Christians: The Social World of the Apostle Paul*. New Haven, 1983.

Meeks, W., and R. L. Wilken. *Jews and Christians in Antioch*. Missoula, MT, 1978.

Mendels, D. *The Media Revolution in Early Christianity*. Grand Rapids, MI, 1999.

Métivier, S. *La Cappadoce (IV–VI siècle): un histoire provinciale de l'empire romain d'orient*. Paris, 2005.

Meunier, B. *Le Christ de Cyrille d'Alexandrie*. Paris, 1997.

Michelson, D. A. "Practice Leads to Theory: Orthodoxy and the Spiritual Struggle in the World of Philoxenos of Mabbug (470–523)." PhD Diss., Princeton University, 2007.

Millar, F. "Ethnic Identity in the Roman Near East, 325–450: Language, Religion and Culture." *Mediterranean Archaeology* 11 (1998): 159–76.

———. *A Greek Roman Empire: Power and Belief under Theodosius II*. Berkeley, 2006.

———. *The Roman Near East 31 BC–AD 337*. Cambridge, MA, 1993.

———. "Theodoret of Cyrrhus: A Syrian in Greek Dress?" In *From Rome to Constantinople: Studies in Honor of Averil Cameron*, edited by H. Amirav and B. ter Haar Romeny, 105–25. Louvain, 2007.

Mitchell, J. C. "Networks, Norms, and Institutions." In *Network Analysis: Studies in Human Interaction*, edited by J. Boissevain and J. C. Mitchell, 2–35. The Hague, 1973.

Mitchell, S. *Anatolia: Land, Men, and Gods in Asia Minor*. 2 vols. Oxford, 1993.

———. "Ethnicity, Acculturation, and Empire in Roman and Late Roman Asia Minor." In *Ethnicity and Culture in Late Antiquity*, edited by S. Mitchell and G. Greatrex, 117–50. London, 2000.

Moeller, C. "Chalcédonisme et le néo-Chalcédonisme en Orient de 451 à la fin du VIe siècle." In *Das Konzil von Chalkedon: Geschichte und Gegenwart*, edited by A. Grillmeier and H. Bacht, 1:637–720. Würzburg, 1951.

Moxnes, H. "Patron-Client Relations and the New Community in Luke-Acts." In *The Social World of Luke-Acts: Models for Interpretation*, edited by J. Neyrey, 241–68. Peabody, MA, 1991.

Mullett, M. "The Classical Tradition in the Byzantine Letter." In *Byzantium and the Classical Tradition*, edited by M. Mullet and R. Scott, 75–93. Birmingham, 1981.

———. *Theophylact of Ochrid: Reading the Letters of a Byzantine Archbishop*. Brookfield, VT, 1997.

Murray, R. *Symbols of Church and Kingdom: A Study in the Early Syriac Tradition.* Cambridge, 1975.

Naaman, P. *Théodoret de Cyr et le monastère de Saint Maroun.* Sin el-Fil, 1971.

Nassif, B. L. "Spritual Exegesis in the School of Antioch." *Anglican Theological Review* 75 (1993): 437–70.

Neusner, J. *Aphrahat and Judaism: The Christian-Jewish Argument in Fourth-Century Iran.* Leiden, 1971.

Nigosian, S. A. *The Zoroastrian Faith: Tradition and Modern Research.* Montreal, 1993.

Norris, R. A. "Christological Models in Cyril of Alexandria." *Studia Patristica* 13 (1975): 255–68.

———. *Manhood and Christ.* Oxford, 1963.

———. "The Problems of Human Identity in Patristic Christological Speculation." *Studia Patristica* 17:1 (1982): 147–59.

Norton, P. *Episcopal Elections 250–600: Hierarchy and Popular Will in Late Antiquity.* Oxford, 2007.

O'Keefe, J. J. "Kenosis or Impassibility: Cyril of Alexandria and Theodoret of Cyrus on the Problem of Divine Pathos." *Studia Patristica* 32 (1997): 358–65.

———. "'A Letter that Killeth': Toward a Reassessment of Antiochene Exegesis, or Diodore, Theodore, and Theodoret on the Psalms." *JECS* 8:1 (2000): 83–104.

Ortiz de Urbina, I. "Das Glaubensymbol von Chalkedon—sein Text, sein Werden, sein dogmatische Bedeutung." In *Das Konzil von Chalkedon: Geschichte und Gegenwart,* edited by A. Grillmeier and H. Bacht, 1:389–418. Würzburg, 1951.

Papadoyannakis, Y. "Christian *Therapeia* and *Politeia:* The Apologetics of Theodoret of Cyrrhus against the Greeks." PhD Diss., Princeton University, 2004.

———. "Defining Orthodoxy in Pseudo-Justin's *Quaestiones et responsiones ad orthodoxos.*" In *Heresy and Identity in Late Antiquity,* edited by E. Iricinischi and H. M. Zellentin, 115–27. Tübingen, 2008.

Pargoire, J. "Un mot sur les Acémètes." *Échos d'Orient* 2 (1899): 304–8, 365–72.

Parmentier, L. *Theodoret Kirchengeschichte.* GCS 5. Berlin, 1998.

Parmentier, M. "A Letter from Theodoret of Cyrus to the Exiled Nestorius (CPG 6270) in a Syriac Version: [facsim]." *Bijdragen* 51 (1990): 234–45.

Pásztori-Kupán, I. *Theodoret of Cyrus.* The Early Church Fathers. New York, 2006.

Patlagean, E. *Pauvreté économique et pauvreté sociale à Byzance 4e-7e siècles.* Paris: 1977.

Paverd, F. J. P. van de. "Anaphoral Intercessions, Epiclesis and Communion-Rites in John Chrysostom." *Orienta christiana periodica* 49:2 (1983): 303–39.

Payne Smith, J. *A Compendious Syriac Dictionary.* Oxford, 1903.

Peeters, P. "Pour l'histoire des origines de l'alphabet arménien." *Revue des études arméniens* 19 (1929): 203–37.

———. "St. Syméon Stylite et ses premiers biographes." *AB* 61 (1943): 29–71.

———. *Le tréfonds oriental de l'hagiographie Byzantine.* Brussels, 1950.

———. "La vie de Rabboula, évêque d'Edesse." *Recherches d'histoire et de philologie orientales,* Subsidia Hagiographica 27, I:139–70. Brussels, 1951.

Penella, R. J. *Greek Philosophers and Sophists in the Fourth Century AD: Studies in Eunapius of Sardis.* Leeds, 1990.

Pericoli-Ridolfini, F. "La controversia tra Cirillo d'Alessandria e Giovanni d'Antiochia nell'epistolario di Andrea di Samosata." *Revisti degli Studi Orientali* 29 (1954): 187–217.

Person, R. E. *The Mode of Theological Decision-Making at the Early Ecumenical Councils: An Inquiry into the Function of Scripture and Tradition at the Councils of Nicaea and Ephesus.* Basel, 1978.

Petit, P. *Les étudiants de Libanius.* Paris, 1956.

———. *Libanius et la vie municipale à Antioche au IV siècle après J-C.* Paris, 1955.

Pollard, N. "The Roman Army as 'Total Institution' in the Near East?: Dura-Europos as a Case Study." In *The Roman Army in the East,* edited by D. Kennedy, 211–27. Ann Arbor, 1996.

Polletta, F. "Contending Stories: Narrative in Social Movements." *Qualitative Sociology* 21:4 (1998): 419–46.

Possekel, U. *Evidence of Greek Philosophical Concepts in the Writings of Ephrem the Syrian.* CSCO Subsidia 102. Louvain, 1999.

Potter, D. S. "Emperors, Their Borders, and Their Neighbors: The Scope of Imperial *mandata.*" In *The Roman Army in the East,* edited by D. Kennedy, 49–66. Ann Arbor, 1996.

Price, R. M. "Holy Men's Letters of Rebuke." *Studia Patristica* 16:2 (1985): 50–53.

Price, R. M., and J. M. Gaddis. *The Acts of the Council of Chalcedon.* Liverpool, 2005.

Pyysiäinen, I. *How Religion Works: Towards a New Cognitive Science of Religion.* Leiden, 2001.

———. *Magic, Miracles and Religion: A Scientist's Perspective.* Walnut Creek, CA, 2004.

———. "Religion and the Counter-Intuitive." In *Current Approaches in the Cognitive Study of Religion,* edited by I. Pyysiäinen and V. Anttonen, 110–32. New York, 2002.

Rajak, T. and D. Noy. "*Archisynagogoi:* Office, Title and Social Status in the Graeco-Jewish Synagogue." *Journal of Roman Studies* 83 (1993): 75–93.

Ramachandran, V. S. *A Brief Tour of Human Consciousness: From Impostor Poodles to Purple Numbers.* New York, 2004.

Rapp, C. "The Elite Status of Bishops in Late Antiquity, in Ecclesiastical, Spiritual and Social Contexts." *Arethusa* 33:3 (2000): 375–401.

———. "'For Next to God You are My Salvation': Reflections on the Rise of the Holy Man in Late Antiquity." In *The Cult of Saints in Late Antiquity and the Middle Ages,* edited by J. Howard-Johnson and P. A. Haywood, 63–81. Oxford, 1999.

———. *Holy Bishops in Late Antiquity: The Nature of Christian Leadership in an Age of Transition.* Berkeley, 2005.

———. "Storytelling as Spiritual Communication in Early Greek Hagiography: The Use of *Diegesis.*" *JECS* 6:3 (1998): 431–48.

Reinink, G. J. "The Quotations from the Lost Works of Theodoret of Cyrus and Theodore of Mopsuestia in an Unpublished East Syrian Work on Christology: ["On the Union" by Simon the Persecuted; Mingana 544 and Cambridge Or 1317]." *Studia Patristica* 33 (1997): 562–67.

Richard, M. "Acace de Mélitène, Proclus de Constantinople et la Grande Arménie." In *Opera Minora,* 2: sec. 50. Turnhout, 1976.

———. "L'activité littéraire de Théodoret avant le concile d'Ephèse." In *Opera Minora,* 2: sec. 45. Turnhout, 1976.

————. "Un écrit de Théodoret sur l'unité de Christ après l'incarnation." In *Opera Minora*, 2: sec. 44. Turnhout, 1976.

————. "La lettre de Théodoret a Jean d'Égées." In *Opera Minora*, 2: sec. 48. Turnhout, 1976.

————. "Notes sur l'évolution doctrinale de Théodoret." In *Opera Minora*, 2: sec. 46. Turnhout, 1976.

————. "Proclus de Constantinople et le Théopaschisme." In *Opera Minora*, 2: sec. 52. Turnhout, 1976.

————. "Théodoret, Jean d'Antioche et les moines de l'orient." In *Opera Minora*, 2: sec. 47. Turnhout, 1976.

Robert, L. *Hellenica: Recueil d'épigraphie de numismatique et d'antiquités grecques.* Amsterdam, 1972.

Roberts, W. J. *Demetrius on Style.* Cambridge, 1902.

Rodriguez Moreno, I. "Les héros comme METAXY l'homme et la divinité dans la pensée grecque." In *Héros et héroïnes dans les mythes et les cultes grecs,* edited by V. Pirenne-Delforge and E. Suárez de la Torre, 91–100. Liège, 2000.

Roey, A. V. "Remarques sur le moine Marcien." *Studia Patristica* 12 (1975): 160–77.

Romanides, J. S. "St Cyril's 'One Physis or Hypostasis of God the Logos Incarnate' and Chalcedon." In *Christ in East and West,* edited by P. Fries and T. Nersoyan, 15–34. Macon, GA, 1987.

Roques, D. *Études sur la correspondance de Synésios de Cyrène.* Brussels, 1989.

Rosenmeyer, P. A. *Ancient Epistolary Fictions: The Letter in Greek Literature.* Cambridge, 2001.

Roueché, C. "Theodosius II, the Cities, and the Date of the *Church History* of Sozomen." *JTS* ns. 37:1 (1986): 130–32.

Rousseau, P. "Ascetics as Mediators and Teachers." In *The Cult of the Saints in Late Antiquity and the Middle Ages,* edited by J. Howard-Johnson and P. A. Haywood, 45–59. Oxford, 1999.

————. "The Identity of the Ascetic Master in the *HR* of Theodoret of Cyrrhus: A New Paideia?" *Mediterranean Archaeology* 11 (1998): 229–44.

————. "Knowing Theodoret: Text and Self." In *The Cultural Turn in Late Ancient Studies,* edited by D. Martin and P. Cox Miller, 278–97. Durham, NC, 2005.

Rouwhorst, G. "Jewish Liturgical Traditions in Early Syriac Christianity." *Vigiliae Christianae* 51 (1997): 72–88.

Ruffini, G. *Social Networks in Byzantine Egypt.* Cambridge, 2008.

Russell, J. "Household Furnishings." In *Antioch: The Lost Ancient City,* edited by C. Kondoleon, 79–89. Princeton, 2000.

Russell, N. *Cyril of Alexandria.* London, 2000.

Russell, P. S. "Ephraim the Syrian on the Utility of Language and the Place of Silence." *JECS* 8:1 (2000): 21–37.

Saller, R. "Patronage and Friendship in Early Imperial Rome: Drawing the Distinction." In *Patronage in Ancient Society,* edited by A. Wallace-Hadrill, 50–62. New York, 1989.

————. *Personal Patronage under the Early Empire.* Cambridge, 1982.

Saltet, M. "Les sources de l'Éranistes de Théodoret." *Revue de l'histoire ecclésiastique* 6 (1905): 289–303, 513–36, 741–54.

Schäublin, C. "Diodor von Tarsus." *Theologische Realenzyklopädie* 8:764–65.

———. *Untersuchungen zu Methode und Herkunft der antiochenischen Exegese.* Cologne, 1974.

Schechner, R. *Performance Theory.* New York, 1988.

Schor, A. M. "Christian Triumph, Christian Peace: The Origenist Controversy and the Historiography of Rufinus of Aquileia." *Byzantine Studies/ Études byzantines* ns. 4 (1999/2001): 126–56.

———. "Patronage Performance and Social Strategy in the Letters of Theodoret, Bishop of Cyrrhus." *JLA* 2.2 (2009): 274–99.

———. "Theodoret on the 'School of Antioch': A Network Approach." *JECS* 15.4 (2007): 517–62.

Schouler, B. *La tradition hellénique chez Libanios.* Paris, 1984.

Schrier, O. "Syriac Evidence for the Roman-Persian War 421–422." *Greek, Roman, and Byzantine Studies* 33 (1992): 75–86.

Schwartz, E. *Acta conciliorum oecumenicorum,* vols. I.1.1–I.5. Berlin, 1914–. (*ACO*)

———. *Codex Vaticanus gr. 1431.* Munich, 1927.

———. *Konzilstudien.* Strasbourg, 1914.

———. "Der Prozess des Eutyches." *Sitzungberichte der bayerischen Akademie de Wissenschaften, philosophisch-historische Klasse Abt.* 5 (1929): 1–52.

Scott, J. *Social Network Analysis: A Handbook.* London, 2000.

Segal, J. *Edessa: The Blessed City.* Oxford, 1970.

Sellers, R. V. *The Council of Chalcedon: An Historical and Doctrinal Survey.* London, 1961.

———. *Two Ancient Christologies.* London, 1940.

Shaw, G. *Theurgy and the Soul: The Neoplatonism of Iamblichus.* University Park, PA, 1995.

Shepardson, C. "Anti-Jewish Rhetoric and Intra-Christian Conflict in the Sermons of Ephrem Syrus." *Studia Patristica* 35 (2001): 502–7.

———. "Controlling Contested Places: John Chrysostom's Adversus Iudaeos Homilies and the Spatial Politics of Religious Controversy." *JECS* 15:4 (2007): 483–516.

Shils, E. *Center and Periphery: Essays in Macrosociology.* Chicago, 1975.

Sillett, H. M. "Culture of Controversy: The Christological Disputes of the Early Fifth Century." PhD Diss., University of California, Berkeley, 1999.

Silva-Tarouca, C. S. *Leonis Magni, Epistulae contra Eutychis haeresim.* 2 parts. *Pontificia universitas Gregoriana Textus et documenta, series theologica* 15, 20. Rome: 1934, 1935.

Silverman, S. "Patronage as Myth." In *Patrons and Clients in Mediterranean Societies,* edited by E. Gellner and L. Waterbury, 7–22. London, 1977.

Simon, M. *Verus Israel: A Study of the Relations between Christians and Jews in the Roman Empire (AD 135–425).* Translated by H. McKeating. New York, 1986.

Somers, M. R. "The Narrative Constitution of Identity: A Relationship and Network Approach." *Theory and Society* 23:5 (1994): 605–60.

Soro, A. B. "La condamnation de Nestorius au concile d'Éphèse." *Istina* 43:2 (1998): 179–213.

Spadavecchia, C. "The Rhetorical Tradition in the Letters of Theodoret of Cyrus." In *From Late Antiquity to Early Byzantium,* edited by V. Vavrínek, 249–52. Prague, 1985.

Spoerl, K. M. "Apollinarian Christology and the Anti-Marcellan Tradition." *JTS* ns. 45:2 (1994): 545–68.

————. "Apollinarius and the Response to Early Arian Christology." *Studia Patristica* 26 (1993): 421–27.

————. "The Schism at Antioch since Cavallera." In *Arianism after Arius,* edited by M. Barnes and D. Williams, 101–26. Edinburgh, 1993.

Stark, R., and W. S. Bainbridge. "Networks of Faith: Interpersonal Bonds and Recruitment to Cults and Sects." *American Journal of Sociology* 85 (1980): 1376–95.

Sterk, A. *Renouncing the World Yet Leading the Church: Monk-Bishops in Late Antiquity.* Cambridge, MA, 2004.

Stewardson, J. L. "Vision of God according to Theodoret of Cyrus." *Studia Patristica* 32 (1997): 371–75.

Stewart, C. *Working the Earth of the Heart: The Messalian Controversy in History, Texts, and Language.* Oxford, 1991.

Stirewalt, M. L. J. *Studies in Ancient Greek Epistolography.* Atlanta, 1993.

Stowers, S. K. *Letter-writing in Greco-Roman Antiquity.* Philadelphia, 1986.

Strack, H., and G. Stemberger. *Introduction to the Talmud and Midrash.* Edinburgh, 1991.

Sullivan, F. A. *The Christology of Theodore of Mopsuestia.* Rome, 1956.

Taft, R. F. "One Bread, One Body: Ritual Symbols of Ecclesial Communion in the Patristic Period." In *Nova Doctrina Vetusque: Essays on Early Christianity in Honor of Frederic W. Schlatter, S. J.,* edited by D. Kries and C. B. Tkacz, 23–50. New York, 1999.

Tambiah, S. J. "A Performative Approach to Ritual." *Proceedings of the British Academy* 65 (1979): 113–69.

Tardieu, M. "Le marcionisme syrien: problèmes de géographie et d'ecclésiologie: 1 Arabie, 2 Cyrrhestique." *Annuaire du Collège de France* 98 (1997–8): 596–605.

Tate, G. *Les campagnes de la Syrie du Nord.* Paris, 1992.

Taylor, M. *Anti-Judaism and Early Christian Identity.* Leiden, 1995.

Tchalenko, G. *Villages antiques de la Syrie du Nord.* Paris, 1953.

Teeter, T. M. "Christian Letters of Recommendation in the Papyrus Record." *Patristic and Byzantine Review* 9:1 (1990): 59–70.

Tilley, M. "No Friendly Letters: Augustine's Correspondence with Women." In *The Cultural Turn in Late Ancient Studies,* edited by D. Martin and P. Cox Miller, 40–62. Durham, NC, 2005.

Thelamon, F. *Païens et Chrétiens au IVe siècle: l'apport de l'"Histoire ecclésiastique" de Rufin d'Aquilée.* Paris, 1981.

Thiessen, G., and M. Kohl. *Social Reality and the Early Christians: Theology, Ethics, and the World of the New Testament.* Edinburgh, 1993.

Tompkins, I. G. "Problems of Dating and Pertinence in Some Letters of Theodoret of Cyrrhus." *Byzantion* 65:1 (1995): 176–95.

————. "The Relations between Theodoret of Cyrrhus and his City and its Territory, with Particular Attention to the Letters and the *Historia Religiosa.*" PhD Diss., University of Oxford, 1993.

Trakatellis, D. M. "Theodoret's Commentary on Isaiah: A Synthesis of Exegetical Traditions." In *New perspectives on historical theology,* edited by B. Nassif, 313–42. Grand Rapids, MI, 1996.

Trapp, M. *Greek and Latin Letters: An Anthology.* Cambridge, 2003.

Treadgold, W. *Byzantium and its Army, 284–1081.* Stanford, 1998.

Trombley, F. "Christian Demography in the *Territorium* of Antioch (4th–5th c.): Observations on the Epigraphy." In *Culture and Society in Later Roman Antioch,* edited by I. Sandwell and J. Huskinson, 59–85. Oxford, 2004.

———. *Hellenic Religion and Christianization 370–529.* 2 vols. Leiden, 1993.

Tsirpanlis, C. N. "The Structure of the Church in the Liturgical Tradition of the First Three Centuries." *Patristic and Byzantine Review* 1:1 (1982): 44–62.

Turcan, R. *Mithra et le Mithraïsme.* Paris, 2004.

Turner, V. "The Anthropology of Performance." In *The Anthropology of Performance,* preface by R. Schechner, 72–98. New York, 1986.

———. *From Ritual to Theater: The Human Seriousness of Play.* New York, 1982.

———. "Images and Reflections: Ritual, Drama, Carnival, Film, and Spectacle in Cultural Performance." In *The Anthropology of Performance,* preface by R. Schechner, 21–32. New York, 1986.

Tyng, D. *Theodore of Mopsuestia as an interpreter of the Old Testament.* Leipzig, 1931.

Ueding, L. "Die Kanones von Chalkedon in ihrer Bedeutung für Mönchtum und Klerus." In *Das Konzil von Chalkedon: Geschichte und Gegenwart,* edited by A. Grillmeier and H. Bacht, 2:569–676. Würzburg, 1951.

Urbainczyk, T. " 'The Devil Spoke Syriac to Me': Theodoret in Syria." In *Ethnicity and Culture in Late Antiquity,* edited by S. Mitchell and G. Greatrex, 253–65. London, 2000.

———. *Socrates of Constantinople.* Ann Arbor, 1997.

———. *Theodoret of Cyrrhus: The Bishop and the Holy Man.* Ann Arbor, 2002.

Vaggione, R. "Some Neglected Fragments of Theodore of Mopsuestia's *Contra Eunomium.*" *JTS* ns. 31:2 (1980): 403–70.

Van Dam, R. *Becoming Christian: The Conversion of Roman Cappadocia.* Philadelphia, 2003.

———. *Families and Friends in Late Roman Cappadocia.* Philadelphia, 2003.

———. *Kingdom of Snow: Roman Rule and Greek Culture in Cappadocia.* Philadelphia, 2002.

———. *Leadership and Community in Late Antique Gaul.* Berkeley, 1985.

———. *The Roman Revolution of Constantine.* Cambridge, 2007.

Vanderspoel, J. *Themistius and the Imperial Court: Oratory, Civic Duty, and Paideia from Constantius to Theodosius.* Ann Arbor, 1995.

Van Esbroeck, M. "Who is Mari, the Addressee of Ibas' Letter?" *JTS* ns. 38:1 (1987): 129–35.

Van Parys, M. "L'évolution de la doctrine christologique de Basile de Séleucie." *Irénikon* 44 (1971): 493–514.

Van Roey, A. "Les débuts de l'Église jacobite." In *Das Konzil von Chalkedon: Geschichte und Gegenwart,* edited by A. Grillmeier and H. Bacht, 2:339–60. Würzburg, 1951.

Vermeule, C. "The Sculptures of Roman Syria." In *Antioch: The Lost Ancient City,* edited by C. Kondoleon, 91–103. Princeton, 2000.

Veyne, P. *Bread and Circuses: Historical Sociology and Political Pluralism.* Translated by B. Pearce. London, 1990.

———. *Did the Greeks Believe in Their Myths?: An Essay on the Constitutive Imagination.* Translated by P. Wissing. Chicago, 1988.

Vogt, H. J. "Unterschiedliches Konzilsverstandnis der Cyrillianer und der Orientalen beim." In *Logos: Festschrift für Luise Abramowski zum 8. Juli 1993*, edited by H. C. Brennecke, E. L. Grasmück, and C. Markschies, 429–445. Berlin, 1993.

Vööbus, A. *A History of Asceticism in the Syrian Orient.* 3 vols. Louvain, 1958–1988.

———. *A History of the School of Nisibis.* Louvain, 1965.

———. *Researches on the Circulation of the Peshitta in the Middle of the Fifth Century.* Pinneberg, 1948.

———. *Studies in the History of the Gospel Text in Syriac.* Louvain, 1951.

Wagner, M. S. "A Chapter in Byzantine Epistolography." *Dumbarton Oaks Papers* 2 (1948): 121–81.

Wallace-Hadrill, A. "Patronage in Roman Society: From Republic to Empire." In *Patronage in Ancient Society,* edited by A. Wallace-Hadrill, 63–75. New York, 1989.

———, ed. *Patronage in Ancient Society.* New York, 1989.

Wallace-Hadrill, D. S. *Christian Antioch: A Study of Early Christian Thought in the East.* Cambridge, 1982.

Ware, K. "The Meaning of 'Pathos' in Abba Isaias and Theodoret of Cyrus." *Studia Patristica* 20 (1989): 315–22.

Wasserman, S., and K. Faust. *Social Network Analysis: Methods and Applications.* Cambridge, 1994.

Watt, E. J. *City and School in Late Antique Athens and Alexandria.* Berkeley, 2006.

Watts, D. *Six Degrees: The Science of a Connected Age.* New York, 2003.

Wessel, S. *Cyril of Alexandria and the Nestorian Controversy: The Making of a Saint and of a Heretic.* Oxford, 2004.

White, C. *Christian Friendship in the Fourth Century.* Cambridge, 1992.

White, H. "The Value of Narrativity in the Representation of Reality." In *On Narrative,* edited by W. J. T. Mitchell, 1–23. Chicago, 1981.

Whittaker, C. R. *Frontiers of the Roman Empire: A Social and Economic Study.* Baltimore, 1994.

———. "Where Are the Frontiers Now?" In *The Roman Army in the East,* edited by D. Kennedy, 25–41. Ann Arbor, 1996.

Wickert, U. *Studien zu den Pauluskommentaren Theodors von Mopsuestia als Beitrag zu Verständnis der antiochischen Theologie.* Beihefte zur Zeitschrift für die neutestamentliche Wissenschaft 27. Berlin, 1962.

Wickham, C. *Framing the Early Middle Ages.* Oxford, 2005.

Wilken, R. L. "Exegesis and the History of Theology: Reflections on the Adam Christ Typology in Cyril of Alexandria." *Church History* 35 (1966): 137–56.

———. *John Chrysostom and the Jews: Rhetoric and Reality in the Late Fourth Century.* Berkeley, 1983.

———. "Tradition, Exegesis, and the Christological Controversies." *Church History* 34 (1965): 123–45.

Winkler, G. "An Obscure Chapter in Armenian Church History (428–439)." *Revue des études arméniens* 19 (1985): 85–179.

Winter, E. "Mithraism and Christianity in Late Antiquity." In *Ethnicity and Culture in Late Antiquity,* edited by S. Mitchell and G. Greatrex, 173–82. London, 2000.

Wipszycka, E. "La chiesa nell' Egitto: Le strutture ecclesiastiche." In *Études sur le Christianisme dans l'Égypt de l'antiquité tardive*, 136–56. Rome, 1996.

———. "Les confréries dans la vie religieuse de l'Egypte chrétienne." In *Études sur le Christianisme dans l'Égypt de l'antiquité tardive*, 257–78. Rome, 1996.

———. "Le monachisme egyptien et les villes." In *Études sur le Christianisme dans l'Égypt de l'antiquité tardive*, 281–336. Rome, 1996.

———. "Les ordres mineurs dans l'église d'Égypte du iv au viii siècle." In *Études sur le Christianisme dans l'Égypt de l'antiquité tardive*, 225–55. Rome, 1996.

———. *Les ressources et les activités économiques des églises en Égypte du IVe au VIIIe siècle.* Brussels, 1972.

Woodward, E. L. *Christianity and Nationalism in the Later Roman Empire.* London, 1916.

Wuyts, A. "Le 28e canon de Chalcédoine et le fondement du primat romain." *Orientalia Christiana Periodica* 17.3 (1951): 265–82.

Young, F. M. *Biblical Exegesis and the Formation of Christian Culture.* Cambridge, 1997.

———. "Christological Ideas in the Greek Commentaries on the Epistle to the Hebrews." *JTS* ns. 20:1 (1969): 150–63.

———. *From Nicaea to Chalcedon.* London, 1983.

———. "Reconsideration of Alexandrian Christology." *Journal of Ecclesiastical History* 22 (1971): 103–14.

Zaharopoulos, D. Z. *Theodore of Mopsuestia on the Bible.* New York, 1989.

INDEX

255n92, 261nn28,38, 261–62n40, 263nn77,81, 264nn86,89,99,101; speeches, 135–36, 161
literal interpretation of Scripture, 23–24, 67, 69, 74, 214n33, 227n72
loans of soldiers, 147, 257n116
local notable class, 5–6, 48, 138–39, 142–43, 153, 158, 251nn23,26,29; relations with Theodoret, 7, 49–50, 49*fig.*, 134, 138–42, 146, 152–53, 157–59, 161–70, 167*fig.*, 169*fig.*; social networks, 7, 14, 136, 138–41, 170. *See also* women, notable
logos (Word, reason): human thought or speech, 142, 162, 165, 182; theological term, 4, 69–70, 85, 93, 120, 162, 182, 186–87, 194, 214n31,, 228n82, 269n39
Longinus of Doliche (archimandrite), 47*fig.*, 177*fig.*, 266n147
Lucian of Antioch, 229n69
Lucian of Samosata, 257n123

Macarius of Laodicea, 44*fig.*, 83*fig.*, 85, 88, 89*fig.*, 92, 95*fig.*, 107, 108*fig.*
Macedonius (hermit), 66*fig.*, 74, 227n62
Magian religion, 6, 135, 151, 257n126
Mani and Manicheans, 6, 24, 27, 54, 150, 152, 217n69
Marana (recluse), 47*fig.*, 118
Maranas (scholasticus), 49*fig.*, 138, 140, 176, 177*fig.*, 223n26, 266n147
Marcellus of Apamea, 72, 225n7, 227n63
Marcellus, archimandrite of the *Akoimetoi*, 115, 177*fig.*
Marcian, Emperor, 5, 66*fig.*, 130, 177*fig.*, 178, 203, 256n110
Marcian (hermit), 47*fig.*, 66*fig.*, 72, 74, 119, 227n62
Marcion and supposed Marcionites, 24, 27, 54, 148–52, 258n131, 259nn141,142
Marinianus of Barbalissus, 44*fig.*, 66*fig.*, 108*fig.*
Maras of Nisus, 44*fig.*, 95*fig.*, 108*fig.*
Maras of Edessa (priest), 123, 124*fig.*
Maris (hermit), 47*fig.*, 118
Mari the Persian, 274n26
Maron (hermit), 47*fig.*, 66*fig.*
Marutha of Martyropolis, 256n114, 274n26
Mary (young woman from N. Africa), 166, 167*fig.*
Mashdotz (Armenian translator), 28, 75, 217n71, 230n120
master of soldiers (*magister utriusque militiae*), 49*fig.*, 50, 114*fig.*, 147–48

Mastoc. *See* Mashdotz
Maximianus of Anazarbus, 44*fig.*, 45; Antiochene leader to 432 A.D., 83*fig.*, 85, 89*fig.*; Antiochene leader from 433 A.D., 95*fig.*, 100–101, 106, 108*fig.*, 239nn150,152, 241n187
Maximianus of Constantinople, 89, 93, 99, 103
Maximianus (decurion), 166, 167*fig.*
Maximus of Antioch, 123, 124*fig.*, 127, 203, 248n121
Maximus of Seleucia in Isauria, 65*fig.*, 227n63
Mazdaean religion. *See* Magian religion
mdabranutha (leadership/flexibility), 27, 204
mediator, 10–11, 173–74; between social networks, 4, 47, 95–96, 98, 116, 121, 175, 203; inside Antiochene network, 14, 40, 48, 50, 82, 84, 102–9, 108*fig.*, 121, 129, 203; of patronage, 14, 133–34, 137, 145, 153–55, 156, 159, 163–66, 170, 179; theological concept, 15, 182–84, 187–90
medical metaphors, 161, 246nn83,91
Meletius of Antioch, 58, 140, 230n117; compromise candidate for bishop, 59–60, 68–69, 215n35, 225nn12,13,14,15, 228n77; exiled Nicene bishop, 60–63, 61*fig.*, 63*fig.*, 71–72, 76–78, 94, 192, 226n31,; memorialized figure, 121, 226n50; sponsor of Nicene coup, 64–65, 65*fig.*, 70, 72–79, 192, 228n78
Meletius of Mopsuestia: core Antiochene member to 432 A.D., 83*fig.*, 85; pro-schism Antiochene leader from 433 A.D., 95*fig.*, 100–103, 107, 108*fig.*, 221nn141,145, 239nn150,152, 240n167
Memnon of Ephesus, 86–88, 234n45
mesiteia (mediation), 135, 153–55, 156–57, 182–88. *See also* mediator
Mesopotamia province, 53, 94, 147, 204, 237n108, 240n157
Messalians, suspected, 74, 119, 150
metaphorical reasoning, 10, 13, 15, 181–84, 188–90, 193
metaphors, deep, 10, 13, 181, 188–90, 193–96, 203
metaphors, stock classical, 161–62, 246n83
metropolitan bishops, 31–32, 50–51, 76, 87, 202, 272n5; in Syria, 45, 50–53, 54*fig.*, 77, 83*fig.*, 84, 98, 103–5, 125, 127, 218n96
miaphyisitism. *See* Cyrillian socio-doctrinal network, doctrinal cues. *See also* Apollinarius

TEXT

10/12.5 Minion Pro

DISPLAY

Minion Pro

COMPOSITOR

Toppan Best-set Premedia Limited